San Francisco

"All you've got to do is decide to go
and the hardest part is over.

So go!"

TONY WHEELER, COFOUNDER – LONELY PLANET

Alison Bing, John A Vlahides, Sara Benson, Ashley Harrell

Contents

(above) Clam chowder served in a bread bowl

(left) The 'Painted Ladies' Victorian mansions at Alamo Square Park (p181)

(right) Crane in Crissy Field (p55)

The Marina,
Fisherman's Wharf
& the Piers
p48

Nob Hill,
Russian Hill
& Fillmore
p128

North Beach
& Chinatown
p112

Downtown,
Civic Center
& SoMa
p74

Golden Gate Park
& the Avenues
p193

The Haight, NoPa
& Hayes Valley
p178

The Mission
& Potrero Hill
p144

The Castro
& Noe Valley
p167

Welcome to San Francisco

Grab your coat and a handful of glitter, and enter the land of fog and fabulousness. So long, inhibitions; hello, San Francisco.

Outlandish Notions

Consider permission permanently granted to be outlandish: other towns may surprise you, but in San Francisco you will surprise yourself. Good times and social revolutions tend to start here, from manic gold rushes to blissful hippie be-ins. If there's a skateboard move yet to be busted, a technology still unimagined, a poem left unspoken or a green scheme untested, chances are it's about to happen here. Yes, right now. This town has lost almost everything in earthquakes and dot-com gambles, but never its nerve.

Food & Drink

Every available Bay Area–invented technology is needed to make dinner decisions in this city, with the most restaurants and farmers markets per capita in North America, supplied by pioneering local organic farms. San Francisco set the gold standard for Wild West saloons, but drinking was driven underground in the 1920s with Prohibition. Today, San Francisco celebrates its speakeasies and vintage saloons – and with Wine Country and local distillers providing a steady supply of America's finest hooch, the West remains wild.

Natural Highs

California is one grand, sweeping gesture – a long arm hugging the Pacific – and the 7-by-7-mile peninsula of San Francisco is a thumb pointed optimistically upwards. Take this as a hint to look up: you'll notice San Francisco's crooked Victorian rooflines, wind-sculpted treetops and fog tumbling over the Golden Gate Bridge.

Heads are perpetually in the clouds atop San Francisco's 43 hills. Cable cars provide easy access to Russian and Nob Hills, and splendid panoramas reward the slog up to Coit Tower – but the most exhilarating highs are earned on Telegraph Hill's garden-lined stairway walks and windswept hikes around Land's End.

Neighborhood Microclimates

Microclimates add magic realism to San Francisco days: when it's drizzling in the outer reaches of Golden Gate Park, it might be sunny in the Mission. A few degrees' difference between neighborhoods grants permission for salted-caramel ice cream in Dolores Park, or a hasty retreat to tropical heat inside the California Academy of Sciences' rainforest dome. This town will give you goose bumps one minute, and warm you to the core the next.

Why I Love San Francisco
By Alison Bing, Writer

On my way from Hong Kong to New York, I stopped in San Francisco for a day. I walked from the Geary St art galleries up Grant Ave to Waverly Pl, just as temple services were starting. The fog was scented with incense and roast duck. In the basement of City Lights bookstore, near the Muckraking section, I noticed a sign painted by a 1920s cult: 'I am the door.' It's true. San Francisco is the threshold between East and West, body and soul, fact and fiction. That was 20 years ago. I'm still here. You've been warned.

For more about our writers, see p320

Top: Cable car with Fisherman's Wharf (p57) in the background

San Francisco's
Top 10

Golden Gate Bridge *(p54)*

1 Other suspension bridges boast impressive engineering, but none can touch the Golden Gate Bridge for showmanship. On sunny days, it transfixes crowds with its radiant glow – thanks to 25 daredevil painters, who reapply 1000 gallons of International Orange paint weekly. When afternoon fog rolls in, the bridge performs its disappearing act: now you see it, now you don't and, abracadabra, it's sawn in half. Return tomorrow for its dramatic unveiling, just in time for the morning commute.

👁 *The Marina, Fisherman's Wharf & the Piers*

Alcatraz *(p50)*

2 From its 19th-century founding to detain Civil War deserters and Native American dissidents until its closure by Bobby Kennedy in 1963, Alcatraz was America's most notorious jail. No prisoner is known to have escaped alive – but, once you enter D-Block solitary and hear carefree city life humming across the bay, the 1.25-mile swim through riptides seems worth a shot. For maximum chill factor, book the spooky twilight jailhouse tour. Freedom never felt so good as it does on the return ferry to San Francisco.

👁 *The Marina, Fisherman's Wharf & the Piers*

PHITHA TANPAIROJ/SHUTTERSTOCK ©

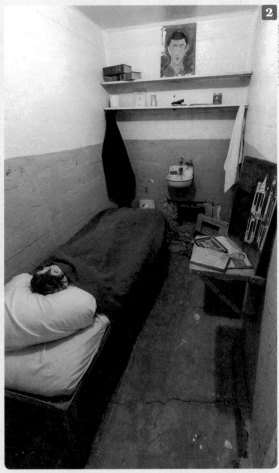

OSCITY/SHUTTERSTOCK ©

Golden Gate Park (p195)

3 You may have heard that SF has a wild streak a mile wide, but that streak also happens to be 4.5 miles long. Golden Gate Park lets locals do what comes naturally: roller-discoing, drum-circling, starfish-petting, orchid-sniffing and stampeding toward the Pacific with a herd of bison. It's hard to believe these lush 1017 acres were once scrubby sand dunes, and that San Franciscans have preserved this stretch of green since 1866, blocking the establishment of casinos and resorts. Today, everything SF needs is here: inspiration, nature and microbrewed beer at the Beach Chalet. BELOW: JAPANESE TEA GARDEN (P197)

⊙ *Golden Gate Park & the Avenues*

Mission Murals (p146)

4 Love changed the course of art history in 1930s San Francisco when modern-art power couple Diego Rivera and Frida Kahlo rekindled their romance here. Kahlo completed some of her first portrait commissions during her time in the city, and Rivera created mural masterpieces that remain vibrant and relevant today. The Mission district is an urban-art showstopper, featuring more than 400 murals. Balmy Alley has some of the oldest, while 24th St and the landmark San Francisco Women's Building are covered with community pride and political dissent. RIGHT: *DEAR FACE* MURAL BY EMILY GLAUBINGER IN CLARION ALLEY (P149)

⊙ *The Mission & Potrero Hill*

SFMOMA *(p76)*

5 Right from its start in 1935, San Francisco Museum of Modern Art envisioned a world of radical new possibilities, starting in San Francisco. SFMOMA was a visionary early investor in then-emerging art forms such as photography, murals, film and installation, and now it's tripled in size and ambition, dedicating entire wings to new media art, room-size paintings, high-tech design and walk-in Richard Serra sculptures. Set aside an afternoon to cover all seven floors, and reserve ahead to enjoy edible art on-site at In Situ, Corey Lee's acclaimed gallery of contemporary cuisine.

⊙ *Downtown, Civic Center & SoMa*

The History-Making Castro (p167)

6 Somewhere over the rainbow crosswalk, you'll realize you've officially arrived in the Castro district. For more than 50 years this has been the most out and proud neighborhood on the planet, as you'll discover walking Castro St's LGBT walk of fame on the way to showtime at the historic Castro Theatre. Learn more at America's first GLBT History Museum, and join history in progress at San Francisco's month-long, million-strong Pride celebrations in June. BELOW: RAINBOW HONOR WALK (P169)

◉ *The Castro & Noe Valley*

Cable Cars (p87)

7 Carnival rides simply can't compare to the time-traveling thrills of cable cars, San Francisco's vintage form of public transit. Novices slide into strangers' laps – cable cars were invented in 1873, long before seat belts – but regulars just grip the leather hand straps, lean back and ride the downhill plunges like pro surfers. Follow their lead, and you'll soon master the San Francisco stance and find yourself conquering the city's hills without even breaking a sweat.

🏃 *Downtown, Civic Center & SoMa*

Coit Tower *(p114)*

8 Wild parrots might mock your progress up Telegraph Hill, but they can't expect to keep scenery like this to themselves. Filbert St Steps pass cliffside cottage gardens to reach SF's monument to independent thinking: Coit Tower. Fire-fighting heiress Lillie Hitchcock Coit commissioned this deco monument honoring fire-fighters, and muralists captured 1930s San Francisco in freshly restored lobby frescoes. Coit Tower's paintings and panoramic viewing platform show San Francisco at its best: a city of broad perspectives, outlandish and inspiring.

⊙ *North Beach & Chinatown*

Barbary Coast Nights (p121)

9 In the mid-19th century, you could start a San Francisco bar crawl with smiles and 10¢ whiskey – and end up two days later involuntarily working on a vessel bound for Patagonia. Now that double-crossing barkeep Shanghai Kelly is no longer a danger to drinkers, revelers can relax at North Beach's once-notorious Barbary Coast saloons. These days, you can pick your own poison: historically correct cocktails at Comstock Saloon (p121), cult California wines and/or enough microbrewed beer to keep you snoring to Patagonia and back.

🍷 *North Beach & Chinatown*

Ferry Building (p79)

10 Global food trends start in San Francisco. To sample tomorrow's menu today, head to the Ferry Building, the city's monument to trailblazing local, sustainable food. Don't miss Saturday farmers markets here, where top chefs jostle for first pick of rare heirloom varietals and foodie babies blissfully teethe on organic California peaches. Picnic on Pier 2 with food-truck finds, feet dangling over the sparkling bay – and let lunch and life exceed expectations. ABOVE: FARMERS MARKET HALL

🍴 *Downtown, Civic Center & SoMa*

What's New

Super-Sized SFMOMA

The half-billion-dollar expansion at the San Francisco Museum of Modern Art is now open, tripling the museum in size and scope. (p76)

Showtime Mid-Market

For about 100 years, showtime on this strip meant the same tired old striptease – but now mid-Market entertainment is constantly surprising, with cutting-edge venues like PianoFight (p103) and Black Cat (p103) – and don't miss breakthrough performances at the Strand Theater (p103), Root Division (p86) and the Warfield (p104).

Mission Paper Trail

Even Silicon Valley techies unplug and go analog in the Mission, with member-supported book collectives, kids writing books at 826 Valencia (p147), epic Litquake (p21) readings in bars, and upstart galleries showcasing original works on paper.

Dogpatch Creative Corridor

Hop on the T streetcar to 22nd St to discover arts workshops, local designers, the Museum of Craft & Design and (oh yes) chocolate factories. (p151)

Dragstravaganzas

San Francisco has entertained in drag since the gold rush, and now SF drags days into nights with historical Drag Me Along Tours (p127), Castro Theatre (p175) movie spoofs, and original drag cabaret at Oasis (p105).

Maker/hackerspaces

The ultimate SF souvenir is a freshly acquired DIY skill, whether that's leather tooling at Workshop (www.workshopsf. org), app making at SoMa hackerspaces (p105), or foraging for seaweed with Sea Foraging Adventures (www.seaforager. com).

Comedy Comeback

Comic geniuses like Woody Allen and Lenny Bruce emerged from North Beach's underground in the '60s, and Punch Line (p103) and Cobb's Comedy Club (p125) launched talents like Ellen DeGeneres and Chris Rock. Now bars citywide are hosting comedy nights, and new clubs like Doc's Lab (p125) and Oasis (p104) are doing their bit to keep SF outrageous.

Potrero Flats Galleries

Potrero's Design District is branching out from sofas into art, with some of SF's best contemporary galleries taking up residence around nonprofit arts hubs SOMArts (p150) and the San Francisco Center for the Book (p166).

Green Rules

America's greenest city already has mandatory composting and recycling citywide, and now bags will cost you 10¢ at stores and restaurants – a fine excuse to score a souvenir tote bag.

For more recommendations and reviews, see **lonelyplanet. com/usa/san-francisco**

Need to Know

For more information, see Survival Guide (p263)

Currency
US dollar ($)

Language
English

Visas
USA Visa Waiver Program (VWP) allows nationals from 38 countries with machine-readable passports to enter without a visa – see the **US Department of State** website (http://travel.state.gov) and register with **US Department of Homeland Security** (https://esta.cbp.dhs.gov/esta).

Money
ATMs are widespread; debit/credit cards are accepted almost everywhere, but it's wise to bring a combination of cash, cards and traveler's checks.

Cell Phones
Most US cell phones besides iPhones operate on CDMA; check with your provider.

Time
Pacific Standard Time (GMT/UTC minus eight hours)

Tourist Information
SF Visitor Information Center (www.sanfrancisco.travel/visitor-information-center) Muni Passports, deals and event calendars.

Daily Costs

Budget: Less than $150
➡ Dorm bed: $33–60
➡ Burrito: $6–9
➡ Food-truck fare: $5–13
➡ Mission and Coit Tower murals: free
➡ Live North Beach music or comedy: free–$15
➡ Castro Theatre show: $12

Midrange: $150–350
➡ Downtown hotel/home-share: $130–180
➡ Ferry Building meal: $18–45
➡ Mission share-plates meal: $20–50
➡ Symphony rush tickets: $20
➡ Muni Passport: $21

Top End: More than $350
➡ Boutique hotel: $180–380
➡ Chef's tasting menu: $60–228
➡ City Pass (Muni, cable cars plus four attractions): $89
➡ Alcatraz night tour: $44.50
➡ Opera orchestra seats: $90–140

Advance Planning

Two months before Make reservations at Benu, Chez Panisse or French Laundry; start walking to build stamina for Coit Tower climbs and Mission bar crawls.

Three weeks before Book Alcatraz tour, Chinatown History Tour or Precita Eyes Mission Mural Tour.

One week before Search for tickets to American Conservatory Theater, SF Symphony, SF Opera and Oasis drag shows – and find out what else is on next weekend.

Useful Websites

SFGate (www.sfgate.com) *San Francisco Chronicle* news and event listings.

7x7 (www.7x7.com) Trend-spotting SF restaurants, bars and style.

Craigslist (http://sfbay.craigslist.org) SF-based source for jobs, dates and free junk.

Lonely Planet (www.lonelyplanet.com/usa/san-francisco) Destination information, hotel bookings, traveler forum and more.

WHEN TO GO

June and July bring fog and chilly 55°F (13°C) weather to SF; August to October offer warm weather, street fairs and harvest cuisine.

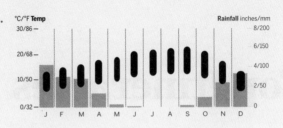

Arriving in San Francisco

San Francisco Airport (SFO) Fast rides to downtown SF on BART (www.bart.gov) cost $8.95; door-to-door shuttle vans cost $17 to $20, plus tip; express bus fare to Temporary Transbay Terminal is $2.50 via SamTrans (p268); taxis cost $40 to $55, plus tip.

Oakland International Airport (OAK) Catch BART from the airport to downtown SF ($10.20); take a shared van to downtown SF for $30 to $40; or pay $60 to $80 for a taxi to SF destinations.

Temporary Transbay Terminal Greyhound buses arrive/depart downtown SF's temporary depot (in use until the permanent Transbay Transit Center opens, scheduled for late 2017) at Howard and Main Sts.

Emeryville Amtrak station (EMY) Located outside Oakland, this depot serves West Coast and nationwide train routes; Amtrak runs free shuttles to/from San Francisco's Ferry Building, Caltrain, Civic Center and Fisherman's Wharf.

For much more on **arrival** see p264

Getting Around

Avoid driving until it's time to leave town. For Bay Area transit options, departures and arrivals, call ☑511 or check www.511.org. *Muni Street & Transit Map* is available free online.

➡ **Cable cars** Frequent, slow and scenic, from 6am to 12:30am daily. Single rides cost $7; for frequent use, get a Muni Passport ($21 per day).

➡ **Muni streetcar and bus** Reasonably fast, but schedules vary by line; infrequent after 9pm. Fares are $2.50.

➡ **BART** High-speed transit to East Bay, Mission St, SF airport and Millbrae, where it connects with Caltrain.

➡ **Taxi** Fares are about $2.75 per mile; meters start at $3.50.

For much more on **getting around** see p265

Sleeping

San Francisco hotels are among the world's most expensive. Plan well ahead to find the rare bargains.

Accommodations Websites

➡ **B&B San Francisco** (www.bbsf.com) Personable, privately owned B&Bs and neighborhood inns.

➡ **Hotel Tonight** (www. hoteltonight.com) SF-based hotel-search app offering discount last-minute bookings.

➡ **Lonely Planet** (www. lonelyplanet.com/usa/sanfrancisco/hotels) Expert author reviews, user feedback, booking engine.

For much more on **sleeping** see p226

Top Itineraries

Day One

North Beach & Chinatown (p112)

 Grab a leather strap on the Powell-Mason cable car and hold on: you're in for hills and thrills. Hop off at **Washington Square Park**, where parrots squawk encouragement for your hike up to **Coit Tower** for Work Projects Administration (WPA) murals and 360-degree panoramas. Take scenic **Filbert Street Steps** to the **Embarcadero** to wander across Fog Bridge and explore the freaky Tactile Dome at the **Exploratorium**.

> **Lunch** Try local oysters and Dungeness crab at the Ferry Building (p79).

The Marina, Fisherman's Wharf & the Piers (p48)

 Catch your prebooked ferry to **Alcatraz**, where D-Block solitary raises goose bumps. Make your island-prison break, taking in **Golden Gate Bridge** views on the ferry ride back. Take the Powell-Mason cable car to North Beach, to take in free-speech landmark **City Lights** and mingle with SF's freest spirits at the **Beat Museum**.

> **Dinner** Reserve North Beach's best pasta at Cotogna (p88) or a Cal-Chinese banquet at Mister Jiu's (p121).

North Beach & Chinatown (p112)

Since you just escaped prison, you're tough enough to handle too-close-for-comfort comics at **Cobb's Comedy Club** or razor-sharp satire at **Beach Blanket Babylon**. Toast the wildest night in the west with potent Pisco sours at **Comstock Saloon** or spiked cappuccinos at **Tosca Cafe**.

Day Two

Golden Gate Park & the Avenues (p193)

 Hop the N Judah to Golden Gate Park to see carnivorous plants enjoying insect breakfasts at the **Conservatory of Flowers** and spiky dahlias wet with dew in the **Dahlia Garden**. Follow Andy Goldsworthy's artful sidewalk fault lines to find Oceanic masks and flawless tower-top views inside the **de Young Museum**, then take a walk on the wild side in the rainforest dome of the **California Academy of Sciences**. Enjoy a moment of Zen with green tea at the **Japanese Tea Garden** and bliss out in the secret redwood grove at the **San Francisco Botanical Garden**.

> **Lunch** Join surfers at Outerlands (p202) for grilled cheese and organic soup.

Golden Gate Park & the Avenues (p193)

Beachcomb **Ocean Beach** up to the **Beach Chalet** to glimpse 1930s WPA murals celebrating Golden Gate Park. Follow the **Coastal Trail** past **Sutro Baths** and Land's End for Golden Gate Bridge vistas and priceless paper artworks at the **Legion of Honor**.

> **Dinner** You've walked the coastline – now savour a seafood feast at Wako (p201).

Nob Hill, Russian Hill & Fillmore (p128)

 Psychedelic posters and top acts make for rock-legendary nights at the **Fillmore**.

Golden Gate Park (p195)

Day Three

North Beach & Chinatown (p112)

 Take the **California cable car** to pagoda-topped Grant St for an eye-opening **Red Blossom** tea tasting and then a jaw-dropping history of Chinatown at the **Chinese Historical Society of America**. Wander temple-lined **Waverly Place** and notorious **Ross Alley** to find your fortune at the **Golden Gate Fortune Cookie Company**.

 Lunch Hail dim-sum carts for dumplings at City View (p120).

The Marina, Fisherman's Wharf & the Piers (p48)

To cover the waterfront, take the Powell-Hyde cable car past zigzagging **Lombard Street** to the **San Francisco Maritime National Historical Park**, where you can see what it was like to stow away on a schooner. Save the world from Space Invaders at **Musée Mécanique** or enter underwater stealth mode inside a real WWII submarine: the **USS Pampanito**. Watch sea lions cavort as the sun fades over **Pier 39**, then hop onto the vintage F-line streetcar.

Dinner Inspired NorCal fare at Rich Table (p186) satisfies and surprises.

The Haight, NoPa & Hayes Valley (p178)

Browse Hayes Valley boutiques before your concert at the **SF Symphony** or **SFJAZZ Center**, and toast your good fortune at **Smuggler's Cove**.

Day Four

The Mission & Potrero Hill (p144)

 Wander 24th St past mural-covered bodegas to **Balmy Alley**, where the Mission muralist movement began in the 1970s. Stop for a 'secret breakfast' (bourbon and cornflakes) ice-cream sundae at **Humphry Slocombe**, then head up Valencia to **Ritual Coffee Roasters**. Pause for pirate supplies and Fish Theater at **826 Valencia** and duck into **Clarion Alley**, the Mission's outdoor graffiti-art gallery. See San Francisco's first building, Spanish adobe **Mission Dolores**, and visit the memorial to the Native Ohlone who built it.

 Lunch Take La Taqueria (p151) burritos to Dolores Park, or dine in at Tacolicious (p153).

The Haight, NoPa & Hayes Valley (p178)

Spot Victorian 'Painted Ladies' around **Alamo Square** and browse **NoPa boutiques**. Stroll tree-lined Panhandle park to Stanyan, then window-shop your way down hippie-historic **Haight Street** past record stores, vintage emporiums, drag designers and **Bound Together Anarchist Book Collective**.

Dinner Early walk-ins may score sensational small plates at Frances (p173).

The Castro & Noe Valley (p167)

Sing along to tunes pounded out on the Mighty Wurlitzer organ before shows at the deco-fabulous **Castro Theatre**. Party boys cruise over to **440 Castro**, while straight-friendly crowds clink glasses at **Blackbird**.

If You Like...

Vista Points

Coit Tower Up Greenwich St stairs, atop Telegraph Hill, inside the 1930s tower, upon the viewing platform: 360-degree panoramas. (p114)

Land's End Shipwrecks, Golden Gate views and Monterey pines line the coastal trail from Sutro Baths to the Legion of Honor. (p205)

George Sterling Park Poetic views of the Golden Gate Bridge from atop Russian Hill. (p130)

Corona Heights Park Rocky outcropping with views over the Haight, Castro and Mission to the silvery bay beyond. (p169)

Dolores Park On the southwestern corner, overlook sunbathers, picnickers and kids swarming the Aztec play pyramid all the way to the bay. (p147)

Alamo Square Park Peek over the shoulders of 'Painted Lady' Victorian mansions to glimpse City Hall and the Transamerica Pyramid. (p181)

Movie Locations

Nob Hill Steve McQueen's muscle car goes flying over the summit in *Bullitt* and somehow lands in SoMa. (p47)

Ocean Beach The windswept beach sets the scene for turbulent romance in Woody Allen's *Blue Jasmine*. (p199)

Sutro Baths San Francisco's splendid ruin sets the scene for a May–December romance in *Harold and Maude*. (p198)

City Hall lit up in honor of Pride Week

Human Rights Campaign Action Center & Store Harvey Milk's camera shop in *Milk* was this real-life Castro location, now home to the LGBT civil-rights organization. (p177)

Bay Bridge Oops: when Dustin Hoffman sets out for Berkeley in *The Graduate*, he's heading the wrong way across the bridge. (p79)

Transamerica Pyramid Godzilla stomps through the Golden Gate Bridge in the 2014 sci-fi remake but mysteriously spares downtown's signature landmark. (p80)

Alcatraz Even America's highest-security prison can't contain Clint Eastwood in *Escape from Alcatraz*. (p50)

Historic Sites

Mission Dolores The first building in SF was this Spanish adobe mission, built by conscripted Ohlone and Miwok. (p149)

Alcatraz 'The Rock' was a Civil War jail, an A-list gangster penitentiary, and territory contested between Native Americans and the FBI. (p50)

City Lights Publishing poetry got City Lights founder Lawrence Ferlinghetti arrested – and won a landmark case for free speech. (p115)

Chinese Historical Society of America California's first licensed woman architect, Julia Morgan, built the elegant, tile-roofed brick Chinese YWCA. (p116)

City Hall Home to the first 1960s sit-in, America's first publicly gay elected official and the first citywide composting law. (p86)

Local Hangouts

Dolores Park Athletes, radical politicos, performance artists and toddlers: on sunny days, they all converge on this grassy hillside. (p147)

Japantown The unofficial living room of film-festival freaks, Lolita Goths, *anime* aficionados and grandmas who fought for civil rights. (p141)

Adobe Books & Backroom Gallery Meet backroom artists-in-residence and talk books with strangers in this community-supported bookshop. (p163)

Coffee to the People The quadruple-shot Freak Out with hemp milk could wake the Grateful Dead at this radical Haight coffeehouse. (p189)

Washington Square Mellow out with poets and tai-chi masters while wild parrots eye your foccacia from the trees. (p116)

Free Stuff

Stern Grove Festival Free concerts at Golden Gate Park's natural amphitheater, from Afro-beat jazz to SF Opera. (p21)

Hardly Strictly Bluegrass Festival Headliners like Elvis Costello, Gillian Welch and banjo legend Béla Fleck plus 100 other acts in Golden Gate Park. (p21)

Cable Car Museum Observe the inner workings of San Francisco's transportation icon, which remains largely unchanged since its 1873 invention. (p130)

Amoeba Music concerts Rockers, DJs and hip-hop heroes give free shows in-store. (p190)

Giants baseball Catch a glimpse of the action and join the party at the Embarcadero

For more top San Francisco spots, see the following:
→ Eating (p25)
→ Drinking & Nightlife (p30)
→ Entertainment (p34)
→ Shopping (p39)
→ Sports & Activities (p42)

waterfront promenade behind left field. (p105)

Golden Gate Bridge Yeah, you've probably heard of this. Walk across, hop a bus or rent a bike. (p54)

Balmy Alley Mural-covered garage doors make colorful political statements along this Mission backstreet. (p146)

City Lights Books A landmark to free speech and free spirits. (p115)

Hidden Alleyways

Balmy Alley Hot topics and artistic talents have surfaced since the 1970s in this backstreet decorated by SF *muralistas*. (p146)

Spofford Alley Revolutions were plotted and bootlegger gun battles waged here – but peace has brought Chinese orchestras and marathon mah-jongg games. (p122)

Jack Kerouac Alley This byway named after the Beat author is inscribed with his poetry, right on the road. (p115)

Bob Kaufman Alley A quiet alley named for the spoken-word artist who kept an anti-war vow of silence for 12 years. (p116)

Ross Alley Ladies who entered this alley once risked their reputations, but now its most colorful characters are in the murals. (p122)

Month By Month

February

Lion dancing, warm days and alt-rock shows provide brilliant breaks in the February drizzle.

Noise Pop

Winter blues, be gone: discover your new favorite indie band and catch roc-kumentary premieres and rockin' pop-up gallery openings during the Noise Pop (www.noisepop.com) festival; last week of February.

Lunar New Year Parade

Chase the 200ft dragon, legions of lion dancers and frozen-smile runners-up for the Miss Chinatown title during Lunar New Year (www.chineseparade.com) celebrations.

April

Reasonable room rates and weekends crammed with cultural events will put some spring in your step.

Perpetual Indulgence in the Park

Easter Sunday is an all-day event with the Sisters of Perpetual Indulgence (www.thesisters.org) in Golden Gate Park, with bonnets and bands galore and the infamous Hunky Jesus Contest.

Cherry Blossom Festival

Japantown blooms and booms in April when the Cherry Blossom Festival (www.nccbf.org) arrives with *taiko* drums, home-grown hip-hop and anime costumes.

San Francisco International Film Festival

The nation's oldest film festival (www.sffs.org) is stellar, with 325 films and 200 directors. Plan ahead for two weeks of screenings at Castro Theatre (p175), Alamo Drafthouse Cinema (p160) and Roxie Cinema (p160).

Art Market SF

Gallerists converge on Fort Mason to showcase contemporary art, and satellite art fairs pop up in motels and parking lots in the Marina.

May

As inland California warms up, fog settles over the Bay Area – but goosebumps don't stopped the naked joggers and conga lines.

Bay to Breakers

Run costumed or naked from Embarcadero to Ocean Beach for Bay to Breakers (p42), while joggers dressed as salmon run upstream. It's held on the third Sunday in May.

Carnaval

Brazilian, or just faking it with glitter and a tan? Shake your tail feathers in the Mission and conga through the fog during Carnaval (www.carnavalsf.com).

June

Since 1970, Pride has grown into a month-long extravaganza, culminating in the million-strong Pride Parade.

✡ Haight Ashbury Street Fair

Free music, tie-dye galore and herbal brownies for sale – the Summer of Love stages a comeback in the Haight every mid-June since 1977, when Harvey Milk helped make the first Haight Ashbury Street Fair (www.haightashburystreet-fair.org) happen.

✡ San Francisco International LGBTQ Film Festival

Here, queer and ready for a premiere since 1976, the San Francisco LGBTQ Film Festival (www.frameline. org) is the biggest lesbian/gay/bisexual/transgender/queer film fest anywhere. Binge-watch up to 300 films from 30 countries.

✡ Dyke March & Pink Party

Starting with a roar from the Dykes on Bikes motor-cycle contingent, the 100,000-strong, Dyke March (www.thedykemarch.org) heads from Dolores Park to the Castro's Pink Party. Castro St and upper Market St are closed to traffic, and festivities last until sunset.

✡ Pride Parade

Come out wherever you are: SF goes wild for LGBTQ pride on the last Sunday of June, with 1.2+ million people, seven stages, and tons of glitter at the Pride Parade (www.sfpride.org). Join crowds cheering for civil-rights pioneers, gays in uniform, proud families and rainbow-flag drag.

July

Wintry summer days make bundling up advisable, but don't miss barbecues and outdoor events, including charity hikes, free concerts and fireworks.

✡ Stern Grove Festival

Music among the redwood trees, every summer since 1938. Free concerts (www. sterngrove.org) include hip-hop and jazz, but biggest events are performances by SF Ballet, SF Symphony and SF Opera; 2pm Sundays July and August.

🏃 AIDS Walk

Until AIDS takes a hike, you can: the 10km fund-raising AIDS Walk (http://sf.aidswalk.net/) through Golden Gate Park benefits 43 AIDS organizations. Over three decades, $88 million has been raised to fight the pandemic and support those living with HIV; third Sunday in July.

August

Finally the fog rolls back and permits sunset views from Ocean Beach, in time for one last glorious summer fling in Golden Gate Park and a harvest feast at Fort Mason.

✡ Outside Lands

Golden Gate Park hosts major marquee acts and gleeful debauchery at Wine Lands, Beer Lands and star-chef food trucks during Outside Lands (www.sfoutsidelands.com). Tickets sell out months in advance.

🍴 Eat Drink SF

Loosen your belt for four days of events celebrating California's bounty, culminating in a Grand Tasting at Fort Mason.

September

Warm weather arrives at last and SF celebrates with outrageous antics, including public spankings and Shakespearean declarations of love.

✡ Folsom Street Fair

Bondage enthusiasts emerge from dungeons worldwide for San Francisco's wild-est street party on Folsom St (www.folsomstreetfair. com), between 7th and 11th Sts. Enjoy leather, beer, and public spankings for local charities.

✡ SF Shakespeare Festival

The play's the thing in the Presidio, outdoors and free of charge on sunny September weekends during the Shakespeare Festival (p34). Kids' summer workshops are also held for budding Bards, culminating in performances throughout the Bay Area.

October

Expect golden sunshine – this is San Francisco's true summer – and music and literature events.

✡ Litquake

Stranger-than-fiction literary events take place during SF's literary festival (www. litquake.org), with authors leading lunchtime sessions and spilling trade secrets over drinks at the legendary Lit Crawl.

✡ Hardly Strictly Bluegrass

The West goes wild for free bluegrass (www.hardly strictlybluegrass.com) at

Golden Gate Park, with three days of concerts and seven stages of headliners.

November

Party to wake the dead and save the planet as San Francisco celebrates its Mexican history, crafty present and green future.

🎊 Día de los Muertos

Zombie brides and Aztec dancers in feathers regalia party like there's no tomorrow on Día de los Muertos (www.dayofthedeadsf.org), paying their respects to altars to the dead along the Mission processional route.

🎊 Green Festival

Energy-saving spotlights are turned on green cuisine, tech and fashion during the three-day, mid-November Green Festival (www.greenfestivals.org).

🎊 West Coast Craft

Get hip, handmade style without lifting a finger at West Coast Craft (http://westcoastcraft.com), featuring 100+ indie makers just in time for the holidays.

December

December days may be overcast, but nights sparkle with holiday lights and events citywide.

☆ Kung Pao Kosher

A San Francisco holiday tradition to rival the San Francisco Ballet's *The Nutcracker*, Kung Pao Kosher (www.koshercomedy.com) is a Jewish comedy marathon held in a Chinese restaurant at Christmas.

(Top) Lunar New Year Parade (p20)

KOBBY DAGAN/SHUTTERSTOCK ©

(Bottom) San Francisco Pride Parade (p21)

SHEILA FITZGERALD/SHUTTERSTOCK ©

With Kids

San Francisco has the fewest kids per capita of any US city and, according to SPCA data, about 10,000 more dogs than children live here. Yet many locals make a living entertaining kids – from Pixar animators to video-game designers – and this town is full of attractions for young people.

ANTON_IVANOV/SHUTTERSTOCK ©

Osher Rainforest Dome, California Academy of Sciences (p196)

Alcatraz & the Piers

Prison tours of Alcatraz (p50) fascinate kids and give them an interesting, safe place to run around. Afterwards, hit the award-winning, hands-on exhibits at the Exploratorium (p60) to investigate the science of skateboarding and glow-in-the-dark animals. Free the world from Space Invaders at Musée Mechanique (p58), then troll the waterfront for fish-wiches. Don't be shy: bark back at the sea lions at Pier 39 (p57), and ride a purple pony on the pier's vintage San Francisco carousel.

Cable Cars & Boats

When junior gearheads demand to know how cable cars work, the Cable Car Museum (p130) lets them glimpse the inner workings for themselves. Take a joyride on the Powell-Hyde cable car to Fisherman's Wharf, where you can enter submarine stealth mode aboard the USS Pampanito (p59) and climb aboard schooners and steamships at the Maritime National Historical Park (p58). Future sea captains will enjoy model-ship weekend regattas at Spreckels Lake in Golden Gate Park (p195).

Freebies

See SF history in motion at the free Cable Car Museum (p130), and take free mechanical pony rides and peeks inside vintage stagecoaches at the Wells Fargo History Museum (p80). Cool kids will want to head to 24th St to see Balmy Alley murals and skaters at Potrero del Sol Skatepark (p43). The free Randall Junior Museum (p172) introduces kids to urban wildlife, earth science and, on Saturdays, the fascinating Golden Gate model railroad. Daredevils can conquer the concrete Seward Street slides (p177) in the Castro and the Winfield Street slides in Bernal Heights. Lunchtime concerts are free at Old St Mary's (p117) and, in summer, at Yerba Buena Gardens (p84) and **Justin Herman Plaza** (Map p301, C2; www.sfrecplaza. org; cnr Market St & the Embarcadero; ☐2, 6, 7, 9, 14, 21, 31, 32, Ⓑ Embarcadero, Ⓜ Embarcadero). Kids can graze on free samples at the Ferry Building (p79), and score free toys in exchange for a bartered song, drawing or poem at 826 Valencia (p147).

Nature Lovers

Penguins, buffalo and white alligators call Golden Gate Park (p195) home. Chase butterflies through the rainforest dome, pet starfish in the petting zoo and squeal in the Eel Forest at the California Academy of Sciences (p196). Get a whiff of insect breath from carnivorous flowers at the Conservatory of Flowers (p197) – pee-eeww! – and brave the shark tunnel at Aquarium of the Bay (p57). San Francisco Zoo (p199) is out of the way but worth the trip for monkeys, lemurs and giraffes.

Sunny Days

On sunny Sundays when Golden Gate Park is mostly closed to traffic, rent paddleboats at Stow Lake (p197) or strap on some rentals at Golden Gate Park Bike & Skate (p205). Crissy Field (p55) and Aquatic Park (p59) are better bets for kid-friendly beaches than Ocean Beach, where fog and strong currents swiftly end sandcastle-building sessions. Hit Chinatown for teen-led Chinatown Alleyway Tours (p127), and cookies at Golden Gate Fortune Cookie Company (p126).

Playgrounds

Golden Gate Park (p195) Swings, monkey bars, play castles with slides, hillside slides and a vintage carousel.

Dolores Park (p147) Jungle gym, Mayan pyramid and picnic tables.

Yerba Buena Gardens (p84) Grassy downtown playground surrounded by museums, cinemas and kid-friendly dining.

Huntington Park (p131) Top-end playground in ritzy hilltop park.

Portsmouth Square (p117) Chinatown's outdoor playroom.

Old St Mary's Square (p117) Skateboarders and play equipment.

Museums & Galleries

The Children's Creativity Museum (p84) allows future tech moguls to design their own video games and animations, while the Exploratorium (p60) has interactive displays that let kids send fog signals and figure out optical illusions. Kids are encouraged to explore art in San Francisco, with free admission for those aged 12 and under at the Asian Art Museum (p78), Legion of Honor (p198), de Young Museum (p196), Museum of the African Diaspora (p84) and Contemporary Jewish Museum (p83). To make your own hands-on fun, hit Paxton Gate kids' store (p165) for shadow puppets and organic playdough.

NEED TO KNOW

Change facilities Best public facilities are at Westfield San Francisco Centre (p107) and **San Francisco Main Library** (☑415-557-4400; www.sfpl.org; 100 Larkin St; ☺10am-6pm Mon & Sat, 9am-8pm Tue-Thu, noon-6pm Fri, noon-5pm Sun; 🛜; ⓂCivic Center).

Emergency care San Francisco General Hospital (p272).

Babysitting Available at high-end hotels or **American Child Care** (Map p294; ☑415-285-2300; www.americanchildcare.com; 71 Stevenson St, Ste 400).

Strollers and car seats Bring your own or hire from a rental agency like **Cloud of Goods** (☑415-741-5056; www.cloudofgoods.com; 2nd fl, 950 Grant Ave).

Diapers and formula Available citywide at Walgreens and CVS stores, and also Safeway grocery stores.

Kiddie menus Mostly in cafes and downtown diners; call ahead about dietary restrictions.

Seafood at Fisherman's Wharf (p57)

 **Eating**

Other US cities boast bigger monuments, but San Francisco packs more flavor. Chef Alice Waters set the Bay Area standard for organic, sustainable, seasonal food back in 1971 at Chez Panisse, and today you'll find California's pasture-raised meats and organic produce proudly featured on the Bay Area's trend-setting, cross-cultural menus. Congratulations: you couldn't have chosen a better time or place for dinner.

Farmers Markets

NorCal idealists who headed back to the land in the 1970s started the nation's organic-farming movement. Today the local bounty can be sampled across SF, the US city with the most farmers markets per capita.

Ferry Plaza Farmers Market (p79) Star chefs, heirloom ingredients, and food trucks at weekends.

Mission Community Market (p152) Nonprofit, neighborhood-run market with 30 local vendors, offering farm-fresh ingredients and artisan-food meals.

Heart of the City Farmers Market (p94) Low-cost, farmer-run market bringing healthy, fresh food to the inner city, including California-grown produce and mom-and-pop food trucks.

Alemany Farmers Market (http://sfgsa.org; 100 Alemany Blvd; ⊘dawn-dusk Sat) California's first farmers market, offering bargain California-grown produce and ready-to-eat artisan food since 1943.

Castro Farmers Market (p177) Local produce and artisan foods at moderate prices, plus charmingly offbeat folk-music groups.

NEED TO KNOW

Price Ranges

The following price ranges refer to a main course, exclusive of drinks, tax and tip:

$ less than $15

$$ $15–25

$$$ more than $25

Tipping

Together, tax and tip add 25% to 35% to the bill. SF follows the US tipping standard: 20% to 25% is generous; 15% is the minimum, unless something went horribly wrong with the service you received.

Surcharges

Some restaurants tack on a 4% surcharge to cover the cost of providing health care to restaurant employees, as required by SF law. If you don't appreciate restaurants passing on their business costs to customers, say so in an online restaurant review. Just don't blame your server, who may not actually be benefiting. In a 2013 scandal, the city found that 50 restaurants were pocketing surcharge fees earmarked for employee health care. The city published the list at www.sfgate.com and fined the restaurants heavily.

A growing number of SF restaurants charge a flat 20% service fee, especially for parties of six or more, even though diners may balk at having tipping decisions made for them. Restaurants argue that the flat fee helps guarantee a living wage to staff in the notoriously pricey Bay Area.

Business Hours

Many restaurants are open seven days a week, though some close Sunday and/or Monday night. Breakfast is served 8am to 10am; lunch is usually 11:30am to 2:30pm; dinner starts around 5:30pm, with last service between 9pm and 9:30pm on weekdays and 10pm at weekends. Weekend brunch is from 10am to 2pm.

Fine Dining

San Francisco is a magnet for award-winning chefs – many of whom just so happen to be women, including Iron Chef Traci des Jardins, James Beard Award–winner Nancy Oakes, Michelin-starred Dominique Crenn and Melissa Perello – and you may recognize their names from TV.

Reservations are a must at popular San Francisco restaurants – the sooner you make them, the better the options you'll have. Most restaurants have online reservations through their websites or OpenTable (www.opentable.com), but if the system shows no availability, call the restaurant directly – some seats may be held for phone reservations and early-evening walk-ins, and there may be last-minute cancellations or room at the bar. Landmark restaurants like French Laundry (p220) and Chez Panisse (p210) and small, celebrated SF bistros like Benu (p92), Rich Table (p186), State Bird Provisions (p138) and Frances (p173) offer limited seating, so call a month ahead and take what's available.

Walk-ins Your best bets are restaurant-dense areas like the Mission, Japantown, the Avenues or North Beach – go early (5pm-ish) or eat late (after 9pm).

Local and sustainable If you don't see sourcing footnotes or mentions of sustainable, organic ingredients on the menu, ask – it's an SF server's job to know where and how your food was sourced.

Dietary restrictions Mention any dietary limitations when reserving, and you should be cheerfully accommodated.

California casual Nice jeans are acceptable and personable interactions appreciated. Service is well informed and friendly, never snooty.

Nontraditional Dining

POP-UP RESTAURANTS

To test out possible restaurant ventures or trial new culinary concepts, guest chefs occasionally commandeer SF bars, cafes and restaurants with creative pop-up menus. Educational community food nonprofit 18 Reasons (p165) hosts pop-ups where chefs share cooking tips with diners. For a four-day pop-up feast, plan your visit to coincide with **Eat Drink SF** (☑415-781-5348; www.eatdrink-sf.com; ☺last weekend Aug).

Look for announcements on EaterSF (http://sf.eater.com), Grub Street San Francisco (http://sanfrancisco.grubstreet.com) and Inside Scoop (http://insidescoopsf.sfgate.com) for upcoming pop-ups. Bring cash and arrive early: most pop-ups don't accept credit cards, and popular dishes run out fast.

Top: Boulette's Larder (p89)

Bottom: Dim sum restaurant

T PHOTOGRAPHY/SHUTTERSTOCK ©

SF CRAVING: DIM SUM

Since one of three San Franciscans has Asian roots, SF's go-to comfort foods aren't just burgers and pizza – though you'll find plenty of those – but also kimchi, tandoori and, above all, dim sum. Dim sum is Cantonese for what's known in Mandarin as *xiao che* ('small eats'); some also call it *yum cha* ('drink tea'). Traditionally, waitstaff roll carts past your table with steaming baskets of dumplings, platters of garlicky greens and, finally, crispy sweet sesame balls.

But at SF's new upscale dim-sum specialists like **China Live** (p120), **Dragon Beaux** (p200) and **Hakkasan** (p91), you'll find succulent duck dumplings worthy of fine-dining tasting menus. For James Beard–acclaimed California twists on dim-sum dining, reserve at fusion sensations **State Bird Provisions** (p138) or **Mister Jiu's** (p121). Expect a queue for traditional dim-sum brunches along Geary St and in Chinatown, and for gourmet *bao* (buns) at the **Chairman** (p28) food truck.

FOOD TRUCKS & CARTS

Feeling hungry and adventurous? You're in the right place. Just be street-food smart: look for prominently displayed permits as a guarantee of proper food preparation, refrigeration and regulated working conditions.

SF's largest gathering of gourmet trucks is Off the Grid (p62), which hosts several events weekly. Sunday brings OTG picnics to the Presidio, Friday sees 30-plus food trucks circle their wagons in Fort Mason, and Thursday is a food-truck hootenanny in the Haight with live music. Trucks and carts are mostly cash-only businesses, and lines for popular trucks can take 10 to 20 minutes.

For the best selection of gourmet food on the go, don't miss the Ferry Building (p79) kiosks and Saturday farmers market. An excellent pre-party option before hitting SoMa clubs is SoMa StrEat Food Park (p91), a permanent food-truck parking lot with over a dozen trucks, picnic tables, beer and DJs.

For the best gourmet to go, try empanadas from **El Sur** (📞415-530-2803; www.elsursf.com; empanadas $3.50-5), clamshell buns stuffed with duck and mango from the **Chairman** (www.thechairmantruck.com; buns $3.75-6, bowls $7-9), free-range herbed roast chicken from **Roli Roti** (www.roliroti.com; mains $8-11), and dessert from Kara's Cupcakes (p65).

You can track food trucks at Roaming Hunger (www.roaminghunger.com/sf/vendors) or on Twitter (@MobileCravings/sf-food-trucks,@streetfoodsf).

Start getting hungry now for August's SF Street Food Festival (www.sfstreetfoodfest.com), featuring hundreds of mom-and-pop food vendors – proceeds provide training and kitchens for low-income culinary entrepreneurs.

Eating by Neighborhood

➡ **The Marina, Fisherman's Wharf & the Piers** (p62) Fusion fare in the Marina; seafood and fast food on Fisherman's Wharf; food trucks in Fort Mason.

➡ **Downtown, Civic Center & SoMa** (p88) Vietnamese and tandoori in the Tenderloin; bar bites, tasting menus and sandwiches in SoMa; business lunches and date-night dinners downtown.

➡ **North Beach & Chinatown** (p118) Pizza, pasta and experimental California fare in North Beach.

➡ **The Mission & Potrero Hill** (p151) Tacos, innovative California food, vegetarian, and Asian soul food.

➡ **The Castro & Noe Valley** (p172) Bistros and burgers in the Castro.

➡ **The Haight & Hayes Valley** (p182) Market-inspired menus, sunny brunches and dessert in Hayes Valley.

➡ **Golden Gate Park & the Avenues** (p200) Dim sum, surfer cuisine and international desserts in the Avenues.

Lonely Planet's Top Choices

In Situ (p92) SFMOMA's gallery of contemporary cuisine serves global top chefs' signature dishes.

Benu (p92) Fine dining meets DJ styling in ingenious remixes of Eastern classics and the best ingredients in the West.

La Taqueria (p151) Serving some of SF's most memorable meals, wrapped in foil and under $9.

Rich Table (p186) Tasty, inventive California fare with French fine-dining finesse makes you feel clever by association.

Cala (p186) Highly original San Francisco soul food celebrates Mexican heritage and local ingredients.

Al's Place (p153) California dreams are shared here, with imaginative plates of pristine seafood and seasonal specialties.

Best NorCal Cuisine

Rich Table (p186) See Top Choices.

Al's Place (p153) See Top Choices.

Chez Panisse (p210) Alice Waters' Berkeley bistro has championed local, sustainable, fabulous food since 1971.

French Laundry (p220) Napa's finest multicourse feasts celebrate the good life and the bounty of California.

Jardinière (p186) Mood-altering, luxuriant meals cater to California's decadent appetites.

Outerlands (p202) Organic surfer fare with hearty flavor to help diners take on big waves.

Serpentine (p156) For flavor-packed brunches, raid farmers markets and spice racks citywide – or just come here.

Best Local Fusion

Benu (p92) See Top Choices.

In Situ (p92) See Top Choices.

Cala (p186) See Top Choices.

Mister Jiu's (p121) Celebrate gold-rush-style, with reinvented Cal-Chinese banquets and killer cocktails.

Acquerello (p136) Spaghetti Western fine dining, with creative handmade pastas and California quail salads.

Liholiho Yacht Club (p90) Hawaiian-inspired fare with sun-drenched flavor and aloha-inducing cocktails.

Brenda's Meat & Three (p182) Cal-Creole brunches bring Southern comfort north of SF's Panhandle.

Ichi Sushi (p156) Sustainable Pacific seafood dressed to impress – no soy sauce necessary.

Best Meals Under $10

La Taqueria (p151) See Top Choices.

Off the Grid (p62) First course: empanadas; next course: pork-belly bun; cupcakes for dessert.

Cinderella Russian Bakery (p200) Piroshki pastry and dumplings bring SF's Russian community to Cinderella's sociable parklet.

Craftsman & Wolves (p152) Not baked goods, but baked greats – try Thai-coconut-curry scones and the ingenious Rebel Within.

Mill (p182) Just-baked bread slathered with fresh California almond butter.

Liguria Bakery (p118) Foccacia hot from the 100-year-old oven.

La Palma Mexicatessen (p152) Beyond tacos: Salvadoran *pupusas* (tortilla pockets) and *huaraches* (stuffed savory pancakes) handmade with organic masa.

Best Al Fresco Frisco

Boulette's Larder (p89) Sunny, market-inspired lunches at the Ferry Building waterfront.

Greens (p65) Sitting on the dock of the bay, with chili that will distract you from the Golden Gate Bridge.

Beach Chalet (p202) Toast the bison with bubbly over brunches in Golden Gate Park's heated backyard.

Mission Cheese (p152) Gloat over your California goat-cheese selections and trend-spot Mission street fashion.

Cafe Flore (p173) Brunch on the glassed-in patio at the center of the gay universe.

Greens (p65) At the to-go counter, get black-bean chili and portobello panini to enjoy with bayfront Golden Gate Bridge views.

Irish coffees at Buena Vista Cafe (p69)

Drinking & Nightlife

No matter what you're having, SF bars, cafes and clubs are here to oblige. But why stick to your usual, when there are California wines, Bay spirits, microbrews and local roasts to try? Adventurous drinking is abetted by local bartenders, who've been making good on gold-rush-saloon history. SF baristas take their cappuccino-foam drawings seriously and, around here, DJs invent their own software.

Cocktails

Tonight you're gonna party like it's 1899. Gone are the mad scientist's mixology beakers of five years ago: today SF drink historians are judged by their Old Tom gin selections and vintage tiki barware displays. All that authenticity-tripping over cocktails may sound self-conscious, but after enjoying strong pours at vintage saloons and speakeasies, consciousness is hardly an issue.

➡ **Cost** Happy-hour specials or well drinks run $5 to $8 and gourmet choices with premium hooch run $9 to $15.

➡ **Trendy tiki** Pacific trade winds blow strong through SF happy hours at SF's trendsetting tiki hot spots Pagan Idol (p95), Liholiho Yacht Club (p90) and Smuggler's Cove (p186) – but the Tonga Room (p138) and Trad'r Sam (p202) still set the standard for old-school tiki.

➡ **Local spirits** Top-shelf SF Bay liquor includes St George gin, 1512 Barbershop white rye, Anchor Old Tom gin, Hangar One vodka, Workhorse rye, Spirit Works sloe gin, Old Potrero whiskey and Emperor Norton absinthe.

➡ **Tips** With $1 to $2 per drink, bartenders return the favor with heavy pours next round – that's why it's called getting tip-sy.

Wine

To get the good stuff, you don't need to commit to a bottle or escape to Wine Country. San Francisco restaurants, wine bars and urban wineries are increasingly offering top-notch, small-production California wines *alla spina* (on tap). Organically grown, sustainable and even biodynamic wines feature on most SF restaurant lists.

➡ **Wine Country deals** Plan your trip to Napa or Sonoma for late fall, when you can taste new releases and score harvest specials.

➡ **SF's warehouse wineries** Toast city living at Bluxome Street Winery (p100) and in Dogpatch, where San Francisco's best vintages are blended and served in industrial warehouses.

➡ **Food-truck pairings** Consult the bar's Twitter feed or Facebook page – or see which trucks are around at www.roaminghunger.com/sf/vendors or @MobileCravings/sf-food-trucks on Twitter.

➡ **Cult wine retailers** Bi-Rite (p162), Ferry Plaza Wine Merchant (p95), Dig (p160) and California Wine Merchant (p69) sell hard-to-find wines at reasonable prices.

Beer

SF's first brewery (1849) was built before the city was, and beer has been a staple ever since.

➡ **Cost** Budget $4 to $7 a pint for draft microbrews, $2 to $3 for Pabst Blue Ribbon (PBR) – plus $1 tip.

➡ **Beer gardens** Drink in the great outdoors at Biergarten (p189), Zeitgeist (p158), Beach Chalet (p202) and Wild Side West (p158).

➡ **House brews** It doesn't get more local than beer brewed on-site at the Anchor Brewing Company (p166), 21st Amendment Brewery (p92), Magnolia Brewpub (p183) and Social (p202).

➡ **Brew it yourself** Attend meet-ups with local brewers at the **SF Brewers' Guild** (www.sf brewersguild.org); pick up trade secrets at City Beer Store & Tasting Room (p99); or take a Workshop (www.workshopsf.org) brewing class.

Cafe Scene

When San Francisco couples break up, the thorniest issue is: who gets the cafe? San Franciscans are fiercely loyal to specific roasts and baristas – especially in the Mission, Hayes Valley and North Beach –

NEED TO KNOW

Opening Hours

Downtown and SoMa bars draw happy-hour crowds from 4pm to 7pm; otherwise, bars are hopping by 9pm, with last call 10:30pm to 11:30pm weekdays and 1:30am weekends. Clubs kick in around 10pm and many close at 2am.

Smoking

Not legal indoors. Some bars have smoking patios, including Rye (p101), Bar Agricole (p98), Hemlock Tavern (p104) and Irish Bank (p95), or backyards El Rio (p158), Wild Side West (p158) and Zeitgeist (p158) – otherwise, you'll be puffing on the sidewalk.

Websites

To find out what's up where this weekend, check **SF Weekly** (www.sfweekly.com) and **Funcheap SF** (http://sf.funcheap.com), and skim calendars at **SF Station** (www.sfstation.com), **UrbanDaddy** (www.urbandaddy.com/home/sfo) and **Thrillist** (www.thrillist.com).

and the majority of first internet dates meet on neutral coffee grounds. When using free cafe wi-fi, remember: order something every hour, deal with interruptions graciously and don't leave laptops unattended.

➡ **Cost** $2 to $4 for American coffee and $3 to $5 for espresso drinks.

➡ **Tip** Leave a buck in the tip jar for espresso drinks, especially when staying a while.

➡ **Cell phones** Texting is fine, but phone calls are many baristas' pet peeve.

Clubbing

DJs set the tone at clubs in SF, where the right groove gets everyone on the dancefloor – blending gay and straight in a giddy motion blur. You'll usually only wait 15 minutes to get in anywhere, unless you're stumbling drunk.

➡ **Cost** Most clubs charge $10 to $25 at the door. For discounted admission, show up before 10pm or sign up to the club's online guest list (look for a VIP or RSVP link). Seating may be reserved for bottle service at high-end clubs.

Bar Agricole (p98)

→ **Dress code** SF is pretty casual, though club bouncers do turn away people wearing flip-flops, shorts or T-shirts (unless they're spiffy), especially at swing and salsa clubs.

→ **Late night** Last call at many clubs is around 11:30pm on weekdays and 1:30am at weekends. Many clubs close around 2am, though a few after-hours clubs like EndUp (p99) rage until the sun rises.

Drinking & Nightlife by Neighborhood

→ **The Marina, Fisherman's Wharf & the Piers** (p68) Straight bars in the Marina.

→ **Downtown, Civic Center & SoMa** (p94) Dives, chichi lounges and old-school gay bars in Civic Center and the Tenderloin; clubs, art lounges, drag showcases and men's cruising bars in SoMa.

→ **North Beach & Chinatown** (p121) Barbary Coast saloons, historic dives, cafes and deco lounges in North Beach and Chinatown.

→ **The Mission & Potrero Hill** (p157) Coffee roasters, hipster saloons, friendly wine bars, salsa clubs, straight-friendly LGBT clubs in the Mission.

→ **The Castro & Noe Valley** (p173) Gay bars in the Castro.

→ **The Haight, NoPa & Hayes Valley** (p186) Cheap whiskey, serious beer and boho lounges in the Haight; wine bars and coffee kiosks in Hayes Valley.

→ **Golden Gate Park & the Avenues** (p202) Irish and tiki bars in the Richmond District; coffee and beer in the Sunset District.

Lonely Planet's Top Choices

Comstock Saloon (p121) Vintage Wild West saloon with potent, period-perfect concoctions and dainty bar bites.

Bar Agricole (p98) Drink your way to a history degree with well-researched cocktails – anything with hellfire bitters earns honors.

Specs (p121) Swill Anchor Steam by the pitcher with salty characters in SF's definitive Merchant Marine dive.

Pagan Idol (p95) Tiki to a T, with Hemingway-esque rum drinks served in skulls and volcano eruptions.

Bourbon & Branch (p101) Not since Prohibition have secret passwords and gin knowledge proved so handy.

Trick Dog (p158) The ultimate theme bar switches up drinks and decor every few months to match SF obsessions: murals, horoscopes, conspiracy theories...

Best Retro Cocktails

Bar Agricole (p98) See Top Choices.

Pagan Idol (p95) See Top Choices.

Comstock Saloon (p121) See Top Choices.

Bourbon & Branch (p101) See Top Choices.

Smuggler's Cove (p186) Roll with the rum punches at this Barbary Coast shipwreck bar.

%ABV (p157) Find hooch happiness downstairs, or hit cocktail-pairing heaven in the upstairs speakeasy.

Local Edition (p95) Extra, extra – read all about specialty cocktails in the Hearst newspaper building's speakeasy.

Best Wine Selections

Hôtel Biron (p189) Walk-in closet wine bar with small, standout selection.

20 Spot (p158) Expect the unexpected: unusual wines and double-deviled eggs in a former punk-record storefront.

Terroir Natural Wine Merchant (p100) Red, white and green: sustainably produced wines from cult winemakers.

Bluxome Street Winery (p100) Sample the latest SF vintages at this SoMa warehouse winery's tasting bar.

Best for Beer

Specs (p121) See Top Choices.

Toronado (p188) Beer for every season and any reason – summer ales, holiday barley wines, Oktoberfest wheats.

Zeitgeist (p158) Surly women bartenders tap 40 microbrews to guzzle in the beer garden.

City Beer Store & Tasting Room (p99) Beer sommeliers earn the title here, with expert-led tastings, brewing and pairing tips.

Biergarten (p189) A shipping-container bar keeps this beer garden well watered.

Plough & Stars (p203) Emerald Isle gem just off the Pacific, with proper Guinness and live bluegrass, Celtic and folk jams.

Best Cafes

Caffe Trieste (p124) Legendary North Beach cafe, fueling epic Beat poetry and weekend accordion jams since the '50s.

Ritual Coffee Roasters (p158) Heady roasts, local art and sociable seating in a cult roastery-cafe.

Réveille (p125) Sunny flatiron cafe with stellar espresso drinks, decadent pastries and sidewalk people-watching.

Sightglass Coffee (p98) This SoMa roastery looks industrial but serves small-batch roasts from family farms.

Blue Bottle Coffee Kiosk (p188) The back-alley garage that kicked off the Third Wave coffee-roastery craze.

Trouble Coffee & Coconut Club (p202) Driftwood seating, espresso in stoneware, and surfers hunched over coconuts.

Best Dance Clubs

EndUp (p99) Epic 24-hour dance sessions in an urban-legendary SoMa gay club since 1973.

DNA Lounge (p106) Known for booty-shaking mash-ups, burlesque, Goth, and roof-raising live acts.

Cat Club (p99) Something for everyone: '80s one-hit wonders, '90s mega-pop and go-go bondage.

El Rio (p158) Get down and funky in the Mission and flirt internationally in the backyard.

Club OMG (p99) Mixed-gender club where the gays come out to play.

Rickshaw Stop (p101) Beats won't quit at this all-ages, all-orientations, all-fabulous shoebox club.

Entertainment

SF is one of the top five US cities for number of creative types per square mile – and when they all take to the stage, look out. Though there's a world-famous orchestra, opera, jazz center, film festival, theater and ballet, the scene isn't all about marquee names: you can see cutting-edge dance, comedy and music for the price of an IMAX movie.

Opera & Classical Music

Between San Francisco Opera (p102) seasons, hear opera by the Grammy-winning, 12-man chorus **Chanticleer** (www.chanticleer.org) and SF's **Pocket Opera Company** (www.pocket opera.org; ⊘Feb-Jun).

Michael Tilson Thomas conducts the nine-time Grammy-winning San Francisco Symphony (p102), and **San Francisco Performances** (www.performances.org) hosts world-class classical performances at the Herbst Theater. Revolution Cafe (p161) hosts chamber music in the Mission at Classical Revolution.

➡ **Symphony and opera season** Typically runs September through June; check **SF Classical Voice** (www.sfcv.org) for dates.

➡ **Free music** SF Opera and SF Symphony perform gratis at the Stern Grove Festival (p21). Stop by Old St Mary's (p117) for regular Tuesday noon concerts, and check http://noontimeconcerts.org for other donation-requested concerts.

➡ **Bargain tickets** SF Opera offers America's least expensive opera tickets (starting from $10); SF Symphony offers rush tickets and SoundBox rehearsal-stage shows ($20 to $35).

Live Music

Eclectic SF clubs host funk, reggae, bluegrass and punk; check online calendars.

➡ **Bluegrass** Hear the original music of SF's gold rush at the Hardly Strictly Bluegrass festival (p21) and at Berkeley's Freight & Salvage Coffeehouse

(p212). Host Peter Thompson brings encyclopedic knowledge of American roots music to KALW's breakthrough bluegrass national public radio program, **Bluegrass Signal** (www.kalw.org; 91.7FM).

➡ **Funk and hip-hop** Oakland has tougher rap and faster beats, but SF plays it loose and funky at Mezzanine (p107) and the Independent (p190).

➡ **Jazz** Major jazz talents are in residence year-round at the SFJAZZ Center (p189), and jazz ensembles regularly play the Revolution Cafe (p161), Chapel (p160), Café Royale (p104), Club Deluxe (p190) and Doc's Lab (p125).

➡ **Punk** Punk's not dead at **Bottom of the Hill** (p161), **Edinburgh Castle** (p101), the **Hemlock Tavern** (p104) and **Slim's** (p105).

➡ **Rock** Psychedelic rock legends played at the Fillmore (p140), but alt-rock storms the stage at Outside Lands (p21), Warfield (p104) and the Great American Music Hall (p103).

Theater

Before winning Tonys and a Pulitzer Prize, *Angels in America* got its wings at the American Conservatory Theater (p103), and you can see the next theatrical breakthrough in progress at the ACT's new Strand Theater (p103). In summer the **San Francisco Mime Troupe** (www.sfmt.org) performs free political-comedy satire in Dolores Park, while the **SF Shakespeare Festival** (www.sfshakes.org; ⊘Sep) is held gratis in the Presidio.

➡ **Theatre Bay Area** (www.theatrebayarea.org) is a comprehensive calendar of 100 Bay Area theater companies.

→ **Broadway shows** See SF listings at SHN (www.shnsf.com).

→ **Tickets** Marquee shows run $35 to $150, but same-day, half-price tickets are often available. Indie theater runs $10 to $35.

Comedy & Spoken Word

For laughs, try drag comedy at Oasis (p104), Marsh (p160) monologues, upstart comics at Doc's Lab (p125), campy Beach Blanket Babylon (p125), HBO headliners at Cobb's Comedy Club (p125) and the Punch Line (p103), or get onstage with BATS Improv (p69) comedy workshops.

This town has tales like you wouldn't believe – hear every eyebrow-raising detail at SF's annual Litquake (p40), the San Francisco Main Library (p85) and Booksmith (p189) author events. For raucous readings, check out Writers with Drinks at the Make-Out Room (p161), storytelling slams at Public Works (p106), Pint-Sized Plays at PianoFight (p103), and Mortified's teen-diary excerpts at the DNA Lounge (p106).

Dance

SF supports the longest-running US ballet company, the San Francisco Ballet (p103), and multiple independent troupes at the Yerba Buena Center for the Arts (p105). Experimental styles are championed at the Oberlin Dance Collective (p160) and Joe Goode Performance Group (p161), and you can invent your own style at Dance Mission (p166). **Dancers' Group** (www.dancersgroup. org) has a comprehensive dance calendar.

Cinema

Cinemaniacs adore SF's vintage movie palaces, including the Roxie (p160), Castro (p175) and Balboa (p203) cinemas. For major releases and film-festival favorites in a certified-green cinema, head to Sundance

NEED TO KNOW

Arts Calendar

Check **KQED's The Do List** (http://ww2. kqed.org/arts/programs/the-do-list/) for an excellent selection of upcoming performing-arts events.

Discounts

Sign up at **Gold Star Events** (www.goldstarevents.com) for discounts on comedy, theater, concerts and opera, or stop by the Tix Bay Area (p104) Union Sq ticket booth for cheap tickets for same-day or next-day shows.

(sidebar text: PLAN YOUR TRIP ENTERTAINMENT)

Kabuki Cinema (p140). Foreign films and award contenders show at the Embarcadero Center Cinema (p104), while IMAX blockbusters screen at AMC Loews Metreon 16 (p107).

→ **Festivals** Beyond the SF International Film Festival (p20), the city hosts LGBT (p21), Jewish and Arab film festivals.

→ **Tickets** Most tickets run $10 to $16, with weekday matinees around $8.

Entertainment by Neighborhood

→ **Downtown, Civic Center & SoMa** (p69) Symphony, opera, theater, punk, jazz, rock and comedy.

→ **North Beach & Chinatown** (p125) Comedy, jazz, folk, blues and spoken word.

→ **The Mission & Potrero Hill** (p160) Dance, alt-bands, punk, bluegrass, experimental theater and spoken word.

→ **Golden Gate Park & the Avenues** (p203) Festivals and free concerts.

Lonely Planet's Top Choices

San Francisco Symphony (p102) Sets the tempo for modern classical, with guests like Metallica and Rufus Wainwright.

SFJAZZ Center (p189) Top talents reinvent standards and create new works inspired by mariachis, skateboarders, Hunter S Thompson and Joni Mitchell.

San Francisco Opera (p102) Divas like Renée Fleming bring down the house with classics and contemporary works including Stephen King's *Dolores Claiborne*.

American Conservatory Theater (p103) Daring theater, from operas by Tom Waits and William S Burroughs to controversial David Mamet plays – plus experimental works at the Strand Theater.

Castro Theatre (p175) Organ overtures and cult classics with enthusiastic audience participation raise the roof at this art-deco movie palace.

Best for Laughs

Oasis (p104) Drag comedy variety acts so outrageously funny, you'll laugh until you cough up glitter.

Cobb's Comedy Club (p125) Comics from the streets to Comedy Central test risky new material.

Beach Blanket Babylon (p125) Laugh your wig off with San Francisco's over-the-top Disney-drag cabaret.

Punch Line (p103) Breakthrough comedians like Ellen Degeneres, Chris Rock and Margaret Cho started here.

Marsh (p160) Monologues range from uproarious to heartbreaking, sometimes in the same act.

Best for Theater & Dance

American Conservatory Theater (p103) See Top Choices.

San Francisco Ballet (p103) Elegant lines and gorgeous original staging from America's oldest ballet company.

Oberlin Dance Collective (p160) Style and substance in balance, with muscular, meaningful original choreography.

Yerba Buena Center for the Arts (p105) Modern dance troupes throw down and represent SF's cutting edge.

Magic Theatre (p69) Original works by major playwrights, performed in a converted army base.

Best Live Music Venues

San Francisco Symphony (p102) See Top Choices.

SFJAZZ Center (p189) See Top Choices.

San Francisco Opera (p102) See Top Choices.

Fillmore Auditorium (p140) Rock-legendary since the '60s, with the psychedelic posters to prove it.

Great American Music Hall (p103) Marquee acts in a historic, intimate venue that was once a bordello.

Slim's (p105) Big names play this smallish club, from punk legends to surprise shows by the likes of Prince.

Best for Movies

Castro Theatre (p175) Organ overtures and cult classics with enthusiastic audience participation raise the roof at this art-deco movie palace.

SF International Film Festival (p20) Breakthrough indies and stealth Oscar favorites premiere here, with directors from Afghanistan to Uganda and movie-star Q&As.

Sundance Kabuki Cinema (p140) Balcony bars, reserved seating and zero ads make great films better.

Roxie Cinema (p160) Offers cult classics, documentary premieres and indie films not yet distributed, in a vintage cinema.

Balboa Theatre (p203) Art-deco cinema features first-run and art-house films, plus family matinees.

Best Free Entertainment

Hardly Strictly Bluegrass (p21) See bluegrass greats like Alison Krauss jam alongside Elvis Costello, Patti Smith and Dwight Yoakam – for free.

Stern Grove Festival (p21) SFJAZZ legends and symphony soloists perform in the great outdoors.

San Francisco Mime Troupe (p34) Social satire, Kabuki and musical comedy make scenes in Dolores Park.

SF Shakespeare Festival (p34) Audiences warm to *The Winter's Tale* at foggy Presidio performances.

Amoeba Music (p190) Free in-store concerts by rock and alt-pop radio favorites, plus oddballs and cult bands.

 LGBT+

It doesn't matter where you're from, who you love or who's your daddy: if you're here and queer, welcome home. San Francisco is America's pinkest city, and though New York Marys may call it the retirement home of the young – the sidewalks roll up early here – there's nowhere easier to be out and proud.

LGBT+ Scene

In San Francisco, you don't need to trawl the urban underworld for a gay scene. The intersection of 18th and Castro is the historic center of the gay world, but dancing queens head to SoMa for thump-thump clubs.

So where are all the ladies? They're busy sunning on the patio at Wild Side West (p158) or El Rio (p158), screening documentaries at the Roxie Cinema (p160), inventing new technologies at SF hackerspaces, working it out on the dancefloor at Rickshaw Stop (p101) or Oasis (p104), and/or raising kids in Noe Valley and Bernal Heights. The Mission remains the preferred 'hood of alt-chicks, dykes, trans female-to-males (FTMs) and flirty femmes.

Gender need not apply in SF, where the DMV officially acknowledges trans-queer identities. Drag shows happen nightly, though you'll never need a professional reason to blur gender lines here – next to baseball, gender-bending is SF's favorite sport.

Party Planning

On Sundays in the 1950s, SF bars held gay old times euphemistically called 'tea dances' – and Sunday afternoons remain a happening time to go out, most notably at the Eagle Tavern (p98) – but most parties happen Thursday through Sunday nights. **Comfort & Joy** (http://playajoy.org), the queer Burning Man collective, lists happening dance parties and creative community events.

NEWS & EVENTS

San Francisco has two gay newspapers, plus a glossy nightlife rag.

➡ **Bay Area Reporter** (www.ebar.com) Released every Wednesday since 1971; news and events.

➡ **San Francisco Bay Times** (http://sfbaytimes.com) News and calendar listings.

➡ **Gloss Magazine** Nightlife and parties.

Women's Community Venues

➡ **Women's Building** (p275) For organizations.

➡ **Lyon-Martin Women's Health Services** (http://lyon-martin.org) For health and support.

➡ **Brava Theater** (p160) For arts.

Support & Activism

➡ **LYRIC** (http://lyric.org) For queer youth.

➡ **Human Rights Campaign Action Center & Store** (p177) For political organizing.

➡ **GLBT History Museum** (p169) For context.

➡ **Transgender Law Center** (http://transgenderlawcenter.org) For civil-rights activism and support.

➡ **Homobiles** (p270) For nonprofit LGBT taxis.

LGBT+ by Neighborhood

➡ **Downtown, Civic Center & SoMa** Raging dance clubs, leather bars, drag shows and men's sex clubs in SoMa; bars, trans venues and queer cabaret in the Tenderloin.

➡ **The Mission & Potrero Hill** Women's and trans-queer bars, arts venues and community spaces in the Mission.

➡ **The Castro & Noe Valley** Gay history, activism and men's cruising bars in the Castro; LGBT family scene in Noe Valley.

Lonely Planet's Top Choices

Pride (p21) The most extravagant celebration on the planet culminates in the Dyke March, Pink Party and an exhilarating 1.2-million-strong Pride Parade.

Human Rights Campaign Action Center & Store (p177) Been there, signed the petition, bought the T-shirt supporting civil rights at Harvey Milk's camera storefront.

Castro Theatre (p175) The San Francisco LGBTQ Film Festival premieres here; also screens audience-participatory cult classics.

Oasis (p104) SF's dedicated drag venue, hostessed by drag icons Heklinka and D'Arcy Drollinger.

GLBT History Museum (p169) Proud moments and historic challenges, captured for posterity.

Best for Women

Wild Side West (p158) Cheers to queers and beers in the herstory-making sculpture garden.

El Rio (p158) Mix it up with world music, salsa, house, live bands and SF's flirtiest patio.

Beaux (p174) The weekly 'Pussy Party' happens Wednesday.

Rickshaw Stop (p101) All-ages parties and all-out estrogen at semi-monthly Cockblock.

Women's Building (p275) Glorious murals crown this community institution.

Brava Theater (p160) Original shows by, for and about lesbians and trans women.

Oasis (p104) Women bring it all to the dancefloor monthly at UHaul.

Best Dancefloors

Aunt Charlie's Lounge (p101) Knock-down, drag-out winner for gender-bending shows and dancefloor freakiness in a tiny space.

Stud (p98) Shows and DJs nightly, plus the tantalizing aroma of bourbon, cologne and testosterone.

Powerhouse (p99) DJs most nights, gogo dancers and strong drinks at the classic SoMa cruise bar.

EndUp (p99) Hit your groove Saturday night and work it until Monday.

Best Daytime Scene

Dolores Park (p147) Sun and cityscapes on hillside 'Gay Beach,' plus protests and the Hunky Jesus Contest.

Baker Beach (p56) Only Baker Beach regulars know you can get goose bumps *there*.

Cafe Flore (p173) Fab gay scene-watching: blind dates, parents with LGBT kids, occasional dogs in drag.

El Rio (p158) Sunday's Daytime Realness brings back-patio drag fabulousness.

Eagle Tavern (p98) At Sunday-afternoon beer busts, leather daddies drink alongside gay scenesters.

Best for Gay Old Times with Straight Friends

Pride (p21) See Top Choices.

GLBT History Museum (p169) See Top Choices.

Castro Theatre (p175) See Top Choices.

AsiaSF (p106) Waitresses serve drinks and sass with a not-so-secret secret: they're in drag.

San Francisco LGBTQ Film Festival (p21) Queer premieres of works from everywhere from Argentina to Vietnam.

Best Places to Stay

Parker Guest House (p235) Top choice for comfort and style.

Inn on Castro (p236) Vintage Victorian styled with disco-era furnishings.

Willows Inn (p235) Best for budgeteers who don't mind sharing a bath.

Beck's Motor Lodge (p235) Upgraded motel rooms in the heart of the Castro.

Piedmont Boutique (p191)

Shopping

All those tricked-out dens, well-stocked spice racks and fabulous ensembles don't just pull themselves together – San Franciscans scour their city for them. Eclectic originality is SF's signature style, and that's not one-stop shopping. But consider the thrill of the hunt: while shopping, you can watch fish theater, make necklaces from zippers and trade fashion tips with professional drag queens.

Adventures in Retail

Indie designers and vintage shops supply original style on SF's most boutique-studded streets: Haight, Valencia, Hayes, upper Grant, Fillmore, Union and Polk.

STYLE SECRETS

➡ **Union Square** Ringed by department stores and megabrands, including Neiman Marcus, Macy's, Saks and Apple.

➡ **Valencia Street** Made-in-SF gifts, West Coast style and scents, pirate supplies.

➡ **Haight Street** Vintage, drag glam, steampunk gear and hats galore – plus anarchist comics, vinyl LPs and skateboards to complete your look.

➡ **Hayes Valley** Local designers, gourmet treats, home decor.

➡ **Powell Street** Lined with flagship stores and cheap glamour from Gap, Uniqlo, H&M and Urban Outfitters.

Retail Events

Want to take your shopping spree up a notch? San Franciscans are a festive bunch with wildly diverse interests – no matter

NEED TO KNOW

Sales Tax

Combined SF city and California state sales taxes tack 8.75% onto the price of your purchase. This tax is not refundable.

Business Hours

Most stores are open daily from 10am to 6pm or 7pm, though hours often run 11am to 8pm Saturday and 11am to 6pm Sunday. Stores in the Mission and the Haight tend to open later and keep erratic hours; many downtown stores stay open until 8pm.

Returns

Try before you buy and ask about return policies. Many stores offer returns for store credit only, so, when in doubt, consider a gift certificate. In California, they never expire – and you can often use them online.

Websites

Check **Urban Daddy** (www.urbandaddy. com) for store openings and pop-ups, **Thrillist** (www.thrillist.com) for gear and gadgets, and **Refinery 29** (www.refinery 29.com) for sales and trends.

what you're looking for, there's an event in San Francisco to celebrate it.

Art Market San Francisco (http://art marketsf.com/; ⊙last weekend Apr) At Fort Mason, San Francisco's signature art fair attracts curators with major museum pieces but also sells affordable original works for as little as $80. For further art action, look for renegade satellite fairs in Fort Mason's parking lot and nearby motels.

West Coast Craft (http://westcoastcraft.com; ⊙mid-Jun & mid-Nov) That laid-back, homespun California look takes handiwork – or you can leave it to the pros at West Coast Craft, featuring 100-plus indie makers. Held at Fort Mason.

Litquake (www.litquake.org; ⊙2nd week Oct) Stranger-than-fiction literary events take place during SF's outlandish literary festival, with authors leading lunchtime story sessions and spilling trade secrets over drinks at the legendary Lit Crawl.

Haight Ashbury Street Fair (www.haight ashburystreetfair.org; ⊙mid-Jun) Free music on two stages, plus macramé, tie-dye and herbal brownies surreptitiously for sale – the Summer of Love stages a comeback in the Haight every year since 1977, when Harvey Milk helped make the first Haight Street Fair happen.

Green Festival (www.greenfestivals.org; ⊙mid-Nov) Energy-saving spotlights are turned on green cuisine, technology and fashion during the three-day Green Festival.

Shopping by Neighborhood

➡ **The Marina, Fisherman's Wharf & the Piers** (p70) Date outfits, girly accessories, wine and design in the Marina.

➡ **Downtown, Civic Center & SoMa** (p107) Department stores, global megabrands, discount retail and Apple's flagship store.

➡ **Nob Hill, Russian Hill & Fillmore** (p140) Home design, stationery, toys, accessories and anime in Japantown; designer clothes, jewelry and decor in Pacific Heights and Russian Hill.

➡ **The Mission & Potrero Hill** (p162) Local makers, community-supported bookstores, indie art galleries, artisan foods, dandy style, vintage whatever.

➡ **The Haight, NoPa & Hayes Valley** (p190) Design boutiques, decor, food and coffee in Hayes Valley; quirky gifts and accessories in NoPa; head shops, music, vintage and skate gear in the Haight.

Lonely Planet's Top Choices

City Lights (p115) If you can't find nirvana in the Poetry Chair upstairs, try Lost Continents in the basement.

826 Valencia (p147) Your friendly neighborhood pirate-supply store and publishing house; proceeds support on-site youth writing programs.

Gravel & Gold (p162) Get good Californian vibrations from G&G's SF-made, feel-good clothing and beach-shack housewares.

Little Paper Planes (p162) Original gifts by indie makers, gallery-ready clothing and works on paper from LPP's artist-residency program.

Heath Ceramics (p164) The local, handmade tableware of choice for SF's star chefs, in essential modern shapes and appetizing earthy colors.

Park Life (p203) Art, books, Aesthetics team T-shirts and design objects make SF seem exceptionally gifted.

Legion (p126) Striking sculptural styles good to go from downtown galleries to SoMa clubs.

Best SF Fashion Designers

Gravel & Gold (p162) See Top Choices.

Paloma (p190) Retro-motorcycle-gang scarves, billiard-ball cocktail rings and handmade leather bags banged out on-site.

Aggregate Supply (p163) Pop-art windbreakers and California tees from Turk+Taylor.

Nooworks (p163) Eighties new-wave designs reinvented with edgy art-schooled graphics.

Amour Vert (p191) Feel-good fashion: flattering silhouettes cut from earth-friendly materials.

Baggu (p163) Carry your shopping in California-made totes and leather bags.

Workshop Residence (p164) SF artists work with local fabricators to produce artistically inspired, limited-edition fashion, decor and more.

Community Thrift (p162) Vintage scores and local designer seconds, with proceeds benefiting local charities.

Best for the Person Who Has Everything

826 Valencia (p147) See Top Choices.

Good Vibrations (p164) Adult toys, with informed staff and zero judgment.

New People (p141) Ninja shoes, Lolita Goth petticoats and the latest in wooden speakers at this Japantown showcase.

Foggy Notion (p203) Presidio hiking-trail scents, un-washing powder for Ocean Beachy hair and other SF beauty secrets.

Piedmont Boutique (p191) Drag like you mean it, honey: boas, fake-fur booty shorts, airplane earrings.

Loved to Death (p191) Goth jewelry, macabre Victoriana and taxidermied everything.

Best for Eclectic SF Decor

Heath Ceramics (p107) Handmade modern stoneware.

Workshop Residence (p164) Limited-edition designs.

Aria (p126) Anatomical heart diagrams, bottled messages and other vintage decor for incorrigible romantics.

Casa Bonampak (p162) *Papel picado* banners and *piñatas* for every occasion, from Pride to Día de los Muertos.

Rare Device (p190) Handcrafted ceramics, toys and other indie decor beyond standard design magazines.

Adobe Books & Backroom Gallery (p163) Art freshly made on-site by the artist in residence, out-of-print books and 'zines galore.

Best for Gourmet Gifts

Heath Ceramics (p107) See Top Choices.

Bi-Rite (p162) SF's best-curated selection of local artisan chocolates, cured meats and small-production wines.

Rainbow Grocery (p164) Vast selection of NorCal's finest coffees, cheeses and organic airplane snacks.

Poco Dolce (p162) Award-winning savory chocolates destined to convert dessert nonbelievers.

Fatted Calf (p192) Heirloom beans, organic chutneys, sustainable cured meats and other California gourmet essentials.

Omnivore (p176) Rare vintage cookbooks and author events with star chefs.

Sports & Activities

San Franciscans love the outdoors, and their historic conservation efforts have protected acres of parks, beaches and woodlands for all to enjoy. This city lives for sunny days spent biking, skating, surfing and drifting on the Bay. Foggy days are spent making art projects, but nights are for dancing and Giants games.

Spectator Sports

See the Giants play baseball on their home turf at the Giants Stadium (p105). You might be able to catch some Giants action for free at the Embarcadero waterfront boardwalk. The Golden State Warriors (p211) play NBA basketball to win in Oakland, as they did in 2015 – but they're moving back to SF in 2018. To see the 49ers (p166) play, you'll need to drive an hour south of SF to Santa Clara, where they now play in Levi's Stadium.

➡ **Tickets** Book through team websites or try **Ticketmaster** (www.ticketmaster.com). If games are sold out, search the 'Tickets' category on www.craigslist.org.

➡ **Sports coverage** The *San Francisco Chronicle* (www.sfgate.com) offers complete coverage, but *The Examiner* (www.sfexaminer.com) also has sports stats and predictions.

Outdoor Activities

On sunny weekends, SF is out kite-flying, surfing or biking. Even on foggy days, don't neglect sunscreen: UV rays penetrate SF's thin cloud cover.

BICYCLING

Every weekend, thousands of cyclists cross Golden Gate Bridge to explore the Marin Headlands and Mt Tamalpais. Since the 1970s 'Mt Tam' has been the Bay Area's ultimate mountain-biking challenge.

Many SF streets have bicycle lanes and major parks have bike paths. The safest places to cycle in SF are Golden Gate Park (car free on Sunday), the Embarcadero and the wooded Presidio. SF bikers' favorite street-biking route is the green-painted, flat bike lane connecting Market St and Golden Gate Park called the **Wiggle** (www.sfbike.org/our-work/street-campaigns/the-wiggle/).

➡ **City biking maps** The **San Francisco Bicycle Coalition** (p266) produces the *San Francisco Bike Map & Walking Guide,* which outlines the Wiggle route and shows how to avoid traffic and hills.

➡ **Route planning** Put your smart phone to work finding the perfect route using the **San Francisco Bike Route Planner** (http://amarpai.com/bikemap).

➡ **Critical Mass** To claim bicyclists' right of way on city streets, join the **Critical Mass** (www.sfcriticalmass.org/) protest parade on the last Friday of the month. Use caution around motorists, who may be unsympathetic to this interruption in rush-hour traffic, and always yield to pedestrians.

➡ **Riding naked** On Earth Day each April, the **World Naked Bike Ride** (www.sfbikeride.org) protests US dependence on fossil fuels.

RUNNING

Crissy Field (p55) has a 2.5-mile jogging track, and trails run 3 miles through Golden Gate Park (p195) from the Panhandle to Ocean Beach. The Presidio (p62) offers ocean breezes through eucalyptus trees. SF's major races, including **Bay to Breakers** (www.baytobreakers.com; race registration from $65; ☉3rd Sun May), are festive – bring a costume, or at least a feather boa.

SKATING & SKATEBOARDING

SF is the home of roller disco and the skateboard magazine *Thrasher*. Inline skaters skate the Embarcadero Friday nights and disco-skate in Golden Gate Park (p195) on Sunday. Golden Gate Park Bike & Skate (p205) rents inline and four-wheeled roller skates in good weather.

Potrero del Sol/La Raza Skatepark (Map p302; cnr 25th & Utah Sts; ☉8am-9pm; ☐9, 10, 27, 33, 48, Ⓑ24th St Mission) has ramps for kids and bowls for pros. Haight St is urban skating at its obstacle-course best, especially the downhill slide from Baker to Pierce.

For signature SF skateboards and skate gear, hit Mission Skateboards (p164) and FTC Skateboarding (p192); for skate fashion and street graphics, check out Upper Playground (p192).

GOLF

Tee up and enjoy mild weather, clipped greens and gorgeous views on SF's top public courses: Lincoln Park Golf Course (p198) and Golden Gate Municipal Golf Course (p205).

Water Sports & Activities

SURFING & WINDSURFING

About a 90-minute drive south of SF, Santa Cruz is NorCal's top surf destination for kooks (newbies) and pros alike. SF's Ocean Beach (p199) is surfed by locals at daybreak in winter, but these Pacific swells are not for beginners. **Mavericks** (http://titansof mavericks.com) big-wave surfing competition is held each February in Half Moon Bay (30 minutes south of SF); it's strictly invitation-only for pros willing to risk it all.

A safer bet is Bay windsurfing and body-surfing off the beach at Crissy Field (p55). Hit up Mollusk (p204) for specialty boards and Aqua Surf Shop (p204) for rental gear. Check the **surf report** (☎415-273-1618) before you suit up.

SAILING

Sailing is best April through August, and classes and rentals are available from Spinnaker Sailing (p111) or City Kayak (p111). Newbies may feel more comfortable on a catamaran with Adventure Cat (p72) or a booze cruise with Red & White Fleet (p73).

Whale-watching season peaks mid-October through December, when the mighty mammals are easy to spot from Point Reyes. Book whale-watching tours through Oceanic Society Expeditions (p72).

SWIMMING

Ocean Beach (p199) is best for walking – the Pacific undertow is dangerous. Don't turn your back on the Pacific: Northern California occasionally gets 'sneaker waves' that whisk unsuspecting strollers and casual waders out to sea. Hardy swimmers brave chilly Bay waters at Aquatic Park (p59) or Baker Beach (p56), which is nude around the northern end.

➡ **Local pools** The Embarcadero YMCA (p111) has a well-kept pool; city pool schedules are listed at http://sfrecpark.org.

➡ **Alcatraz Sharkfest Swim** Swim 1.5 miles from Alcatraz to Aquatic Park. Entry is $250; check **Envirosports** (www.envirosports.com) for info.

Sports & Activities by Neighborhood

➡ **The Marina, Fisherman's Wharf & the Piers** (p72) Running, biking, windsurfing, kayaking, skating and yoga in the Marina.

➡ **Downtown, Civic Center & SoMa** (p111) Swimming, kayaking and sailing in SoMa.

➡ **The Mission & Potrero Hill** (p165) Arts, dance, skateboarding and yoga in the Mission.

➡ **Golden Gate Park & the Avenues** (p205) Surfing, biking, archery, golf, disc golf and lawn bowling in the Avenues.

Lonely Planet's Top Choices

➡ **Golden Gate Park** (p195) Perfect for cycling, especially on car-free Sundays.

➡ **Potrero del Sol Skatepark** (p43) Skate the bowl if you've got the skills.

➡ **Stow Lake** (p205) Glide across the lake by paddleboat.

➡ **Spinnaker Sailing** (p111) Sail across the bay.

➡ **Crissy Field** (p55) Kitesurfing with a Golden Gate Bridge backdrop.

➡ **Ocean Beach** (p199) Only hardcore surfers brave these riptides.

➡ **Golden Gate Park** (p195) Lawn bowl at the park's historic club.

Explore San Francisco

SAN FRANCISCO'S TOP SIGHTS

Neighborhoods at a Glance

① The Marina, Fisherman's Wharf & the Piers p48

Since the gold rush this waterfront has been the point of entry for new arrivals – and it remains a major attraction for sea-lion antics and getaways to and from Alcatraz. To the west, the Marina has chic boutiques in a former cow pasture and organic dining along the waterfront. At the adjoining Presidio,

you'll encounter Shakespeare on the loose and public nudity on a former army base.

② Downtown, Civic Center & SoMa p74

Downtown has all the urban amenities: art galleries, swanky hotels, first-run theaters, malls and XXX cinemas. Civic Center is a zoning conundrum, with great performances

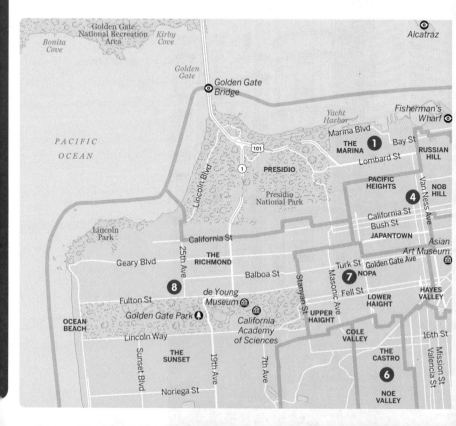

and Asian art treasures on one side of City Hall and dive bars and soup kitchens on the other. Some head to South of Market (SoMa) for high-tech deals, others for high art, but everyone gets down and dirty on the dancefloor.

❸ North Beach & Chinatown p112

Wild parrots circle over Italian cafes and bohemian bars in North Beach. Dumplings and rare teas are served under pagoda roofs on Chinatown's main streets – but its historic back alleys are filled with temple incense, mah-jongg tile clatter and distant echoes of revolution.

❹ Nob Hill, Russian Hill & Fillmore p128

Russian and Nob Hills are the stomping grounds of millionaires and urban hikers,

with cable cars delivering customers to hill-top bars and high-fashion boutiques. When you see sushi picnics, anime-inspired fashion and the legendary Fillmore auditorium, you'll know you've arrived in Japantown.

❺ The Mission & Potrero Hill p144

The best way to enjoy the Mission is with a book in one hand and a burrito in the other, amid murals, sunshine and the usual crowd of filmmakers, techies, grocers, skaters and novelists. Calle 24 (24th St) is SF's designated Latino Cultural District, and the Mission is also a magnet for Southeast Asians, lesbians and dandies. Silicon Valley refugees take to Potrero Hill, while barflies and artists lurk in the valleys below.

❻ The Castro & Noe Valley p167

Rainbow flags wave their welcome to party boys, career activists and leather daddies in the Castro, while over the hill in Noe Valley megastrollers brake for bakeries and boutiques, as parents load up on sleek shoes and strong coffee.

❼ The Haight, NoPa & Hayes Valley p178

Hippie idealism lives in the Haight, with street musicians, anarchist comic books and psychedelic murals galore. Browse local designs and go gourmet in Hayes Valley, where Zen monks and jazz legends drift down the sidewalks.

❽ Golden Gate Park & the Avenues p193

Hardcore surfers and gourmet adventurers meet in the foggy Avenues around Golden Gate Park. This is one totally chill global village, featuring bluegrass and Korean BBQ, disc golf and tiki cocktails, French pastries and cult-movie matinees.

The Marina, Fisherman's Wharf & the Piers

THE MARINA | COW HOLLOW | FISHERMAN'S WHARF | THE PIERS | PRESIDIO

Neighborhood Top Five

❶ Golden Gate Bridge (p54) Strolling across just after the fog clears, revealing magnificent views of downtown San Francisco with sailboats plying the waves below.

❷ Alcatraz (p72) Feeling cold winds blow and imagining the misery of prison life.

❸ Pier 39 (p57) Giggling at the shenanigans of braying and barking sea lions.

❹ Union St (p70) Poking into hidden courtyards and discovering indie boutiques.

❺ Musée Mécanique (p58) Marveling at 19th-century arcade games.

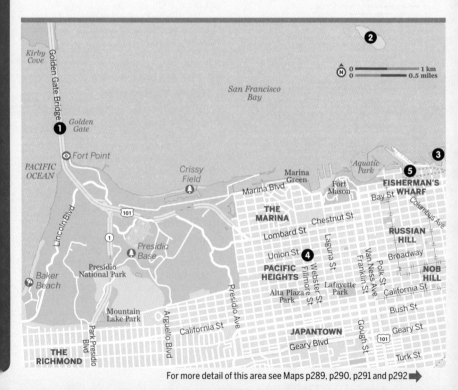

For more detail of this area see Maps p289, p290, p291 and p292 ➡

Explore: the Marina, Fisherman's Wharf & the Piers

Fisherman's Wharf is the epicenter of tourism in San Francisco; the few remaining fishermen moor their boats around Pier 47. Locals don't usually visit the Wharf because it's entirely geared to tourists. Budget two hours to a half-day maximum. Weekends it gets packed by early afternoon: come first thing in the morning to avoid crowds. Summertime fog usually clears by midday (if it clears at all), so visit the Golden Gate Bridge during early afternoon – but be warned that the afternoon fog blows in around 4pm. Carry a jacket and don't wear shorts, unless you're here during a rare heat wave (locals spot the tourists by their short pants). Most people walk further than they anticipate: wear comfortable shoes and sunscreen. Cow Hollow and the Marina have good boutique-shopping strips, bars and restaurants. Explore them later in the day, after working hours but while the shops are still open, when the busy sidewalks provide a glimpse of the fancy-pants Marina crowd.

Local Life

→**Nature walks** San Franciscans love the outdoors – joggers and dog walkers flock to the waterfront trails at Crissy Field and to the hills of the Presidio for wooded trails and site-specific art installations.

→**Barhopping** The Marina District bars on Fillmore St, from Union St to Chestnut St, are ground zero for party-girl sorority sisters and the varsity jocks who love them. Not all locals approve.

→**City views** For dramatic views of Fisherman's Wharf and the San Francisco skyline – and a break from the crowds – hop on a ferry at Pier 41.

Getting There & Away

→**Streetcar** Historic F Market streetcars run along Market St, then up the Embarcadero waterfront to Fisherman's Wharf.

→**Cable car** The Powell-Hyde and Powell-Mason lines run up Powell St to the Wharf; the Mason line is quicker, but the hills are better on the Hyde line.

→**Bus** Major routes to the Wharf and/or the Marina from downtown include the 19, 30, 47 and 49.

→**Car** At the Wharf, there are parking garages at Pier 39 and Ghiradelli Sq (enter on Beach St, between Larkin and Polk Sts). At the Marina, there's parking at Crissy Field and Fort Mason. The Presidio is the only place where it's easy – and free – to park.

→**Ferry** Ferries (p72) run from the Wharf and Ferry Building to Angel Island, Sausalito, Tiburon and Vallejo.

Lonely Planet's Top Tip

To escape the crowds, head west of Ghirardelli Sq. FIrst, make your way on foot or by bike to Aquatic Park, then cut west along the waterfront path, through Fort Mason to Marina Green. Aim for the bobbing masts of the yacht club along Marina Blvd, stopping to explore the piers but keeping your eye on the prize: the Golden Gate Bridge.

◉ Best Waterfront Vistas

→ Golden Gate Bridge (p54)

→ Warming Hut (p64)

→ Crissy Field (p55)

→ Aquatic Park (p59)

→ Pier 39 (p57)

✖ Best Places to Eat

→ Gary Danko (p68)

→ In-N-Out Burger (p65)

→ Off the Grid (p62)

→ Greens (p65)

For reviews, see p62 ➡

▤ Best Places to Drink

→ Interval Bar & Cafe (p69)

→ Buena Vista Cafe (p69)

→ Gold Dust Lounge (p69)

→ Pier 23 (p69)

→ West Coast Wine & Cheese (p69)

For reviews, see p68 ➡

TOP SIGHT
ALCATRAZ

Alcatraz: for over 150 years, the name has given the innocent chills and the guilty cold sweats. Over the decades it's been the nation's first military prison, a forbidding maximum-security penitentiary and disputed territory between Native American activists and the FBI. So it's no surprise that the first step you take onto 'the Rock' seems to cue ominous music: dunh-dunh-dunnnnh!

Early History

It all started innocently enough back in 1775, when Spanish lieutenant Juan Manuel de Ayala sailed the *San Carlos* past the 22-acre island that he called Isla de Alcatraces (Isle of the Pelicans). In 1859 a new post on Alcatraz became the first US West Coast fort and it soon proved handy as a holding pen for Civil War deserters, insubordinates and the court-martialed. Among the prisoners were Native American scouts and 'unfriendlies,' including 19 Hopis who refused to send their children to government boarding schools, where speaking Hopi and practicing their religion were punishable by beatings. By 1902 the four cell blocks of wooden cages were rotting, unsanitary and ill-equipped for the influx of US soldiers convicted of war crimes in the Philippines. The army began building a new concrete military prison in 1909, but upkeep was expensive and the US soon had other things to worry about: WWI, financial ruin and flappers.

DON'T MISS

➡ Introductory films and self-guided audio tour

➡ D-Block solitary-confinement cells

➡ Any site-specific temporary art installations

➡ Waterfront vistas along the (seasonal) Agave Trail

PRACTICALITIES

➡ Map p216, H4

➡ ☑ Alcatraz Cruises 415-981-7625

➡ www.nps.gov/alcatraz

➡ tours adult/child 5-11yr day $37.25/23, night $44.25/26.50

➡ ⊘ call center 8am-7pm, ferries depart Pier 33 half-hourly 8:45am-3:50pm, night tours 5:55pm & 6:30pm

Prison Life

In 1922, when the 18th Amendment to the Constitution declared selling liquor a crime, rebellious Jazz Agers weren't prepared to give up their tipple – and gangsters kept the booze coming. Authorities were determined to make a public example of criminal ringleaders and in 1934 the Federal Bureau of Prisons took over Alcatraz as a prominent showcase for its crime-fighting efforts. The Rock averaged only 264 inmates, but its roster read like a list of America's Most Wanted. A-list criminals doing time on Alcatraz included Chicago crime boss Al 'Scarface' Capone, dapper kidnapper George 'Machine Gun' Kelly, hot-headed Harlem mafioso and sometime poet 'Bumpy' Johnson, and Morton Sobell, the military contractor found guilty of Soviet espionage along with Julius and Ethel Rosenberg.

Today, first-person accounts of daily life in the Alcatraz lockup are included on the excellent self-guided audio tour. But take your headphones off for just a moment and you'll notice the sound of carefree city life traveling from across the water: this is the torment that made perilous escapes into riptides worth the risk. Although Alcatraz was considered escape-proof, in 1962 the Anglin brothers and Frank Morris stuffed their beds with dummies, floated away on a makeshift raft and were never seen again. Security and upkeep proved prohibitively expensive and finally the island prison was abandoned to the birds in 1963.

Native American Occupation

Native Americans claimed sovereignty over the island in the '60s, noting that Alcatraz had long been used by the Ohlone people as a spiritual retreat. But federal authorities refused their proposal to turn Alcatraz into a Native American study center. Then, on the eve of Thanksgiving 1969, 79 Native American activists swam to the island and took it over. During the next 19 months, some 5600 Native Americans would visit the occupied island. Public support eventually pressured President Richard Nixon in 1970 to restore Native territory and strengthen self-rule for Native nations. Each Thanksgiving Day since 1975, an 'Un-Thanksgiving' ceremony has been held at dawn on Alcatraz, with Native leaders and supporters showing their determination to reverse the course of colonial history. After the government regained control of the island, it became a national park and by 1973 it had already become a major tourist draw. Today, the cell blocks' 'free Indian land' water-tower graffiti and rare wildlife are all part of the attraction.

NEED TO KNOW

When visiting by day, to avoid crowds book the day's first or last boat. You need only reserve the outbound boat, not the return, so take your time.

The weather changes fast and it's often windy and much colder on Alcatraz, so wear extra layers, long pants and a cap.

Visiting Alcatraz means walking – a lot. The ferry drops you off at the bottom of a 130ft-high hill, which you'll have to ascend to reach the cell block. The quarter-mile path is paved, but if you're not fully fit you'll be panting by the top. For people with mobility impairment, there's a twice-hourly tram from dock to cell house. Wear sturdy shoes, as you may want to explore some of the unpaved bird-watching trails.

Find out if there's a site-specific art installation during your visit, and plan to see it. They're included in your ticket price but may have limited hours.

Alcatraz

A HALF-DAY TOUR

Book a ferry from Pier 33 and ride 1.5 miles across the bay to explore America's most notorious former prison. The trip itself is worth the money, providing stunning views of the city skyline. Once you've landed at the **❶ Ferry Dock & Pier**, you begin the 580-yard walk to the top of the island and prison; if you need assistance to reach the top, there's a twice-hourly tram.

As you climb toward the **❷ Guardhouse**, notice the island's steep slope; before it was a prison, Alcatraz was a fort. In the 1850s, the military quarried the rocky shores into near-vertical cliffs. Ships could then only dock at a single port, separated from the main buildings by a sally port (a drawbridge and moat in what became the guardhouse). Inside, peer through floor grates to see Alcatraz' original prison.

Volunteers tend the brilliant **❸ Officer's Row Gardens** an orderly counterpoint to the overgrown rose bushes surrounding the burned-out shell of the **❹ Warden's House**. At the top of the hill, by the front door of the **❺ Main Cellhouse**, beautiful shots unfurl all around, including a view of the **❻ Golden Gate Bridge**. Above the main door of the administration building, notice the **❼ historic signs & graffiti**, before you step inside the dank, cold prison to find the **❽ Frank Morris cell**, former home to Alcatraz' most notorious jail-breaker.

TOP TIPS

➡ Book at least one month prior for self-guided daytime visits, longer for ranger-led night tours. For info on garden tours, see www.alcatraz gardens.org.

➡ Be prepared to hike; a steep path ascends from the ferry landing to the cell block. Most people spend two to three hours on the island. You need only reserve for the outbound ferry; take any ferry back.

➡ There's no food (just water) but you can bring your own; picnicking is allowed at the ferry dock only. Dress in layers as weather changes fast and it's usually windy.

Historic Signs & Graffiti
During their 1969–71 occupation, Native Americans graffitied the water tower: 'Home of the Free Indian Land.' Above the cellhouse door, examine the eagle-and-flag crest to see how the red-and-white stripes were changed to spell 'Free.'

Warden's House
Fires destroyed the warden's house and other structures during the Indian Occupation. The government blamed the Native Americans; the Native Americans blamed agents provocateurs acting on behalf of the Nixon Administration to undermine public sympathy.

Parade Grounds

Officer's Row Gardens
In the 19th century soldiers imported topsoil to beautify the island with gardens. Well-trusted prisoners later gardened – Elliott Michener said it kept him sane. Historians, ornithologists and archaeologists choose today's plants.

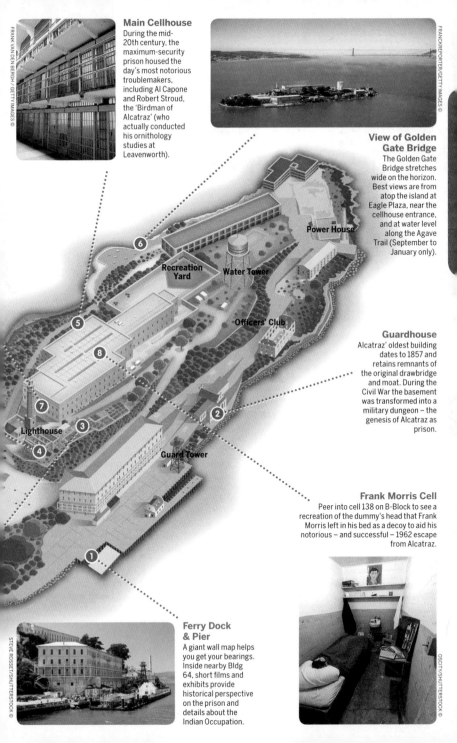

Main Cellhouse
During the mid-20th century, the maximum-security prison housed the day's most notorious troublemakers, including Al Capone and Robert Stroud, the 'Birdman of Alcatraz' (who actually conducted his ornithology studies at Leavenworth).

View of Golden Gate Bridge
The Golden Gate Bridge stretches wide on the horizon. Best views are from atop the island at Eagle Plaza, near the cellhouse entrance, and at water level along the Agave Trail (September to January only).

Power House

Recreation Yard

Water Tower

Officers' Club

Guardhouse
Alcatraz' oldest building dates to 1857 and retains remnants of the original drawbridge and moat. During the Civil War the basement was transformed into a military dungeon – the genesis of Alcatraz as prison.

Lighthouse

Guard Tower

Frank Morris Cell
Peer into cell 138 on B-Block to see a recreation of the dummy's head that Frank Morris left in his bed as a decoy to aid his notorious – and successful – 1962 escape from Alcatraz.

Ferry Dock & Pier
A giant wall map helps you get your bearings. Inside nearby Bldg 64, short films and exhibits provide historical perspective on the prison and details about the Indian Occupation.

TOP SIGHT
GOLDEN GATE BRIDGE, THE MARINA & PRESIDIO

The city's most spectacular icon towers 80 stories above the roiling waters of the Golden Gate, the narrow entrance to San Francisco Bay. It's hard to believe that SF's northern gateway lands not into a tangle of city streets but into the Presidio, an army base turned national park where forested paths and grassy promenades look largely as they have since the 19th century.

SF's Iconic Bridge

San Francisco's famous suspension bridge, painted a signature shade called International Orange, was almost nixed by the Navy in favor of concrete pylons and yellow stripes. Joseph B Strauss rightly receives praise as the engineering mastermind behind this iconic marvel, but without the aesthetic intervention of architects Gertrude and Irving Murrow and incredibly quick work by daredevil laborers, this 1937 landmark might have been just another traffic bottleneck.

How the Bridge was Built

Nobody thought it could happen. Not until the early 1920s did the City of San Francisco seriously investigate building a bridge over the treacherous, windblown strait. The War Department owned the land on both sides and didn't want to take chances with ships: safety and solidity were its goals. But the green light was given to the counter-proposal by Strauss and the Murrows for a subtler suspension span, economic in form, that harmonized with the natural environment. Before the War Department could insist on an eyesore, laborers dove into the treacherous riptides of the bay and got the bridge under way in 1933. Just four years later workers balancing atop swaying cables completed what was

DON'T MISS

- ➡ Fort Point
- ➡ Cross-section of suspension cable, behind Bridge Pavilion visitors center
- ➡ Bridge towers emerging as fog clears
- ➡ Municipal pier behind Warming Hut

PRACTICALITIES

- ➡ Map p216, F5
- ➡ ☑toll information 877-229-8655
- ➡ www.goldengate bridge.org/visitors
- ➡ Hwy 101
- ➡ northbound free, southbound $6.50-7.50
- ➡ 🚌28, all Golden Gate Transit buses

then the world's longest suspension bridge – nearly 2 miles long, with 746ft suspension towers, higher than any construction west of New York.

Crossing the Bridge

For on-site information, stop into the **Bridge Pavilion Visitors Center** (Map p291; ☑415-426-5220; www.ggnpc.org; Golden Gate Bridge toll plaza; ⊗9am-7pm Jun-Aug, to 6pm Sep-May).

Pedestrians take the eastern sidewalk. Dress warmly! From the parking area and bus stop (off Lincoln Blvd), a pathway leads past the toll plaza, then it's 1.7 miles across. If 3.4 miles round-trip seems too much, take a bus to the north side via Golden Gate Transit, then walk back (for exact instructions, see www.goldengatebridge.org/visitors). Note: pedestrian access is open 5am to 9pm summer, to 6:30pm winter.

By bicycle, from the toll-plaza parking area ride toward the Roundhouse, then follow signs to the western sidewalk, reserved for bikes only. (Caution: locals pedal fast; avoid collisions.) Bicycles can cross 24 hours but travel the eastern sidewalk certain hours; see www.goldengatebridge.org.

From the toll plaza, it's 4.5 miles to Sausalito; ferry back to SF via Golden Gate Ferry (p267; to downtown) or Blue & Gold Fleet (p72; to Fisherman's Wharf). Bikes are allowed on ferries.

Muni bus 28 runs west from Fort Mason (corner Marina Blvd and Laguna St) to the bridge parking lot, then cuts south down 19th Ave, intersecting with the N-Judah metro line at Judah St. Marin County–bound Golden Gate Transit buses (10, 70/71 and 101; $5 one way) are the fastest, most comfortable way from downtown; alert the driver and disembark at the toll plaza *just before* the bridge. On Sunday only, Muni bus 76 travels from downtown, crosses the bridge and loops through the spectacular Marin Headlands.

Parking at the toll plaza is extremely limited. Find additional parking west along Lincoln Blvd.

Crissy Field

War is for the birds at **Crissy Field** (Map p291; ☑415-561-4700; www.crissyfield.org; 1199 East Beach; ℗; ☐30, PresidiGo Shuttle), a military airstrip turned waterfront nature preserve with knockout Golden Gate views. Where military aircraft once zoomed in for landings, bird-watchers now huddle in the silent rushes of a reclaimed tidal marsh. Joggers pound beachside trails and the only security alerts are raised by puppies suspiciously sniffing surfers. On foggy days, stop by the certified-green Warming Hut (p64) to browse regional-nature books and warm up with fair-trade coffee.

Hitchcock had it right: seen from below at Fort Point, the bridge induces a thrilling case of Vertigo. For wider vistas, explore the headlands just southwest of the toll plaza, atop high bluffs dotted with wildflowers. Crissy Field reveals the span's entirety, with windsurfers and kite-fliers adding action to snapshots.

Fog aficionados prefer the lookout at Vista Point, in Marin, on the bridge's sunnier northern side, to watch gusting clouds rush through the bridge cables. Better still, find your way up the Marin Headlands to look down upon the span. On the foggiest days, up to one million gallons of water, in the form of fog, blow through hourly.

City Guides (☑415-557-4266; www.sfcityguides.org; donations/tips welcome) **FREE** offers free tours of the bridge, departing Sunday and Thursday at 11am, from the statue of Joseph Strauss by the visitor center on the bridge's SF side; plan to tip $5 per person.

You'll find refreshments only at the SF end of the bridge by the Bridge Pavilion. Otherwise, there's nothing nearby for food or drink.

Fort Point

Fort Point (Map p291; ☑415-556-1693; www.nps.gov/fopo; Marine Dr; ☺10am-5pm Fri-Sun; P; ☐28) FREE – a triple-decker, brick-walled US military fortress – was completed in 1861, with 126 cannons, just in time to protect the bay against certain invasion during the Civil War...or not, as it turned out. Without a single shot having been fired, Fort Point was abandoned in 1900. When the bridge was built overhead, engineers added an extra span to preserve it. Alfred Hitchcock saw deadly potential in Fort Point, and shot the trademark scene from *Vertigo* of Kim Novak leaping from the lookout to certain death into the bay...or not, as it turned out. Fort Point has since given up all pretense of deadliness and now showcases Civil War displays and knockout panoramic viewing decks.

Saturdays once monthly March through October, staff demonstrate crabbing from the pier, available by lottery only (see website); November to February, inquire about spooky Saturday-night candlelight tours (reservations required).

Baker Beach

Picnic amid wind-sculpted pines, fish from craggy rocks or frolic nude at mile-long **Baker Beach** (Map p291; ☑10am-5pm 415-561-4323; www.nps.gov/prsf; ☺sunrise-sunset; P; ☐29, PresidiGo Shuttle), with spectacular views of the bridge. Crowds come weekends, especially on fog-free days; arrive early. For nude sunbathing (mostly straight girls and gay boys), head to the northern end. Families in clothing stick to the southern end, nearer the parking lot. Mind the currents and the c-c-cold water.

Presidio Base

What began in 1776 as a Spanish fort, built by conscripted Ohlone people, is now a treasure trove of surprises, set in an urban national park, the Presidio of San Francisco (p62).

Begin at the Main Post parade grounds to gather maps and shuttle schedules at the **visitor center** (Map p291; ☑415-561-4323; www.presidio.gov; 210 Lincoln Blvd; ☺10am-5pm; ☐PresidiGo Shuttle), then explore the free Officers' Club (p62) to learn the Presidio's checkered history, and warm up on fireside sofas, cozy on foggy days. Mickey Mouse fans head to the Walt Disney Family Museum (p62); fans of the macabre hike to the **Pet Cemetery**, off Crissy Field Ave, where handmade tombstones mark the final resting places of hamsters and kitties. East of the parade grounds, toward the Palace of Fine Arts, lies the **Letterman Campus**, home to nonprofits and *Star Wars* creator George Lucas' Lucas Arts (now owned by Disney) – offices are closed to visitors, but you can pay your respects to the Yoda statue outside. Sunday afternoons April to October, Off the Grid (p62) sets up food trucks on the parade grounds.

There's excellent hiking, too. To find exciting site-specific sculptures by environmental artist Andy Goldsworthy, **Presidio Trust** (Map p291; ☑415-561-5300; www.presidio.gov; Montgomery St, bldg 103, cnr Lincoln Blvd; ☺info 8am-5pm Mon-Fri, gallery 11am-5pm Wed-Sun; ☐PresidiGo Shuttle) publishes good maps to scenic overlooks; they're available free at the visitor center.

Free **PresidiGo** (☑415-561-2739; www.presidio.gov/shuttle) buses loop the park, via two routes, from the **Presidio Transit Center** (Map p291; www.presidio.gov/places/presidio-transit-center; 215 Lincoln Blvd). Service runs every 30 minutes 5:45am to 9pm weekdays, 9am to 7pm weekends. There's weekday-only service to downtown, free to the public 9:30am to 4pm and 7:30pm to 9:30pm. Download maps, pass information and schedules from the PresidiGo website.

TOP SIGHT
FISHERMAN'S WHARF

TUPUNGATO/SHUTTERSTOCK ©

You won't find many fishermen at Fisherman's Wharf – though some still moor here, they're difficult to spot beyond the blinking neon and side-by-side souvenir shops. The Wharf may not be the 'real San Francisco,' but it's lively and holds a few surprises. Stick near the waterfront, where sea lions bray, street performers scare unsuspecting passersby, and an aquarium and carousel entice kids.

Pier 39

The focal point of Fisherman's Wharf isn't the waning fishing fleet but the carousel, carnival-like attractions, shops and restaurants of **Pier 39** (Map p289; ☏415-705-5500; www.pier39.com; cnr Beach St & the Embarcadero; 🅿🛜♿; 🚌47, 🚋Powell-Mason, Ⓜ E, F). Developed in the 1970s to revitalize tourism, the pier draws thousands of tourists daily, but it's really just a big outdoor shopping mall. On the plus side, its visitor center rents strollers, stores luggage and has free phone-charging stations.

By far the best reason to walk the pier is to spot the famous **sea lions** (Map p289; www.pier39.com; Pier 39, cnr Beach St & the Embarcadero; ⏰24hr; ♿; 🚌15, 37, 49, Ⓜ E, F), who took over this coveted waterfront real estate in 1989. These unkempt squatters have been making a public display ever since and now they're San Francisco's favorite mascots. The valuable boat slips accommodate as many as 1300 sea lions that 'haul out' onto the docks between January and July. Follow signs along the pier's western edge – you can't miss 'em.

Aquarium of the Bay

Sharks circle overhead, manta rays sweep by and seaweed sways all around at the **Aquarium of the Bay** (Map p289; ☏415-623-5300; www.aquariumofthebay.org; Pier 39; adult/

DON'T MISS

➡ Sea lions at Pier 39
➡ Musée Mécanique
➡ San Francisco Maritime National Historical Park
➡ Aquatic Park

PRACTICALITIES

➡ Map p289, C2
➡ www.fishermans wharf.org
➡ admission free
➡ ♿
➡ 🚌19, 30, 47, 49, 🚋Powell-Mason, Powell-Hyde, Ⓜ F

Above: Crab sculpture, by topiary artist Jeff Brees

It's hard to resist waterfront restaurants and their breathtaking views, but you really should, unless you go only for drinks and appetizers. Wharf restaurants are generally way overpriced and the food can't compare to what's available in nearby neighborhoods. Go simple – maybe a cup of chowder or some crab Louis from the fish stands at the foot of Taylor St.

A few third- and fourth-generation fishermen remain in the bay, but to survive the drop in salmon and other local stocks some now use their boats for tours, surviving off the city's new lifeblood: tourism. Find the remaining fleet around Pier 47.

The Wharf is the only place in San Francisco where you won't see many San Franciscans. Once you've explored tall ships, consulted mechanical fortune tellers and eaten the obligatory clam chowder in a sourdough-bread bowl, hightail it away to more authentic neighborhoods, where you will discover the real soul of the city.

child/family $24.95/14.95/70; ⏰9am-8pm late May-early Sep, shorter hours low season; 🚻; 🚌49, 🚋Powell-Mason, ⓂE, F), where you wander through glass tubes surrounded by sea life from San Francisco Bay. Not for the claustrophobic, perhaps, but the thrilling fish-eye view leaves kids and parents wide eyed. Kids love the critters and touch pools upstairs.

San Francisco Carousel

A chariot awaits to whisk you and the kids past the Golden Gate Bridge, Alcatraz and other SF landmarks hand-painted onto this Italian **carousel** (Map p289; www.pier39.com; Pier 39; rides $3; ⏰11am-7pm; 🚻; 🚌47, 🚋Powell-Mason, ⓂE, F), twinkling with 1800 lights, at the bayside end of Pier 39.

Musée Mécanique

A flashback to penny arcades, the **Musée Mécanique** (Map p289; 📞415-346-2000; www.musee mechanique.org; Pier 45, Shed A; ⏰10am-8pm; 🚻; 🚌47, 🚋Powell-Mason, Powell-Hyde, ⓂE, F) houses a mind-blowing collection of vintage mechanical amusements. Sinister, freckle-faced Laughing Sal has creeped out kids for over a century, but don't let this manic mannequin deter you from the best arcade west of Coney Island. A quarter lets you start brawls in Wild West saloons, peep at belly dancers through a vintage Mutoscope and even learn a cautionary tale about smoking opium.

San Francisco Maritime National Historical Park

Four historic Bay Area ships are floating museums at the **Maritime National Historical Park** (Map p289; 📞415-447-5000; www.nps.gov/safr; 499 Jefferson St, Hyde St Pier; 7-day ticket adult/child $10/free; ⏰9:30am-5pm Oct-May, to 5:30pm Jun-Sep; 🚻; 🚌19, 30, 47, 🚋Powell-Hyde, ⓂF), the Wharf's most authentic attraction. Moored along the Hyde St Pier, standouts include the elegant 1891 schooner *Alma* and the large 1890 steamboat *Eureka*. For more mariner action, check out the paddle-wheel tugboat *Eppleton Hall* and the iron-hulled *Balclutha*, which brought coal to San Francisco and took grain back to Europe via the dreaded Cape Horn. It's free to walk out along the pier; you pay only to board ships.

National Park Visitors Center

San Francisco grew from its docks. This 10,000-sq-ft **visitor center** (Map p289; 📞415-447-5000; www.nps. gov/safr; 499 Jefferson St; ⏰9:30am-5:30pm; 🚻; 🚌19, 30, 47, 🚋Powell-Hyde, ⓂE, F) FREE for the nearby maritime national historical park details how it happened, in a permanent exhibit that recreates the

19th-century waterfront. Also on display is a rich collection of maritime artifacts, from a giant 1850s first-order lighthouse lens to scale models of 19th-century schooners. Kids love running around the vast space. Rangers provide maps and information about the surrounding area's trails and walks, as well as all national parks and monuments of the American West, including Yosemite.

USS Pampanito

The **USS Pampanito** (Map p289; ✆415-775-1943, tickets 855-384-6410; www.maritime. org/pamphome.htm; Pier 45; adult/child/family $20/10/45; ⏰9am-8pm Thu-Tue, to 6pm Wed; 👫; 🚌19, 30, 47, 🚋Powell-Hyde, ⓂE, F), a WWII-era US Navy submarine, completed six wartime patrols, sank six Japanese ships, battled three others and lived to tell the tale. Submariners' stories of tense moments in underwater stealth mode will have you holding your breath, and all those cool brass knobs and mysterious hydraulic valves will make 21st-century technology seem overrated.

SS Jeremiah O'Brien

It's hard to believe that the historic 10,000-ton **SS Jeremiah O'Brien** (Map p289; ✆415-554-0100; www.ssjeremiahobrien.org; Pier 45; adult/child/family $20/10/40; ⏰9am-4pm; 👫; 🚌19, 30, 47, 🚋Powell-Hyde, ⓂE, F) was turned out by San Francisco's shipbuilders in under eight weeks. Harder still to imagine how she dodged U-boats on a mission delivering supplies to Allied forces on D-Day. Of the 2710 Liberty ships launched during WWII, only this one is still fully operational. Check the website for upcoming four-hour cruises.

Aquatic Park Bathhouse (Maritime Museum)

The **Maritime Museum** (Aquatic Park Bathhouse; Map p292; www.maritime.org; 900 Beach St; ⏰10am-4pm; 👫; 🚌19, 30, 47, 🚋Powell-Hyde) FREE was built as a casino and public bathhouse in 1939 by the Depression-era Works Progress Administration (WPA). Beautifully restored murals depict the mythical lands of Atlantis and Mu and the handful of exhibits include maritime ephemera and dioramas. Note the entryway slate carvings by celebrated African American artist Sargent Johnson and the back verandah's sculptures by Beniamino Bufano.

Aquatic Park

Fisherman's Wharf's eccentricity is mostly staged, but at **Aquatic Park** (Map p289; ✆415-561-7000; www.nps.gov/safr; 👫; 🚌19, 30, 47, 🚋Powell-Hyde) FREE it's the real deal: extreme swimmers dive into the bone-chilling waters of the bay in winter, while oblivious old men cast fishing lines and listen to AM-radio sports. Aside from being the city's principal swimming beach (with bathrooms, but no lifeguard), the park is ideal for people-watching and sandcastle building. For perspective on the Wharf, wander out along the enormous Municipal Pier at the foot of Van Ness Ave.

Cartoon Art Museum

Introducing the **Cartoon Art Museum** (Map p289; ✆415-227-8666; http://cartoonart. org; 781 Beach St; adult/student $10/7; ⏰11am-5pm Tue-Sat; 🚌19, 30, 47, 🚋Powell-Hyde) to comic fans would be an insult: of course you recognize John Romita's amazing Spiderman cover drawings and you were probably raised on Edward Gorey's Gashlycrumb Tinies, starting with 'A is for Amy who fell down the stairs/B is for Basil assaulted by bears...' But even fans will learn something from lectures about 1930s efforts to unionize overworked women animators and shows on underground cartoonist legends like Spain Rodriguez and Trina Robbins.

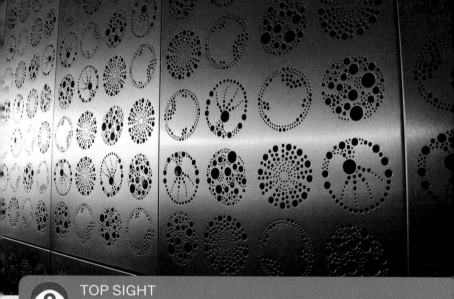

TOP SIGHT
EXPLORATORIUM

Is there a science to skateboarding? Is it true that toilets flush counterclockwise in Australia? Combining science with art, San Francisco's dazzling hands-on Exploratorium nudges you to question how you know what you know. As thrilling as the exhibits is the setting: a 9-acre, glass-walled pier jutting over San Francisco Bay, with vast outdoor portions you can explore for free.

Covering 330,000 sq ft of indoor-outdoor space, the 600-plus exhibits have buttons to push, cranks to ratchet and dials to adjust, all made by artists and scientists at the in-house building shop. Try a punk hairdo, courtesy of the static-electricity station. Turn your body into the gnomon of a sundial. Slide, climb and feel your way – in total darkness – through the labyrinth of the **Tactile Dome** (reservation & separate ticket required; $15; ☺10am-5pm Tue-Sun, over 18yr only 6-10pm Thu).

In 2013 the Exploratorium moved to its purpose-built solar-powered space, constructed in concert with scientific agencies, including NOAA, which hardwired the pier with sensors delivering real-time data on weather, wind, tides and the bay.

Frank Oppenheimer founded the Exploratorium in 1969. He'd been a physicist on the atom bomb, was black-balled during the McCarthy era, then reemerged as a high-school teacher, eschewing secret scientific study in favor of public education. The Exploratorium is his lasting legacy.

Above: Planktonwall © Exploratorium, www.exploratorium.edu

DON'T MISS

➡ Tactile Dome (reservations required)
➡ Visualizing the Bay
➡ Tinkering Studio
➡ Plankton exhibit
➡ Everyone Is You and Me (mirror)

TOP TIPS

➡ Make reservations and plan your day around your visit.
➡ To avoid crowds, come early in the day.

PRACTICALITIES

➡ Map p290, A5
➡ ☎415-528-4444
➡ www.exploratorium.edu
➡ Pier 15
➡ adult/child $30/20, 6-10pm Thu $15
➡ ☺10am-5pm Tue-Sun, over 18yr only 6-10pm Thu
➡ Ⓜ E, F

⊙ SIGHTS

Sights along Fisherman's Wharf are geared entirely to tourists, particularly to families, and it's easy to get stuck with so much vying for your attention. Stick to the waterside and keep moving. Once you're west of Van Ness Ave, locals supplant tourists and you get a better sense of how people actually live along the waterfront. Though everything looks close together on the map, on the ground you'll do a lot of walking.

⊙ The Marina & Cow Hollow

FORT MASON CENTER   AREA
Map p292 (☎415-345-7500; www.fortmason.org; cnr Marina Blvd & Laguna St; ℗; 📵22, 28, 30, 43, 47, 49) San Francisco takes subversive glee in turning military installations into venues for nature, fine dining and out-there experimental art. Evidence: Fort Mason, once a shipyard and embarkation point for WWII troops, now a vast cultural center and gathering place for events, drinking and eating. Wander the waterfront, keeping your eyes peeled for fascinating outdoor art-and-science installations designed by the Exploratorium.

The mess halls are replaced by vegan-friendly Greens, a Zen-community-run restaurant, and also the Long Now Foundation, whose compelling exhibits reconsider extinction and the future of time. Warehouses contain cutting-edge theater at the Magic (p69) and improvised comedy workshops at BATS Improv (p69). The Herbst Pavilion counts major arts events and fashion shows among its arsenal – see the website for upcoming events. Hidden art exhibits include the 'Tasting the Tides' water fountain, which lets you taste, with the touch of a button, the varying salinity of the bay – it's next to the firehouse, with glorious water views.

WAVE ORGAN   MONUMENT
Map p292 (www.exploratorium.edu/visit/wave-organ; Marina Small Craft Harbor jetty; ☉daylight hours; ♿; 📵22, 30) FREE A project of the Exploratorium, the Wave Organ is a sound sculpture of PVC tubes and concrete pipes capped with found marble from San Francisco's old cemetery, built into the tip of the yacht-harbor jetty. Depending on the waves, winds and tide, the tones emitted sound like nervous humming from a dinnertime line cook or spooky heavy breathing over the phone in a slasher film.

OCTAGON HOUSE   HISTORIC BUILDING
Map p292 (☎415-441-7512; http://nscda-ca.org/octagon-house; 2645 Gough St; admission by donation $3; ☉noon-3pm 2nd & 4th Thu & 2nd Sun of month, closed Jan; 📵41, 45) Crafty architects are always trying to cut corners on clients, and architect William C McElroy has done so splendidly with this house. This is among the last examples of a brief San Franciscan vogue for octagonal houses in the 1860s, when some believed that catching direct sunlight from eight angles was healthful. Three afternoons monthly, you can peruse collections of colonial antiques and peek inside a time capsule that McElroy hid under the stairs.

GHIRARDELLI SQUARE   SQUARE
Map p289 (☎415-775-5500; www.ghirardellisq.com; 900 North Point St; ☉10am-9pm; 📵19, 30, 47, 🚋Powell-Hyde) Willy Wonka would tip his hat to Domingo Ghirardelli (gear-ar-deli), whose business became the West's largest chocolate factory in 1893. After the company moved to the East Bay, two sweet-talking developers reinvented the factory as a mall and landmark ice-cream parlor in 1964. Today, the square is entering its third incarnation as a boutique luxury time-share/spa complex with wine-tasting rooms – care for a massage and some merlot with your Ghirardelli chocolate sundae?

⊙ Fisherman's Wharf & the Piers

FISHERMAN'S WHARF   PIER
See p57.

EXPLORATORIUM   MUSEUM
See p60.

⊙ Presidio

GOLDEN GATE BRIDGE   BRIDGE
See p54.

ALCATRAZ   HISTORIC SITE
See p50.

PALACE OF FINE ARTS MONUMENT

Map p291 (☑510-599-4651; www.lovethepalace. org; Palace Dr; ☺24hr; ☐28, 30, 43) FREE Like a fossilized party favor, this romantic, ersatz Greco-Roman ruin is the city's memento from the 1915 Panama-Pacific International Exposition. The original, designed by celebrated Berkeley architect Bernard Maybeck, was of wood, burlap and plaster, then later reinforced. By the 1960s it was crumbling. The structure was recast in concrete so that future generations could gaze at the rotunda relief to glimpse 'Art under attack by materialists, with idealists leaping to her rescue.' A glorious spot to wander day or night.

SWEDENBORGIAN CHURCH CHURCH

Map p291 (☑415-346-6466; www.sfswedenbor gian.org; 2107 Lyon St; ☺10am-6pm Mon-Fri, services 11am Sun; ☐3, 43) Radical ideals in the form of distinctive buildings make beloved SF landmarks; this standout 1894 example is the collaborative effort of 19th-century Bay Area progressive thinkers, such as naturalist John Muir, California Arts and Crafts leader Bernard Maybeck and architect Arthur Page Brown. Inside, nature is everywhere – in hewn-maple chairs, in mighty madrone trees supporting the roof and in scenes of northern California that took muralist William Keith 40 years to complete.

PRESIDIO OF SAN FRANCISCO PARK

Map p291 (☑415-561-4323; www.nps.gov/prsf; ☺dawn-dusk; ℗; ☐28, 43) Explore that splotch of green on the map between Baker Beach and Crissy Field and you'll find parade grounds, Yoda, a centuries-old adobe wall and some thrilling site-specific art installations. What started as a Spanish fort built by Ohlone conscripts in 1776 is now a treasure hunt of surprises. Begin your adventures at the Main Post to get trail maps at the visitor center (p56) and inquire about site-specific art installations by Andy Goldsworthy.

WALT DISNEY FAMILY MUSEUM MUSEUM

Map p291 (☑415-345-6800; www.waltdisney.org; 104 Montgomery St (Presidio); adult/student/ child $25/20/12; ☺10am-6pm Wed-Mon, last entry 5pm; ℗ 🖘; ☐43, PresidiGo shuttle) An 1890s military barracks in the Presidio houses 10 galleries that chronologically tell the exhaustively long story of Walt Disney's life. Opened in 2009, the museum gets high marks for design, integrating 20,000 sq ft of contemporary glass-and-steel exhibition space with the original 19th-century brick building, but it's definitely geared toward grown-ups and will bore kids after an hour.

PRESIDIO OFFICERS' CLUB HISTORIC BUILDING

Map p291 (☑415-561-4165; www.presidio.gov/ officers-club-internal; 50 Moraga Ave; ☺10am-6pm Tue, Wed, Sat & Sun, to 8pm Thu & Fri; 🖘; ☐PresidiGo shuttle) FREE The Presidio's oldest building dates to the late 1700s, and was fully renovated in 2015, revealing gorgeous Spanish-Moorish adobe architecture. The free **Heritage Gallery** shows the history of the Presidio, from Native American days to the present. Moraga Hall – the former officers'-club lounge – is a lovely spot to sit fireside and also has free wi-fi. Thursday and Friday evenings the club hosts a lineup of events and lectures; check the website.

EATING

Mid-November to June, the specialty is Dungeness crab. Wharf restaurants are generally mediocre and expensive: if you're a serious foodie, explore the Wharf before lunch, west to east (if you're arriving by cable car, ride the Powell-Hyde line), then go to the Ferry Building, on foot (1-mile/20-minute walk) or via the F-Market streetcar. In the Marina, good restaurants line Chestnut St, from Fillmore to Divisadero Sts, and Union St, between Fillmore St and Van Ness Ave. There's also good-priced ethnic fare on Lombard St, if you're willing to hunt. Greens (p65) gives reason to trek to Fort Mason.

★OFF THE GRID FOOD TRUCK $

Map p292 (www.offthegridsf.com; Fort Mason Center, 2 Marina Blvd; items $6-14; ☺5-10pm Fri Apr-Oct; 🖘; ☐22, 28) Spring through fall, some 30 food trucks circle their wagons at SF's largest mobile-gourmet hootenannies on Friday night at Fort Mason Center, and 11am to 4pm Sunday for Picnic at the Presidio on the Main Post lawn. Arrive early for the best selection and to minimize waits. Cash only.

These weekly parties are a great way to appreciate the breadth of the SF food scene while rubbing elbows with locals. Some favorites: the Chairman's clamshell buns stuffed with duck and mango, Roli Roti's free-range herbed roast chicken and, on Friday, A16's pizza and meatballs. Beer,

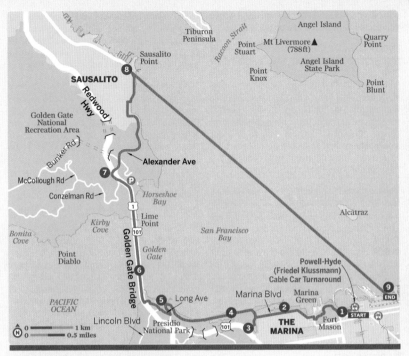

Neighborhood Walk
Freewheeling Over the Bridge

START MARITIME MUSEUM
FINISH PIER 41
LENGTH 8 MILES; TWO TO FOUR HOURS

Built in Streamline Moderne style, the 1939 **①Maritime Museum** (p59) resembles an art-deco ocean liner. Head behind the building to the sandy shore along Aquatic Park and dip your toes into the icy bay.

Joggers, Frisbee throwers and kite fliers congregate at **②Marina Green**. A right turn bisects two boat marinas; at the end is the curious Wave Organ. Flash back to the 1915 Panama–Pacific International Expo at the **③Palace of Fine Arts** (p62). Hear how your voice echoes inside. Watch kids chase swans, while you pose for photos beside gorgeous Greco-Roman arches.

Head to **④Crissy Field** (p55) to watch windsurfers and kiteboarders attempt one of SF's windiest beaches. Take the Golden Gate Promenade, a foot-and-bike path skirting the field, toward Fort Point. Fuel up on organic sandwiches and coffee at **⑤Warming Hut** (p64). Afterwards, back-

track to Long Ave and hang a right up super-steep Lincoln Blvd toward the bridge. This is the steepest part of the route. If all else fails, you can walk and push your bike.

With everyone craning their necks, it's no surprise bicycles sometimes collide on the **⑥Golden Gate Bridge** (p54); keep your eyes peeled. Before crossing, stop at the visitor center and see the exhibits. You'll be grateful you brought a tight-fitting hat and windbreaker if the fog suddenly blows in.

Just across the bridge, turn left onto Conzelman Rd and ascend the **⑦Marin Headlands** to look down on the bridge from a former WWII bunker, Battery Spencer – you can either pedal up the giant hill or walk your bike. Or just enjoy the views and pedal past. Swanky **⑧Sausalito**, with bayside vistas and galleries aplenty, is ideal for a stroll, but first get the ferry schedule at the dock to coordinate your timing.

Take the ferry from Sausalito back to **⑨Pier 41** at Fisherman's Wharf or, if you're headed downtown, board a boat to the Ferry Building.

wine and cocktails (Fort Mason only) warm you up for dancing to live music and DJs.

LUCCA DELICATESSEN DELI $

Map p292 (☑415-921-7873; www.luccadeli.com; 2120 Chestnut St; sandwiches $9-12; ☺9am-6pm; ☐28, 30, 43) Open since 1929, this classic Italian deli is an ideal spot to assemble picnics for Marina Green. Besides perfect prosciutto and salami, nutty cheeses and fruity Chiantis, expect made-to-order sandwiches on fresh-baked Acme bread, including yummy meatball subs. There's hot homemade soup from 11am to 3pm.

BLUE BARN GOURMET SANDWICHES $

Map p292 (☑415-896-4866; www.bluebarngourmet.com; 3344 Steiner St; salads & sandwiches $11-16; ☺11am-8:30pm Mon-Fri, to 8pm Sat & Sun; � ☑ ☑; ☐22, 28, 30, 43) ☑ Toss aside ordinary salads. For $12.95, build a mighty mound of organic produce, topped with six fixings, including artisan cheeses, heirloom tomatoes, candied pecans and pomegranate seeds; add extra for grilled organic meats and seafood. For something hot, try the grilled cheese with *soppressata* salami, *manchego* cheese and Mission-fig jam.

WARMING HUT CAFE $

Map p291 (☑415-561-3042; www.parksconservancy.org/visit/eat/warming-hut.html; 983 Marine Dr; items $4-9; ☺9am-5pm; ☐ ☑; ☐PresidiGo shuttle) ☑ At the Warming Hut, wet-suited windsurfers and Crissy Field kite fliers recharge with fair-trade coffee, organic pastries and hot dogs while browsing field guides and sampling honey from Presidio honeybees. Ingeniously insulated with recycled denim, this eco-shack below the Golden Gate Bridge evolved from a heartwarming concept: all purchases fund Crissy Field's ongoing conversion from US Army airstrip to wildlife preserve.

FISHERMAN'S WHARF
CRAB STANDS SEAFOOD $

Map p289 (Taylor St; mains $5-15; ☐F) Brawny men stir steaming cauldrons of Dungeness crab at several side-by-side takeout crab stands at the foot of Taylor St, the epicenter of Fisherman's Wharf. Crab season typically runs winter through spring, but you'll find shrimp and other seafood year-round.

Instead of dining on the giant, crowded plaza, head east along the waterfront to the Pier 43 promenade to find benches where you can sit, or – if you don't mind standing

to eat – look behind the crab stalls between numbers 8 and 9 Fisherman's Wharf for swinging glass doors marked 'Passageway to the Boats' and amble out the docks to eat in view of the craft that hauled in your lunch.

ITALIAN HOMEMADE ITALIAN $

Map p292 (☑415-655-9325; www.italianhomemadecompany.com; 1919 Union St; mains $12-15; ☺11am-9:30pm; ☑; ☐22, 41, 45) You'd be hard-pressed to find pasta fresher than this – cooks roll out sheets of dough right in the window. The formula is simple: pick your pasta, add a sauce. The Bolognese is most popular and, because the proprietor's from Bologna, you can bet on its quality. Kids love seeing how their dinner is made.

TANGUITO FOOD TRUCK $

Map p289 (☑415-577-4223; 2850 Jones St; dishes $4-13; ☺11:30am-6:30pm; ☐47, ☐Powell-Mason, ☐F) Parked permanently at Fisherman's Wharf, the Tanguito food truck makes exceptional Argentine empanadas with chicken or steak, stellar saffron rice and even paella (if you can wait 45 minutes). Note the early closing time at dinner.

CODMOTHER FISH & CHIPS FOOD TRUCK $

Map p289 (☑415-606-9349; 2824 Jones St; mains $5-10; ☺11:30am-5pm Mon & Wed-Sat, to 2:30pm Sun; ☐47, ☐Powell-Mason, ☐F) If being at Fisherman's Wharf makes you crave fish and chips, skip the expensive restaurants lining the water and instead find this little food truck, which makes delicious fried cod, Baja-style fish tacos and several varieties of flavored French fries. Note the early closing times.

ROOSTER & RICE THAI $

Map p292 (☑415-776-3647; www.roosterandrice.com; 2211 Filbert St; mains $11-14; ☺11:30am-8pm Mon-Sat; ☐22, 41, 45) ☑ This quick-eats hole-in-the-wall place makes one dish (with a vegetarian variation) – *khao mun gai* (Thai-style chicken and rice), made with organic poached chicken, white or brown rice, and flavor-packed chili sauce on the side. Add $2 for veggies. The only drawback is limited seating; consider getting it to go.

PLUTO'S FRESH FOOD AMERICAN $

Map p292 (☑415-775-8867; www.plutosfreshfood.com; 3258 Scott St; mains $7-13; ☺11am-10pm; ☑ ☑; ☐28, 30, 43) When you're hungry for a wholesome meal but don't want to fuss, Pluto's serves good food fast, with build-your-own salads, stick-to-your-ribs mac 'n' cheese and carved-to-order roast beef and turkey with all the fixings. Order at the counter, then snag a seat. Kids' meals cost just $5.25.

IN-N-OUT BURGER
BURGERS $

Map p289 (☎800-786-1000; www.in-n-out.com; 333 Jefferson St; meals under $10; ⏱10:30am-1am Sun-Thu, to 1:30am Fri & Sat; ♿; ☐30, 47, ☐Powell-Hyde) Gourmet burgers have taken SF by storm, but In-N-Out has had a good thing going for 60 years: prime chuck beef processed on site, plus fries and shakes made with ingredients you can pronounce, all served by employees you paid a living wage. Consider ordering yours off the menu 'Animal style,' cooked in mustard with grilled onions.

SEED & SALT
VEGAN $

Map p292 (☎415-872-9173; http://seedandsalt. com; 2240 Chestnut St; dishes $7-14; ⏱8am-8pm Mon-Fri, to 7pm Sat, 10am-7pm Sun; ♥; ☐30, 43) 🍃 Vegans, rejoice! This tiny cafe, with just two shared tables, exclusively serves organic, vegan, gluten-free foods, including great collard-green wraps, scratch-made veggie burgers, homemade pastries, and fresh-pressed green drinks and smoothies.

KARA'S CUPCAKES
BAKERY, DESSERTS $

Map p292 (☎415-563-2253; www.karascupcakes. com; 3249 Scott St; cupcakes $2-3.75; ⏱10am-8pm Sun-Thu, to 10pm Fri & Sat; ☐28, 30, 43) 🍃 Proustian nostalgia washes over fully grown adults as they bite into cupcakes that recall childhood magician-led birthday parties. Varieties range from yummy chocolate marshmallow to classic carrot cake with cream-cheese frosting, all calculated for maximum glee – there's even gluten-free.

LITE BITE
CAFE, AMERICAN $

Map p292 (☎415-931-5483; www.litebite.com; 1796 Union St; items $5-10; ⏱8:30am-8:30pm Mon-Thu, 8am-7pm Fri, 9am-7pm Sat & Sun; ♥; ☐41, 45, 47, 49) 🍃 Just because you're traveling doesn't mean you have to give up your diet. Lite Bite keeps you in check with quality fast food, made with organic ingredients. Expect dishes like whole-wheat turkey lasagna and shepherd's pie, with minimal fat, sugar and salt – plus fresh green drinks, cold-pressed juices and prepared foods to go.

★GREENS
VEGETARIAN, CALIFORNIAN $$

Map p292 (☎415-771-6222; www.greensrestaurant. com; Fort Mason Center, 2 Marina Blvd, Bldg A; mains lunch $16-19, dinner $20-28; ⏱11:45am-2:30pm & 5:30-9pm; ♿♨; ☐22, 28, 30, 43, 47, 49) 🍃 Career carnivores won't realize there's zero meat in the hearty black-bean chili, or in Greens' other flavor-packed vegetarian dishes, made using ingredients from a Zen farm in Marin. And, oh, what views! The Golden Gate rises just outside the window-lined dining room. The on-site cafe serves to-go lunches, but for sit-down meals, including Sunday brunch, reservations are essential.

MAMACITA
MEXICAN $$

Map p292 (☎415-346-8494; www.mamacitasf. com; 2317 Chestnut St; mains $20-25; ⏱5:30-9pm Mon-Thu, 5-10pm Fri-Sun; ☐30, 43) One of the city's best for sit-down Mexican, Mamacita makes everything from scratch – tortillas, tamales and two dozen fresh-daily sauces for wide-ranging dishes, from spit-roasted goat to duck *carnitas*. The knockout cocktail menu lists 60 tequilas, which explains the room's deafening roar. Make reservations.

BELGA
BELGIAN $$

Map p292 (☎415-872-7350; http://belgasf.com; 2000 Union St; mains lunch $12-17, dinner $21-26; ⏱11am-3pm & 5-9:30pm Mon-Fri, 10am-3pm & 5-9:30pm Sat & Sun; ☐22, 41, 45) Happening and swank, Belga resembles a European brasserie, with side-by-side tables flanking red-leather banquettes – fitting for northern French and Belgian specialties like mussels and fries, wood-fired roasts and sausages, *spaetzle* (boiled dumplings) and cabbage, gratins and *carbonnade* (beef stew in beer), all made with a lighter Californian sensibility. Reservations essential.

ROSE'S CAFÉ
ITALIAN, CALIFORNIAN $$

Map p292 (☎415-775-2200; www.rosescafesf. com; 2298 Union St; mains lunch $10-17, dinner $17-30; ⏱8am-9pm; ♥; ☐22, 41, 45) 🍃 The ideal refueling spot while you're browsing Union St boutiques. Follow your salads and house-made soups with rich organic polenta with gorgonzola and thyme, or a simple grass-fed beef burger, then linger over espresso or tea. Shop if you must, but return to this sunny corner cafe from 4pm to 6pm for half-price wine by the glass. Great breakfasts, too.

ARGUELLO
MEXICAN $$

Map p291 (☎415-561-3650; www.arguellosf.com; 50 Moraga Ave; mains $18-25; ⏱11am-4pm Tue, to 9pm Wed-Fri, 11am-3pm & 5-9pm Sat, 11am-4pm Sun; 📶; ☐43, PresidiGo shuttle) Inside the Presidio Officers' Club, this lively Mexican restaurant by James Beard Award—winner

1

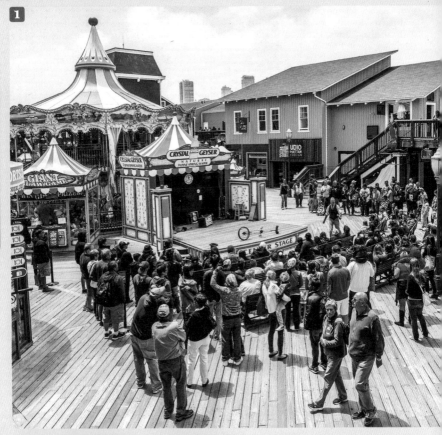

4

MIKA ELDRITCH/SHUTTERSTOCK ©

1. Pier 39 (p57)
The focal point of Fisherman's Wharf draws thousands of people each day to stroll and spot sea lions.

2. Aquarium of the Bay (p57)
Get up close and personal with sea life from San Francisco Bay.

3. Golden Gate Bridge (p54)
It's hard to find a bad angle on this incredibly photogenic landmark.

4. Sea lions at Fisherman's Wharf (p57)
In season, more than a thousand sea lions can occupy the Pier 39 boat slips at one time, making for quite the public spectacle.

BLUEBEAT76/GETTY IMAGES ©

2

ETHAN DANIELS/SHUTTERSTOCK ©

3

ALESSANDRO COLLE/SHUTTERSTOCK ©

Traci Des Jardins features small dishes good for sharing, plus several mains, including standout caramelized pork shoulder. The bar makes great margaritas, which you can sip fireside in the adjoining Moraga Hall, the former officers'-club lounge.

BALBOA CAFE
GASTROPUB $$

Map p292 (☑415-921-3944; www.balboacafe. com/san-francisco; 3199 Fillmore St; mains lunch $14-20, dinner $14-30; ☺kitchen 11:30am-10pm Sun-Wed, to 11pm Thu-Sat, bar to 2am; ☐22, 28, 30, 43) Equal parts bar and grill, Balboa is a mainstay for classic cooking in a pub operational since 1913. The decor retains an old-world look, with massive oak bar, wood-paneled walls and brass trim – a fitting backdrop for well-wrought cocktails and dishes like crab cakes, Caesar salad, steaks and burgers. Local luminaries frequent the bar. Good brunch. Make reservations.

CARMEL PIZZA CO
FOOD TRUCK $$

Map p289 (☑415-676-1185; www.carmelpizzaco. com; 2826 Jones St; pizzas $13-21; ☺11:30am-3:30pm & 5-8pm Mon, Tue & Thu, noon-8pm Fri & Sat, to 6pm Sun; ☐47, ☐Powell-Mason, ☒F) It's remarkable that a food truck could contain a wood-burning oven, but herein lies the secret to Carmel's remarkably good single-serving blistered-crust pizzas. Note the early closing time at dinner.

EAGLE CAFE
AMERICAN $$

Map p289 (☑415-433-3689; www.eaglecafe.com; Pier 39, 2nd fl, suite 103; mains $10-20; ☺7:30am-9pm; ☒; ☐47, ☐Powell-Mason, ☒F) Good for breakfast or a no-fuss lunch, the Eagle's straightforward fare includes pancakes and omelets, crab-salad sandwiches, burgers etc. The views are good, the prices are right for families and it takes reservations, which you should definitely make at weekends to spare yourself (long) waits.

★GARY DANKO
CALIFORNIAN $$$

Map p289 (☑415-749-2060; www.garydanko. com; 800 North Point St; 3-/5-course menu $86/124; ☺5:30-10pm; ☐19, 30, 47, ☐Powell-Hyde) Gary Danko wins James Beard Awards for his impeccable California *haute cuisine*. Smoked-glass windows prevent passersby from tripping over their tongues at the exquisite presentations – roasted lobster with blood oranges, blushing duck breast with port-roasted grapes, lavish cheeses and trios of crèmes brûlées. Reservations a must.

FORBES ISLAND
GRILL $$$

Map p289 (☑415-951-4900; www.forbesisland. com; Pier 41; 4-course menu $79; ☺5pm-late; ☒; ☐47, ☒F) No man is an island, except for eccentric millionaire Forbes Thor Kiddoo. A miniature lighthouse, a thatched hut, a waterfall, a sandy beach and swaying palms transformed his houseboat into the Hearst Castle of the bay. Today this bizarre domicile is a gently rocking, romantic restaurant, strong on grilled meats and atmosphere – consider the lamb. Reservations essential.

Take the put-put boat taxi from the western side of Pier 39; landlubbers dining below deck should bring motion-sickness meds.

SCOMA'S
SEAFOOD $$$

Map p289 (☑415-771-4383; www.scomas.com; Pier 47; mains $28-40; ☺11:30am-9:30pm; ☐; ☐Powell-Hyde, ☒F) Enjoy a flashback to the 1960s, with waiters in white dinner jackets, pine-paneled walls decorated with signed photographs of forgotten celebrities, and plate-glass windows overlooking the docks – Scoma's is the Wharf's long-standing staple for seafood. Little changes, except the prices. Expect classics like *cioppino* (seafood stew) and lobster thermidor – never groundbreaking, always good – that taste better when someone else buys.

IZZY'S STEAKS & CHOPS
STEAK $$$

Map p292 (☑415-644-5330; www.izzyssteaks. com; 3345 Steiner St; mains $20-35; ☺5-9:30pm Mon-Fri, 4-9:30pm Sat & Sun; ☐22, 28, 30, 43) Izzy's casual dining room is a throwback to Barbary Coast saloons, with old-time memorabilia and trophy heads lining the walls. Of all the steak houses in SF, this one's the most relaxed, with no dress code. It has all the usual classics, like rib-eye steak and creamed spinach. Reservations essential.

🍷 DRINKING & NIGHTLIFE

Fisherman's Wharf bars cater almost entirely to tourists but can be good fun, if pricey. If you're at a Wharf hotel but prefer a local nightlife scene, head a mile up Polk St from the waterfront. Clustered around Fillmore and Greenwich Sts, Marina watering holes – which author Armistead Maupin called 'breeder bars' – cater to a frat-boy crowd.

★ **INTERVAL BAR & CAFE** BAR

Map p292 (www.theinterval.org; Fort Mason Center, 2 Marina Blvd, Bldg A; ☺10am-midnight; 🚇10, 22, 28, 30, 47, 49) Designed to stimulate discussion of philosophy and art, the Interval is a favorite spot in the Marina for cocktails and conversation. It's inside the Long Now Foundation, with floor-to-ceiling bookshelves, which contain the canon of Western lit, rising above a glorious 10,000-year clock – a fitting backdrop for a daiquiri, gimlet or aged Tom Collins, or single-origin coffee, tea and snacks.

★ **BUENA VISTA CAFE** BAR

Map p289 (📞415-474-5044; www.thebuena vista.com; 2765 Hyde St; ☺9am-2am Mon-Fri, 8am-2am Sat & Sun; 🛜; 🚇19, 47, 🚋Powell-Hyde) Warm your cockles with a prim little goblet of bitter-creamy Irish coffee, introduced to America at this destination bar that once served sailors and cannery workers. That old Victorian floor manages to hold up carousers and families alike, served community-style at round tables overlooking the cable-car turnaround at Victoria Park.

GOLD DUST LOUNGE BAR

Map p289 (📞415-397-1695; www.golddustsf.com; 165 Jefferson St; ☺9am-2am; 🚇47, 🚋Powell-Mason, Ⓜ E, F) The Gold Dust is so beloved by San Franciscans that, when it lost its lease on the Union Sq building it had occupied since the 1930s, then reopened in 2013 at the Wharf – with the same precarious Victorian brass chandeliers and twangy rockabilly band – the mayor declared it 'Gold Dust Lounge Day.'

WEST COAST WINE & CHEESE WINE BAR

Map p292 (www.westcoastsf.com; 2165 Union St; ☺4-10pm Mon & Tue, to 11pm Wed, to midnight Thu & Fri, 2pm-midnight Sat, to 10pm Sun; 🚇22, 41, 45) A rack of 720 bottles frames the wall at this austerely elegant storefront wine bar, which pours wines exclusively from California, Oregon and Washington, 26 by the glass. All pair with delectable small bites (dishes $8 to $16), including house-made charcuterie and cheese plates.

CALIFORNIA WINE MERCHANT WINE BAR

Map p292 (📞415-567-1639; www.californiawine merchant.com; 2113 Chestnut St; ☺11am-midnight Mon-Wed, to 1:30am Thu-Sat, to 11pm Sun; 🚇22, 30, 43) Part wine store, part wine bar, this small shop on busy Chestnut St caters to neighborhood wine aficionados, with a daily-changing list of 50 wines by the glass, available in half pours. Arrive early to score a seat, or stand and gab with the locals.

MATRIXFILLMORE LOUNGE

Map p292 (📞415-598-9222; www.matrixfillmore. com; 3138 Fillmore St; ☺5pm-2am Wed-Sun; 🚇22, 28, 30, 43) The neighborhood's most notorious upmarket pick-up joint provides a fascinating glimpse of the lives of swank Marina singletons. Treat it as a comic sociological study, while enjoying stellar cocktails and sexy beats – if you can get past the door. There's dancing after 10pm.

⭐ **ENTERTAINMENT**

MAGIC THEATRE THEATER

Map p292 (📞415-441-8822; www.magictheatre. org; Fort Mason Center, cnr Marina Blvd & Laguna St, Bldg D, 3rd fl; tickets $30-85; 🚇22, 28, 30, 43, 47, 49) The Magic is known for taking risks and staging provocative plays by playwrights such as Bill Pullman, Terrence McNally, Edna O'Brien, David Mamet and Sam Shepard. If you're interested in seeing new theatrical works and getting under the skin of the Bay Area theater scene, the Magic is an excellent starting point. Check the calendar online.

BATS IMPROV THEATER

Map p292 (📞415-474-8935; www.improv.org; Fort Mason Center, cnr Marina Blvd & Laguna St, Bldg B, 3rd fl; $17-20; ☺shows 8pm Fri & Sat; 🚇22, 28, 30, 43) Bay Area Theater Sports explores all things improv, from audience-inspired themes to whacked-out musicals at completely extemporaneous weekend shows. Or take center stage yourself at a three-hour improv-comedy workshop (held weekday nights and weekend afternoons). Think fast: classes fill quickly. Admission prices vary depending on the show/workshop.

PIER 23 LIVE MUSIC

Map p290 (📞415-362-5125; www.pier23cafe. com; Pier 23; cover free-$10; ☺shows 5-7pm Tue, 6-8pm Wed, 7-10pm Thu-Sat, 5-8pm Sun; Ⓜ E, F) It resembles a surf shack, but this old waterfront restaurant regularly features R&B, reggae, Latin bands, mellow rock and the occasional jazz pianist – and most shows are free. Wander out to the bayside patio to soak in the views. The dinner menu features pier-worthy options like batter-fried oysters and whole roasted crab.

LOU'S FISH SHACK
LIVE MUSIC

Map p289 (☑415-771-5687; http://lousfish shacksf.com; 300 Jefferson St; ⊙shows 7-11pm Fri & Sat, 4-8pm Sun; 🚻; 🚌30, 47, 🚋Powell-Mason, M F) FREE Lou's presents live blues on Friday and Saturday nights and Sunday afternoons. Primarily a restaurant, it also has a few bar tables near the bandstand and a tiny dance floor, making it a good backup when you're staying nearby and want to hear live music but don't want to travel. And, unlike bona fide blues bars, Lou's welcomes kids.

SHOPPING

Wharf shopping yields T-shirts, fridge magnets and miniature cable cars – the latter are perfect souvenirs; best are wood or metal. There's better shopping on Polk St (Russian Hill) and the Marina. First choice is Cow Hollow – Union St between Gough and Fillmore Sts – where indie boutiques flank upmarket chains. Second choice is Chestnut St, between Fillmore and Divisadero Sts, where chains and boutiques cater to wealthy stay-at-home parents.

★EPICUREAN TRADER
FOOD & DRINKS

(☑415-780-1628; www.theepicureantrader.com; 1909 Union St; ⊙10am-9pm Sun-Tue, to 10pm Wed-Sat; 🚌22, 41, 45, 47, 49) 🖋 A must-visit for discerning bartenders and anyone wanting under the skin of the artisanal foods movement, this grocery, liquor store and deli carries only small-batch products, many locally made, with an emphasis on bar supplies – grass-flavored gin with elderflower tonic, anyone? The deli makes perfect paninis on bread from Tartine; for dessert there's Humphry Slocombe ice cream by the scoop.

★ATYS
HOMEWARES

Map p292 (☑415-441-9220; www.atysdesign. com; 2149b Union St; ⊙11am-6:30pm Mon-Sat, noon-6pm Sun; 🚌22, 41, 45) Tucked in a courtyard, this design showcase is like a museum store for exceptional, artistic household items – to wit, a mirrored coat rack, a rechargeable flashlight that turns a wineglass into a lamp, and a zero-emissions, solar-powered toy airplane. Expect sleek,

modern designs of superior quality that you won't find anywhere else.

★SUI GENERIS ILLA
CLOTHING

Map p292 (☑415-800-4584; www.suigeneris consignment.com; 2147 Union St; ⊙11am-7pm Mon-Sat, to 5pm Sun; 🚌22, 41, 45) *Sui generis* is Latin for one of a kind – which is what you'll find at this high-end designer consignment shop that features recent seasons' looks, one-of-a-kind gowns and a few archival pieces by key couturiers from decades past. No jeans, no pants – unless they're leather or superglam. Yes, it's pricey, but far cheaper than you'd pay shopping retail.

EXPLORATORIUM STORE
GIFTS & SOUVENIRS

Map p290 (☑415-528-4390; www.exploratorium. edu/visit/store; Pier 17; ⊙10am-5:30pm Fri-Wed, to 10:30pm Thu; 🚻; M E, F) Bring home gifts for the kids that you won't find anywhere else. The shop at the Exploratorium – the city's famous art and science museum – carries unique novelties, games, books and artworks, many made in San Francisco, all designed to inspire imagination.

FLAX ART & DESIGN
DESIGN

Map p292 (☑415-530-3510; http://flaxart.com; 2 Marina Blvd, Bldg D; ⊙10am-6:30pm Mon-Sat, to 6pm Sun; 🚌22, 28, 30, 43) The city's finest art-supply store carries a dizzying array of ink, paints, brushes, pens, pencils, markers, glues and gums, plus paper in myriad varieties, from stationery and wrapping to drawing pads and sketch tablets. If you're a serious designer or artist, Flax is a must-visit.

SPORTS BASEMENT
SPORTS & OUTDOORS

Map p291 (☑415-437-0100; www.sportsbase ment.com; 610 Old Mason St; ⊙9am-9pm Mon-Fri, 8am-8pm Sat & Sun; 🚌30, 43, PresidiGo shuttle) Specializing in odd lots of sporting goods at closeout prices, this 80,000-sq-ft sports-and-camping emporium is also the best place to rent wet suits for swims at Aquatic Park, gear for last-minute trips to Yosemite, or bikes to cross the nearby Golden Gate Bridge – and free parking makes it easy to trade your rental car for a bike.

ANOMIE
FASHION & ACCESSORIES

(☑415-872-9943; www.shopanomie.com; 2149 Union St; ⊙11am-7pm; 🚌22, 41, 45) An essential stop on a Union St shopping raid, Anomie carries multiple small-production, independent designers of casual women's clothing, all subtly fashion forward, plus a changing lineup of accessories, jewelry, candles and bath supplies. Many pieces are in the online shop, so you can get a sense for featured designers before you trek to the Marina.

PLUMPJACK WINES — WINE

Map p292 (☑415-346-9870; www.plumpjackwines. com; 3201 Fillmore St; ⊙11am-8pm Mon-Sat, to 6pm Sun; ☑22, 28, 30, 43) Discover new favorite California vintages for under $25 at the distinctive boutique that won part-owner and former mayor Gavin Newsom respect even from Green Party gourmets. A more knowledgeable staff is hard to find anywhere in SF, and they'll set you up with the right bottles to cross party lines. PlumpJack Wines also has a store in **Noe Valley** (Map p311; ☑415-282-3841; 4011 24th St; ⊙11am-8pm Mon-Thu, to 9pm Fri & Sat, to 6pm Sun; ☑24, 28).

MY ROOMMATE'S CLOSET — CLOTHING

Map p292 (☑415-447-7703; www.shopmrc.com; 3044 Fillmore St; ⊙11am-7pm Mon-Sat, noon-6pm Sun; ☑22, 41, 45) All the half-off bargains and none of the clawing dangers of a sample sale. Stocks constantly change but have included cloud-like Catherine Malandrino chiffon party dresses, executive Diane von Furstenberg wrap dresses and designer denim at prices approaching reality.

ELIZABETHW — PERFUME

Map p289 (☑415-441-8354; www.elizabethw.com; 900 North Point St; ⊙10am-6pm Mon-Thu, to 9pm Fri & Sat, to 8pm Sun; ☑19, 30, 47, ☑Powell-Hyde) Local scent maker elizabethW supplies the tantalizing aromas of changing seasons without the sweaty brows or frozen toes. 'Sweet Tea' smells like a Georgia porch in summertime, 'Vetiver' like autumn in Maine. For a true SF fragrance, 'Leaves' is as audaciously green as Golden Gate Park in January.

AMBIANCE — FASHION & ACCESSORIES

Map p292 (☑415-923-9796; www.ambiancesf. com; 1858 Union St; ⊙11am-7pm Sun-Fri, 10am-7pm Sat; ☑41, 45) The Union St outpost of this three-store SF-based chain showcases midrange designers, with a good mix of trendy and classic cuts in jeans, dresses, shirts, shoes and locally made jewelry. Half the store is devoted to sale items with prices at least 20% below retail.

KIT & ACE — CLOTHING

(☑844-528-6223; www.kitandace.com; 3108 Fillmore St; ⊙11am-6pm; ☑22, 41, 45) Kit and Ace makes 'technical cashmere,' a blend

of cashmere and cotton you can throw in the washing machine. Designs are simple, nothing fancy. What's remarkable is the fabric's softness and drape. There's a whole line of basics – mostly T-shirts and pants – plus some items entirely of dense, plush 100% cashmere (the hoodies are fab).

FOG CITY LEATHER — CLOTHING

Map p292 (☑415-567-1996; http://fogcity leather.com; 2060 Union St; ⊙11:30am-6pm; ☑22, 41, 45) Nothing screams San Francisco quite as much as a new leather outfit – it's what Hillary Clinton wore in SF the first time she spoke publicly after losing the election – and Fog City's clothes are made to be statement pieces. Though it carries practical motorcycle jackets, too, what's great here are the fashion styles – buttery soft and in a rainbow of colors.

SF SALT CO — HOMEWARES

Map p289 (☑800-480-4540; www.sfsalt.com; Pier 39; ⊙10am-9pm; ☑47, ☑Powell-Mason, Ⓜ E, F) Here's an unusual gift: bring back the bay to those who couldn't join you. SF Salt mines salt from San Francisco Bay to make bath salts, adding only essential oils and/or fragrances. The 'detox soak,' made with lavender oil and sea kelp, is especially appealing. After being surrounded by dense crowds at the Wharf, you're gonna need it.

HOUDINI'S MAGIC SHOP — TOYS

Map p289 (☑415-433-1422; www.houdini.com; Pier 39; ⊙9am-9pm Mon-Thu, to 10pm Fri & Sat, 10am-9pm Sun; ⊛; ☑47, ☑Powell-Mason, Ⓜ E, F) For the prankster in your life, Houdini's stocks all the classic gags – rubber chickens, exploding caps, marked cards, escapable handcuffs – plus sophisticated sleight-of-hand tricks and a surprisingly good collection of vintage and modern books on magic. A staff of well-suited magicians will teach you, in the privacy of a 'magic-teaching booth,' how to deploy your new tricks.

BOOKS INC — BOOKS

Map p292 (☑415-931-3633; www.booksinc.net; 2251 Chestnut St; ⊙10am-10pm Mon-Sat, to 9pm Sun; ☑22, 28, 30, 43) One of the city's best remaining independent bookstores, Books Inc carries new-release hardcovers, good fiction, extensive magazines and travel books. Check the bulletin boards for readings and literary events.

BENEFIT
COSMETICS

Map p292 (☑415-567-1173; www.benefitcosmetics. com; 2219 Chestnut St; ⊙10am-7pm Sun-Tue, to 8pm Wed-Fri, 9am-7pm Sat; ☐28, 30, 43) Founded in San Francisco by twin sisters, Benefit offers memorably named makeup – Brow Zings, Ooh La Lift – that draws a cult following. There's a branch on Fillmore St.

ITOYA TOP DRAWER
GIFTS & SOUVENIRS

Map p292 (☑415-771-1108; www.kolo.com; 1840 Union St; ⊙11am-7pm; ☐41, 45) The first boutique outside Japan of Japanese brand Itoya showcases ingenious gadgets for travel you never knew you needed, including pocket-sized hotel-room humidifiers, reversible house slippers, collapsible bottles, travel alarms and portable bento boxes, plus pouches and totes to carry them home.

Y & I BOUTIQUE
FASHION & ACCESSORIES

Map p292 (☑415-202-0775; www.shopyandi.com; 2101 Chestnut St; ⊙10:30am-7pm Mon-Wed & Fri, to 8pm Thu, 10am-7pm Sat, to 6pm Sun; ☐22, 30, 43) When Marina girls need an outfit that won't break the bank, they shop Y and I for their cute dresses, priced at $50 to $200, by brands including Everly and Yumi Kim, plus fun sandals and shoes under $100 and a big selection of handmade jewelry starting at just $20.

JACK'S
CLOTHING

Map p292 (☑415-409-6114; www.jackssf.com; 2260 Chestnut St; ⊙10:30am-6:30pm; ☐28, 30, 43) Jack's dresses Marina dudes in sexy denim by Hudson, Agave and J Brand. But best are the screen-printed T-shirts, emblazoned with the logos of Bay Area sports teams, present and past, from the A's to the Seals – not cheap at $40 but perfect souvenirs for fans.

🏃 SPORTS & ACTIVITIES

★ OCEANIC SOCIETY EXPEDITIONS
CRUISE

Map p292 (☑415-256-9604; www.oceanicsociety. org; 3950 Scott St; whale-watching trips per person $128; ⊙office 9am-5pm Mon-Fri, to 2pm Sat; ☐30) The Oceanic Society runs top-notch, naturalist-led, ocean-going weekend boat trips – sometimes to the Farallon Islands – during both whale-migration seasons. Cruises depart from the yacht harbor

and last all day. Kids must be 10 years or older. Reservations required.

ALCATRAZ CRUISES
TOURS

Map p290 (☑415-981-7625; www.alcatrazcruises. com; tours day adult/child/family $37.25/ 23/112.75, night adult/child $44.25/26.50; Ⓜ E, F) The only transportation to Alcatraz (p50) requires advance bookings; reserve at least a week to a month ahead for first choice of departure times (there's no need to book the return boat, just the outbound one).

ADVENTURE CAT
CRUISE

Map p289 (☑415-777-1630; www.adventurecat. com; Pier 39; adult/child $45/25, sunset cruise $60; ♿; ☐47, Ⓜ E, F) There's no better view of San Francisco than from the water, especially at twilight on a fogless evening aboard a sunset cruise. Adventure Cat uses catamarans, with a windless indoor cabin for grandparents and a trampoline between hulls for bouncy kids. Three daily cruises depart March to October; weekends only in November.

HOUSE OF AIR
TRAMPOLINING

Map p291 (☑415-345-9675; www.houseofairsf. com; 926 Old Mason St; adult $20; ⊙10am-8pm Sun & Mon, 2-9pm Tue-Thu, 10am-10pm Fri & Sat; ♿; ☐28) If you resented your gym teacher for not letting you jump on the trampoline, you can finally have your way at this incredible Crissy Field trampoline park, with multiple jumping areas where you can literally bounce off the walls on 42 attached trampolines. Kids get dedicated areas. Reservations strongly recommended – book three days ahead, especially at weekends.

BLUE & GOLD FLEET
CRUISE

Map p289 (☑415-705-8200; www.blueandgold fleet.com; Pier 41; adult/child 60min ferry tour $31/21, 30min Rocketboat ride $28/20; ♿; ☐47, Ⓜ E, F) See the bay up close aboard a one-hour round-trip cruise to the Golden Gate Bridge or on a 30-minute high-speed thrill ride aboard the fleet's *Rocketboat* (May to October only). Blue & Gold also operates regular ferry services to Sausalito, Tiburon and Angel Island, departing from Pier 41 at Fisherman's Wharf and (some) from the Ferry Building.

PLANET GRANITE
CLIMBING

Map p291 (☑415-692-3434; www.planetgranite. com/sf; 924 Old Mason St; day use adult $18-22, child $15; ⊙6am-11pm Mon-Fri, 8am-8pm Sat, to 6pm Sun; ☐28) Take in spectacular bay views

THE BAY BY BOAT

Some of the best views of San Francisco are from the water – if the weather's fair, be sure to take a boat ride. Following is a list of tours and ferries that will get you out on the bay and provide some stellar photo ops too. Be warned: it's always at least 10 degrees cooler on the bay's chilly waters. Bring a jacket.

Bay cruises The quickest way to familiarize yourself with the view from the bay is aboard a narrated one-hour cruise that loops beneath the Golden Gate Bridge. Red & White Fleet (p73) operates multiple trips from Pier 43½; Blue & Gold Fleet (p72) operates from Pier 41 and also offers 30-minute trips aboard its high-speed *Rocketboat*. (Note: Blue & Gold's Alcatraz-themed cruise only sails *around* the island, not to it.)

Sailboat tours If you prefer sailboats to ferries, hit the bay aboard the Adventure Cat (p72) – a catamaran with a trampoline between its hulls – for a 90-minute bay cruise or sunset sail. Or charter a private sailboat, with or without skipper, from Spinnaker Sailing (p111).

Paddle tours Explore the bay's calm eastern shoreline in a canoe or kayak from City Kayak (p111), which guides tours, including full-moon paddles, and rents boats to experienced paddlers.

Whale-watching tours To go beyond the Golden Gate and on to the open ocean, take one of the excellent trips operated by the Oceanic Society (p72).

Sausalito and Tiburon trips It's a quick, inexpensive ferry ride to these neighboring waterside villages across the bay from SF (p214). Golden Gate Ferry (p267) and Blue & Gold Fleet (p72) operate services.

Angel Island trips Spend the day exploring this state park in the middle of the bay, featuring California's historic immigration station. From San Francisco, take Blue & Gold Fleet (p72).

Oakland trips Ferries land at Jack London Sq, where you can eat bayside and have a beer at historic Heinold's First & Last Chance Saloon, whose sloping bar has been operating since 1883. Take San Francisco Bay Ferry (p266).

THE MARINA, FISHERMAN'S WHARF & THE PIERS SPORTS & ACTIVITIES

as you ascend false-rock structures inside this kick-ass 25,000-sq-ft glass-walled climbing center at Crissy Field – ideal for training before climbs at Yosemite. Master top ropes of 45ft or test your strength ascending giant boulders and vertical-crack climbing walls; finish in the full gym or stretch in a yoga session. Check the website for schedules.

BLAZING SADDLES   CYCLING
Map p289 (☏415-202-8888; www.blazingsaddles. com/san-francisco; 2715 Hyde St; bicycle rental per hour $8-15, per day $32-88, electric bikes per day $48-88; ☉8am-8pm; 🚲; 🚋Powell-Hyde) Blazing Saddles is tailored to visitors, with a main shop on Hyde St and six rental stands around Fisherman's Wharf, convenient for biking the Embarcadero or to the Golden Gate Bridge. It also rents electric bikes and offers a 24-hour return service – a big plus. Reserve online for a 20% discount; rental includes all extras (bungee cords, packs etc).

PRESIDIO GOLF COURSE   GOLF
Map p291 (☏415-561-4661; www.presidiogolf. com; cnr Arguello Blvd & Finley Rd; 18 holes SF resident $67-82, non-resident $125-145; ☉sunrise-sunset; 🚌33) Whack balls with military-style precision on the course once reserved for US forces. The Presidio course, now operated by Arnold Palmer Enterprises, overlooks the bay and is considered one of the country's best. Book up to 30 days in advance on the website, which sometimes lists specials too. Rates include cart.

RED & WHITE FLEET   CRUISE
Map p289 (☏415-673-2900; www.redandwhite. com; Pier 43½; adult/child $38/26; 🚲; 🚌47, Ⓜ E, F) A one-hour bay cruise with Red & White lets you see the Golden Gate Bridge from the water. Brave the wind and sit on the outdoor upper deck. Audio tours in multiple languages provide narrative. On-board alcohol subdues naysayers.

Downtown, Civic Center & SoMa

FINANCIAL DISTRICT | JACKSON SQUARE | UNION SQUARE | SOMA | CIVIC CENTER | THE TENDERLOIN

Neighborhood Top Five

1 Ferry Building (p79) Grazing the Northern California food scene with incredible bay views at this showcase for the Bay Area's food purveyors and organic farmers.

2 San Francisco Museum of Modern Art (p76) Getting lost in mesmerizing installation art at the new triple-sized SFMOMA – and discussing it over museum-quality meals at In Situ.

3 Riding a cable car (p82) Squealing with glee during the trip and congratulating yourself for not wearing shorts and shivering the whole way.

4 San Francisco Symphony (p102) Watching impresario Michael Tilson Thomas conduct Beethoven from the tips of his toes at the Grammy-winning Symphony.

5 Asian Art Museum (p78) Seeing all the way across the Pacific via the museum's priceless treasures.

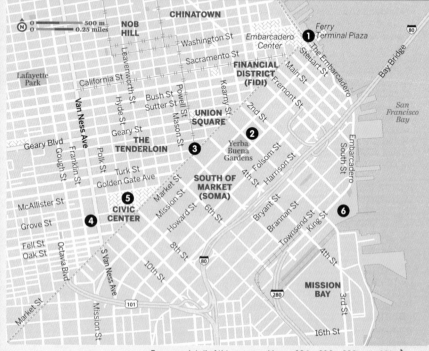

For more detail of this area see Maps p294, p296, p298 and p301

Explore: Downtown, Civic Center & SoMa

The cluster of monumental stone buildings and plazas around City Hall is called Civic Center. Start your day at the Asian Art Museum (p78), then take your pick of dozens of local food stalls at Heart of the City Farmers Market (p94) or the Twitter building marketplace (p86). North and east of Civic Center is the less-than-savory Tenderloin, which most first-time visitors are advised to skip – though adventurous gallery-goers brave Market St between 8th and 6th for groundbreaking arts nonprofits. Hop the F line to Powell St for shopping around Union Sq, or head onward to Montgomery to discover splendid architecture among the Financial District's mighty temples of money. Come nightfall, SoMa bars, nightclubs and drag cabarets encourage outrageousness. If you scored tickets to the SF Symphony or Opera, catch the California cable car to Van Ness and stroll downhill to your show.

Local Life

➡**Markets** Ferry Building and Civic Center farmers-market days are foodie magnets, with heirloom produce, local artisan foods and free samples galore.

➡**Arts revival** The blighted blocks of SoMa and Market St west of Powell may not be much to look at from the outside, but inside they're full of ideas: arts nonprofits stage provocative shows in many formerly derelict dives.

➡**Happy hours** You're spoiled for choice downtown – and weekday drink specials beckon.

Getting There & Away

➡**Streetcar** Historic F-Market streetcars run above Market St, between the Castro and Fisherman's Wharf.

➡**Cable car** Powell-Hyde and Powell-Mason lines link downtown with the Wharf (Mason is shorter, Hyde more scenic); the California St line runs over Nob Hill.

➡**Bus** Market St–bound Muni lines serve downtown: 2, 5, 6, 7, 14, 21, 30, 31, 38, 41, 45. In SoMa the 30 and 45 run down 4th St from the Marina and Union Sq; the 14 runs through SoMa to the Mission along Mission St. The 27 runs from the Mission to Nob Hill via SoMa; the 47 runs along Harrison St through SoMa, up Van Ness to Fisherman's Wharf; the 19 runs up 8th and Polk Sts to the Wharf.

➡**Metro** J, K/T, L, M and N metro lines run under Market St. The N continues to the Caltrain station, connecting SoMa to the Haight and Golden Gate Park. The T runs from downtown, via SoMa, stopping along 3rd St.

➡**BART** Downtown stations are Embarcadero, Montgomery, Powell and Civic Center.

Lonely Planet's Top Tip

Most tourists begin cable-car trips at Powell St but often get stuck waiting in the long lines at the cable-car turnaround at Powell and Market Sts – and subjected to panhandlers and clamorous street performers. Either queue up for the Powell St cable car before noon, or hop the lesser-traveled, more historic California St line near the Embarcadero.

DOWNTOWN, CIVIC CENTER & SOMA

 Best Places to Eat

➡ In Situ (p92)

➡ Ferry Building (p79)

➡ Benu (p92)

➡ Tout Sweet (p90)

➡ Cotogna (p88)

For reviews, see p88 ➡

 Best Places to Drink

➡ Bar Agricole (p98)

➡ Bourbon & Branch (p101)

➡ Pagan Idol (p95)

➡ Aunt Charlie's (p101)

➡ Eagle Tavern (p98)

➡ Local Edition (p95)

➡ Stud (p98)

For reviews, see p94 ➡

☆ Best Entertainment

➡ San Francisco Symphony (p102)

➡ American Conservatory Theater (p103)

➡ San Francisco Opera (p102)

➡ Oasis (p104)

➡ Yerba Buena Center for the Arts (p105)

For reviews, see p102 ➡

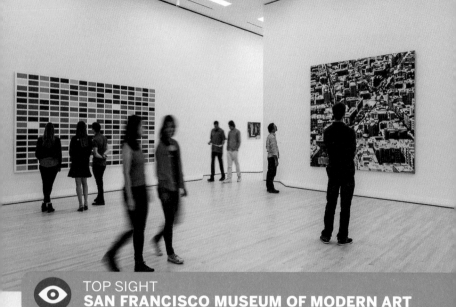

The expanded SFMOMA is a mind-boggling feat, tripled in size to accommodate a sprawling collection of modern masterworks and 19 concurrent exhibitions over 10 floors – but, then again, SFMOMA has defied limits ever since its 1935 founding. SFMOMA was a visionary early investor in then-emerging art forms including photography, installations, video, performance art, digital art and industrial design.

New Galleries, Expanding Collections

Ever since the Great Depression, SFMOMA envisioned a world of vivid possibilities, starting in San Francisco. The collection has outgrown its home twice since, and the 2016 expansion offers free access to ground-floor galleries and a dramatic entrance via Richard Serra's mammoth rusted-steel maze – a truly inspired alternative to shrubbery. The unprecedented donation of over 1100 major modern works by the Fisher family (founders of SF-based clothiers the Gap, Old Navy and Banana Republic) was the catalyst behind Snøhetta architects' half-billion-dollar extension, which has added ship-shape galleries around Mario Botta's original periscope-shaped atrium.

Design

Architecture and design are showcased on the 6th floor and you can start your own collection of SFMOMA design objects, statement jewelry and art catalogs at the ground-floor Museum Store.

Above: German Art after 1960, the Fisher Collection exhibition at SFMOMA. Image courtesy SFMOMA.

DON'T MISS

➡ Photography collection

➡ Video and new-media installations

➡ Richard Serra lobby maze

➡ 7th-floor experimental art

➡ In Situ (p92)

PRACTICALITIES

➡ SFMOMA

➡ Map p298, E3

➡ ☎415-357-4000

➡ www.sfmoma.org

➡ 151 3rd St

➡ adult/under 18yr/student $25/free/$19

➡ ⊙10am-5pm Fri-Tue, to 9pm Thu, public spaces from 9am

➡ ♿

➡ 🚌5, 6, 7, 14, 19, 21, 31, 38, ⓂMontgomery, ⒷMontgomery

Suggested Itinerary

There are free gallery tours, but exploring on your own gives you the thrill of discovery, which is what SFMOMA is all about. Following this itinerary, you should be able to cover collection highlights in two to four hours. Start on the 3rd floor with SFMOMA's standout **photography** collection, featuring great postwar Japanese photographers Shomei Tomatsu and Daido Moriyama alongside pioneering West Coast photographers Ansel Adams, Edward Weston, Imogen Cunningham, Dorothea Lange, Pirkle Jones and Larry Sultan. Meditate amid sunwashed, subtle tone-on-tone paintings in the Agnes Martin room surrounded by 4th floor **Minimalists** then get an eyeful of Warhol's silver Elvis in **Pop Art** on the 5th floor.

The 6th floor hosts poignant **video art** by Shirin Neshat and William Kentridge, while the top floor reaches peak art freak with **experimental works** by the likes of SF's own Matthew Barney – who launched his career at SFMOMA with poetic performances involving industrial quantities of Vaseline. Head down via the atrium to see how SFMOMA began, with colorful local characters admiring equally colorful characters by Diego Rivera, Frida Kahlo and Henri Matisse.

Above: Alexander Calder gallery at SFMOMA. Image courtesy SFMOMA.

For weekend visits and special exhibits, book tickets ahead online.

Visitors under age 18 enjoy free admission, but they must have a ticket for entry.

Reserve weeks/months ahead to dine at In Situ, SFMOMA's acclaimed gallery of world cuisine.

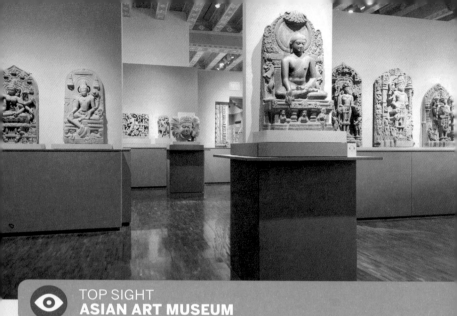

TOP SIGHT
ASIAN ART MUSEUM

The Asian Art Museum's distinguished collection of 18,000 Asian treasures does San Francisco proud, reflecting the city's 150-year history as America's gateway to Asia. The museum's curators have performed diplomatic wonders under this roof, bringing Taiwan, China and Tibet together, uniting Pakistan and India, and striking a harmonious balance among artifacts from Japan, Korea and China.

Suggested Itinerary

The Asian Museum's curatorial concept is to follow the evolution of Asian art from West to East toward San Francisco, along Buddhist pilgrimage trails and trade routes – all in under three hours. Start on the 3rd floor, where you'll find a treasure trove of **Indian miniatures**. Detour through dizzying **Iranian geometric tiles** and **Javanese shadow puppets**, and turn a corner to find **Tibetan prayer wheels**. Downstairs on the 2nd floor are **Chinese calligraphy**, **Korean celadon bowls** and an entire **Japanese tea-ceremony room**.

Throughout your treasure hunt, look for artworks by contemporary artists responding to ancient masterpieces. Parents can pick up Explorer Cards for kids to find favorite animals and characters in the galleries.

Events & Evenings at the Asian

Don't miss special exhibits on the ground floor, featuring major artists and topical themes. Hands-on workshops for kids, artists' demonstrations in Samsung Hall and free yoga classes draw intergenerational crowds. On Thursday evenings from 5pm to 9pm February through September, hipsters flock to the Asian for $10 entry with free evening events hosted by major contemporary artists.

DON'T MISS

➡ South Asian and Persian miniatures

➡ Japanese tea-house artifacts

➡ 3000-year-old Chinese bronze rhinoceros wine vessel with a twinkle in its eye

➡ Breakthrough contemporary Asian art

➡ Thursday-night live artist-led events

PRACTICALITIES

➡ Map p296, B5

➡ ☏415-581-3500

➡ www.asianart.org

➡ 200 Larkin St

➡ adult/student/child $15/10/free, 1st Sun of month free

➡ ⊘10am-5pm Tue-Sun, to 9pm Thu

➡ Ⓜ Civic Center, ⒷCivic Center

TOP SIGHT
FERRY BUILDING & SURROUNDS

Other towns have gourmet ghettos, but San Francisco puts its love of food front and center at the Ferry Building. The once-grand port was overshadowed by a 1950s elevated freeway – until the overpass collapsed in 1989's Loma Prieta earthquake. The Ferry Building survived and became a symbol of San Francisco's reinvention, marking your arrival onto America's forward-thinking food frontier.

Ferry Building

The Ferry Building's trademark 240ft clocktower has greeted ferries daily since 1898 – but today the kiosk-lined grand arrivals hall and award-winning restaurants tempt commuters to miss the boat and get on board with SF's latest culinary trends instead.

Join SF's legions of professional chefs and semiprofessional eaters and sample 50 to 100 local food purveyors catering to hometown crowds three times a week. The Saturday morning **farmers market** (Map p301; ☎415-291-3276; www.cuesa.org; cnr Market St & the Embarcadero; street food $3-12; ⊙10am-2pm Tue & Thu, from 8am Sat; 🖉 🚻; Ⓜ Embarcadero) 🖉 offers the best selection – but arrive early, before those pesky *Top Chef* contestants snap up the best finds.

Bay Bridge Lights

The Bay Bridge looms large on the horizon south of the Ferry Building, especially at night. Artist Leo Villareal strung 25,000 LED lights onto the western span, programming Bay Bridge Lights to blink in never-repeating patterns – one second it looks like bubbly champagne, then a lava-lamp forest, then Vegas-style fountains spraying 50 stories high. The installation was meant to be temporary, but thanks to hypnotized local donors, it was permanently installed in 2016.

DON'T MISS

➡ Ferry Plaza Farmers Market (p79) picnics by the bay
➡ Food kiosks in the Ferry Building's grand arrivals hall
➡ Bay Bridge views along the Embarcadero waterfront promenade

PRACTICALITIES

➡ Map p301, D2
➡ ☎415-983-8030
➡ www.ferrybuilding marketplace.com
➡ cnr Market St & the Embarcadero
➡ ⊙10am-7pm Mon-Fri, 8am-6pm Sat, 11am-5pm Sun
➡ 🚌2, 6, 9, 14, 21, 31, Ⓜ Embarcadero, Ⓑ Embarcadero

◉ SIGHTS

The Financial District centers on Montgomery St – the 'Wall St of the West' – and stretches to Jackson Square, the city's oldest neighborhood, with low-slung brick buildings and high-end antiquarians. The term Union Sq refers to the square *and* the surrounding retail-shopping and hotel district. Tech and biotech are converting South of Market (SoMa) into a second downtown. Museums and galleries cluster around 3rd and Mission, but otherwise SoMa's long, industrial blocks are gritty and tedious. Civic Center is the area around City Hall bordered north and east by the seedy Tenderloin district – best avoided without a mapped route to a specific destination.

◉ Financial District & Jackson Square

FERRY BUILDING LANDMARK
See p79.

**TRANSAMERICA PYRAMID
& REDWOOD PARK** NOTABLE BUILDING
Map p301 (www.thepyramidcenter.com; 600 Montgomery St; ☺9am-6pm Mon-Fri; MEmbarcadero, BEmbarcadero) The defining feature of San Francisco's skyline is this 1972 pyramid, built atop a whaling ship abandoned in the gold rush. A half-acre redwood grove sprouted out front, on the site of Mark Twain's favorite saloon and the newspaper office where Sun Yat-sen drafted his Proclamation of the Republic of China. Although these transplanted redwoods have shallow roots, their intertwined structure helps them reach dizzying heights – Twain himself couldn't have penned a more perfect metaphor for San Francisco.

**DIEGO RIVERA'S ALLEGORY OF
CALIFORNIA FRESCO** PUBLIC ART
Map p294 (www.sfcityguides.org/desc.html?tour=96; 155 Sansome St; tours free; ☺tours by reservation with SF City Guides 3pm 1st & 3rd Mon of month; BMontgomery, MMontgomery) FREE Hidden inside San Francisco's Stock Exchange tower is a priceless treasure: Diego Rivera's 1930–31 *Allegory of California* fresco. Spanning a two-story stairwell between the 10th and 11th floors, the fresco shows California as a giant golden goddess offering farm-fresh produce, while gold miners toil beneath her and oil refineries loom on the horizon. Rivera's *Allegory* is glorious, but cautionary – while Californian workers, inventors and dreamers go about their business, the pressure gauge in the left-hand corner is entering the red zone.

AP HOTALING WAREHOUSE HISTORIC BUILDING
Map p301 (451-55 Jackson St; MEmbarcadero, BEmbarcadero) 'If, as they say, God spanked the town/For being over-frisky/Why did He burn His churches down/And spare Hotaling's whiskey?' This saloon-goers' retort was the snappiest comeback in SF history after Hotaling's 1866 whiskey warehouse survived the 1906 earthquake and fire. A bronze plaque bearing the ditty graces the resilient Italianate building.

WELLS FARGO HISTORY MUSEUM MUSEUM
Map p301 (☎415-396-2619; www.wellsfargo history.com/museums; 420 Montgomery St; ☺9am-5pm Mon-Fri; ♿; MMontgomery, BMontgomery) FREE Gold miners needed somewhere to stash and send cash, so Wells Fargo opened in this location in 1852. Today, this storefront museum covers gold rush–era innovations, including the Pony Express, transcontinental telegrams and statewide stagecoaches. Wells Fargo was the world's largest stagecoach operator c 1866, and you can climb aboard a preserved stagecoach to hear pioneer-trail stories while kids ride a free mechanical pony. Notwithstanding the blatant PR for Wells Fargo, the exhibits are well researched, fascinating and free.

SUN TERRACE VIEWPOINT
Map p301 (343 Sansome St; ☺10am-6pm Mon-Fri; MEmbarcadero, BEmbarcadero) Enjoy knockout vistas of the Financial District and Transamerica Pyramid from atop a slender art-deco skyscraper. Take the elevator to the 15th floor.

JACKSON SQUARE AREA
Map p301 (www.jacksonsquaresf.com; around Jackson & Montgomery Sts; MEmbarcadero, BEmbarcadero) Today upscale Jackson Sq is framed by Washington, Columbus, Pacific and Sansome Sts – but before the gold rush filled in the area with abandoned ships, this was a notorious waterfront dock area. Behind the iron shutters of these Italianate brick buildings, whiskey dealers, loan sharks, madams, lawyers and other hustlers plied their trades.

⊙ Union Square

ANGLIM GILBERT GALLERY   GALLERY

Map p294 (☎415-433-2710; www.gallerypaule anglim.com; 14 Geary St; ⏱10am-5:30pm Tue-Fri, 10:30am-5pm Sat; ☐5, 6, 7, 15, 21, 31, 38, 71, F, J, K, L, M, N, Ⓑ Montgomery) **FREE** For more than 30 years, this SF gallery has launched break-through works like Bruce Conner's punk stage-dive photos, Deborah Butterfield's driftwood stallions and Enrique Chagoya's subversive paintings of indigenous char-acters wearing modernist masterpieces as fashion. See what's on the minds of SF artists now, from Lynn Hershman Leeson's eerie cy-borg nudes to Tomas Nakada's mesmerizing paintings of bacterial migration patterns. Don't miss the gallery's experimental exten-sion at the Minnesota Street Project.

49 GEARY   GALLERY

Map p294 (www.sfada.com; 49 Geary St; ⏱10:30am-5:30pm Tue-Fri, 11am-5pm Sat; ☐5, 6, 7, 9, 21, 31, 38, Ⓜ Powell, Ⓑ Powell) **FREE** Pity the collectors silently nibbling endive in austere Chelsea galleries – at 49 Geary, openings mean unexpected art, popcorn and outspo-ken crowds. Four floors of galleries feature standout international and local works, including photography at Fraenkel Gallery and Scott Nichols Gallery, Ai Weiwei instal-lations at Haines Gallery, and Christian May-chack's architectural excess at Gregory Lind. For quieter contemplation, visit weekdays.

PACIFIC TELEPHONE & TELEGRAPH COMPANY BUILDING   NOTABLE BUILDING

Map p298 (140 New Montgomery St; ☐14, Ⓑ Mont-gomery, Ⓜ Montgomery) Recently renovated and gilt to the hilt indoors, this 1925 build-ing made architect Timothy Pflueger's reputation with its black-marble deco lobby and soaring, streamlined shape. Winston Churchill made his first transatlantic tele-phone call here in 1929, but ironically the tower now seems to interfere with cell-phone coverage. Notice the cable-like lines running right up the building, past stylized telegraph insulators to fierce stone eagles. Today it's the headquarters of review site Yelp, and home to Morocco-moderne restaurant Mourad.

450 SUTTER ST   NOTABLE BUILDING

Map p294 (450 Sutter St; ☐38, ☐ Powell-Mason, Powell-Hyde) A 26-story deco dental build-ing fit for the gods, this 1929 Mayan-revival

KIOSK MUSEUM

Ever since the web was invented in the Bay Area, San Francisco has been circulating news online, rendering newspaper kiosks on downtown street corners largely obsolete. Community Arts International is working with the city to upcycle them into mini muse-ums, turning long waits for traffic lights into opportunities to illuminate and delight passersby. The **Kiosk Museum** (www.kioskmuseum.com) showcases San Francisco history in five kiosks: at Geary and Powell, Post and Stockton, another across Stockton, Maiden Lane and Grant Ave, and the last on Kearny at Vermehr Pl. Theatrical scenes are created in kiosk windows, where newspaper sellers once announced the day's headlines. A recent show focused on circus-themed toys from around the world, and *The Streets of San Francisco* saw each kiosk feature an SF photo-grapher from a different era in the city's history. Check the website for current kiosk shows and a route map.

stone skyscraper has a lobby covered floor to ceiling with cast-bronze snakes represent-ing healing, grimacing figures apparently in need of dentistry, and panels covered with mystifying glyphs – early insurance forms, perhaps? With glowing inverted-pyramid lights, this Timothy Pflueger–designed landmark makes getting a cavity filled seem like a spiritual experience.

RUTH ASAWA'S SAN FRANCISCO FOUNTAIN   FOUNTAIN

Map p294 (www.ruthasawa.com; 355 Stock-ton St, on Grand Hyatt steps; ☐ Powell-Mason, Mason-Hyde, Ⓜ Powell, Ⓑ Powell) Covered in local landmarks and colorful SF charac-ters – burlesque icon Carol Doda, psyche-delic rockers Jefferson Airplane, protestors declaring themselves 'Jewish Diabetics for Peace' – Ruth Asawa's 1973 San Francisco Fountain captures the city's spirit. Asawa collected favorite city sights from 250 San Franciscans, sculpted them in bread dough, then cast them in bronze. Apple designed its flagship store for this spot, but, after a public outcry defending the fountain, it eventually redesigned the building and re-stored the fountain.

POWELL ST CABLE CAR TURNAROUND
LANDMARK

Map p294 (www.sfmta.com; cnr Powell & Market Sts; 🚋Powell-Mason, Mason-Hyde, Ⓜ Powell, Ⓑ Powell) Peek through the passenger queue at Powell and Market Sts to spot cable-car operators leaping out, gripping the chassis of each trolley and slooowly turning the car atop a revolving wooden platform. Cable cars can't go in reverse, so they need to be turned around by hand here at the terminus of the Powell St lines. Riders queue up midmorning to early evening here to secure a seat, with raucous street performers and doomsday preachers on the sidelines as entertainment.

UNION SQUARE
SQUARE

Map p294 (btwn Geary, Powell, Post & Stockton Sts; 🚋Powell-Mason, Powell-Hyde, Ⓜ Powell, Ⓑ Powell) High-end stores ring Union Sq now, but this people-watching plaza has been a hotbed of protest, from pro-Union Civil War rallies to AIDS vigils. Atop the central pillar is the Goddess of Victory, who's apparently having a wardrobe malfunction. This bare-breasted deity is modeled after Big Alma Spreckles, who volunteered her nude-modeling services when she heard sugar-baron Adolph Spreckels was heading the monument committee.

Spreckles became her 'sugar daddy,' and Alma donated her fortune to build the Legion of Honor.

LOTTA'S FOUNTAIN
MONUMENT

Map p294 (cnr Market & Kearny Sts; 🚋5, 6, 7, 9, 21, 31, Ⓜ Montgomery, Ⓑ Montgomery) Lotta Crabtree made fortunes as San Francisco's diminutive opera diva, and she never forgot the city that paid for her trademark cigars. In 1875 she donated this cast-metal spigot fountain (thrice her size) to San Francisco. Her gift came in handy during the April 18, 1906, earthquake and fire, when it became downtown's sole water source, as corrupt officials had pocketed funds intended to hook up fire hydrants. Descendants of earthquake survivors meet here each April 18 at 5:12am for rousing sing-alongs.

PALACE HOTEL
HISTORIC BUILDING

Map p294 (📞415-512-1111; www.sfpalace.com; 2 New Montgomery St; Ⓜ Montgomery, Ⓑ Montgomery) A true SF survivor, the Palace opened in 1875 but was gutted during the 1906 earthquake. Opera star Enrico Caruso was jolted from his Palace bed by the quake and fled San Francisco, never to return. The Palace reopened by 1909 and it was here that Woodrow Wilson gave his League

TIMOTHY PFLUEGER'S JAWDROPPING SKYSCRAPERS

When a downtown skyscraper makes you stop, stare and crane your neck, it's probably Timothy Pflueger's fault. San Francisco's prolifically fanciful architect was responsible for downtown's most jaw-dropping buildings from 1925 to 1948, in styles ranging from opulent art deco to monumental minimalism. Movie buffs and architecture aficionados will want to hop the F line to catch a movie in Pflueger's 1922 palatial Mexican-baroque Castro Theatre, then take BART to Oakland to see how his 1931 glittering mosaic deco Paramount Theatre inspired *Wizard of Oz* Emerald City sets. But first, stop and stare at these Pflueger masterpieces downtown.

Pacific Telephone & Telegraph Company Building (p81) Art deco reaches new heights in this 1925 skyscraper, banded with carved-stone telegraph cables and topped by eagles screaming into the wind – anyone trying to find cell reception in San Francisco's overloaded grid can definitely relate. Peek inside at SF's most magnificent lobby, where Chinese-inspired golden clouds float over black marble walls.

450 Sutter St (p81) Grimacing gods are inauspicious omens lining the lobby of Pflueger's 1929 Mayan Revival dentists' office building, sticking up 26 floors above downtown like a giant's long-lost molar.

I Magnin Store (p83) Pflueger's radical stripped-down design for a clothing store caused a scandal when revealed in 1948 – but his stark naked expanse of white marble stands the test of time and changing fashions as Pflueger's final work.

Pflueger's legacy includes a dozen other Bay Area landmarks, including the Bay Bridge and the arts institution he co-founded: the **San Francisco Museum of Modern Art** (p76).

of Nations speech 10 years later. Visit by day to see the Garden Court stained-glass ceiling, then peek into the **Pied Piper Bar** to see Maxfield Parrish's *Pied Piper* mural.

I MAGNIN BUILDING   NOTABLE BUILDING

Map p294 (cnr Stockton & Geary Sts; ▣38, ▣Powell-Mason, Powell-Hyde) When Timothy Pflueger's radical design was revealed on Union Sq in 1948, SF society was shocked: San Francisco's flagship clothing store appeared completely naked. Stripped of deco adornment, Pflueger's avant-garde white-marble plinth caused consternation – until Christian Dior himself pronounced it '*magnifique*.' Today it's a Macy's with new interiors – only the original 6th-floor women's bathroom remains intact. Pflueger's daring building remains Union Sq's most timeless fashion statement, and was his final work before his untimely death of a heart attack at 54.

JAMES FLOOD BUILDING   HISTORIC BUILDING

Map p294 (cnr Market & Powell Sts; ▣Powell, ▣Powell) This 1904 stone building survived the 1906 earthquake and retains its original character, notwithstanding the Gap flagship downstairs. Upstairs, labyrinthine marble hallways are lined with frosted-glass doors, just like a noir movie set. No coincidence: in 1921 the SF office of infamous Pinkerton Detective Agency hired a young investigator named Dashiell Hammett, author of the 1930 noir classic *The Maltese Falcon*.

FRANK LLOYD WRIGHT BUILDING   NOTABLE BUILDING

Map p294 (VC Morris Store; 140 Maiden Lane; ▣38, ▣Powell, ▣Powell) Shrink the Guggenheim, plop it inside a yellow-brick box with a round Romanesque entryway and put it where you'd least expect it: on a shady SF alley that was once a backstreet brothel. Groundbreaking American architect Frank Lloyd Wright designed this as the VC Morris Gift Store in 1948; this is his only San Francisco building. It's changed hands since and was up for sale in early 2017. If it's open, duck inside to see Wright's signature nautilus-shell atrium ramp.

◉ SoMa

SAN FRANCISCO MUSEUM OF MODERN ART   MUSEUM

See p76.

★CONTEMPORARY JEWISH MUSEUM   MUSEUM

Map p294 (☏415-344-8800; www.thecjm.org; 736 Mission St; adult/student/child $14/12/free; after 5pm Thu $5; ⊙11am-5pm Mon, Tue & Fri-Sun, to 8pm Thu; ▣; ▣14, 30, 45, ▣Montgomery, ▣Montgomery) That upended blue-steel box miraculously balancing on one corner isn't sculpture but the Yerba Buena Lane entry to the Contemporary Jewish Museum – an institution that upends conventional ideas about art and religion. Exhibits here are compelling explorations of Jewish ideals and visionaries, including writer Gertrude Stein, rock promoter Bill Graham, cartoonist Roz Chast and filmmaker Stanley Kubrick.

Architect Daniel Libeskind designed this museum to be rational, mystical and powerful: building onto a 1907 brick power station, he added blue-steel elements to form the Hebrew word *l'chaim* (life). But it's the contemporary art commissions that truly bring the building to life, from Anthony Discenza's spiritual road signs warning of 'Wafting Music' ahead, to Elisabeth Higgins O'Connor's giant trickster *golem* (monsters), built of scavenged rags and packing crates. Stick around for events such as desert filmmaking with *Star Wars* set designer Erik Tiemens, Bay Area artists discussing the impact of AIDS activism and interpretive dance for elders with choreographer Joe Goode. Artistic and theological debates are further fueled by respectable pastrami, served on-site 11am to 2pm daily by SF's own Wise Sons deli.

SAN FRANCISCO MURALS AT RINCON ANNEX POST OFFICE   PUBLIC ART

Map p298 (101 Spear St; ⊙8:30am-5:30pm Mon-Fri; ▣2, 6, 7, 14, 21, 31, ▣Embarcadero, ▣Embarcadero) FREE Only in San Francisco could a post office prove so controversial. This art-deco landmark is lined with vibrant Works Project Administration murals of SF history, begun by Russian-born painter Anton Refregier in 1941 – but WWII and political squabbles ensued. After 92 changes to satisfy censors, Refregier concluded these murals in 1948 with *War & Peace*, pointedly contrasting Nazi book-burning scenes with postwar promises of 'freedom from fear/want/of worship/speech.' Initially denounced by McCarthyists, Refregier's masterpiece is now a National Landmark.

CALIFORNIA
HISTORICAL SOCIETY MUSEUM
Map p298 (☑415-357-1848; www.california
historicalsociety.org; 678 Mission St; adult/child
$5/free; ☺gallery & store 11am-5pm Tue-Sun,
library noon-5pm Wed-Fri; ♿; MMontgomery,
BMontgomery) Enter a Golden State of en-
lightenment at this Californiana treasure
trove, featuring themed exhibitions drawn
from the museum's million-plus California
photographs, paintings and ephemera. Recent exhibits have unearthed Prohibition-
era wine labels, protest posters from the
Summer of Love and 1971 instructions for
interpretive-dancing your way through San
Francisco by dance pioneer Anna Halprin.
Events are rare opportunities to discuss
1970s underground comix, 1940s SF gay
bars and gold rush–era saloon menu staples
(whiskey, opium and tamales).

MUSEUM OF THE
AFRICAN DIASPORA MUSEUM
Map p298 (MoAD; ☑415-358-7200; www.moadsf.
org; 685 Mission St; adult/child/student $10/
free/$5; ☺11am-6pm Wed-Sat, noon-5pm Sun;
P♿; ➎14, 30, 45, MMontgomery, BMontgomery) MoAD assembles an international
cast of characters to tell the epic story of
diaspora, including a moving video of slave
narratives told by Maya Angelou. Standouts among quarterly changing exhibits
have included homages to '80s New Wave
icon Grace Jones, architect David Adjaye's
photographs of contemporary African
landmarks and Alison Saar's sculptures of
figures marked by history. Public events
include poetry slams, Yoruba spiritual music celebrations and lectures examining the
legacy of the Black Panthers' free-school-
breakfast program.

CHILDREN'S CREATIVITY
MUSEUM MUSEUM
Map p298 (☑415-820-3320; http://creativity.
org/; 221 4th St; $12; ☺10am-4pm Wed-Sun;
♿; ➎14, MPowell, BPowell) No velvet ropes
or hands-off signs here: kids rule, with
high-tech displays double-daring them to
make music videos, film claymation movies
and construct play castles. Jump into live-
action video games and sign up for workshops with Bay Area superstar animators,
techno whizzes and robot builders. For low-
tech fun, take a spin on the vintage-1906
Loof Carousel outside, operating 10am to
5pm daily; one $4 ticket covers two rides
($1 discount with museum admission).

YERBA BUENA GARDENS PARK
Map p298 (☑415-820-3550; www.yerbabuena
gardens.com; cnr 3rd & Mission Sts; ☺sunrise-
10pm; ♿; MMontgomery, BMontgomery)
Breathe a sigh of relief: you've found the
lush green getaway in the concrete heart
of SoMa, between Yerba Buena Center for
the Arts and Metreon entertainment complex. This is a prime spot to picnic, hear free
noontime summer concerts (see website)
or duck behind the fountain for a smooch.
Martin Luther King Jr Memorial Fountain
is a wall of water that runs over the Reverend's immortal words: '...until justice rolls
down like water and righteousness like a
mighty stream.'

CROWN POINT PRESS GALLERY
Map p298 (☑415-974-6273; www.crownpoint.
com; 20 Hawthorne St; ☺10am-5pm Mon, to 6pm
Tue-Sat; ➎14, BMontgomery, MMontgomery)
FREE Bet you didn't think anyone could
capture Chuck Close's giant portraits, Robert Bechtle's hyperrealistic street scenes or
Kiki Smith's painstaking wall paintings
on paper – yet here they are. Crown Point
Press printmakers work with international
artists to turn singular visions into large-
scale, limited-edition woodblocks and
etchings. When master printmakers are at
work, you're often invited to watch – and if
you're inspired to make your own, you can
pick up how-to books and tools here.

SF ARTS COMMISSION GALLERY GALLERY
Map p296 (☑415-252-2244; www.sfartscommis
sion.org; War Memorial Veterans Bldg, Suite 126,
401 Van Ness Ave; ☺11am-6pm Tue-Sat; MVan
Ness) ✐ Get in on the ground floor of the
next SF art movement at this public showcase for local talent, from Susan O'Malley's
silk-screened words of advice from San
Franciscans to rock photographer Jim
Marshall's iconic shots of Jimi and Janis.
Beyond gallery exhibitions, the commission
also shows art in City Hall and in an empty
storefront at 155 Grove St.

SOUTH PARK PARK
Map p298 (S Park St; MN, T) 'Dot-com' was
coined in mid-'90s San Francisco, when
venture capitalists and tattooed cyber-
punks plotted website launches in South
Park cafes. But speculation is nothing new
to South Park, planned by an 1850s real-
estate speculator as a bucolic gated community. The development foundered, but
South Park became a breeding ground for

wild ideas: a plaque at 601 3rd St marks the birthplace of Jack London, author of *The Call of the Wild*, *White Fang* and other Wild West adventure stories.

SPUR URBAN CENTER GALLERY CENTER
Map p298 (☑415-781-8726; www.spur.org; 654 Mission St; ☺11am-5pm Tue-Fri; ☑12, 14, ⓑMontgomery, ⓜMontgomery) FREE Cities are what you make of them, and urban-planning nonprofit SPUR invites you to reimagine San Francisco (and your own hometown) with gallery shows that explore urban living, from soundscapes to elder-housing design. Exhibitions are free, thought-provoking and visually appealing, featuring local and international artists. For the ultimate SF treasure hunt, check out SPUR's interactive map to hidden downtown 'privately owned public spaces' (POPOs), which are actually open to the public (www.spur.org/blog/2012-08-27/get-spurs-guide-public-spaces-your-smart-phone).

◉ Civic Center & the Tenderloin

ASIAN ART MUSEUM MUSEUM
See p78.

★LUGGAGE STORE GALLERY GALLERY
Map p296 (☑415-255-5971; www.luggagestoregallery.org; 1007 Market St; ☺noon-5pm Wed-Sat; ☑5, 6, 7, 21, 31, ⓜCivic Center, ⓑCivic Center) Like a dandelion pushing through sidewalk cracks, this plucky nonprofit gallery has brought signs of life to one of the Tenderloin's toughest blocks for two decades. By giving SF street artists a gallery platform, the Luggage Store helped launch graffiti-art star Barry McGee, muralist Rigo and street photographer Cheryl Dunn. Find the graffitied door and climb to the 2nd-floor gallery, which rises above the street without losing sight of it.

★SF CAMERAWORK GALLERY
Map p296 (☑415-487-1011; www.sfcamerawork.org; 1011 Market St, 2nd fl; ☺noon-6pm Tue-Sat; ☑6, 7, 9, 21, ⓑCivic Center, ⓜCivic Center) FREE Since 1974, this nonprofit art organization has championed experimental photo-based imagery beyond classic B&W prints and casual digital snapshots. Since moving into this spacious new Market St gallery, Camerawork's far-reaching exhibitions

DOWNTOWN ROOFTOP GARDENS

Above the busy sidewalks, there's a serene world of unmarked public rooftop gardens that grant perspective on downtown's skyscraper canyons. They're called 'privately owned public-open spaces' (POPOS). Local public-advocacy urbanist group **SPUR** (p112) publishes a downloadable app that lists them all. Local favorites:

One Montgomery Terrace (50 Post St/1 Montgomery St; ☺10am-6pm Mon-Sat; ⓜMontgomery, ⓑMontgomery) has great Market St views of old and new SF. Enter through Crocker Galleria, take the elevator to the top, then ascend the stairs; or enter Wells Fargo at One Montgomery and take the elevator to 'R.'

Sun Terrace (p108) has knockout vistas of the Financial District and Transamerica Pyramid from atop a slender art-deco skyscraper. Take the elevator to the 15th floor.

have examined memories of love and war in Southeast Asia, taken imaginary holidays with slide shows of vacation snapshots scavenged from the San Francisco Dump and showcased SF-based Iranian American artist Sanaz Mazinani's mesmerizing Islamic-inspired photo montages made of tiny Trumps.

SAN FRANCISCO MAIN LIBRARY CULTURAL CENTER
Map p296 (☑415-557-4400; www.sfpl.org; 100 Larkin St; ☺10am-6pm Mon & Sat, 9am-8pm Tue-Thu, noon-6pm Fri, noon-5pm Sun; 🛜♿; ☑5, 6, 7, 19, 21, 31, ⓜCivic Center, ⓑCivic Center) FREE A grand light well illuminates SF's favorite subjects: poetry in the Robert Frost Collection, civil rights in the Hormel LGBTQIA Center, SF music 'zines in the Little Maga/Zine Center and comic relief in the Schmulowitz Collection of Wit and Humor. Check out the 2nd-floor wallpaper made from the old card catalog – artists Ann Chamberlain and Ann Hamilton invited 200 San Franciscans to add multilingual commentary to 50,000 cards. The library quietly hosts high-profile basement lectures, plus enlightening Skylight Gallery ephemera exhibits.

GLIDE MEMORIAL UNITED
METHODIST CHURCH
CHURCH

Map p296 (☑415-674-6090; www.glide.org; 330 Ellis St; ⊙celebrations 9am & 11am Sun; ♿; ☐38, MPowell, BPowell) When the rainbow-robed Glide gospel choir enters singing their hearts out, the 2000-plus congregation erupts in cheers, hugs and dance moves. Raucous Sunday Glide celebrations capture San Francisco at its most welcoming and uplifting, embracing the rainbow spectrum of culture, gender, orientation, ability and socioeconomics. After the celebration ends, the congregation keeps the inspiration coming, serving a million free meals a year and providing housing for 52 formerly homeless families – and, yes, Glide welcomes volunteers.

TENDERLOIN NATIONAL FOREST
PARK

Map p296 (www.luggagestoregallery.org/tnf; Ellis St, btwn Leavenworth & Hyde Sts; ⊙noon-5pm; ☐27, 31, 38, BPowell, MPowell) ♿ **FREE** Urban blight is interrupted by bucolic splendor on one of the Tenderloin's grittiest blocks. Once littered with hypodermic needles and garbage, dead-end Cohen Alley has been transformed by a nonprofit artists' collective. A grove of trees is taking root, concrete walls are covered with murals by local artists, and asphalt has been replaced with mosaic pathways and koi ponds. If you feel so inspired – and, really, who wouldn't? – garden tools are available to help maintain SF's scrappiest natural wonder.

This forest is a project of the nonprofit Luggage Store gallery in cooperation with the city of San Francisco, which allows the nonprofit to lease the alley for $1 a year. See the Luggage Store's website for upcoming events in the Tenderloin National Forest, including free clothes mending by artist Michael Swain on the 15th of each month (weather permitting) and occasional community pizza-making in the garden-patio oven.

CITY HALL
HISTORIC BUILDING

Map p296 (☑tour info 415-554-6139; http://sfgov.org/cityhall/city-hall; 400 Van Ness Ave; ⊙8am-8pm Mon-Fri, tours 10am, noon & 2pm; ♿; MCivic Center, BCivic Center) **FREE** Rising from the ashes of the 1906 earthquake, this beaux arts landmark echoes with history. Demonstrators protesting red-scare McCarthy hearings on City Hall steps in 1960 were blasted with fire hoses – yet America's first sit-in worked. America's first openly

gay official supervisor, Harvey Milk, was assassinated here in 1978, along with Mayor George Moscone – but, in 2004, 4037 same-sex couples were legally wed here. Recently, City Hall has made headlines for approving pioneering environmental initiatives and citywide sanctuary status.

Designed in 1915 to outdo Paris for flair and outsize the capitol in Washington, DC, the world's fifth-largest dome was unsteady until its retrofit after the 1989 earthquake, when ingenious technology enabled it to swing on its base without raising alarm. The dome's gilded exterior is a reminder of 1990s dot-com excess, when the city squandered a short-lived windfall on gold leafing – but at least its foundations are solid. Don't miss ground-floor exhibitions, which range from portraits of iconic LGBT performers to photographs from western railroad journeys.

TWITTER HEADQUARTERS
LANDMARK

Map p296 (Western Furniture Exchange & Merchandise Mart; https://about.twitter.com/company; 1355 Market St; ☐6, 7, 21, MCivic Center, BCivic Center) ♿ Market St's traffic-stopping 1937 Mayan deco landmark was built to accommodate 300 wholesale furniture-design showrooms – but, a decade ago, fewer than 30 remained. The city offered tax breaks to Twitter to move here from its South Park (p84) headquarters, and after a $1.2-million LEED-certified green makeover, including a rooftop farm, Twitter nested here. Only employees can access Twitter's free video arcade and Bird-feeder cafeteria, but the ground-floor public **Marketplace** offers 22,000 sq ft of local gourmet fare.

ROOT DIVISION
GALLERY

Map p298 (☑415-863-7668; www.rootdivision.org; 1131 Mission St; donations welcome; ⊙gallery 2-6pm Wed-Sat; ♿; ☐6, 9, 71, BCivic Center, streetcar F, MCivic Center) **FREE** Get back to your creative roots at this arts nonprofit, which hosts curated shows on themes ranging from garden art to calligraphy made with human-hair brushes. Root Division keeps the inspiration coming, offering artists subsidized studio space in exchange for providing community art classes ranging from felt sculpture to electronic art – see the schedule for upcoming workshops for youth and adults. Don't miss events like the annual Misfit Toy Factory, where artists create works live for sale.

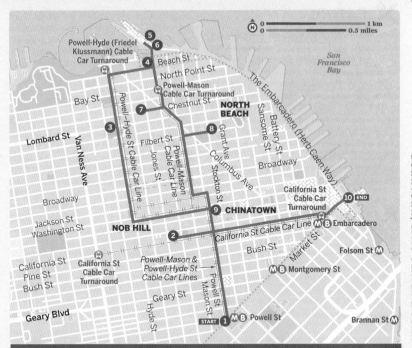

Neighborhood Tour
San Francisco by Cable Car

Carnival rides can't compare to cable cars, San Francisco's vintage public transit. Novices slide into strangers' laps, but regular commuters just grip leather hand straps, lean back and ride downhill slides like pro surfers. On this trip, you'll master the San Francisco stance.

At the ① **Powell St Cable Car Turnaround**, you'll see operators turn the car atop a revolving wooden platform and a vintage kiosk where you can buy an all-day Muni Passport for $21, instead of paying $7 per ride. Board the red-signed Powell-Hyde cable car and begin your 338ft ascent of Nob Hill.

Nineteenth-century city planners were skeptical of inventor Andrew Hallidie's 'wire-rope railway' – but after more than a century of near-continuous operation, his wire-and-hemp cables have seldom broken. Hallidie's cable cars even survived the 1906 earthquake and fire that destroyed 'Snob Hill' mansions, returning the faithful to the rebuilt ② **Grace Cathedral** (p130).

Enjoy Bay views as you careen past crooked ③ **Lombard Street** (p130) toward ④ **Fisherman's Wharf** (p57). The terminus is named for Friedel Klussmann, who saved cable cars from mayoral modernization plans in 1947. She did the math: cable cars brought in more tourism dollars than they cost in upkeep. The mayor demanded a vote – and lost to 'the Cable Car Lady' by a landslide.

At the wharf, emerge from the submarine ⑤ **USS Pampanito** (p59) to glimpse SF as sailors used to. Witness saloon brawls in vintage arcade games at the ⑥ **Musée Mécanique** (p58) before hitching the Powell-Mason cable car to North Beach.

Hop off to see Diego Rivera's 1934 cityscape at the ⑦ **San Francisco Art Institute** (p130), or follow your rumbling stomach directly to ⑧ **Liguria Bakery** (p118). Stroll through North Beach and Chinatown alleyways, or take the Powell-Mason line to time-travel through the ⑨ **Chinese Historical Society of America** (p116). Nearby, catch a ride on the city's oldest line: the California St cable car. The terminus is near the ⑩ **Ferry Building** (p79), where champagne-and-oyster happy hour awaits.

EATING

Make reservations whenever possible for downtown restaurants. Downtown and South of Market (SoMa) are best known for high-end restaurants, but lunchtime eateries in the neighborhood cater to office workers, with meals around $12 to $25. The Financial District is dead at night, when only midrange and top-end joints stay open. The Tenderloin (west of Powell St, south of Geary St, north of Market St) feels sketchy and rough but, as always in San Francisco, bargain eats reward the adventurous.

Financial District & Jackson Square

MIJITA
MEXICAN $

Map p301 (☎415-399-0814; www.mijitasf.com; 1 Ferry Bldg, cnr Market St & the Embarcadero; dishes $4-10; ☺10am-7pm Mon-Thu, to 8pm Fri, 9am-8pm Sat, 9am-3pm Sun; ⚑👶; ⓂEmbarcadero, ⒷEmbarcadero) ⚑ Jealous seagulls circle above your outdoor bayside table, eying your sustainable fish tacos and tangy jicama and grapefruit salad. James Beard Award–winning chef Traci Des Jardins honors her Mexican grandmother's cooking at this sunny taqueria – the Mexico City–style quesadilla is laced with *epazote* (Mayan herbs) and the *agua fresca* (fruit punch) is made from just-squeezed juice.

EL PORTEÑO EMPANADAS
ARGENTINE $

Map p301 (☎415-513-4529; www.elportenosf. com; 1 Ferry Bldg, cnr Market St & the Embarcadero; empanadas $4.50; ☺9am-7pm Mon-Sat, 10am-5pm Sun; ⚑👶; ⒷEmbarcadero, ⓂEmbarcadero) ⚑ Pocket change left over from farmers-market shopping scores Argentine pocket pastries packed with local flavor at El Porteño. Vegetarian versions like *acelga* (organic swiss chard and Gruyère) and *humita* (Brentwood sweet corn and caramelized onions) are just as mouthwatering as classic *jamon y queso* (prosciutto and fontina). Save room for *dulce de leche alfajores* (cookies with gooey caramel centers).

GOLDEN WEST
SANDWICHES $

Map p294 (☎415-216-6443; http://theauwest. com; 8 Trinity Pl; lunch $9-12; ☺8am-2pm Mon-Fri; 🚍3, 8, 30, 45, ⒷMontgomery, ⓂMontgomery) Eureka! Wedged between brokerage firms under the glowing sign that says Au

(the periodic-table symbol for gold) is an elusive FiDi find: a memorable lunch with top-notch California-grown ingredients that won't break the bank. Menu items are seasonal, but look for short-rib sandwiches with caramelized onions and house-made mayo or spicy chicken salads with mango, organic greens and pumpkin seeds.

GOTT'S ROADSIDE
BURGERS $

Map p301 (www.gotts.com; 1 Ferry Bldg, cnr Market St & the Embarcadero; burgers $8-11; ☺10am-10pm; 👶; ⓂEmbarcadero, ⒷEmbarcadero) ⚑ Gott's keeps it simple with juicy hamburgers made from local, sustainably farmed Niman Ranch beef, plus tasty Cobb salads, mini corn dogs for kids, and irresistible gourmet fries – go with sweet potato or garlic. Order at the counter and relax with local wine, beer or thick milkshakes at a sunny picnic table until your order's ready for pickup.

MIXT
HEALTH FOOD $

Map p301 (☎415-296-8009; www.mixtgreens. com; 475 Sansome St; salads & bowls $10-15; ☺10:30am-3pm Mon-Fri; ⚑; 🚋California, ⓂMontgomery, ⒷMontgomery) ⚑ Stockbrokers and Paleo dieters line up for organic salads with zingy dressings and bowls of farro or quinoa heaped with locally sourced vegetables – don't worry, the line moves fast. Sustainable sushi-grade tuna and grass-fed steak are pricey but tasty additions. Grab a stool or get takeout to enjoy in the Transamerica Pyramid redwood grove (p80). Multiple locations; this one's the cleanest.

★COTOGNA
ITALIAN $$

Map p301 (☎415-775-8508; www.cotognasf. com; 490 Pacific Ave; mains $19-35; ☺11:30am-10:30pm Mon-Thu, to 11pm Fri & Sat, 5-9:30pm Sun; ⚑; 🚋10, 12) Chef-owner Michael Tusk racks up James Beard Awards for a quintessentially Italian culinary balancing act: he strikes ideal proportions among a few pristine flavors in rustic pastas, woodfired pizzas and salt-crusted branzino. Reserve, especially for bargain $55 four-course Sunday suppers with $35 wine pairings – or plan a walk-in late lunch/early dinner. Top-value Italian wine list (most bottles $55).

SLANTED DOOR
VIETNAMESE $$

Map p301 (☎415-861-8032; www.slanteddoor. com; 1 Ferry Bldg, cnr Market St & the Embarcadero; mains $18-42; ☺11am-4:30pm & 5:30-10pm Mon-Sat, 11:30am-10pm Sun; ⓂEmbarcadero, ⒷEmbarcadero) ⚑ Live the dream at this bayfront bistro, where California-fresh, Vietnamese-inspired dishes are served with sparkling waterfront views. Chinatown-raised chef-owner Charles Phan is a James Beard Award winner and a local hero for championing California-grown ingredients in signature dishes like garlicky grass-fed 'shaking beef' and Dungeness crab heaped atop cellophane noodles. Book weeks ahead, or settle for Out the Door takeout.

**HOG ISLAND
OYSTER COMPANY**   SEAFOOD **$$**
Map p301 (🖉415-391-7117; www.hogisland oysters.com; 1 Ferry Bldg, cnr Market St & the Embarcadero; 4 oysters $14; ⏱11am-9pm; Ⓜ Embarcadero, ⒷEmbarcadero) 🍴 Slurp the bounty of the North Bay with East Bay views at this local, sustainable oyster bar. Get them raw, grilled with chipotle-bourbon butter, or Rockefeller (cooked with spinach, Pernod and cream). Not the cheapest oysters in town, but consistently the best – with excellent wines. Stop by Hog Island's farmers-market stall 8am to 2pm Saturday for $2 oysters.

**BOULETTE'S LARDER
& BOULIBAR**   MEDITERRANEAN, CALIFORNIAN **$$**
Map p301 (🖉415-399-1155; www.boulettes lar der.com; 1 Ferry Bldg, cnr Market St & the Embarcadero; mains $18-24; ⏱Larder 8-10:30am & 11:30am-3pm Tue-Sat, 10am-2:30pm Sun, Boulibar 11:30am-9:30pm Tue-Fri, to 8pm Sat; Ⓜ Embarcadero, ⒷEmbarcadero) Dinner can't beat brunch at Boulette's communal table, strategically placed inside a working kitchen amid a swirl of chefs with views of the Bay Bridge. At adjoining Boulibar, get tangy Middle Eastern mezze platters, beautifully blistered wood-fired pizzas and flatbreads at indoor picnic-style tables – perfect for people-watching, despite sometimes rushed service. Get inspiration to go with Larder spice mixes.

BOCADILLOS   BASQUE **$$**
Map p301 (🖉415-982-2622; www.bocasf.com; 710 Montgomery St; mains $8-19; ⏱11am-2:30pm Mon, to 9pm Tue-Thu, to 10pm Fri, 5-10pm Sat; 🚌8, 10, 12, 41) Forget multipage menus and giant portions: for lunch, choose two small sandwiches on toasted rolls with a side salad for $14 at this little bistro with mighty Mediterranean flavors. Juicy lamb burgers, halibut ceviche and crispy brussels sprouts are just-right Basque bites for light dinners. Weekday happy hours bring $7 wine and

$5-to-$7 snacks – though also sometimes deafening noise.

⭐**KUSAKABE**   SUSHI, JAPANESE **$$$**
Map p301 (🖉415-757-0155; http://kusakabe-sf. com; 584 Washington St; prix fixe $95; ⏱5-10pm, last seating 8:30pm; 🚌8, 10, 12, 41) Trust chef Mitsunori Kusakabe's *omakase* (tasting menu). Sit at the counter while chef adds a herbal hint to tuna with the inside of a *shiso* leaf. After you devour the menu – mostly with your hands, 'to release flavors' – you can special-order Hokkaido sea urchin, which chef perfumes with the *outside* of the *shiso* leaf. Soy sauce isn't provided – or missed.

COI   CALIFORNIAN **$$$**
Map p301 (🖉415-393-9000; www.coirestaurant. com; 373 Broadway; set menu $250; ⏱5:30-10pm Thu-Mon; Ⓟ; 🚌8, 10, 12, 30, 41, 45, 🚋Powell-Mason) 🍴 Entire beach vacations are condensed into chef Matthew Kirkley's artful nine-course modern seafood menu. Expect waves of surf, with scant turf – a truffle here, bone marrow there, sunny splashes of California citrus everywhere. Seasonal standouts include Dungeness crab, fluke with caviar, and – nodding to North Beach – mussels morphed into cannoli. Lavish wine pairings ($180); 20% service added.

KOKKARI   GREEK **$$$**
Map p301 (🖉415-981-0983; www.kokkari.com; 200 Jackson St; mains $18-49; ⏱11:30am-2:30pm & 5:30-10pm Mon-Thu, 11:30am-2:30pm & 5:30-11pm Fri, 5-11pm Sat, 5-10pm Sun; 🚗; 🚌8, 10, 12, 41) This is one Greek restaurant where you'll want to lick your plate instead of break it, with starters like chargrilled octopus with a zing of lemon and oregano, and a signature lamb, eggplant and yogurt moussaka as rich as the Pacific Stock Exchange. Reserve to avoid waits, or make a meal of hearty Mediterranean appetizers at the happening bar.

QUINCE   CALIFORNIAN **$$$**
Map p301 (🖉415-775-8700; www.quincerestau rant.com; 470 Pacific Ave; 11-course tasting menu $250, 9-course menu Mon-Thu $210; ⏱5:30-9:30pm Mon-Thu, from 5pm Fri & Sat; 🚌3, 10) 🍴 Chef Michael Tusk's tasting menu of Northern California bounty is an adventure and an investment – if you're not sold on this season's menu (see online), go à la carte in the salon instead. It's slightly more affordable and no less swanky, with seasonal fare like

foie gras with kumquat, abalone with green garlic, or lobster and wild mushroom pasta. Reservations essential.

WAYFARE TAVERN
AMERICAN $$$

Map p301 (☑415-772-9060; www.wayfaretavern. com; 558 Sacramento St; mains lunch $18-28, dinner $18-43; ☺11am-10:30pm Mon-Wed, to 11pm Thu & Fri, 11:30am-11pm Sat, to 10pm Sun; ☐1, 8, 10, ☐California, ☐Montgomery) All signs say San Francisco: barkeeps wear white jackets over their tats, couples canoodle around a fireplace salvaged from the 1906 earthquake, and lunch crowds toast to venture capital. Here American classics get the California treatment – gooey Marin brie tops burgers, California pistachio crumble graces all-American apple pie, and herb-laced fried chicken is addictive.

✕ Union Square

★TOUT SWEET
BAKERY $

Map p294 (☑415-385-1679; www.toutsweetsf. com; Macy's, 3rd fl, cnr Geary & Stockton Sts; baked goods $2-8; ☺11am-6pm Sun-Wed, to 8pm Thu-Sat; ☎☝; ☐2, 38, ☐Powell-Mason, Powell-Hyde, ☐Powell) Mango with Thai chili or peanut butter and jelly? Choosing your favorite California-French macaron isn't easy at Tout Sweet, where *Top Chef Just Desserts* champion Yigit Pura keeps outdoing his own inventions – he's like the love child of Julia Child and Steve Jobs. Chef Pura's sweet retreat on Macy's 3rd floor offers unbeatable views overlooking Union Sq, excellent teas and free wi-fi.

SUSHIRRITO
JAPANESE, FUSION $

Map p294 (☑415-544-9868; www.sushirrito. com; 226 Kearny St; dishes $9-13; ☺11am-4pm Mon-Thu, to 7pm Fri & Sat; ☝; ☐30, 45, ☐Montgomery, ☐Montgomery) ✐ Ever get a sushi craving, but you're hungry enough for a burrito? Join the crowd at Sushirrito, where fresh Latin and Asian ingredients are rolled in rice and nori seaweed, then conveniently wrapped in foil. Pan–Pacific Rim flavors shine in Geisha's Kiss, with line-caught yellowfin tuna and *piquillo* peppers, and vegetarian Buddha Belly, with spicy Japanese eggplant, kale and avocado.

BOXED FOODS
SANDWICHES $

Map p294 (☑415-981-9377; www.boxedfoods company.com; 245 Kearny St; sandwiches & salads $11-12; ☺10:30am-3pm Mon-Fri; ☝; ☐8, 30,

45, ☐Montgomery, ☐Montgomery) ✐ Local, seasonal, sustainable ingredients make outrageously flavorful lunches, whether you choose the free-range flank-steak salad with feta, tomatoes and mint or the BLTA with crunchy applewood-smoked bacon, lettuce, heirloom tomato and Hass avocado spread. Get yours to go to the Transamerica Pyramid redwood grove (p80).

BIO
CAFE $

Map p294 (☑415-362-0255; www.biologiquesf. com; 75 O'Farrell St; dishes $5-10; ☺8am-6pm; ☝; ☐Powell, ☐Powell) ✐ Dietary constraints are no barrier to tasty, fast French fare here. Quiches and cookies are gluten free, split-pea soup is vegetarian, many sandwiches and soups are vegan and coffee is fair trade. California cranberry-turmeric kombucha is an acquired taste – but you're going to crave that baguette with prosciutto, goat cheese and house-made jam. No seating; picnic at Union Sq.

EMPORIO RULLI
CAFE $

Map p294 (☑415-433-1122; www.rulli.com; Union Sq; pastries $4-8; ☺8am-7pm; ☝; ☐Powell, ☐Powell) Food is secondary to people-watching at this glass-pavilion cafe perched atop Union Sq – stake out a prime outdoor table and order snacks at the counter. On sunny days, this is a welcome midday stop for gelato, Italian pastries or ham or prosciutto croissants – plus powerful espresso drinks or wine.

★LIHOLIHO YACHT CLUB
HAWAIIAN, CALIFORNIAN $$

Map p296 (☑415-440-5446; http://lycsf.com; 871 Sutter St; dishes $11-37; ☺5-10:30pm Mon-Thu, to 11pm Fri & Sat; ☐2, 3, 27, 38, ☐California) Who needs yachts to be happy? Aloha abounds over Liholiho's pucker-up-tart cocktails and gleefully creative Calwaiian/Hawafornian dishes – surefire mood enhancers include spicy beef-tongue *bao*, duck-liver mousse with pickled pineapple on brioche, and Vietnamese slaw with tender squid and crispy tripe. Reservations are impossible; arrive early/late for bar dining, or head downstairs to Louie's Gen-Gen Room speakeasy for shamelessly tasty bone-marrow-butter waffles.

FARMERBROWN
SOUTHERN US $$

Map p294 (☑415-409-3276; www.farmer brownsf.com; 25 Mason St; mains $13-27; ☺10am-2:30pm & 5-9pm Sun-Wed, to 10pm

Thu-Sat; 🚌8, 27, 31, 45, Ⓜ Powell, Ⓑ Powell) 🐾 This rebel from the wrong side of the block dishes ribs that'll stick to yours, as well as authentic stone-ground grits with Louisiana Cajun shrimp and 16oz mason jars of bourbon-spiked iced tea. Chef-owner Jay Foster works with local organic and African American farmers to provide heartfelt, homegrown soul food. Buffet brunches ($25) feature fried chicken and waffles; rambunctious happy hours 3pm to 6pm weekdays.

CAFE CLAUDE   FRENCH $$

Map p294 (📞415-392-3505; www.cafeclaude. com; 7 Claude Lane; mains $15-26; ⏱11:30am-10:30pm Mon-Sat, 5:30-10:30pm Sun; 🚌30, 45, Ⓜ Montgomery, Ⓑ Montgomery) Escape down an SF alleyway to a sleek French cafe, with zinc bar, umbrella tables outside and staff chattering *en français*. Lunch is served 'til a civilized 4:30pm and jazz combos play Thursday to Saturday dinnertimes. Expect classics like *coq au vin* and gently garlicky *escargots*, always good, if not great – but wine and romance make it memorable.

GITANE   MEDITERRANEAN $$

Map p294 (📞415-788-6686; www.gitanerestau rant.com; 6 Claude Lane; share plates $16-29; ⏱5-10pm Tue-Thu, to 10:30pm Fri & Sat; 🍴; 🚌30, 45, Ⓜ Montgomery, Ⓑ Montgomery) Slip out of the Financial District and into something more comfortable at this sultry Mediterranean bistro, where the decor is cushioned, curtained, mirrored and decadently date worthy. Andalucian-accented share plates include wood-fired octopus, sherry-laced brussels sprouts, *albondigas* (meatballs) in romesco sauce, and the obligatory *patatas bravas* (potatoes) with *pimentón* aioli. Dress sharp and mingle over craft cocktails; reserve for dinner.

HAKKASAN   DIM SUM $$$

Map p294 (📞415-829-8148; http://hakkasan.com; 1 Kearny St; mains $20-38; ⏱11:30am-2:30pm & 5:30-11pm Tue-Sat, to 10pm Mon; Ⓜ Montgomery, Ⓑ Montgomery) Bootstrapping start-ups and venture capitalists alike hit Hakkasan for three-course lunch specials ($31) or elegant dim sum (get XO brandy scallop dumplings and prawn and chive dumplings). Celebrate birthdays and IPOs in style with generous bartender pours and decadent mains like Peking duck with sustainable California caviar. For dinner, count on two to three dishes per person; $15 parking available.

✗ SoMa

SENTINEL   SANDWICHES $

Map p298 (📞415-284-9960; www.thesentinelsf. com; 37 New Montgomery St; sandwiches $9-12; ⏱7:30am-2:30pm Mon-Fri; 🚌12, 14, Ⓜ Montgomery, Ⓑ Montgomery) Rebel SF chef Dennis Leary revolutionizes the humble sandwich with top-notch seasonal ingredients: lamb gyros get radical with pesto and eggplant, and corned beef crosses borders with Swiss cheese and housemade Russian dressing. Check the website for daily menus and call in your order, or expect a 10-minute wait – sandwiches are made to order. Enjoy in nearby Yerba Buena Gardens (p84).

DOTTIE'S TRUE
BLUE CAFÉ   AMERICAN, BREAKFAST $

Map p298 (📞415-885-2767; 28 6th St; mains $9-17; ⏱7:30am-3pm Thu-Mon; Ⓑ Powell, Ⓜ Powell) Consider yourself lucky if you wait less than half an hour and get hit up for change only once – but fresh-baked goods come to those who wait at Dottie's. Cinnamon-ginger pancakes, grilled chili-cheddar cornbread, scrambles with whiskey-fennel sausage and other breakfast staples hot off Dottie's griddle are tried and true blue.

AMAWELE'S SOUTH
AFRICAN KITCHEN   SOUTH AFRICAN $

Map p298 (📞415-536-5900; www.amawelessouth africankitchen.com; 101 Spear St; mains $8-11; ⏱10:30am-2:30pm Mon-Fri; 🍴🚶; 🚌6,9,14,21,31, Ⓑ Embarcadero, Ⓜ Embarcadero) Salads alone won't power you through downtown days – follow techies sneaking away from their corporate cafeterias and duck into the Rincon Center (p83) for hearty, home-style South African lunches with tangy punch. Get 'bunny chow' (chicken curry) with pickled carrots, or vinegary slap fries with a *frikadella* (meatballs) roti wrap – equally tasty in a vegetarian version with butter-bean curry.

SOMA STREAT FOOD PARK   FOOD TRUCK $

Map p298 (http://somastreatfoodpark.com; 428 11th St; dishes $5-12; ⏱11am-3pm & 5-9pm Mon-Fri, 11am-9pm Sat, to 5pm Sun; 🚌9, 27, 47) Your posse is hungry, but one of you is vegan, another demands tacos with beer, and another craves Korean fried chicken. So what do you do? First: recognize that you and your friends belong in San Francisco. Second: head to this SoMa parking lot, where gourmet food trucks will satisfy your every whim. The area gets sketchy – mind your wallet.

ZERO ZERO
PIZZA $$

Map p298 (☑415-348-8800; www.zerozerosf. com; 826 Folsom St; pizzas $13-20; ☺11:30am-10pm Sun-Thu, to 11pm Fri & Sat; ⓂPowell, ⒷPowell) The name is a throw-down of pizza credentials – '00' flour is the secret to puffy-edged Neapolitan crust – and these pies deliver on that promise, with inspired SF-themed toppings. The Geary is a cross-cultural adventure involving Manila clams, bacon and Calabrian chilies, but the real crowd pleaser is the Castro, which is fittingly loaded with house-made sausage.

COCKSCOMB
CALIFORNIAN $$

Map p298 (☑415-974-0700; http://cockscomb sf.com; 564 4th St; mains $14-26; ☺11:30am-1:30pm & 5-11pm Mon-Fri, 5-11pm Sat; ⍾; ⍰30, 45, 47, ⓂN, T) ⌁ Rules need not apply in San Francisco: concrete warehouses can become cozy bistros, duck-fat cauliflower and oysters are daily dietary requirements, and veggie burgers are served rare and 'bleeding' plant-based heme juice. Cockscomb's rebel chef-owner Chris Cosentino is a *Top Chef* regular and a champion of nose-to-tail dining – even the faint of heart will be converted by his beef-heart tartare.

1601 BAR & KITCHEN
CALIFORNIAN, FUSION $$

Map p298 (☑415-552-1601; http://1601sf.com; 1601 Howard St; mains $13-23; ☺6-10pm Tue-Thu, to 11pm Fri & Sat; ⍰9, 12, 47, ⓂVan Ness) ⌁ Rising-star-chef alert: Brian Fernando is turning Sri Lankan inspirations into Californian cravings. Velvety halibut ceviche in coconut milk is an instant obsession, Marin Sun Farms goat stew with red basmati rice for two is date worthy, and you'll want the house-smoked turmeric salmon and fenugreek-chile-vinegar home fries again for breakfast. Ingenuity without pretension, and well-priced tasting menu ($76).

BUTLER & THE CHEF
FRENCH $$

Map p298 (☑415-896-2075; http://butlerand thechef.com; 155a S Park St; mains $14-18; ☺8am-3pm Tue-Sat, 10am-3pm Sun; ⍰10, 30, 45, ⓂN,T) Find authentic French-cafe classics among the SoMa warehouses at this lunch-only South Park favorite. Tables are tiny: mind your elbows or they'll wind up in your French onion soup, made properly with rich beef stock and a real crouton

topped with melting Gruyère. Quiche and niçoise salads are also no-fail classics.

TROPISUEÑO
MEXICAN $$

Map p298 (☑415-243-0299; www.tropisueno.com; 75 Yerba Buena Lane; mains lunch $7-12, dinner $12-21; ☺10am-10pm Sun-Thu, to 10:30pm Fri & Sat, 11am-10pm Sun; ⍰8, 14, 30, 45, ⓂPowell, ⒷPowell) Last time you enjoyed casual Mexican dining this much, there were probably balmy ocean breezes and hammocks involved. Instead, you're steps away from SoMa museums, savoring *al pastor* (marinated pork) burritos with mesquite salsa and grilled pineapple, and sipping margaritas with chili-salted rims. Despite the prime downtown location, prices are down to earth – especially during happy hour (4pm to 6pm).

21ST AMENDMENT BREWERY
AMERICAN $$

Map p298 (☑415-369-0900; http://21st-amend ment.com; 563 2nd St; mains $10-20; ☺kitchen 11:30am-10pm Mon-Sat, 10am-10pm Sun, bar to midnight; ⍾⏸; ⍰10, ⓂN,T) Perfectly placed before Giants games, 21st Amendment brews stellar IPA and Hell or High Watermelon wheat beer. The vegetarian-friendly bar-and-grill menu – pizza, beef and veggie burgers, and signature tot-chos (tater-tot nachos) – checks your buzz, but the cavernous space is so loud, nobody'll notice you're shouting. Kids get ice-cream floats made with homemade root beer.

★IN SITU
CALIFORNIAN, INTERNATIONAL $$$

Map p298 (☑415-941-6050; http://insitu.sf moma.org; SFMOMA, 151 3rd St; mains $14-34; ☺11am-3:30pm Mon & Tue, 11am-3:30pm & 5-9pm Thu-Sun; ⍰14, ⒷMontgomery, ⓂMontgomery) The landmark gallery of modern cuisine attached to SFMOMA also showcases avant-garde masterpieces – but these ones you'll lick clean. Chef Corey Lee collaborates with star chefs worldwide, scrupulously recreating their signature dishes with California-grown ingredients so that you can enjoy Harald Wohlfahrt's impeccable anis-marinated salmon, Hiroshi Sasaki's decadent chicken thighs and Albert Adrià's gravity-defying cocoa-bubble cake in one unforgettable sitting.

★BENU
CALIFORNIAN, FUSION $$$

Map p298 (☑415-685-4860; www.benusf.com; 22 Hawthorne St; tasting menu $285; ☺6-9pm seatings Tue-Sat; ⍰10, 12, 14, 30, 45) SF has pioneered Asian fusion cuisine for 150 years, but the pan-Pacific innovation chef-owner Corey

Lee brings to the plate is gasp-inducing: foie-gras soup dumplings – what?! Dungeness crab and truffle custard pack such outsize flavor into Lee's faux–shark's fin soup, you'll swear Jaws is in there. Benu dinners are investments, but don't miss star sommelier Yoon Ha's ingenious pairings ($185).

There's a 20% service charge.

BOULEVARD   CALIFORNIAN $$$

Map p298 (☑415-543-6084; www.boulevard restaurant.com; 1 Mission St; mains lunch $15-29, dinner $29-51; ☺11:30am-2pm & 5:30-9:30pm Mon-Thu, to 10pm Fri, 5:30-10pm Sat, 5:30-9:30pm Sun; ⓜEmbarcadero, ⒷEmbarcadero) The 1889 belle epoque Audiffred Building once housed the Coast Seamen's Union, but for 20-plus years James Beard Award–winning chef Nancy Oakes has made culinary history here. Reliably tasty, effortlessly elegant dishes include juicy wood-oven-roasted Kurobuta pork chops, crisp California quail, and grilled Pacific salmon with wild morels, plus decadent, nostalgia-inducing cakes and ice cream, and SF's best service.

SALT HOUSE   CALIFORNIAN $$$

Map p298 (☑415-543-8900; www.salthousesf. com; 545 Mission St; mains lunch $15-25, dinner $24-47; ☺11am-10pm Mon-Thu, to 11pm Fri, 5:30-11pm Sat; ⓺6, 7, 10, 14, 21, 31, 71, ⒷMontgomery, ⓜF, J, K, L, M, N) For a business lunch that feels like a spa getaway, Salt House offers casual yet swanky meals of satiny yuzu-avocado tuna tartare and shrimp salad with a jalapeño kick. Late lunches here have a way of turning into early happy hours (2pm to 6pm), with bargain oysters, decadent poutine and absinthe-laced Corpse Reviver cocktails that'll seal any deal.

✗ Civic Center & the Tenderloin

★ FARM:TABLE   AMERICAN $

Map p296 (☑415-292-7089; www.farmtablesf. com; 754 Post St; dishes $6-9; ☺7:30am-2pm Tue-Fri, 8am-3pm Sat & Sun; ✐; ⓺2, 3, 27, 38) ⚘ A ray of sunshine in the concrete heart of the city, this plucky little storefront showcases seasonal California organics in just-baked breakfasts and farmstead-fresh lunches. Check the menu on Twitter (@farmtable) for today's homemade cereals, savory tarts and game-changing toast – mmmm, ginger peach and mascarpone on whole-wheat

AL FRESCO DINING DOWNTOWN

During the odd heat wave in SF, when it's too hot to stay indoors without air-con (which nobody in SF has) and warm enough to eat outside, two downtown streets become go-to destinations for dining alfresco: **Belden Place** (www. belden-place.com) and Claude Lane. Both are pedestrian alleyways lined with European-style restaurants and convivial sidewalk seating. The food is marginally better on Claude Lane, notably at Gitane (p91) and Cafe Claude (p91). Belden is sunnier and more color-ful – the restaurants here make up for average Francophone fare with big smiles and generous wine pours.

sourdough. Tiny space, but immaculate kitchen and great coffee. Cash only.

HOOKER'S SWEET TREATS   DESSERTS

Map p296 (☑415-441-4628; www.hookers sweettreats.com; 442 Hyde St; ☺8am-3pm Tue-Fri, 10am-2pm Sat; ⓺2, 3, 19, 27, 38, 47, 49) ⚘ Bring your sweet tooth and twisted sense of humor – Hooker's name winks knowingly at other businesses conducted on nearby street corners, but the decadent desserts on offer are no joke. Get bread pudding for here and award-winning caramels to go – Town S'Mhore caramels tempt with marsh-mallows and pecans, but get 3rd Nut with fair-trade chocolate, pistachios and sea salt.

RED CHILLI   NEPALI $

Map p296 (☑415-931-3529; www.redchillisf.com; 522 Jones St; mains $8-11; ☺11:30am-10:30pm; ⓺2, 3, 27, 38) Mt Everest is for amateurs – gourmet adventurers brave the Tenderloin's mean streets for Red Chilli's bargain butter chicken, Kathmandu rolls (naan wraps) and pickle-spice lamb *achar*. Can't decide? Get rice-plate combos, but don't skip the *momos* (Nepalese dumplings). This family-run storefront diner is welcoming, charmingly kitschy and convenient before/after Bourbon & Branch (p101) cocktails – otherwise, get delivery.

SAIGON SANDWICH SHOP   VIETNAMESE $

Map p296 (☑415-474-5698; 560 Larkin St; sand-wiches $3.75-4.25; ☺7am-5:30pm; ⓺19, 31) Don't get distracted by Tenderloin street scenes while you wait – be ready to order your *banh mi* (Vietnamese sandwiches) when the Saigon boss ladies call 'Next!' or you'll get skipped. Act fast and be rewarded with a baguette piled high with your choice of roast pork, chicken, pâté, meatballs or tofu, plus pickled carrots, cilantro, jalapeño and thinly sliced onion.

HEART OF THE CITY FARMERS MARKET
MARKET **$**

Map p296 (www.hotcfarmersmarket.org; United Nations Plaza; ⊙7am-5:30pm Wed, to 5pm Sun; ⛟; ⎕6, 7, 9, 21, Ⓜ Civic Center, Ⓑ Civic Center) Bringing farm freshness to the city's concrete-paved center since 1981, this nonprofit, farmer-operated market is on a mission to provide local, affordable, healthy food to low-income inner-city communities. Seasonal scores include organic berries from Yerena Farms, Buddha's-hand citrus from De Santis Farms and pesticide-free salad greens from Ortiz Brothers. Prepared-food vendors include RoliRoti free-range rotisserie chicken and All-Star Tamales. Bargain prices.

LERS ROS
THAI **$**

Map p296 (✑415-931-6917; www.lersros.com/larkin; 730 Larkin St; mains $10-17; ⊙11am-midnight; ⎕19, 31, 38, 47, 49) Most Thai eateries stick to familiar favorites, but Lers Ros imports regional Thai cooking with bold spicing and wild ingredients – house specialties include boar, coconut venison, garlic-pepper rabbit and quail with on-the-vine green peppercorns. Good wine and late hours make this a magnet after the movies or symphony, never mind the sketchy neighborhood.

SHALIMAR
PAKISTANI **$**

Map p296 (✑415-928-0333; 532 Jones St; dishes $5-10; ⊙noon-3pm & 5-11:30pm; ⎕27, 38) Brave a grim Tenderloin block to score tandoori chicken straight off the skewer and naan bread still bubbling from the oven at this fluorescent-lit, linoleum-floored Pakistani mainstay. Watch and learn as foodies who demand five-star service elsewhere meekly fetch their own water pitchers and tamarind sauce from the fridge. Vegetable dishes are heavy and bland; stick to the tasty meats.

CAFE ZITOUNA
MOROCCAN **$**

Map p296 (✑415-673-2622; www.sfcafezitouna.com; 1201 Sutter St; mains $12-19; ⊙11:30am-9pm Tue-Thu & Sat & Sun, 2-9pm Fri; ⎕2, 3, 19, 47, 49) Surprise: this classic storefront diner serves home-style Moroccan cooking, from kebabs and falafel to savory lentil soup and slow-cooked lamb tagine stews. Friendly chef-owner Najid hails from Tunisia, his wife from Morocco – and everything, from *merguez* (lamb sausage) to mint tea, is made from scratch from family recipes. They sometimes close early: call ahead.

BRENDA'S FRENCH SOUL FOOD
CREOLE **$$**

Map p296 (✑415-345-8100; www.frenchsoulfood.com; 652 Polk St; mains $11-17; ⊙8am-3pm Mon & Tue, to 10pm Wed-Sat, to 8pm Sun; ⎕19, 31, 38, 47, 49) Chef-owner Brenda Buenviaje blends New Orleans–style Creole cooking with French technique to invent 'French soul food.' Expect updated classics like cayenne-spiked crawfish beignets, fluffy cream biscuits, impeccable Hangtown Fry (eggs, bacon and cornmeal-crusted oysters) and fried chicken with collard greens and hot-pepper jelly. Long waits on sketchy sidewalks are unavoidable – but you can order takeout two doors down.

🍷 DRINKING & NIGHTLIFE

Most nightclubs are in SoMa, but they're spread across a large area – don't get stuck walking in heels. The highest concentration of bars and clubs is around 11th and Folsom Sts. The SoMa scene pops weekends and shrivels weekdays. Financial District bars pack 5pm to 8pm Wednesday through Friday, empty suddenly and close by midnight. Braggadocious bro-grammers and after-hours office drama spoil the scene, and things get sloppy on Fridays. For cheaper drinks, brave the Tenderloin to swill with hipsters, free spirits and career drinkers. Prices rise as you go toward the Financial District, exceeding $12 east of Powell St.

🍷 Financial District & Jackson Square

BIX
BAR

Map p301 (✑415-433-6300; www.bixrestaurant.com; 56 Gold St; ⊙bar 4:30-10pm Mon-Thu, 11:30am-midnight Fri, 5:30pm-midnight Sat, 5:30-10pm Sun; ⎕1, 8, 10, 12, 41) Head down a Jackson Square alleyway and back in time at Bix, a speakeasy-style supper club with white-jacketed staff shaking martinis at the mahogany bar. The restaurant's good – order the steak tartare or the potato pillow with caviar – but the bar is great, with nightly live piano and jazz combos. Look sharp and swagger; reserve.

FERRY PLAZA WINE MERCHANT WINE BAR

Map p301 (☑415-391-9400; www.fpwm.com; 1 Ferry Bldg, cnr Market St & the Embarcadero; ⊗11am-7pm Mon, 10am-8pm Tue, 10am-9pm Wed-Fri, 8am-8pm Sat, 10am-7pm Sun; Ⓜ Embarcadero, Ⓑ Embarcadero) Are you feeling flinty or flirty? With 25 wines available to try by 2oz taste or 5oz pour, you're bound to find a flavor profile to match your mood with ready assistance from Ferry Plaza Wine Merchant's well-informed staff. The bar is jammed Saturdays, but otherwise staff take time to introduce exciting new California releases.

TAVERNA AVENTINE BAR

Map p301 (☑415-981-1500; www.aventinesf. com; 582 Washington St; ⊗11:30am-10pm Mon & Tue, to 11pm Wed, to midnight Thu, to 2am Fri, 7pm-midnight Sat; ☐1, 8, 10, 12, 41) Back in SF's wild Barbary Coast days, the Aventine's 150-year-old building fronted the bay – you can still see salt-water marks on the brick walls downstairs. Now bartenders hit a high-water mark during happy hours (3pm to 7pm weekdays), mixing bourbon and whiskey cocktails fit for a sailor.

🍺 Union Square

★ PAGAN IDOL LOUNGE

Map p294 (☑415-985-6375; www.paganidol.com; 375 Bush St; ⊗4pm-1am Mon-Fri, 6pm-1:30am Sat; Ⓑ Montgomery, Ⓜ F, J, K, L, M) Volcanoes erupt inside Pagan Idol every half hour, or until there's a virgin sacrifice...what, no takers? Then order your island cocktail and brace for impact – these tiki drinks are no joke. Flirt with disaster over a Hemingway Is Dead: rum, bitters and grapefruit, served in a skull. Book online to nab a hut for groups of four to six.

★ LOCAL EDITION BAR

Map p294 (☑415-795-1375; www.localeditionsf. com; 691 Market St; ⊗5pm-2am Mon-Thu, from 4:30pm Fri, from 7pm Sat; Ⓜ Montgomery, Ⓑ Montgomery) Get the scoop on the SF cocktail scene at this speakeasy in the basement of the historic Hearst newspaper building. The lighting is so dim you might bump into typewriters, but that's no excuse to dodge a Good Question: a cocktail of hibiscus-infused sherry, genever, thyme, salt, pepper and mystery. Book tables ahead for swinging live-music nights (Tuesday to Thursday).

RICKHOUSE BAR

Map p294 (☑415-398-2827; www.rickhousebar. com; 246 Kearny St; ⊗5pm-2am Mon, 3pm-2am Tue-Fri, 6pm-2am Sat; ☐8, 30, 45, Ⓜ Montgomery, Ⓑ Montgomery) Like a shotgun shack plunked downtown, Rickhouse is lined floor to ceiling with repurposed whiskey casks imported from Kentucky and backbar shelving from an Ozarks nunnery that once secretly brewed hooch. Cocktails are strong on whiskey and bourbon – but the Californio with gold-dust bitters does rye proud. Round up a posse to help finish that vast bowl of Admiral's Whiskey Punch.

PACIFIC COCKTAIL HAVEN COCKTAIL BAR

Map p296 (PCH; ☑415-744-5000; www.pacific cocktailsf.com; 580 Sutter St; ⊗5pm-midnight Mon, 5pm-2am Tue-Thu, 4pm-2am Fri & Sat; ☐1, ☐ Powell-Mason, Powell-Hyde, California) Sip your way around the Pacific Rim from the comfort of your downtown San Francisco barstool. Expand your hooch horizons to the South Pacific with Lime in da Coconut (vodka, coconut, salted pistachio, lime and crushed ice) and sail off into the sunset with Eastern Promises (Bombay Sapphire East gin, pink pepper and lemongrass bitters).

BURRITT ROOM LOUNGE

Map p294 (☑415-400-0561; www.mystichotel. com; 417 Stockton St, 2nd fl; ⊗5pm-midnight Sun-Thu, to 2am Fri & Sat; ☐2, 3, 8, 30, 38, Ⓜ Montgomery, Ⓑ Montgomery) Upstairs at the Mystic Hotel, enter a decadent Victorian parlor bar with century-old tile floors, red-velvet sofas and gaudy chandeliers – as though Victorian burlesque troupes might arrive any moment, demanding champagne, Guilty Pleasures rye and Genepy cocktails. Celebrity chefowner Charlie Palmer expanded the place with a tavern and a meat-heavy menu, but the bar remains the star attraction.

IRISH BANK PUB

Map p294 (☑415-788-7152; www.theirishbank. com; 10 Mark Lane; ⊗11:30am-2am; ☐2, 3, 30, 45, Ⓜ Montgomery, Ⓑ Montgomery) Perfectly pulled pints and thick-cut fries with malt vinegar are staples at this cozy Irish pub, hidden in

TINNAPORN SATHAPORNNANONT/SHUTTERSTOCK ©

1. Union Square (p82)
The Goddess of Victory statue, by Robert Ingersoll Aitken, atop the Dewey Monument.

2. Hotel Utah Saloon (p107)
An entertainment institution for more than a century.

3. Powell-Hyde cable car (p82)
Cars rattle past some of San Francisco's top sights on this picturesque line.

4. Ferry Plaza Farmers Market (p79)
The best place to equip yourself for picnics by the bay.

an alleyway near the Chinatown gate. Settle into your snug for juicy burgers, brats and anything else you could want with lashings of mustard. Sociable tables beneath the alley awning are ideal for easy banter and stigma-free smoking – rare in California.

111 MINNA
BAR, CLUB

Map p298 (📞415-974-1719; www.111minna gallery.com; 111 Minna St; free-$20; ⏰7:30-9pm Mon-Thu, to 2am Fri, 10pm-2am Sat; Ⓜ︎Montgomery, Ⓑ︎Montgomery) Minna St is named after a gold rush–era madam, and today 111 Minna works three jobs on this street corner: art gallery–cafe (7:30am to 3:30pm weekdays), happy-hour scene (3:30pm to as late as 9pm weekdays) and weekend club. Don't miss '90s hip-hop nights or Trap x Art, when art-partiers make their mark on blank canvas and the dance floor.

GASPAR BRASSERIE & COGNAC ROOM
BAR

Map p294 (📞415-576-8800; http://gasparbras serie.com; 185 Sutter St; ⏰bar 3-10pm Mon-Sat; Ⓑ︎Montgomery, Ⓜ︎Montgomery) When gold-rush prospectors struck it rich, they upgraded from rotgut rye to fine French cognac – and history repeats itself nightly at Gaspar's. SF's biggest, best selection of cognac cocktails features the drop-dead-delicious Corpse Reviver #1 (cognac, calvados, vermouth, orange). Come boom or bust, don't miss weekday 4pm-to-6pm happy hours for $1 oysters and half-price cocktails.

TUNNEL TOP
BAR

Map p294 (📞415-235-6587; 601 Bush St; ⏰5pm-2am Mon-Sat, to 2am Sun; Ⓛ︎2, 3, 8, 30, 45, Ⓜ︎Montgomery, Ⓑ︎Montgomery) You can't tell who's local and who's not in this happening hilltop bar with exposed beams, a steampunk chandelier and a rickety mezzanine where you can spy on the crowd. Head up the Stockton St staircase to find the place and you'll be rewarded with craft beer on tap and $2 off cocktails before 7:30pm.

JOHN'S GRILL
BAR

Map p294 (www.johnsgrill.com; 63 Ellis St; ⏰11am-10pm; Ⓛ︎Powell-Mason, Powell-Hyde, Ⓜ︎Powell, Ⓑ︎Powell) 'She was a real gone gal, until she double-crossed me...' Tough-guy martinis at Dashiell Hammett's favorite bar will get you talking like a noir-movie villain, telling tales of lost love and true crimes while chewing toothpicks. Cocktails are strictly classic and the food greasy-spoon – nothing fancy here, except for the golden *Maltese Falcon* movie-prop statuette upstairs.

🍷 SoMa

⭐BAR AGRICOLE
BAR

Map p298 (📞415-355-9400; www.baragricole. com; 355 11th St; ⏰6-10pm Mon-Thu, 5:30-11pm Fri & Sat, 10am-2pm & 6-9pm Sun; Ⓛ︎9, 12, 27, 47) 🍸 Drink your way to a history degree with well-researched cocktails: Whiz Bang with house bitters, whiskey, vermouth and absinthe scores high, but El Presidente with white rum, farmhouse curaçao and California-pomegranate grenadine takes top honors. This overachiever wins James Beard Award nods for spirits and eco-savvy design, plus popular acclaim for $1 oysters and $5 aperitifs 5pm to 6pm Monday to Saturday.

⭐SIGHTGLASS COFFEE
CAFE

Map p298 (📞415-861-1313; www.sightglass coffee.com; 270 7th St; ⏰7am-7pm; Ⓛ︎12, 14, 19, Ⓑ︎Civic Center, Ⓜ︎Civic Center) Follow cult coffee aromas into this sunny SoMa warehouse, where family-grown, high-end bourbon-shrub coffee is roasted daily. Aficionados sip signature Owl's Howl Espresso downstairs or head directly to the mezzanine Affogato Bar to get ice cream with that espresso. Daredevils should try the powerfully dark cocoa or sparkling coffee cascara shrub – soda made with the cherry fruit of coffee plants.

⭐STUD
GAY, CLUB

Map p298 (www.studsf.com; 399 9th St; $5-8; ⏰noon-2am Tue, 5pm-3am Thu-Sat, 5pm-midnight Sun; Ⓛ︎12, 19, 27, 47) Rocking the gay scene since 1966, the Stud makes history nightly as America's first worker-owned co-op club. Theme nights run amok, from Heavy Metal Yoga Mondays to Sunday's '70s singer-songwriter drag act Broni Mitchell. Red Hots Burlesque shows make Fridays blush, DJs and visual artists amp up Saturday's freak factor, and monthly Pink Escalade leaves skid marks on the dance floor.

⭐EAGLE TAVERN
GAY, BAR

Map p298 (www.sf-eagle.com; 398 12th St; $5-10; ⏰2pm-2am Mon-Fri, from noon Sat & Sun; Ⓛ︎9, 12, 27, 47) Sunday afternoons, all roads in the gay underground lead to the historic Eagle for all-you-can-drink beer busts ($15) from 3pm to 6pm. Wear leather – or flirt shamelessly – and blend right in; arrive before 3pm to beat long lines and score free BBQ. Thursdays bring mixed crowds for rockin' bands; Fridays and Saturdays range from bondage to drag. Check online.

BLOODHOUND   BAR
Map p298 (☑415-863-2840; www.bloodhoundsf. com; 1145 Folsom St; ◷4pm-2am; 🚍12, 14, 19, 27, 47) The murder of crows painted on the ceiling is an omen: nights at Bloodhound often assume mythic proportions. Vikings would feel at home amid these antler chandeliers, while bootleggers would appreciate barnwood walls and top-shelf hooch served in mason jars. Shoot pool or chill on leather couches until your jam comes on the jukebox.

CAT CLUB   CLUB
Map p298 (www.sfcatclub.com; 1190 Folsom St; free-$12; ◷9pm-3am Tue-Sat; 🚍12, 19, 27, 47, Ⓜ Civic Center, Ⓑ Civic Center) You never really know your friends till you've seen them belt out A-ha's 'Take on Me' at Class of '84, Cat Club's Thursday-night retro dance party, where the euphoric bi/straight/gay/undefinable scene seems like an outtake from some John Hughes art-school flick. Tuesdays it's free karaoke, Wednesdays Bondage-a-Go-Go, Fridays Goth and Saturdays '80s and '90s power pop – dress the part and rock out.

LONE STAR SALOON   GAY, BAR
Map p298 (☑415-863-9999; http://lonestarsf. com; 1354 Harrison St; ◷4pm-2am Mon-Fri, from 2pm Fri, from noon Sat & Sun; 🚍9, 12, 27, 47) Like California grizzlies to a honeycomb, big guys with bushy beards pack the legendary Lone Star. There's a huge back patio and a competitive pool table, perpetually thronged by manly men and their admirers since 1989 – this is SF's original all-male bear bar. Owner-bartenders Charlie and Bruce sling $3 beer during weekday 2pm-to-8pm happy hours; Sundays are jammed.

POWERHOUSE   GAY, BAR
Map p298 (☑415-522-8689; www.powerhouse-sf. com; 1347 Folsom St; free-$10; ◷4pm-2am; 🚍9, 12, 27, 47) Thursdays through Sundays are best at Powerhouse, a sweaty SoMa bar for leathermen, shirtless gym queens and the occasional porn star. Draft beer is cheap

and specials keep the crowd loose, and dance erupts around the pool table at weekends. Smokers grope on the smoky back patio, while oddballs lurk in corners. Powerhouse is a gay men's scene – no gawkers.

CITY BEER STORE & TASTING ROOM   BAR
Map p298 (☑415-503-1033; www.citybeerstore. com; 1168 Folsom St; ◷noon-10pm; 🚍12, 14, 19) Sample exceptional local and Belgian microbrews in 6oz to 20oz pours at SF's top beer store. Mix and match a six-pack of stouts or ales to go, or join the crowd enjoying featured craft brews of the day on draft. Learn to discern sours and IPAs at brewery-hosted sipping sessions – and pace yourself with grass-fed beef jerky or bacon caramel corn.

COIN-OP GAME ROOM   BAR
Map p298 (☑628-444-3277; http://coinopsf. com; 508 4th St; ◷4pm-2am; 🚍30, 45, 47, Ⓜ N, T) Finally, someplace where introverts can extroverts can drink, flirt shyly over shuffleboard and fight off nefarious ninjas together. Pinball wizards compete for high scores, while retro video-gamers take on Street Fighter, Tron and Super Mario Brothers at throwback 1980s prices. Prepare to be wowed by the bar made of vintage TVs and California craft beer selection during happy hour (4pm to 7pm).

CLUB OMG   CLUB, GAY
Map p298 (☑415-896-6473; www.clubomgsf. com; 43 6th St; free-$10; ◷5pm-2am Tue-Fri & Sun, 7pm-2am Sat; Ⓜ Powell, Ⓑ Powell) Minuscule but magnetic OMG lures 20s-to-40ish gays to San Francisco's skid row to get down, drink up and strip to skivvies. Latin-diva DJs make Wednesdays and Scandalous Saturdays *muy caliente*, and the undress code is strict on Underwear Party Tuesdays. Drag shows and comedy get the party started weeknights; come early to claim two-for-one drinks at the glowing bar.

ENDUP   GAY, CLUB
Map p298 (☑415-646-0999; www.facebook. com/theendup; 401 6th St; $10-25; ◷11pm Fri-8am Sat, 10pm Sat-4am Mon; 🚍12, 19, 27, 47) Forget Golden Gate Bridge – once you EndUp watching the sunrise over the 101 freeway ramp, you've officially arrived in SF. Dance sessions are marathons fueled by EndUp's 24-hour license, so Saturday nights have a way of turning into Monday mornings. Straight people sometimes End

Up here – but the gay Sunday tea dances have been legendary since 1973. Laughable bathrooms; serious weapon/drug checks.

HOLE IN THE WALL
GAY, BAR

Map p298 (☏415-431-4695; www.holeinthewall saloon.com; 1369 Folsom St; ⊙2pm-2am Mon-Fri, noon-2am Sat & Sun; 🚌9, 12, 47) Filthy bikers and loudmouth punks proudly call this Hole their home. The tangle of neon and bike parts hanging over the bar sets the mood amid walls plastered with vintage party handbills and erotica. Tattooed regulars give the pool table a workout. Check online for beer busts and Thursday drink specials for shirtless men.

BLUXOME STREET WINERY
WINE BAR

Map p298 (☏415-543-5353; www.bluxome winery.com; 53 Bluxome St; ⊙1-8pm Tue-Sun; Ⓜ N, T) Rolling vineyards seem overrated once you've visited SoMa's finest back-alley winery. Grab a barrel-top stool and glimpse winemakers at work in the adjoining warehouse while you sip Sonoma viognier. For best results, pair velvety Russian River Pinot Noir with a cheese plate or pork-belly tacos on food-truck Fridays. Call ahead or you might accidentally crash a start-up launch.

WATERBAR
BAR

Map p298 (☏415-284-9922; www.waterbarsf. com; 399 The Embarcadero; ⊙11:30am-9:30pm Sun & Mon, to 10pm Tue-Sat; Ⓑ Embarcadero, Ⓜ N, T) Waterbar's glass-column aquariums and Bay Bridge vistas are SF's surest way to impress a date over drinks. Leave the dining room to Silicon Valley start-up founders trying to impress investors and head for the oval oyster bar, where wine is $7 from 2pm to 5:30pm and oysters just $1.05 – including 5¢ donated to environmental nonprofits that keep the Bay sparkling.

TERROIR NATURAL WINE MERCHANT
WINE BAR

Map p298 (☏415-558-9946; 1116 Folsom St; ⊙5pm-midnight Mon-Thu, 4pm-2am Fri, 5pm-2am Sat, 4-9pm Sun; 🚌12, 19, 27, 47, Ⓑ Civic Center) 🌿 Whether it's red or white, your wine is green here – Terroir specializes in natural-process, organic and biodynamic wines, with impressive lists from French and Italian producers. Order at the counter and retreat to the loft, or park at the reclaimed-wood bar for cult-wine flights captained by knowledgeable, bossy somme-

liers. The eclectic crowd and vinyl collection complete your evening's entertainment.

DADA
BAR

Map p298 (☏415-357-1367; www.dadasf.com; 65 Post St; ⊙2pm-2am; 🚌14, Ⓜ Montgomery, Ⓑ Montgomery) Downstairs from the Mechanics Institute Library, surreal scenes unfold over vintage sofas and free-flowing California beer and wine. Dada takes the commercial edge off Financial District crowds and restores downtown's art-freak factor with rotating local art, ranging from Rana Horesh's fish-tank installation art to Jason Mercier's junk celebrity portraits – Amy Schumer's is made of antacid boxes and dental dams.

MONARCH
BAR, CLUB

Map p298 (☏415-284-9774; www.monarchsf. com; 101 6th St; ⊙5:30pm-2am Mon-Thu, 5:30pm-4am Fri, 9pm-4am Sat & Sun; 🚌6, 7, 9, 14, Ⓑ Powell, Ⓜ Powell) A boom-town club on a skid-row block, Monarch has a plush parlor bar and a cozy library bar on the main floor, plus a downstairs dance hall with killer sound system and party-ready DJs (entry $5 to $20; cash only). Upgrade from merely happy to 'amazing hours' 5:30pm to 8:30pm weekdays, when contortionists and circus burlesque acts perform in the air over the bar.

HOUSE OF SHIELDS
BAR

Map p298 (www.thehouseofshields.com; 39 New Montgomery St; ⊙2pm-2am Mon-Fri, from 3pm Sat & Sun; Ⓜ Montgomery, Ⓑ Montgomery) Flash back 100 years at this gloriously restored mahogany bar with original 1908 chandeliers and old-fashioned cocktails without the frippery. You won't find any TVs or clocks, so it's easy to lose all track of time. This is one bar Nob Hill socialites and downtown bike messengers can agree on – especially over potent Sazeracs in dimly lit corners.

BUTTER
BAR

Map p298 (☏415-863-5964; www.smoothas butter.com; 354 11th St; ⊙6pm-2am Wed-Sat, from 8pm Sun; 🚌9, 12, 27, 47) Lowbrow and loving it: everyone's wailing to rock anthems and swilling 100% artificially flavored soda-pop cocktails here. For a cheap date, you can't beat a Shotgun Wedding (shot and PBR) with Butter's standout selection of 'trailer treats' – including Tater Tots, mini corn dogs and deep-fried PB&J.

Check the website for raucous events, including retro FUBAR Fridays and genuinely sloppy Sunday karaoke.

1015 FOLSOM
CLUB

Map p298 (www.1015.com; 1015 Folsom St; $10-30; ⏰10pm-3am Fri & Sat; 🚌12, 27) Among the city's biggest clubs, Ten Fifteen packs for marquee EDM DJs and hip-hop acts like Mos Def. Five dance floors and bars mean you'll lose your posse if you're distracted. Prepare for entry pat-downs; there's a serious no-drugs (or weapons) policy. For a smaller, more laid-back scene, try little-sister club 103 Harriet next door. Sketchy block, but pricey drinks.

83 PROOF
BAR

Map p298 (📞415-296-8383; www.83proof.com; 83 1st St; ⏰2pm-midnight Mon & Tue, to 2am Wed & Thu, noon-2am Fri, 8pm-2am Sat; 🚌14, Ⓜ Montgomery, Ⓑ Montgomery) On average weeknights when the rest of downtown is dead, you may have to shout to be heard over 83's flirtatious, buzzing crowd. High ceilings make room for five shelves of top-notch spirits behind the bar – including 200-plus whiskeys – so trust your bartender to make an old-fashioned that won't hurt at work tomorrow. Arrive early for loft seating.

🍷 Civic Center & the Tenderloin

★ BOURBON & BRANCH
BAR

Map p296 (📞415-346-1735; www.bourbonandbranch.com; 501 Jones St; ⏰6pm-2am; 🚌27, 38) 'Don't even think of asking for a cosmo' read the House Rules at this Prohibition-era speakeasy, recognizable by its deliciously misleading Anti-Saloon League sign. For award-winning cocktails in the liquored-up library, whisper the password ('books') to be ushered through the bookcase secret passageway. Reservations required for front-room booths and Wilson & Wilson Detective Agency, the noir-themed speakeasy-within-a-speakeasy (password supplied with reservations).

★ AUNT CHARLIE'S LOUNGE
GAY, CLUB

Map p296 (📞415-441-2922; www.auntcharlieslounge.com; 133 Turk St; free-$5; ⏰noon-2am Mon-Fri, from 10am Sat, 10am-midnight Sun; 🚌27, 31, Ⓜ Powell, Ⓑ Powell) Vintage pulp-fiction covers come to life when the Hot Boxxx Girls storm the battered stage at Aunt Charlie's on Friday and Saturday nights at 10pm ($5; call for reservations). Thursday is Tubesteak Connection ($5; free before 10pm), when bathhouse anthems and '80s disco draw throngs of art-school gays. Other nights bring guaranteed minor mayhem, seedy glamour and Tenderloin dive-bar shenanigans.

STOOKEY'S CLUB MODERNE
LOUNGE

Map p306 (📞415-771-9695; www.stookeysclubmoderne.com; 895 Bush St; ⏰4:30pm-2am Mon-Sat, to midnight Sun; 🚋1, 🚋Powell-Hyde, Powell-Mason, California) Dangerous dames lure unsuspecting sailors into late-night intrigues over potent hooch at this art-deco bar straight out of a Dashiell Hammett thriller (Dashiell Hammett St is just down the block). Chrome-lined 1930s Streamline Moderne decor sets the scene, and wise-cracking white-jacketed bartenders shake the stiffest Corpse Reviver cocktails in town. Ready to live dangerously? Cocktails are $2 off 4:30pm to 6pm.

EDINBURGH CASTLE
PUB

Map p296 (📞415-885-4074; www.thecastlesf.com; 950 Geary St; ⏰5pm-2am; 🚌19, 38, 47, 49) Bagpiper murals on the walls, the *Trainspotting* soundtrack on the jukebox, ale on tap, Tuesday pub quiz and vinegary fish and chips until 9pm provide all the Scottish authenticity you could ask for, short of haggis. This flag-waving bastion of drink comes fully equipped with dartboard, pool tables, DJs on Saturday and the Quiet Lightning reading series on Monday.

RICKSHAW STOP
CLUB

Map p296 (📞415-861-2011; www.rickshawstop.com; 155 Fell St; $5-35; 🚌21, 47, 49, Ⓜ Van Ness) Welcome to the high-school prom you always wanted: indie bands, DIY decor, glitter drag and '90s getups in a former TV studio. Regular events include Popscene indie bands, Brazilian breakbeat nights, Nerd Nite lecture mixers and monthly gay Asian house party GAMeBoi. Some nights welcome ages 18-plus, others 21-plus; doors open around 8pm and main acts kick off around 10pm.

RYE
LOUNGE

Map p296 (📞415-474-4448; www.ryesf.com; 688 Geary St; ⏰5:30pm-2am Mon-Fri, from 6pm Sat, from 7pm Sun; 🚌2, 3, 27, 38) Swagger into this sleek sunken lounge for cocktails that

LOCAL KNOWLEDGE

SOMA'S LEGENDARY LGBT SCENE

Sailors have cruised Polk St and Tenderloin gay/trans joints since the 1940s, Castro bars boomed in the 1970s and women into women have been hitting Mission dives since the '60s – but SoMa warehouses have been the biggest weekend gay scene for decades now. From leather bars and drag cabarets to full-time LGBT clubs, SoMa has it all. True, internet cruising has thinned the herd, many women still prefer the Mission and some nights are slow starters – but the following fixtures on the gay drinking scene pack at weekends.

Eagle Tavern (p98) Legendary leather bar with Sunday beer busts.

Oasis (p104) SF's dedicated drag cabaret mounts outrageous shows, sometimes literally.

Lone Star Saloon (p99) The original bear bar makes manly men warm and fuzzy at happy hour.

Stud (p98) The freaks come out at night for surreal, only-in-SF theme events.

Powerhouse (p99) Major men-only back-patio action.

Hole in the Wall (p100) Spiritual home to gay bikers and loudmouth punks.

Club OMG (p99) Dance in your skivvies on Skid Row.

look sharp and pack more heat than Steve McQueen in *Bullitt*. The soundtrack is '80s and the drinks strictly old school – bartenders mix their own rye Pimm's No 5 Cup with ginger and proper English cucumber. Come early to sip at your leisure on leather couches and leave before the smokers' cage overflows.

WHISKEY THIEVES BAR
Map p296 (☑415-506-8331; 839 Geary St; ⊙1pm-2am; 🚌19, 27, 38) The scene outside this Tenderloin dive makes whiskey seem like a comparatively harmless drug of choice, and this joint has whiskey galore, including rare rye and aged single malts. The back bar is subdivided by category – Irish, Scotch, Bourbon and Rye – and $7 buys a bartender's-choice shot plus a PBR. Feed the jukebox between rounds of pool and pinball.

LUSH LOUNGE GAY, BAR
Map p296 (☑415-771-2022; www.lushloungesf. com; 1221 Polk St; ⊙3pm-2am Mon-Fri, 1pm-2am Sat & Sun; 🚌2, 3, 19, 38, 47, 49) Snag a wooden table by the steel-front fireplace and order anything in stemware – here the lemon drops, blueberry martinis and other fruity drinks pack a punch. Lush Lounge marks the line on Polk where grit ends and hip begins, and sexual orientations blur. During its generous happy hours (weekdays 3pm to 7pm, weekends 1pm to 7pm), everyone becomes a lush.

 ENTERTAINMENT

☆ Financial District, Union Square & Civic Center

⭐SAN FRANCISCO
SYMPHONY CLASSICAL MUSIC
Map p296 (☑box office 415-864-6000, rush-ticket hotline 415-503-5577; www.sfsymphony. org; Grove St, btwn Franklin St & Van Ness Ave; tickets $20-150; 🚌21, 45, 47, Ⓜ Van Ness, 🅑 Civic Center) From the moment conductor Michael Tilson Thomas bounces up on his toes and raises his baton, the audience is on the edge of their seats for another thunderous performance by the Grammy-winning SF Symphony. Don't miss signature concerts of Beethoven and Mahler, live symphony performances with such films as *Star Trek*, and creative collaborations with artists from Elvis Costello to Metallica.

⭐SAN FRANCISCO OPERA OPERA
Map p296 (☑415-864-3330; www.sfopera.com; War Memorial Opera House, 301 Van Ness Ave; tickets $10-350; 🚌21, 45, 47, 🅑 Civic Center, Ⓜ Van Ness) Opera was SF's gold-rush soundtrack – and SF Opera rivals the Met, with world premieres of original works ranging from Stephen King's *Dolores Claiborne* to *Girls of the Golden West*, filmmaker Peter Sellars' collaboration with composer John Adams.

Expect haute couture costumes and radical sets by painter David Hockney. Score $10 same-day standing-room tickets at 10am; check website for Opera Lab pop-ups.

★AMERICAN CONSERVATORY THEATER
THEATER

Map p294 (ACT; ☑415-749-2228; www.act-sf.org; 405 Geary St; ⊗box office 10am-6pm Mon, to curtain Tue-Sun; ☒8, 30, 38, 45, ☒Powell-Mason, Powell-Hyde, ⒷPowell, ⓂPowell) Breakthrough shows launch at this turn-of-the-century landmark, which has hosted ACT's productions of Tony Kushner's *Angels in America* and Robert Wilson's *Black Rider*, with William S Burroughs' libretto and music by Tom Waits. Major playwrights like Tom Stoppard, Dustin Lance Black, Eve Ensler and David Mamet premiere work here, while the ACT's new Strand Theater (p103) stages experimental works.

★GREAT AMERICAN MUSIC HALL
LIVE MUSIC

Map p296 (☑415-885-0750; www.gamh.com; 859 O'Farrell St; shows $20-45; ⊗box office 10:30am-6pm Mon-Fri & show nights; ▣; ☒19, 38, 47, 49) Everyone busts out their best sets at this opulent 1907 bordello turned all-ages venue – indie rockers like the Band Perry throw down, international legends like Salif Keita grace the stage, and John Waters hosts Christmas extravaganzas. Pay $25 extra for dinner with prime balcony seating to watch shows comfortably, or rock out with the standing-room scrum downstairs.

SAN FRANCISCO BALLET
DANCE

Map p296 (☑tickets 415-865-2000; www.sfballet.org; War Memorial Opera House, 301 Van Ness Ave; tickets $22-141; ⊗ticket sales 10am-4pm Mon-Fri; ☒5, 21, 47, 49, ⓂVan Ness, ⒷCivic Center) America's oldest ballet company is looking sharp in more than 100 shows annually, from *The Nutcracker* (the US premiere was here) to modern originals. Performances are mostly at the War Memorial Opera House January to May, and occasionally at the Yerba Buena Center for the Arts. Score $15-to-$20 same-day standing-room tickets at the box office (from noon Tuesday to Friday, 10am weekends).

STRAND THEATER
THEATER

Map p296 (☑415-749-2228; www.act-sf.org/home/box_office/strand.html; 1127 Market St; ☒F, ⒷCivic Center, ⓂCivic Center) What a comeback: this 1917 theater has shed its 1970s porn-palace notoriety and reclaimed the limelight as the American Conservatory Theater (p103) venue for commissioned pieces by cutting-edge playwrights – though the scarlet decor winks knowingly at its red-light past. Upstairs is a prime performance space for jazz and cabaret, with vast windows letting in moonlight and the Strand's neon marquee glow.

PIANOFIGHT
THEATER, CABARET

Map p296 (☑415-816-3691; www.pianofight.com; 144 Taylor St; free-$30; ⊗5-10pm Mon & Tue, to midnight Wed & Thu, to 2am Fri & Sat; ☒5, 6, 7, 21, 31, ☒Powell-Mason, Powell-Hyde, ⓂPowell St, ⒷPowell St) Watch SF make merciless fun of itself at PianoFight supper club, featuring an unruly line-up of lectures with drunken experts at WasTED Talks, smart-phone-hacker murder mysteries, midnight Friday comedy showcases, ukelele-for-your-life Variety Show Death Matches, and Pint-Sized Plays timed to last as long as your beer. Come for happy hour (5pm to 6:30pm), stay 'til mayhem erupts – repeatedly. All ages welcome.

BLACK CAT
JAZZ

Map p296 (☑415-358-1999; www.blackcatsf.com; 400 Eddy St; $10-20; ⊗5:30pm-2am, shows 8pm & 10pm; ☒27, 31) Jazz cats have stalked the Tenderloin ever since Miles Davis, Billie Holiday, Charlie Parker and Dave Brubeck played underground clubs here – and Black Cat is out to restore the laid-back, lowdown glory of the capital of West Coast cool. Upstairs is a bar-restaurant, but downstairs is where the action is nightly, from gypsy-klezmer be-bop to brass-band rebellion.

PUNCH LINE
COMEDY

Map p301 (☑415-397-7573; www.punchlinecomedyclub.com; 444 Battery St; $15-25, plus 2-drink minimum; ⊗shows 8pm Tue-Thu & Sun, 8pm & 10pm Fri, 7:30pm & 9:30pm Sat; ⓂEmbarcadero, ⒷEmbarcadero) Known for launching big talent (including Robin Williams, Chris Rock, Ellen DeGeneres and David Cross), this historic stand-up venue is small enough for you to hear sighs of relief backstage when jokes kill, and teeth grind when they bomb. Strong drinks loosen up the crowd, but you might not be laughing tomorrow.

SOUNDBOX
CLASSICAL MUSIC

Map p296 (☑415-503-5299; http://sfsoundbox.com; 300 Franklin St; $25-35; ⊗9pm-midnight Fri & Sat, doors open 8pm; ☒5, 7, 21, ⓂVan Ness) Once only musicians were allowed backstage at the Symphony's cavernous rehearsal space, because the acoustics weren't fit for audiences – but with digital upgrades supplying sublime sound, club-style multimedia projections, and craft cocktails, one-off performances here threaten to upstage polished Symphony Hall performances. Arrive at least 30 minutes early to nab a cocktail table; latecomers mingle on leather benches.

HEMLOCK TAVERN   LIVE MUSIC

Map p296 (☏415-923-0923; www.hemlocktavern. com; 1131 Polk St; free-$10; ☺4pm-2am; ☐2, 3, 19, 47, 49) When you wake up tomorrow with peanut shells in your hair (weren't they on the floor?) and a stiff neck from rocking too hard to the Lucky Eejits (weren't they insane?), you'll know it was another successful, near-lethal night at the Hemlock. Blame it on cheap drink at the oval bar, pogo-worthy punk and a sociable smoker's room (yes, in California).

COMMONWEALTH CLUB   LIVE PERFORMANCE

Map p294 (☏415-597-6700; www.common wealthclub.org; 595 Market St; $20-50; Mont-gomery St, ⒷMontgomery St) For ideas too big to squeeze into 10-minute TED talks, count on the Commonwealth Club. America's most influential public-affairs forum hosts 400 annual events, where public figures as diverse as conservationist Jane Goodall, former Mexico president Vicente Fox and transgender celebrity Caitlyn Jenner address current cultural and political issues. Many programs are broadcast on public radio, including KQED-FM (88.5).

WARFIELD   LIVE MUSIC

Map p296 (☏888-929-7849; www.thewarfield theatre.com; 982 Market St; ☺box office 10am-4pm Sun & 90min before shows; MPowell, ⒷPow-ell) Big acts with international followings play this former vaudeville theater. Marquee names like Wu-Tang Clan, Iggy Pop, Kanye West and Sarah Silverman explain the line down this seedy Tenderloin block and the packed, pot-smoky balconies. Beer costs $9 to $10 and water $4, so you might as well get cocktails. Street parking isn't advisable – try the garage at 5th and Mission.

EMBARCADERO CENTER CINEMA   CINEMA

Map p301 (☏415-267-4893; www.landmark theatres.com; 1 Embarcadero Center, Promenade Level; adult/child $12.50/10.50; MEmbarcadero, ⒷEmbarcadero) Forget blockbusters – here

San Franciscans catch the latest art-house flick or whatever won best foreign film at the Oscars with reserved seating in cushy pleather recliners. Don't miss the lobby beer/wine bar and gourmet concession stand.

BISCUITS & BLUES   LIVE MUSIC

Map p294 (☏415-292-2583; www.biscuitsand blues.com; 401 Mason St; free-$30; ☺shows 7:30pm & 9:30pm Tue-Thu, 7:30pm & 10pm Fri & Sat, 7pm & 9pm Sun, restaurant 5:30-10:30pm Tue-Sun; 🚼; ☐8, 30, 38, 45, ⒼPowell-Mason, Powell-Hyde, ⒷPowell) With a steady lineup of top-notch regional and national blues and jazz talent, this intimate place off Union Sq earns its reputation as the Bay Area's top blues club. The name isn't a gimmick – the joint serves biscuits, California catfish and Southern fried chicken ($15 minimum food purchase at 8pm weekend shows). Check calendar and reserve online; all ages welcome.

TIX BAY AREA   BOOKING SERVICE

Map p294 (http://tixbayarea.org; 350 Powell St; ⒼPowell-Mason, Powell-Hyde, ⒷPowell, MPow-ell) Line up at Union Sq's discount-ticket booth to score half-price seats for unsold day-of (or next-day) shows. Check the website first, because some tickets are available only online and others only at the booth.

CAFÉ ROYALE   LOUNGE, JAZZ

Map p296 (☏415-441-4099; www.theroyalesf. com; 800 Post St; ☺4pm-midnight Sun-Wed, to 2am Thu-Sat; ☐2, 3, 27, 38) The pool table and TV are mostly ignored at this artsy Parisian-style cafe-bar, where the local crowd roars for free live jazz, hip-hop DJs, author readings, vintage soul and reggae plus art openings. Royale's bartender-owners pour mean craft cocktails and local beer, and conversationalists get served first – so switch off your phone and make a night of it.

☆ SoMa

★OASIS   CABARET

Map p298 (☏415-795-3180; www.sfoasis.com; 298 11th St; tickets $15-35; ☐9, 12, 14, 47, MVan Ness) Forget what you've learned about drag on TV – at this dedicated dragstrava-ganza venue, the shows are so fearless, freaky-deaky and funny you'll laugh until it stops hurting. In a former gay bathhouse, drag-legendary owners Heklina and D'Arcy

SOMA'S SPIRIT OF INVENTION

Few San Francisco visitors realize that most of the personal technology they use every day was invented within 50 miles of where they're standing – all those handy search engines, websites and apps, plus the smart phones, glasses and watches they run on. But even fewer people realize how many of the most widely used apps were invented within the half-sq-mile area of SoMa District – including Instagram, Twitter, Pinterest and Airbnb.

Is there something in the water in SoMa? No, but there may be something in the beer. By joining techies for downtime in SoMa start-up hubs, you can get a sneak preview of the next big technology. Several of Silicon Valley's most important start-up incubator spaces are in SoMa, including RocketSpace (http://rocketspace.com), PARISOMA (www.parisoma.com) and Impact Hub (https://bayarea.impacthub.net). Check their websites for happy hours, meet-ups and pitch nights, where you can hear technology ideas and beta-test the next big tech launch and/or flop.

When you are seized with your own technology breakthrough – yep, it happens to everyone in SF eventually – you're in the right place to make it happen. San Francisco has several hackerspaces where you can socialize over circuitry with people who could probably break into your bank account but who instead graciously share pointers. Two hackerspaces that host events open to nonmembers are the Mission's non-profit women's maker/hackerspace, Double Union (https://www.doubleunion.org; check online for open-house hack sessions and workshops), and anarchically creative nonprofit Mission hackerspace Noisebridge (https://www.noisebridge.net; donations welcome).

Don't be discouraged if your invention doesn't turn out as planned. As the Silicon Valley saying goes: if at first you don't succeed, fail better. Most technologies become obsolete eventually – some just do it faster than others. On Friday afternoons you can pay your respects to bygone blogs and glimpse the inner workings of the Wayback Machine at the Internet Archive, housed in a converted 1927 neoclassical temple in the Richmond District.

So what else is left to invent in San Francisco? Time machines, for starters. Drink to the future at the Interval, the Long Now Foundation (http://longnow.org) bar where you can participate in ongoing experiments in 4D engineering directed by artist Brian Eno and internet pioneer Stewart Brand.

Drollinger mount original shows (sometimes literally), host drag-star DJs like Sharon Needles, and perform *Star Trek*, *Three's Company* and *Sex and the City* in drag.

★ **GIANTS STADIUM** BASEBALL
Map p298 (AT&T Park; ☑415-972-2000, tours 415-972-2400; http://sanfrancisco.giants.mlb. com; 24 Willie Mays Plaza; tickets $14-349, stadium tour adult/child/senior $22/12/17; ⊘tours 10:30am & 12:30pm; ♿; ⓂN, T) Baseball fans roar April to October at the Giants' 81 home games. As any orange-blooded San Franciscan will remind you, the Giants have won three World Series since 2010 – and you'll know the Giants are on another winning streak when superstitious locals sport team colors (orange and black) and bushy beards (the Giants' rallying cry is 'Fear the Beard!').

SLIM'S LIVE MUSIC
Map p298 (☑415-255-0333; www.slimspresents. com; 333 11th St; tickets $15-30; ⊘box office 10:30am-6pm Mon-Fri & show nights; ☐9, 12, 27, 47) Guaranteed good times by Gogol Bordello, New Found Glory, Shiny Toy Guns and female Stones tribute band Chick Jagger fit the bill at this intimate club, owned by R&B star Boz Scaggs. Shows are all-ages, though shorties may have a hard time seeing once the floor starts bouncing. Reserve dinner for an additional $25 to score balcony seats.

YERBA BUENA CENTER FOR THE ARTS PERFORMING ARTS
Map p298 (YBCA; ☑415-978-2700; www.ybca. org; 700 Howard St; tickets free-$35; ⊘box office noon-6pm Sun, Tue & Wed, to 8pm Thu-Sat, galleries closed Mon & Tue; ♿; ☐14, ⓂPowell, ⒷPowell) Rock stars would be jealous of art

❶ GIANTS GAME SEATS

The downside of the Giants' winning streak is that **Giants** (p105) games often sell out, even though the stadium is among America's most expensive ballparks – the average cost for a family of four, including hot dogs and beer, is $239. Don't despair: season-ticket holders sell unwanted tickets through the team's Double Play Ticket Window (see http://sanfrancisco.giants.mlb.com).

If you can't find tickets, head to the park's eastern side along the waterfront, where you may be able to stand at the archways and watch innings for free. You'll need to show up hours early with die-hard local fans for a decent view – or be prepared to just glimpse the game and enjoy the party instead. Go Giants!

stars at YBCA openings, which draw overflow crowds of art-school groupies with shows ranging from cyberpunk video art to hip-hop showdowns and Indian kathak-American tap-dance-fusion freestyle. Most touring dance and jazz companies perform at YBCA's main theater (across the sidewalk from the gallery).

ALONZO KING'S LINES BALLET   DANCE
Map p298 (📞415-863-3040; www.linesballet.org; Yerba Buena Center for the Arts, 700 Howard St; 🚇14, Ⓑ Montgomery, Ⓜ Montgomery) Long, lean dancers perform complicated, angular movements that showcase impeccable technical skills. Original works include dance set to songs in endangered languages, and collaborations with poet Bob Holman and Grateful Dead drummer Mickey Hart. King also offers classes and workshops.

ASIASF   CABARET
Map p298 (📞415-255-2742; www.asiasf.com; 201 9th St; from $39; ⏰5-10pm Wed, 7-10pm Thu & Sun, 7pm-2am Fri, 5pm-2am Sat; 🚇12, 14, 19, Ⓜ Civic Center, Ⓑ Civic Center) First ladies of the world, look out: these dazzling Asian divas can out-hostess you in half the time and half the clothes. Cocktails and Asian-inspired dishes are served with sass by AsiaSF's transgender stars. Hostesses rock the bar/runway hourly, and at weekends everyone hits the downstairs dance floor.

Three-course dinners run $39 to $75 – and, honey, those tips are well earned.

PUBLIC WORKS   LIVE MUSIC
Map p298 (📞415-496-6738; http://publicsf.com; 161 Erie St; 🚇14, 49, Ⓑ16th St Mission) Go Public for story-slam nights with NPR's the Moth, appearances by Questlove, European electronica fascinators like Jan Blomqvist, SF Opera pop-up nights, and DJ sets ranging from euphoric bhangra to Honey Soundsystem queer dance parties. On-site Roll Up Gallery art shows celebrate such enduring SF obsessions as hydroponics, science fiction, Burning Man and sourdough bacteria. Cash only, despite sketchy alleyway entry.

SMUIN BALLET   DANCE
Map p298 (📞415-912-1899; www.smuinballet.org; Yerba Buena Center for the Arts, 700 Howard St; ⏰box-office phone line 1-5pm Tue-Fri; 🚇14, Ⓑ Montgomery, Ⓜ Montgomery) Not your grandma's ballet, Smuin debuts original balletic works inspired by cartoons, cello prodigies and Dr Martin Luther King's civil rights speeches. Performances are witty and poignant, with mass appeal – ideal for those who find ballet too stiff but interpretive dance too precious. Also performs at ODC and Palace of Fine Arts; see website for dates and venues.

LISS FAIN DANCE   DANCE
Map p298 (📞415-380-9433; www.lissfaindance.org; Yerba Buena Center for the Arts, 700 Howard St; 🚇14, Ⓑ Montgomery, Ⓜ Montgomery) Holding your breath is instinctual as you watch this classically trained modern-dance troupe throw themselves into precise, muscular choreography, with original soundscapes and spoken texts by writers ranging from novelist William Faulkner to poet Jane Hirschfield. The troupe's home season is hosted by Yerba Buena Center for the Arts; see website for performances and dances staged in non-traditional venues.

DNA LOUNGE   LIVE PERFORMANCE
Map p298 (📞415-626-1409; www.dnalounge.com; 375 11th St; $9-35; ⏰9pm-5am; 🚇9, 12, 27, 47) SF's reigning megaclub hosts bands, literary slams and big-name DJs, with two floors of late-night dance action just seedy enough to be interesting. Original Saturday mash-up party Bootie brings Justin/Justin (Bieber/Timberlake) jams; Fridays are for Hubba-Hubba Burlesque revues and writers reading teenage diaries at Mortified;

Mondays mean Goth/industrial bands at 18-plus Death Guild. Check calendar; early arrivals may hear crickets.

HOTEL UTAH SALOON LIVE MUSIC

Map p298 (☑415-546-6300; www.hotelutah. com; 500 4th St; free–$10; ☷11:30am-2am; ☐30, 47, Ⓜ N, T) This Victorian saloon ruled SF's '70s underground scene, when upstairs Whoopi Goldberg and Robin Williams took to the stage – and fresh talents surface here during Monday open-mike nights, indie-label debuts and twangy weekend show-cases. In the '50s the bartender graciously served Beats and drifters but snipped off suits' ties; now you can wear whatever, but there's a $20 credit-card minimum.

MEZZANINE LIVE MUSIC

Map p298 (☑415-625-8880; www.mezzanine sf.com; 444 Jessie St; $20-60; Ⓜ Powell, Ⓑ Pow-ell) Big nights come with bragging rights at Mezzanine, with one of the city's best sound systems and crowds hyped for breakthrough shows by hip-hop greats like Wyclef and Mystikal, pop powerhouses like Lupe Fiasco, and Saturday Contro-vrsy dance-offs (spoiler alert for Rihanna-versus-Beyonce nights: B wins, every time). No in/out privileges.

BRAINWASH COMEDY

Map p298 (☑415-861-3663; www.brainwash.com; 1122 Folsom St; ☷7am-9pm Mon-Thu, to 11pm Fri, 8am-8pm Sat & Sun; ☏; ☐12, 19, Ⓜ Civic Center, Ⓑ Civic Center) The barfly's eternal dilemma between going out or doing laundry is solved at this bar-cafe-launderette featur-ing live music and stand-up comedy open mics – comedians Ali Wong, Al Madrigal and Hannibal Buress got their start here. Last wash is at 8pm and happy hour is 4pm to 7pm, so plan your presoaking and orders of beer and Wash Load Nachos accordingly.

AMC METREON 16 CINEMA

Map p298 (☑415-369-6201; www.amctheatres. com; 101 4th St; adult/child $14.49/11.49; ☐14, Ⓜ Powell, Ⓑ Powell) Sprawling across the top floor of the Metreon mall complex, the 16-screen Metreon cinema has comfortable stadium seats with clear views of digital-projection screens, plus 3D screenings ($4 extra per ticket) and a 3D IMAX theater ($7 for 3D screenings). For dinner before show-time, there's a passable ground-floor food court and a Super Duper Burger out front at 783 Mission St.

🛍 SHOPPING

Union Sq is the city's principal shop-ping district, with flagship stores and department stores, including inter-national chains. Downtown shopping-district borders are (roughly) Powell St (west), Sutter St (north), Kearny St (east) and Market St (south), where the Westfield mall (Map p294; www.westfield. com/sanfrancisco; 865 Market St; ☷10am-8:30pm Mon-Sat, 11am-7pm Sun; ☏; ☐ Pow-ell-Mason, Powell-Hyde, Ⓜ Powell, Ⓑ Powell) **sprawls. The epicenter of the Union Sq shopping area is around Post St, near Grant Ave. Stockton St crosses Mar-ket St and becomes 4th St, flanked by flagship stores and Metreon cinema and mall (p107). For boutique offerings, head toward Jackson Sq (p80) along Commercial St.**

🏙 Financial District

★ HEATH CERAMICS HOMEWARES

Map p301 (☑415-399-9284; www.heathcera mics.com; 1 Ferry Bldg, cnr Market St & the Em-barcadero; ☷10am-7pm Mon-Fri, 8am-6pm Sat, 11am-5pm Sun; Ⓜ Embarcadero, Ⓑ Embarca-dero) Odds are your favorite SF meal was served on Heath Ceramics, Bay Area chefs' tableware of choice ever since Alice Wa-ters started using Heath's modern, hand-thrown dishes at Chez Panisse. Heath's muted colors and streamlined, mid-century designs stay true to Edith Heath's originals c 1948. Pieces are priced for fine dining, ex-cept studio seconds, sold here at weekends.

★ RECCHIUTI CHOCOLATES FOOD & DRINKS

Map p301 (☑415-834-9494; www.recchiuticon fections.com; 1 Ferry Bldg, cnr Market St & the Embarcadero; ☷10am-7pm Mon-Fri, 8am-6pm Sat, 10am-5pm Sun; Ⓜ Embarcadero, Ⓑ Em-barcadero) No San Franciscan can resist award-winning Recchiuti: Pacific Heights parts with old money for its *fleur de sel* caramels; Noe Valley's foodie kids prefer S'more Bites to the campground variety; North Beach toasts to the red-wine-pairing chocolate box; and the Mission approves SF-landmark chocolates designed by Crea-tivity Explored – proceeds benefit the Mis-sion arts-education nonprofit for artists with developmental disabilities.

★ WILLIAM STOUT ARCHITECTURAL BOOKS BOOKS

Map p301 (☑415-391-6757; www.stoutbooks.com; 804 Montgomery St; ☺10am-6:30pm Mon-Fri, to 5:30pm Sat; ☑1, 10, 12, 41, ☑California) You can't fit SFMOMA into your pocket, but you can put it on your coffee table – California architectural obsessions begin at William Stout, with 1st-edition catalogs for SFMOMA designers Snøhetta and retro classics like *Cabins, Love Shacks and Other Hide-outs*. This is SF's best-kept design secret, where Apple designers and skateboard makers alike find inspiration at reasonable prices.

PRATHER RANCH MEAT COMPANY FOOD

Map p301 (☑415-391-0420; www.prmeatco.com; 1 Ferry Bldg, cnr Market St & the Embarcadero; ☺10am-7pm Sun-Fri, 8am-6pm Sat) For carnivores this is the highest-quality outlet in the Bay Area. Look no further for humanely raised, all-natural, dry-aged organic beef.

JAPONESQUE HOMEWARES

Map p301 (☑415-391-8860; http://japonesque gallery.com; 824 Montgomery St; ☺10:30am-5:30pm Tue-Fri, 11am-5pm Sat; ☑10, 12, 41) *Wabi-sabi* is the fine appreciation for imperfect, organic forms and materials, and the stock in trade of Japonesque. Owner Koichi Hara arranges antique Japanese bamboo baskets and contemporary ceramics alongside Kaname Higa's post-apocalyptic ballpoint-pen landscapes and Hiromichi Iwashita's graphite-coated, chiseled-wood panels that look like bonfire embers.

FOG CITY NEWS BOOKS, CHOCOLATE

Map p301 (☑415-543-7400; www.fogcitynews. com; 455 Market St; ☺10am-7pm Mon-Fri, 11am-6pm Sat; ☑Embarcadero, ☑Embarcadero) The perfect stop before a long flight, Fog City stocks a vast variety of domestic magazines and newspapers, plus 700 international titles from 25 countries – plus a chocolate selection so big it has its own database, featuring 200-plus candy bars. Historic photos of SF line the walls between the wooden magazine racks and fridges stocked with old-fashioned bottled soda pop.

MCEVOY RANCH FOOD

Map p301 (☑415-291-7224; www.mcevoyranch. com; 1 Ferry Bldg, cnr Market St & the Embarcadero; ☺9am-6pm Mon-Sat, 10am-5pm Sun) In addition to its famous olive oils, this marketplace inside the Ferry Building sells organic treats and potted olive trees.

🅰 Union Square

★ BRITEX FABRICS ARTS & CRAFTS

Map p294 (☑415-392-2910; www.britexfabrics. com; 146 Geary St; ☺10am-6pm Mon-Sat; ☑38, ☑Powell-Mason, Powell-Hyde, ☑Powell, ☑Powell) Runways can't compete with Britex' fashion drama since 1952. First floor: designers bicker over dibs on caution-orange chiffon. Second floor: glam rockers dig through velvet goldmines. Third floor: Hollywood costumers make vampire-movie magic with jet buttons and hand-dyed ribbon. Top floor: fake fur flies and remnants roll as costumers prepare for Burning Man, Halloween and your average SF weekend.

JOHN VARVATOS CLOTHING

Map p294 (☑415-986-0138; www.johnvarvatos. com; 152 Geary St; ☺11am-7pm Mon-Sat, noon-6pm Sun; ☑38, ☑Powell, ☑Powell) America's most wanted men's look is classic California outlaw – and nobody does it better than designer John Varvatos. Western jackets, waxed jeans and pick-stitched waistcoats make any dude seem destined to rob a bank, or at least steal a few hearts. Cuts are slim, prices steep and colors dark, but you're in the right place to live and dress dangerously.

MARGARET O'LEARY FASHION & ACCESSORIES

Map p294 (☑415-391-1010; www.margareto leary.com; 1 Claude Lane; ☺10am-5pm Tue-Sat; ☑8, 30, 45, ☑Montgomery, ☑Montgomery) Ignorance of the fog is no excuse in San Francisco – but should you confuse SF for LA (the horror!) and neglect to pack the obligatory sweater, Margaret O'Leary will sheathe you in knitwear, no questions asked. The SF designer's warm yet whisper-light signatures include Scottish-cashmere cardigans, nubby linen ponchos and Ocean Beachy tie-dyed cotton pullovers.

WINGTIP FASHION & ACCESSORIES

Map p294 (☑415-765-0993; http://wingtip.com; 550 Montgomery St; ☺10am-6pm Mon-Sat; ☑Montgomery, ☑Montgomery) Get the look of an outdoorsy professor who invested early in Apple at this old-school men's store in the handsome 1908 Bank of Italy building. Visiting power brokers will find FiDi wardrobe basics and accessories from cigars to fly-fishing lures, and score perks: commit to spend $1200 in-store or online and gain access to a swanky top-floor clubhouse.

LOCAL KNOWLEDGE

SAN FRANCISCO'S HOMELESS

It's inevitable: panhandlers will ask you for spare change during your visit to San Francisco, especially around Union Sq and downtown tourist attractions.

If it seems as though more people are homeless in San Francisco than in other cities, you're not wrong. Homelessness exists across America, but police crackdowns and a lack of appropriate social services in cities nationwide have created a 'weed and seed' effect: homeless populations forced out of other cities come to San Francisco for its milder climate, history of tolerance and safety-net services. San Francisco's homeless population is now estimated to exceed 10,000 – the highest per capita in the US – despite the city's limited shelter capacity of around 3000 beds.

Some historians date San Francisco's challenges with homelessness to the 1940s, when shell-shocked WWII Pacific Theater veterans were discharged here without sufficient support. Local homeless advocates say the real crisis in California started in the 1960s, when then-governor Ronald Reagan slashed funding to mental hospitals, drug-rehab programs and low-income-housing programs – policies he continued as president in the 1980s.

San Francisco City Hall schemes to address homelessness have had minimal success. Former mayor Willie Brown proposed seizing homeless people's shopping carts – a notorious failure. Ex-mayor Gavin Newsom's controversial 2002 'Care Not Cash' policy replaced cash payments with social services, which left some San Franciscans unable to pay rent. The equally controversial 2010 'Sit/Lie Ordinance' made daytime sidewalk loitering punishable by fines, which has been disproportionately enforced with vulnerable homeless teens in the Haight. Current mayor Ed Lee seems to be skirting the problem; he discontinued the City Hall position of 'Homeless Czar,' focusing instead on downtown business development. But, given San Francisco's growing income inequality, the city can't ignore homelessness.

So you may well sympathize with homeless San Franciscans who ask you to share food or spare change. Whether you choose to or not, know that there are also other ways you can make an immediate difference. You can volunteer with or make a donation to an SF homeless-services organization like Glide (p86), or you could offer your services to an organization back home. Homelessness isn't a uniquely San Franciscan problem – it's a global human tragedy.

LEVI'S FLAGSHIP STORE CLOTHING

Map p294 (☑415-501-0100; www.us.levi.com; 815 Market St; ⊙9am-9pm Mon-Sat, 10am-8pm Sun; 🚋Powell-Mason, Powell-Hyde, ⓂPowell, ⒷPowell) The flagship store in Levi Strauss' hometown sells classic jeans that fit without fail, plus limited-edition Japanese selvage pairs and remakes of Levi's original copper-riveted miner's dungarees. Scour discount racks for limited-edition Levi's Made & Crafted shirts (30% to 60% off), but don't count on sales lasting – rare lines like 1950s prison-model denim jackets sell fast. Hemming costs $10.

BARNEYS DEPARTMENT STORE

Map p294 (☑415-268-3500; www.barneys.com; 77 O'Farrell St; ⊙10am-7pm Mon-Sat, noon-7pm Sun; 🚋Powell-Mason, Powell-Hyde, ⓂPowell, ⒷPowell) The West Coast outpost of the high-end New York fashion landmark has similar signatures, including inspired window displays and up-to-70%-off sales. But Barneys SF feels more boutique than department store, showcasing emerging designers upstairs, cult fragrances downstairs, and a sprawling double-floor men's shop with shoes, jackets and manbags galore.

UNIQLO CLOTHING

Map p294 (www.uniqlo.com; 111 Powell St; ⊙10am-9pm Mon-Sat, 11am-8pm Sun; ⓂPowell, ⒷPowell) Ever since Japanese retailer Uniqlo landed on the West Coast here, SF has been rocking pop-art tees, cashmere in rainbow colors and down jackets that scrunch to the size of a coffee mug. Uniqlo's wardrobe basics may not be built to last, but the color, price and fit are on point.

MACY'S
DEPARTMENT STORE

Map p294 (www.macys.com; 170 O'Farrell St; ⊙10am-9pm Mon-Sat, 11am-8pm Sun; 🚇Powell-Mason, Powell-Hyde, Ⓜ Powell, Ⓑ Powell) Five floors of name brands spanning a city block and the historic marble I Magnin building (p83) offer charming old-school amenities – including actual powder rooms and the delightful 3rd-floor Tout Sweet patisserie (p90). The strong-willed brave perfume police and slightly insulting free-makeover offers to reach shoe sales (totally worth it), but those SPCA holiday windows will totally convince anyone to adopt a kitten.

GUMP'S
JEWELRY, HOMEWARES

Map p294 (🖉415-982-1616; www.gumps.com; 135 Post St; ⊙10am-6pm Mon-Sat, noon-5pm Sun; Ⓜ Montgomery, Ⓑ Montgomery) San Francisco's original department store opened in 1861, importing luxury items from the Far East. Today it's famous for jade, silk, rugs, porcelain and homewares – if you're a guest in a San Franciscan home and want to express your gratitude with a high-end host gift, something from Gump's will always impress.

🏛 SoMa

MR S LEATHER
ADULT

Map p298 (🖉415-863-7764; www.mr-s-leather. com; 385 8th St; ⊙11am-8pm; 🚌12, 19, 27, 47) Only in San Francisco would you find an S&M superstore, with such musts as suspension stirrups, latex hoods and, for that special someone, a chrome-plated codpiece. If you've been a very bad puppy, there's an entire doghouse department catering to you here, and gluttons for punishment will find home-decor inspiration in dungeon furniture.

SAN FRANCISCO RAILWAY MUSEUM GIFT SHOP
GIFTS & SOUVENIRS

Map p298 (🖉415-974-1948; www.streetcar.org/ museum; 77 Steuart St; ⊙10am-5pm Tue-Sun; 🚇Embarcadero, Ⓑ Embarcadero) The next best thing to taking an SF cable car home with you is getting a scale-model streetcar from this tiny, free Municipal Railway museum showcasing SF public transit. Earn instant SF street cred with baseball caps and T-shirts emblazoned with Muni slogans, including everyone's favorite: 'Information gladly given, but safety requires avoiding unnecessary conversation.'

🏛 Civic Center & the Tenderloin

GENERAL BEAD
JEWELRY, GIFTS

Map p298 (🖉415-621-8187; https://generalbead sanfrancisco.com; 637 Minna St; ⊙noon-6pm; 🚌14, 19, Ⓜ Civic Center, Ⓑ Civic Center) Wild beading ambitions strike suddenly within these walls lined with bulk beads, inducing visions of DIY drag and handmade holiday gifts like sparkling mirages: multi-tiered necklaces, sequined samba costumes, mosaic frames, fringed lampshades that double as hats...To practice restraint, order smaller quantities downstairs from bead-bedecked staff behind the counter, who will ring up your sale on bejeweled calculators.

THE MAGAZINE
BOOKS

Map p296 (www.themagazinesf.com; 920 Larkin St; ⊙noon-7pm Mon-Sat; 🚌19, 38, 47, 49) The mother lode of magazines since 1973. The Magazine's old wooden shelves barely contain all the 1940s pinup mags, 1950s *Vogue*, trippy 1960s underground hippie newspapers, 1970s Italian boxing fanzines and '80s new-wave music 'zines – plus a back room packed with early issues of *Playboy* and vintage gay erotica. Many titles cost under a buck, and few are over $15.

HERO SHOP
FASHION & ACCESSORIES

Map p296 (🖉415-829-3129; http://heroshopsf. com; 982 Post St; ⊙11am-7pm Tue-Fri, from 10am Sat, noon-5pm Sun; 🚌2, 3, 19, 27, 38, 47, 49) On the cutting edge of the Tenderloin, Hero transforms casual browsers into SF fashionistas with statement pieces by rising-star local designers: Stevie Howell's boho silk tunics, Future Glory's handmade marbled-leather handbags, psychedelic Never Elsewhere tees. It's no accident Hero's selection seems unusually well edited – owner Emily Holt left her job as *Vogue*'s fashion-trend editor to open this boutique.

SAN FRANCYCLE
FASHION & ACCESSORIES

Map p296 (🖉415-872-5014; www.wearesfc.com; 702 Larkin St; ⊙11am-5pm Mon, to 6:30 Thu & Fri, to 4pm Sat; 🚌19, 31, 38, 47, 49) Keep those muscles warm and show local-loco cyclist pride as you whip through downtown streets wearing San Francycle's California-bear-on-a-bicycle tee and SF bike-district hoodie (Mission is represented by fixies, Castro by exercise bikes). Designer/owner/

cyclist Tommy Pham prints his designs here in SF, so your souvenir tee has neighborhood street cred that earns bike-messenger nods, if not right of way.

GYPSY ROSALIE'S
FASHION & ACCESSORIES

Map p296 (☑415-771-8814; 1222 Sutter St; ☺10am-6pm Mon-Sat; ☐2, 3, 19, 38, 47, 49) Costuming is a competitive sport in SF, and Rosalie's will help you find a head-to-toe ensemble that will have the whole city gagging on your glamour. Choose from SF's most fabulous lace-front wig selection and try out over-the-top looks, from slinky Marilyn Monroe numbers to Marie Antoinette velvet frock coats that will make heads roll.

🏃 SPORTS & ACTIVITIES

CITY KAYAK
KAYAKING

Map p298 (☑415-294-1050, 888-966-0953; www.citykayak.com; Pier 40, South Beach Harbor; kayak rentals per hour $35-125, 3hr lesson & rental $49, tours $59-75; ☺rentals noon-3pm, return by 5pm Thu-Mon; ☐30, 45, Ⓜ N, T) You haven't seen San Francisco until you've seen it from the water. Newbies to kayaking can take lessons and paddle calm waters near the Bay Bridge; experienced paddlers can rent kayaks to brave currents near the Golden Gate (conditions permitting; get advice first). Sporty romantics: twilight tours past the Bay Bridge lights are ideal for proposals. Check website for details.

ONSEN BATH
BATHHOUSE

Map p296 (☑415-441-4987; www.onsensf.com; 466 Eddy St; 1¾hr bath $35; ☺3:30-10pm Mon & Wed, from 11am Thu, noon-11pm Fri, 10:30am-11pm Sat & Sun; ☐19, 31, 38, Ⓑ Civic Center, Ⓜ Civic Center) Hot-tubbing is a California custom that predates the swinging '70s and hippie '60s, with Victorian-era Sutro Baths and *onsen* (spa baths) founded by SF's Japanese American pioneers. Cultivate your own California glow in Onsen's redwood saunas, communal tubs, cold plunge pools and cozy teahouse. Bathing suits required on co-ed days (Friday to Monday), optional

on men-only Wednesdays and women-only Thursdays.

SPINNAKER SAILING
BOATING

Map p298 (☑415-543-7333; www.spinnakersailing.com; Pier 40, South Beach Harbor; skippered charters from $445, lessons from $450; ☺10am-5pm; ☐30, 45, Ⓜ N, T) Do 'luff,' 'cringle' and 'helms-a-lee' mean anything to you? If yes, captain a boat from Spinnaker and sail into the sunset. If not, charter a skippered vessel or take classes and learn to talk like a sailor – in a good way.

YERBA BUENA ICE SKATING & BOWLING CENTER
SKATING, BOWLING

Map p298 (☑415-820-3532; www.skatebowl.com; 750 Folsom St; skating adult/child $12/10, skate rental $4, bowling per lane per hour $22-48, shoe rental $4.75; ☺10am-9pm Sun-Wed, to 10pm Thu-Sat; ☒; ☐14, Ⓜ Powell, Ⓑ Powell) While the suits are working the floor at Moscone Convention Center, upstairs you can skate carefree figure eights or throw strikes at this rooftop family-fun center. Book bowling lanes ahead – especially for glow-in-the-dark Ultra Bowling. Check website or call for availability and deals, including Family Bowling specials (Sunday to Monday).

EMBARCADERO YMCA
HEALTH & FITNESS

Map p298 (☑415-957-9622; www.ymcasf.org/embarcadero; 169 Steuart St; day pass $20; ☺5:30am-9:45pm Mon-Fri, 8am-7:45pm Sat, 9am-5:45pm Sun; ☒; Ⓜ Embarcadero, Ⓑ Embarcadero) The Embarcadero YMCA gym has knockout bay views with no distractions – no blaring TVs, amplified music or cell phones here. The full-service facility includes 25m pool, co-ed hot tub, basketball courts, extensive gym equipment, and separate men's and women's sauna and steam. Towels included. Bring a lock or use the free small lockers outside the locker rooms.

BLAZING SADDLES
CYCLING

Map p294 (☑415-202-8888; www.blazingsaddles.com; 433 Mason St; bike hire per hour $8-15, per day $32-88, electric bikes per day $48-88; ☺8am-8pm; ☐Powell-Hyde, Powell-Mason, Ⓑ Powell, Ⓜ Powell) Rent bicycles near Union Sq to cover downtown in a day – just mind the traffic. Reserve online for 20% off rates.

North Beach & Chinatown

NORTH BEACH | CHINATOWN

Neighborhood Top Five

❶ Chinatown alleyways
(Map p308; btwn Grant Ave,
Stockton St, California St &
Broadway; 🚃1, 30, 45, 🚋Powell-
Hyde, Powell-Mason, California)
Hearing mah-jongg tiles,
temple gongs and Chinese
orchestras as you wander
the backstreets.

❷ Coit Tower (p114)
Climbing Filbert Street
Steps past heckling parrots
and fragrant gardens to
this panoramic, mural-lined
tower.

❸ City Lights Books
(p115) Reflecting in the
Poet's Chair and celebrating
free speech.

**❹ Chinese Historical
Society of America** (p116)
Time traveling through the
old Chinatown at this mu-
seum, housed in the historic
Julia Morgan–designed
Chinatown YWCA.

❺ Li Po (p124) Picking up
where Jack Kerouac left off at
a historic Beat hangout.

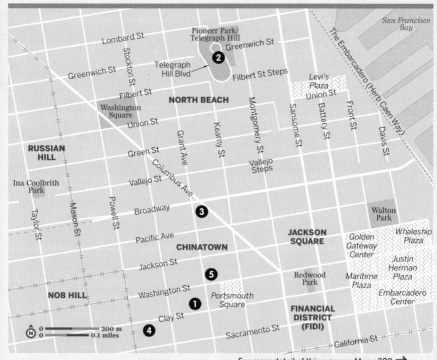

For more detail of this area see Map p308 ➡

Explore: North Beach & Chinatown

From downtown, enter Dragon's Gate (p118) onto Chinatown's main tourist drag, Grant Ave. It's hard to believe this pagoda-topped, souvenir-shopping strip was once notorious brothel-lined Dupont St – at least until you see the fascinating displays at the Chinese Historical Society of America (p116). Duck into Chinatown's historic alleyways to glimpse a neighborhood that's survived against daunting odds, then detour for dim sum at City View (p120). Cross into North Beach via Jack Kerouac Alley (p115) and City Lights (p115), birthplace of Beat literature. Fuel up with espresso at Caffe Trieste (p124) for your North Beach Beat walking tour and hike the garden-lined Filbert Street Steps (p115) to giddy panoramas and daring murals at Coit Tower (p114). Descend for a bar crawl and a hot slice at Golden Boy (p118) or a proper feast at Mister Jiu's (p121).

Local Life

➡**Hangouts** Join regular crowds of poets at Caffe Trieste (p124), martial-arts masters at Washington Square (p116) and skaters at Old St Mary's Square (p117).

➡**Foodie discoveries** Even been-there, tried-that San Franciscans find new taste sensations at Z & Y (p121), Mister Jiu's (p121) and China Live (p120).

➡**Local celebrity sightings** Keep an eye out for Sean Penn at Tosca Cafe (p120), Francis Ford Coppola at Columbus Tower (p115), Tom Waits and Carlos Santana at 101 Music (p126) and Countess Lola Montez reincarnated at Drag Me Along Tours (p127).

➡**Five-buck bargains** Fly a butterfly kite from Chinatown Kite Shop (p127), carbo-load at Liguria Bakery (p118) and catch a show at Doc's Lab (p125).

Getting There & Away

➡**Bus** Key routes passing through Chinatown and North Beach are 1, 10, 12, 30, 39, 41 and 45.

➡**Cable car** From downtown or Fisherman's Wharf, take the Powell-Mason or the Powell-Hyde line through Chinatown and North Beach. The California St cable car passes through the southern end of Chinatown.

Lonely Planet's Top Tip

Wild hawks and parrots circle above North Beach as though looking for a parking spot. The weekend parking situation is so dire that locals avoid North Beach and Chinatown – forgetting there's public parking underneath Portsmouth Sq and at Good Luck Parking Garage, where spots are stenciled with fortune-cookie wisdom: 'You have found the love of your life. Stop looking.'

 Best for Artistic Inspiration

➡ City Lights Books (p115)
➡ Coit Tower (p114)
➡ Chinese Culture Center (p116)
➡ Bob Kaufman Alley (p116)
➡ Jack Kerouac Alley (p115)

✕ **Best Places to Eat**

➡ Molinari (p118)
➡ Liguria Bakery (p118)
➡ Mister Jiu's (p121)
➡ Tosca Cafe (p120)
➡ Z & Y (p121)

For reviews, see p118 ➡

🍸 **Best Places to Drink**

➡ Specs (p121)
➡ Comstock Saloon (p121)
➡ Li Po (p124)
➡ Vesuvio (p124)
➡ Devil's Acre (p124)

For reviews, see p121

TOP SIGHT
COIT TOWER & TELEGRAPH HILL

The exclamation point on San Francisco's skyline is Coit Tower, the stark white deco building that firefighting heiress Lillie Hitchcock Coit left a fortune to build as a monument to SF firefighters.

The tower's lobby **murals** depict city life during the Depression: people lining up at soup kitchens, organizing dockworkers' unions, partying despite Prohibition and reading books – including Marxist manifestos – in Chinese, Italian and English.

When they were completed in 1934, these federally funded artworks were controversial. Authorities denounced the 26 artists that painted them as communists and demanded that radical elements be removed. The artists refused and in a last-minute compromise, park employees painted over one hammer-and-sickle symbol.

The censors shouldn't have bothered: San Franciscans embraced the murals as symbols of the city's openness. In 2012 voters passed a measure to preserve them, and today the murals are freshly restored – and as bold as ever.

In the 19th century, a ruthless entrepreneur began quarrying and blasting away roads on the side of **Telegraph Hill**. City Hall eventually stopped the quarrying, but the view of the bay from the **Filbert Street Steps** is still dynamite. The steep climb leads past hidden cottages along Napier Lane, sweeping Bay Bridge vistas and colorful wild-parrot flocks.

Above: Christopher Columbus statue, by sculptor Vittorio di Colbertaldo. Collection of the City and County of San Francisco.

DON'T MISS

➡ Once-censored, bold murals that show SF as it was

➡ 360-degree viewing-platform panorama

➡ Bay views and sculpture gardens along Filbert Street Steps

➡ Secret murals revealed on free stairway tours

PRACTICALITIES

➡ Map p308, D2

➡ 415-249-0995

➡ www.coittowertours.com

➡ Telegraph Hill Blvd

➡ free, nonresident elevator fee adult/child $8/5

➡ ⊙10am-6pm Apr-Oct, to 5pm Nov-Mar

➡ ▣39

⊙ SIGHTS

Standing atop the Filbert Street Steps, you can understand what Italian fishermen, Beat poets and wild parrots saw in North Beach: more sky than ground, social but never entirely tamed. Coit Tower punctuates the scenery, lifting North Beach out of the fog of everyday life. Across Columbus Ave is Chinatown, survivor of gold booms and busts, anti-Chinese riots, bootlegging wars and trials by fire and earthquake. Yet Chinatown repeatedly made history, providing labor for America's first cross-country railroad, rebuilding San Francisco and leading the charge for China's revolution and US civil rights.

⊙ North Beach

COIT TOWER
PUBLIC ART

See p114.

★CITY LIGHTS BOOKS
CENTER

Map p308 (☑415-362-8193; www.citylights.com; 261 Columbus Ave; ☉10am-midnight; 🚻; 🚌8, 10, 12, 30, 41, 45, 🚋Powell-Mason, Powell-Hyde) Free speech and free spirits have flourished here since 1957, when City Lights founder and poet Lawrence Ferlinghetti and manager Shigeyoshi Murao won a landmark ruling defending their right to publish Allen Ginsberg's magnificent epic poem *Howl*. Celebrate your freedom to read freely in the designated Poet's Chair upstairs overlooking Jack Kerouac Alley, load up on 'zines on the mezzanine and entertain radical ideas downstairs in the new Pedagogies of Resistance section.

Idle browsing is highly encouraged, too – Ferlinghetti's hand-lettered sign describes City Lights as 'A Kind of Library Where Books Are Sold.' On the main floor, City Lights publications include titles by Angela Davis, Charles Bukowski, Diane di Prima and Noam Chomsky, proving the point on another of Ferlinghetti's signs: 'Printer's Ink Is the Greater Explosive.' The nonfiction cellar is unconventionally organized by book buyer Paul Yamazaki according to countercultural themes like Stolen Continents, Muckraking and Commodity Aesthetics. This cellar was once the lair of the paper dragon used in Chinatown's lunar new year celebrations, and enigmatic slo-gans on the walls like 'I am the door' were left behind by a cult that worshipped here in the 1930s. For readers everywhere, City Lights remains a cause for celebration and a source of continuing revelation.

BEAT MUSEUM
MUSEUM

Map p308 (☑800-537-6822; www.kerouac.com; 540 Broadway; adult/student $8/5, walking tours $25; ☉museum 10am-7pm, walking tours 2-4pm Sat; 🚌8, 10, 12, 30, 41, 45, 🚋Powell-Mason) The closest you can get to the complete Beat experience without breaking a law. The 1000-plus artifacts in this museum's literary-ephemera collection include the sublime (the banned edition of Ginsberg's *Howl*, with the author's own annotations) and the ridiculous (those Kerouac bobblehead dolls are definite head-shakers). Downstairs, watch Beat-era films in ramshackle theater seats redolent with the odors of literary giants, pets and pot. Upstairs, pay your respects at shrines to individual Beat writers.

FILBERT STREET STEPS
ARCHITECTURE

Map p308 (🚌39) Halfway through the steep climb up the Filbert Street Steps to Coit Tower, you might wonder if it's all worth the trouble. Take a breather and notice what you're passing: hidden cottages along Napier Lane's wooden boardwalk, sculpture-dotted gardens in bloom year-round and sweeping Bay Bridge vistas. If you need further encouragement, the wild parrots in the trees have been known to interject a few choice words your gym trainer would probably get sued for using.

JACK KEROUAC ALLEY
STREET

Map p308 (btwn Grant & Columbus Aves; 🚌8, 10, 12, 30, 41, 45, 🚋Powell-Mason) 'The air was soft, the stars so fine, the promise of every cobbled alley so great...' This ode by the *On the Road* and *Dharma Bums* author is embedded in his namesake alley, a fittingly poetic, streetwise shortcut between Chinatown and North Beach via the writer's haunts City Lights (p115) and Vesuvio (p124) – Kerouac took literature, Buddhism and beer seriously.

COLUMBUS TOWER
HISTORIC BUILDING

Map p308 (Sentinel Building; 916 Kearny St; 🚌8, 10, 12, 30, 41, 45, 🚋California) If these copper-clad walls could talk, they'd name-drop shamelessly. The tower's original occupant was political boss Abe Rueff, ousted in 1907 and sent to San Quentin for bribing city supervisors. Grammy-winning folk group the Kingston Trio bought the tower in the 1960s, and the Grateful Dead recorded in the basement. Since 1972 it's been owned by *Godfather* director Francis Ford Coppola, who shares offices with *Joy Luck Club* director Wayne Wang and Oscar-winning actor-director Sean Penn. Coppola runs ground-floor Cafe Zoetrope (p124).

MULE GALLERY   GALLERY
Map p308 (✆415-543-2789; http://mulegallery.com; 80 Fresno St; ☉1-6pm Wed-Fri, noon-6pm Sat; ☐8, 10, 12, 41, ☐Powell-Mason) FREE Upstart San Francisco artists buck art-world trends and kick out brave new work at the backstreet Mule Gallery. In recent shows, Kathryn Clark's hand-embroidered tapestries traced the journeys of Syrian refugees via news stories and Google Earth data, and Oakland's Western Edition paid homage to SF's women-run cooperative's Lusty Lady peep show with bawdy posters raising funds for Planned Parenthood. Check the website for salon conversations with SF artists and activists.

WASHINGTON SQUARE   PARK
Map p308 (http://sfrecpark.org/destination/washington-square; cnr Columbus Ave & Union St; ☐8, 30, 39, 41, 45, ☐Powell-Mason) Wild parrots, tai chi masters and nonagenarian churchgoing *nonnas* (grandmothers) are the company you'll keep on this lively patch of lawn. This was the city's earliest official park, built in 1850 on the ranchland of pioneering businesswoman Juana Briones – there's a bench dedicated to her. The parrots keep their distance in the treetops, but, like anyone else in North Beach, they can probably be bribed into friendship with a focaccia from Liguria Bakery (p118), on the square's northeastern corner.

BOB KAUFMAN ALLEY   STREET
Map p308 (☐8, 10, 12, 30, 41, 45, ☐Powell-Mason) What's that – your hometown *doesn't* have a street named after an African American Catholic-Jewish-voodoo anarchist street poet? Revered in France as the 'American Rimbaud,' Bob Kaufman co-founded legendary *Beatitudes* magazine in 1959 and was a spoken-word jazz artist. Yet he took a Buddhist vow of silence after John F Kennedy's assassination that he kept until the Vietnam War ended – 12 years later. This hidden alleyway (off Grant Ave near Filbert St) duly honors him: it's offbeat, streetwise and often profoundly silent.

◉ Chinatown

CHINESE HISTORICAL SOCIETY
OF AMERICA   MUSEUM
Map p308 (CHSA; ✆415-391-1188; www.chsa.org; 965 Clay St; adult/student/child $15/10/free; ☉noon-5pm Tue-Fri, 10am-4pm Sat & Sun; ☻; ☐1, 8, 30, 45, ☐California, Powell-Mason, Powell-Hyde) FREE Picture what it was like to be Chinese in America during the gold rush, transcontinental railroad construction or Beat heyday in this 1932 landmark, built as Chinatown's YWCA by Julia Morgan (chief architect of Hearst Castle). CHSA historians unearth fascinating artifacts, from 1920s silk *qipao* dresses to Chinatown miniatures created by set designer Frank Wong. Exhibits reveal once-popular views of Chinatown, including the sensationalist opium-den exhibit at San Francisco's 1915 Panama-Pacific International Expo inviting fairgoers to 'Go Slumming' in Chinatown.

TIN HOW TEMPLE   TEMPLE
Map p308 (Tien Hau Temple; 125 Waverly Pl; donation customary; ☉10am-4pm, except holidays; ☐1, 8, 30, 45, ☐California, Powell-Mason, Powell-Hyde) There was no place to go but up in Chinatown in the 19th century, when laws restricted where Chinese San Franciscans could live and work. Atop barber shops, laundries and diners lining **Waverly Place** (Map p308; ☐1, 30, ☐California, Powell-Mason), you'll spot lantern-festooned temple balconies. Tin How Temple was built in 1852; its altar miraculously survived the 1906 earthquake. To pay your respects, follow sandalwood aromas up three flights of stairs. Entry is free, but offerings are customary for temple upkeep. No photography inside, please.

CHINESE CULTURE CENTER   GALLERY
Map p308 (✆415-986-1822; www.cccsf.us; Hilton Hotel, 3rd fl, 750 Kearny St; suggested donation $5; ☉during exhibitions 10am-4pm Tue-Sat; ☻; ☐1, 8, 10, 12, 30, 41, 45, ☐California, Powell-Mason, Powell-Hyde) You can see all the way to China from the Hilton's 3rd floor inside this cultural center, which hosts exhibits ranging from showcases of contemporary Chinese ink-brush painters to installations of kung-fu punching bags studded with fighting words. In odd-numbered years, don't miss the Present Tense Biennial, where 30-plus Bay Area artists present personal takes on Chinese culture. Visit the satellite gallery at 41 Ross Alley solo or on the center's

CHINATOWN'S CLINKER-BRICK ARCHITECTURE

As you walk through Chinatown, take a close look at the brick buildings around you. Some of the bricks are blackened, twisted and bubbled. You might notice bricks jutting out from the wall at odd angles, because they're not flat enough to be laid flush. You've spotted clinker bricks, warped and discolored by fire over a century ago.

Clinker bricks are part of Chinatown's extraordinary survival story. Chinatown was originally largely built by non-Chinese landlords in cheap, unreinforced brick – and when the great 1906 earthquake hit, those buildings toppled. Fire swept Chinatown at such high temperatures that the bricks began to melt and turn glassy, becoming clinker bricks. Many residents returned to find they had lost everything – their homes, workplaces, social centers, churches and temples were reduced to rubble. The streets were choked with clinker bricks.

Bricklayers typically toss out over-fired clinker bricks as defective, because they're hard to lay straight and don't insulate well – but Chinatown couldn't wait for better materials to start rebuilding. Ruthless developers like Abe Ruef – of **Columbus Tower** (p115) fame – with the backing of City Hall, were conspiring to relocate Chinatown outside San Francisco. When Chinatown residents caught wind of the plan, they marched back into their still-smoking neighborhood, cleared the streets, and started rebuilding Chinatown, brick by brick. They made ingenious use of warped bricks others would consider useless, turning them on their ends to create decorative patterns.

Chinatown not only stood its ground – it made an architectural statement. Architect Julia Morgan incorporated clinker bricks as a poignant decorative motif for Chinatown's 1908 Donaldina Cameron House (920 Sacramento St), a refuge for women and children who escaped indentured servitude. Chinatown's architecture of survival soon became a signature of California's 1920s Arts and Crafts movement, and today clinker bricks can be seen on religious buildings and family homes across the state.

Chinatown Heritage Walking Tours, led by resident Chinatown historians.

CHINESE TELEPHONE EXCHANGE
HISTORIC BUILDING

Map p308 (743 Washington St; 1, 30, 45, California, Powell-Hyde, Powell-Mason) California's earliest high-tech adopters weren't Silicon Valley programmers but Chinatown switchboard operators in 1894. To connect callers, operators had to speak six languages fluently and memorize 1500-plus Chinatown residents by name, residence and occupation. Managers lived at the pagoda-topped exchange, operating the switchboard 365 days a year until 1949. Since people born in China were prohibited from entering the US during the 1882–1943 Chinese Exclusion era, the exchange provided Chinatown residents with their only family contact for 60 years.

PORTSMOUTH SQUARE
PARK

Map p308 (http://sfrecpark.org/destination/portsmouth-square; cnr Washington St & Walter Lum Pl; P; 1, 8, 10, 12, 30, 41, 45, California, Powell-Hyde, Powell-Mason) Chinatown's unofficial living room is named after John B Montgomery's sloop, which staked the US claim on San Francisco in 1846. SF's first city hall moved into Portsmouth Sq's burlesque Jenny Lind Theater in 1852, and today the square is graced by the Goddess of Democracy, a bronze replica of the statue Tiananmen Sq protesters made in 1989. Tai chi practitioners greet the dawn, toddlers rush the playground at noon, and chess players plot moves well into the night.

OLD ST MARY'S CATHEDRAL & SQUARE
CHURCH

Map p308 (415-288-3800; www.oldsaintmarys.org; 660 California St; cathedral 11am-6pm Mon & Tue, to 7pm Wed-Fri, 9am-6:30pm Sat, to 4:30pm Sun; 1, 30, 45, California) California's first cathedral was started in 1854 by an Irish entrepreneur determined to give wayward San Francisco some religion – despite the cathedral's location on brothel-lined Dupont St. The 1906 earthquake miraculously spared the church's brick walls but destroyed a bordello across the street, making room for St Mary's Sq. Today, skateboarders do tricks of a different sort in the park, under the eye of Beniamino Bufano's 1929 pink-granite-and-steel statue of Chinese revolutionary Sun Yat-sen.

GOOD LUCK PARKING GARAGE   LANDMARK

Map p308 (www.sfmta.com/getting-around/parking/parking-garages/north-beach-garage; 735 Vallejo St; parking per hour $3.50; 🚃10, 12, 30, 41, 45, 🚋Powell-Mason) Each parking spot at this garage comes with fortune-cookie wisdom stenciled onto the asphalt: 'The time is right to make new friends' or 'Stop searching forever: happiness is just next to you.' These omens are supplied by artists Harrell Fletcher and Jon Rubin, who also gathered the local residents' photographs of their Chinese and Italian ancestors that grace the parking-lot entry – fitting heraldic emblems for this cross-cultural neighborhood.

DRAGON'S GATE   MONUMENT

Map p308 (cnr Grant Ave & Bush St; 🚃1, 8, 30, 45, 🚋California) Enter through the Dragon archway, donated by Taiwan in 1970, and you'll find yourself on the street formerly known as Dupont in its notorious red-light heyday. The pagoda-topped 'Chinatown deco' architecture beyond this gate was innovated by Chinatown merchants, led by Look Tin Ely, in the 1920s – a pioneering initiative to lure tourists with a distinctive modern look. It worked: dragon streetlights chased away the shady ladies and now light the way to bargain souvenirs and tea shops.

✕ EATING

✕ North Beach

★GOLDEN BOY   PIZZA $

Map p308 (📞415-982-9738; www.goldenboypizza.com; 542 Green St; slices $2.75-3.75; ⏰11:30am-11:30pm Sun-Thu, to 2:30am Fri & Sat; 🚃8, 30, 39, 41, 45, 🚋Powell-Mason) Looking for the ultimate post-bar-crawl or morning-after slice? Here you're golden. Since 1978, Sodini family *pizzaioli* (pizza makers) have perfected Genovese-style focaccia-crust pizza, achieving that mystical mean between chewy and crunchy with the ideal amount of olive oil. Go for Genovese toppings like clam and garlic or pesto.

★LIGURIA BAKERY   BAKERY $

Map p308 (📞415-421-3786; 1700 Stockton St; focaccia $4-6; ⏰8am-1pm Tue-Fri, from 7am Sat; 🖊🖰; 🚃8, 30, 39, 41, 45, 🚋Powell-Mason) Bleary-eyed art students and Italian grandmothers are in line by 8am for cinnamon-raisin focaccia hot out of the 100-year-old oven, leaving 9am dawdlers a choice of tomato or classic rosemary and garlic, and 11am stragglers out of luck. Take yours in waxed paper or boxed for picnics – but don't kid yourself that you're going to save some for later. Cash only.

★MOLINARI   DELI $

Map p308 (📞415-421-2337; www.molinarisalame.com; 373 Columbus Ave; sandwiches $10-13.50; ⏰9am-6pm Mon-Fri, to 5:30pm Sat; 🚃8, 10, 12, 30, 39, 41, 45, 🚋Powell-Mason) Observe quasi-religious North Beach noontime rituals: enter Molinari, and grab a number and a crusty roll. When your number's called, wisecracking staff pile your roll with heavenly fixings: milky buffalo mozzarella, tangy sun-dried tomatoes, translucent sheets of prosciutto di Parma, slabs of legendary house-cured salami, drizzles of olive oil and balsamic. Enjoy hot from the panini press at sidewalk tables.

TONY'S COAL-FIRED PIZZA & SLICE HOUSE   PIZZA $

Map p308 (📞415-835-9888; http://tonyscoalfired.com; 1556 Stockton St; slices $4.50-6; ⏰11:30-11pm Wed-Sun, to 8pm Mon & Tue; 🚃8, 30, 39, 41, 45, 🚋Powell-Mason) Fuggedaboudit, New York pizza loyalists: in SF, you can grab a cheesy, thin-crust slice from nine-time world-champion pizza-slinger Tony Gemignani. What, you were expecting kosher-salt shakers and bottled Coke from a vintage machine? Done. Difference is, here you can take that slice to sunny Washington Sq and watch tai chi practice and wild parrots year-round. Sorry, Manhattan – whaddayagonnado?

MAMA'S   BRUNCH $

Map p308 (📞415-362-6421; www.mamas-sf.com; 1701 Stockton St; brunch mains $10-14; ⏰8am-3pm Tue-Sun; 🖊🖰; 🚃8, 30, 39, 41, 45, 🚋Powell-Mason) Generations of North Beachers have entrusted the most important meal of the day to Mama and Papa Sanchez, whose Victorian storefront diner has soothed barbaric Barbary Coast hangovers for 50 years. Local farm-egg omelets and *kugelhopf* (house-baked brioche) French toast are cure-alls, but weekend specials like Dungeness-crab eggs Benedict make waits down the block worthwhile. Cash only.

MARIO'S BOHEMIAN CIGAR STORE CAFE   CAFE $

Map p308 (📞415-362-0536; 566 Columbus Ave; sandwiches $7-13.50; ⏰10am-11pm; 🚃8, 30, 39, 41, 45, 🚋Powell-Mason) A boho North

🏃 Neighborhood Walk
North Beach Beat

START CITY LIGHTS BOOKS
END LI PO
LENGTH 1.5 MILES; TWO HOURS

At ❶**City Lights Books** (p115), home of Beat poetry and free speech, pick up something to inspire your journey into literary North Beach – Ferlinghetti's *San Francisco Poems* and Ginsberg's *Howl* make excellent company.

Head to ❷**Caffe Trieste** (p124) for opera on the jukebox and potent espresso in the back booth, where Francis Ford Coppola allegedly drafted *The Godfather* screenplay.

At ❸**Washington Square** (p116), you'll spot parrots in the treetops and octogenarians in tai chi tiger stances on the lawn – pure poetry in motion. At the corner, ❹**Liguria Bakery** (p118) will give you something to write home about: focaccia hot from a 100-year-old oven.

Peaceful ❺**Bob Kaufman Alley** (p116) was named for the legendary street-corner poet, who broke a 12-year vow of silence that lasted until the Vietnam War ended, whereupon he finally walked into a North Beach cafe and recited his poem 'All Those Ships That Never Sailed': 'Today I bring them back/Huge and transitory/And let them sail/Forever.'

Dylan jam sessions erupt in the bookshop, Allen Ginsberg spouts poetry nude in backroom documentary screenings, and onlookers grin beatifically at it all. Welcome to the ❻**Beat Museum** (p115), where visitors are all (to quote Ginsberg's *Howl*) 'angelheaded hipsters burning for the ancient heavenly connection.'

The obligatory literary bar crawl begins at ❼**Specs** (p121) amid merchant-marine memorabilia, tall tales and pitchers of Anchor Steam. *On the Road* author Jack Kerouac once blew off Henry Miller to go on a bender across the street at ❽**Vesuvio** (p124), until bartenders ejected him into the street now named for him: ❾**Jack Kerouac Alley** (p115). Note the words of Chinese poet Li Po embedded in the alley: 'In the company of friends, there is never enough wine.'

Follow the lead of Kerouac and Ginsberg and end your night under the laughing Buddha at ❿**Li Po** (p124) – there may not be enough wine, but there's plenty of beer.

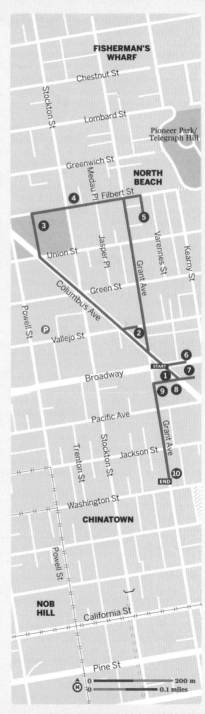

Beach holdout on Washington Sq, Mario's gave up smoking in the 1970s and turned to piping-hot panini. Generations of artistic movements have been fueled by Mario's oven-baked onion-focaccia sandwiches with meatballs or eggplant. This is a prime corner for people-watching over carafes of Chianti or pints of Anchor Steam.

★TOSCA CAFE   ITALIAN $$

Map p308 (☑415-986-9651; www.toscacafesf. com; 242 Columbus Ave; mains $15-22; ☺5pm-2am; ☐8, 10, 12, 30, 41, 45, ☐Powell-Mason) When this historic North Beach speakeasy was nearly evicted in 2012, devotees like Sean Penn, Robert De Niro and Johnny Depp rallied, and New York star chef April Bloomfield took over. Now the 1930s murals and red-leather banquettes are restored and the revived kitchen serves rustic Italian classics (get the meatballs). Jukebox opera and spiked house cappuccino here deserve SF-landmark status. Reservations essential.

CHINA LIVE   CHINESE $$

Map p308 (☑415-788-8188; http://chinalivesf. com; 644 Broadway; small plates $11-22; ☺11:30am-10pm Sun-Wed, to 11pm Thu-Sat; ☐10, 12, ☐Powell-Hyde) San Francisco has steadily craved Chinese food since 1848, and this fancy food hall delivers regional Chinese taste sensations with Californian flair – it's San Francisco chef George Chen's Asian version of New York's Mario Batali–imported Eataly emporium. The upscale main restaurant serves slurp-worthy Shanghai *xiao long bao* (soup dumplings), lip-buzzing-spicy Szechuan wontons, aromatic Cantonese lobster and fragrant kumquat-glazed Peking duck.

E' TUTTO QUA   ITALIAN $$

Map p308 (☑415-989-1002; www.etuttoqua.com; 270 Columbus Ave; mains $16-30; ☺5pm-midnight; ☐8, 10, 12, 30, 41, 45, ☐Powell-Mason) The Colosseum is 6000 miles from the corner of Columbus and Broadway, but you'll eat like a gladiator at E' Tutto Qua (translation: It's All Here). Boisterous Roman service and over-the-top decor create a party atmosphere – but they're serious about homemade pasta, grilled meats and top-flight Italian wines. Order the lamb chops and truffled *paccheri* (tube pasta) and emerge victorious.

RISTORANTE IDEALE   ITALIAN $$

Map p308 (☑415-391-4129; www.idealerestaurant. com; 1309 Grant Ave; pasta $16-22; ☺5:30-10:30pm Mon-Thu, to 11pm Fri & Sat, 5-10pm Sun;

☐8, 10, 12, 30, 41, 45, ☐Powell-Mason) Other North Beach restaurants fake Italian accents, but this trattoria has Italians in the kitchen, on the floor and at the table. Roman chef-owner Maurizio Bruschi serves authentic, al dente *bucatini amatriciana* (tube pasta with tomato-pecorino sauce and house-cured pancetta) and ravioli and gnocchi handmade in-house ('of course!'). North Beach's best-value Italian wine list ensures everyone goes home with Italian accents.

NAKED LUNCH   SANDWICHES $$

Map p308 (☑415-577-4951; www.nakedlunchsf. com; 504 Broadway; sandwiches $11-19; ☺11:30am-2pm & 4:40-11pm Tue-Fri, 11:30am-2am Sat, noon-8pm Sun; ☐8, 10, 12, 30, 41, ☐Powell-Mason) Utterly decadent cravings worthy of a William S Burroughs novel are satisfied by this patio pub tucked between XXX venues. The fried (free-range) chicken sandwich is plenty indulgent – but duck breast with foie gras and truffle salt followed by chocolate bread pudding is the stuff of literary legend. Browse the Beat Museum (p115) until happy hour (4pm to 7pm).

CAFE JACQUELINE   FRENCH $$$

Map p308 (☑415-981-5565; 1454 Grant Ave; soufflés per person $15-30; ☺5:30-11pm Wed-Sun; ☑; ☐8, 30, 39, 41, 45, ☐Powell-Mason) The terror of top chefs is the classic French soufflé – but since 1979 Chef Jacqueline has been turning out perfectly puffy creations that float across the tongue like fog over the Golden Gate Bridge. With the right person to share that seafood soufflé, dinner could hardly get more romantic...until you order the chocolate version for dessert.

✗ Chinatown

CITY VIEW   DIM SUM $

Map p308 (☑415-398-2838; http://cityviewdimsum.com; 662 Commercial St; dishes $3-8; ☺11am-2:30pm Mon-Fri, from 10am Sat & Sun; ☑; ☐1, 8, 10, 12, 30, 45, ☐California) Take a seat in the sunny dining room and make way for carts loaded with delicate shrimp and leek dumplings, garlicky Chinese broccoli, tangy spareribs, coconut-dusted custard tarts and other tantalizing dim sum. Arrive before the midday lunch rush to nab seats in the sunny upstairs room and get first dibs on passing carts.

HOUSE OF NANKING
CHINESE $

Map p308 (☑415-421-1429; http://houseof nanking.net; 919 Kearny St; mains $9-15; ☉11am-9pm Mon-Fri, noon-9:30pm Sat & Sun; ☐8X, 10, 12, 30, 45, ☐Powell-Mason) Meekly suggest an interest in seafood, nothing deep-fried, perhaps some greens, and your server will nod brusquely, grab the menu and return laden with Shanghai specialties: gingery greens with poached scallops, garlicky noodles and black-bean-glazed eggplant. Expect bossy service and a wait for a shared table – but also bold flavors at reasonable prices.

★MISTER JIU'S
CHINESE $$

Map p308 (☑415-857-9688; http://misterjius. com; 28 Waverly Pl; mains $14-45; ☉5:30-10:30pm Tue-Sat; ☐30, ☐California) Ever since the gold rush, San Francisco has craved Chinese food, powerful cocktails and hyperlocal specialties – and Mister Jiu's satisfies on all counts. Build your own banquet of Chinese classics with California twists: chanterelle chow mein, Dungeness-crab rice noodles, quail and Mission-fig sticky rice. Cocktail pairings are equally inspired – try jasmine-infused-gin Happiness ($13) with tea-smoked Sonoma-duck confit.

★Z & Y
CHINESE $$

Map p308 (☑415-981-8988; www.zandyrestau rant.com; 655 Jackson St; mains $9-20; ☉11am-9:30pm Sun-Thu, to 11pm Fri & Sat; ☐8, 10, 12, 30, 45, ☐Powell-Mason, Powell-Hyde) Graduate from ho-hum sweet-and-sour and middling *mu-shu* to sensational Szechuan dishes that go down in a blaze of glory. Warm up with spicy pork dumplings and heat-blistered string beans, take on the housemade *tan-tan* noodles with peanut-chili sauce, and leave lips buzzing with fish poached in flaming chili oil and buried under red Szechuan chili peppers. Go early; worth the inevitable wait.

TRESTLE
CALIFORNIAN $$

Map p308 (☑415-772-0922; http://trestlesf. com; 531 Jackson St; 3-course meal $35; ☉5:30-10:30pm Mon-Thu, to 11pm Fri & Sat, to 10pm Sun; ☐8, 10, 12, 30, 45) If you're on a start-up budget with social-media-mogul tastes, you're in luck here: $35 brings three courses of tasty, rustic comfort food. You get two options per course – typically soup or salad, meat or seafood, fruity or chocolatey dessert – so you and your date can taste the entire menu. Get the bonus handmade-pasta course ($10). Seating is tight, but the mood's friendly.

LAI HONG LOUNGE
DIM SUM $$

Map p308 (☑415-397-2290; www.lhklounge. com; 1416 Powell St; dim sum $4-15; ☉10am-2:30pm & 5:30-8:30pm Mon-Fri, from 9am Sat & Sun; ☐8, 10, 12, 30, 41, 45, ☐Powell-Hyde) Like a greatest-hits album, Lai Hong's menu features remastered dim-sum classics: properly plump shrimp dumplings, crisp Peking duck, baked barbecue-pork buns with the right ratio of savory-sweet pork to meltaway bun. Choose from the menu – no carts – and bide your time while the food is cooked to order. Expect a wait outdoors.

GREAT EASTERN RESTAURANT
CHINESE $$

(☑415-986-2500; http://greateasternrestaurant. net; 649 Jackson St; mains $8-22; ☉10am-11pm Mon-Fri, from 9am Sat & Sun; ☐; ☐8, 10, 12, 30, 45, ☐Powell-Mason, Powell-Hyde) Eat your way across China, from northern Peking duck to southern pan-fried shrimp and Cantonese shrimp-chive dumplings. Weekend dim-sum throngs around noon could mean you'll get seated in the basement, if at all – call ahead for reservations or come around 1pm as brunch crowds stagger out satisfied.

🍷 DRINKING & NIGHTLIFE

🍷 North Beach

★SPECS
BAR

Map p308 (Specs Twelve Adler Museum Cafe; ☑415-421-4112; 12 William Saroyan Pl; ☉5pm-2am; ☐8, 10, 12, 30, 41, 45, ☐Powell-Mason) The walls here are plastered with merchant-marine memorabilia, and you'll be plastered too if you try to keep up with the salty characters holding court in back. Surrounded by seafaring mementos – including walrus genitalia over the bar – your order seems obvious: pitcher of Anchor Steam, coming right up. Cash only.

★COMSTOCK SALOON
BAR

Map p308 (☑415-617-0071; www.comstocksaloon. com; 155 Columbus Ave; ☉4pm-midnight Sun-Mon, to 2am Tue-Thu & Sat, noon-2am Fri; ☐8, 10, 12, 30, 45, ☐Powell-Mason) Relieving yourself in the marble trough below the bar is no longer advisable – Emperor Norton is watching from above – but otherwise this 1907 Victorian saloon brings back the Barbary Coast's glory days with authentic pisco

Chinatown Alleyways

Forty-one historic alleyways packed into Chinatown's 22 blocks have seen it all since 1849: gold rushes and revolution, incense and opium, fire and icy receptions. These narrow backstreets are lined with towering buildings because there was nowhere to go but up in Chinatown after 1870, when laws limited immigration, employment and housing.

Waverly Place

Off Sacramento St are the flag-festooned balconies of Chinatown's historic temples, where services have been held since 1852 – even after the 1906 earthquake and fire, while the altar was still smoldering at **Tin How Temple** (p116). Downstairs are noodle shops, laundries and traditional Chinese apothecaries.

Ross Alley

Ross Alley was known as Mexico, Spanish and Manila St, after the women who staffed its back-parlor brothels. Colorful characters now fill alleyway murals, and anyone can make a fortune the easy way at **Golden Gate Fortune Cookie Company** (p126). You may luck into a concert at Jun Yu's barbershop at 32 Ross Alley, where the octogenarian barber often plays the *erhu* (lap violin) between customers on weekends.

Spofford Alley

As sunset falls on Spofford Alley, you'll hear clicking mah-jongg tiles and a Chinese orchestra warming up. But, generations ago, you might have overheard Sun Yat-sen and his conspirators at number 36 plotting the 1911 overthrow of China's last dynasty.

Commercial St

Across Portsmouth Sq from San Francisco's City Hall, this euphemistically named hot spot caught fire in 1906. City Hall moved across town - and so did the bordellos.

Tours

Chinatown Alleyway Tours (p127) and **Chinatown Heritage Walking Tours** (p127) offer community-supporting, time-traveling strolls through defining moments in American history.

1. Fortune cookies 2. Dragon's Gate, the entrance to Chinatown
3. Lanterns 4. Waverly Place

punch and martini-precursor Martinez (gin, vermouth, bitters, maraschino liqueur). Reserve booths or back-parlor seating to hear on nights when ragtime-jazz bands play.

★CAFFE TRIESTE   CAFE

Map p308 (☑415-392-6739; www.caffetrieste. com; 601 Vallejo St; ☺6:30am-10pm Sun-Thu, to 11pm Fri & Sat; 🛜; 🚊8, 10, 12, 30, 41, 45) Poetry on bathroom walls, opera on the jukebox, live accordion jams and sightings of Beat poet-laureate Lawrence Ferlinghetti: this is North Beach at its best, since the 1950s. Linger over legendary espresso and scribble your screenplay under the Sardinian fishing mural just as young Francis Ford Coppola did. Perhaps you've heard of the movie: *The Godfather*. Cash only.

★VESUVIO   BAR

Map p308 (☑415-362-3370; www.vesuvio.com; 255 Columbus Ave; ☺8am-2am; 🚊8, 10, 12, 30, 41, 45, 🚋Powell-Mason) Guy walks into a bar, roars and leaves. Without missing a beat, the bartender says to the next customer, 'Welcome to Vesuvio, honey – what can I get you?' Jack Kerouac blew off Henry Miller to go on a bender here and, after you've joined neighborhood characters on the stained-glass mezzanine for microbrews or Kerouacs (rum, tequila and OJ), you'll see why.

DEVIL'S ACRE   BAR

Map p308 (☑415-766-4363; www.thedevilsacre. com; 256 Columbus Ave; ☺5pm-2am Tue, from 3pm Wed-Sat, 5pm-midnight Sun & Mon; 🚊8, 10, 12, 30, 41, 45, 🚋Powell-Mason) Magic potions and quack cures are proudly served by this apothecary-style Barbary Coast saloon. Tartly quaffable Lachlan's Antiscorbutic (lime, sea salt, two kinds of gin) is a surefire cure for scurvy and/or sobriety; if you're feeling flush, get the Prospector (pisco, armagnac, Gold Rush bitters). There's happy hour until 7pm, but no food – take your medicine.

15 ROMOLO   BAR

Map p308 (☑415-398-1359; www.15romolo.com; 15 Romolo Pl; ☺5pm-2am Mon-Fri, from 11:30am Sat & Sun; 🚊8, 10, 12, 30, 41, 45, 🚋Powell-Mason) Strap on your spurs: it's gonna be a wild Western night at this back-alley Basque saloon squeezed between burlesque joints. The strong survive the Suckerpunch (bourbon, sherry, hibiscus, lemon, Basque bitters), but the Basque Firing Squad (mezcal, Basque Patxaran liqueur, grenadine, lime, bitters) ends the night with a bang. Bask in

$20 sangria pitchers at the 5:30pm-to-7pm happy hours.

SALOON   BAR

Map p308 (☑415-989-7666; www.sfblues.net/ Saloon.html; 1232 Grant Ave; live music free-$5; ☺noon-2am; 🚊8, 10, 12, 30, 41, 45, 🚋Powell-Mason) Blues in a red saloon that's been a dive since 1861 – this is North Beach at its most colorful. Legend has it that, when the city caught fire in 1906, loyal patrons saved the Saloon by dousing it with buckets of hooch. Today it's SF's oldest bar, and blues and rock bands perform nightly plus weekend afternoons. Cash only.

TONY NIK'S   LOUNGE

Map p308 (☑415-693-0990; www.tonyniks.com; 1534 Stockton St; ☺4pm-2am Mon-Fri, from 2pm Sat & Sun; 🚊8, 30, 39, 41, 45, 🚋Powell-Mason) Vintage neon points the way to Tony Nik's, keeping North Beach nicely naughty since 1933. This tiny cocktail lounge is co-owned by the original Tony 'Nik' Nicco's grandson, who has preserved the glass-brick entry, deco wood paneling and Rat Pack–worthy martini recipe. Aim for the vintage banquettes in back, or hang with neighborhood characters at the mosaic bar.

CAFE ZOETROPE   CAFE, BAR

(☑415-291-1700; www.cafecoppola.com/cafezoetrope; Columbus Tower, 916 Kearny St; ☺11:30am-10pm Tue-Fri, noon-10pm Sat, noon-9pm Sun; 🚊8, 10, 12, 30, 41, 45) During Prohibition, historic Columbus Tower (p115) housed a speakeasy – but now you can drink here in plain sight, at filmmaker Francis Ford Coppola's ground-floor sidewalk bistro. Sip Coppola's Napa wines surrounded by *Godfather* movie memorabilia, and consider the Caesar salad – first served at Columbus Tower in 1924 – but, whatever you do, take the cannoli.

🍷 Chinatown

★LI PO   BAR

Map p308 (☑415-982-0072; www.lipolounge.com; 916 Grant Ave; ☺2pm-2am; 🚊8, 30, 45, 🚋Powell-Mason, Powell-Hyde) Beat a hasty retreat to red-vinyl booths where Allen Ginsberg and Jack Kerouac debated the meaning of life under a golden Buddha. Enter the 1937 faux-grotto doorway and dodge lanterns to place your order: Tsingtao beer or a sweet, sneaky-strong Chinese mai tai made with *baijiu* (rice liquor). Brusque bartenders, basement bathrooms, cash only – a world-class dive bar.

RÉVEILLE CAFE
Map p308 (☑415-789-6258; http://reveillecoffee.com; 200 Columbus Ave; ⏱7am-6pm Mon-Fri, 8am-5pm Sat & Sun; ☐8, 10, 12, 30, 41, 45, ⬚Powell-Mason) If this sunny flat-iron storefront doesn't lighten your mood, cappuccino with a foam-art heart will. Réveille's coffee is like San Francisco on a good day: nutty and uplifting, without a trace of bitterness. Check the circular marble counter for just-baked chocolate-chip cookies and sticky buns. No wi-fi makes for easy conversation, and sidewalk-facing counters offer some of SF's best people-watching.

PLENTEA TEAHOUSE
Map p308 (☑415-757-0223; www.plenteasf.com; 341 Kearny St; ⏱11am-11pm; ☐1, 8, 30, 45, ⬚California) ✐ Chinatown's latest, greatest import is Taiwanese bubble tea: milky iced tea polka-dotted with *boba* (chewy, gently sweet tapioca pearls). PlenTea fills vintage milk bottles with just-brewed organic bubble tea in your choice of flavors: green, black or oolong, plus fresh seasonal mango, peach or strawberry. For only-in-SF flavor, get the bittersweet matcha latte or decadent oolong tea with sea-salt cream.

BUDDHA LOUNGE BAR
Map p308 (☑415-362-1792; 901 Grant Ave; ⏱1pm-2am; ☐8, 30, 45, ⬚Powell-Mason, Powell-Hyde) Vintage red neon promises evenings worthy of WWII sailors on shore leave. Drink in the atmosphere, but stick to basic well drinks and beer straight from a laughing-Buddha bottle. Cue selections on the eclectic jukebox (Dylan, Outkast, The Clash), ask the bartender for dice and you're in for the duration. Cash only.

ENTERTAINMENT

★BEACH BLANKET BABYLON CABARET
Map p308 (BBB; ☑415-421-4222; www.beachblanketbabylon.com; 678 Green St; $25-130; ⏱shows 8pm Wed, Thu & Fri, 6pm & 9pm Sat, 2pm & 5pm Sun; ☐8, 30, 39, 41, 45, ⬚Powell-Mason) Snow White searches for Prince Charming in San Francisco: what could go wrong? The Disney-spoof comedy cabaret has been running since 1974, but topical jokes keep it outrageous and wigs big as parade floats are gaspworthy. Spectators must be over 21, except at

cleverly sanitized Sunday matinees. Reservations essential; arrive early for best seats.

COBB'S COMEDY CLUB COMEDY
Map p308 (☑415-928-4320; www.cobbscomedyclub.com; 915 Columbus Ave; $13-45; ☐8, 30, 39, 41, 45, ⬚Powell-Mason) There's no room to be shy at Cobb's, where bumper-to-bumper shared tables make the audience cozy – and vulnerable. The venue is known for launching local talent and giving big-name acts (Louis CK, John Oliver, Ali Wong) a place to try risky new material. Check the website for shows and showcases like Really Funny Comedians (Who Happen to Be Women). Two-drink minimum.

BIMBO'S 365 CLUB LIVE MUSIC
Map p308 (☑415-474-0365; www.bimbos365club.com; 1025 Columbus Ave; from $20; ⏱box office 10am-4pm; ☐8, 30, 39, 41, 45, ⬚Powell-Mason) Get your kicks at this 1931 speakeasy with stiff drinks, bawdy vintage bar murals, parquet dance floors for high-stepping like Rita Hayworth (she was in the chorus line here) and intimate live shows by the likes of Beck, Pinback, Guided by Voices and Nouvelle Vague. Dress snazzy and bring cash to tip the ladies'-powder-room attendant. Two-drink minimum; cash only.

DOC'S LAB LIVE PERFORMANCE
Map p308 (☑415-649-6191; www.docslabsf.com; 124 Columbus Ave; free-$20; ☐8, 10, 12, 30, 41, 45, ⬚Powell-Mason) Social experiments begin in this subterranean venue, where potent drinks are concocted with mad-scientist beakers and the daring bill upholds North Beach traditions of experimental jazz, outthere comedy, boom-boom burlesque and anything-goes Americana. Doc's Lab occupies the space left by the legendary Purple Onion, home of breakout performances from everyone from Maya Angelou to Zach Galifianakis – and fills the void.

SHOPPING

🛍 North Beach

★SAN FRANCISCO ROCK POSTERS & COLLECTIBLES ANTIQUES
Map p308 (☑415-956-6749; www.rockposters.com; 1851 Powell St; ⏱10am-6pm Mon-Sat; ☐8, 30, 39, 41, 45, ⬚Powell-Mason) Are you ready

to rock? Enter this trippy temple to classic rock gods – but leave your lighters at home, because these concert posters are valuable. Expect to pay hundreds for first-run psychedelic Fillmore concert posters featuring the Grateful Dead – but you can score bargain handbills for San Francisco acts like Santana, the Dead Kennedys and Sly and the Family Stone.

ARIA   ANTIQUES
Map p308 (☑415-433-0219; 1522 Grant Ave; ⊙11am-6pm Mon-Sat; ☐8, 30, 39, 41, 45, ☐Powell-Mason) Find inspiration for your own North Beach epic poem on Aria's weathered wood counters, piled with anatomical drawings of starfish, castle keys lost in gutters a century ago, rusty numbers pried from French village walls and 19th-century letters still in their wax-sealed envelopes. Hours are erratic whenever owner and chief scavenger Bill Haskell is treasure-hunting abroad, so call ahead.

101 MUSIC   MUSIC
Map p308 (☑415-392-6368; 1414 Grant Ave; ⊙10am-8pm Mon-Sat, from noon Sun; ☐8, 30, 39, 41, 45, ☐Powell-Mason) You'll have to bend over those bins to let DJs and hard-core collectors pass (and, hey, wasn't that Tom Waits?!), but among the $8-to-$25 discs are obscure releases (*Songs for Greek Lovers*) and original recordings by Nina Simone, Janis Joplin and San Francisco's own anthem-rockers, Journey. At the sister shop (513 Green St), don't knock your head on vintage Les Pauls.

EDEN & EDEN   GIFTS & SOUVENIRS
Map p308 (☑415-983-0490; www.edenandeden. com; 560 Jackson St; ⊙10am-7pm Mon-Fri, to 6pm Sat; ☐8, 10, 12, 41) Detour from reality at Eden & Eden, a Dadaist design boutique where bats with outstretched wings serve as necklaces, galaxies twinkle on dresses, shaggy tea cozies make teapots look bearded, and those suede lips are coin purses that swallow loose change. Prices are surprisingly reasonable for far-out, limited-edition and repurposed-vintage finds from local and international designers.

ARTIST & CRAFTSMAN SUPPLY   ARTS & CRAFTS
Map p308 (☑415-931-1900; www.artistcraftsman. com; 555 Pacific Ave; ⊙8:30am-7:30pm Mon-Fri, 10am-7pm Sat, 11am-6pm Sun; ☐; ☐8, 10, 12, 41) Ditch your day job and take up painting at this employee-owned art-supply store,

housed in the former Hippodrome burlesque theater. This Barbary Coast hot spot became the Gay Nineties club – check out the figures cavorting in the entry reliefs and peek into the original speakeasy tunnel downstairs. Two floors of supplies anticipate every SF inspiration and rainy-day kids' project.

AL'S ATTIRE   FASHION & ACCESSORIES
Map p308 (☑415-693-9900; www.alsattire.com; 1300 Grant Ave; ⊙11am-7pm Mon-Sat, noon-6pm Sun; ☐8, 10, 12, 30, 41, 45, ☐Powell-Mason) Hepcats and slick chicks get their handmade threads at Al's, where vintage styles are reinvented in noir-novel twill, dandy high-sheen cotton and mid-century flecked tweeds. Prices aren't exactly bohemian for these bespoke originals, but turquoise wing tips are custom-made to fit your feet and svelte hand-stitched jackets have silver-screen star quality. Ask about custom orders for weddings and other shindigs.

LYLE TUTTLE TATTOO ART MUSEUM & SHOP   COSMETICS
Map p308 (☑415-255-2473; www.lyletuttle.com; 841 Columbus Ave; ⊙noon-10pm Sun-Wed, to midnight Thu-Sat; ☐8, 30, 39, 41, 45, ☐Powell-Mason) Tattooed ladies are the life's work of icon Lyle Tuttle, who inked women across seven continents – including Janis Joplin, Cher and Joan Baez. Since the maestro's retirement, his shop's become a working museum, with vintage photos and American traditional tattoos inked by his protégés. You're in good hands – Tuttle championed safe, sanitary tattooing practices with SF's health department.

🏮 Chinatown

⭐ GOLDEN GATE FORTUNE COOKIE COMPANY   FOOD & DRINKS
Map p308 (☑415-781-3956; 56 Ross Alley; ⊙9am-6pm; ☐8, 30, 45, ☐Powell-Mason, Powell-Hyde) Make a fortune at this bakery, where cookies are stamped from vintage presses just as in 1909, when fortune cookies were invented for SF's Japanese Tea Garden (p197). Write your own custom cookies (50¢ each), or get cookies with regular or risqué fortunes (pro tip: add 'in bed' to regular ones). Cash only; 50¢ tip for photos.

⭐ LEGION   FASHION & ACCESSORIES
Map p308 (☑415-733-7900; www.legionsf.com; 678 Commercial St; ⊙11am-6pm Tue-Fri, to 5pm Sat; ☐1, 8, 41, ☐California) This cool-girl

boutique may be tiny, but its fans are legion. Legion's curator-owners specialize in laid-back West Coast looks with smart details: Kowtow fair-trade-cotton dresses with pockets, Ilana Kohn's Ocean Beachy cloud-pattern tanks, and pot-print knee-high socks. Legion's creatively inclined getups go the distance from farmers markets to gallery openings – including the compelling art shows hosted here.

RED BLOSSOM TEA COMPANY TEA

Map p308 (☑415-395-0868; www.redblossom tea.com; 831 Grant Ave; ☉10am-6:30pm Mon-Sat, to 6pm Sun; ☐1, 10, 12, 30, 35, 41, ☐Powell-Mason, Powell-Hyde, California) Crook your pinky: it's always teatime at Red Blossom, featuring 100-plus specialty teas imported by second-generation tea merchants Alice and Peter Luong. Sniff shiny canisters lining wooden shelves, ask about seasonal offerings and try premium blends before you buy. For gourmet gifts, go with the namesake blossoms – tightly wound balls of tea that unfurl into flowers in hot water.

CHINATOWN KITE SHOP GIFTS & SOUVENIRS

Map p308 (☑415-989-5182; www.chinatownkite. com; 717 Grant Ave; ☉10am-8pm; ☀; ☐1, 10, 12, 30, 35, 41, ☐Powell-Hyde, Powell-Mason, California) Be the star of Crissy Field and wow any kids in your life with a fierce 9ft-long flying dragon, a pirate-worthy wild parrot (SF's city bird), surreal floating legs or a flying panda that looks understandably stunned. Pick up a two-person, papier-mâché lion-dance costume and invite a date to bust ferocious moves with you next lunar new year.

🏃 SPORTS & ACTIVITIES

⭐CHINATOWN ALLEYWAY TOURS WALKING
Map p308 (☑415-984-1478; www.chinatown alleywaytours.org; Portsmouth Sq; adult/student $26/16; ☉tours 11am Sat; ☀; ☐1, 8, 10, 12, 30, 41, 45, ☐California, Powell-Mason, Powell-Hyde) Teenage Chinatown residents guide you on two-hour tours through backstreets that have seen it all – Sun Yat-sen plotting China's revolution, '49ers squandering fortunes on opium, services held in temple ruins after the 1906 earthquake. Your presence here helps the community remember its history and shape its future – Chinatown Alleyway Tours are a nonprofit youth-led

program of the Chinatown Community Development Center.

Credit cards are accepted for advance online reservations only; drop-ins must pay with exact change.

DRAG ME ALONG TOURS WALKING

(☑415-857-0865; www.dragmealongtours.com; Portsmouth Sq; $20; ☉tours usually 11am-1pm Sun; ☐1, 8, 10, 12, 30, 41, 45, ☐California, Powell-Mason, Powell-Hyde) Explore San Francisco's bawdy Barbary Coast with a bona-fide legend: gold-rush burlesque star Countess Lola Montez, reincarnated in drag by SF historian Rick Shelton. Her Highness leads you through Chinatown alleyways where Victorian ladies made and lost reputations, and past North Beach saloons where sailors were shanghaied. Barbary Coast characters gambled, loved and lived dangerously. Adult content; reservations required; cash only.

CHINATOWN HERITAGE WALKING TOURS WALKING

Map p308 (☑415-986-1822; www.cccsf.us; Chinese Culture Center, Hilton Hotel, 3rd fl, 750 Kearny St; group tour adult $25-30, student $15-20, private tour (1-4 people) $60; ☉tours 10am, noon & 2pm Tue-Sat; ☀; ☐1, 8, 10, 12, 30, 41, 45, ☐California, Powell-Mason, Powell-Hyde) Local-led Chinatown Heritage Walking Tours pack discoveries into a kid-friendly, school-accredited program. One-hour Public Art walks explore Chinatown's history through its murals – including new Wentworth Alley murals. Two-hour Democracy Walks reveal Chinatown's role in US civil rights and international human-rights movements. Proceeds support the nonprofit Chinese Culture Center; book online or by phone three days ahead.

BASICALLY FREE BIKE RENTALS CYCLING

Map p289 (☑415-741-1196; www.sportsbase ment.com/annex; 1196 Columbus Ave; half-/full-day bike rentals adult from $24/32, child $15/20; ☉9am-7pm Mon-Fri, 8am-7pm Sat & Sun; ☀; ☐F, 30, 47, ☐Powell-Mason, Powell-Hyde) This quality bike-rental shop cleverly gives you the choice of paying for your rental or taking the cost as credit for purchases (valid for 72 hours) at sporting-goods store Sports Basement (p70), in the Presidio en route to the Golden Gate Bridge. (If you buy too much to carry, Sports Basement staff will mount panniers or mail your stuff home.)

Nob Hill, Russian Hill & Fillmore

RUSSIAN HILL | NOB HILL | JAPANTOWN | PACIFIC HEIGHTS

Neighborhood Top Five

1 **Lombard St** (p130) Stepping off the Powell-Hyde cable car and thrilling to spectacular hilltop vistas, before descending the hill's famous switchbacks.

2 **George Sterling Park** (p130) Marveling at afternoon fog blowing through the Golden Gate from this elevated park, a lovely spot for a picnic.

3 **Kabuki Springs & Spa** (p143) Soaking naked in silence in communal Japanese baths – a cozy hideaway on a cold, foggy day.

4 **Vallejo Street Steps** (p130) Standing at the top of the steps and seeing North Beach unfurl below you, framed by the Bay Bridge and downtown skyscrapers.

5 **Japan Center** (p131) Shopping for Japanime and kooky ephemera at a vintage '60s mall, then slurping on a bowl of hot noodles.

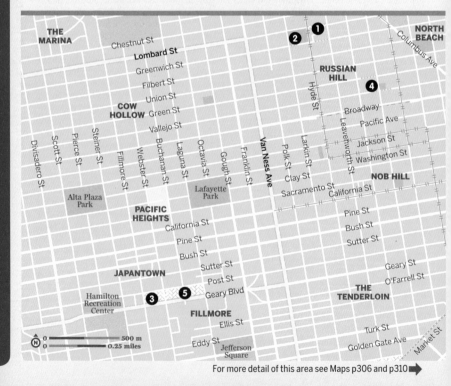

For more detail of this area see Maps p306 and p310 ➡

Explore: Nob Hill, Russian Hill & Fillmore

Tackle Japantown and Pacific Heights together – they're adjacent, connected via Fillmore St. Start at Geary Blvd and Fillmore St, wander east through Japantown, then go north on Fillmore to window-shop spiffy boutiques. Continue uphill till the street becomes residential, around Jackson St, then walk west to Alta Plaza Park for knock-out city-view picnics – there's a fantastic playground, too.

Russian and Nob Hills are likewise adjacent, but their ultra-steep gradients render them harder to explore on foot unless you're in good shape. Fortunately they're accessible via cable car. Nob Hill stands between downtown and Chinatown; Russian Hill abuts Fisherman's Wharf and North Beach. Consider exploring the hills with these other neighborhoods. Polk St is the happening shopping and nightlife strip near Russian Hill; Fillmore St, in Pacific Heights, is swankier by day, quieter by night.

Local Life

→**Music** Several live-music venues lie near Geary and Fillmore Sts – the famous Fillmore Auditorium, plus a couple of intimate jazz clubs.

→**Cinema** Locals come to Japantown for dinner and a movie at Sundance Kabuki Cinema, which serves food and wine in its main theater.

→**Shopping** Most visitors only see the inside of the mall at the Japan Center, but there's also shopping *outside* the mall, along Post St, from Webster St to Laguna St.

→**Canines** Dog lovers flock to Alta Plaza Park for a pug parade – awww! – on the first Sunday of the month, 1pm to 4pm.

Getting There & Away

→**Bus** Buses 1, 2, 3 and 38 connect downtown with Japantown and Pacific Heights; the 22 connects Japantown and Pacific Heights with the Marina and the Mission. Buses 10 and 12 link downtown with Russian and Nob Hills; the 10 continues to Pacific Heights. Bus 27 connects the Mission, SoMa and Downtown to Nob Hill. Buses 41 and 45 connect downtown to Russian Hill and Cow Hollow.

→**Cable car** The Powell-Hyde cable car serves Russian and Nob Hills; the Powell-Mason line serves Nob Hill; and the California line runs between downtown, Nob Hill and the easternmost edge of Pacific Heights.

→**Car** Street parking is difficult but possible. Find garages at the Japan Center on Fillmore St (between Geary and Post Sts) and Post St (between Webster and Buchanan Sts).

Lonely Planet's Top Tip

Cable cars serve Russian and Nob Hills, but the Powell St lines have notoriously long waits at their terminuses. Alternatively, take the California St line, which rarely has queues. Ride west from the foot of Market St to Van Ness Ave, then walk to Pacific Heights and Japantown. Instead of taking busy California St west of Van Ness, walk along pretty Sacramento St (one block north of California), detouring through lovely Lafayette Park.

Best Shopping

→ Japan Center (p131)
→ Margaret O'Leary (p142)
→ Molte Cose (p141)
→ Nest (p142)
→ New People (p141)
→ Relove (p141)

For reviews, see p140.

Best Places to Eat

→ Acquerello (p136)
→ Seven Hills (p136)
→ Swan Oyster Depot (p135)
→ State Bird Provisions (p138)
→ La Folie (p136)

For reviews, see p135. →

Best Places to Drink

→ Tonga Room (p138)
→ Amélie (p139)
→ Hi-Lo Club (p139)
→ 1300 on Fillmore (p138)
→ Social Study (p140)

For reviews, see p138.

⊙ SIGHTS

⊙ Russian & Nob Hills

★**CABLE CAR MUSEUM** HISTORIC SITE
Map p306 (☎415-474-1887; www.cablecarmuseum.org; 1201 Mason St; donations appreciated; ⊙10am-6pm Apr-Sep, to 5pm Oct-Mar; ⛟; ☖Powell-Mason, Powell-Hyde) FREE Hear that whirring beneath the cable-car tracks? That's the sound of the cables that pull the cars, and they all connect inside the city's long-functioning cable-car barn. Grips, engines, braking mechanisms...if these warm your gearhead heart, you'll be besotted with the Cable Car Museum.

★**LOMBARD STREET** STREET
Map p306 (☖Powell-Hyde) You've seen the eight switchbacks of Lombard St's 900 block in a thousand photographs. The tourist board has dubbed it 'the world's crookedest street,' which is factually incorrect: Vermont St in Potrero Hill deserves that award, but Lombard is much more scenic, with its redbrick pavement and lovingly tended flowerbeds. It wasn't always so bent; before the arrival of the car it lunged straight down the hill.

VALLEJO STREET STEPS ARCHITECTURE
Map p306 (Vallejo St, btwn Mason & Jones Sts; ☖Powell-Mason, Powell-Hyde) This glorious high staircase connects North Beach with Russian Hill – ideal for working off a pasta dinner. Ascend Vallejo toward Mason St; stairs rise toward Jones St, passing Ina Coolbrith Park (p131). Sit at the top for brilliant views of the Bay Bridge lights, then continue west to Polk St for nightlife.

GRACE CATHEDRAL CHURCH
Map p306 (☎415-749-6300; www.gracecathedral.org; 1100 California St; suggested donation adult/child $3/2, services free; ⊙8am-6pm Mon-Sat, to 7pm Sun, services 8:30am, 11am & 6pm Sun; ☖1, ☖California) The city's Episcopal cathedral has been rebuilt three times since the gold rush; the current French-inspired, cathedral took 40 years to complete. The spectacular stained-glass windows include a series dedicated to human endeavor, including Albert Einstein uplifted in swirling nuclear particles. Check the website for events on the indoor and outdoor labyrinths, including candlelit meditation services and yoga,

plus inclusive weekly spiritual events, such as Thursday Evensong.

Grace's commitment to pressing social issues is embodied in its AIDS Memorial Chapel, with a bronze altarpiece by artist-activist Keith Haring depicting his signature figures as angels taking flight – especially powerful since this was his last work before his 1990 death from AIDS. Day and night, spot yogis walking the outdoor, inlaid-stone labyrinth, meant to guide restless souls through three spiritual stages: releasing, receiving and returning.

GEORGE STERLING PARK PARK
Map p306 (www.sfparksalliance.org; cnr Greenwich & Hyde Sts; ⛟; ☖19, 41, 45, ☖Powell-Hyde) 'Homeward into the sunset/Still unwearied we go/Till the northern hills are misty/With the amber of afterglow.' Poet George Sterling's 'City by the Sea' is almost maudlin – that is, until you watch the sunset over the Golden Gate Bridge from his namesake hilltop park – the perfect vantage point over the 'cool grey city of love.'

Sterling was a great romancer of all San Francisco offered – nature, idealism, free love and opium – and was frequently broke. But, as he was the toast of the secretive, elite Bohemian Club, San Francisco's high society indulged the poet in his eccentricities, which included carrying a lethal dose of cyanide as a reminder of life's transience. Broken by his ex-wife's suicide and the loss of his best friend, novelist Jack London, the 'King of Bohemia' apparently took this bitter dose in 1926 inside his apartment at the club. Afterward, his influential friends named this park – with zigzagging paths and stirring, Sterling views – for him.

If you're not breathless from these hilltop vistas, play tennis on the adjacent public court named after San Francisco's Alice Marble, the 1930s tennis champ who recovered from tuberculosis to win Wimbledon and serve during WWII as a US secret agent among Nazis. Sure puts a little posttennis panting into perspective, doesn't it?

SAN FRANCISCO ART INSTITUTE GALLERY
Map p306 (☎415-771-7020; www.sfai.edu; 800 Chestnut St; ⊙Walter & McBean Galleries 11am-7pm Tue, to 6pm Wed-Sat, Diego Rivera Gallery 9am-5pm; ☖30, ☖Powell-Mason) FREE Founded during the 1870s, SFAI was at the vanguard of 1960s Bay Area abstraction, 1970s conceptual art and 1990s new-media art – glimpse what's next in the Walter and

McBean Gallery. Diego Rivera's 1931 *The Making of a Fresco Showing the Building of a City* is a *trompe l'oeil* fresco within a fresco, showing the artist himself pausing to admire his work, as well as the work in progress that is San Francisco. The fresco covers an entire wall in the **Diego Rivera Gallery** (Map p306; ☑415-771-7020; www.sfai.edu; 800 Chestnut St; ☉9am-7pm; ☐30, ☐Powell-Mason) FREE.

For a memorable SF aspect, head to the terrace cafe for espresso and panoramic bay views.

INA COOLBRITH PARK PARK
Map p306 (cnr Vallejo & Taylor Sts; ☐10, 12, ☐Powell-Mason) On San Francisco's literary scene, all roads eventually lead to Ina Coolbrith, California's first poet laureate; colleague of Mark Twain and Ansel Adams; mentor to Jack London, Isadora Duncan, George Sterling and Charlotte Perkins Gilman; and lapsed Mormon (she kept secret that her uncle was Mormon prophet Joseph Smith). The tiny park is a fitting honor – long on romance and exclamation-inspiring vistas. Climb past gardens, decks and flower-framed apartments and, when the fog blows, listen for the whooshing in the treetops.

MASONIC AUDITORIUM
& TEMPLE NOTABLE BUILDING
Map p306 (☑415-292-9137; www.masonic heritage.org; 1111 California St; ☉lobby 9am-5pm Mon-Fri, museum 10am-3pm Mon-Thu & by appointment; ☐; ☐1, ☐California) FREE Conspiracy theorists and rock aficionados fetishize the Masonic – a major concert venue and the Masons' main temple for all California and formerly Hawaii, too. Freemasonry venerates architecture, and this 1958 structure gloriously embodies that philosophy with perfect mid-century-modern style. The marble lobby's focal point is a massive stained-glass window (actually made of crushed colored glass) that depicts Freemasonry's symbols and charmingly simple, sometimes amusing images of early California settlement. The museum focuses on California's Masonic history.

HUNTINGTON PARK PARK
Map p306 (http://sfrecpark.org; California St, btwn Mason & Taylor Sts; ☐; ☐1, ☐California) San Francisco's poshest park, Huntington's 1.3 acres mark the crest of Nob Hill. At the center rises the four-sided 'Fountain of the Tortoises,' a century-old recreation of a 400-year-old limestone fountain in Rome. If you're staying down the hill and don't have a lot of time to explore, the park makes a perfect picnic destination – especially with kids, who love the little playground, kitted out with spongy-soft ground cover.

FILBERT STREET HILL HILL
Map p306 (☐41, 45, ☐Powell-Hyde) The honor for steepest street in San Francisco is tied between Filbert St and 22nd St in the Castro. What Filbert lacks in its stubby length (22nd St is longer) it makes up for with views. From the tippy top, by Hyde St, you look down upon North Beach churches, with Coit Tower rising dead ahead, framed by the glittering lights of the Bay Bridge. The hill occupies the 1100 block of Filbert St, between Hyde and Leavenworth Sts.

JACK KEROUAC'S LOVE SHACK HISTORIC SITE
Map p306 (29 Russell St; ☐41, 45, ☐Powell-Hyde) This modest house on a quiet alley was the source of major literature *and* drama from 1951 to 1952, when Jack Kerouac shacked up with Neal and Carolyn Cassady and their baby daughter to pound out his 120ft-long scroll draft of *On the Road*.

Jack and Carolyn became lovers at her husband Neal's suggestion, but Carolyn frequently kicked them both out – though Neal was allowed to move back for the birth of their son, John Allen Cassady (named for Jack, and Allen Ginsberg).

◉ Japantown & Pacific Heights

JAPAN CENTER NOTABLE BUILDING
Map p310 (www.sfjapantown.org; 1737 Post St; ☉10am-midnight; ☐; ☐2, 3, 22, 38, 38L) The center still looks much the way it did when it opened in 1968, with indoor wooden pedestrian bridges, ikebana (flower arranging) displays and *maneki-neko* (waving cat) figurines beckoning from restaurant entryways.

HAAS-LILIENTHAL HOUSE HISTORIC BUILDING
(☑415-441-3000; www.sfheritage.org/haas-lilienthal-house; 2007 Franklin St; adult/child $8/5; ☉noon-3pm Wed & Sat, 11am-4pm Sun; ☐; ☐1, 10, 12, 19, 27, 47, 49) A grand Queen Anne–style Victorian, its original 1886 splendor intact, this family mansion looks like a Clue game come to life – Colonel Mustard could certainly have committed mur-

HERMAN AU PHOTOGRAPHY/GETTY IMAGES ©

1. Japantown (p136)
Slurp ramen in one of this neighborhood's many Japanese eateries.

2. Lombard Street (p130)
This street's dizzying switchbacks are one of San Francisco's most iconic sights.

3. City & bay views
The view to Coit Tower (p114) and the bay, from the top of Lombard Street.

4. Nob Hill (p128)
A stroll in this neighborhood is not for the faint-hearted.

LOCAL KNOWLEDGE

STAIRWAY WALKS

Appreciating San Francisco's brilliant vistas means ascending her hills. Sure, you could ride a cable car, but you'd miss all those marvelous staircases hidden behind hedgerows and the backyard gardens with their cascades of fragrant flowers. Better to walk.

Here's a short list of our favorite staircases. Add some to your itinerary and be rewarded with knockout views – and strong thighs. Take care on damp days, when wet leaves render some routes slippery. And keep your eyes peeled for the famous wild parrots zipping between hilltops – you'll hear them before you see them.

Filbert Street Steps (p115)

Francisco Street Steps (Map p308; 🚋30, 🚋Powell-Mason)

Lyon Street Steps (Map p291; Lyon St)

Baker Street Steps (Map p292; Baker St; 🚋3)

Vallejo Street Steps (p130)

---

der with a rope in the dark-wood ballroom, or Miss Scarlet with a candlestick in the red-velvet parlor. One-hour tours are led by docents devoted to Victoriana. Kids get to play with Victorian toys and a vintage toy train. Sundays the society leads neighborhood **walking tours** (🖉415-441-3000; www.sfheritage.org/walking-tours; adult/child $8/5; ⊙12:30pm Sun).

COTTAGE ROW   STREET

Map p310 (🚋2, 3, 22, 38) Detour to days of yore, when San Francisco was a sleepy seaside fishing village, before houses got all uptight, upright and Victorian. Easygoing 19th-century California clapboard cottages hang back along a brick-paved pedestrian promenade, where plum trees and bonsai take center stage. Homes are private but the mini-park is public, good for sushi picnics. Cottage Row is off Bush St, between Webster and Fillmore Sts.

RUTH ASAWA FOUNTAINS   MONUMENT

Map p310 (Buchanan St Pedestrian Mall, cnr Post St; 🚋2, 3, 38) During drought years you'll have to imagine how they look with water flowing, but, even without, they're a sight to behold. Celebrated sculptor and former WWII internee Ruth Asawa designed these fountains to be lived in, not observed from a polite distance. Bronze origami dandelions sprout from polished-pebble pools, with built-in benches for bento-box picnics, never mind the breeze along this wind-tunnel pedestrian block.

MACONDRAY LANE   STREET

Map p306 (btwn Jones & Leavenworth Sts; 🚋41, 45, 🚋Powell-Mason, Powell-Hyde) The scenic route down from Ina Coolbrith Park – via steep stairs, past gravity-defying wooden cottages – is so charming, it looks like something from a novel. And so it is: Armistead Maupin used this as the model for Barbary Lane in his *Tales of the City* series.

AUDIUM   SCULPTURE

Map p310 (🖉415-771-1616; www.audium.org; 1616 Bush St; $20; ⊙performances 8:30pm Fri & Sat, arrive by 8:15pm; 🚋2, 3, 19, 38, 47, 49, 🚋California) Sit in total darkness as Stan Shaff plays compositions of sounds emitted by his sound chamber, which sometimes degenerate into 1970s sci-fi sound effects before resolving into oddly endearing Moog-synthesizer wheezes. The Audium was specifically sculpted in 1962 to produce bizarre acoustic effects and eerie soundscapes that only a true stoner could enjoy for two solid hours.

PEACE PAGODA   MONUMENT

Map p310 (Peace Plaza, Japan Center; 🅿; 🚋22, 38) When in 1968 San Francisco's sister city of Osaka, Japan, made a gift of Yoshio Taniguchi's five-tiered concrete stupa, the city seemed stupefied about what to do with the minimalist monument, clustering boxed shrubs around its stark nakedness. But, with well-placed cherry trees and low, hewn-rock benches in the plaza, the pagoda is finally in its element, *au naturel*.

KONKO CHURCH   CHURCH

Map p310 (🖉415-931-0453; www.konkofaith.org; 1909 Bush St; ⊙8:30am-6pm Mon-Sat, to 1pm Sun; 🚋1, 2, 3) Inside this low-roofed, high-modernist church, you'll find a handsome blond-wood sanctuary with lofty beamed ceiling, vintage photographs of Konko events dating back 80 years, and friendly Reverend Joanne Tolosa, who'll answer questions about spirituality, the church or its Shinto-inspired beliefs, then leave you to contemplation. On New Year's Day, visitors jot down an appreciation, an apology and a request on a slip of paper, affix it to a tree and receive blessings with sacred rice wine.

EATING

Japan Center is packed with satisfactory Japanese restaurants; noodle shops line the Buchanan Street Mall (outdoors), north of Post St. Upper Fillmore St has diverse, quality restaurants north of Sutter St. Along Hyde St, on Russian Hill, climb to prime picnic spots and neighborhood bistros, and hop a cable car on the way down.

Nob & Russian Hills

ZA PIZZA $

Map p306 (☎415-771-3100; www.zapizzasf.com; 1919 Hyde St; slices $4-5; ⊙noon-10pm Sun-Wed, to 11pm Thu-Sat; 🚌41, 45, 🚋Powell-Hyde) You don't get gourmet, cornmeal-dusted, thin-crust slices like this every day. Pizza-lovers brave uphill climbs for pizza piled with fresh toppings, a pint of Anchor Steam and a cozy bar setting – all for under $10.

CHEESE PLUS DELI $

Map p306 (www.cheeseplus.com; 2001 Polk St; sandwiches $9; ⊙10am-7pm; 🚌10, 12, 19, 27, 47, 49) Foodies, rejoice: here's one deli where they won't blink if you request aged, drunken chèvre instead of provolone on your sandwich. The specialty is classic grilled cheese, made with artisan *fromage du jour*, but for $11.50 get the Crissy Field, loaded with oven-roasted turkey and sustainable Niman Ranch bacon.

SWENSEN'S ICE CREAM $

Map p306 (www.swensensicecream.com; 1999 Hyde St; cones from $3.75; ⊙noon-10pm Tue-Thu & Sun, to 11pm Fri & Sat; 🚌41, 45, 🚋Powell-Hyde) Bite into your ice-cream cone and get an instant brain freeze and a hit of nostalgia. Oooh-ouch, that peppermint stick really takes you back, doesn't it? The 16oz root-beer floats are the 1950s version of Prozac, but the classic hot-fudge sundae is pure serotonin with sprinkles on top. Cash only.

★SWAN OYSTER DEPOT SEAFOOD $$

Map p306 (☎415-673-1101; 1517 Polk St; dishes $10-25; ⊙10:30am-5:30pm Mon-Sat; 🚌1, 19, 47, 49, 🚋California) Superior flavor without the superior attitude of typical seafood restaurants – Swan's downside is an inevitable wait for the few stools at its vintage lunch counter, but the upside of high turnover is incredibly fresh seafood.

Sunny days, place your order to go, browse Polk St boutiques, then breeze past the line to pick up crab salad with Louie dressing and the obligatory top-grade oysters with mignonette sauce. Hike or bus up to George Sterling Park (p130) for superlative seafood with ocean views.

UNION LARDER GASTROPUB $$

Map p306 (☎415-323-4845; http://unionlarder.com; 1945 Hyde St; dishes $15-25; ⊙5-10:30pm Tue & Wed, 4-10:30pm Thu, noon-10:30pm Fri & Sat, 5-9pm Sun; 🚋Powell-Hyde) Part wine bar, part restaurant, Union Larder's sexy industrial design features walls of backlit bottles rising to the ceiling and enormous vaulted windows overlooking the cable-car line. The short, diverse menu features oysters, charcuterie meats (some house made), succulent stinky cheeses, composed salads and knockout sandwiches, plus some 50 wines by the glass. Seating at shared tables and the bar. No reservations.

ZARZUELA TAPAS $$

Map p306 (☎415-346-0800; 2000 Hyde St; mains $16-24; ⊙5:30-10pm Tue-Thu, to 10:30pm Fri & Sat; 🚌41, 45, 🚋Powell-Hyde) One of Russian Hill's longtime stars, Zarzuela's real Spanish tapas include terrific paella and garlic prawns, plus unusual dishes like braised quail and Madrid-style tripe. Ochre-washed walls and terracotta tile set a simple backdrop for the dynamic cooking. It gets noisy. No reservations: come early or put your name on the list and wander lovely Hyde St.

LEOPOLD'S GERMAN $$

Map p306 (www.leopoldssf.com; 2400 Polk St; mains $19-25; ⊙dinner 5:30-10pm Sun-Thu, to 10:30pm Fri & Sat, brunch noon-2:30pm Sat & Sun; 🚌19, 41, 45, 47, 49) Polk St was traditionally called Polkstrasse by German immigrants. Leopold's pays homage with lip-schmacking Austrian-German alpine cooking, served beer-hall style in pinewood booths. The 20-something crowd gets deafeningly loud, but after a boot full of beer you'll hardly notice. Hearty specialties include chicken soup with dumplings, goulash, schnitzel, flatbread and house-made *salumi* – *lecker*!

★**ACQUERELLO** CALIFORNIAN, ITALIAN $$$

Map p306 (☑415-567-5432; www.acquerello.com; 1722 Sacramento St; 3-/4-/5-course menu $95/120/140; ☺5:30-9:30pm Tue-Sat; ☐1, 19, 47, 49, ☐California) A converted chapel is a fitting location for a meal that'll turn Italian culinary purists into true believers in Cal-Italian cuisine. Chef Suzette Gresham's generous pastas and ingenious seasonal meat dishes include heavenly quail salad, devilish lobster *panzerotti* and venison loin chops. Suave *maître d'hôtel* Giancarlo Paterlini indulges every whim, even providing black-linen napkins if you're worried about lint.

★**SEVEN HILLS** ITALIAN $$$

Map p306 (☑415-775-1550; www.sevenhillssf.com; 1550 Hyde St; mains $19-31; ☺5:30-9:30pm Sun-Thu, to 10pm Fri & Sat; ☐10, 12, ☐Powell-Hyde) Anthony Florian studied with great chefs of California and Italy, and he's expert at taking several seasonal ingredients and making them shine. His short, market-driven menu features house-made pastas with elements like rabbit and house-cured pancetta. The four mains showcase quality California meats. Tables are close in the elegant little storefront, but brilliant sound-canceling technology eliminates noise. Stellar service, too.

★**LA FOLIE** FRENCH $$$

Map p306 (☑415-776-5577; www.lafolie.com; 2316 Polk St; 3-/4-/5-course menu $100/120/140; ☺5:30-10pm Tue-Sat; ☐19, 41, 45, 47) Casually sophisticated La Folie remains one of SF's top tables – even after 30 years. Its success lies in the French-born chef-owner's uncanny ability to balance formal and playful. He's a true artist, whose cooking references classical tradition but also nods to California sensibilities. The colorful flourishes on the plate are mirrored in the *très professionnel* staff. Book a week ahead.

STONE'S THROW CALIFORNIAN $$$

Map p306 (☑415-796-2901; http://stonesthrowsf.com; 1896 Hyde St; mains brunch $13-18, dinner $16-29; ☺5:30-10:30pm Tue-Thu, to 11pm Fri & Sat, 11am-2pm & 5:30-10pm Sun; ☑; ☐41, 45, ☐Powell-Hyde) This New American storefront bistro has great service (staff are alums of some of SF's top houses) and, in keeping with the latest style, no one dresses up. It's famous for Sunday brunch – yum, those mimosas and lavender-glazed dough-nuts! – but it's great at dinner, too, when dishes include standout duck-liver paté with warm pretzels, and squid-ink pasta. Alas, the room's loud.

VENTICELLO ITALIAN $$$

Map p306 (☑415-922-2545; http://venticello.com; 1257 Taylor St; mains $19-33; ☺5:30-10pm; ☐1, ☐Powell-Hyde) To enter Venticello's two-story-high dining room, you descend via a staircase – which may be why so many of the Nob Hill regulars dress up for this otherwise casual neighborhood Italian bistro: everyone sees you arrive. Standout menu items include spaghetti carbonara, risotto and anything from the wood-fired oven, especially pizzas. Perfect for date night.

✖ Japantown & Pacific Heights

B. PATISSERIE BAKERY $

(☑415-440-1700; http://bpatisserie.com; 2821 California St; dishes $4-12; ☺8am-6pm Tue-Sun; ☐1, 24) 🍴 A spin on the classic French tea salon, with marble tables and a line out the door, b makes some of SF's most elegant pastries – hence its multiple James Beard Award nominations. One bite of b's perfect all-butter croissants and you'll be covered in crumbs – just like in Paris. Across the street, it operates a similarly terrific sandwich shop.

BENKYODO JAPANESE $

Map p310 (☑415-922-1244; www.benkyodocompany.com; 1747 Buchanan St; mochi $1.40; ☺8am-4pm Mon-Sat, closed 1st & 3rd Mon of month; ☐2, 3, 22, 38) The perfect retro lunch counter cheerfully serves an old-school egg-salad sandwich or pastrami for around $5, but the real draw is the $1.40 *mochi* (chewy Japanese cakes with savory or sweet fillings) made in-house daily – come early for the popular green-tea and chocolate-filled-strawberry varieties. Cash only.

IZAKAYA KOU JAPANESE $

Map p310 (☑415-441-9294; 1560 Fillmore St; dishes $8-18; ☺5:30-11pm Tue-Thu, to midnight Sat, to 10pm Sun; ☐22, 38) Finding good sushi means leaving the Japan Center mall. This nearby favorite has a lively bar and artful presentations of sushi, small plates and rice bowls, which integrate Western ingredients like bacon and parsley for a different spin on classic beer-hall food.

NIJIYA SUPERMARKET
JAPANESE, SUPERMARKET $

Map p310 (📞415-563-1901; www.nijiya.com; 1737 Post St; ⊙10am-8pm; 🚌2, 3, 22, 38) Picnic under the Peace Pagoda (p134) with sushi or teriyaki bento boxes fresh from the deli counter, swig Berkeley-brewed Takara Sierra Cold sake from the drinks aisle and have change from a $20 for mango-ice-cream-filled *mochi* (chewy Japanese cakes with savory or sweet fillings). Tip: by the door, there's a microwave for customers' use.

BUN MEE
VIETNAMESE, SANDWICHES $

Map p310 (📞415-800-7696; www.bunmee.co; 2015 Fillmore St; sandwiches $8-9; ⊙11am-9pm; 🛜; 🚌1, 3, 22) Lines out the door are evidence of Bun Mee's delicious, if tiny, Vietnamese sandwiches: order two. Five-spice chicken is the classic, but the pork belly is sublime. Rice bowls and salads ($10 to $12) round out the menu. The tiny storefront packs; consider picnicking at nearby Alta Plaza Park.

CROWN & CRUMPET
CAFE $

Map p310 (📞415-771-4252; www.crownandcrumpet.com; 1746 Post St; dishes $10-12, afternoon tea $30; ⊙11am-6pm; 🛜📶; 🚌2, 3, 22, 38) In this cafe inside the New People emporium (p141), designer style and rosy cheer usher teatime into the 21st century: girlfriends rehash hot dates over scones with strawberries, and dads and daughters clink porcelain cups after choosing from 24 kinds of tea. Weekend reservations recommended.

WISE SONS BAGEL & BAKERY
BAKERY $

Map p310 (📞415-872-9046; http://wisesonsdeli.com; 1520 Fillmore St; dishes $3-11; ⊙7am-3pm Mon-Sat, 8am-3pm Sun; 🚌22, 38) Filling a hole in SF's food scene, this order-at-the-counter bakery and deli makes real New York City–style bagels, with the classic cream-cheese *schmears* and smoked salmon, plus good bagel sandwiches made with quality ingredients. Limited seating.

ROAM ARTISAN BURGER
BURGERS $

Map p310 (www.roamburgers.com; 1923 Fillmore St; ⊙11:30am-10pm; 📶; 🚌1, 3, 22) Obsessive about ingredients, Roam's burgers feature locally grown, sustainably farmed beef, bison and turkey. Buns are freshly baked and the pickles are made in-house. House-made organic sodas and top-notch milkshakes (with ice cream from Sonoma) round out

the menu. There's also a branch in the **Marina** (Map p292; 📞415-440-7626; www.roamburgers.com; 1785 Union St; burgers $9-11; ⊙11:30am-10pm; 📶; 🚌41, 45) 🌱.

BLACK BARK BBQ
BARBECUE $

Map p310 (📞415-848-9055; http://blackbarkbbq.com; 1325 Fillmore St; mains $9-15; ⊙11:30am-10pm; 📶; 🚌22, 38) 🌱 This modern barbecue joint cool-smokes meats longer than average to develop a signature smoky crust. Tangy sauces, all made in-house using quality organic ingredients, punctuate the meats' intense smokiness. A fat list of sides rounds out the menu (mmm, that macaroni and cheese). Skip the hard-to-eat sandwiches, made inexplicably with chunked, not sliced, meat.

TATAKI
JAPANESE $$

(📞415-931-1182; www.tatakisushibar.com; 2815 California St; dishes $12-20; ⊙5-10pm Sun-Thu, to 10:30pm Fri & Sat; 🚌1, 24) 🌱 Pioneering sushi chefs Kin Lui and Raymond Ho rescue the oceans with sustainable delicacies: silky Arctic char drizzled with yuzu-citrus replaces at-risk wild salmon; the Golden State roll is a local hero, featuring spicy, line-caught scallop, Pacific tuna, organic-apple slivers and edible 24-karat gold. It's tiny, off the beaten path and accepts no reservations, but the quality is way better than in Japantown.

LOCAL KNOWLEDGE

DINING ON THE CABLE CAR LINE

For a romantic, only-in-SF night on the town, book a table at one of several cozy neighborhood restaurants along the cable-car lines on Nob Hill or Russian Hill. Make reservations where possible, and leave plenty of time for travel– cable-car service can be erratic. If you're running late, taxi there, cable home. Just make sure you board the correct line, going in the right direction.

Stone's Throw (p136)

Seven Hills (p136)

Zarzuela (p135)

Venticello (p136)

Union Larder (p135)

Za (p135)

NOB HILL, RUSSIAN HILL & FILLMORE EATING

1300 ON FILLMORE
SOUTHERN US **$$**

Map p310 (☑415-771-7100; www.1300fillmore. com; 1300 Fillmore St; mains dinner $20-29, brunch $13-19; ☺4:30-10pm Sun-Thu, to midnight Fri & Sat, live music 8:30pm Fri & Sat, gospel brunch 11am-2:30pm Sun; ☐22, 31, 38) Reviving swank south of Geary, 1300 on Fillmore's enormous heavy doors open into a double-high living-room space, with exotic rugs, tufted-leather sofas and floor-to-ceiling, black-and-white portraits of jazz luminaries. Friday and Saturday evenings there's live music. The Southern-inspired food can be heavy – but, oh, that fried chicken. Sunday there's gospel brunch (reservations required), when church ladies arrive all dressed up.

It's also a lovely spot for cocktails on your own.

PIZZERIA DELFINA
PIZZA **$$**

Map p310 (☑415-440-1189; www.pizzeria delfina.com; 2406 California St; pizzas $13-19; ☺11:30am-10pm Sun, Mon, Wed & Thu, 5-10pm Tue, 11:30am-11pm Fri & Sat; ☑; ☐1, 3, 22) Pizzeria Delfina derives success from simplicity: fresh-from-the-farm ingredients in copious salads and house-cured meats on tender-to-the-tooth, thin-crusted pizzas – this is one place you actually *want* anchovies on your pizza. Inside gets loud; sit on the sidewalk. Expect waits at peak times.

★STATE BIRD PROVISIONS
CALIFORNIAN **$$$**

Map p310 (☑415-795-1272; http://statebirdsf. com; 1529 Fillmore St; dishes $9-30; ☺5:30-10pm Sun-Thu, to 11pm Fri & Sat; ☐22, 38) Even before winning back-to-back James Beard Awards, State Bird attracted lines for 5:30pm seatings not seen since the Dead played neighboring Fillmore Auditorium (p140). The draw is a thrilling play on dim sum, wildly inventive with seasonal-regional ingredients and esoteric flavors, like fennel pollen and garum. Plan to order multiple dishes. Book exactly 60 days ahead. The staff couldn't be lovelier.

PROGRESS
CALIFORNIAN **$$$**

Map p310 (☑415-673-1294; https://theprogress-sf.com; 1525 Fillmore St; 4-course meal $62; ☺5:30-10pm Sun-Thu, to 11pm Fri & Sat; ☐22, 38) Winner of the James Beard Award for Best Restaurant in 2015, the Progress is the evolution of co-chef-owners Stuart Brioza and Nicole Krasinski's work at their adjoining restaurant – also a James Beard winner – State Bird Provisions (p138). Choose four courses to share with the table for a bona fide banquet. Book exactly 30 days ahead, or sit in the bar.

OUT THE DOOR
VIETNAMESE **$$$**

Map p310 (☑415-923 9575; www.outthedoors. com; 2232 Bush St; mains lunch $14-22, dinner $20-36; ☺11am-2:30pm & 5:30-9:30pm Mon-Fri, 9am-2:30pm & 5:30-9:30pm Sat & Sun; ☐2, 3, 22) Offshoot of the famous Slanted Door (p88), this casual outpost jump-starts afternoon shopping with stellar Dungeness-crab noodles, five-spice chicken and rice plates and Vietnamese coffee. At dinner, rice plates and noodles are replaced with savory claypot meats and fish – an evening you won't soon forget. Make reservations.

DRINKING & NIGHTLIFE

Bars and pubs are spread around the flanks of Nob Hill as it drops toward downtown and Union Sq. More bars are concentrated on Polk St – the main business district for Russian Hill – and along Fillmore St, where you'll find fancy restaurant bars and a couple of jazz clubs and nightclubs around Geary Blvd.

🍷 Nob & Russian Hills

★TONGA ROOM
LOUNGE

Map p306 (☑reservations 415-772-5278; www. tongaroom.com; Fairmont San Francisco, 950 Mason St; cover $5-7; ☺5-11:30pm Sun, Wed & Thu, to 12:30am Fri & Sat; ☐1, ☐California, Powell-Mason, Powell-Hyde) Tonight's San Francisco weather: 100% chance of tropical rainstorms every 20 minutes, but only on the top-40 band playing on the island in the middle of the indoor pool – you're safe in your grass hut. For a more powerful hurricane, order one in a plastic coconut. Who said tiki bars were dead? Come before 8pm to beat the cover charge.

BIG 4
BAR

Map p306 (www.big4restaurant.com; 1075 California St; ☺bar 11:30am-midnight; 🛜; ☐1, ☐California) A classic for swank cocktails, the Big 4 is named for the railroad barons who once dominated Nob Hill society, and its decor pays tribute with opulence – oak-paneled walls, studded green leather and a big mahogany bar that makes great martinis. Service isn't fab, but the room's lovely. Live piano weekend evenings.

HI-LO CLUB
BAR

Map p306 (http://hilosf.com; 1423 Polk St; ⊙4pm-2am Mon-Sat; ☐1, 19, 47, 49, ☐California) A must-visit on any Polk St pub crawl, the Hi-Lo plays trashy-fancy, with peeling paint, tarnished-tin ceilings and distressed-wood floors that make it resemble a candle-lit squat. The classic cocktails showcase lesser-known craft spirits, never brand names – don't ask for Absolut! – and the soundtrack is vintage soul, rock and punk. Come early; otherwise it's packed – and deafeningly loud.

TOP OF THE MARK
BAR

Map p306 (www.topofthemark.com; 999 California St; cover $10-15; ⊙4:30-11.30pm Sun-Thu, to 12.30am Fri & Sat; ☐1, ☐California) So what if it's touristy? Nothing beats twirling in the clouds in a little cocktail dress on the city's highest dance floor. Thursday to Saturday evenings are best, when a full jazz band plays; Wednesday there's piano music. Sunday to Tuesday it's quiet, but, oh, the views! Remarkably, it's often empty at sunset – and gorgeous on fog-free evenings. Expect $15 drinks.

FINE MOUSSE
WINE BAR

Map p306 (☑415-908-1988; http://thefine mousse.com; 1098 Jackson St; ⊙5-11pm Mon-Wed, to midnight Thu-Sat, to 10pm Sun; ☐Powell-Hyde) Champagne and French fries are what to order at this decidedly un-fancy wine bar on the cable-car line, whose menu showcases five by the glass and 35 by the bottle. And, oh, those duck-fat fries – a luxurious spin on classic comfort food that underscores the fact that you need no special occasion to enjoy a good glass of bubbles.

HOPWATER DISTRIBUTION
BEER HALL

Map p306 (http://hopwaterdistribution.com; 850 Bush St; ⊙5-11pm Sun-Wed, to 1am Thu-Sat; ☐30, 45, ☐Powell-Hyde, Powell-Mason) Beer drinkers are spoiled for choice here, with a changing menu of 30 on-tap ales, IPAs, pilsners and lagers, plus yummy bar bites, notably Humboldt Fog cheese plates, buttermilk-fried-chicken sandwiches and pulled-pork sliders. Sit upstairs for bird's-eye views of the scene. It's noisy at peak hours, but, in classic pub tradition, it's over by midnight.

AMÉLIE
BAR

Map p306 (☑415-292-6916; www.ameliewine bar.com; 1754 Polk St; ⊙5pm-1am; ☐1, 10, 12, 19, 27, 47, 49, ☐Powell-Hyde, California) This *très*-cool neighborhood wine bar with sexy lipstick-red counters serves well-priced vintages – happy-hour (5pm to 7pm) flights of three cost just $10 – and delish cheese and charcuterie plates. Weekends get terribly crowded (make reservations!); weekdays it's an ideal spot to cozy up with your sweetheart.

HARPER & RYE
COCKTAIL BAR

Map p306 (http://web.harperandrye.com; 1695 Polk St; ⊙4pm-2am; ☐1, 19, 47, 49, ☐California) Small-batch rye, craft cocktails and artisanal beers are the specialties at this Polk St bar, styled with floor-to-ceiling weathered wood and exposed steel. The upstairs mezzanine provides a stellar vantage point over an often shoulder-to-shoulder crowd of well-heeled 20- and 30-somethings. Try the punch jars, but be careful: they serve four, not one.

CINCH
GAY

Map p306 (http://cinchsf.com; 1723 Polk St; ⊙9am-2am Mon-Fri, from 6am Sat & Sun; ☐1, 19, 27, 47, 49, ☐California) The last of the old-guard Polk St gay bars still has an old-timey saloon vibe, with pool, pinball, free popcorn and a big smokers patio where you get yelled at if you spark a joint (but people do it anyway).

🍷 Japantown & Pacific Heights

BOBA GUYS
TEAHOUSE

Map p310 (www.bobaguys.com; 1522 Fillmore St; ⊙11am-9pm Tue-Thu, noon-11pm Fri & Sat, to 6pm Sun; ☐22, 38) 🌱 Using premium leaves and local organic milk, Boba Guys makes sweet-milk tea drinks ($4 to $6) and Asian-inspired pastries for chai fetishists not the least bit hesitant to queue up for 20 minutes for service. Quality ingredients and luxe extras like homemade jellies (almost) justify absurd weekend waits.

JANE
CAFE

Map p310 (www.itsjane.com; 2123 Fillmore St; ⊙7am-6pm; 🔊; ☐1, 3, 22) Pac Heights girl-friends sit at side-by-side tables and chat over fair-trade coffee and chai, house-made pastries and gorgeous salads, and freelance workers hunch over their laptops at this upbeat and happening cafe, a great spot for a quick nosh before shopping at the surrounding boutiques.

SOCIAL STUDY   BAR
Map p310 (http://thesocialstudysf.com; 1795 Geary Blvd; ⊙5-10:30pm Mon, noon-11pm Tue-Thu, to 1am Fri & Sat; 🛜; 🚌22, 38) Part cafe, part bar, Social Study draws an upbeat collegiate crowd for strong coffee and good beer, wi-fi and board games. An alternative to booze bars, it's ideal for a post-movie tête-à-tête or catch-up time with friends.

HARRY'S BAR   BAR
Map p310 (www.harrysbarsf.com; 2020 Fillmore St; ⊙4pm-2am Mon-Fri, from 11am Sat & Sun; 🚌1, 3, 22) Cap off a shopping trip at Harry's mahogany bar with freshly muddled mojitos or Bloody Marys made properly with horseradish. A Pacific Heights mainstay, Harry's appeals to those who like to get politely hammered.

PALMER'S TAVERN   BAR
Map p310 (☑415-732-7777; www.palmerssf.com; 2298 Fillmore St; ⊙4pm-midnight Mon-Fri, noon-midnight Sat & Sun; 🚌3, 10, 22) Palmer's revives the classic mid-century-American bar and grill, with wood-paneled walls, tufted red-leather booths and a buzzing neon sign outside. It doubles as a restaurant, with better-than-average food, but the bar's the pick for its craft cocktails and knockout Bloody Marys, made with a strip of bacon protruding from the glass, ideal for a hair-of-the-dog Sunday.

☆ ENTERTAINMENT

Fillmore St was once the epicenter of the West Coast jazz scene. Now only a few places remain, all concentrated on Fillmore St, near Geary Blvd.

FILLMORE AUDITORIUM   LIVE MUSIC
Map p310 (☑415-346-6000; http://thefillmore.com; 1805 Geary Blvd; tickets from $20; ⊙box office 10am-3pm Sun, plus 30min before doors open to 10pm show nights; 🚌22, 38) Jimi Hendrix, Janis Joplin, the Doors – they all played the Fillmore. Now you might catch the Indigo Girls, Willie Nelson or Tracy Chapman in the historic 1250-capacity, standing-room-only theater (if you're polite and lead with

the hip, you might squeeze up to the stage). Don't miss the priceless collection of psychedelic posters in the upstairs gallery.

BOOM BOOM ROOM   LIVE MUSIC
Map p310 (☑415-673-8000; www.boomboomblues.com; 1601 Fillmore St; cover varies; ⊙4pm-2am Tue-Sun; 🚌22, 38) Jumping since the '30s, the Boom Boom is a relic from the Fillmore's heyday – dig the old photos lining the walls. The black-box room ain't fancy – just bar, stage, tables and dance floor – but it rocks six nights a week with blues, soul and New Orleans funk played by top touring talent. Shows start around 9pm.

SUNDANCE KABUKI CINEMA   CINEMA
Map p310 (☑415-346-3243; www.sundancecinemas.com; 1881 Post St; adult $11-16.50; 🚌2, 3, 22, 38) 🍴 Cinema-going at its best. Reserve a stadium seat, belly up to the bar and order wine and surprisingly good food to enjoy during the film. A multiplex initiative by Robert Redford's Sundance Institute, Kabuki features big-name flicks and festivals – and it's green, with recycled-fiber seating, reclaimed-wood decor and local chocolates and booze (hence the 21-plus designation most shows). Validated parking.

Note: expect a $1.50 to $3 surcharge to see a movie not preceded by commercials.

SHEBA PIANO LOUNGE   JAZZ
Map p310 (☑415-440-7414; www.shebapianolounge.com; 1419 Fillmore St; ⊙5pm-1am; 🚌22, 31, 38) One of the last remaining jazz clubs on Fillmore, Sheba doubles as a good Ethiopian restaurant, but it's the bar that's the best, where combos perform nightly from 8pm. Arrive early to score the little table by the fireplace.

🛍 SHOPPING

Near Russian Hill, Polk St (from California St to Broadway) is great for browsing indie boutiques. Japantown is packed with kitschy-fun gift shops and authentic Japanese wares. Fillmore St, in Pacific Heights, caters to an upmarket demographic (hence its nickname, Specific Whites); there's fab shopping between Bush and Jackson Sts – continue to Broadway for brilliant bay views. For more high-end indie

boutiques, head to Presidio Heights – Sacramento St, west of Presidio Ave.

Russian & Nob Hills

VELVET DA VINCI   JEWELRY, ART
Map p306 (www.velvetdavinci.com; 2015 Polk St; 11am-6pm Tue-Sat, to 4pm Sun; 10, 12, 19, 27, 47, 49, Powell-Hyde) At this jewelry and sculpture gallery, you can see the ideas behind the handiwork: Lynn Christiansen channels food obsession into a purse resembling whipped cream, and Tom Hill makes evident his fascination with birds in wire sculptures (note the fire escape outside). Eight annual shows bring an ever-changing collection of contemporary-art jewelry from around the world.

★PICNIC   CLOTHING, HOMEWARES
Map p306 (www.picnicsf.com; 1808 Polk St; 11am-6pm Mon, to 8pm Tue-Sat, noon-6pm Sun; 19, 27, 47, 49, Powell-Hyde) The kind of boutique young moms hope to find when they're out for a girly-girl afternoon, Picnic caters to women who say *c-u-u-u-t-e!* to the pretty tops, smart skirts, baby clothes, children's toys, handmade jewelry, cozy home decor, stationery, hand-crafted woodwork and SF-specific gifts emblazoned with images of the GG Bridge.

STUDIO   ART
Map p306 (415-931-3130; www.studiogallerysf.com; 1641 Pacific Ave; 11am-7pm Mon, Thu & Fri, to 6pm Sat & Sun, by appointment Tue & Wed; 1, 19, 47, 49, California) Spiff up your pad with locally made art at great prices. For a memento of your visit to SF, Studio is the place to come, with a mix of prints and fine art by Elizabeth Ashcroft depicting local haunts, and architectural etchings by Alice Gibbons, plus paintings of local land- and city-scapes. Monthly receptions are open to the public.

RELOVE   VINTAGE
Map p306 (415-800-8285; http://shoprelove.com; 1815 Polk St; 11am-7pm Tue-Sat, to 6pm Sun, noon-6pm Mon; 1, 10, 12, 19, 27, 47, 49, California) Find a snappy new outfit at this fab vintage store, noteworthy for its colorful, eccentric collection. Expect fur, spiked leather, silk kimonos, vintage tees, formal party dresses – looks that spice yours up, without ruining your economy.

MOLTE COSE   FASHION & ACCESSORIES
Map p306 (www.moltecose.com; 2036 Polk St; 11am-6:30pm Mon-Fri, to 6pm Sat, noon-5pm Sun; 10, 12, 19, 47, 49) Thrilling for browsers, Molte Cose's imaginative, unpredictable collection of vintage bric-a-brac ranges from French stemware to Royal typewriters that double as set decoration for displays of pretty-frilly dresses, elegant accessories, cuff links, shaving kits, hip flasks, supercute kids' gear, plus locally made candles by elizabethW.

CRIS   FASHION & ACCESSORIES
Map p306 (415-474-1191; www.crisconsignment.com; 2056 Polk St; 11am-6pm Mon-Sat, from noon Sun; 10, 12, 19, 47, 49, Powell-Hyde) The sharpest windows on Polk St are consistently at Cris, a consignment shop specializing in contemporary high-end fashion by big-name designers like Balenciaga, Lanvin, Marni, Alexander Wang and Chloé, all in beautiful condition and at amazing prices, carefully curated by an elegant Frenchwoman with an eagle's eye and a duchess' taste. Also great for handbags by Prada, Dolce & Gabbana...

JOHNSON LEATHERS   CLOTHING
Map p306 (www.johnsonleather.com; 1833 Polk St; 11am-6pm Tue-Sat; 10, 12, 19, 27, 47, 49) If you've been looking for a new leather jacket – the ideal garment in chilly SF – Johnson custom-tailors classic cuts, built to last. Its materials and craftsmanship are so reliable and durable that it outfits both the SFPD's motorcycle patrol *and* the Hells Angels. These jackets last decades.

Japantown & Pacific Heights

★NEW PEOPLE   CLOTHING, SHOES
Map p310 (415-345-1975; www.newpeopleworld.com; 1746 Post St; noon-7pm Mon-Sat, to 6pm Sun; 2, 3, 22, 38) A three-story emporium devoted to Japanese pop culture, New People carries Japantown's most interesting clothing. At **Maruq**, find Japanese street wear from Tokyo's Shibuya and Harajuku districts (locale of independent-designer boutiques), plus Rilakkuma bear toys. Try on Lolita fashions (imagine *Alice in Wonderland*) at 2nd-floor **Baby the Stars Shine Bright** and traditional Japanese footwear

emblazoned with contemporary graphics at **Sou-Sou**.

Afterward, recharge over tea at Crown & Crumpet (p137).

SOKO HARDWARE   HOMEWARES

Map p310 (☏415-931-5510; 1698 Post St; ☺9am-5:30pm Mon-Sat; ☐2, 3, 22, 38) Folks love Soko for its exceptional selection of ikebana, bonsai, tea-ceremony and Zen rock-garden supplies, and also for its properly tuned wind chimes and quality Japanese bath products.

KINOKUNIYA BOOKS
& STATIONERY   BOOKS

Map p310 (☏415-567-7625; www.kinokuniya.com/us; 1581 Webster St, Japan Center; ☺10:30am-8pm; ☐22, 38) Like warriors in a showdown, the bookstore, stationery and *manga* divisions of Kinokuniya compete for your attention. Only you can decide where your loyalties lie: with stunning photography books and Harajuku fashion mags upstairs, vampire comics downstairs or the stationery department's *washi* paper, super-smooth Sakura gel pens and pig notebooks with the motto 'what lovely friends, they will bring happy.'

BENEFIT   COSMETICS

Map p310 (www.benefitcosmetics.com; 2117 Fillmore St; ☺9am-7pm Mon-Sat, 10am-6pm Sun; ☐1, 3, 22) Get cheeky with BeneTint (dab-on liquid blush from roses) or raise eyebrows with Brow Zings tinted wax – two of Benefit's signature products invented in San Francisco by a twin-sister team. Surgery is so LA: in SF, dark eye circles are cured with Ooh La Lift. There's another branch in the Marina (p72).

MARGARET O'LEARY   CLOTHING

Map p310 (☏415-771-9982; www.margaretoleary.com; 2400 Fillmore St; ☺10am-6pm Mon-Sat, 11am-6pm Sun; ☐1, 3, 10, 22, 24) At her flagship store, San Francisco local Margaret O'Leary showcases whisper-light cardigans of cashmere, organic cotton or eco-minded bamboo yarn, perfect for that moment when the fog blows in.

NEST   HOMEWARES

Map p310 (☏415-292-6199; www.nestsf.com; 2300 Fillmore St; ☺10:30am-6:30pm Mon-Fri, to 6pm Sat, 11am-6pm Sun; ☢; ☐1, 3, 10, 22, 24) Make your nest cozier with one-of-a-kind accessories from this well-curated collec-

tion, including Provençal quilts, beaded jewelry, craft kits and papier-mâché trophy heads for the kids' room, as well as mesmerizing century-old bric-a-brac and toys that will amaze any serious browser.

BITE BEAUTY   COSMETICS

Map p310 (☏628-444-3770; http://bitebeauty.com; 2142 Fillmore St; ☺11am-7pm Mon-Sat, to 6pm Sun; ☐3, 22) For the woman who thought she had everything, at last there's custom-blended, organic lipstick. Specialists find the color for you, from over 200 shades, or they'll custom-blend something new. All come in three finishes: matte, gloss and – wait for it – *amuse bouche*. Make an appointment.

FREDA SALVADOR   SHOES

Map p310 (☏415-872-9690; www.fredasalvador.com; 2416 Fillmore St; ☺11am-7pm Mon-Sat, to 6pm Sun; ☐3, 10, 22) Indulge your inner shoe fetishist with footwear designed right here in Sausalito – by women, for women – and made by hand in Spain. Dig the easy-to-wear styles that pair well with different looks, and also their functionality: these shoes were made for walking, not posing.

SANKO KITCHEN
ESSENTIALS   CERAMICS, HOMEWARES

Map p310 (1758 Buchanan St; ☺10am-5:30pm Mon-Sat, 11:30am-5pm Sun; ☐2, 3, 22, 38) Browse aisle upon aisle of Japanese ceramics, teapots, sake sets, tableware and cookware at this extraordinary Japantown shop that sources quality products from Japan and also from artisans in the Bay Area.

CROSSROADS   FASHION & ACCESSORIES

Map p310 (www.crossroadstrading.com; 1901 Fillmore St; ☺11am-8pm Mon-Sat, to 7pm Sun; ☐2, 3, 22, 38) Pssst, fashionistas: you know those designers you see lining Fillmore St? Many of their creations wind up at Crossroads for a fraction of retail, thanks to Pacific Heights clotheshorses who ditch last season's wardrobe here. That's why this Crossroads is better than others in the city. For better deals, trade in your old clothes for credit.

KOHSHI   GIFTS & SOUVENIRS

Map p310 (☏415-931-2002; www.kohshisf.com; 1737 Post St, Suite 355, West Mall, Japan Center; ☺11am-7pm Wed-Mon; ☐2, 3, 22, 38) Fragrant Japanese incense for every purpose, from long-burning sandalwood for meditation to cinnamon-tinged Gentle Smile to atone for laundry left too long, plus lovely gift ideas: mild charcoal soap, cups that look like crumpled paper, and purple Daruma figurines for making wishes.

KATSURA GARDEN
BONSAI

Map p310 (☑415-931-6209; 1825 Post St, Japan Center; ⊘10am-6pm Mon-Sat, 11am-5:30pm Sun; 🚇2, 3, 22, 38) For a special gift, consider a bonsai. Katsura Garden will set you up with a miniature juniper that looks like it grew on a windswept molehill, or a stunted maple that next autumn will shed five tiny, perfect red leaves. It also has limited ikebana supplies.

BROOKLYN CIRCUS
CLOTHING, SHOES

Map p310 (https://thebkcircus.com; 1521 Fillmore St; ⊘noon-7pm Tue-Sat, to 6pm Sun; 🚇22, 38) Stylish men who skew casual appreciate Brooklyn Circus' classic American aesthetic. Find wool-and-leather varsity-letter jackets, snappy shirts and hats and quality US-made shoes, including high-top leather PF Flyers and Red Wing boots.

JONATHAN ADLER
HOMEWARES

Map p310 (☑415-563-9500; www.jonathan adler.com; 2133 Fillmore St; ⊘10am-6pm Mon-Sat, noon-5pm Sun; 🚇1, 3, 22) Vases with handlebar mustaches and cookie jars labeled 'Quaaludes' may seem like holdovers from a Big Sur bachelor pad c 1974, but they're snappy interior inspirations from California pop potter (and *Top Design* judge) Jonathan Adler. Don't worry whether that leather pig footstool matches your mid-century couch – as Adler says, 'Minimalism is a bummer.'

ICHIBAN KAN
GIFTS & SOUVENIRS

Map p310 (☑415-409-0472; www.ichiban kanusa.com; 22 Peace Plaza, Suite 540, Japan Center; ⊘10am-8pm; 🚇2,3,22,38) It's a wonder you got this far in life without penguin soy-sauce dispensers, 'Men's Pocky' chocolate-covered pretzels, extra-spiky Japanese hair wax, soap dishes with feet and the ultimate in gay gag gifts, the handy 'Closet Case' – all here for under $5.

ZINC DETAILS
HOMEWARES

Map p310 (☑415-776-2700; www.zincdetails. com; 1633 Fillmore St; ⊘11am-6pm Mon-Sat, noon-6pm Sun; 🚇2, 3, 22) Pacific Heights chic meets Japantown mod at Zinc Details, with items like orange-lacquerware salad tossers, a sake dispenser that looks like a Zen garden boulder and bird-shaped soy dispensers, all noteworthy for their smart design and artful presentation, qualities reflected in the retail prices.

🏃 SPORTS & ACTIVITIES

★ KABUKI SPRINGS & SPA
SPA

Map p310 (☑415-922-6000; www.kabuki springs.com; 1750 Geary Blvd; adult $25; ⊘10am-9:45pm, co-ed Tue, women only Wed, Fri & Sun, men only Mon, Thu & Sat; 🚇22, 38) This favorite urban retreat recreates communal, clothing-optional Japanese baths. Salt-scrub in the steam room, soak in the hot pool, then cold-plunge and reheat in the sauna. Rinse and repeat. Silence is mandatory, fostering a meditative mood – if you hear the gong, it means Shhhh! Men and women alternate days, except on co-ed Tuesdays (bathing suits required Tuesdays).

The look befits the location – slightly dated Japanese modern, with vaulted lacquered-wood ceilings, tile mosaics and low lighting. Plan on two hours minimum, plus a 30- to 60-minute wait at peak times (add your name to the waiting list, then go next door to slurp noodles or shop; they'll text you when your key is ready). Communal bathing is discounted with massage appointments; book ahead and come on the gender-appropriate day.

PLAYLAND JAPAN
VIDEO ARCADE

Map p310 (☑510-501-6546; 1737 Post St, unit 323; ⊘2:30-8:30pm Mon-Thu, 12:30-10pm Fri, 11am-10pm Sat, to 8pm Sun; ♿; 🚇2, 3, 22, 38) A godsend when you're with kids in Japantown, this tiny arcade is packed with Japanese games. Dance Dance Revolution competes for attention with the Takoyaki Catcher claw game, promising plush anime prizes to the successful. Attendants help make sense of the all-Japanese instructions printed on machines.

REAL ESCAPE GAME
GAME

(http://realescapegame.com; 1746 Post St; tickets $34-39; ⊘by reservation; ♿; 🚇2, 3, 22, 38) Gamers put down their screens for this real-life puzzle, developed in Japan and imported to SF. You and your teammates get locked in a room, portal to a mysterious somewhere – maybe a time-travel laboratory or a cursed forest – and you've got 90 minutes to find hidden clues to discover the key to escape. Few succeed. Will you?

The Mission & Potrero Hill

Neighborhood Top Five

1 Mission murals (p146) Seeing garage doors, billboards and storefronts transformed into canvases with over 400 artworks.

2 826 Valencia (p147) Watching puffer fish completely immersed in a role inside the Fish Theater.

3 Dolores Park (p147) Playing, tanning, picnicking and protesting entire days away.

4 Mission Dolores (p149) Getting a handle on California history at San Francisco's oldest building.

5 Potrero Flats (p150) Exploring the repurposed industrial buildings that house an exuberant artistic community.

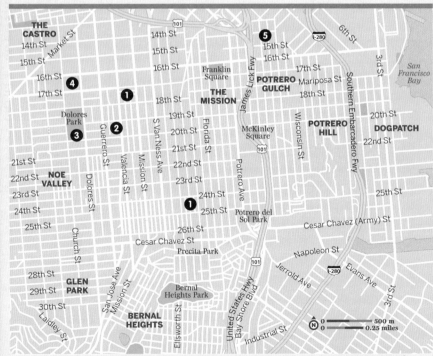

For more detail of this area see Maps p302 and p305 ➡

Explore: The Mission & Potrero Hill

Get to know San Francisco from the inside out, from pirate stores to mural-covered Mission alleys. Score new looks and old books at Mission stores, and book ahead at local venues for the ultimate SF souvenir: a new talent, discovered at a hands-on cooking class, crafts workshop, or dancing or rock-climbing lesson. Combine epic bar crawls with taco tastings and end up salsa dancing with suave strangers at Mission clubs.

Local Life

➡ **Learning something new** Upcycle office supplies into art at SCRAP (p164), hone knife skills at 18 Reasons (p165), vogue at Dance Mission (p166) and tell likely stories at 826 Valencia (p147).

➡ **Doing dessert** After another lap of Mission murals, you're ready for Mission Pie (p153), boozy ice cream at Humphry Slocombe (p152), tea cakes from Tartine (p152) and salted-caramel eclairs from Craftsman & Wolves (p152).

➡ **Looking the part** Define your own streetwise Mission style with local designers at Gravel & Gold (p162), Betabrand (p164), Nooworks (p163), Baggu (p163) and Aggregate Supply (p163).

Getting There & Away

➡ **Bus** Bus 14 runs from downtown to the Mission District along Mission St. Bus 22 runs from Dogpatch and the Mission through the Haight to the Marina. Bus 49 follows Mission St and Van Ness Ave to Fisherman's Wharf, while bus 33 links Potrero and the Mission to the Castro, the Haight and Golden Gate Park.

➡ **Streetcar** The J streetcar heads from downtown through the Mission. The T Muni line from downtown via SoMa stops along 3rd St between 16th and 22nd, in Potrero's Dogpatch district.

➡ **BART** Stations at 16th and 24th Sts serve the Mission.

Lonely Planet's Top Tip

The Mission is packed with bars, boutiques, galleries and clubs, and while you should be fine in the daytime, it's not always the safest area to walk alone in at night. Recruit a friend and be alert in the Mission east of Valencia, in Potrero Hill below 18th St and around deserted Dogpatch warehouses. Don't bring the bling – this isn't LA – and don't leave belongings unattended.

✖ Best Places to Eat

➡ La Taqueria (p151)
➡ La Palma Mexicatessen (p152)
➡ Al's Place (p153)
➡ Craftsman & Wolves (p152)
➡ Serpentine (p156)

For reviews, see p151

🍷 Best Places to Drink

➡ El Rio (p158)
➡ Trick Dog (p158)
➡ %ABV (p157)
➡ 20 Spot (p158)
➡ Elixir (p158)

For reviews, see p157

🛍 Best Shopping

➡ Adobe Books & Backroom Gallery (p163)
➡ Gravel & Gold (p162)
➡ Poco Dolce (p162)
➡ Community Thrift (p162)
➡ Little Paper Planes (p162)

For reviews, see p162

THE MISSION & POTRERO HILL

TOP SIGHT
MISSION MURALS

Diego Rivera and Frida Kahlo have no idea what they started here. In the 1930s, the Mexican maestro was invited to paint murals for the San Francisco Stock Exchange and SF Art Institute, and Frida joined Diego here for a working honeymoon – and soon launched her career with soulful portraits of dedicated San Francisco General Hospital (p272) doctors. The radical painting power couple continues to inspire generations of Mission muralists, who have covered alleys and community institutions with 400-plus murals in a splendid show of political dissent, community pride and street-art bravado.

When 1970s Mission *muralistas* objected to US foreign policy in Latin America, they took to the streets with paintbrushes – beginning with Balmy Alley. Bodegas, taquerias, churches and community centers lining 24th St are now covered with murals of mighty Mayan goddesses and Aztec warriors, honoring the district's combined native and Mexican origins. Aztec serpent-god Quetzalcoatl has kept watch over 24th & York Mini Park (p150) since 1972, and neighboring Galería de la Raza (p149) has repurposed billboards for such Digital Mural Project proclamations as 'Abolish borders!'

In 1993–94 an all-star team of seven women *muralistas* and local volunteers covered the Women's Building (p147) with *Maestrapeace*, featuring icons of female strength. Before artists Barry McGee, Clare Rojas and Chris Johansen sold out shows at international art fairs, they could be found around the corner at Clarion Alley (p149), gripping spray-paint cans. Atop literary nonprofit 826 Valencia (p147) is a gold-leafed mural celebrating human attempts to communicate, created by Pulitzer Prize–winning graphic novelist Chris Ware.

DON'T MISS

➜ Balmy Alley
➜ Clarion Alley
➜ *Maestrapeace* at the Women's Building
➜ 826 Valencia mural by Chris Ware
➜ Digital Mural Project at Galería de la Raza

PRACTICALITIES

➜ Map p302, E7
➜ ☎415-285-2287
➜ www.precitaeyes.org
➜ btwn 24th & 25th Sts
➜ 🚍10, 12, 14, 27, 48,
Ⓑ24th St Mission

Above: Generator Mural, by artists Aaron Noble & Andrew Schoultz

⊙ SIGHTS

The Mission is a crossroads of contradictions and at its heart is Mission St, SF's faded 'miracle mile' of deco cinemas now occupied by 99¢ stores and shady characters, surrounded by colorful murals and trend-setting restaurants. West of Mission St, Valencia St has quirky boutiques, reasonable restaurants and seven-figure condos. Calle 24 (24th St) is SF's designated Latino cultural district, with community centers, churches, bodegas, *panaderias* and taquerias all swathed in murals. Further east, Potrero Hill has become a bedroom community for Silicon Valley tech execs – but, just downhill, culinary schools and art studios have creatively repurposed warehouses in Potrero Flats and waterfront Dogpatch.

★ **826 VALENCIA**   CULTURAL CENTER
Map p302 (✆415-642-5905; www.826valencia. org; 826 Valencia St; ◷noon-6pm; 🚼; 🚌14, 33, 49, Ⓑ16th St Mission, ⓂJ) Avast, ye scurvy scalawags! If ye be shipwrecked without yer eye patch or McSweeney's literary anthology, lay down ye doubloons and claim yer booty at this here nonprofit Pirate Store. Below decks, kids be writing tall tales for dark nights a'sea, and ye can study writing movies and science fiction and suchlike, if that be yer dastardly inclination. Arrrr!

This eccentric pirate-supply store selling eye patches, spyglasses and McSweeney's literary magazines fronts a nonprofit offering free writing workshops and tutoring for youth. 'No buccaneers! No geriatrics!' warns the sign above the vat of sand where kids rummage for buried pirates' booty. Found treasure is theirs to keep, in exchange for barter at the front counter – a drawing, maybe, or a knock-knock joke. Yank open wooden drawers organized according to pirate logic: a drawer marked 'illumination' holds candles; 'thump' is full of mallets. But leave the stinky tub o' lard well enough alone, or you might get mopped – a pirate hazing ritual that involves a trap door, a mop and the element of surprise.

Before you leave, step behind the velvet curtain into the Fish Theater, where a blue-eyed and smirking (yes, smirking) puffer fish is immersed in Method acting. The ichthyoid antics may not be quite up to Sean Penn standards, but, as the sign says, 'Please don't judge the fish.'

For further fishy shenanigans, visit King Karl's Emporium at 826's new nautically themed satellite center in the **Tenderloin** (180 Golden Gate). Check the calendar for evening writing workshops, from perfume-inspired fiction to neighborhood oral-history projects.

★ **WOMEN'S BUILDING**   NOTABLE BUILDING
Map p302 (✆415-431-1180; www.womensbuild ing.org; 3543 18th St; 🚼; 🚌14, 22, 33, 49, Ⓑ16th St Mission, ⓂJ) The nation's first women-owned-and-operated community center has quietly done good work with 170 women's organizations since 1979, but the 1994 addition of the *Maestrapeace* mural showed the Women's Building for the landmark it truly is. An all-star team of *muralistas* covered the building with images of cross-cultural goddesses and women trailblazers, including Nobel Prize winner Rigoberta Menchú, poet Audre Lorde, artist Georgia O'Keeffe and former US Surgeon General Dr Joycelyn Elders.

★ **DOLORES PARK**   PARK
Map p302 (http://sfrecpark.org/destination/ mission-dolores-park; Dolores St, btwn 18th & 20th Sts; ◷6am-10pm; 🚼🐾; 🚌14, 33, 49, Ⓑ16th St Mission, ⓂJ) Semiprofessional tanning, taco picnics and a Hunky Jesus Contest at Easter: welcome to San Francisco's sunny side. Dolores Park has something for everyone, from street ball and tennis to the Mayan-pyramid playground (sorry, kids: no blood sacrifices allowed). Political protests and other favorite local sports happen year-round, and there are free movie nights and Mime Troupe performances in summer. Climb to the upper southwestern corner for superb views of downtown, framed by palm trees.

Dolores Park was built on the site of a former Jewish cemetery that was used as a staging ground by Barnum & Bailey Circus and sold to the city in 1905. San Francisco's 1906 earthquake and fire violently interrupted park planning, and it remained bumpy, squishy and poorly drained until its 2015 regrading. At the corner of 20th and Church Sts, note the **gold-painted fire hydrant**: this little fireplug was the Mission's main water source during the 1906 earthquake and fire, and stopped the fire from spreading south of 20th St. Flat patches further down are generally reserved for soccer games, cultural festivals, candlelight vigils and ultimate Frisbee. Fair warning:

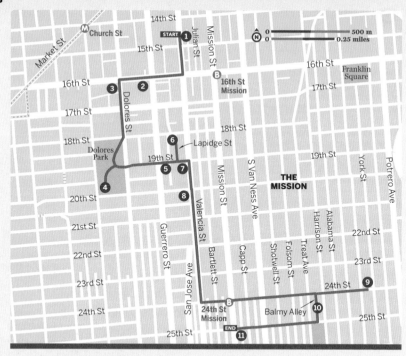

Neighborhood Walk
Colorful Mission Characters

START FOUR BARREL
END MISSION PIE
LENGTH 2.8 MILES; THREE HOURS

Fuel up with house roast in the parklet at **1 Four Barrel** (p159) and buzz right past boutiques to **2 Creativity Explored** (p149), which showcases works by developmentally disabled artists. Ahead is the city's first building: adobe **3 Mission Dolores** (p149), built by some 5000 native Ohlone and Miwok. You can glimpse the Miwok memorial hut through the mission fence on Chula Lane.

Climb to the upper southwestern corner of **4 Dolores Park** (p147) for panoramic views – and pay your respects to the golden fire hydrant that saved much of the Mission from the 1906 fire. Walking down 19th St, you'll pass Daniel Doherty's impressionist-inspired 2009 mural **5 Dejeuner Dolores**, showing Dolores Park's regular cast of characters, including frolicking pugs, handlebar-mustachioed men in their speedoes and families in their Sunday best. Swing left on Lapidge St to spot Georgia O'Keeffe

and goddesses galore in the **6 Women's Building** (p147) murals.

Back on Valencia St, you'll see the Chris Ware mural and storefront art installation of **7 826 Valencia** (p147); duck inside for pirate supplies. Down the street, pause to pay your respects at **8 Dog-Eared Books** (p163) – the front window features hand-drawn obituary cartoons of luminaries from Liz Taylor to Susan Sontag. Window-shop down Valencia, and hang a left onto 24th St, San Francisco's Latino cultural district. You'll pass mural-covered bodegas, taquerias and *panaderias* all the way to **9 24th & York Mini Park** (p150), where serpent-god Quetzalcoatl rears his mighty mosaic head from the playground.

Double back along 24th St, cross over and swing down to **10 Balmy Alley** (p146), where you may recognize recently beatified activist Archbishop Romero and surrealist painter Frida Kahlo among the colorful characters illuminating garage doors along this mural-covered backstreet. After this slice of Mission life, join locals for some strawberry-rhubarb pie at **11 Mission Pie** (p153).

secondhand highs copped near the refurbished bathroom may have you chasing the *helados* (ice-cream) cart.

★CREATIVITY EXPLORED   GALLERY
Map p302 (☑415-863-2108; www.creativity explored.org; 3245 16th St; donations welcome; ☺10am-3pm Mon-Wed & Fri, to 7pm Thu, noon-5pm Sat & Sun; 🚻; 🚌14, 22, 33, 49, 🅱16th St Mission, ⓂJ) Brave new worlds are captured in celebrated artworks destined for museum retrospectives, international shows, and even Marc Jacobs handbags and CB2 pillowcases – all by the local developmentally disabled artists who create at this nonprofit center. Intriguing themes range from monsters to Morse code. Openings are joyous celebrations with the artists, their families and rock-star fan base.

BALMY ALLEY   PUBLIC ART
See p146.

★ANGLIM GILBERT GALLERY   GALLERY
(☑415-528-7258; http://anglimgilbertgallery. com; 1275 Minnesota St, 2nd fl; ☺11am-6pm Tue-Sat; 🚌48, 🚆T) FREE The Bay Area hits the big time here, with gallerist Ed Gilbert continuing Anglim's 30-year legacy of launching art movements from Beat assemblage to Bay Area conceptualists. Major gallery artists range from political provocateur Enrique Chagoya to sublime sculptor Deborah Butterfield, yet shows here maintain a hair-raising edge – an upraised fist pushed through gallery walls in David Huffman's *Panther*. Check the website for concurrent Anglim Gilbert shows at the gallery's downtown location at 14 Geary St.

★CLARION ALLEY   PUBLIC ART
Map p302 (btwn 17th & 18th Sts; 🚌14, 22, 33, 🅱16th St Mission, ⓂJ) Most graffiti artists shun broad daylight – but not in Clarion Alley, SF's open-air street-art showcase. You'll spot artists touching up pieces and making new ones, with the full consent of neighbors and Clarion Alley Collective's curators. Only a few pieces survive for years, such as Megan Wilson's daisy-covered *Tax the Rich* or Jet Martinez' glimpse of Clarion Alley inside a forest spirit. Incontinent art critics often take over the alley's eastern end – pee-eew! – so topical murals usually go up on the western end.

★GALERÍA DE LA RAZA   GALLERY
Map p302 (☑415-826-8009; www.galeria delaraza.org; 2857 24th St; donations welcome; ☺during exhibitions noon-6pm Wed-Sat; 🚻; 🚌10, 14, 33, 48, 49, 🅱24th St Mission) Art never forgets its roots at this nonprofit that has showcased Latino art since 1970. Culture and community are constantly being redefined here, from contemporary Mexican photography and group shows exploring Latin gay culture to performances capturing community responses to Mission gentrification. Outside is the Digital Mural Project, where, in place of the usual cigarette advertisements, a billboard features slogans like 'Abolish borders!' in English, Arabic and Spanish.

MISSION DOLORES   CHURCH
Map p302 (Misión San Francisco de Asís; ☑415-621-8203; www.missiondolores.org; 3321 16th St; adult/child $5/3; ☺9am-4pm Nov-Apr, to 4:30pm May-Oct; 🚌22, 33, 🅱16th St Mission, ⓂJ) The city's oldest building and its namesake, whitewashed adobe Misión San Francisco de Asís was founded in 1776 and rebuilt from 1782 with conscripted Ohlone and Miwok labor – a graveyard memorial hut commemorates 5000 Ohlone and Miwok laborers who died in mission measles epidemics in the early 19th century. Today the modest adobe structure is overshadowed by the ornate adjoining 1913 basilica, featuring stained-glass windows which depict California's 21 missions.

The building's nickname, Mission Dolores (Mission of the Sorrows), was taken from a nearby lake – but it turned out to be tragically apt for native conscripts who were exposed to harsh living conditions and who had little resistance to introduced diseases. Their work survives them in the original adobe mission. The ceiling is patterned after native baskets, and recent restorations have revealed a hidden **Ohlone mural** behind the altar showing a sacred heart pierced by a sword and dripping with blood.

Surrounding the Ohlone memorial in the mission **graveyard** are graves dating from the gold rush. Alongside mission founders are buried Don Luis Antonio Arguello, the first governor of Alta California under Mexican rule, and Don Francisco de Haro, the first mayor of San Francisco. Hitchcock fans looking for the grave of Carlotta Valdes

THE MISSION & POTRERO HILL SIGHTS

POTRERO FLATS' CREATIVE UPSTARTS

San Francisco's historic Design District has rediscovered its edge with the arrival of avant-garde galleries, showing art that easily upstages beige sofas. Between SoMa and Potrero Hill is a flat expanse dotted with warehouse design-trade showrooms long overlooked, unless you were in the business of selecting window treatments. But ever since the **California College of the Arts** (Wattis Institute for Contemporary Arts; Map p302; ✆Wattis Institute 415-355-9673; www.cca.edu/calendar/wattis-institute; 360 Kansas St; ⊗during school sessions noon-7pm Tue-Fri, noon-5pm Sat; ☐10, 19, 22, 33) FREE creatively repurposed the neighborhood's old bus depot for its campus, the emerging Potrero Flats district (also called 'SoMissPo,' for SoMa, Mission and Potrero) is becoming an eye-catcher. Stop at CCA's campus to discover fresh provocations in student-curated **PLAySPACE** and the **Wattis Institute for Contemporary Arts**, which has featured Brazilian artist Cinthia Marcelle's sketches created while watching art lectures.

Head under the highway overpass to discover **SOMArts** (Map p298; ✆415-863-1414; www.somarts.org; 934 Brannan St; ⊗gallery noon-7pm Tue-Fri, to 5pm Sat; ☐8, 9, 10, 19, 27, 47), a nonprofit community hub for creative thinking that hosts shows featuring edible murals, global street dance-offs, and new meanings for old words supplied by the pop-up Bureau of Linguistical Reality. Just down the street, the **San Francisco Center for the Book** (p166) features shows of handmade pop-up books and matchbook-sized 'zines, plus workshops for making your own.

The creative pull of Potrero Flats is irresistible now that several of San Francisco's leading galleries have moved to the neighborhood. The **Catharine Clark Gallery** (Map p302; ✆415-399-1439; www.cclarkgallery.com; 248 Utah St; ⊗11am-6pm Tue-Sat; ☐9, 10, 19, 22, 27, 33) FREE instigates art revolutions with Masami Teraoka's monumental paintings of geisha superheroines fending off wayward priests, while the **Hosfelt Gallery** (Map p302; ✆415-495-5454; http://hosfeltgallery.com; 260 Utah St; ⊗10am-5:30pm Tue, Wed & Sat, 11am-7pm Thu; ☐9, 10, 22, 27, 33) mesmerizes visitors with Emil Lukas' drawings made by thousands of fly larvae dragging ink across paper. Meanwhile, collage artists at the **Jack Fischer Gallery** bring intriguing interior worlds to life inside a warehouse space off Hwy 101. Friendly art debates continue around the corner at **Thee Parkside** (Map p305; ✆415-252-1330; www.theeparkside.com; 1600 17th St; ⊗11am-2am; ☐10, 19, 22), where bikers and art students converge for cheap drinks, parking-lot BBQ and vintage photo-booth photo-ops. But once alt-rock and punk bands start playing at **Bottom of the Hill** (p161), artistic differences are set aside and mosh-pit mayhem reigns supreme.

will be disappointed: the tomb was only a prop for the film *Vertigo*.

Next door to the mission is the grand Churrigueresque **basilica**, built after the 1876 brick Gothic cathedral collapsed in the 1906 earthquake. The front doors are usually only open during services, so you'll need to pass through the original adobe structure and cross a courtyard to enter the basilica's side door.

Your eyes may take a moment to adjust once you're inside, because most of the light is filtered through the basilica's splendid **stained-glass windows**. The choir windows show St Francis beaming beatifically against an orange background. Lower windows along the nave feature 21 California missions from Sonoma to San Diego, plus mission builders Father Junípero Serra and Father Francisco Palou. True to Mission Dolores' name, seven panels depict the Seven Sorrows of Mary: one above the main door and three on each of the side balconies.

24TH & YORK MINI PARK   PARK

Map p302 (www.sfparksalliance.org/our-parks/parks/24th-and-york-mini-park; cnr York & 24th Sts; ⊗sunrise-sunset; ⛲; ☐9, 12, 27, 48, ⓑ24th St) Take a ride on dazzling mosaic serpent-god Quetzalcoatl, who raises his fierce head from the rubberized ground of this pioneering pocket park. Quetzalcoatl has been lurking around this corner in murals since 1972, when neighbors first rallied to turn a derelict vacant lot into a point of Mission pride. His recently restored mosaic back is irresistible to toddlers, and his transformative powers are irrefutable – since Quetzalcoatl first appeared here, San Franciscans have created 40 more mini parks citywide.

MUSEUM OF
CRAFT & DESIGN   MUSEUM
Map p305 (☑415-773-0303; www.sfmcd.org; 2569 3rd St; adult/student $8/6; ☉11am-6pm Tue-Sat, noon-5pm Sun; ♿; ☐22, 48, Ⓜ T) Elephants sewn together from maps, benches made from repurposed shovel handles, factory-floor scenes recreated entirely in duct tape: one-off original works not meant for mass production reignite wonder at the Museum of Craft & Design. Check the online schedule for hands-on workshops where accomplished artisans lead projects related to museum shows, from upcycled-book furnishings to block-printed tea towels.

SOUTHERN EXPOSURE   GALLERY
Map p302 (☑415-863-2141; www.soex.org; 3030 20th St; donations welcome; ☉noon-6pm Thu-Sat; ☐12, 22, 27, 33, Ⓑ16th St Mission) Art really ties the room together at this nonprofit arts center, where works are carefully crafted not just with paint and canvas but a sense of community. Past projects featured science-fiction visions of a near future envisioned by artists of color, and 24 artists making artworks according to other artists' instructions. Don't miss SoEx's annual auction, where major Bay Area artists create installations and the audience snaps up museum-worthy bargains.

ELEANOR HARWOOD GALLERY   GALLERY
(☑415-867-7770; www.eleanorharwood.com; 1275 Minnesota St, 2nd fl; ☉1-5pm Tue, 11am-5pm Wed-Sat & by appointment; ☐10, 27, 33, 48, Ⓑ24th St Mission) FREE A curiosity cupboard of major Bay Area talents. Works showcased here are entrancing and meticulous – recent shows have featured Dana Hemenway's dazzling extension-cord macramé wall lamps, and Francesca Pastine's plaster planets sculpted out of intricately folded and carved issues of *Artforum* magazine.

CASEMORE KIRKEBY   GALLERY
(☑415-851-9808; http://casemorekirkeby.com; 1275 Minnesota St, 1st fl; ☉11am-6pm Tue-Sat; ☐48, Ⓜ T) FREE Ever since gold-rush miners set about capturing their newfound wealth

with ferrotype portraits, San Francisco has staked claims to artistic fame with photography – and Casemore Kirkeby continues to push the boundaries. Group shows explore techniques ranging from Aspen Mays' photograms to Sean McFarland's manufactured landscapes; Todd Hido retrospectives showcase his color-photography mastery in eerie suburban nocturnes.

DEARBORN
COMMUNITY GARDEN   GARDENS
Map p302 (www.sfparksalliance.org/our-parks/parks/dearborn-community-garden; Dearborn St, btwn 17th & 18th Sts; ☉sunrise-sunset; ♿; ☐33) ✐ Welcome to paradise in a parking lot. When the local Pepsi bottling plant closed its doors, neighbors wouldn't let urban blight take over the block – they rolled up their sleeves, dug up parking spaces and started planting. Twenty-five years later, the Dearborn Community Garden provides fresh produce for 40-plus Mission families and garden benches where anyone can stop and smell the roses.

AESTHETIC UNION   GALLERY
Map p302 (www.theaestheticunion.com; 555 Alabama St; ☉11am-6pm Tue-Fri, to 5pm Sat & Sun; ☐12, 22, 33, 37) FREE Upgrade from kitten posters to frame-worthy original SF artworks hand-printed in this working printmakers' studio. Watch prints pulled from a vintage Heidelberg machine, and find inspiration with no words at all (in James L Tucker's sublime California coastal landscapes or Maria Forde's Hwy 1 bikers) or a few choice letterpressed ones ('Let's Be Humans Together,' 'Can't believe we still have to protest this shit,' or the quiet but firmly embossed 'enough') printed as posters and/or greeting cards.

EATING

★ LA TAQUERIA   MEXICAN $
Map p302 (☑415-285-7117; 2889 Mission St; items $3-11; ☉11am-9pm Mon-Sat, to 8pm Sun; ♿; ☐12, 14, 48, 49, Ⓑ24th St Mission) SF's definitive burrito has no saffron rice, spinach tortilla or mango salsa – just perfectly grilled meats, slow-cooked beans and tomatillo or mesquite salsa wrapped in a flour tortilla. They're purists at James Beard Award–winning La Taqueria – you'll pay extra to go without beans, because they add

more meat – but spicy pickles and *crema* (sour cream) bring burrito bliss. Worth the wait, always.

★LA PALMA MEXICATESSEN
MEXICAN $

Map p302 (☑415-647-1500; www.lapalmasf.com; 2884 24th St; tamales, tacos & huarache $3-5; ⏲8am-6pm Mon-Sat, to 5pm Sun; ☑⛽; 🚌12, 14, 27, 48, Ⓑ24th St Mission) ✎ Follow the applause: that's the sound of organic tortilla-making in progress at La Palma. You've found the Mission mother lode of handmade tamales, *pupusas* (tortilla pockets) with potato and *chicharones* (pork crackling), *carnitas* (slow-roasted pork), *cotija* (Oaxacan cheese) and La Palma's own tangy tomatillo sauce. Get takeout, or bring a small army to finish that massive meal at sunny sidewalk tables.

★CRAFTSMAN & WOLVES
BAKERY, CALIFORNIAN $

Map p302 (☑415-913-7713; http://craftsman-wolves.com; 746 Valencia St; pastries $3-8; ⏲7am-6pm Mon-Fri, from 8am Sat & Sun; 🚌14, 22, 33, 49, Ⓑ16th St Mission, ⓂJ) Breakfast routines are made to be broken by the infamous Rebel Within: a sausage-spiked Asiago-cheese muffin with a silken soft-boiled egg baked inside. SF's surest pick-me-up is a Highwire macchiato with matcha (green tea) cookies; a Thai coconut-curry scone enjoyed with pea soup and rosé is lunch perfected. Exquisite hazelnut cube-cakes and vanilla-violet cheesecakes are ideal for celebrating unbirthdays and imaginary holidays.

★HUMPHRY SLOCOMBE
ICE CREAM $

Map p302 (☑415-550-6971; www.humphry slocombe.com; 2790 Harrison St; ice creams $4-6; ⏲1-11pm Mon-Fri, from noon Sat & Sun; ⛽; 🚌12, 14, 49, Ⓑ24th St Mission) ✎ Indie-rock organic ice cream may permanently spoil you for Top 40 flavors. Once 'Elvis: The Fat Years' (banana and peanut butter) and Hibiscus Beet Sorbet have rocked your taste buds, cookie dough seems so basic – and ordinary sundaes can't compare to 'Secret Breakfast' (bourbon and cornflakes) and Blue Bottle Vietnamese Coffee drizzled with hot fudge, California olive oil and sea salt.

★MISSION COMMUNITY MARKET
MARKET $

Map p302 (http://missioncommunitymarket.org; Bartlett St, btwn 21st & 22nd Sts; ⏲4-8pm Thu mid-Jan–mid-Dec; ☑⛽; 🚌14, 48, 49, Ⓑ24th St Mission) ✎ Back-alley bounty brings ravenous crowds Thursdays to this nonprofit, neighborhood-run market, come rain or shine. More than 30 local farmers and food artisans offer California produce and inspired SF street food – look for Coastside Farms' smoked albacore, Tomatero Farms' heirloom green-zebra tomatoes, Flour Chylde pastries and Chaac Mool's *cochinita pibil* (slow-roasted pork). Enjoy shade, seating and mariachis at mural-lined La Placita.

★MITCHELL'S ICE CREAM
ICE CREAM $

(☑415-648-2300; www.mitchellsicecream.com; 688 San Jose Ave; ice cream $3.50-6; ⏲11am-11pm; ⛽; 🚌14, 49, Ⓑ24th St Mission, ⓂJ) When you see happy dances break out on Mission sidewalks, you must be getting close to Mitchell's. One glance at the day's flavors induces gleeful gluttony: classic Kahlua mocha cream, exotic tropical *macapuno* (young coconut)...or *both*?! Avocado and *ube* (purple yam) are acquired tastes, but they've been local favorites for generations – Mitchell's has kept SF coming back for seconds since 1953.

TARTINE MANUFACTORY
BAKERY, CALIFORNIAN $

Map p302 (☑415-757-0007; www.tartinemanu factory.com; 595 Alabama St; mains $9-18; ☑; 🚌12, 22, 27, 33) Rise and shine at Tartine Manufactory, the baking powerhouse that awakens Mission barflies and bleary-eyed engineers religiously early on Sunday to claim spots near the front of the line. Sure, you could skip the queue to buy bread at the kiosk, but you're here for breakout brunch sensations: mozzarella-pepperoni biscuits, huckleberry-pecan grits, butternut-squash danishes and Dungeness-crab Louie sandwiches.

MISSION CHEESE
CHEESE $

Map p302 (☑415-553-8667; www.mission cheese.net; 736 Valencia St; ⏲11am-9pm Tue-Thu & Sun, to 10pm Fri & Sat; ☑; 🚌14, 22, 33, 49, 🚌J, Ⓑ16th St Mission) ✎ Smile and say wine at this cheese bar serving sublime pairings with expert advice and zero pretension. The all-domestic cheese menu ranges from triple creamy to extra stinky, raw cow's milk to sheep's milk, and California wines reign supreme. When in dairy doubt, let 'mongers choice' surprise-cheese platters with pickles, nuts and dried fruit. Order at the bar; note early closing.

UDUPI PALACE   SOUTH INDIAN $
Map p302 (☑415-970-8000; www.udupipalaceca. com; 1007 Valencia St; mains $8-12; ☺11:30am-10pm Sun-Thu, to 10:30pm Fri & Sat; ⚡; ▣12, 14, 33, 49, Ⓑ24th St Mission) Tandoori in the Tenderloin is for novices – SF foodies queue for the bright, clean flavors of Udupi's South Indian *dosa* (light, crispy lentil-flour pancake) dipped in *sambar* (vegetable stew) and coconut chutney. Marathoners may need help finishing the 2ft-long paper *dosa* – save room for pea-and-onion *uthappam* (lentil-flour pancake) and *bagala bhath* (yogurt rice with nutty toasted mustard seeds).

MISSION PIE   AMERICAN, BAKERY $
Map p302 (☑415-282-1500; http://missionpie. com; 2901 Mission St; pie slice $4-5.50; ☺7am-10pm Mon-Fri, from 8am Sat, from 9am Sun; ⊡⚡⒟; ▣12, 14, 48, 49, Ⓑ24th St Mission) ⊘ Like mom used to make, only better: hot-from-the-oven pies at this certified-green bakery range from savory organic-chicken pot pies ($7) to all-American heirloom-apple pies ($4 per slice with free organic whipped cream). The sunny Victorian storefront doubles as a neighborhood hangout, with board games, blocks for kids and a library of conscientious cookbooks to inspire your own food revolution.

TACOLICIOUS   MEXICAN $
Map p302 (☑415-649-6077; http://tacolicious. com; 741 Valencia St; tacos $4; ☺11:30am-midnight; ⚡; ▣14, 22, 33, 49, Ⓑ16th St Mission, ⓂJ) Never mind the name: once you've sampled the *carnitas* (slow-roasted pork) tacos and passion-fruit-habañero margaritas, you'll be in no position to debate authenticity or grammar – or say anything besides *uno mas, por favor* (another, please). Choose four tacos for $14, including seasonal vegetarian options. No reservations, but while you wait you can work through the 100-tequila menu at the bar.

OLD JERUSALEM   MIDDLE EASTERN $
Map p302 (☑415-642-5958; 2976 Mission St; mains $8-13; ☺noon-10pm Mon-Sat, to 9pm Sun; ⚡; ▣12, 14, 48, 49, Ⓑ24th St Mission) Foodies scouring the Mission for the ultimate taco shouldn't overlook this outpost of Middle Eastern authenticity, complete with Dome of the Rock poster and pristine hummus that doesn't overdo the tahini. Get the classic falafel, *shwarma* (spit-roasted lamb) or *shish taouk* (marinated grilled chicken) with all the fixings: hummus, onion, eggplant, potato and tangy purple sumac, with optional *shatta* (hot-pepper paste).

PANCHO VILLA   MEXICAN $
Map p302 (☑415-864-8840; www.sfpancho villa.com; 3071 16th St; burritos $5-10; ☺10am-midnight; ⚡⒟; ▣14, 22, 33, 49, Ⓑ16th St Mission) The hero of the downtrodden and burrito deprived, Pancho Villa supplies tinfoil-wrapped burritos the girth of your forearm and lets you add ammunition at the fresh, heaping salsa bar. The line moves fast going in and, as you leave, the door is held open for you and your newly acquired Pancho's paunch. Stick around for serenades by roving mariachis.

DYNAMO DONUTS   BAKERY $
Map p302 (☑415-920-1978; www.dynamodonut. com; 2760 24th St; donuts $3.50-5; ☺7am-5pm Tue-Sat, 9am-4pm Sun; ⒟; ▣9, 10, 33, 47, 48) ⊘ Wrapping your head around chef Sara Spearin's freak flavors may take a hot minute – but your taste buds immediately grasp the appeal of raspberry-black-pepper glaze, lemon pistachio, and the flavor that launched a thousand cravings: maple-glazed bacon. Hot-cross donuts are a bundonut mash-up made in heaven, especially with Four Barrel Coffee. Not light fare but conscientious, with local and organic ingredients.

★AL'S PLACE   CALIFORNIAN $$
Map p302 (☑415-416-6136; www.alsplacesf.com; 1499 Valencia St; share plates $15-19; ☺5:30-10pm Wed-Sun; ⚡; ▣12, 14, 49, ⓂJ, Ⓑ24th St Mission) ⊘ The Golden State dazzles on Al's plates, featuring homegrown heirloom ingredients, pristine Pacific seafood, and grass-fed meat on the side. Painstaking preparation yields sun-drenched flavors and exquisite textures: crispy-skin cod with frothy preserved-lime dip, grilled peach melting into velvety foie gras. Dishes are half the size but thrice the flavor of mains elsewhere – get two or three, and you'll be California dreaming.

If everyone wants to try everything – because, really, who wouldn't at Al's? – get

FOTOVOYAGER/GETTY IMAGES ©

JUDY BELLAH/GETTY IMAGES ©

1. Mission Dolores (p149)
This modest adobe building is the city's oldest structure, built with conscripted Ohlone and Miwok labor.

2. Carnaval (p20)
The last weekend of May sees feathered and bejewelled hordes take to the streets of the Mission for a celebration of Latin American culture.

3. La Taqueria (p151)
Search no longer: this is the home of San Francisco's definitive burrito.

4. Dolores Park (p147)
The Mission's green patch has something for everyone, from tanning and tennis to protests and street theater.

JEJIM/GETTY IMAGES ©

the family-style tasting menu (four courses $65) with optional wine pairings (add $45).

★ **SERPENTINE**   CALIFORNIAN **$$**

Map p305 (☑415-252-2000; www.serpentinesf. com; 2495 3rd St; mains $10-26; ⏱11:30am-2:30pm & 5-10pm Mon-Thu, to 11pm Fri, 10am-2:30pm & 5-11pm Sat, 10am-2:30pm Sun; ☐22, ⓂT) The best brunch you'll ever have in a boiler room – or, really, anywhere in San Francisco – is Serpentine's Dungeness-crab Benedict, with extra-frothy hollandaise and audaciously fried lemon and capers, served in a lofty converted tin-can factory. Chef Deepak Kaul ditched med school to master precision spicing; now his ancho-chile osso bucco will cure whatever ails you.

★ **ICHI SUSHI**   SUSHI **$$**

(☑415-525-4750; www.ichisushi.com; 3369 Mission St; sushi $4-8; ⏱11:30am-2pm & 5:30-10pm Mon-Thu, to 11pm Fri & Sat, 5:30-9:30pm Sun; ☐14, 24, 49, Ⓑ24th St Mission, ⓂJ) ✒ Alluring on the plate and positively obscene on the tongue, Ichi Sushi is a sharp cut above other seafood joints. Chef Tim Archuleta slices silky, sustainably sourced fish with a jeweler's precision, balances it atop well-packed rice, and tops it with tiny but powerfully tangy dabs of gelled *yuzu* and microscopically cut spring onion and chili daikon that make soy sauce unthinkable.

PIZZERIA DELFINA   PIZZA **$$**

Map p302 (☑415-437-6800; www.delfinasf. com; 3621 18th St; pizzas $14-19; ⏱5-10pm Tue, 11:30am-10pm Mon, Wed & Thu, to 11pm Fri, noon-11pm Sat, to 10pm Sun; ☐14, 22, 33, 49, ⓂJ, Ⓑ16th St Mission) ✒ One bite explains why SF is obsessed with pizza lately: Delfina's thin crust heroically supports the weight of fennel sausage and fresh mozzarella without drooping or cracking. On sauce-free white pizzas, chefs freestyle with California ingredients such as broccoli rabe, Maitake mushrooms and artisan cheese. No reservations; sign the chalkboard and wait with a glass of wine at next-door Delfina bar.

NAMU GAJI   KOREAN, CALIFORNIAN **$$**

Map p302 (☑415-431-6268; www.namusf.com; 499 Dolores St; share plates $10-19; ⏱5:30-10pm Tue, 11:30am-3pm & 5:30-10pm Wed-Fri, 10:30am-4pm & 5-10pm Sat & Sun; ☐14, 22, 33, 49, ⓂJ, Ⓑ16th St Mission) ✒ SF's unfair culinary advantages – organic local ingredients, Pacific Rim roots, and street-skater,

try-anything attitude – are showcased in Namu's Korean-inspired soul food. Bold flavors abound in ultra-savory shiitake-mushroom dumplings, meltingly tender marinated beef tongue, and Namu's version of *bibimbap:* Marin Sun Farm's grass-fed steak, organic vegetables, spicy *gojuchang* (Korean chili sauce) and Sonoma farm egg atop rice, served sizzling in a stone pot.

FARMHOUSE KITCHEN THAI CUISINE   THAI **$$**

Map p302 (☑415-814-2920; http://farmhousesf. com; 710 Florida St; share plates $10-24; ⏱11am-2pm & 5-10pm Mon-Thu, to 10:30pm Fri, noon-10:30pm Sat, to 10pm Sun; ✒ ♿; ☐22, 27) California farm-to-table gets Thai street smarts in this warehouse restaurant showcasing organic, local ingredients and regional Thai street-food inspirations. Skewered Sonoma BBQ chicken marinated in fresh turmeric packs a savory punch, but spicy eggplant with blue rice teaches your taste buds Thai kickboxing. Pricey for lunch, but worth it – embrace the decadence with local wines and croissant-bread pudding.

BURMA LOVE   BURMESE **$$**

Map p302 (☑415-861-2100; www.burmalovesf. com; 211 Valencia St; shared mains $13-25; ⏱11:30am-3pm & 5-10pm Sun-Thu, to 10:30pm Fri & Sat; ✒; ☐F, Ⓑ16th St Mission) For flavors that hug your tongue, then deliver a swift kick, it must be Burma Love. Salad gets upgraded to the main event here, with garlic chips, nutty toasted split peas and tangy fermented tea-leaf dressing. Profoundly spiced vegetables make star turns across the menu – especially caramelized eggplant – and coconut sticky rice adds decadence. Top-notch cocktails offset the haphazard service.

MISSION CHINESE   FUSION **$$**

Map p302 (Lung Shan; ☑415-863-2800; www. missionchinesefood.com; 2234 Mission St; mains $11-25; ⏱11:30am-3pm & 5-10:30pm Thu-Mon, 5-10:30pm Tue & Wed; ☐14, 33, 49, Ⓑ16th St Mission) ✒ Mission barflies and globe-trotting gourmands find common ground at Danny Bowien's cult-food dive. *Kung pao* pastrami burritos, lamb dumplings with Greek tzatziki, and tiki pork belly with pickled pineapple are mind-bending, border-crossing taste sensations – though not for the salt shy – and they satisfy your conscience, too: 75¢ from each main is donated to the San Francisco Food Bank.

LOCANDA
ITALIAN $$

Map p302 (☑415-863-6800; www.locandasf. com; 557 Valencia St; mains $17-31; ☺5:30-10pm Wed & Thu, to 11pm Fri & Sat, 5-10pm Sun, brunch 10:30-2pm Sat & Sun; ☐14, 22, 33, 49, ⒷI16th St Mission) Friends, Romans, San Franciscans – join the crowd for Roman fried artichokes, pizza bianca and prosciutto, blood-orange and beet salads, and scrumptious tripe melting into rich tomato-mint sauce. Pasta dishes are less adventurous than the small plates and mains created with market-fresh organic ingredients, like the whole fish of the day (served head on) and roast meats worthy of imperial feasts.

PRUBECHU'
PACIFIC, CALIFORNIAN $$

Map p302 (☑415-952-3654; www.prubechu. com; 2847 Mission St; mains $16-28; ☺5-10pm Tue-Sat; ☐12, 14, 48, 49, ⒷI24th St Mission) Yes, there's someplace more far-out than San Francisco: Guam, that speck in the Pacific's eye that's been a port of call for Spain, Japan, the Philippines and the US. With fresh, bright, deeply satisfying flavors, Guam's *chamorro* cuisine goes Californian in dishes like greens with turmeric and green garlic, coconut-braised beef with asparagus and handmade pasta, and red rice with pork belly and pickled vegetables.

EL TECHO
LATIN AMERICAN $$

Map p302 (Lolinda Rooftop; ☑415-550-6970; http://eltechosf.com; 2516 Mission St; small plates $8-13; ☺4-10:30pm Mon-Thu, to 12:30am Fri, 11am-12:30am Sat, to 10:30pm Sun; ☐14, 33, 49, ⒷI24th St Mission) Savor Latin street food six floors above Mission St, with views over cinema marquees, palm trees and bodegas all the way downtown. Sunny brunches call for eggs Benedict with jalapeño cornbread, a Chilcano (pisco, lime, ginger, passion fruit and bitters) and sunblock; foggy days require empanadas, La Avenida (rum, lemon and vermouth) and a windbreaker. Kitchen closes 10pm weekdays, 11pm weekends.

CALIFORNIOS
LATIN AMERICAN $$$

Map p302 (☑415-757-0994; www.californios sf.com; 3115 22nd St; 16-course tasting menu $150; ☐12, 14, 49, ⒷI24th St Mission) Parades – from Carnaval to Día de los Muertos – are a Mission specialty, and the parade of Latin-inspired flavors nightly at Californios does justice to the neighborhood's roots and unbridled creativity. Chef Val Cantu collaborates with local farms and artisan producers to reinvent staples according to

the seasons: imagine sourdough tortillas, foie-gras tamales, Dungeness-crab ceviche and wild-strawberry flan. Reserve ahead.

FOREIGN CINEMA
CALIFORNIAN $$$

Map p302 (☑415-648-7600; www.foreign cinema.com; 2534 Mission St; mains $22-33; ☺5:30-10pm Sun-Wed, to 11pm Thu-Sat, brunch 11am-2:30pm Sat & Sun; ☐12, 14, 33, 48, 49, ⒷI24th St Mission) 🍴 Chef Gayle Pirie's acclaimed California classics such as velvety Pacific *poke* (marinated tuna) and crisp sesame fried chicken are the star attractions here – but subtitled films by Luis Buñuel and François Truffaut screening in the courtyard are mighty handy when conversation lags with first dates or in-laws. Get the red-carpet treatment with valet parking ($15) and a well-stocked oyster bar.

COMMONWEALTH
CALIFORNIAN $$$

Map p302 (☑415-355-1500; www.common wealthsf.com; 2224 Mission St; small plates $15-22; ☺5:30-10pm Sun-Thu, to 11pm Fri & Sat; ☑; ☐14, 22, 33, 49, ⒷI16th St Mission) Wildly imaginative farm-to-table dining where you'd least expect it: in a converted cinderblock Mission dive. Chef Jason Fox serves adventurous compositions like *uni* and bone-marrow cream with nasturtium flowers, and lamb with beets and seaweed on a redwood plank. Dishes are dainty but pack wallops of earthy flavor. Savor the six-course tasting menu ($80) knowing that a portion benefits local charities.

🍷 DRINKING & NIGHTLIFE

★%ABV
COCKTAIL BAR

Map p302 (☑415-400-4748; www.abvsf.com; 3174 16th St; ☺2pm-2am; ☐14, 22, ⒷI16th St Mission, ⓂJ) As kindred spirits will deduce from the name (the abbreviation for 'percent alcohol by volume'), this bar is backed by cocktail crafters who know their Rittenhouse rye from their Japanese malt whisky. Top-notch hooch is served promptly and without pretension, including excellent Cali wine and beer on tap and original historically inspired cocktails like the Sutro Swizzle (Armagnac, grapefruit shrub, maraschino liqueur).

For drinks with a plot twist, choose a bargain $50 four-course dinner with cocktail pairings upstairs at Overproof. The featured spirit, accompanying menu and decor change every three months, and two seatings nightly are limited to 24 total at communal tables – reserve ahead.

★ TRICK DOG BAR

Map p302 (📞415-471-2999; www.trickdogbar.com; 3010 20th St; ⏰3pm-2am; 🚌12, 14, 49) Drink adventurously with ingenious cocktails inspired by local obsessions: San Francisco muralists, Chinese diners or conspiracy theories. Every six months, Trick Dog adopts a new theme and the entire menu changes – proof that you can teach an old dog new tricks, and improve on classics like the Manhattan. Arrive early for bar stools or hit the mood-lit loft for high-concept bar bites.

Trick Dog has collaborated with SF muralists to create cocktails based on their artwork, and proceeds from the resulting *Trick Dog Murals* cocktail-recipe book benefit the Mission's own Precita Eyes (p165) and Creativity Explored (p149) arts nonprofits.

★ EL RIO CLUB

Map p302 (📞415-282-3325; www.elriosf.com; 3158 Mission St; cover free-$8; ⏰1pm-2am; 🚌12, 14, 27, 49, 🚇24th St Mission) Work it all out on the dance floor with SF's most down and funky crowd – the full rainbow spectrum of colorful characters is here to party. Calendar highlights include Salsa Sunday, free oysters from 5:30pm Friday, drag-star DJs, backyard bands and ping-pong. Expect knockout margaritas and shameless flirting on a patio that's seen it all since 1978. Cash only.

★ 20 SPOT WINE BAR

Map p302 (📞415-624-3140; www.20spot.com; 3565 20th St; ⏰5pm-midnight Mon-Thu, to 1am Fri & Sat; 🚌14, 22, 33, 🚇16th St Mission) Find your California mellow at this neighborhood wine lounge in a 1895 Victorian building. After decades as Force of Habit punk-record shop – note the vintage sign – this corner joint has earned the right to unwind with a glass of Berkeley's Donkey and Goat sparkling wine and not get any guff. Caution: oysters with pickled persimmon could become a habit.

★ ELIXIR BAR

Map p302 (📞415-522-1633; www.elixirsf.com; 3200 16th St; ⏰3pm-2am Mon-Fri, from noon Sat, from 10am Sun; 🚌14, 22, 33, 49, 🚇16th St Mission, Ⓜ J) 🍸 Do the planet a favor and have another drink at SF's first certified green bar, in an actual 1858 Wild West saloon. Elixir expertly blends farm-fresh seasonal mixers with local small-batch, organic, biodynamic

spirits – Meyer-lemon and rye sours and Mission Pimm's Cup with pisco and cucumber vodka get everyone air-guitar rocking to the killer jukebox. Proceeds from drink-for-a-cause Wednesdays support local charities.

★ WILD SIDE WEST GAY & LESBIAN

(📞415-647-3099; www.wildsidewest.com; 424 Cortland Ave; ⏰2pm-2am; 🚌24) Lesbian-owned since 1964, Wild Side West has kept its clientele busy making herstory in the beer garden and making out on the pool table (Janis Joplin started it). The sculpture garden began in the 1970s, when killjoy neighbors chucked junk over the fence to protest women enjoying themselves – but cast-offs upcycled into art became the pride of the Wild Side.

★ DALVA & HIDEOUT LOUNGE

Map p302 (📞415-252-7740; http://dalvasf.com; 3121 16th St; ⏰4pm-2am; 🚌14, 22, 33, 49, 🚇24th St Mission) SF's best bars are distinguished not just by their drinks but by the conversations they inspire – and by both measures Dalva is top shelf. Here Roxie (p160) movie critiques drip with Irony Pinot Noir, politics invoke Russian River Damnation ale, and Dolores Park gossip spills over Dirty Pigeons (mezcal, lime, grapefruit, gentian-flower bitters) at back-room Hideout (from 7pm; cash only). Happy hour 4pm to 7pm; karaoke on Sunday.

★ ZEITGEIST BAR

Map p302 (📞415-255-7505; www.zeitgeistsf. com; 199 Valencia St; ⏰9am-2am; 🚌14, 22, 49, 🚇16th St Mission) You've got two seconds flat to order from tough-gal barkeeps used to putting macho bikers in their place – but with 48 beers on draft, you're spoiled for choice. Epic afternoons unfold in the graveled beer garden, with folks hanging out and smoking at long picnic tables. SF's longest happy hour lasts 9am to 8pm weekdays. Cash only; no photos (read: no evidence).

RITUAL COFFEE ROASTERS CAFE

Map p302 (📞415-641-1011; www.ritualroasters. com; 1026 Valencia St; ⏰6am-8pm Mon-Sat, from 7am Sat & Sun; 🚌14, 49, 🚇24th St Mission) Cults wish they inspired the same devotion as Ritual, where regulars solemnly queue for house-roasted cappuccino with ferns drawn in foam and specialty drip coffees with highly distinctive flavor profiles – descriptions comparing roasts to grapefruit peel or hazelnut aren't exaggerating.

Electrical outlets are limited to encourage conversation, so you can eavesdrop on dates and political-protest plans.

BISSAP BAOBAB   CLUB

Map p302 (☑415-826-9287; www.bissapbaobab. com; 3372 19th St; cover free-$5; ☺club 9pm or 10pm-2am Thu-Sat; ☒14, 22, 33, 49, Ⓑ16th St Mission) A Senegalese restaurant early in the evening, Baobab brings on the DJ or live act around 10pm – and before you can say 'tamarind margarita,' tables are shoved out of the way to make room on the dance floor. Midweek Cuban timba salsa, occasional flamenco and gypsy jazz shows, and Friday and Saturday Paris-Dakar Afrobeat get the Mission in a universal groove.

BORDERLANDS   CAFE

Map p302 (☑415-970-6998; www.borderlands-cafe.com; 870 Valencia St; ☺8am-8pm; ☒14, 33, 49, Ⓑ16th St Mission) West Coast coffeehouse culture is staging a comeback at this membership-supported neighborhood bookstore-cafe, complete with hairless cats, creaky wooden floors, top-notch hot chocolate and sofas encouraging offline chats. Mysterious yet sociable Borderlands limits wi-fi (9am to 5pm weekdays) to keep conversation flowing and thoughtfully provides racks of paperback mysteries for browsing – or buying at the 1950s purchase price of 50¢. Cash only.

HOMESTEAD   BAR

Map p302 (☑415-282-4663; www.homesteadsf. com; 2301 Folsom St; ☺2pm-2am; ☒12, 14, 22, 33, 49, Ⓑ16th St Mission) Your friendly Victorian corner dive c 1893, complete with carved-wood bar, pressed-tin ceiling, salty roast peanuts in the shell, Mission characters and their sweet dogs. SF's creative contingent packs the place to celebrate art openings, grants and writing assignments with cheap draft beer – and when Iggy Pop or David Bowie hits the jukebox, stand back.

FOUR BARREL COFFEE   CAFE

Map p302 (☑415-896-4289; www.fourbarrel coffee.com; 375 Valencia St; ☺7am-8pm; ☒14, 22, Ⓡ16th St Mission) Surprise: the hippest cafe in town is also the friendliest, with upbeat baristas and no outlets or wi-fi to hinder conversation. Drip roasts are complex and powerful; the fruity espresso is an acquired taste. The front-bar Slow Pour comes with coffee-geek explanations of growing, roasting and cupping methods. Caffeinating

crowds mingle in the sunny parklet with bike parking and patio seating.

ROCK BAR   BAR

(☑415-550-6664; http://rockbarsf.com; 80 29th St; ☺4pm-2am Mon-Sat, from noon Sun; ☒14, 24, 49, ⓂJ) Eureka! Inside these rock-veneer walls, you're golden with original concoctions made of craft spirits and priced to move ($9 to $12). Get fancy with house-specialty cocktails like the Gold Digger (gin, champagne, peach, ginger) or go 4pm to 7pm weekdays for $6 old-fashioneds. Order fried chicken across the street at Front Porch and they'll deliver to your stool. Cash only.

YIELD   WINE BAR

Map p305 (☑415-401-8984; www.yieldandpause. com; 2490 3rd St; ☺3:30-11pm Mon-Sat; ☒22, 48, ⓂT) 🌿 It's easy being green at Yield, a storefront wine bar with a rotating list of sustainably farmed vintages served at rough-hewn wooden tables. Pull up an ottoman and settle in with a bottle or glass, and maybe some tasty flatbread and California cheeses, and kick it with the convivial crowd that gets downright rowdy on Tuesday trivia nights.

DOC'S CLOCK   BAR

Map p302 (☑415-824-3627; www.docsclock.com; 2575 Mission St; ☺5pm-2am Mon-Thu, 4pm-2am Fri & Sat, 3pm-2am Sun; ☒12, 14, 49, Ⓑ24th St Mission) 🌿 Tickle in your throat? Time to see the Doc – head directly to the Prescriptions Counter at this gruffly lovable green-certified dive for local craft brews and spirits, free shuffleboard, Barbie Mutilation Nights, tricky pinball and easy conversation. Dog-friendly happy hours run 5pm to 9pm daily, with a percentage of proceeds supporting city dog rescues. Cash only.

LATIN AMERICAN CLUB   BAR

Map p302 (☑415-647-2732; 3286 22nd St; ☺6pm-2am Mon-Fri, from 3pm Sat & Sun; ☒12, 14, 49, Ⓑ24th St Mission) Margaritas served in beer glasses go the distance here – just don't stand up too fast. Ninja *piñatas* and *papel picado* (cut-paper banners) add a festive atmosphere, and rosy lighting and generous pours enable shameless flirting. Cash only.

PHONE BOOTH   BAR

Map p302 (☑415-648-4683; 1398 S Van Ness Ave; ☺2pm-2am; ☒14, 49, Ⓑ24th St Mission) Classic SF dive celebrating defunct technology, with naked Barbie chandeliers and year-round Christmas lights. Art-school students mingle with sundry techies (oh, hi, Mark Zuckerberg) over pool tables and make out in dark corners. Cheap beer, Jameson and Bloody Marys flow freely, and the jukebox is perpetually on fire.

DIG WINE BAR

Map p305 (☎415-648-6133; http://digwinesf.com; 1005 Minnesota St; ⊙noon-7pm Tue-Fri, to 5pm Sat; ☐22, 48, ⓂT) Great wines that won't break the bank: San Francisco's dedicated wine drinkers totally Dig it. Enter a well-curated wine library featuring the work of small producers in France and Italy, with most bottles priced for easy drinking under $50. Ask about illuminating and dangerously generous weekend wine tastings, held at the shop bar or on the 1859 Yellow Building's patio.

☆ ENTERTAINMENT

★**ALAMO DRAFTHOUSE CINEMA** CINEMA

Map p302 (☎415-549-5959; https://drafthouse. com/sf; 2550 Mission St; tickets $9-20; 🍴; ☐14, Ⓑ24th St Mission) The landmark 1932 New Mission cinema, now restored to its original Timothy Pfleuger–designed art-deco glory, has a new mission: to upgrade dinner-and-a-movie dates. Staff deliver microbrews and tasty fare to plush banquette seats, so you don't miss a moment of the premieres, cult revivals (especially Music Mondays) or SF favorites from *Mrs Doubtfire* to *Dirty Harry* – often with filmmaker Q&As.

★**OBERLIN DANCE COLLECTIVE** DANCE

Map p302 (ODC; ☎box office 415-863-9834, classes 415-549-8519; www.odctheater.org; 3153 17th St; drop-in classes from $15, shows $20-50; ☐12, 14, 22, 33, 49, Ⓑ16th St Mission) For 45 years, ODC has been redefining dance with risky, raw performances and the sheer joy of movement. ODC's season runs September to December, but its stage presents year-round shows featuring local and international artists. ODC Dance Commons is a hub and hangout for the dance community offering 200-plus classes a week, from flamenco to vogue; all ages and skill levels welcome.

★**ROXIE CINEMA** CINEMA

Map p302 (☎415-863-1087; www.roxie.com; 3117 16th St; regular screening/matinee $11/8; ☐14, 22, 33, 49, Ⓑ16th St Mission) This vintage 1909

cinema is a neighborhood nonprofit with an international reputation for distributing documentaries and showing controversial films banned elsewhere. Tickets to film-festival premieres, rare revivals and raucous Oscars telecasts sell out – get tickets online – but if the main show's packed, discover riveting documentaries in teensy next-door Little Roxy instead. No ads, plus personal introductions to every film.

★**CHAPEL** LIVE MUSIC

Map p302 (☎415-551-5157; www.thechapelsf. com; 777 Valencia St; cover $15-40; ⊙bar 7pm-2am; ☐14, 33, ⓂJ, Ⓑ16th St Mission) Musical prayers are answered in a 1914 California Craftsman landmark with heavenly acoustics. The 40ft roof is regularly raised by shows by New Orleans brass bands, folkYEAH! Americana groups, legendary rockers like Peter Murphy and hip-hop icons such as Prince Paul. Many shows are all ages, except when comedians like W Kamau Bell test edgy material.

★**BRAVA THEATER** THEATER

Map p302 (☎415-641-7657; www.brava.org; 2781 24th St; 🍴; ☐12, 27, 33, 48) Brava's been producing women-run theater for 30-plus years, hosting acts from comedian Sandra Bernhard to V-day monologist Eve Ensler, and it's the nation's first company with a commitment to producing original works by women of color and LGBTQIA playwrights. Brava honors the Mission's Mexican heritage with Latinx music and dance celebrations, plus hand-painted show posters modeled after Mexican cinema billboards.

BRICK & MORTAR LIVE MUSIC

Map p302 (☎415-800-8782; http://brickand mortarmusic.com; 1710 Mission St; cover $10-20; ☐14, 49, Ⓑ16th St Mission) Some bands are too outlandish for regular radio – to hear them, you need San Francisco's Brick & Mortar. The bill here features national acts from brass-band showcases to the US air-guitar championships, plus homegrown SF upstarts like post-punk Magic Bullet, ironic 'indie-rock avalanche' the Yellow Dress and psychedelically groovy Loco Tranquilo.

MARSH THEATER, COMEDY

Map p302 (☎415-282-3055; www.themarsh.org; 1062 Valencia St; tickets $15-35; ⊙box office 1-4pm Mon-Fri; ☐12, 14, 48, 49, Ⓑ24th St Mission) Choose your seat wisely: you may spend the evening on the edge of it. One-acts and

WORTH A DETOUR

BOTTOM OF THE HILL

Quite literally at the bottom of Potrero Hill, **Bottom of the Hill** (Map p305; ☑415-621-4455; www.bottomofthehill.com; 1233 17th St; $5-20; ◎shows generally 9pm Tue-Sat; ◻10, 19, 22) is always top of the list for alt-rocking out with punk legends the Avengers, Pansy Division and Nerf Herder, and newcomers worth checking out for their names alone (Summer Salt, the Regrettes, Sorority Noise). The smokers' patio is covered in handbills and ruled by a cat that enjoys music more than people – totally punk rock. There's Anchor Steam on tap at the cash-only bar; check the website for lineups.

monologues here involve the audience in the creative process, from comedian W Kamau Bell's riffs to live tapings of National Public Radio's *Philosophy Talk*. Sliding-scale pricing allows everyone to participate, and a few reserved seats are sometimes available (tickets $55).

MAKE-OUT ROOM   LIVE PERFORMANCE

Map p302 (☑415-647-2888; www.makeoutroom. com; 3225 22nd St; cover free-$10; ◎6pm-2am; ◻12, 14, 49, Ⓑ24th St Mission) Velvet curtains and round booths invite you to get comfortable under the disco ball for an evening of utterly unpredictable entertainment, ranging from Toychestra performances on kids' instruments to dance-hall and cumbia DJ mash-ups and painfully funny readings at Writers with Drinks. Booze is a bargain, especially during happy hour (6pm to 8pm weeknights; drinks $5!) – but the bar is cash only.

AMNESIA   LIVE MUSIC

Map p302 (☑415-970-0012; www.facebook. com/amnesiaSF; 853 Valencia St; cover free-$10; ◎4pm-2am Mon-Fri, from noon Sat & Sun; ◻14, 33, 49, Ⓑ16th St Mission) Forget standard playlists – this closet-sized boho dive will make you lose your mind for Monday bluegrass jams, Tuesday Troubled Comedy sessions, Wednesday gaucho jazz, random readings and breakout dance parties. Shows are cheap and often sliding scale, so the crowd is pumped and the beer flows freely. Check Facebook or just go with the flow; $5 craft beer from 4pm to 7pm.

REVOLUTION CAFE   LIVE PERFORMANCE

Map p302 (☑415-642-0474; www.revolution cafesf.com; 3248 22nd St; suggested donation $5-20; ◎9am-midnight Sun-Thu, to 2am Fri & Sat; ☏; ◻12, 14, 49, Ⓑ24th St Mission) Musicians, you're among friends: classically trained musicians and jazz artists jam here daily. Hot days call for iced coffee and live Latin

jazz, and Mondays are redeemed with Belgian brews and Classical Revolution's rollicking chamber music. Arrive by 7pm to snag a table, or hang on the sidewalk with free wi-fi. Bring cash for drinks and musicians' tip jars.

RED POPPY ART HOUSE   ARTS CENTER

Map p302 (☑650-731-5383; http://redpoppy arthouse.org; 2698 Folsom St; shows free-$25; ◎11am-5pm Tue, Wed & Fri, noon-4pm Thu, evening shows 7:30-10pm; ◻12, 48, Ⓑ24th St Mission) San Francisco's underground arts scene has taken up residence in a sunny Mission loft. Red Poppy hosts artist residencies, live jazz and roots music and initiatives like the Mission Stoop Fest, a roaming storytelling spectacle. More than a backdrop to events, Red Poppy installation art shows make the scene – artist Michelle Morby recently installed an audience of 70 watercolor portraits.

JOE GOODE PERFORMANCE GROUP   DANCE

Map p302 (☑415-561-6565; www.joegoode.org; 499 Alabama St; ◻22, 33) Combining performance art and dance, maverick Joe Goode's troupe tours internationally – but it all begins in the Mission's Joe Goode Annex, where you can see shows and take workshops. In Joe Goode's original works, dancers often use their voices and movements to create immersive experiences – *The Resilience Project* includes original songs composed from Iraq war veterans' interview excerpts.

RITE SPOT CAFE   LIVE MUSIC

Map p302 (☑415-552-6066; www.ritespotcafe. net; 2099 Folsom St; donation appreciated; ◎shows 9pm; ◻12, 22, 33, Ⓑ16th St Mission) The vintage dive-bar neon in the middle of warehouse nowhere-land is pointing you in the Rite direction for offbeat performances banged out on a tinkling house piano. Check the online calendar for enchantingly kooky acts like Mr Lucky and the Cocktail

Party, the Misery Index comedy night, or live-band Beatles karaoke – or just follow a hunch and discover the next Tom Waits.

🔒 SHOPPING

★ GRAVEL & GOLD · CLOTHING, HOMEWARES
Map p302 (☑415-552-0112; www.gravelandgold. com; 3266 21st St; ⊘noon-7pm Mon-Sat, to 5pm Sun; 📵12, 14, 49, 🅱24th St Mission) ✐ Get back to the land and in touch with California's roots without leaving sight of a Mission sidewalk. Gravel & Gold celebrates California's hippie homesteader movement with hand-printed smock-dresses, signature boob-print totes and wiggly stoner-striped throw pillows. It's homestead California-style with hand-thrown stoneware mugs, silk-screened '60s Osborn/Woods ecology posters, and rare books on '70s beach-shack architecture – plus DIY maker workshops.

★ COMMUNITY THRIFT · CLOTHING, VINTAGE
Map p302 (☑415-861-4910; www.community thriftsf.org; 623 Valencia St; ⊘10am-6:30pm; 📵14, 22, 33, 49, 🅱16th St Mission) ✐ When local collectors and retailers have too much of a good thing, they donate it to nonprofit Community Thrift, where proceeds go to 200-plus local charities – all the more reason to gloat over your $5 totem-pole teacup, $10 vintage windbreaker and $14 disco-era glitter romper. Donate your cast-offs (until 5pm daily) and show some love to the Community.

★ POCO DOLCE · CHOCOLATE
Map p305 (☑415-817-1551; http://pocodolce. com; 2419 3rd St; ⊘11am-5:30pm Mon, to 6pm Tue-Fri, noon-5:30pm Sat; 📵22, 48, Ⓜ T) ✐ People who swear they're not into dessert can't get enough Poco Dolce, San Francisco's award-winning, sustainably sourced chocolates with a touch of sea salt. Popcorn-toffee chocolates upgrade movie nights, and Aztec chili-chocolate tiles are ideal with Dogpatch wine tastings – but the Legion of Honor (p198) art-inspired bars with silky California olive oil are a reason to leave your heart in San Francisco.

★ LITTLE PAPER PLANES · GIFTS & SOUVENIRS
Map p302 (☑415-643-4616; http://littlepaper planes.com; 855 Valencia St; ⊘noon-7pm Mon-Sat, to 6pm Sun; 📵14, 33, 49, 🅱16th St Mission, Ⓜ J) Explore fresh gift possibilities at this purveyor of essential SF oddities: SF artist Kelly Lynn Jones' ocean-print scarves,

Oakland-made cacti-print wallets, eco-friendly glossy black nail polish made in California and house-published manifestos (including *Art as a Muscular Principle* and *Bay Area Women Artists*). The place is tiny, but it thinks big – LPP's artists' residency yields original works like Hannah Perrine's paper-airplane prints.

★ RECCHIUTI AT THELAB · CHOCOLATE
Map p305 (☑415-489-2881; www.recchiuti.com; 801 22nd St; ⊘noon-7pm Mon-Fri, 11am-6pm Sat, noon-5pm Sun; 📵22, 48, Ⓜ T) Star chocolatier Michael Recchiuti sells confections at the Ferry Building (p79) but invents them in Dogpatch – try his latest concoctions here first: dark-chocolate cocoa in winter, brownie sundaes in summer, or whatever oddity is on the menu – recent standouts include chocolate stout beer, verrine cream cakes, and trippy swirled bars made in the Wonka-esque spinning 'chocolate art' machine.

★ CASA BONAMPAK · GIFTS & SOUVENIRS
Map p302 (☑415-642-4079; www.casabonam pak.com; 1051 Valencia St; ⊘11am-7pm Tue-Thu, to 9pm Fri & Sat, noon-6pm Sun; ♿; 📵12, 14, 48, 49, 🅱24th St Mission) Celebrate every conceivable holiday the Mission way: with fair-trade, artisan-made *papel picado* (cut-paper banners), paper flowers, and *piñatas* to smack with a broom until candy falls out. Stock up on *papel picado* for Pride and Hanukkah, paper rosebud bouquets for *quinceañeras*, and kits to make your own Day of the Dead sugar skulls.

★ BI-RITE · FOOD & DRINKS
Map p302 (☑415-241-9760; www.biritemarket. com; 3639 18th St; ⊘8am-9pm; ♿; 📵14, 22, 33, 49, 🅱16th St Mission, Ⓜ J) ✐ Diamond counters can't compare to the foodie dazzle of Bi-Rite's sublime wall of local artisan chocolates, treasure boxes of organic fruit, and California wine and cheese selections expertly curated by upbeat, knowledgeable staff. Step up to the altar-like deli counter to provision five-star Dolores Park picnics. An institution since 1940, Bi-Rite champions good food for all through its nonprofit 18 Reasons (p165). The jaw-dropping, mouthwatering experience continues at Bi-Rite's second location (500 Divisadero St).

★ MISSION COMICS & ART · COMICS, ART
Map p302 (☑415-695-1545; www.missioncomic sandart.com; 2250 Mission St; ⊘noon-8pm Mon, Tue & Thu-Sat, from 11am Wed, noon-6pm Sun;

THE MISSION'S COMMUNITY-SUPPORTED BOOKSTORE SCENE

San Francisco may be the global hub for all things digital, but an analog revolution is afoot in the Mission. The district has rallied around the once-struggling **Adobe Books** (Map p302; ☑415-864-3936; www.adobebookshop.com; 3130 24th St; ⊘noon-8pm Mon-Fri, from 11am Sat & Sun; ☐12, 14, 48, 49, Ⓑ24th St Mission), now reinvented as a member-supported collective hosting raucous readings and Backroom Gallery art openings with a track record of launching Whitney Biennial stars. Down 24th St from Adobe, **Alley Cat Books** (Map p302; ☑415-824-1761; www.alleycatbookshop.com; 3036 24th St; ⊘10am-9pm Mon-Sat, to 8pm Sun; ☑; ☐12, 14, 48, 49, Ⓑ24th St Mission) is part bookstore, part community center, with bilingual books in the front, art shows in the middle, and events and a ping-pong table in back. On Valencia St, Alley Cat's sibling bookstore **Dog-Eared Books** (Map p302; ☑415-282-1901; www.dogearedbooks.com; 900 Valencia St; ⊘10am-10pm; ☐12, 14, 33, 49) supports new releases and small presses with author readings and commemorates bygone cultural figures in hand-drawn obituaries. Further along Valencia, member-supported **Borderlands** (p159) upholds San Francisco's noir-novel reputation, selling 50¢ mysteries to read in the convivial cafe.

☐12, 14, 33, 49, Ⓑ16th St Mission) Heads will roll, fists will fly and furious vengeance will be wreaked inside this mild-mannered shop stocking big-name and indie comics. Staff picks range from marquee (*Walking Dead, Star Wars*) to niche (*Snotgirl, Head Lopper*), and artists headlining signings and gallery shows here have included *Supergirl* writer Mariko Tamaki, *Ancestor* surrealist artist Matt Sheean and *New Yorker* constructivist cartoonist Roman Muradov.

★ TIGERLILY PERFUMERY   PERFUME

Map p302 (☑510-230-7975; www.tigerlilysf.com; 973 Valencia St; ⊘noon-6:30pm Wed-Fri, to 7pm Sat, noon-5pm Sun; ☐14, 33, 49, Ⓑ24th St Mission) If you want to bottle San Francisco and take it home with you, you've come to the right place. Tigerlily stocks an intoxicating variety of local perfumers' creations, which will transport you from beach days to Barbary Coast nights. Options range from Yosh Han's California-sunbeam scent, appropriately called U4EAHH!, to Ikiryo's kinky, leather-bound Bad Omen. Check out the calendar for in-person perfume events.

★ NEEDLES & PENS   ARTS & CRAFTS

Map p302 (☑415-872-9189; www.needles-pens. com; 1173 Valencia St; ⊘noon-7pm; ☐14, 33, 49, Ⓑ24th St Mission) This scrappy 'zine shop/ how-to source/art gallery/publisher delivers inspiration to create your own artworks, 'zines and repurposed fashion statements. Nab limited-edition printings of Xara Thustra's manifesto *Friendship Between Artists Is an Equation of Love and Survival* and H Finn Cunningham's *Mental Health Cook-*

book – plus alphabet buttons to pin your own credo onto a handmade messenger bag.

★ NOOWORKS   CLOTHING

Map p302 (☑415-829-7623; www.nooworks.com; 395 Valencia St; ⊘11am-7pm Tue-Sat, to 5pm Sun & Mon; ☐14, 22, 33, 49, Ⓑ16th St Mission) Get a streetwise Mission edge with Nooworks' locally designed, US-made fashions, most under $100. Nooworks' open-mouth shirts are ideal for Pancho-Villa-burrito-and-Roxie-documentary dates, and 'Muscle Beach' maxi dresses are Dolores Park ready with psychedelic rainbows and Schwarzenegger-esque flexing bodybuilders. Kids are good to go to any Mission gallery opening in soft leggings and tees in feather-, forest- and desert-inspired graphic prints.

★ BAGGU   FASHION & ACCESSORIES

Map p302 (☑800-605-0759; https://baggu. com; 911 Valencia St; ⊘noon-7pm; ☐12, 14, 33, 49, Ⓜ J) Plastic bags are banned in San Francisco, which is a perfect excuse to stock up on SF designer Baggu's reusable Ripstop nylon totes in bright colors and quirky prints: sharks, alpacas, and, ay, chihuahuas. They're durable, lightweight and crushable – totes fabulous. Striped canvas backpacks are destined for hauling Adobe Books (p163), and little leather circle purses hold Mission Lit Crawl essentials.

★ AGGREGATE SUPPLY   CLOTHING, HOMEWARES

Map p302 (☑415-474-3190; www.Aggregate SupplySF.com; 806 Valencia St; ⊘11am-7pm Mon-Sat, noon-6pm Sun; ☐14, 33, 49, Ⓑ16th St

Mission) Wild West modern is the look at Aggregate Supply, purveyors of California-cool fashion and home decor. Local designers and indie makers get pride of place, including vintage Heath stoneware mugs, Turk+Taylor's plaid shirt-jackets, and SF artist Tauba Auerbach's 24-hour clocks. Souvenirs don't get more authentically local than Aggregate Supply's own op-art California graphic tee and NorCal-forest-scented organic soaps.

RAINBOW GROCERY FOOD & DRINKS

Map p302 (☑415-863-0620; www.rainbow.coop; 1745 Folsom St; ⊙9am-9pm; ☐9, 12, 33, 47) 🍃 This legendary cooperative attracts crowds to buy eco/organic/fair-trade products in bulk, sample the bounty of local cheeses and flirt in the artisan-chocolate aisle. To answer your questions about where to find what in the Byzantine bulk section, ask a fellow shopper – staff can be elusive. Small though well-priced wine and craft-beer selections; no meat products.

GOOD VIBRATIONS ADULT

Map p302 (☑415-503-9522; www.goodvibes. com; 603 Valencia St; ⊙10am-10pm Sun-Thu, to 11pm Fri & Sat; ☐14, 22, 33, 49, ⓑ16th St Mission) 'Wait, I'm supposed to put that where?' The understanding salespeople in this worker-owned cooperative are used to giving rather explicit instructions, so don't hesitate to ask. Margaret Cho is on the board here, so you know they're not shy. Check out the display of antique vibrators, including one that looks like a floor waxer – thank goodness for modern technology.

WORKSHOP RESIDENCE DESIGN

Map p305 (☑415-285-2050; http://workshop residence.com; 833 22nd St; ⊙10am-6pm Tue-Sat; ☐22, 48, Ⓜ T) Cottage industry is alive at Workshop Residence, where artists and designers collaborate with Bay Area fabricators to produce limited-edition designs – Ann Hamilton's welcome mats quote the children's book *Heidi*, Bruno Fazzolari's scents are inspired by drying oil paintings, and Lauren DiCioccio's nylon bags are embroidered with the slogan 'Thank you – have a nice day.' Check out the website for upcoming artist talks.

SCRAP ARTS & CRAFTS

(Scroungers' Center for Re-Usable Art Parts; ☑415-647-1746; www.scrap-sf.org; 801 Toland St; ⊙10am-6pm Mon-Fri, to 5pm Sat; 🚻; ☐9, 15, 23, 24, 44) 🍃 Renew, recycle and rediscover your creativity with post-industrial arts and crafts materials from SCRAP. Take a workshop for inspiration and make your own upcycled dollhouse, repurposed-glass mosaic or recycled shag rug. DIY classes are held most Saturdays (see website for listings); the entrance to SCRAP is at the confluence of Hwys 101 and 280.

MISSION SKATEBOARDS FASHION & ACCESSORIES

Map p302 (☑415-647-7888; 3045 24th St; ⊙11am-7pm; 🚻; ☐12, 14, 48, 49, ⓑ24th St Mission) Street cred comes easy with locally designed Mission decks, custom tees to kick-flip over and cult skate shoes at this shop owned by SF street-skate legend Scot Thompson. Cool deal: kids who show report cards with GPAs over 3.0 get discounts. This shop is handy to Potrero del Sol/La Raza Skatepark (p43) and, for newbies too cool for kneepads, SF General (p272).

BETABRAND CLOTHING

Map p302 (☑415-400-9491; www.betabrand. com; 780 Valencia St; ⊙11am-7pm Mon-Fri, to 8pm Sat, noon-6pm Sun; ☐14, 22, 33, 49, ⓑ16th St Mission) Crowdsource fashion choices at Betabrand, where experimental designs are put to an online vote and winners are produced in limited editions. Recent approved designs include office-ready dress yoga pants, disco-ball windbreakers and sundresses with a smiling-poo-emoji print. Some styles are clunkers – including the 'chillmono,' a kimono-style down puffer jacket – but at these prices you can afford to take fashion risks.

BLACK & BLUE TATTOO BODY ART

Map p302 (☑415-626-0770; www.blackandblue tattoo.com; 381 Guerrero St; ⊙noon-7pm; ☐14, 22, 33, 49, ⓑ16th St Mission) This women-owned tattoo parlor gets it in ink with designs ranging from honeycomb-pattern bicep graphics to shoulder-to-shoulder Golden Gate Bridge spans. Check out artists' work at the shop or online, then book a consultation. Once you've talked over the design, you can book your tattoo – you'll need to show up sober, well fed, fragrance free and clear headed.

HEATH CERAMICS & NEWSSTAND CERAMICS

Map p302 (☑415-361-5552; www.heathceramics. com; 2900 18th St; ⊙8am-6pm Sun-Wed, to 7pm Thu-Sat; ☐12, 22, 27, 33) No local, artisan SF restaurant decor is complete without earthy Heath stoneware, including the hand-glazed tiles found at this Mission studio-showroom. New Heath models are sold here alongside a design-mag newsstand, artisan pop-ups and jewelry trunk shows. Factory tours are available weekends at 11:30am; working tours are held the first and third Fridays of each month at 11:15am.

TRIPLE AUGHT DESIGN CLOTHING
Map p305 (☑415-520-3214; www.tripleaught design.com; 660 22nd St; ☺11am-7pm Tue-Sun; ☐22, 48, Ⓜ T) Whether you're a social-media millionaire who runs Parkour or you just rock that look, Triple Aught has your back, with zip-up paramilitary sweaters and multi-functional pants too stylish for standard cargo. Key features in these SF-designed, US-made garments include hidden pockets, and the sleek Stealth hoodie, which transitions from TED conferences to off-the-grid weekends, is a unisex favorite.

VOYAGER FASHION & ACCESSORIES
Map p302 (☑415-779-2712; www.thevoyagershop.com; 365 Valencia St; ☺11am-7pm; ☐14, 22, 33, 49, Ⓑ16th St Mission) Post-apocalyptic art-school surf shack is the vibe inside this curated storefront, featuring the work of sundry indie makers on plywood planks. Items for sale range from cultish denim shirts and sculptural ninja pants to surf wear and art books in the geodesic submarine gallery. Monthly pop-ups showcase statement jewelry, minimalist dresses and artistically inclined office supplies by SF makers.

PAXTON GATE GIFTS & SOUVENIRS
Map p302 (☑415-824-1872; https://paxtongate.com; 824 Valencia St; ☺11am-7pm Sun-Wed, to 8pm Thu-Sat; ☐12, 14, 33, 49, Ⓑ16th St Mission) Salvador Dalí probably would've shopped here for all his taxidermy and gardening needs. Get a surrealist home makeover with animal-skull puppets, terrariums sprouting from lab beakers and teddy-bear heads mounted like hunting trophies. The kids' shop down the street (at 766 Valencia) maximizes playtime with volcano-making kits, shadow-puppet theaters and solar-powered dollhouses. Check DIY taxidermy and amulet-making workshop dates online.

TINA FREY HOMEWARES
(☑415-223-4710; www.tinafreydesigns.com; 1278 Minnesota St; ☺9am-5pm Mon-Fri; ☐48, Ⓜ T) Popsicles, tide pools, stained glass: Tina Frey's hand-cast vessels light up rooms and fire up neurons with their hypnotic, translucent color. If the urge to lick them becomes overwhelming, don't worry: they're made of food-safe resin. You may spot her work at Barneys and other exclusive retailers, but at Tina's studio you can snap up limited-edition works and sought-after copper-resin designs.

🏃 SPORTS & ACTIVITIES

⭐**PRECITA EYES MISSION MURAL TOURS** WALKING
Map p302 (☑415-285-2287; www.precitaeyes.org; 2981 24th St; adult $15-20, child $3; ♿; ☐12, 14, 48, 49, Ⓑ24th St Mission) Muralists lead weekend walking tours covering 60 to 70 Mission murals within a six- to 10-block radius of mural-bedecked Balmy Alley (p146). Tours last 90 minutes to two hours and 15 minutes. Proceeds fund mural upkeep at this community arts nonprofit.

⭐**18 REASONS** COOKING
Map p302 (☑415-568-2710; www.18reasons.org; 3674 18th St; classes & dining events $12-125; ♿; ☐22, 33, Ⓜ J) 🍴 Go gourmet at this Bi-Rite-affiliated community food nonprofit offering deliciously educational events: wine tastings, knife-skills and cheese-making workshops, and chef-led classes. Mingle with fellow foodies at family-friendly, $12 community suppers and multi-course winemaker dinners ($95 to $125). Check the website for bargain guest-chef pop-ups and low-cost classes with cookbook authors. Spots fill quickly for excellent hands-on cooking classes – book early.

⭐**URBAN PUTT** MINIGOLF
Map p302 (☑415-341-1080; www.urbanputt.com; 1096 S Van Ness Ave; adult/child $12/8; ☺4pm-midnight Mon-Thu, to 1am Fri, 11am-1am Sat, 11am-midnight Sun; ☐14, Ⓑ24th St Mission) Leave it to the town that brought you Burning Man and the Exploratorium to turn innocent mini-golf games into total trips. Urban Putt's course looks like a Tim Burton hallucination, from tricky windmill Transamerica Pyramid hole 5 to Día de los Muertos–themed hole 9. Enjoy big beers with wee snacks while putting, including mini corndogs and tiny chicken-and-waffle stacks on sticks.

SAN FRANCISCO 49ERS

The **49ers** (☑415-656-4900; www.sf49ers.com; Levi's Stadium, Santa Clara; tickets $43-569; ▣CalTrain Santa Clara Station) were the National Football League's dream team from 1981 to1994, claiming five Super Bowl championships. But after decades of chilly, fumbled games at foggy Candlestick Park, the 49ers moved to Santa Clara's **Levi's Stadium** in 2014. Some fans argue the team should be renamed, since Santa Clara is 38 miles from San Francisco. Locals hoped the move would lift the jinx, but the 49ers still lost when Levi's Stadium hosted Super Bowl 50 in 2016. To reach the stadium, take CalTrain one hour south to Santa Clara station, then catch the game-day shuttle. Since Levi's Stadium is in Silicon Valley, it's tricked out with technology, from the power-generating solar roof to wi-fi–enabled concessions. Maybe there's hope yet: in a super-stitious effort to align the team with the San Francisco Giants' bearded winning streak, the team's bread-loving mining mascot Sourdough Sam now sports a beard.

MISSION CULTURAL CENTER
FOR LATINO ARTS   ART
Map p302 (☑415-643-5001; www.mission culturalcenter.org; 2868 Mission St; ⊙5-10pm Mon, 10am-10pm Tue-Fri, to 5:30pm Sat; ➍; ▣14, 49, ⓑ24th St Mission) Join a class in tango, take up the congas, get crafty with your kids or silkscreen a protest poster at the printmaking studio at the Mission's Latino arts hub. Teachers are friendly and participants range from *niños* (kids) to *abuelos* (grandparents). Check the online calendar for upcoming gallery openings, and don't miss November's Día de los Muertos altar displays.

ANCHOR BREWING COMPANY   BREWERY
Map p305 (☑415-863-8350; www.anchorbrewing. com; 1705 Mariposa St; tours adult $20-25, child free; ⊙tours 10am & 1pm Mon-Fri, 11am & 1pm Sat; ▣10, 19, 22) Beer-lovers, here's your best-ever excuse for daytime drinking: the Anchor Brewing Company shares its steam-brewing secrets on tours with extensive tastings. The 45-minute tour covers Anchor's landmark 1937 building, shiny-copper equipment and 2017 extension, followed by a 45-minute tasting featuring several half-pints of Anchor brews. Reserve via website; pre-lunch tours are $5 off.

DANCE MISSION   DANCING
Map p302 (☑415-826-4441; www.dancemission. com; 3316 24th St; ➍; ▣12, 14, 48, 49, ⓑ24th St Mission) Find your niche at this nonprofit Mission dance hub, featuring contact improv, dance jams and classes in styles from Afro-Haitian to vogue – there's a class here for every interest and skill level. Check the web for dance showcases in the 140-seat theater, plus events and guest-artist workshops from beginner taiko drumming to dancing in stilts. To see how the pros get down, check out upcoming shows at the Dance Mission Theater (3316 Mission St).

SAN FRANCISCO
CENTER FOR THE BOOK   ART
Map p305 (☑415-565-0545; www.sfcb.org; 300 De Haro St; gallery free; ⊙gallery 10am-5:30pm Mon-Sun; ▣8, 10, 19, 22, 33) Bookish beauty is redefined daily at San Francisco's community press. Beyond traditional binding workshops, this nonprofit offers hands-on classes that teach you to make books that fit into matchboxes, pop up into theaters and store secret treasures. SFCB also hosts September's **Roadworks Street Fair**, where artists use a three-ton construction steamroller to make prints on the street.

MISSION BOWLING CLUB   BOWLING
Map p302 (☑415-863-2695; www.missionbowl ingclub.com; 3176 17th St; ⊙3-11pm Mon-Wed, to midnight Thu & Fri, 11am-midnight Sat, to 11pm Sun; ▣12, 22, 33, 49, ⓑ16th St Mission) Try bowling Mission style: six lanes in a mood-lit warehouse, where the bar pours smokey mezcal sours and Sonoma saison ales, and $1 of happy-hour orders of crispy brussels sprouts gets donated to local nonprofits. Book in advance online or bide your time for walk-in lanes at the bar. Under-21s allowed only at weekends before 7pm.

THE MISSION & POTRERO HILL SPORTS & ACTIVITIES

The Castro & Noe Valley

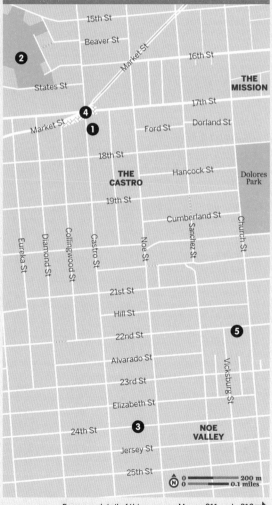

15th St

Beaver St

Market St

16th St

States St

THE
MISSION

Market St

17th St

Ford St

Dorland St

18th St

THE
CASTRO

Hancock St

Dolores
Park

19th St

Cumberland St

Eureka St

Diamond St

Collingwood St

Castro St

Noe St

Sanchez St

Church St

21st St

Hill St

22nd St

Alvarado St

Vicksburg St

23rd St

Elizabeth St

24th St

Jersey St

25th St

NOE
VALLEY

0   200 m
0   0.1 miles

Neighborhood Top Five

1 **Castro Theatre** (p175) Catching an evening film and hearing the Mighty Wurlitzer's pipes roar before showtime.

2 **Corona Heights** (p169) Climbing to the top at sunset and watching Market St light up below.

3 **24th Street** (p176) Dodging baby strollers as you window-shop indie stores.

4 **Jane Warner Plaza** (p169) Watching for kooky naked dudes.

5 **22nd Street** (p172) Not going over the handlebars while biking down SF's steepest street.

For more detail of this area see Maps p311 and p312 ➡

Lonely Planet's Top Tip

Historic streetcars run like toy trains along the waterfront and up Market St, from Fisherman's Wharf to the Castro, via downtown. Trouble is, trains sometimes get stuck in traffic and you can wait forever. Check arrival times at www.nextmuni.com, which uses GPS tracking; use the 'live map' to determine trains' exact locations. If the F-Market service is far away or running slow, take underground-metro K, L or M trains, which move (much) faster beneath Market St – same ticket, same price.

✖ Best Places to Eat

➡ Frances (p173)

➡ Starbelly (p172)

➡ Anchor Oyster Bar (p173)

➡ Lovejoy's Tea Room (p173)

➡ Poesia (p173)

For reviews, see p172 ➡

☕ Best Places to Drink

➡ Cafe Flore (p173)

➡ Blackbird (p174)

➡ 440 Castro (p174)

➡ Moby Dick (p175)

➡ Twin Peaks Tavern (p174)

For reviews, see p173 ➡

🔒 Best Shopping

➡ Sui Generis (p176)

➡ Artisana (p176)

➡ Podolls (p176)

➡ Local Take (p176)

➡ Cliff's Variety (p176)

For reviews, see p176 ➡

Explore: the Castro & Noe Valley

The Castro's main crossroads is at the intersection of Market, 17th and Castro Sts. Noe Valley extends along 24th St, a scant mile down Castro, over the (gigantic) 21st St hill. You can explore both neighborhoods in a few hours.

Mornings are quiet. The Castro is busiest afternoons and evenings, especially weekends, when crowds come to people-watch, shop and drink; at night expect to see 20-somethings stumbling down the wide sidewalks. Noe Valley is best midday and in the afternoon – there's not much open after 7pm, just some bars and restaurants.

If the 21st St Hill atop Castro St proves too daunting, bus 24-Divasadero connects the two neighborhoods, but it's notorious for gaps in service: expect to wait, or check www.nextmuni.com for real-time arrivals. In Noe Valley, shops on 24th St extend between Diamond and Church Sts; and on Church St, the restaurants and shops continue until the last stop on the J-Church line, around 29th St. Castro-area shops line Market St, between Church and Castro Sts, and Castro St itself, from Market to 19th Sts, with a few scattered along 18th St. Both neighborhoods are surrounded by residential streets, good for strolling, with many pretty Victorians.

Local Life

➡**Hangouts** The Wednesday-afternoon Castro Farmers Market (March through November) provides the best glimpse of locals, especially from sidewalk tables at Cafe Flore (p173).

➡**Drinking** The Castro is packed with bars, but most don't get going till evening. For listings, pick up a copy of *BarTab* magazine – supplement to the local, gay *Bay Area Reporter* newspaper.

➡**Paying homage** When a friend of the community dies, locals lay flowers and post pictures on the wall of the Bank of America building at 18th and Castro – always a touching sight.

➡**What (not) to wear** You may be tempted to flaunt your gym-toned physique in the sexy Castro, but once the afternoon fog blows, carry a jacket or shiver – locals spot tourists by their shorts and tank tops.

Getting There & Away

➡**Metro** K, L and M trains run beneath Market St to Castro Station. J trains serve Noe Valley.

➡**Streetcar** Vintage streetcars operate on the F-Market line, from Fisherman's Wharf to Castro St.

➡**Bus** Buses 24 and 33 go to the Castro, but there may be long waits between services. Buses 24 and 48 serve Noe Valley.

👁 SIGHTS

The principal sights are scattered around the intersection of Castro and Market Sts, with several up the surrounding hills. Start with the Castro, then cross the hill to Noe Valley if time allows.

★**CASTRO THEATRE** THEATER
Map p312 (☑415-621-6120; www.castrotheatre.com; 429 Castro St; ⊕Tue-Sun; Ⓜ Castro St) The city's grandest movie palace opened in 1922. The Spanish-Moorish exterior yields to mishmash styles inside, from Italianate to Oriental. Ask nicely and staff may let you peek, or come for the nightly cult or classic films (p175), or one of the many film festivals – check calendars online. At evening shows, arrive early to hear the organist play before the curtain rises.

GLBT HISTORY MUSEUM MUSEUM
Map p312 (☑415-621-1107; www.glbthistory.org/museum; 4127 18th St; $5, 1st Wed of month free; ⊕11am-7pm Mon-Sat, noon-5pm Sun, closed Tue fall-spring; Ⓜ Castro St) America's first gay-history museum cobbles ephemera from the community – Harvey Milk's campaign literature, matchbooks from long-gone bathhouses, photographs of early activists – together with harder-hitting installations that focus on various aspects of queer history, incorporating electronic media to tell personal stories that illuminate the evolution of the struggle to gain rights and acceptance into the larger culture.

RAINBOW HONOR WALK LANDMARK
Map p312 (http://rainbowhonorwalk.org; Castro St, btwn 18th & 20th Sts; Ⓜ Castro St) Castro St got a major makeover in 2014, when the city doubled the width of the sidewalks, painted rainbow crosswalks at 18th St and laid into the concrete 20 3ft-square plaques honoring LGBT+ heroes – as diverse as Oscar Wilde and Sylvester, Gertrude Stein and Keith Haring – whose portraits are acid-etched in bronze and captioned with illuminating text. They look particularly fab at night, when new LED lights, mounted on the streetlamps above, cast changing colors onto the sidewalk.

HARVEY MILK & JANE WARNER PLAZAS SQUARE
Map p312 (cnr Market & Castro Sts; Ⓜ Castro St) A huge rainbow flag flaps above Castro and Market Sts, officially Harvey Milk Plaza.

Look closer and spot a plaque honoring the man whose legacy is gay civic pride and political clout. Across Castro, by the F-train terminus, is Jane Warner Plaza, where ragtag oddballs and kids too young for the bars congregate at public tables and chairs.

For more on Milk, wander down the Muni-metro stairs to see text and images of his life. Jane Warner was a much-loved lesbian police officer. Compared with loudmouth Harvey, Jane was modest – which makes it doubly ironic that in 2012 her namesake plaza attracted international attention for public nudity. Several flagrant exhibitionists lollygagged here dawn till dusk, casually splaying their legs at oncoming traffic. Their passive-aggressive behavior incited such an outcry that public nudity in SF was eventually dubbed illegal – but not a sex crime, just an infraction. Now it's legal to strip only at a handful of public events, like the Folsom Street Fair. You can still often spot the 'naked guys' at the plaza, only now they wear socks on their penises, posing for pictures with tourists by the F-Market streetcar turnaround.

CORONA HEIGHTS PARK PARK
Map p312 (btwn 16th St & Roosevelt Way; 🚌37, Ⓜ Castro St) Scramble up the rocky 520ft Corona Heights summit (aka Museum Hill or Red Rocks) for jaw-dropping, eastward 180-degree views. Come evening, the city unfurls below in a carpet of light. Take tiny Beaver St uphill to the steps through the bushes, then cut right of the tennis courts and up the trail. For an easier hike, enter via the Roosevelt Way side.

HUMAN RIGHTS CAMPAIGN ACTION CENTER HISTORIC SITE
Map p312 (☑415-431-2200; http://shop.hrc.org/san-francisco-hrc-store; 575 Castro St; ⊕10am-8pm Mon-Sat, to 7pm Sun; Ⓜ Castro St) Harvey Milk's former camera storefront is now home to a civil rights advocacy group, where supporters converge to sign petitions and score special editions of T-shirts by designers great and small.

BARBIE-DOLL WINDOW PUBLIC ART
Map p312 (4099 19th St; 🚌24, Ⓜ Castro) No first-time loop through the Castro would be complete without a peek at the Barbie-Doll Window – better called the Billy-Doll Window, a gay spin-off of Barbie, notable for its shockingly huge penis. Dolls are dressed – well, some of them – in outrageous

DAN HENSON/SHUTTERSTOCK ©

1. Castro Theatre (p169)
The city's grandest movie palace plays host to cult classics and festivals.

2. House in Noe Valley (p167)
The rainbow Pride flag is everywhere in San Francisco, and invented in the Castro.

3. Pride Parade (p21)
More than 1.2 million people participate in this Pride parade, the world's leading LGBT+ event.

4. Rainbow Honor Walk (p169)
The rainbow crosswalks at 18th St are part of the Rainbow Honor Walk, a permanent installation celebrating LGBT heroes.

costumes and arranged in miniature protest lines, complete with signs. One of them says it best: 'It's Castro, Bitch.'

RANDALL JUNIOR MUSEUM
MUSEUM

Map p312 (☑415-554-9600; www.randallmuseum.org; 199 Museum Way; ⊙10am-5pm Tue-Sat; P 🚻; 🚌24, 37, Ⓜ Castro St) FREE Kids go cuckoo for live-animal exhibits of urban wildlife – raccoons, owls, more raccoons – and earth-science exhibits at this oh-so-cute nature museum near the summit of Corona Heights Park (p169). Don't miss the Golden Gate Model Railroad Club, a thrilling display of vintage Lionel toy trains. Check the website for wonder-inspiring hands-on workshops. Call ahead; the museum was under renovation at the time of writing.

GOLDEN GATE MODEL RAILROAD CLUB
MUSEUM

Map p312 (☑415-554-9600; www.ggmrc.org; 199 Museum Way; ⊙10am-5pm Tue-Sat; P; Ⓜ Castro St) FREE Downstairs at the Randall Junior Museum, the Golden Gate Model Railroad Club showcases an eye-popping array of vintage Lionel trains.

22ND ST HILL
STREET

Map p311 (22nd St, btwn Church & Vicksburg Sts; Ⓜ J) The prize for the steepest street is shared between two SF streets: Filbert St (between Hyde and Leavenworth) and here. Both have 31.5% grades (17-degree slope), but this one's longer and there's barely any traffic on 22nd. Nothing quite beats the thrill of cycling down it, grabbing two fistfuls of brakes, trying not to go over the bars.

🍴 EATING

Most Castro restaurants lie on Market St, from Church to Castro Sts, and around the intersection of Castro and 18th Sts. In Noe Valley, find quick lunch spots along 24th St, between Church and Diamond Sts.

MEKONG KITCHEN
VIETNAMESE $

Map p312 (☑415-346-9701; http://mekongkitcheneatery.com; 4039 18th St; dishes $8-11; ⊙11am-2pm & 5:30-10pm Mon-Fri, 11am-10pm Sat & Sun; ☑; 🚌33, Ⓜ Castro St) A favorite spot for quick eats, Mekong adds a California spin to classic Vietnamese dishes, specifically pho (noodle soup) and rice-noodle bowls. In addition to the classic ingredients, it throws in an excess of fresh veggies, which lend a healthful crunch to every bite. Standouts include imperial rolls and five-spice chicken, plus good fried tofu for vegetarians.

SUPER DUPER BURGER
BURGERS $

Map p312 (www.superdupersf.com; 2304 Market St; burgers $5.50-7.50; ⊙11am-11pm; 🚻; Ⓜ Castro St) 🍃 Delicious greasy burgers made with top-quality beef, and fantastic milkshakes made with organic, locally sourced cream.

DINOSAURS
SANDWICHES $

Map p312 (☑415-503-1421; http://dinosaursrestaurant.com; 2275 Market St, lower level; sandwiches $7; ⊙10am-10pm; Ⓜ Castro St) Stellar Vietnamese sandwiches on crusty French bread – a fave for quick eats.

MYRIAD
STREET FOOD $

Map p312 (☑415-608-2220; www.themyriad.com; 2175 Market St; ⊙9am-10pm; 🛜🚻; 🚌F, J, Ⓜ L, M, N) When you're between meals and out of ideas to satisfy your pack of picky eaters, the Myriad is mighty handy. Inside the chilly warehouse storefront, rainbow-colored kiosks cover the spectrum from coffee to cocktails, baked goods to raw food. Spicy Hawaiian *poke* (raw-fish salad) is a welcome addition to the Castro's burger-or-burrito dining scene; DJs and piano players entertain at weekends.

NOE VALLEY BAKERY
BAKERY $

Map p311 (www.noevalleybakery.com; 4073 24th St; dishes $4-8; ⊙7am-7pm Mon-Fri, to 6pm Sat & Sun; 🚻; 🚌24, 48) Croissants, éclairs, and sandwiches on house-baked bread.

THAI HOUSE EXPRESS
THAI $

Map p312 (☑415-864-5000; www.thaihousesf.com; 599 Castro St; dinner mains $10-16; ⊙noon-10pm; 🚌24, Ⓜ Castro St) Of the many Castro Thai joints, this one's best for quality. And at lunch, good-value rice plates cost just $8 to $10. All hard surfaces makes it loud at peak times, but between lunch and dinner, when other restaurants close, Thai House remains open – ideal when you're jet-lagged and hungry between mealtimes. Expect the usual classics and nothing fussy.

STARBELLY
CALIFORNIAN, PIZZA $$

Map p312 (☑415-252-7500; www.starbellysf.com; 3583 16th St; dishes $8-25; ⊙11:30am-11pm Mon-Thu, to midnight Fri, 10am-midnight Sat, to 11pm Sun; Ⓜ Castro St) 🍃 The seasonal small plates at always-busy Starbelly include standout *salumi*, market-fresh salads, scrumptious pâté, roasted mussels with house-made sausage and thin-crusted pizzas. The barn-like rooms get loud; sit on the heated patio for quieter conversation.

ANCHOR OYSTER BAR — SEAFOOD $$

Map p312 (www.anchoroysterbar.com; 579 Castro St; mains $18-28; ⏰11:30am-10pm Mon-Sat, 4-9:30pm Sun; Ⓜ️Castro St) Since its founding in 1977, Anchor's formula has been simple: seafood classics, like local oysters, crab cakes, Boston clam chowder and copious salads. The nautical-themed room seats just 24 at stainless-steel tables; you can't make reservations, but for faster service sit at the marble-top bar. Or wait outside with vino on the bench until you're called.

ANCHOR OYSTER BAR — MIDDLE EASTERN $$

Map p312 (☑415-431-7210; www.lamednoe.com; 288 Noe St; mains $12-18; ⏰11am-10pm Mon-Thu, to 10:30pm Fri & Sat, 11am-9pm Sun; 🖉🚼; Ⓜ️Castro St) Zesty, lemon-laced Lebanese fare at friendly prices makes La Méd the Castro's meet-up spot. Chicken kebabs on rice pilaf are pleasingly plump; the *kibbe* harmoniously blends pine nuts, ground lamb and cracked wheat; and the smoky eggplant in the baba ghanoush was roasted for hours and isn't the least bit bitter about it. On rare warm nights, sit outside.

FINN TOWN TAVERN — AMERICAN $$

Map p312 (☑415-626-3466; www.finntownsf.com; 2251 Market St; mains $17-25; ⏰dinner 5-11pm; Ⓜ️Castro St) Owned by TV chef Ryan Scott, Finn Town reimagines classic American dishes – duck-confit pot pies, oysters Rockefeller, iceberg wedge with Stilton and dates – with big flavors and handsome presentation. The room nods to the *Mad Men*–inspired cocktail-lounge craze, with wood paneling, tufted leather, and honeyed light flattering to all. Reservations advised. Also a happening bar scene.

LOVEJOY'S TEA ROOM — BAKERY $$

Map p311 (☑415-648-5895; www.lovejoystearoom.com; 1351 Church St; high tea $16-29; ⏰11am-6pm Wed-Sun, last seating 4:30pm; 🚼; Ⓜ️J) All the chintz you'd expect from an English tearoom but with a San Francisco crowd: curators talk video-installation art over Lapsang souchong, scones and clotted cream, while dual dads take their daughters and dolls out for 'wee tea' of tiny sandwiches, petits fours and hot chocolate. Make reservations.

★FRANCES — CALIFORNIAN $$$

Map p312 (☑415-621-3870; www.frances-sf.com; 3870 17th St; mains $26-34; ⏰5-10pm Sun & Tue-Thu, to 10:30pm Fri & Sat; Ⓜ️Castro St) Chef-owner Melissa Perello earned a Michelin star for fine dining, then ditched downtown to start this market-inspired neighborhood bistro. Daily menus showcase bright, seasonal flavors and luxurious textures: cloud-like sheep's-milk ricotta gnocchi with crunchy breadcrumbs and broccolini, grilled calamari with preserved Meyer lemon, and artisan wine served by the ounce, directly from Wine Country.

★POESIA — ITALIAN $$$

Map p312 (☑415-252-9325; http://poesiasf.com; 4072 18th St; mains $19-31; ⏰5-10:30pm Mon-Sat, to 10pm Sun; Ⓜ️Castro St) An all-Italian staff flirts with diners at this unpretentious 2nd-floor bistro with a sunny yellow interior and comfy banquettes good for lingering long after a hearty dinner. Expect dishes you don't typically see at American-Italian restaurants, with standout house-made pastas and a stellar *branzino* (sea bass) cooked in parchment. Fun fact: this is where Oprah ate when she visited the Castro.

L'ARDOISE — FRENCH $$$

Map p312 (☑415-437-2600; www.ardoisesf.com; 151 Noe St; mains $19-39; ⏰5:30-10pm Tue-Thu, to 10:30pm Fri & Sat; Ⓜ️F, K, L, M, N) For date night with an all-local crowd, this storefront neighborhood charmer on a leafy side street is perfectly placed for some strolling hand-in-hand after dining on classic French-bistro fare, including perfect *steak-frites*. Dim lighting adds sex appeal, but the room gets noisy – especially at weekends – when the cheek-by-jowl tables fill. Make reservations.

🍷 DRINKING & NIGHTLIFE

Castro bars open earlier than in other neighborhoods; on weekends most open at noon.

CAFE FLORE — CAFE

Map p312 (☑415-621-8579; www.cafeflore.com; 2298 Market St; ⏰10am-10pm Mon-Fri, 9am-10pm Sat & Sun; 🛜; Ⓜ️Castro St) You haven't done the

Castro till you've idled on the sun-drenched patio at the Flore – everyone winds up here sooner or later. Weekdays present the best chance to meet neighborhood regulars, who colonize the tables outside, especially during the Wednesday-afternoon Castro farmers market. Expect good coffee drinks and great cocktails. The food's OK, too. Wi-fi weekdays only; no electrical outlets.

BLACKBIRD   GAY

Map p312 (☏415-503-0630; www.blackbirdbar. com; 2124 Market St; ☉3pm-2am Mon-Fri, from 2pm Sat & Sun; ⓜChurch St) The Castro's first-choice lounge-bar draws an unpretentious mix of guys in tight T-shirts and their gal pals for seasonally changing cocktails made with bitters and tinctures, good wine and craft beer by the glass, billiards and – everyone's favorite bar amenity – the photo booth. Ideal on a Castro pub crawl, but crowded – and earsplittingly loud – at weekends.

TWIN PEAKS TAVERN   GAY

Map p312 (☏415-864-9470; www.twinpeaks tavern.com; 401 Castro St; ☉noon-2am Mon-Fri, from 8am Sat & Sun; ⓜCastro St) Don't call it the glass coffin. Show some respect! Twin Peaks was the world's first gay bar with windows open to the street. The jovial crowd skews (way) over 40, but they're not chicken hawks (or they wouldn't hang here) and they love it when happy kids show up to join the party.

Ideal for a tête-à-tête after a film at the Castro, or for cards, Yahtzee or backgammon (BYO).

SWIRL   WINE BAR

Map p312 (☏415-864-2262; www.swirloncastro. com; 572 Castro St; ☉2-8pm Mon-Thu, 1-9pm Fri, noon-9pm Sat, to 8pm Sun; ☐33, ☐F, ⓜK, L, M) Other Castro bars are niche driven, but this wine shop–bar has universal appeal: reliably delicious wine at fair prices in friendly company. Come as you are – pinstripes or leather, gay, straight or whatever – to toast freedom with sublime bubbly after GLBT History Museum (p169) visits, or find liquid courage for sing-alongs at the Castro Theatre (p175) in flights of bold reds.

BEAUX   GAY & LESBIAN

Map p312 (www.beauxsf.com; 2344 Market St; cover free-$5; ☉4pm-2am Mon-Fri, noon-2am Sat & Sun; ⓜCastro St) Part lounge, part dance bar, Beaux has a changing lineup of live en-

tertainment, theme nights and DJ parties, including Pussy Party Wednesdays (for the ladies), Throwback Thursdays ('80s night), Manimal Fridays (plucked and primped go-go boys) and disco Saturdays (tip: find the mezzanine for best views over the floor). Arrive before 10pm to beat the cover.

440 CASTRO   GAY

Map p312 (☏415-621-8732; www.the440.com; 440 Castro St; ☉noon-2am; ⓜCastro St) The most happening bar on the street, 440 draws bearded, gym-fit 30- and 40-something dudes – especially weekend nights when go-go boys twirl – and an odd mix of Peter Pans for Monday's underwear night.

HITOPS   SPORTS BAR

Map p312 (http://hitopssf.com; 2247 Market St; ☉11:30am-midnight Mon-Wed, to 2am Thu & Fri, 10am-2am Sat & Sun; ⓜCastro St) If you thought homosexuality and team sports were incompatible, you haven't spent Sunday at Castro's first gay sports bar doing shots with softball leaguers, scarfing down fries and screaming at giant-screen TVs. It's hard not to love its collegial pub vibe, full-length shuffleboard table and fat, comfy bar stools – but, damn, it's loud.

LOOKOUT   GAY

Map p312 (☏415-431-0306; www.lookoutsf. com; 3600 16th St; ☉3:30pm-2am Mon-Fri, from 12:30pm Sat & Sun; ⓜCastro St) A favorite for its street-view balcony, Lookout packs in gym-fit 30-somethings. Monday's karaoke provides fun on the Castro's quietest night; DJs spin other evenings. Hot rugby players come by on Sunday afternoons for Jock. No cat-calling from the balcony, please!

THE CAFE   GAY & LESBIAN

Map p312 (☏415-523-0133; www.cafesf.com; 2369 Market St; cover free-$5; ☉5pm-2am Mon-Fri, from 3pm Sat & Sun; ⓜCastro St) The Cafe draws a just-over-21 crowd to its upstairs dance floor with kick-ass sound and high-tech lighting. Parties range from Latino to lesbian; check the calendar. If you're not dancing, cruise the open-air smokers lounge or shoot pool beneath trippy changing LED lights that make it hard to aim after your second cocktail.

MIDNIGHT SUN   GAY

Map p312 (☏415-861-4186; www.midnightsunsf. com; 4067 18th St; ☉2pm-2am; ⓜCastro St) Midnight Sun got a makeover in 2014, and the once dark and gloomy video bar has become one of the Castro's A-list places, especially for Friday's always-packed bear happy hour and on Monday evenings, when drag queen extraordinaire Honey Mahogany hosts her 10pm show. Other nights it's a reliable spot for strong drinks and good videos.

MOBY DICK   GAY
Map p312 (☎415-861-1199; www.mobydicksf.com; 4049 18th St; Wed night cover $5; ☺noon-2am; ⓂCastro St) The name over-promises, but not regarding the giant fish tank behind the bar, which provides a focal point for shy boys who would otherwise look at their shoes. Weekdays it's a mellow spot for pool, pinball and meeting neighborhood 20- to 40-somethings. Wednesdays at 11pm local bearded drag-celeb Grace Towers packs the joint for Dick at Nite.

MIX   GAY
Map p312 (☎415-431-8616; www.sfmixbar.com; 4086 18th St; ☺7am-2am Mon-Fri, from 6am Sat & Sun; ⓂCastro St) The last Castro bar to open at 6am, Mix is a must on a pub crawl. The low-ceilinged pool and bar area is appealing, but the open-roofed smokers patio has a better vibe. Expect gal-next-door lesbians, 20-something gay boys, trans pals and the odd stumbling drag queen. Great drink specials keep everyone happy.

EDGE   GAY
Map p312 (www.edgesf.com; 4149 18th St; ☺noon-2am; ⓂCastro St) When you're feeling kinda ratty and you're looking for a daddy, it's the Edge. And who says drag queens and leather men can't be friends? See how close they draw to one another on Musical Sundays, Mondays and Wednesdays, when everyone sings along to standards and show tunes.

HEARTH COFFEE ROASTERS   CAFE
Map p312 (www.hearthcoffee.com; 3985 17th St; ☺7am-3pm Mon & Tue, to 5:30pm Wed-Fri, 8am-5:30pm Sat & Sun, brunch 9am-2pm Wed-Sun; 🛜; ⓂCastro St) 🌱 At the F-Market terminus, Hearth is an ideal place to wait for the train on a foggy day, with a strong cup of single-origin house-roasted coffee or a big glass of Californian wine. Mornings they make outstanding pastries, notably croissants, and at lunchtime there's a daily-changing menu of terrific soups, organic salads and sandwiches.

BADLANDS   GAY
Map p312 (☎415-626-9320; www.sfbadlands.com; 4121 18th St; ☺2pm-2am; ⓂCastro St) The Castro's long-standing dance bar gets packed with gay college boys, their screaming straight girlfriends and chicken hawks. If you're over 30, you'll feel old (unless you're a chicken hawk). Expect lines at weekends.

TOAD HALL   GAY
Map p312 (☎415-621-2811; 4146 18th St; ☺2pm-2am, to midnight Sun; ⓂCastro St) Posses of pals get their drink on fast with Toad Hall's two-for-one happy hour till 8:30pm. You'll dig the smokers patio and little dance floor. The name derives from the Castro's original gay bar, forgotten until the film *Milk*, but this bears no resemblance to it.

☆ ENTERTAINMENT

Most of the shops lining Market and Castro Sts sell clothing, souvenirs and sex toys. For more family-friendly shopping, cross the hill to Noe Valley.

★CASTRO THEATRE   CINEMA
Map p312 (☎415-621-6120; www.castrotheatre.com; 429 Castro St; adult/child $11/8.50; ⓂCastro St) The Mighty Wurlitzer organ rises from the orchestra pit before evening performances and the audience cheers for the Great American Songbook, ending with: 'San Francisco open your Golden Gate/You let no stranger wait outside your door...' If there's a cult classic on the bill – say, *Whatever Happened to Baby Jane?* – expect participation. Otherwise, crowds are well behaved and rapt.

CAFE DU NORD/SWEDISH AMERICAN HALL   LIVE MUSIC
Map p312 (☎415-471-2969; www.cafedunord.com; 2170 Market St; ☺5pm-2am; ⓂChurch St) Rockers, chanteuses and other musicians perform at this former basement speakeasy with bar, restaurant and showroom, and the joint still looks like it did in the '30s. At midnight, look for half-price oysters and champagne. The Swedish-American Hall, upstairs, with balcony seating and Scandinavian woodwork, hosts bigger concerts. Check the online calendar at www.swedishamericanhall.com.

🔒 SHOPPING

⭐ **LOCAL TAKE** — GIFTS & SOUVENIRS

Map p312 (☑415-556-5300; http://localtakesf.com; 3979b 17th St; ⊙11am-7pm; Ⓜ Castro St) 🛋 This fab little shop next to the F-Market terminus carries perfect gifts to take home: SF-specific merchandise, all made locally. Favorite items include a miniature scale model of Sutro Tower; T-shirts emblazoned with iconic SF locales; cable-car and Golden Gate Bridge jewelry; woodcut city maps; knit caps; and snappy one-of-a-kind belt buckles.

⭐ **SUI GENERIS** — FASHION & ACCESSORIES

Map p312 (www.suigenerisconsignment.com; 2265 Market St; ⊙11am-7pm Mon-Sat, 11am-5pm Sun; Ⓜ Castro St) Emerge with confidence from this designer boutique certain that nobody but you will be working your new look. The well-curated collection of contemporary and vintage clothing skews towards dressy – best for those with fat wallets who fit runway-model sizes – but because it's mostly secondhand, prices are way lower than normal retail and occasionally even negotiable.

⭐ **CHARLIE'S CORNER** — BOOKS

Map p311 (☑415-641-1104; https://charlies-corner.com; 4102 24th St; ⊙9:30am-6:30pm Mon-Fri, 10am-5pm Sat & Sun; 🚼; 🚌24, 48, Ⓜ J) More than a bookstore, Charlie's Corner is a place for kids to explore ideas, creativity and storytelling. The playfully designed space is scaled to children, with a giant magic tree rising to the ceiling and munchkin-sized toadstools to sit on during daily story hours – given in English, Spanish and French, some with live music. See website for current calendar.

⭐ **ARTISANA** — ART, JEWELRY

Map p311 (☑415-500-2257; www.artisanafunctionalart.com; 3927 24th St; ⊙10:30am-6pm Mon-Sat, to 5pm Sun; 🚌24, 48, Ⓜ J) 🛋 Artisana sells functional artworks designed for daily use – or at least daily admiration. And they're made exclusively by small-batch artisans, some of them local. Look for stitched-leather hip flasks, sterling and turquoise jewelry, hand-thrown pottery, small-scale sculpture, beeswax candles, block-print note cards and other quality, gift-ready items and accessories that will mark you as a person of distinction and taste.

CLIFF'S VARIETY — HOMEWARES

Map p312 (www.cliffsvariety.com; 479 Castro St; ⊙10am-8pm Mon-Sat, to 6pm Sun; Ⓜ Castro St) None of the hardware maestros at Cliff's will raise an eyebrow if you express a dire need for a jar of rubber nuns, some silver body paint and a case of cocktail toothpicks, though they might angle for an invitation. The window displays here, a community institution since 1936, are a local landmark.

OMNIVORE — BOOKS

Map p311 (☑415-282-4712; www.omnivorebooks.com; 3885a Cesar Chavez St; ⊙11am-6pm Mon-Sat, noon-5pm Sun; Ⓜ J) Salivate over signed cookbooks by chef-legend Alice Waters and James Beard winner Charles Phan of Slanted Door; get a signed copy of *The Omnivore's Dilemma* by Michael Pollan. Check the calendar for standing-room-only in-store events with star chefs. Don't miss the collection of vintage cookbooks and rarities, such as a Civil War–era recipe book written in longhand.

PODOLLS — CLOTHING

Map p311 (☑415-529-1196; http://shopthepodolls.com; 3985 24th St; ⊙11am-6pm Mon-Fri, 10am-6pm Sat, noon-5pm Sun; 🚌24, 48, Ⓜ J) 🛋 Husband-and-wife team Josh and Lauren Podoll design and manufacture in SF their own line of clothing – easy-to-wear tops, bottoms and dresses, with snappy prints on sand-washed silk and handwoven cotton, plus a fab line of kids clothing – all sustainability manufactured. They also carry the work of other eco-conscious local designers, plus jewelry, gifts and ceramics made in the Bay Area.

DOG EARED BOOKS — BOOKS

Map p312 (www.dogearedbooks.com; 489 Castro St; ⊙10am-10pm; Ⓜ Castro St) The Castro's essential general-interest bookstore carries a mishmash of new and used books, with an emphasis on San Francisco literature, social justice, gay studies and small-press works. For a window on local activism and literary events, peruse the bulletin board at the back of the store.

GIDDY — CHOCOLATE

Map p312 (☑415-857-4198; www.giddycandy.com; 2299 Market St; ⊙11:30am-9pm Sun-Thu, to 10pm Fri & Sat; 🚼; 🚇F, Ⓜ K, L, M) Nothing compares to being a kid in a candy store, except being a Giddy adult. Every treat your mom used as bribery is here, with upgrades: Whoopie pies and s'mores are embedded in chocolate bars, and gummy Swedish fish come in regular red, extra-sour and chocolate-covered varieties. Host-gift hint: the Compartes' California Love dark-chocolate-covered-pretzel candy bar never disappoints.

HUMAN RIGHTS CAMPAIGN ACTION CENTER & STORE
FASHION & ACCESSORIES

Map p312 (http://shop.hrc.org; 575 Castro St; ☺10am-8pm Mon-Sat, to 7pm Sun; ⓂCastro St) Make more than a fashion statement in signature HRC tees, designed by Marc Jacobs, Kenneth Cole and other fashion-forward thinkers, with proceeds supporting LGBT civil-rights initiatives. Hopeful romantics shop for sterling-silver rings, while activists scan the bulletin board and petitions.

If this storefront seems familiar, you're right: this was once Harvey Milk's camera shop and one of the locations used in the Academy Award–winning *Milk*.

CASTRO FARMERS MARKET
MARKET

Map p312 (www.pcfma.com; Market St, cnr Noe St; ☺4-8pm Wed Mar-Dec; ⓂCastro St) Find local and organic produce and artisan foods at moderate prices, plus charmingly offbeat folk music March through December.

KENNETH WINGARD
HOMEWARES

Map p312 (⏻415-431-6900; www.kenneth wingard.com; 2319 Market St; ☺noon-8pm Mon-Fri, 11am-7pm Sat & Sun; ⓂCastro St) Upgrade from ho-hum IKEA to mod housewares that are positively scrumptious. The inventory changes often, but expect things like glossy tangerine vases, vintage tiki-fabric cushions and mood-setting, ecofriendly cork-shaded lamps, all priced for mass consumption.

WORN OUT WEST
FASHION & ACCESSORIES

Map p312 (⏻415-556-9378; http://worn-out-west-2nd-generation.myshopify.com; 2352 Market St; ☺noon-7pm Sun-Wed, 10am-midnight Thu-Sat; ⓂCastro St) Left your gear at home and want to dress like a slutty local? Find leathers, original-cut Levi's 501s, cockrings and tanks at this old-school-Castro used-clothing store. Good fetish wear at great prices. Not much for gals, alas.

RABAT
SHOES, CLOTHING

Map p311 (⏻415-282-7861; http://rabatshoes.com; 4001 24th St; ☺10:30am-7pm Mon-Sat, 11am-6pm Sun; ◻24, 48, ⓂJ) With frenetic collections of high-end and local designers – some of whom work in-store – Rabat offers style without sacrificing function, with Michael Stars tees and pieces from wrinkle-free Canadian brand Simply. The owner hits Europe's shows to personally select the bounce-in-your-step men's shoes and snazzy-but-flat women's shoes and boots.

UNIONMADE
CLOTHING

Map p312 (⏻415-861-3373; www.unionmade goods.com; 493 Sanchez St; ☺11am-7pm Mon-Sat, noon-6pm Sun; ⓂCastro St) Upgrade your casual-Friday look with Unionmade's gender-fluid mix of classic quality labels – American-heritage brands like Pendleton and Levi's Vintage, plus European staples like Il Bisonte leather goods and a fab array of handmade shoes by Red Wing and Alden. Be warned: prices are high (except for quality shoe polish), but the selection is smart.

AMBIANCE
FASHION & ACCESSORIES

Map p311 (⏻415-647-6800; www.ambiancesf.com; 3979 24th St; ☺11am-7pm Sun-Fri, 10am-7pm Sat; ◻24, 48, ⓂJ) Expect to find some super-cute outfit here that requires you to hit the town. Dresses are particularly good, emphasizing girly-girl casual. For bargains, start next door at the shoe-and-sale store. Shop sister locations at 1458 Haight St for teen-appropriate prom dresses, and 1858 Union St (p71) in the Marina for cocktail attire.

 ## SPORTS & ACTIVITIES

SEWARD STREET SLIDES
PLAYGROUND

Map p312 (Seward St, cnr Douglass St; ☺daylight hours; ♿; ◻33, ⓂCastro St) Like a mini luge, two parallel concrete slides snake down the steep hill at this tiny park in a residential area (where the neighbors don't appreciate hearing your squeals of joy). Bring kids: a park sign reads, 'No adults unless accompanied by children.' There's usually cardboard by the slides, necessary for descents, but BYO waxed paper for faster speeds. Wheeee!

The Haight, NoPa & Hayes Valley

Neighborhood Top Five

1 **Haight Street** (p180) Bringing back the Summer of Love: wearing flowers, making a manifesto, singing freestyle folk songs on the corner of Haight and Ashbury Sts, and following in the footsteps of psychedelic rock gods.

2 **SFJAZZ** (p189) Toasting jazz giants between sets in front of Sandow Birk's tiled music-history mural.

3 **Alamo Square Park** (p181) Admiring Victorian mansions that have hosted earthquake refugees and hippie communes, speakeasies and satanic rites.

4 **Patricia's Green** (p181) Browsing local designs, downing coffee and pints, and catching free movies in this shipping-container social hub.

5 **Bound Together Anarchist Book Collective** (p190) Check out the *Anarchists of the Americas* mural, peruse prison lit and browse radical comics at this volunteer-run outpost of Left Coast ideas.

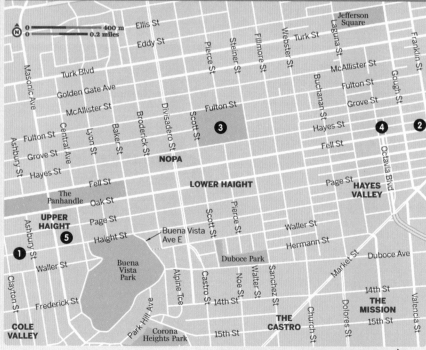

For more detail of this area see Maps p314 and p316 ➡

Explore: The Haight, NoPa & Hayes Valley

Pick up picnic fixings for lunch amid Victorians atop Alamo Square Park (p181) – or, in case of fog, brunch in NoPa. Take a **tour of hippie history** (Map p314; ☑415-863-1621; www.haightashburytour.com; adult/under 10yr $20/free; ☺10:30am Tue & Sat, 2pm Fri; ♿; ▣6, 7, ⓂN) in the upper Haight, then go highbrow with Hayes Valley boutiques and fine dining, or hunker down in the Lower Haight with skate-art openings, Rosamunde (p183) sausages and Toronado (p188) beer. Overcome powerful bar-stool inertia for world-class SFJAZZ (p189) shows or epic mosh-pit action at the Independent (p190).

Local Life

➡**Cheap eats with fancy drinks** Go high/low with Rosamunde sausages (p183) and Toronado Belgian ales (p188), oyster po' boy sliders and rare bourbon at Alembic (p188), DragonEats (p183) duck *banh mi* and agricole-rum drinks at Smuggler's Cove (p186).

➡**Hangouts** Aspiring flower children and original-issue hippies gather at Coffee to the People (p189), skaters hit Haight St's downhill slide to Upper Playground (p192) street-art shows, and hipsters grab bites in NoPa before shows at the Independent (p190).

➡**Musical stylings** Go acoustic on the corner of Haight and Ashbury Sts, improvise at SFJAZZ (p189) workshops, belt it out at the **Mint** (☑415-626-4726; www.the mint.net; 1942 Market St; ☺3pm-2am Mon-Fri, from 2pm Sat & Sun; ⓂF, J, K, L, M), sing along at Martuni's (p189) or rock out at free concerts at Amoeba Music (p190).

Getting There & Away

➡**Bus** Market St buses 6 and 7 run up Haight St to Golden Gate Park. The 22 links Lower Haight to the Mission and Japantown/Marina. Bus 24 runs along Divisadero, connecting NoPa and the Haight to the Castro and Pacific Heights. Bus 37 connects the Haight and the Castro, bus 43 goes from the Upper Haight to the Marina, and bus 33 runs through the Upper Haight between the Richmond District and the Mission. Buses 21 and 5 connect Hayes Valley with downtown and Golden Gate Park.

➡**Streetcar** The N line offers a shortcut from downtown and the Lower Haight to the Upper Haight, and onward to Ocean Beach.

➡**BART** Civic Center BART station is four blocks east of Hayes Valley.

Lonely Planet's Top Tip

Dinnertime can divide friends into warring factions – one party insists on Chinese, a splinter group wants Mexican and a rogue element demands doughnuts. From 5pm to 9pm Thursday, there's a diplomatic solution at the corner of Stanyan and Waller: **Off the Grid** (www. offthegridsf.com). A dozen food trucks pull into the lot across from McDonald's – and, for little more than the price of a McMeal, you can get all three options. There's live music too.

Best Places to Eat

➡ Rich Table (p186)
➡ Cala (p186)
➡ Souvla (p182)
➡ Jardinière (p186)
➡ Brenda's Meat & Three (p182)

For reviews, see p182 ➡

Best Place to Drink

➡ Smuggler's Cove (p186)
➡ Toronado (p188)
➡ Alembic (p188)
➡ Aub Zam Zam (p188)
➡ Riddler (p188)

For reviews, see p186 ➡

Best Shopping

➡ Amoeba Music (p190)
➡ Bound Together Anarchist Book Collective (p190)
➡ Paloma (p190)
➡ Nancy Boy (p190)
➡ Tantrum (p191)

For reviews, see p190 ➡

 TOP SIGHT
HAIGHT STREET

Was it the fall of 1966 or the winter of '67? As the saying goes, if you can actually remember the Summer of Love, man, you probably weren't there. The fog was laced with pot, sandalwood incense and burning draft cards, and the corner of Haight and Ashbury Sts became the turning point for an entire generation.

Flashbacks are a given in the Haight, which still has its '60s tendencies. The fog remains fragrant downwind of neighborhood marijuana dispensaries, and tie-dyes and ideals have never entirely gone out of fashion – hence the prized vintage rock tees on the wall at Wasteland (p192) and organic-farming manuals in their umpteenth printing at Bound Together Anarchist Book Collective (p190). Ever since the Summer of Love, bummer trips and unfortunate itches have been mercifully treated gratis at the **Haight-Ashbury Free Clinic** (HealthRIGHT 360; ☎415-746-1950; www.healthright360.org; 558 Clayton St; ⊗by appointment 8:45am-noon & 1-5pm; ☐6, 7, 33, 37, 43, Ⓜ N). To see where rock-star residents lived and loved freely, take a self-guided Flashback Walking Tour (p187). And at the corner of Haight and Cole, Joana Zegri's 1967 *Evolution Rainbow* mural shows how life forms evolved from the Pleistocene era to the Age of Aquarius.

Since the '60s, Haight St has separated into two camps, divided by the Divisadero St strip of indie boutiques, trendy bars and restaurants now called **NoPa** (North of the Panhandle). The **Upper Haight** specializes in potent coffee, radical literature and retail therapy for rebels, while the **Lower Haight** has better beer selections and more economic and ethnic diversity.

Above: Amoeba Music (p190)

DON'T MISS

➜ Mysterious 4:20 clock at Haight and Ashbury Sts

➜ *Anarchists of the Americas* mural at Bound Together Anarchist Book Collective

PRACTICALITIES

➜ Map p314, C4

➜ Haight St, btwn Fillmore & Stanyan Sts

➜ ☐7, 22, 33, 43, Ⓜ N

👁 SIGHTS

Weekends are a major scene in the Upper Haight, with hippies reminiscing about glory days, suburban punks wearing too much aftershave, earnest Green Party candidates campaigning steadily and street musicians playing a mean banjo. Wedged between the Lower Haight and Civic Center, Hayes Valley packs in many of the city's best restaurants, design boutiques and two low-key landmarks: the Zen Center and SFJAZZ.

HAIGHT STREET   STREET
See p180.

ZEN CENTER   HISTORIC BUILDING
Map p316 (📞415-863-3136; http://sfzc.org; 300 Page St; ⏰9:30am-12:30pm & 1:30-4pm Mon-Fri, 8:30am-noon Sat; 🚌6, 7, 21, 22) With its sunny courtyard and generous cased windows, this uplifting 1922 Italianate brick building is an interfaith landmark. Since 1969 it's been home to the largest Buddhist community outside Asia. Before she built Hearst Castle, Julia Morgan (California's first licensed woman architect) designed this Italianate brick structure to house the Emanu-El Sisterhood, a residence for low-income Jewish working women – note the ironwork stars of David on the 1st-floor loggia. Today the Zen Center opens to the public for visits, meditation, introductions to Zen practice and other Zen workshops.

ALAMO SQUARE PARK   PARK
Map p314 (www.sfparksalliance.org/our-parks/parks/alamo-square; cnr Hayes & Steiner Sts; ⏰sunrise-sunset; 👶🐾; 🚌5, 21, 22, 24) Hippie communes and Victorian bordellos, jazz greats and opera stars, earthquakes and Church of Satan services: these genteel 'Painted Lady' Victorian mansions have hosted them all since 1857, and survived elegantly intact. Pastel Postcard Row mansions along Alamo Sq's eastern side pale in comparison with the colorful characters along the northwestern end of this hilltop park. The northern side features Barbary Coast baroque mansions at their most bombastic, bedecked with fish-scale shingles and gingerbread trim dripping from peaked roofs.

PATRICIA'S GREEN   PARK
Map p316 (http://proxysf.net; cnr Octavia Blvd & Fell St; 🚌5, 21) The social center of hip, walkable, tree-lined Octavia Blvd is this pocket park, featuring Burning Man–inspired temporary sculpture installations flanked by picnic tables and a playground. At the eastern end is the PROXY project, a car-parking lot that's become a people lot with the inspired addition of shipping containers to serve as eating, drinking and shopping venues. Spring through fall, PROXY shows free Friday-night movies on an outdoor screen; see the website for showtimes.

HAIGHT & ASHBURY   LANDMARK
Map p314 (🚌6, 7, 33, 37, 43) This legendary intersection was the epicenter of the psychedelic '60s, and 'Hashbury' remains a counterculture magnet. On average Saturdays here you can sign Green Party petitions, commission a poem and hear Hare Krishna on keyboards and Bob Dylan on banjo. The clock overhead always reads 4:20 – better known in herbal circles as International Bong-Hit Time. A local clockmaker recently fixed the clock; within a week it was stuck again at 4:20.

GRATEFUL DEAD HOUSE   NOTABLE BUILDING
Map p314 (710 Ashbury St; 🚌6, 7, 33, 37, 43) Like surviving members of the Grateful Dead, this purple Victorian sports a touch of gray – but, during the Summer of Love, this was where Jerry Garcia and bandmates blew minds, amps and brain cells. After their 1967 drug bust, the Dead held a press conference here arguing for decriminalization, claiming that, if everyone who smoked marijuana were arrested, San Francisco would be empty. Point taken, eventually – in 2016, California legalized adult recreational marijuana use in private (read: not this sidewalk, dude).

BUENA VISTA PARK   PARK
Map p314 (http://sfrecpark.org; Haight St, btwn Central Ave & Baker St; ⏰sunrise-sunset; 🐾; 🚌6, 7, 37, 43) True to its name, this park, founded in 1867, offers splendid vistas over the city to Golden Gate Bridge. Consider them your reward for hiking up the steep hill, ringed by stately, century-old California oaks. Take Buena Vista Ave West downhill to spot Victorian mansions that survived the 1906 earthquake and fire. Note that after-hours boozing or cruising here is risky, given petty criminal activity.

LOCAL KNOWLEDGE

THE WESTERFELD MANSION

On the northwestern corner of Alamo Square Park (p181), you can't miss Westerfeld House, a gilded green Stick Italianate Victorian capped by a spooky watchtower. An extraordinary San Francisco survivor, the confectionary mansion was built by candy baron William Westerfeld in 1889, and miraculously survived subsequent incarnations as a czarist Russian speakeasy, Fillmore jazz musicians' flophouse, and the 50-strong hippie commune described in Tom Wolfe's psychedelic '60s chronicle *The Electric Kool-Aid Acid Test*. Filmed rituals held in the tower by Church of Satan founder Anton LaVey were psychedelic indeed, and hard work – hundreds of candles needed to be lit without catching the house on fire, and a grumpy lion somehow coaxed up four flights of stairs. The house's legacy of reinvention continues – today it's been painstakingly restored to Victorian glory by steampunk aficionado Jim Siegel, the former Haight teenage runaway who now owns Distractions (p192) on Haight St.

✖ EATING

Hayes Valley is SF's new culinary hot spot – reserve for memorable feasts, especially if you've got SFJAZZ, Opera or Symphony tickets. Haight St is a cheap-eats destination – worth the detour if you're on a budget.

★ SOUVLA   GREEK $

Map p316 (☑415-400-5458; www.souvlasf.com; 517 Hayes St; sandwiches & salads $11-14; ⊙11am-10pm; ☐5, 21, 47, 49, ⓂVan Ness) Ancient Greek philosophers didn't think too hard about lunch, and neither should you at Souvla's. Get in line and make no-fail choices: pita or salad, wine or not. Instead of go-to gyros, try roast lamb atop kale with yogurt dressing, or tangy chicken salad with pickled onion and *mizithra* cheese. Go early/late for skylit communal seating, or head to Patricia's Green (p181) with takeout.

★ BRENDA'S MEAT & THREE   SOUTHERN US $

(☑415-926-8657; http://brendasmeatandthree.com; 919 Divisadero St; mains $8-15; ⊙8am-10pm Wed-Mon; ☐5, 21, 24, 38) The name means one meaty main course plus three sides – though only superheroes finish ham steak with Creole red-eye gravy and exemplary grits, let alone cream biscuits and eggs. Chef Brenda Buenviaje's portions are defiantly Southern, which explains brunch lines of marathoners and partiers who forgot to eat last night. Arrive early, share sweet-potato pancakes, and pray for crawfish specials.

★ MILL   BAKERY $

Map p314 (☑415-345-1953; www.themillsf.com; 736 Divisadero St; toast $4-7; ⊙7am-7pm Tue-Thu, to 8pm Fri-Sun, to 9pm Mon; ☑🚼; ☐5,

21, 24, 38) Baked with organic whole grain stone-ground on-site, hearty Josey Baker Bread sustains Haight skaters and start-uppers alike. You might think SF hipsters are gullible for queuing for pricey toast, until you taste the truth: slathered in house-made hazelnut spread or California-grown almond butter, it's a meal. Monday is pizza night, and any time's right for made-in-house granola with Sonoma yogurt.

INDIAN PARADOX   INDIAN $

Map p314 (☑415-593-5386; http://indianparadox sf.com; 258 Divisadero St; share plates $7-14; ⊙5-10pm Tue & Wed, to 11pm Thu-Sat, 4-9:30pm Sun; ☑; ☐6, 7, 24, ⓂN) Hit the high-low sweet spot between the Upper and Lower Haight at this cozy storefront serving zesty Indian street food with inspired wine pairings. Coconut chutney melting into fluffy lentil pancakes deserves bubbles; paper cones of spicy mango and mint chutney on puffed-rice crackers require refreshing rosé; and masala-laced Sonoma lamb will have you waxing rhapsodic over deep red Refosco.

THREE TWINS ICE CREAM   ICE CREAM $

Map p314 (☑415-487-8946; www.threetwins icecream.com; 254 Fillmore St; cones $3-5.75; ⊙2-10pm Tue-Thu, to 11pm Fri, 1-11pm Sat, 1-10pm Sun, 3-10pm Mon; 🚼; ☐6, 7, 22, ⓂN) 🌱 For local flavor, join the motley crowd of Lower Haighters lining up for extra-creamy organic ice cream in local, seasonal flavors. To guess who gets what, here's a cheat sheet: Wiggle bikers brake for Dad's cardamom, foodie babies coo over lemon cookie and stoned skaters feast on California clichés (two scoops, pistachios, olive oil, sea salt, caramel and whipped cream).

DRAGONEATS
VIETNAMESE **$**

Map p316 (☎415-795-1469; http://dragoneats.
com; 520 Gough St; sandwiches & bowls $6-7;
⊙11am-6pm; ✐; ☐5, 21, 47, 49, ⓂCivic Center)
Velvety roast-duck *banh mi* gives opera
stars something to sing about at this sunny
Vietnamese deli, right around the corner
from San Francisco's opera house and symphony hall. Hungry divas order theirs with a
shrimp-roll side, while tenors in tight corsets
opt for five-spice-chicken 'fresh bowls.

LITTLE CHIHUAHUA
MEXICAN **$**

Map p314 (☎415-255-8225; www.thelittlechihua
hua.com; 292 Divisadero St; tacos $5-5.50, burritos
$8.50-12.50; ⊙11am-11pm Mon-Fri, from 10pm Sat
& Sun; ✐🖶; ☐6, 7, 21, 24) ✒ Who says sustainable, organic food has to be expensive
or French? Grass-fed meats and organic veggies and beans are packed into organic tortillas, all washed down with $4 draft beer.
Burritos are a two-meal deal, especially the
decadent *al pastor* (grilled pork with pineapple salsa and jack cheese) and garlic shrimp
(sustainably sourced). Kids menu available.

ROSAMUNDE SAUSAGE GRILL
FAST FOOD **$**

Map p314 (☎415-437-6851; http://rosamunde
sausagegrill.com; 545 Haight St; sausages $8-
8.50; ⊙11:30am-10pm Sun-Wed, to 11pm Thu-Sat;
☐6, 7, 22, ⓂN) Impress a dinner date on the
cheap: load up Coleman Farms pork Brats or
free-range duck links with complimentary
roasted peppers, grilled onions, whole-grain
mustard and mango chutney, and enjoy with
your choice of 45 seasonal draft brews at Toronado (p188) next door. To impress a local
lunch date, call ahead or line up by 11:30am
Tuesday for massive $6 burgers.

CHEZ MAMAN WEST
FRENCH **$**

Map p316 (☎415-355-9067; www.chezmamansf.
com; 401 Gough St; mains $9-22; ⊙11:30am-11pm
Mon-Fri, from 10:30am Sat & Sun; ☐5, 21, 47,
49, ⓂVan Ness) Quit pretending you're con-
sidering the sensible Niçoise salad and go
for the restorative brunch everyone needs
mid-shopping spree: crepes plumped with
decadent fillings, like prosciutto béchamel
or chicken with creamy mustard sauce. Bubbly by the glass and cinnamon-laced berry
pain perdu for dessert will leave you ready
to take Hayes Valley sales racks by storm.

RAGAZZA
PIZZA **$$**

Map p314 (☎415-255-1133; www.ragazzasf.com;
311 Divisadero St; pizzas $14-19; ⊙5-10pm Sun-
Thu, to 10:30pm Fri & Sat; 🖶; ☐6, 7, 21, 24) 'Girl'

is what the name means, as in, 'Oooh, *girl*,
did you try the wild-nettle pizza?!' Artisan
salumi is the star of many Ragazza pizzas,
from the Amatriciana with pecorino, pan-
cetta and egg to the Moto with Calabrian
chili and sausage – best with carafes of rus-
tic Tuscan reds or Fort Point beer.

LITTLE GEM
CALIFORNIAN **$$**

Map p316 (www.littlegem.restaurant; 400 Grove
St; $10-25; ⊙11am-9pm Mon-Thu, to 10pm Fri,
9am-10pm Sat, to 9pm Sun; ✐; ☐5, 21, 49) ✒
Sunny Golden State flavors and easygoing
elegance make Little Gem a true San Francisco treasure. Chef David Cruz combines
fine-dining trade craft honed at French
Laundry with a Californian devotion to
cross-cultural soul food: he gives equal,
heartfelt attention to every julienned veg-
etable in Korean bibimbap, and slathers
Wagyu beef brisket with BBQ sauce that
tastes like a Napa summer's day.

NOJO RAMEN TAVERN
JAPANESE **$$**

Map p316 (☎415-896-4587; www.nojosf.com; 231
Franklin St; noodle bowls $16-18.50; ⊙5-11pm
Tue-Sat, 11:30am-2:30pm & 4-7pm Sun; ☐5,
6, 7, 21, 47, 49, ⓂVan Ness) Find moments of
clarity on foggy Hayes Valley nights with
restorative, eye-opening bowls of proper ra-
men. Housemade broth brings bottomless
flavor to modest bowls of noodles, topped
by house-specialty chicken any way you
want it – shredded, slow-braised, in meat-
balls or ground with spice. Get the optional
'spice bomb' and well-priced local beer and
wine by the glass.

MAGNOLIA BREWERY
CALIFORNIAN **$$**

Map p314 (☎415-864-7468; www.magnoliapub.
com; 1398 Haight St; mains $14-26; ⊙11am-11pm
Mon-Thu, to midnight Fri, 10am-midnight Sat, to
11pm Sun; ☐6, 7, 33, 43) ✒ Organic pub grub
and home-brew samplers keep conversation flowing at communal tables, while
grass-fed burgers satisfy stoner appetites
in booths – it's like the Summer of Love all
over again, only with better food. Morning-
after brunches of housemade sausage-and-
egg sandwiches and Thursday-night fried
chicken are plenty curative, but Cole Porter
pints are powerful enough to revive the
Grateful Dead.

BAR CRUDO
SEAFOOD **$$**

Map p314 (☎415-409-0679; www.barcrudo.
com; 655 Divisadero St; share plates $13-24;
⊙5-10pm Tue-Thu & Sun, to 11pm Fri & Sat; ☐5,

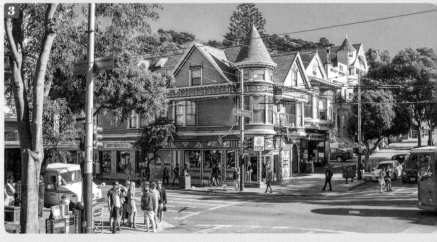

HAYK SHALUNTS/SHUTTERSTOCK ©

1. Alamo Square Park (p181)
Sun yourself while catching glimpses of the Transamerica Pyramid between the 'Painted Lady' mansions.

2. Shopping in the Haight (p190)
Head this way for anarchist literature, vintage concert tees or tasty goat cheeses.

3. Haight Street (p180)
Tie-dyes and Summer of Love idealism have never entirely gone out of fashion here.

VICTORIA R/SHUTTERSTOCK ©

6, 7, 21, 24) An international idea that's pure California: choice seafood served raw in the Italian style, with pan-Asian condiments and East–West beers. Start with Japanese Hitachino white ale with velvety avocado-*uni* (sea urchin) toast and graduate to potent Belgian Tripel ales with crudo platters featuring horseradish-spiked Arctic char. Happy-hour specials include $1 oysters, $6 chowder and $6 wine (5pm to 6:30pm).

★CALA   MEXICAN, CALIFORNIAN $$$
Map p296 (📋415-660-7701; www.calarestaurant. com; 149 Fell St; ⏰5-10pm Mon-Wed, to 11pm Thu-Sat, 11am-3pm Sun; taco bar 11am-2pm Mon-Fri; 🚌6, 7, 21, 47, 49, Ⓜ Van Ness) Like discovering a long-lost twin, Cala's Mexico Norte cuisine is a revelation. San Francisco's Mexican-rancher roots are deeply honored here: silky bone-marrow salsa and fragrant heritage-corn tortillas grace a sweet potato slow-cooked in ashes. Brace yourself with mezcal margaritas for the ultimate California surf and turf: sea urchin with beef tongue.

Service is set at 20% so that staff receive a steady paycheck – key to Cala's pioneering partnership with the city to employ former prisoners. Chef-owner Gabriela Cámara first gained renown for her upscale Mexico City restaurant Contramar – but here, at her first US restaurant, she's committed to upholding SF's time-honored Mexican-street-food traditions, with $3.50 tacos served in the back-alley bar at lunchtime. Mmmm – or, as the note on your receipt says, 'Immigrants make America great.'

★RICH TABLE   CALIFORNIAN $$$
Map p316 (📋415-355-9085; http://richtablesf. com; 199 Gough St; mains $17-36; ⏰5:30-10pm Sun-Thu, to 10:30pm Fri & Sat; 🚌5, 6, 7, 21, 47, 49, Ⓜ Van Ness) 🖋 Impossible cravings begin at Rich Table, inventor of porcini doughnuts, miso-marrow-stuffed pasta and fried-chicken madeleines with caviar. Married cochefs and owners Sarah and Evan Rich playfully riff on seasonal California fare, freestyling with whimsical off-menu amuse-bouches like trippy beet marshmallows or the Dirty Hippie: nutty hemp atop silky goat-buttermilk *pannacotta*, as offbeat and entrancing as Hippie Hill drum circles.

★JARDINIÈRE   CALIFORNIAN $$$
Map p316 (📋415-861-5555; www.jardiniere.com; 300 Grove St; mains $20-36; ⏰5-9pm Sun-Thu, to 10:30pm Fri & Sat; 🚌5, 21, 47, 49, Ⓜ Van Ness) 🖋 *Iron Chef* winner, *Top Chef Masters* finalist

and James Beard Award–winner Traci Des Jardins champions sustainable, salacious California cuisine. She has a way with California's organic produce, sustainable meats and seafood that's probably illegal in other states, slathering sturgeon with buttery chanterelles and lavishing root vegetables with truffles and honey from Jardinière's rooftop hives. Mondays bring $55 three-course dinners with wine pairings.

PETIT CRENN   CALIFORNIAN, FRENCH $$$
Map p316 (📋415-864-1744; www.petitcrenn. com; 609 Hayes St; mains $16-40; ⏰11am-2pm & 5-9:15pm Tue-Sat; 🚌5, 21) Leave gimmicky star-chef flagships behind on the waterfront and find higher ground in Hayes Valley with rustic French flavors and easy social graces. Michelin-starred chef Dominique Crenn offers her Brittany-inspired à la carte menu 5pm to 7pm daily, and serves a communal seven-course 'dinner party' from 6pm to 9pm ($87). Optional $65 wine pairings ensure easy conversation; service included in meal price.

ZUNI CAFE   AMERICAN $$$
Map p316 (📋415-552-2522; www.zunicafe.com; 1658 Market St; mains $12-33; ⏰11:30am-11pm Tue-Thu, to midnight Fri & Sat, 11am-11pm Sun; 🚌6, 71, 47, 49, Ⓜ Van Ness) 🖋 Gimmickry is for amateurs – Zuni has been turning basic menu items into gourmet staples since 1979. Reservations and fat wallets are key for oyster-and-martini lunches, but the see-and-be-seen seating is a kick and the local, sustainably sourced signatures beyond reproach: Caesar salad with house-cured anchovies, brick-oven-roasted free-range chicken with Tuscan bread salad, and mesquite-grilled organic-beef burgers on focaccia

🍷 DRINKING & NIGHTLIFE

Hayes Valley is high-rolling wine bars and sneaky rum punches, while Haight St is a beer bonanza.

★SMUGGLER'S COVE   BAR
Map p298 (📋415-869-1900; www.smugglers covesf.com; 650 Gough St; ⏰5pm-1:15am; 🚌5, 21, 47, 49, Ⓜ Civic Center, Ⓑ Civic Center) Yo-ho-ho and a bottle of rum...wait, make that a Dead Reckoning (Nicaraguan rum, port, pineapple and bitters), unless you'll split

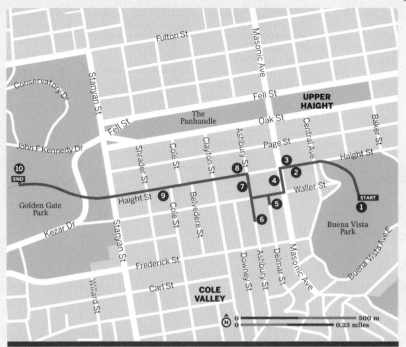

🏃 Neighborhood Walk
Haight Flashback

START BUENA VISTA PARK
END GOLDEN GATE PARK
LENGTH 1.3 MILES; ONE HOUR

Start in ❶**Buena Vista Park** (p181), with panoramic city views that moved San Franciscans to tears after the 1906 earthquake.

Heading west up Haight St, you may recognize Emma Goldman and Sacco and Vanzetti in the *Anarchists of the Americas* mural at ❷**Bound Together Anarchist Book Collective** (p190) – if you don't, staff can provide you with some comics by way of introduction. Continuing west, you can't miss ❸**Magnolia Brewery** (p183), named after a Grateful Dead song.

Neighborhood old-timers claim that the Symbionese Liberation Army used ❹**1235 Masonic Ave** as a safe house to hold kidnapped-heiress-turned-revolutionary-bankrobber Patty Hearst.

Turning right onto Waller St, you'll notice a narrow lane. The apartment at ❺**32 Delmar St** was the site of the Sid Vicious overdose that broke up the Sex Pistols in 1978.

A block over, pay your respects to the flophouse of Jerry Garcia, Bob Weir and Pigpen at the ❻**Grateful Dead House** (p181), site of a scandalous 1967 drug bust – and a landmark press conference demanding the decriminalization of marijuana. Fifty years later, California is finally complying.

Down the block, ❼**635 Ashbury St** is one of many SF addresses for Janis Joplin, who had a hard time hanging onto leases in the 1960s – but, as she sang, 'Freedom's just another word for nothin' left to lose.'

At the corner of Haight and Ashbury, you'll notice that the ❽**clock** overhead always reads 4:20, better known in 'Hashbury' as International Bong-Hit Time. At the corner of Haight and Cole Sts – across from the apartment where Charles Manson once lived – you'll spot a Summer of Love relic: Joana Zegri's 1967 ❾**Evolution Rainbow mural**. Follow your bliss to the drum circle at ❿**Hippie Hill in Golden Gate Park**, where free spirits have gathered since the '60s to tune in, turn on and flail to the beat.

the flaming Scorpion Bowl? Pirates are bedeviled by choice at this Barbary Coast–shipwreck tiki bar, hidden behind tinted-glass doors. With 550 rums and 70-plus cocktails gleaned from rum-running around the world – and $2 off 5pm to 6pm daily – you won't be dry-docked long.

★ BLUE BOTTLE COFFEE KIOSK   CAFE

Map p316 (www.bluebottlecoffee.net; 315 Linden St; ☺7am-6pm Mon-Sat, from 8am Sun; ⬛5, 21, 47, 49, ⓂVan Ness) Don't mock SF's coffee geekery until you've tried the elixir emerging from this back-alley garage-door kiosk. The Bay Area's Blue Bottle built its reputation with microroasted organic coffee – especially Blue Bottle–invented, off-the-menu Gibraltar, the barista-favorite drink with foam and espresso poured together into the eponymous short glass. Expect a (short) wait and seats outside on creatively repurposed traffic curbs.

★ TORONADO   PUB

Map p314 (☎415-863-2276; www.toronado.com; 547 Haight St; ☺11:30am-2am; ⬛6, 7, 22, ⓂN) Glory hallelujah, beer-lovers: your prayers are answered. Genuflect before the chalkboard altar that lists 40-plus beers on tap and hundreds more bottled, including sensational seasonal microbrews. Bring cash for all-day happy hours and score sausages from Rosamunde (p183) to accompany ale made by Trappist monks. It sometimes gets too loud to hear your date talk, but you'll hear angels sing.

★ AUB ZAM ZAM   BAR

Map p314 (☎415-861-2545; 1633 Haight St; ☺3pm-2am Mon-Fri, 1pm-2am Sat & Sun; ⬛6, 7, 22, 33, 43, ⓂN) Persian arches, *One Thousand and One Nights* murals, 1930s jazz on the jukebox and top-shelf cocktails at low-shelf prices have brought Bohemian bliss to Haight St since 1941. Legendary founder Bruno used to throw people out for ordering a vodka martini, but he was a softie in the end, bequeathing his beloved bar to regulars who had become friends. Cash only.

★ RIDDLER   WINE BAR

Map p316 (www.theriddlersf.com; 528 Laguna St; ☺4-10pm Sun & Tue-Thu, to 11pm Fri & Sat; ⬛5, 6, 7, 21) Riddle me this: how can you ever thank the women in your life? As the Riddler's all-women sommelier-chef-investor team points out, champagne makes a fine start. Bubbles begin at $12 and include

Veuve Cliquot, the brand named after the woman who invented riddling, the process that gives champagne its unclouded sparkle.

ALEMBIC   BAR

Map p314 (☎415-666-0822; www.alembicbar.com; 1725 Haight St; ☺4pm-midnight Mon & Tue, to 2am Wed-Fri, 2pm-2am Sat, 2pm-midnight Sun; ⬛6, 7, 33, 37, 43, ⓂN) The tin ceilings are hammered and the floors stomped, but drinks expertly crafted from 250 specialty spirits aren't made for pounding – hence the 'No Red Bull/No Jägermeister' sign and the dainty duck-heart bar snacks. 'Blood In, Blood Out' cocktails (rye, blood-orange shrub, egg white) prompt eternal Haight debates (Janis or Jimi?), but everyone loves the Sourdough (rum, grapefruit bitters, sourdough).

RITUAL COFFEE   CAFE

Map p316 (www.ritualroasters.com; PROXY, 432b Octavia St; ☺7am-7pm; ⬛5, 21, 47, 49) The Hayes Valley shipping-container outpost of the Mission roastery offers creamy single-origin espresso and powerful pour-overs to rival those at Blue Bottle around the corner...but beware: those are fighting words among SF's hard-core coffee loyalists.

MADRONE ART BAR   BAR

Map p314 (☎415-241-0202; www.madroneartbar.com; 500 Divisadero St; cover free-$5; ☺4pm-2am Tue-Sat, 3pm-1:30am Sun; ⬛5, 6, 7, 21, 24) Drinking becomes an art form at this Victorian parlor crammed with graffiti installations and absinthe fountains. Motown Mondays feature the Ike Turner drink special (Hennessy served with a slap) but nothing beats Purple Thriller mash-ups at the monthly Prince versus Michael Jackson throw-down. Performers redefine genres: punk-grass (bluegrass and punk), blunt-funk (reggae and soul) and church, no chaser (Sunday-morning jazz organ). Cash only.

NOC NOC   BAR

Map p314 (☎415-861-5811; www.nocnocs.com; 557 Haight St; ☺5pm-2am Mon-Thu, from 3:30pm Fri, from 3pm Sat & Sun; ⬛6, 7, 22, 24, ⓂN) Who's there? Steampunk hackers, anarchist graffiti artists, electronica DJs practicing for Burning Man and other San Francisco characters straight out of an R Crumb comic, that's who. Happy hour from 5pm to 7pm daily brings $3 local drafts, but mixing black-and-tans with potent house sake will Noc-knock you off your junkyard-art stool.

MARTUNI'S
GAY & LESBIAN

Map p316 (☎415-241-0205; 4 Valencia St; ⏰2pm-2am; ☒6, 7, Ⓜ Van Ness) Slip behind the velvet curtains to see who's tickling the ivories at the city's top piano bar, where the rainbow spectrum of regulars seem to have memorized every lyric in the great American songbook. Comedy nights are a blast and sing-alongs a given – especially after a couple of top-notch watermelon, pepper-cucumber, lemon-drop or chocolate martinis under $10.

COFFEE TO THE PEOPLE
CAFE

Map p314 (☎415-626-2435; 1206 Masonic Ave; ⏰6am-7pm Mon-Fri, 7am-7:30pm Sat & Sun; ☎; ☒6, 7, 33, 37, 43) ✐ The people united will never be decaffeinated at this radical coffee house – dairy-free hemp milk and vegan cookies are optional. Choose a bumper-sticker-covered table to match your politics, admire hippie macramé on the walls and browse consciousness-raising books. Just beware the quadruple-shot Freak Out, which has enough fair-trade espresso to revive the Sandinista movement. Free wi-fi.

HÔTEL BIRON
WINE BAR

Map p316 (☎415-703-0403; www.hotelbiron.com; 45 Rose St; ⏰5pm-2am; ☒6, 7, 21, 47, 49, Ⓜ Van Ness) Duck into the alley to find this walk-in wine closet, with standout Californian, French and Italian vintages and a cork-studded ceiling. The vibe is French underground, with exposed-brick walls, surreal romantic art, a leather couch and just a few tables for two. Barkeeps let you keep tasting until you find what you like; pair with decadent cheese and *salumi* platters.

BIERGARTEN
BEER GARDEN

Map p316 (http://biergartensf.com; 424 Octavia St; ⏰3-9pm Mon-Sat, 1-7pm Sun; ☒5, 21, 47, 49) The faintest ray of sunshine brings lines down the block for beer on draft and bratwurst at Biergarten – wear sunblock, order two rounds of seasonal Fort Point brews at once and get the pickled deviled eggs and pretzels to share with newfound friends at communal picnic tables.

KITTEA
CAFE

Map p316 (☎415-658-7888; www.kitteasf.com; 96 Gough St; per hour $25; ⏰noon-4pm Mon, to 7pm Wed & Thu, to 8pm Fri, 10am-8pm Sat, 10am-7pm Sun; ☒6, 7, 21, 47, 49, Ⓜ Van Ness) San Francisco's cat café serves Japanese tea and feline cuteness for a good cause: all the kitties you'll meet are being socialized for adoption in partnership with Give Me Shelter, a nonprofit cat-rescue organization (volunteer sign-up online). Get *genmaicha* (toasted-rice tea) for here and that tubby tabby to go.

☆ ENTERTAINMENT

★ SFJAZZ CENTER
JAZZ

Map p316 (☎866-920-5299; www.sfjazz.org; 201 Franklin St; tickets $25-120; ♿; ☒5, 6, 7, 21, 47, 49, Ⓜ Van Ness) ✐ Jazz legends and singular talents from Argentina to Yemen are showcased at America's newest, largest jazz center. Hear fresh takes on classic jazz albums and poets riffing with jazz combos in the downstairs Joe Henderson Lab, and witness extraordinary main-stage collaborations ranging from Afro-Cuban All Stars to roots legends Emmylou Harris, Rosanne Cash and Lucinda Williams.

★ BOOKSMITH
LIVE PERFORMANCE

Map p314 (☎415-863-8688; www.booksmith.com; 1644 Haight St; ⏰10am-10pm Mon-Sat, to 8pm Sun; ♿; ☒6, 7, 43, Ⓜ N) Throw a stone in SF and you'll probably hit a writer (ouch) or reader (ouch again) headed to/from Booksmith. Literary figures organize Booksmith book signings, mass giveaways of George Orwell's *1984*, boozy book swaps and politician-postcard-writing marathons. At monthly Shipwreck events, local writers wreck innocent classics by turning them into hastily written erotica, read with theatrical flourish – expect heaving below decks.

★ INDEPENDENT
LIVE MUSIC

Map p314(☑415-771-1421; www.theindependentsf. com; 628 Divisadero St; tickets $12-45; ⊗box office 11am-6pm Mon-Fri, to 9:30pm show nights; 🚇5, 6, 7, 21, 24) Bragging rights are earned with breakthrough shows at the small but mighty Independent, featuring indie dreamers (Magnetic Fields, Death Cab for Cutie), music legends (Steel Pulse, Guided by Voices), alt-pop (the Killers, Imagine Dragons) and international bands (Tokyo Chaotic, Australia's Airbourne). Ventilation is poor in this max-capacity-800 venue, but the sound is stellar, drinks reasonable and bathrooms improbably clean.

CLUB DELUXE
JAZZ

Map p314 (☑415-552-6949; www.clubdeluxe.co; 1511 Haight St; cover free-$10; ⊗4pm-2am Mon-Fri, 3pm-2am Sat & Sun; 🚇6, 7, 33, 37, 43) Blame it on the bossa nova or the Deluxe Spa Collins (gin, cucumber, ginger, mint, lemon and soda) – you'll be swinging before the night is through. Nightly jazz combos bring the zoot suits and lindy-hoppers to the dance floor. Expect mood lighting, cats who wear hats well and dames who can swill highballs without losing their matte red lipstick.

🛍 SHOPPING

Discover local designers in Hayes Valley and vintage signature pieces in the Upper Haight.

★ BOUND TOGETHER
ANARCHIST BOOK COLLECTIVE
BOOKS

Map p314 (☑415-431-8355; http://bound togetherbooks.wordpress.com; 1369 Haight St; ⊗11:30am-7:30pm; 🚇6, 7, 33, 37, 43) Since 1976 this volunteer-run, nonprofit anarchist bookstore has kept free thinkers supplied with organic-permaculture manuals, prison literature and radical comics, while coordinating the annual spring Anarchist Book Fair and restoring its *Anarchists of the Americas* storefront mural – makes us tools of the state look like slackers.

★ AMOEBA MUSIC
MUSIC

Map p314 (☑415-831-1200; www.amoeba.com; 1855 Haight St; ⊗11am-8pm; 🚇6, 7, 33, 43, Ⓜ N) 🍃 Enticements are hardly necessary to lure the masses to the West Coast's most eclectic collection of new and used music and video, but Amoeba offers listening sta-

tions, free 'zines with uncannily accurate staff reviews, and a free concert series that recently starred the Violent Femmes, Kehlani, Billy Bragg and Mike Doughty – plus a foundation that's saved one million acres of rainforest.

★ PALOMA
FASHION & ACCESSORIES

Map p316 (https://instagram.com/paloma hayesvalley; 112 Gough St; ⊗noon-7pm Tue-Sat; 🚇5, 6, 7, 21, 47, 49, Ⓜ Van Ness) Like raiding a surrealist's attic, this SF maker collective yields highly unlikely, imaginatively reinvented finds. Don't be surprised to discover billiard-ball cocktail rings, hand-patched indigo scarves, or real buffalo nickels adorning handbags made on-site by artisan Laureano Faedi. On SF-history T-shirts, Faedi emblazons insignias from bizarre bygone businesses, from Playland at the Beach to Topsy's Roost, SF's chicken-themed speakeasy.

★ NANCY BOY
COSMETICS

Map p316 (☑415-552-3636; www.nancyboy.com; 347 Hayes St; ⊗11am-7pm Mon-Sat, to 6pm Sun; 🚇5, 21, 47, 49) All you closet pomaders and after-sun balmers: wear those potions with pride, without feeling like the dupe of some cosmetics conglomerate. Clever Nancy Boy knows you'd rather pay for the product than for advertising campaigns featuring the starlet du jour, and delivers locally made wares with effective plant oils that are tested on boyfriends, never animals.

★ RARE DEVICE
GIFTS & SOUVENIRS

Map p314 (☑415-863-3969; www.raredevice.net; 600 Divisadero St; ⊗noon-8pm Mon-Fri, 11am-7pm Sat & Sun; 🚇5, 6, 7, 21, 24) Sly San Francisco wit is the rare device that makes this well-curated selection of gifts for all ages so irresistible. Charcoal chef soap scrubs off leftover burrito, SF-map play mats let babies drool all over the Golden Gate Bridge, Saguaro macramé statement necklaces bring uptown fashion down to earth, and Little Otsu's un-planner finds time for joy in start-up schedules.

★ ISOTOPE
COMICS

Map p316 (☑415-621-6543; www.isotopecomics. com; 326 Fell St; ⊗11am-7pm Tue-Fri, to 6pm Sat & Sun; 🖤; 🚇5, 21, 47, 49) Toilet seats signed by famous cartoonists over the front counter show just how seriously Isotope takes comics. Newbies tentatively flip through superhero serials, while fanboys eye the latest limited-edition graphic novels and head upstairs to lounge with local cartoonists – some of whom teach comics classes here. Don't miss signings and epic over-21 launch parties.

★AMOUR VERT
FASHION & ACCESSORIES

Map p316 (415-800-8576; https://amourvert.com; 437 Hayes St; 11am-7pm Mon-Wed & Sat, to 8pm Thu & Fri, to 6pm Sun; 5, 21, 47, 49, Van Ness) Looking smart comes easy with effortless wardrobe essentials that casually blend style, comfort and sustainability. Wear your heart on your sleeve with feel-good fabrics ingeniously engineered from renewable sources, including Italian flax linen, eucalyptus-tree Tencel and Peruvian cooperative-grown organic cotton. Find soft, flattering pieces at down-to-earth prices, designed in San Francisco and US-made to last a lifetime.

★TANTRUM
TOYS

(415-504-6980; www.shoptantrum.com; 858 Cole St; 10am-7pm; ; 6, 7, 33, 37, 43, Van Ness) Overbooked kids and overworked adults deserve a time-out for Tantrum, delightfully stocked with musical otters, wooden ducks on wheels, and a mechanical seal kids can ride for a quarter. Mid-century-modern circus is the design aesthetic in new and vintage items, including stuffed circus elephants, magic bunny lamps and vintage pinafores worthy of *Alice in Wonderland*.

MAC
FASHION & ACCESSORIES

Map p316 (415-863-3011; www.modernappealingclothing.com; 387 Grove St; 11am-7pm Mon-Sat, noon-6pm Sun; 5, 21, 47, 49) 'Modern Appealing Clothing' is what it promises and it's what it delivers for men and women alike, with streamlined chic from Engineered Garments, luxe Dries Van Noten jackets, splashy graphic Minä Perhonen shifts and gallery-ready limited-edition tees by developmentally disabled artists at Oakland's Creative Growth. Fashion-forward-thinking staff are on your side, finding perfect fits and scores from the 40%-to-75%-off sales rack.

PIEDMONT BOUTIQUE
FASHION & ACCESSORIES

Map p314 (415-864-8075; www.piedmontboutique.com; 1452 Haight St; 11am-7pm; 6, 7, 33, 37, 43) 'No food, no cell phones, no playing in the boas,' says the sign at the door – but that last rule is gleefully ignored by drag stars, pageant dropouts, strippers and people who take Halloween dead seriously (read: all SF). Since 1972 Piedmont's signature getups have been designed and sewn in the city, so they're not cheap – but those airplane earrings are priceless.

COVE
GIFTS & SOUVENIRS

Map p314 (415-863-8199; www.covertcove.com; 683 Haight St; noon-7pm; 6, 7, 22, N) Sand-cast cocktail rings, succulents dripping from sea-urchin shells, scented candles in the shape of a doll's hand: such unique gifts lead grateful recipients to believe you've spent weeks combing San Francisco's curiosity shops. Owner Jean regularly stocks rare finds at reasonable prices and will wrap them for you, too. Call ahead; hours can be erratic.

GREEN ARCADE
BOOKS

Map p316 (415-431-6800; www.thegreenarcade.com; 1680 Market St; noon-8pm Mon-Sat, to 7pm Sun; 6, 7, 47, 49, Van Ness) Everything you always wanted to know about mushroom foraging, worm composting and running for office on an environmental platform – plus poetry and noir novels by SF authors. This bookstore emphasizes visionary possibility over eco-apocalypse doom, so you'll leave with a rosier outlook on making the world a greener place. Check website for author events, covering invasive species to electronic art.

ACRIMONY
FASHION & ACCESSORIES

Map p316 (415-861-1025; www.shopacrimony.com; 333 Hayes St; 5, 21, 47, 49, Van Ness) Working rooms is easy with Acrimony, purveyor of effortless California cool and subversive San Francisco humor. Start conversations with Rachel Comey's art-schooled graffiti tops, wisecrack in Gitman Bros' vintage pagoda-pattern shirts, match wits in his-and-hers bomber jackets and always get in the last word with 'As If' stud earrings.

LOVED TO DEATH
GIFTS & SOUVENIRS

Map p314 (415-551-1036; www.lovedtodeath.net; 1681-1685 Haight St; noon-7pm; 6, 7, 33, 37, 43, N) Stuffed deer exchange glassy stares with caged baby dolls over rusty dental tools: the signs are ominous, and for sale. Head upstairs for Goth gifts, including Victorian hair lockets and portable last-rites kits. Not for the faint of heart, vegans or shutterbugs – no photos allowed, though you might recognize staff from the Science Channel's *Oddities: San Francisco* reality show.

LOCAL KNOWLEDGE

HOMELESS KIDS IN THE HAIGHT

Ever since the '60s, America's youth have headed to the Haight as a place to fit in, no questions asked. But in 2010 San Francisco passed the controversial Sit/Lie Ordinance, making 7am-to-11pm sidewalk loitering punishable by $50-to-$100 fines. Critics note that the law has been primarily enforced in the Haight, ticketing homeless teens – but with 1145 shelter beds to accommodate 6400 to 13,000 homeless people citywide, many youths have no place else to go. Spare change is a short-term fix; consider donations to youth-service nonprofits instead.

RELIQUARY   FASHION & ACCESSORIES

Map p316 (☑415-431-4000; www.reliquarysf.com; 544 Hayes St; ⏱11am-7pm Mon-Sat, noon-6pm Sun; 🚌5, 21, 47, 49) Enter the well-traveled wardrobe of Leah Bershad, a former Gap designer whose folksy jet-set aesthetic is SF's antidote to khaki-and-fleece global domination. Hand-crafted and vintage items – peasant blouses, hand-knitted ponchos, silver jewelry banged together by Humboldt hippies – share the spotlight with cult-brand finds like orSlow selvedge denim, artfully draped Humanoid shifts and DS Durga's sexy unisex scents (Cowboy Grass, mmm).

BRAINDROPS PIERCING
& TATTOO STUDIO   BODY ART

Map p314 (☑415-621-4162; www.braindrops.net; 1324 Haight St; ⏱noon-7pm Sun-Thu, to 8pm Fri & Sat; 🚌6, 7, 33, 37, 43) Stick that stud where the sun doesn't shine with gentle assistance from SF's body-manipulation specialists. Braindrops' experienced professionals use laser-like precision instead of wobbly piercing guns, and the vast selection of body jewelry ranges from subtle opal nose studs to fossilized mammoth-bone ear spools. ID is required for all clients, plus accompaniment by legal guardian for minors.

WASTELAND   VINTAGE, CLOTHING

Map p314 (☑415-863-3150; www.shopwasteland. com; 1660 Haight St; ⏱11am-8pm Mon-Sat, noon-7pm Sun; 🚌6, 7, 33, 37, 43, Ⓜ N) 🕭 Take center stage in this converted-cinema vintage superstore in barely worn Marc Jacobs frocks, vintage concert tees and a steady supply of platform go-go boots. Hip occasionally verges on hideous with sequined sweaters and '80s power suits, but, at reasonable (not bargain) prices, anyone can afford fashion risks. If you've got excess baggage, Wasteland buys clothes noon to 6pm daily.

FATTED CALF   FOOD & DRINKS

Map p316 (☑414-400-5614; www.fattedcalf.com; 320 Fell St; ⏱10am-8pm; 🚌5, 21, 47, 49, Ⓜ Van Ness) Host gifts that earn return invitations to SF dinner parties come from Fatted Calf. This Bay Area *salumi* maker's showcase is a one-stop shop for California artisan foods, including goat cheeses, jams and heirloom beans – plus meaty house specialties from mortadella to duck confit. Don't miss Wednesday Butcher's Happy Hour (5:30pm to 7pm) for free bites, drinks and butchery demos.

UPPER PLAYGROUND   FASHION & ACCESSORIES

Map p314 (☑415-861-1960; www.upperplayground.com; 220 Fillmore St; ⏱11am-7pm; 🚌6, 7, 22, Ⓜ N) Blend into the SF scenery with a locally designed 'Left Coast' hoodie, bragadocious 'Hella Fresh' tee, handy BART-map smartphone case, and SF snap-back caps in classic canvas, badass leather and smart-ass tweed. Men's gear dominates, but there are women's tees on side racks, kids' tees in the back room and slick graffiti art in UP's Fifty24SF Gallery next door.

DISTRACTIONS   FASHION & ACCESSORIES

Map p314 (☑415-252-8751; 1552 Haight St; ⏱11am-7pm Sun-Fri, to 8pm Sat; 🚌6, 7, 33, 37, 43) Strap on goggles and hang onto your top hat: with steampunk styling from Distractions, tonight you're gonna party like it's 1899. This gold-rush mad-inventor look is SF's go-to alt-party style, from historically correct Edwardian-ball ensembles to postapocalyptic Burning Man getups. So hang a compass from your lace corset and rock that creepy whaler's mask – you're among friends here.

FTC SKATEBOARDING   SPORTS & OUTDOORS

Map p314 (☑415-626-0663; www.ftcsf.com; 1632 Haight St; ⏱11am-7pm; 🚌6, 7, 33, 37, 43, Ⓜ N) Big air and big style are the tip at this local skateboard outfitter, featuring artist-designed Western Edition decks by local guest artists. Show insider flair as you grab air on Mike Giant's SF Victorian deck or the Carlos Santana concert-photo deck, and rock the SF look with FTC chore jackets and caps. Ask staff about upcoming SF street games.

Golden Gate Park & the Avenues

THE RICHMOND | THE SUNSET

Neighborhood Top Five

① Golden Gate Park (p195) Doing what comes naturally: skipping, lolling or lindy-hopping through America's most outlandish stretch of urban wilderness, and racing bison toward the Pacific Ocean.

② de Young Museum (p196) Following Andy Goldsworthy's sidewalk fault lines to discover ground-breaking global art from Oceania to South Africa, Afghanistan to Alaska.

③ California Academy of Sciences (p196) Enjoying sunsets on the wildflower-topped roof and wild nights at kids-only Academy sleepovers and 21-plus NightLife events.

④ Coastal Trail (p205) Glimpsing seals, sunsets and shipwrecks along San Francisco's wild waterfront walk.

⑤ Ocean Beach (p199) Numbing your toes in the Pacific and expanding your horizons to Asia over bonfires in artist-designed fire pits.

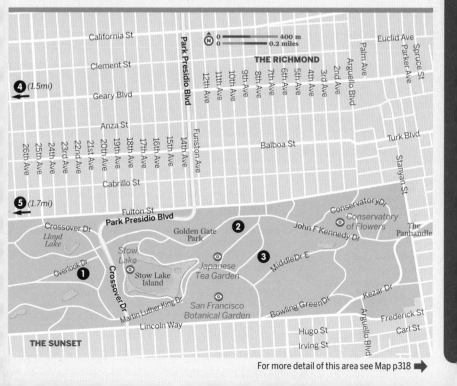

For more detail of this area see Map p318 ➡

Lonely Planet's Top Tip

Hear that echo across Golden Gate Park? It's probably a concert – and quite possibly a free one. Opera divas, indie acts, bluegrass greats and hip-hop heavies take turns rocking SF gratis, from the wintry days of June through golden October afternoons. Most concerts are held in Sharon Meadow or Polo Fields at weekends; for upcoming events, consult the park calendar at www.golden-gate-park.com.

◉ Best for Urban Wildlife

➡ Golden Gate Park (p195)

➡ Fort Funston (p199)

➡ Ocean Beach (p199)

➡ California Academy of Sciences (p196)

✖ Best Places to Eat

➡ Wako (p201)

➡ Dragon Beaux (p200)

➡ Outerlands (p202)

➡ Spruce (p201)

➡ Cinderella Russian Bakery (p200)

For reviews, see p200 ➡

♟ Best Places to Drink

➡ Plough & Stars (p203)

➡ Trad'r Sam (p202)

➡ Trouble Coffee (p202)

➡ Tommy's Mexican Restaurant (p202)

➡ Beach Chalet (p202)

For reviews, see p202 ➡

Explore: Golden Gate Park & the Avenues

Civilization is overrated, with its traffic jams and office blocks – but once you reach the Conservatory of Flowers (p197) in Golden Gate Park, that's all behind you. Hang out with blue butterflies in the rainforest dome at the California Academy of Sciences (p196), or globe-trot from Oceanic masks to James Turrell light installations in the worldly arts exhibits of the de Young Museum (p196). Enjoy a moment of Zen and green tea in the Japanese Tea Garden (p197), then summit Strawberry Hill for views past Stow Lake to the Pacific as red-tailed hawks swoop past.

Wander to San Francisco Botanical Garden (p197) for respite in the redwood grove before hopping the N streetcar all the way to Ocean Beach (p199). Stroll the 4-mile stretch of sand to the Richmond for decadent sushi at Wako (p201) and dangerous Hurricanes at Trad'r Sam (p202), or stay put in the Sunset for surf-shopping at Mollusk (p204) and organic Cali comfort food at Outerlands (p202). With food and fog like this, you must be in heaven.

Local Life

➡**Foggy days** Stay warm with Trouble Coffee (p202), matinees at Balboa Theatre (p203), noir-movie fedoras at Paul's Hat Works (p204), and sultry rainforest strolls inside the California Academy of Sciences (p196) and the Conservatory of Flowers (p197).

➡**Goose bumps, guaranteed** Get delicious chills with bare feet on Ocean Beach (p199), eerily lifelike masks at the de Young Museum (p196), cliff's-edge views along the Coastal Trail (p205) and steep concrete slides at the Children's Playground (p197).

➡**Out-there art outposts** Outlandishness is an SF way of life; take in the scene with Park Life (p203) art openings, original '60s Pop Art at Legion of Honor (p198) and gnarly surf photography at Mollusk (p204).

Getting There & Away

➡**Bus** Buses 1, 31 and 38 run from downtown through the Richmond, while 7 and 6 head from downtown to the Sunset. Buses 5 and 21 skirt the northern edge of Golden Gate Park, while north–south buses 28, 29 and 44 cut across the park. Bus 2 covers Clement St, 33 connects to the Haight and Castro, and 18 spans the Great Hwy.

➡**Streetcar** The N line runs from downtown through the Sunset to Ocean Beach.

TOP SIGHT
GOLDEN GATE PARK

When San Franciscans refer to 'the park,' there's only one that gets the definite article: Golden Gate Park. Everything San Franciscans hold dear is here: free spirits, free music, redwoods, Frisbee, protests, fine art, bonsai and bison. Thanks to SF's microclimates and multiculturalism, the park blooms year-round and lures visitors with world-class attractions.

Today you can cover more than 150 years of SF history with a stroll through the park's eastern end. Next to the grandly elegant Victorian Conservatory of Flowers (p197), the tiny Dahlia Garden (p198) is spikier than an SF mosh pit – and just uphill are the restored 1926 art-deco **Horseshoe Pits** (Map p318; https://goldengatepark.com/horseshoe-pits.html; ). West of Hippie Hill drum circles on Sharon Meadow are the quietly quaint Lawn Bowling Club (p205) and the contemplative valley of the National AIDS Memorial Grove (p197). Since 1887, the park's southeastern end has hosted the city's biggest children's playground (p197), complete with 1912 carousel and 1970s concrete slides.

Clustered around 9th Avenue are the de Young Museum (p196), California Academy of Sciences (p196) and Japanese Tea Garden (p197), plus some unexpected hidden finds: Druid altars in Monarch Bear Grove behind the baseball diamond, the ruins of a Spanish monastery in the San Francisco Botanical Garden (p197; pictured above), an island pagoda on Stow Lake (p197), and the Shakespeare Garden (p198) – a collection of 200 plants mentioned in Shakespeare's writings.

West around Martin Luther King Jr Dr are the Polo Fields, where the 1967 Human Be-In took place and free concerts are still held during Hardly Strictly Bluegrass. At the park's wild western edge, bison stampede quixotically in the Buffalo Paddock (p199) toward windmills and Ocean Beach (p199) sunsets.

DON'T MISS

- ➡ de Young Museum
- ➡ California Academy of Sciences
- ➡ San Francisco Botanical Garden
- ➡ Japanese Tea Garden
- ➡ Conservatory of Flowers

PRACTICALITIES

- ➡ Map p318, E4
- ➡ www.golden-gate-park.com
- ➡ btwn Stanyan St & Great Hwy
- ➡ admission free
- ➡ 🅿 👷 🎿
- ➡ 🚌 5, 7, 18, 21, 28, 29, 33, 44, Ⓜ N

EXCESS HUGGING

Though a local newspaper once cautioned that Golden Gate Park's scenic benches led to 'excess hugging,' San Franciscans have flocked to the park since its inception. On a single sunny day in 1886, almost a fifth of the city's entire population made the trip to the park – canoodling shamelessly, no doubt.

PLANNING

To plan a picnic, concert or protest in the park and get detailed maps, check in at **McLaren Lodge** (Map p318; ☏415-831-2700; www. golden-gate-park.com; 501 Stanyan St, cnr Fell St; ☉8am-5pm Mon-Fri; ☐5, 7, 21, 33) at the eastern entrance, under the splendid cypress that's the city's official tree.

ROAD CLOSURES

John F Kennedy Dr is closed to motor vehicles east of Crossover Dr (around 8th Ave) all day Sunday and Saturday mornings to accommodate runners, skateboarders, unicyclists and meandering dreamers.

De Young Museum

The oxidized-copper building keeps a low profile, but there's no denying the park's all-star attraction: the **de Young Museum** (Map p318; ☏415-750-3600; http:// deyoung.famsf.org; 50 Hagiwara Tea Garden Dr; adult/ child $15/free, 1st Tue of month free; ☉9:30am-5:15pm Tue-Sun, to 8:45pm Fri Apr-Nov; ☒; ☐5, 7, 44, ⓂN). The cross-cultural collection featuring African masks and Turkish kilims alongside California crafts and avant-garde American art has been broadening artistic horizons for a century, and its acclaimed building by Swiss architects Herzog & de Meuron (of Tate Modern fame) is suitably daring.

The 144ft sci-fi observation **tower** is one futuristic feature that seems incongruous with the park setting – but access to the 360-degree tower viewing room is free, and Ruth Asawa's mesmerizing filigreed pods make elevator waits worthwhile.

Upstairs, don't miss 19th-century **Oceanic collection** ceremonial oars and stunning Afghani rugs from the 11,000-plus **textile collection**. **Blockbuster basement shows** range from psychedelic hand-sewn hippie fashions to Ed Ruscha paintings of Route 66 gas stations – but rotating **main-floor installations** are just as riveting and diverse, from early Inuit carvings to documentary prison photography.

Access to the **garden cafe** is free, as is entry to the **Osher Sculpture Garden** and its low-profile star attraction built into a hill: James Turrell's **Skyspace**.

California Academy of Sciences

Leave it to San Francisco to dedicate a glorious four-story monument entirely to freaks of nature: the **California Academy of Sciences** (Map p318; ☏415-379-8000; www.calacademy.org; 55 Music Concourse Dr; adult/student/child $35/30/25; ☉9:30am-5pm Mon-Sat, from 11am Sun; Ⓟ☒; ☐5, 6, 7, 21, 31, 33, 44, ⓂN) ☏. The Academy's tradition of weird science dates from 1853, with thousands of live animals and 60 research scientists now under a 2.5-acre wildflower-covered roof. Butterflies alight on visitors in the glass **Osher Rainforest Dome**, penguins paddle the tank in the **African Hall**, and Claude the albino alligator stalks the **mezzanine swamp**.

In the basement **Steinhart Aquarium**, kids duck inside a glass bubble to enter an **Eel Forest**, find Dorys in the tropical-fish tanks and pet starfish in the hands-on **Discovery Tidepool**. Glimpse infinity in the **Morrison Planetarium** and ride the elevator to the blooming **Living Roof** for park panoramas.

The penguins nod off to sleep, but night owls party on at after-hours events. At the over-21 **NightLife**, nature-themed cocktails are served and strange mating rituals observed among shy internet daters (ID required; $15 entry; 6pm to 10pm Thursday). Kids may not technically sleep during Academy Sleepovers, but they might jump-start careers as scientists (ages five to 17, plus adult chaperones; $109 per person including snack and breakfast; events 6pm to 8am). Book online.

San Francisco Botanical Garden

Sniff your way around the world inside the 55-acre **San Francisco Botanical Garden** (Strybing Arboretum; Map p318; ☑415-661-1316; www.strybing.org; 1199 9th Ave; adult/child $8/2, before 9am daily & 2nd Tue of month free; ☺7:30am-7pm Mar-Sep, to 6pm Oct–mid-Nov & Feb, to 5pm mid-Nov–Jan, last entry 1hr before closing, bookstore 10am-4pm; ⛨; ☐6, 7, 44, Ⓜ N) ◢, from South African savanna grasses to Japanese magnolias. Don't miss the California native-plant meadow, redwood grove and **Ancient Planet Garden**, with plants dating back to California's dinosaur days. **Free tours** take place daily; for details, stop by the bookstore inside the entrance.

Japanese Tea Garden

Since 1894 this 5-acre **garden** (Map p318; ☑415-752-1171; www.japaneseteagardensf.com; 75 Hagiwara Tea Garden Dr; adult/child $8/2, before 10am Mon, Wed & Fri free; ☺9am-6pm Mar-Oct, to 4:45pm Nov-Feb; Ⓟ⛨; ☐5, 7, 44, Ⓜ N) has blushed pink with cherry blossoms in spring, turned flaming red with maple leaves in fall and induced visitors to lose all track of time in its meditative **Zen Garden**. The century-old **bonsai grove** was cultivated by the Hagiwara family, who returned from WWII Japanese American internment camps to discover that many of their prized miniature evergreens had been sold – and spent decades recovering the precious trees.

Stop by the **Tea House** for traditional green tea and fortune cookies – first introduced to the US right here, over 120 years ago.

Conservatory of Flowers

Flower power is alive and well at SF's **Conservatory of Flowers** (Map p318; ☑info 415-831-2090; www.conservatoryofflowers.org; 100 John F Kennedy Dr; adult/student/child $8/6/2, 1st Tue of month free; ☺10am-4pm Tue-Sun; ⛨; ☐5, 7, 21, 33, Ⓜ N). Inside this gloriously restored 1878 Victorian greenhouse, orchids command center stage like opera divas, lilies float in ponds and gluttonous carnivorous plants gulp insects.

Stow Lake

A park within the park, **Stow Lake** (Map p318; www.sfrecpark.org; ☺sunrise-sunset; ⛨; ☐7, 44, Ⓜ N) offers waterfall views, picnics in the **Taiwanese pagoda** and birdwatching on a picturesque island called **Strawberry Hill**. Pedal boats, rowboats and electric boats are available daily in good weather at the 1946 boathouse (p205). Ghost-hunters come at night seeking the **White Lady** – legend has it she has haunted Stow Lake for a century, searching these shores for her lost child.

National AIDS Memorial Grove

This tranquil, 10-acre **memorial grove** (Map p318; ☑volunteer info & tours 415-765-0497; www.aidsmemorial.org; Bowling Green Dr; ☺sunrise-sunset; ⛨; ☐44, 71, Ⓜ N) ◢FREE graced with poetic paving-stone tributes was founded in 1991 to commemorate millions of lives lost to the AIDS epidemic and to strengthen national resolve for compassionate care and a lasting cure.

Children's Playground

Kids have had the run of the park's southeastern end since 1887. Highlights of this historic **children's playground** (Koret Children's Quarter; Map p318; ☑415-831-2700; www.golden-gate-park.com/childrens-playground.html; carousel per ride adult/child $2/1; ☺sunrise-sunset, carousel 10am-4:15pm; Ⓟ⛨; ☐7,33, Ⓜ N) include 1970s concrete slides, a new climbing wall and a vintage 1912 carousel.

◉ SIGHTS

◉ The Richmond

GOLDEN GATE PARK PARK
See p195.

INTERNET ARCHIVE ARCHIVES
Map p318 (☑415-561-6767; https://archive.org/index.php; 300 Funston Ave; ☺events only; ☐2, 38) **FREE** Follow trails of deleted White House tweets, lost Grateful Dead tapes and defunct Nintendo gamer magazines to this 1923 Greek Revival landmark. In a former Christian Science church, the nonprofit Internet Archive hosts 20 petabytes (that's 200 million gigabytes) of bygone media, and counting. The archive is run by 100-plus dedicated volunteer archivists, depicted in ceramic sculptures by artist Nuala Creed. Check website for Friday visits (1pm to 2pm) and tours, often led by founder, internet pioneer and Alexa inventor Brewster Kahle.

LEGION OF HONOR MUSEUM
Map p318 (☑415-750-3600; http://legionofhonor.famsf.org; 100 34th Ave; adult/child $15/free, discount with Muni ticket $2, 1st Tue of month free; ☺9:30am-5:15pm Tue-Sun; ♿; ☐1, 2, 18, 38) A museum as eccentric and illuminating as San Francisco itself, the Legion showcases a wildly eclectic collection ranging from Monet water lilies to John Cage soundscapes, ancient Iraqi ivories to R Crumb comics. Upstairs are blockbuster shows of old masters and Impressionists, but don't miss selections from the Legion's Achenbach Foundation of Graphic Arts collection of 90,000 works on paper, ranging from Rembrandt to Ed Ruscha. Ticket price includes free same-day entry to the de Young Museum (p196).

SUTRO BATHS PARK
Map p318 (www.nps.gov/goga/historyculture/sutro-baths.htm; 680 Point Lobos Ave; ☺sunrise-sunset, visitor center 9am-5pm; ℙ; ☐5, 31, 38) **FREE** It's hard to imagine from these ruins, but Victorian dandies and working stiffs once converged here for bracing baths in itchy woolen rental swimsuits. Millionaire Adolph Sutro built hot and cold indoor pools to accommodate 10,000 unwashed souls in 1896, but the masses apparently preferred dirt – despite added attractions including trapezes and Egyptian mummies, the baths went bust in 1952. At low tide, follow the steep path past the now-ruined baths and through the sea-cave tunnel to find sublime Pacific panoramas.

Above the baths are the **Lands End Lookout** visitor center and cafe, plus the **Sutro Heights Park** public gardens, built in 1885 and splendidly restored with native plants.

DAHLIA GARDEN GARDENS
Map p318 (www.conservatoryofflowers.org; ☺sunrise-sunset; ♿; ☐5, 21, 33) **FREE** Leave it to San Francisco to plant a dell that's totally punk rock, featuring spiky, in-your-face neon blooms cultivated by the city's many hardcore dahlia devotees. The flowers burst onto the park scene next to the Conservatory of Flowers (p197) each June and reach peak mosh-pit glory in August or September. Find them off John F Kennedy Dr.

LINCOLN PARK PARK
Map p318 (http://sfrecpark.org; Clement St; ☺sunrise-sunset; ☐1, 18, 38) ♿ America's legendary coast-to-coast Lincoln Hwy officially ends at 100-acre Lincoln Park, which served as San Francisco's cemetery until 1909. The city's best urban hike leads through Lincoln Park around **Lands End**, following a partially paved coastline trail with glorious Golden Gate views and low-tide sightings of coastal shipwrecks. Pick up the trailhead north of the Legion of Honor, or head up the newly tiled **Lincoln Park Steps** near 32nd Ave.

CLIFF HOUSE LANDMARK
Map p318 (☑415-386-3330; www.cliffhouse.com; 1090 Point Lobos Ave; ☺9am-11pm Sun-Thu, to midnight Fri & Sat; ☐5, 18, 31, 38) **FREE** Populist millionaire Adolph Sutro imagined the Cliff House as a working man's paradise in 1863, but Sutro's dream has been rebuilt three times. The latest reworking, a $19-million 2004 facelift, turned the Cliff House into a sadly generic, if panoramic, restaurant complex. Two key attractions remain: sea lions barking on **Seal Rocks** and the **Camera Obscura**, a vintage 1946 attraction projecting sea views onto a parabolic screen.

SHAKESPEARE GARDEN PARK
Map p318 (Garden of Shakespeare's Flowers; www.golden-gate-park.com/garden-of-shakespeares-flowers.html; Martin Luther King Jr Dr, cnr Middle Dr E; ☺sunrise-sunset; ☐7, 44, Ⓜ N) **FREE** Sonnets dot the flower beds in this romantic gated garden, home since 1928 to more than 200 plants mentioned in Shakespeare's writings. With all the poetry and perfume, this is

an ideal secluded spot for a smooch – and a favorite spot for weddings.

COLUMBARIUM
NOTABLE BUILDING

Map p318 (☏415-771-0717; www.neptune-society. com/columbarium; 1 Loraine Ct; ⊙8am-6pm; 🚌5, 31, 33, 38) FREE Art-nouveau stained-glass windows and a dome skylight illuminate more than 8000 niches honoring dearly departed San Franciscans and their beloved pets. San Francisco's Columbarium revived the ancient Roman custom of sheltering cremated remains in 1898, when burial grounds crowded the Richmond district. The Columbarium was neglected from 1934 until its 1979 restoration by the Neptune Society, a cremation advocacy group. Today visitors admire the neoclassical architecture and pay their respects to the niche of pioneering gay city supervisor Harvey Milk.

HUNTER S THOMPSON
CRASH PAD
NOTABLE BUILDING

Map p318 (318 Parnassus Ave; 🚌6, Ⓜ N) On the stuccoed facade, you might notice patched bullet holes – mementos of Hunter S Thompson's 1960s tenancy, when parties degenerated into Hells Angels orgies and shoot-outs. Thompson narrowly survived to write *Hell's Angels: The Strange and Terrible Saga of the Outlaw Motorcycle Gang*, founding Gonzo journalism with this motto: 'When the going gets weird, the weird turn pro.'

WINDMILLS
LANDMARK

Map p318 (Dutch & Murphy Windmills; www. golden-gate-park.com/windmills.html; ⊙sunrise-sunset; 🚌5, 18, 21, Ⓜ N) Surfers aiming for Ocean Beach tilt quixotically toward these twin landmarks on Golden Gate Park's extreme western edge. The 1902 Dutch windmill at the northwestern end of the park is closed due to structural concerns, but photographers swarm its magnificent Queen Wilhelmina Tulip Garden February to April. At the park's southwestern end, the restored 95ft-tall 1908 Murphy Windmill has resumed its original irrigation function. The windmills are off the Great Hwy near John F Kennedy and Martin Luther King Jr Drs.

⊙ The Sunset

OCEAN BEACH
BEACH

Map p318 (☏415-561-4323; www.parksconservancy.org; Great Hwy; ⊙sunrise-sunset; 🅿 ♿ 🐾; 🚌5, 18, 31, Ⓜ N) The sun sets over the Pacific just beyond the fog at this blustery beach. Most days are too chilly for bikini-clad clambakes but fine for hardy beachcombers and hardcore surfers braving riptides (casual swimmers, beware). The original site of Burning Man, Ocean Beach now allows bonfires only in 16 artist-designed fire pits until 9:30pm; no alcohol permitted. Stick to paths in the fragile southern dunes, where skittish snowy plover shorebirds shelter in winter.

FORT FUNSTON
PARK

(☏415-561-4323; www.parksconservancy.org; Fort Funston Rd; ⊙sunrise-sunset; 🅿 ♿ 🐾; Ⓜ L) 🐾 Grassy dunes up to 200ft high at Fort Funston give an idea of what the Sunset District looked like until the 20th century. A defunct military installation, Fort Funston still has 146-ton WWII guns aimed seaward and abandoned Nike missile silos near the parking lot. Nuclear missiles were never launched from Fort Funston, but flocks of hang gliders launch and land here. Butterflies and shorebirds flock to the fort, which is now part of the Golden Gate National Recreation Area.

Loop trails and hang-glider launch areas are wheelchair and stroller accessible, and dogs are allowed off the leash in many areas. The National Park Service is gradually replacing invasive ice plants with native vegetation, and volunteers are welcome to join the effort at the **Fort Funston Native Plant Nursery** (see website for details). The park entrance is on your right off Skyline Blvd, past Lake Merced.

BUFFALO PADDOCK
PARK

Map p318 (www.golden-gate-park.com/buffalo-paddock.html; ⊙sunrise-sunset; 🚌5, 21) FREE Since 1899, this is Golden Gate Park's home where the buffalo roam – though technically, they're bison. SF's mellow herd rarely moves – but when their tails point upwards, you may be about to witness bison bucking. On the very rare occasion of a stampede, they can reach speeds up to 30mph. The paddock is off John F Kennedy Dr, near 39th Ave.

SAN FRANCISCO ZOO
ZOO

(☏415-753-7080; www.sfzoo.org; 1 Zoo Rd; adult/ child 4-14yr/0-3yr $19/13/free; ⊙10am-4pm incl holidays, last entry 3pm; 🅿 ♿; 🚌18, 23, Ⓜ L) Crafty kids find ways to persuade parents to brave traffic and chilly fog to reach SF Zoo – but everyone ends up enjoying the well-kept habitats, including the Lemur Forest and the Savanna (featuring giraffes, zebras and ostriches). Star attractions include Bear Country, the Gorilla Preserve, the barnyard-style petting zoo, the Dentzel carousel (rides $3) and the miniature steam train (rides $5). Interactive storybook features are activated with a keepsake Zoo Key ($3); strollers and wheelchairs available ($10 to $12 and $15, respectively).

EATING

✖ The Richmond

★CINDERELLA RUSSIAN BAKERY RUSSIAN $

Map p318 (☑415-751-6723; www.cinderellabakery. com; 436 Balboa St; pastries $1.50-3.50, mains $7-13; ☉7am-7pm; 👹; ☖5, 21, 31, 33) Fog banks and cold wars are no match for the heart-warming powers of the Cinderella, serving treats like your *baba* used to make since 1953. Join SF's Russian community in Cinderella's new parklet near Golden Gate Park for scrumptious, just-baked egg-and-green-onion piroshki, hearty borscht and decadent dumplings – all at neighborly prices.

PRETTY PLEASE BAKESHOP BAKERY $

Map p318 (☑415-347-3733; www.prettypleasesf. com; 291 3rd Ave; baked goods $3-6; ☉11am-6pm Tue-Sat; 👹; ☖1, 2, 33, 38, 44) Since you asked nicely, pastry chef Alison Okabayashi will hand over your choice of all-American treats: mini apple pies, carrot cupcakes and sculpted Star Wars character cakes. Best of all are upscale, preservative-free versions of Hostess cakes: Ding Dongs are butter-cream-filled chocolate cakes dipped in Guittard ganache, and Twinks are cream-filled sponge cakes in vanilla, pumpkin spice or red velvet.

HALU JAPANESE $

Map p318 (☑415-221-9165; 312 8th Ave; yakitori $5-10, ramen $12-15; ☉5-10pm Tue-Sat; ☖1, 2, 38, 44) Nibbling creative yakitori (skewers) at this snug five-table joint plastered with Beatles memorabilia is like dining aboard the Yellow Submarine. Chef-owner Shig was a drummer with John Lennon's Plastic Ono Band, and though he rocks ramen, sticks are still his specialty. Get anything skewered – yuzu chicken thighs, trumpet mushrooms – and, if you're up for offal, have a heart.

ORSON'S BELLY TURKISH, CAFE $

Map p318 (☑415-340-3967; www.orsonsbelly. com; 1737 Balboa St; mains $8-14; ☉8am-7pm Mon-Thu, to 9pm Fri, 9am-9pm Sat, 9am-5pm Sun; 👹👹👹; ☖5, 18, 31, 38) The fastest way to a San Franciscan's heart is through Orson's Belly, where Coastal Trail-blazers devour Turkish breakfasts of feta, organic eggs and freshly baked pita and Balboa movie-goers debate cafe-namesake Orson Wells' best film over flaky, spinach-stuffed *borek* pastry and garlicky *haydari* cucumber-yogurt dip. Laze days away over wine and Turkish coffee, served with Turkish delight on owl platters.

GENKI DESSERTS $

Map p318 (☑415-379-6414; www.genkicrepes. com; 330 Clement St; crepes $4-7; ☉11am-11:30pm Mon, 10:30am-11:30pm Tue-Thu & Sun, 10:30am-12:30am Fri & Sat; 👹; ☖1, 2, 33, 38) Life is always sweet at Genki, with aisles of packaged Japanese gummy candies nonsensically boasting pineapple flavor 'imposing as a southern island king,' a dozen variations on tapioca bubble tea, and French crepes by way of Tokyo with green-tea ice cream and Nutella. Stock up in the beauty-supply and Pocky aisle to satisfy sudden hair-dye or snack whims.

WING LEE DIM SUM $

Map p318 (☑415-668-9481; 503 Clement St; dim sum $1.60-3.50; ☉8am-6pm; 👹; ☖1, 2, 38, 44) To feed two famished surfers for $10, just Wing Lee it. Line up with small bills and walk away loaded with shrimp-and-leek dumplings, BBQ-pork buns (baked or steamed), chicken *shumai* (open-topped dumplings), pot stickers and crispy sesame balls with red-bean centers. Fluorescent-lit lunch tables aren't made for dates, but these dumplings won't last long anyway.

★DRAGON BEAUX DIM SUM $$

Map p318 (☑415-333-8899; www.dragonbeaux. com; 5700 Geary Blvd; dumplings $4-9; ☉11:30am-2:30pm & 5:30-10pm Mon-Thu, to 10:30pm Fri, 10am-3pm & 5:30-10pm Sat & Sun; 👹; ☖2, 38) Hong Kong meets Vegas at SF's most decadent Cantonese restaurant. Say yes to cart-loads of succulent roast meats – hello, roast duck and pork belly – and creative dumplings, especially XO dumplings with plump, brandy-laced shrimp in spinach wrappers. Expect premium teas, sharp service and impeccable Cantonese standards, like Chinese doughnuts, *har gow* (shrimp dumplings) and Chinese broccoli in oyster sauce.

BURMA SUPERSTAR
BURMESE $$

Map p318 (☑415-387-2147; www.burmasuperstar.
com; 309 Clement St; mains $11-28; ⊙11:30am-
3:30pm & 5-9:30pm Sun-Thu, to 10pm Fri & Sat;
☑; 🚌1, 2, 33, 38, 44) Yes, there's a wait, but do
you see anyone walking away? Blame it on
fragrant *moh hinga* (catfish curry), tangy
vegetarian *samusa* soup, and traditional
Burmese green-tea salads tarted up with
lime and fried garlic. Reservations aren't
accepted – ask the host to call you so you
can browse Burmese cookbooks at Green
Apple Books (p204) while you wait.

CASSAVA
BAKERY, CALIFORNIAN $$

Map p318 (☑415-640-8990; www.cassavasf.
com; 3519 Balboa St; mains breakfast & lunch
$7-12, dinner $13-21; ⊙8:30am-2:30pm Mon,
8:30am-2:30pm & 5:30-9pm Wed-Fri, 10am-
2:30pm & 5:30-9pm Sat, 10am-2:30pm Sun; ☑;
🚌5, 18, 31, 38) Early risers and park joggers
are rewarded with SF-roasted Ritual coffee
and Cassava's house-made, multilingual
breakfasts – choose from Japanese miso-
poached egg, pomegranate-glazed short-rib
hash, or Californian farm egg with avocado
and Meyer-lemon aioli on toast. Book ahead
for brunch before a Balboa Theatre (p203)
matinee, and return to debrief over four-
course dinners ($42). Communal seating.

★ WAKO
SUSHI, JAPANESE $$$

Map p318 (☑415-682-4875; www.sushiwakosf.
com; 211 Clement St; 9-course menu $95; ⊙5:30-
10pm Mon-Thu; 🚌1, 2, 33, 38, 44) Tiny yet
mighty in fascination, chef-owner Tomo-
haru Nakamura's driftwood-paneled bistro
is as quirkily San Franciscan as the bonsai
grove at the nearby Japanese Tea Garden
(p197). Each *omakase* (chef's choice) dish
is a miniature marvel of Japanese seafood
with a California accent – Santa Cruz aba-
lone *nigiri*, seared tuna belly with Cali-
fornia caviar, crab *mushimono* with yuzu
grown by a neighbor. *Domo arigato*, dude.

SPRUCE
CALIFORNIAN $$$

Map p291 (☑415-931-5100; www.sprucesf.com;
3640 Sacramento St; mains $19-44; ⊙11:30am-
2:30pm & 5-10pm Mon-Fri, 5-11pm Sat, 10am-2pm
& 5-9pm Sun; 🚌1, 2, 33, 43) 🌿 VIP all the way:
chandeliers, tawny leather chairs, lobster
rolls and 2500 wines. Ladies who lunch
dispense with polite conversation, tearing
into grass-fed burgers on house-baked English muffins loaded with pickled onions,
heirloom tomato grown on the restaurant's
own organic farm and optional foie gras.

✕ The Sunset

POKI TIME
SEAFOOD, HAWAIIAN $

Map p318 (☑415-702-6333; http://pokitime.com;
549 Irving St; poke bowl $10-12; ⊙11am-9pm; 👶;
🚌6, 7, 43, 44, Ⓜ N) For fresh, wallet-friendly
meals, it's always Poki Time. Order a bowl-
ful of kale or brown rice, plus your choice
of marinated sushi-grade fish (the house
sesame tuna is a winner), topping (dare
you try the spicy Seoul sauce?) and fixings
(sesame, seaweed salad and mango are recommended). After all those healthy choices,
you deserve a passion-fruit ice-cream *mo-
chi* (rice ball).

REVENGE PIES
DESSERTS $

Map p318 (www.revengepies.com; 1248 9th Ave;
pie $5-8, picecream $3-6; ⊙9am-9pm; 👶; 🚌6,
7, 43, 44, Ⓜ N) Living well is only the second-
best revenge – a face full of pecan Revenge
Pie is far more satisfying. Here's the compen-
sation for every skimpy à la mode serving
you've suffered through: picecream (home-
made frozen custard with flakes of buttery
pie crust). The chocolate-almond Revenge
pie is a crowd-pleaser – but the key-lime
picecream could make, break and remake
friendships. Inside San Franpsycho (p204).

MANNA
KOREAN $

Map p318 (☑415-665-5969; http://mannasf.com;
845 Irving St; mains $11-15; ⊙11am-9:30pm Tue-
Sun; 🚌6, 7, 43, 44, Ⓜ N) As Korean grandmothers and other Sunset District dwellers will tell
you, nothing cures fog chills like home-style
Korean cooking. Manna's *kalbi* (barbecue
short ribs) and *dol-sot bibimbap* (rice, vegetables, steak and egg in a sizzling stone pot)
are surefire toe-warmers, especially with addictive *gojujang* (sweetly spicy Korean chili
sauce). Weekday lunch specials $2 off; parties
of four maximum; expect waits.

MASALA DOSA
INDIAN $

Map p318 (☑415-566-6976; www.masaladosasf.
com; 1375 9th Ave; mains $10-17; ⊙11am-11pm;
☑ 👶; 🚌6, 7, 33, 43, 44, Ⓜ N) Warm up on
Golden Gate Park's south side with South
Indian fare in a mood-lit storefront bistro.
The house specialty is paper dosa, a massive crispy lentil-flour pancake served with
sambar (spicy soup) and chutney – but
onion-and-pea *uthappam* is heartier and
equally gluten free. Standout mains include
chicken Madras rich with coconut milk and
fragrant wild-salmon masala.

UNDERDOG
HOT DOGS **$**

Map p318 (☑415-665-8881; www.underdog organic.com; 1634 Irving St; hot dogs $5-7; ⊙11am-4pm Thu & Fri, 10am-4pm Sat & Sun; ☑☑; ☑7, 28, 29, MN) ☑ For bargain organic meals on the run in a bun, Underdog is a winner. Meats are USDA-certified organic, and smoky veggie-chipotle hot dogs could make carnivores into fans of fake meat. The organic condiment options can be overwhelming, but the off-the-menu staff-favorite combo is no-fail: any hot dog with barbecue sauce and house-made coleslaw. Gluten-free and vegan options available.

★ OUTERLANDS
CALIFORNIAN **$$**

Map p318 (☑415-661-6140; www.outerlandssf. com; 4001 Judah St; sandwiches & small plates $8-14, mains $15-27; ⊙9am-3pm & 5-10pm; ☑☑; ☑18, MN) ☑ When windy Ocean Beach leaves you feeling shipwrecked, drift into this beach-shack bistro for organic Californian comfort food. Brunch demands Dutch pancakes in iron skillets with housemade ricotta, lunch brings cast-iron-grilled artisan cheese on house-baked levain bread with citrusy Steely Dan–themed beach cocktails, and dinner means creative coastal fare like hazelnut-dusted California salmon with black-eyed peas. Reserve.

NOPALITO
MEXICAN **$$**

Map p318 (☑415-233-9966; www.nopalitosf.com; 1224 9th Ave; mains $13-21; ⊙11:30am-10pm; ☑☑; ☑6, 7, 43, 44, MN) ☑ Head south of Golden Gate Park's border for upscale, sustainably sourced Cal-Mex, including succulent Sonoma-duck empanadas, melt-in-your-mouth *carnitas* (beer-braised pork) with handmade organic-corn tortillas, and cinnamon-laced Mexican hot chocolate. Reservations aren't accepted, but at sunny weekends when every parkgoer craves margaritas and ceviche, call to join the waiting list an hour ahead or pre-order online.

🍷 DRINKING & NIGHTLIFE

TROUBLE COFFEE & COCONUT CLUB
CAFE

Map p318 (4033 Judah St; ⊙7am-7pm; ☑18, MN) ☑ Coconuts are unlikely near blustery Ocean Beach, but here comes Trouble with the 'Build Your Own Damn House' breakfast special: coffee, thick-cut cinnamon-laced toast and an entire young coconut.

Join surfers sipping house roasts on driftwood perches outside, or toss back espresso in stoneware cups at the reclaimed-wood counter. Featured on National Public Radio, but not Instagram – sorry, no indoor photos.

TRAD'R SAM
BAR

Map p318 (☑415-221-0773; 6150 Geary Blvd; ⊙9am-2am; ☑1, 29, 31, 38) Island getaways at this vintage tiki dive will make you forget that Ocean Beach chill. Sailor-strength hot buttered rum will leave you three sheets to the wind, and five-rum Zombies will leave you wondering what happened to your brain. Kitsch-lovers order the Hurricane, which comes with two straws for a reason: drink it solo and it'll blow you away.

BEACH CHALET
BREWERY, BAR

Map p318 (☑415-386-8439; www.beachchalet. com; 1000 Great Hwy; ⊙9am-10pm Mon-Thu, to midnight Fri, 8am-midnight Sat, to 11pm Sun; ☑5, 18, 31) Microbrews with views: watch Pacific sunsets through pint glasses of the Beach Chalet's Riptide Red ale, with live music most Fridays and Saturdays. Downstairs, splendid 1930s Works Project Administration (WPA) frescoes celebrate the building of Golden Gate Park. The backyard Park Chalet hosts raucous Taco Tuesdays, lazy Sunday brunch buffets, and $1 oysters during happy hour (3pm to 6pm Wednesday to Friday).

TOMMY'S MEXICAN RESTAURANT
BAR

Map p318 (☑415-387-4747; http://tommys mexican.com; 5929 Geary Blvd; ⊙noon-11pm Wed-Mon; ☑1, 29, 31, 38) Welcome to SF's temple of tequila since 1965. Tommy's serves enchiladas as a cover for day drinking until 7pm, when margarita pitchers with *blanco, reposado or añejo* tequila rule. Cuervo Gold is displayed 'for educational purposes only' – it doesn't meet Tommy's strict criteria of unadulterated 100% agave, preferably aged in small barrels. Luckily for connoisseurs, 311 tasty tequilas do.

SOCIAL
BREWERY

Map p318 (☑415-681-0330; www.socialkitchen andbrewery.com; 1326 9th Ave; ⊙4pm-midnight Mon-Thu, to 1am Fri, 11:30am-2am Sat, 11:30am-midnight Sun; ☑6, 7, 43, 44, MN) In every Social situation, there are troublemakers – specifically the bitter Belgian blonde Rapscallion and Freak Scene oatmeal amber house brews. This snazzy, skylit loft looks like an architect's office but tastes like a neighborhood brewpub, dishing addictive sweet-potato tempura fries and lime-laced brussels-sprout chips – but, hey, hogging the bowl is anti-Social. Weekdays, score $10 brews and bites 4pm to 10pm.

HOLLOW
CAFE

Map p318 (☑415-242-4119; 1435 Irving St; ⊙8am-5pm Mon-Fri, 9am-6pm Sat & Sun; ☑7, 28, 29, MN) An enigma wrapped in a mystery inside a garage espresso bar, Hollow serves cultish Ritual coffee and Guinness cupcakes alongside beard conditioner and arsenic-scented perfume. The ideal retreat on foggy Golden Gate Park days, Hollow packs surprisingly ample seating into its snug single-car-garage space – plus arty shopping in the next-door annex that rivals the de Young Museum (p196) store.

540 CLUB
BAR

Map p318 (☑415-752-7276; www.540-club.com; 540 Clement St; ⊙11am-2am; ☎; ☑1, 2, 38, 44) Bank on bargain booze in this converted savings-and-loan office – just look for the pink elephant over the archway. Come for weekday happy hours (4pm to 7pm), Sunday trivia nights, tiki Tuesdays featuring Californian spirits, and infamous punk karaoke. Loosen up for darts and pool with a dozen beers on tap. Free wi-fi; cash only.

☆ ENTERTAINMENT

PLOUGH & STARS
LIVE MUSIC

Map p318 (☑415-751-1122; www.theploughand-stars.com; 116 Clement St; ⊙3pm-2am Mon-Thu, from 2pm Fri-Sun, shows 9pm; ☑1, 2, 33, 38, 44) Bands who sell out shows from Ireland to Appalachia and headline SF's Hardly Strictly Bluegrass festival (p21) jam here on weeknights, taking breaks to clink pint glasses of Guinness at long union-hall tables. Mondays compensate for no live music with an all-day happy hour, plus free pool and blarney from regulars; expect modest cover charges ($6 to $14) for barnstorming weekend shows.

NECK OF THE WOODS
LIVE MUSIC

Map p318 (☑415-387-6343; http://neckofthe woodssf.com; 406 Clement St; ⊙6pm-2am; ☑1, 2, 33, 38, 44) A vast yet cozy venue with all the right moves, including Monday salsa dance classes, Russian karaoke (no language skills required), monthly women's Cotton Pony dance parties, and indie rock acts regularly pounding the upstairs stage (listen to the line-up online). Downstairs the lounge

serves $4 happy-hour well drinks and beer, and hosts unpredictable open-mic nights.

BALBOA THEATRE
CINEMA

Map p318 (☑415-221-8184; www.balboamovies. com; 3630 Balboa St; adult/child $11/8, matinees $8; ☷; ☑5, 18, 31, 38) First stop, Cannes; next stop, Balboa and 37th, where film-fest favorites split the bill with Bogart noir classics, family-friendly Saturday-morning matinees and B-movie marathons with in-person director commentary and free Fort Point beer. This 1926 movie palace is run by the nonprofit San Francisco Neighborhood Theater Foundation, which keeps tickets affordable and programming exciting.

FOUR STAR THEATER
CINEMA

Map p318 (☑415-666-3488; www.lntsf.com; 2200 Clement St; adult/child & matinee $10.50/ 8.50; ☑1, 2, 29, 38) Before John Woo, Ang Lee and Wong Kar-wai hit multiplex marquees, they brought down the house in the Four Star's tiny screening rooms. Running since 1964, this international neighborhood cinema still shows Jackie Chan action flicks alongside international film-festival favorites – see website for showtimes.

🛍 SHOPPING

★ PARK LIFE
GIFTS & SOUVENIRS

Map p318 (☑415-386-7275; www.parklifestore. com; 220 Clement St; ⊙11am-8pm Mon-Sat, to 6pm Sun; ☑1, 2, 33, 38, 44) The Swiss Army knife of hip SF emporiums, Park Life is design store, indie publisher and art gallery all in one. Browse presents too clever to give away, including toy soldiers in yoga poses, Tauba Auerbach's reprogrammed Casio watches, Park Life catalogs of Shaun O'Dell paintings of natural disorder and sinister Todd Hido photos of shaggy cats on shag rugs.

★ FOGGY NOTION
GIFTS & SOUVENIRS

Map p318 (☑415-683-5654; www.foggy-notion. com; 275 6th Ave; ⊙11am-7pm Mon-Sat, to 6pm Sun; ☑1, 2, 38, 49) ✍ You can't take Golden Gate Park home with you – the city would seem naked without it – but Foggy Notion specializes in sense memories of SF's urban wilderness. The all-natural, all-artisan gift selection includes Juniper Ridge's hiking-trail scents, Golden Gate Park honey, SF artist Julia Canright's hand-printed canvas backpacks, and Wildman beard conditioner for scruff soft as fog.

★ **PAUL'S HAT WORKS**   HATS

Map p318 (☑415-221-5332; www.hatworksbypaul.
com; 6128 Geary Blvd; ☺11am-6pm Wed-Sat; ☒1,
38) Psst...keep this SF style secret under your
hat: there is no Paul. Started in 1918 by a Peruvian hatmaker named Napoleon, Paul's Fog
Belt mystique is maintained today by two
women handcrafting noir-novel fedoras on-
site. Head downtown in Paul's jazz-standard
porkpie, social-climb Nob Hill in Paul's
stovepipe top hat or storm Trad'r Sam down
the block in Paul's classic panama.

★ **JADE CHOCOLATES**   FOOD

Map p318 (☑415-350-3878; www.jadechocolates.
com; 4207 Geary Blvd; ☺11am-7pm Tue-Sat; ☒2,
31, 38, 44) SF-born chocolatier Mindy Fong
hits the sweet spot between East and West
with only-in-SF treats like passion-fruit
caramels, Thai-curry hot chocolate and the
legendary peanut Buddha with mango jam.
Fusion flavors originally inspired by Fong's
pregnancy cravings have won national acclaim, but Jade keeps its SF edge with experimental chocolates featuring sriracha,
California's own Asian-inspired chili sauce.

GREEN APPLE BOOKS   BOOKS

Map p318 (☑415-742-5833; www.greenapple-
books.com; 506 Clement St; ☺10am-10:30pm;
☒2, 38, 44) Stagger out of this literary
opium den while you still can, laden with
remaindered art books, used cookbooks
and just-released novels signed by local authors. If three floors of bookish bliss aren't
enough, check out more new titles, in-store
readings and film events at Green Apple
Books on the Park (1231 9th Ave).

SAN FRANPSYCHO   GIFTS & SOUVENIRS

Map p318 (☑415-213-5442; http://sanfranpsycho.
com; 1248 9th Ave; ☺10am-9pm; ☒; ☒6, 7, 43,
44, ⓂN) Blow minds with souvenirs that get
visitors mistaken for locals. Be the toast of
Golden Gate Park concerts with California
origami-bear flasks, and go from downtown protests to beach bonfires in tees
featuring the city's unofficial slogan: 'Build
bridges, not walls.' Complete Cali-casual
looks with driftwood jewelry and matching
hoodies for you and your dog.

GENERAL STORE   GIFTS & SOUVENIRS

Map p318 (☑415-682-0600; http://shop-general
store.com; 4035 Judah St; ☺11am-7pm Mon-Fri,
from 10am Sat & Sun; ☒18, ⓂN) Anyone born
in the wrong place or time to be a NorCal
hippie architect can still look the part,
thanks to General Store. Pine-lined walls
showcase handcrafted indigo scarves,
slingshots, stoneware pots, smudge sticks,
surfer salve and beach checker sets. To impress sustainability-minded SF hosts, give
them succulents from the backyard greenhouse instead of cut flowers.

WHERE TO GEAR UP FOR OCEAN BEACH

Mollusk (Map p318; ☑415-564-6300; www.mollusksurfshop.com; 4500 Irving St; ☺10am-
6:30pm Mon-Sat, to 6pm Sun; ☒18, ⓂN) The geodesic-dome tugboat marks the spot
where ocean meets art in this surf gallery. Legendary shapers (surfboard makers)
create limited-edition boards for Mollusk, and signature big-wave T-shirts and hoodies win nods of recognition on Ocean Beach. Kooks (newbies) get vicarious thrills from
coffee-table books on California surf culture, Thomas Campbell ocean collages and
other works by SF surfer-artists.

Aqua Surf Shop (Map p318; ☑415-242-9283; www.aquasurfshop.com; 3847 Judah St;
rental per day bodyboard/wetsuit $10/15, surfboard $25-35; ☺10am-5:30pm Sun-Tue, to 7pm
Wed-Sat; ☒18, ⓂN) Earn Sunset street cred the hardcore way, with Aqua's rental surf
gear plus referrals for surf instructors (see website). Ocean Beach riptides are challenging, so Aqua only offers rentals when conditions are safe. For instant cool without
getting wet, join Aqua pop-up events and Monday sunset yoga ($10) sporting new
Aqua tees designed by SF artist Ferris Plock.

On the Run (Map p318; ☑415-682-2042; www.ontherunshoes.com; 1310 9th Ave; ☺10am-
7pm Mon-Fri, to 6pm Sat, 11am-6pm Sun; ☒6, 7, 43, 44, ⓂN) If your morning jog leaves
your feet or shins hurting, get your gait checked here before you hit Ocean Beach
or Golden Gate Park trails. The pros will recommend the right orthopedic inserts or
shoes to relieve the pressure for free – and if you choose to buy inserts here, they'll
mold them to fit while you wait.

LAST STRAW
GIFTS & SOUVENIRS

Map p318 (☑415-566-4692; 4540 Irving St; ⊙noon-6pm Tue-Sat; ☐7, 18, Ⓜ N) Gifts come from the heart inside this front-parlor gift shop, packed with outer-avenues necessities: *haori* jackets, indigo beach totes and fisherman's scarves knitted on a nearby houseboat. Open jewelry chests to find hidden treasures under $50, including Amano's Sonoma-made chiseled-silver *señorita* hoops. No credit cards, but owner Marge accepts cash, checks and – proof that SF idealism lives – IOUs.

🏃 SPORTS & ACTIVITIES

★ COASTAL TRAIL
HIKING

Map p318 (www.californiacoastaltrail.info; ⊙sunrise-sunset; ☐1, 18, 38) Hit your stride on this 10.5-mile stretch, starting at Fort Funston, crossing 4 miles of sandy Ocean Beach and wrapping around the Presidio to the Golden Gate Bridge. Casual strollers can pick up the freshly restored trail near Sutro Baths and head around the Lands End bluffs for end-of-the-world views and glimpses of shipwrecks at low tide. At Lincoln Park, duck into the Legion of Honor or descend the gloriously tiled Lincoln Park Steps.

LAWN BOWLING CLUB
BOWLING

Map p318 (☑415-487-8787; www.golden-gate-park.com; Bowling Green Dr; ⊙11am-4pm Apr-Oct, weather permitting Nov-Mar; ☐5, 7, 21, 33, Ⓜ N) Pins seem ungainly and bowling shirts unthinkable once you've joined enthusiasts on America's first public lawn-bowling green. Free lessons are available from volunteers on Wednesday at noon and occasional evenings in spring and summer. Flat-soled shoes are mandatory, but otherwise bowlers dress for comfort and the weather – though all-white clothing has been customary at club social events since 1901.

SAN FRANCISCO DISC GOLF
SPORTS

Map p318 (www.sfdiscgolf.org; 900 John F Kennedy Dr; ⊙sunrise-sunset; ☐5, 28, 29, 31, 38) FREE Wander the tranquil fairy-tale woods of outer Golden Gate Park and you'll find fierce Frisbee golf games in progress at a permanent 18-hole disc-golf course. Rent tournament discs at Golden Gate Park Bike & Skate (p205) and register online to mingle with disc-tossing singles on Sunday (8:30am to 10am; $5) or join Tuesday doubles tournaments (5pm; $5) – winners take home cash.

GOLDEN GATE MUNICIPAL GOLF COURSE
GOLF

Map p318 (☑415-751-8987; www.goldengatepark golf.com; 970 47th Ave; adult/child Mon-Thu $18/9, Fri-Sun $22/11; ⊙7am-dusk; ♿; ☐5, 18, 31) With sunlight filtering through majestic Monterey cypress trees, even the rough is glorious at this challenging nine-hole, par-27 public course sculpted from park sand dunes in 1951. Equipment rental (adult/child $15/6) and practice range available; kids welcome. Book ahead online, especially before 9am weekdays, weekends and after school. At the clubhouse, score wood-fired BBQ sandwiches (sauce secret: Anchor Steam beer).

STOW LAKE BOATHOUSE
BOATING

Map p318 (☑415-386-2531; http://stowlakeboat house.com; 50 Stow Lake Dr; boats per hour $21-37; ⊙10am-5pm; ☐5, 7, 29, 44) ⌁ Push off from the dock of this vintage 1948 boathouse in a pedal-powered, electric or rowing boat to glide across Stow Lake (p197), and return for organic Three Twins ice cream at the renovated boathouse cafe (11am to 4pm).

GOLDEN GATE JOAD
ARCHERY

Map p318 (www.goldengatejoad.com; Golden Gate Park Archery Range, cnr Fulton St & 47th Ave; 2hr lesson incl archery-gear rental $20; ⊙classes morning Sat; ♿; ☐5, 18, 31) Blockbusters like *The Avengers*, *The Hunger Games* and *Brave* have revived San Francisco's Victorian-era archery craze, and you can take aim Saturday mornings in Golden Gate Park with SF's nonprofit Junior Olympic Archery Division (JOAD). Patient, certified coaches offer traditional bow archery classes for adults and kids aged eight and up (with guardian consent). Book online; beginner classes fill quickly.

GOLDEN GATE PARK BIKE & SKATE
CYCLING

Map p318 (☑415-668-1117; www.goldengate parkbikeandskate.com; 3038 Fulton St; skates per hour $5-6, per day $20-24, bikes per hour $3-5, per day $15-25, tandem bikes per hour/day $15/75, discs $6/25; ⊙10am-6pm Mon-Fri, to 7pm Sat & Sun; ♿; ☐5, 21, 31, 44) Besides bikes (for kids and adults) and skates (four-wheeled and inline), this rental shop just outside Golden Gate Park rents disc putters and drivers for the park's free Frisbee golf course. Bargain rates; helmets included with rentals. Call to confirm it's open if the weather looks iffy.

Day Trips from San Francisco

Berkeley & Oakland p207
The legendary counterculture hubs of 'Bezerkely' and 'Oaktown' keep busy reinventing music, art, history and politics – but dinnertime is sacred in this culinary hub.

Muir Woods to Stinson Beach p212
Some of the world's tallest trees reach skyward in primordial forests near windblown beaches, just across the Golden Gate Bridge.

Sausalito & Tiburon p214
Picturesque bayside towns, perfect for strolling, are a fast ferry ride away in Marin County. Meet for sunset drinks and seafood by the water.

Napa Valley p218
Sun-washed valleys and cool coastal fog have turned Napa into California's most iconic wine-growing region – but redwood groves, pioneering organic farms and natural hot springs keep things diverse.

Sonoma Valley p223
With its 19th-century California mission town, farm-to-table kitchens and pastoral wineries that welcome picnicking, Sonoma retains its folksy ways.

Berkeley & Oakland

Explore

Berkeley and Oakland are what most San Franciscans think of as the East Bay, though the area covers industrial bayside flats to exclusive enclaves in the hills. Even the most die-hard San Franciscans are eventually lured over to the sunny side of the bay by fascinating museum shows and historical sites, ground-breaking restaurants and bars, a booming arts scene, offbeat shopping, idyllic parks and a world-famous university.

The Best...

➡**Sight** University of California, Berkeley
Place to Eat Chez Panisse (p210)
➡**Entertainment** Fox Theater (p211)

Top Tip

The **Bay Bridge Path** (www.baybridgeinfo.org/path; ⊙hours vary) is a pedestrian and bicycle route along the new eastern span of the Bay Bridge between Oakland and Yerba Buena Island. To reach Yerba Buena Island, it's about 5 miles from Emeryville or 3.5 miles from West Oakland.

Getting There & Away

➡**BART** (www.bart.gov) Trains run approximately every 10 to 20 minutes from around 4:30am to midnight on weekdays, with more limited service from 6am on Saturday and from 8am on Sunday and holidays.

➡**Bus** AC Transit (www.actransit.org) operates a number of buses from San Francisco's Transbay Temporary Terminal to the East Bay (one-way fare $4.20, or $2.10 if you buy a $5 day pass valid on local buses).

➡**Car** Approach the East Bay from San Francisco by taking the Bay Bridge. Driving back westbound to San Francisco, the bridge toll is $4 to $6.

➡**Ferry** Offering splendid views, the San Francisco Bay Ferry (p266) is the most enjoyable way of traveling between San Francisco and the East Bay, though also the slowest and most expensive.

Need to Know

➡**Area Code** ☑510
➡**Location** Berkeley is 11 miles northeast of San Francisco; Oakland is 8 miles west.
➡**Visit Berkeley** (☑510-549-7040, 800-847-4823; www.visitberkeley.com; 2030 Addison St; ⊙9am-1pm & 2-5pm Mon-Fri; Ⓑ Downtown Berkeley)
➡**Visit Oakland** (☑510-839-9000; www.visitoakland.com; 481 Water St; ⊙9am-5pm Mon-Fri, 10am-4pm Sat & Sun)

◉ SIGHTS

UNIVERSITY OF CALIFORNIA, BERKELEY
UNIVERSITY

(☑510-642-6000; www.berkeley.edu; ⊙hours vary; Ⓟ �🛜; Ⓑ Downtown Berkeley) 'Cal' is one of the country's top universities, California's oldest university (1866), and home to 40,000 diverse, politically conscious students. Next to **California Memorial Stadium** (☑510-642-2730; www.californiamemorialstadium.com; 2227 Piedmont Ave; ⊙hours vary; 🚻; ☒AC Transit 52), the **Koret Visitor Center** (☑510-642-5215; http://visit.berkeley.edu; 2227 Piedmont Ave; ⊙8:30am-4:30pm Mon-Fri, 9am-1pm Sat & Sun; ☒AC Transit 36) has information and maps, and leads free campus walking tours (reservations required). Cal's landmark is the 1914 **Campanile** (Sather Tower; ☑510-642-6000; http://campanile.berkeley.edu; adult/child $3/2; ⊙10am-3:45pm Mon-Fri, 10am-4:45pm Sat, 10am-1:30pm & 3-4:45pm Sun; 🚻; Ⓑ Downtown Berkeley), with elevator rides ($3) to the top and carillon concerts. The **Bancroft Library** (☑510-642-3781; www.lib.berkeley.edu/libraries/bancroft-library; University Dr; ⊙archives 10am-4pm or 5pm Mon-Fri; 🛜; Ⓑ Downtown Berkeley) ████ displays the small gold nugget that started the California gold rush in 1848.

UC BERKELEY ART MUSEUM
MUSEUM

(BAMPFA; ☑510-642-0808; www.bampfa.berkeley.edu; 2155 Center St, Berkeley; adult/child $12/free; ⊙11am-7pm Sun, Wed & Thu, to 9pm Fri & Sat; 🛜; Ⓑ Downtown Berkeley) With a stainless-steel exterior wrapping around a 1930s printing plant, the museum's new location holds multiple galleries showcasing a limited number of artworks, from ancient Chinese to cutting-edge contemporary. The complex also houses a bookstore, cafe and the much-loved **Pacific Film Archive** (PFA; ☑510-642-5249; www.bampfa.berkeley.edu; 2155

East Bay

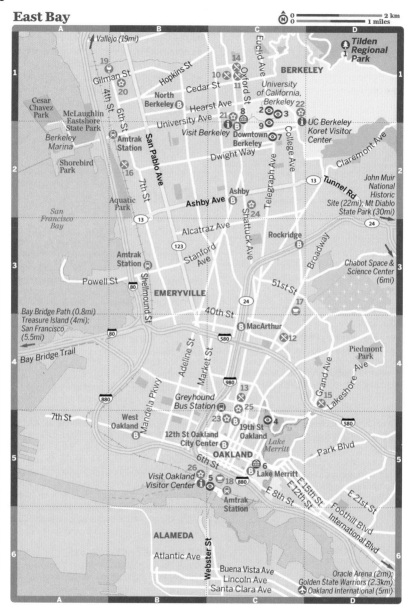

Center St; adult/child from $12/8; ⊙hours vary; ⓖ; Ⓑ Downtown Berkeley).

OAKLAND MUSEUM OF CALIFORNIA

MUSEUM

(OMCA; ☎888-625-6873, 510-318-8400; http://museumca.org; 1000 Oak St; adult/child $16/7, free 1st Sun each month; ⊙11am-5pm Wed-Thu, 11am-9pm Fri, 10am-6pm Sat & Sun; ⓟⓢⓖ; ⒷLake Merritt) Near the southern end of Lake Merritt, this museum has rotating exhibitions on artistic and scientific themes, and permanent galleries dedicated to the state's diverse ecology and history, as well as California art. Admission is steeply discounted on Friday nights (after 5pm), when DJs, food trucks and free art workshops for kids make it a fun hangout.

⭐**TILDEN REGIONAL PARK** PARK
(☎888-327-3757, 510-544-2747; www.ebparks.org/parks/tilden; ⊙5am-10pm; P🚻🐾; 🚌AC Transit 67) ⫸FREE This 2079-acre park, up in the hills east of town, is Berkeley's best. It has nearly 40 miles of hiking and multi-use trails of varying difficulty, from paved paths to hilly scrambles, including part of the magnificent Bay Area Ridge Trail. There's also a miniature steam train ($3), a children's farm and environmental education center, a wonderfully wild-looking botanical garden and an 18-hole golf course. Lake Anza is good for picnics and from spring through fall you can swim ($3.50).

⭐**CHABOT SPACE & SCIENCE CENTER** MUSEUM
(☎510-336-7300; www.chabotspace.org; 10000 Skyline Blvd, Oakland; adult/child $18/14; ⊙10am-5pm Wed-Sun, also Tue Jun-Aug; P🚻; 🚌AC Transit 339) ⫸ Stargazers will go gaga over this kid-oriented science and technology center in the Oakland Hills with loads of exhibits on subjects such as space travel and eclipses, as well as cool planetarium shows. When the weather's good, check out the free Friday and Saturday evening viewings (7:30pm to 10:30pm) using a 20in refractor telescope.

TELEGRAPH AVENUE STREET
(⊙shop & restaurant hours vary; P; 🚌AC Transit 6) Telegraph Ave has traditionally been the throbbing heart of studentville in Berkeley, the sidewalks crowded with undergrads, postdocs and youthful shoppers squeezing their way past throngs of vendors, buskers and panhandlers. Street stalls hawk everything from crystals to bumper stickers to self-published tracts. Several cafes and budget eateries cater to students.

JACK LONDON SQUARE SQUARE
(☎510-645-9292; www.jacklondonsquare.com; Broadway & Embarcadero, Oakland; ⊙24hr, shop, restaurant & bar hours vary; P; 🚌Broadway Shuttle) The area where writer and adventurer Jack London once raised hell now bears his name. The pretty waterfront location is worth a stroll, especially when the Sunday **farmers market** (☎415-291-3276; www.cuesa.org; Jack London Sq; ⊙10am-3pm Sun; 🚸🚻) ⫸ takes over, or get off your feet and kayak around the harbor. Contemporary redevelopment has added a cinema complex, condo development and popular restaurants and bars.

A replica of Jack London's Yukon cabin stands at the end of the square. Oddly, people throw coins inside as if it's a fountain.

CHILDREN'S FAIRYLAND AMUSEMENT PARK
(☎510-452-2259; http://fairyland.org; 699 Bellevue Ave, Oakland; $10, child under 1yr free; ⊙10am-4pm Mon-Fri, to 5pm Sat & Sun Jun-Aug, off-season hours vary; ▣ ♿; ▣AC Transit 12) Lakeside Park, on the northern side of Lake Merritt, includes this 10-acre kiddie attraction, which dates from 1950 and has a charming fairy-tale-themed train, carousel and mini Ferris wheel.

✖ EATING & DRINKING

VIK'S CHAAT CORNER INDIAN $
(☎510-644-4412; www.vikschaatcorner.com; 2390 4th St, Berkeley; mains $6-12; ⊙11am-6pm Mon-Thu, to 8pm Fri-Sun; ▱ ♿; ▣AC Transit 80) Off in West Berkeley, this longtime, popular *chaat* house gets mobbed at lunchtime by regulars that include equal numbers of hungry office workers, students and Indian families. Order samosas or a puffy *bhature* (flatbread) with *chole* (chickpea curry), an *uttapam* (savory pancake) or one of many filling *dosas* (savory crepes). Colorful Indian sweets, sold by the piece or pound, are irresistible.

★OAKLAND–GRAND LAKE FARMERS MARKET MARKET $
(☎415-472-6100; https://agriculturalinstitute.org; Lake Park Ave, at Grand Ave; ⊙9am-2pm Sat; ▱ ♿; ▣AC Transit 12) ✦ A rival to San Francisco's Ferry Plaza Farmers Market, this bountiful weekly market hauls in bushels of fresh fruit, vegetables, seafood, ranched meats, artisanal cheese and baked goods from as far away as Marin County and the Central Valley. The northern side of the market is cheek-to-jowl with food trucks and hot-food vendors – don't skip the dim-sum tent.

NORTH BERKELEY FARMERS MARKET MARKET $
(☎510-548-3333; www.ecologycenter.org; Shattuck Ave, at Rose St; ⊙3-7pm Thu; ▱ ♿; ▣AC Transit 79) ✦ Pick up some organic produce or tasty prepared food at North Berkeley's weekly farmers market.

CHEESE BOARD COLLECTIVE PIZZA $
(☎510-549-3055; www.cheeseboardcollective. coop; 1504 & 1512 Shattuck Ave, Berkeley; slice/half-pizza $2.75/11; ⊙shop 7am-1pm Mon, to 6pm Tue-Fri, to 5pm Sat, pizzeria 11:30am-3pm & 4:30-8pm Tue-Sat; ▱ ♿; ▣AC Transit 7) Stop in to take stock of more than 300 cheeses available at this worker-owned business and scoop up some fresh bread to make a picnic lunch. Or sit down for a slice of the crispy veggie pizza just next door, where live music's often featured.

IPPUKU JAPANESE $$
(☎510-665-1969; www.ippukuberkeley.com; 2130 Center St, Berkeley; shared plates $5-20; ⊙5-10pm Tue-Thu, to 11pm Fri & Sat; ▣Downtown Berkeley) Japanese expats gush that Ippuku reminds them of *izakaya* (Japanese gastropubs) back in Tokyo. Choose from a menu of yakitori (skewered meats and vegetables) and handmade soba noodles as you settle in at one of the traditional tatami tables (no shoes, please) or cozy booth perches. Order *shōchū*, a distilled alcohol usually made from rice or barley. Reservations essential.

GATHER CALIFORNIAN $$
(☎510-809-0400; www.gatherrestaurant.com; 2200 Oxford St, Berkeley; dinner mains $16-30; ⊙lunch 11:30am-2pm Mon-Fri, brunch 10am-2pm Sat & Sun, dinner 5-9pm Sun-Thu, to 10pm Fri & Sat; ▱; ▣Downtown Berkeley) ✦ When vegan foodies and passionate farm-to-table types dine out together, they often end up here. Inside a salvaged-wood interior punctuated by green vines streaking down over an open kitchen, dishes are created from locally sourced ingredients and sustainably raised meats. Reservations recommended.

KINGSTON 11 CARIBBEAN $$
(☎510-465-2558; http://kingston11eats.com; 2270 Telegraph Ave, Oakland; mains $13-20; ⊙11am-2pm & 5-10pm Tue-Fri, 5-10pm Sat, 11am-4pm Sun; ♿; ▣19th St Oakland) The wait will be worth it at this raucous Caribbean bar with a groovy soundtrack, where oxtail stew, salt-fish fritters, fried plantains and goat curry are succulent delights. Swing by for 'Irie Hour' (5pm to 7pm Tuesday through Friday) to sip out-of-this-world cocktails such as the Rise Up (cold-brew coffee, coconut milk, spiced rum and Angostura bitters). Reservations recommended.

★CHEZ PANISSE CALIFORNIAN $$$
(☎cafe 510-548-5049, restaurant 510-548-5525; www.chezpanisse.com; 1517 Shattuck Ave, Berkeley; cafe dinner mains $22-35, restaurant prix-fixe dinner $75-125; ⊙cafe 11:30am-2:45pm & 5-10:30pm Mon-Thu, 11:30am-3pm & 5-11:30pm Fri & Sat, restaurant seatings 5:30pm & 8pm Mon-Sat; ▱; ▣AC Transit 7) ✦ Foodies come to worship here at the

church of Alice Waters, inventor of California cuisine. It's in a lovely arts-and-crafts house in Berkeley's 'Gourmet Ghetto,' and you can choose to pull out all the stops with a prix-fixe meal downstairs, or go less expensive and a less formal in the upstairs cafe. Reservations accepted one month ahead.

★**COMMIS**   CALIFORNIAN **$$$**
(☑510-653-3902; http://commisrestaurant.com; 3859 Piedmont Ave, Oakland; 8-course dinner $149, with wine & beer pairings $229; ⊘5:30-9:30pm Wed-Sat, 5-9pm Sun; 🚌AC Transit 51A) The East Bay's only Michelin-starred restaurant, the signless and discreet dining room counts a minimalist decor and some coveted counter real estate where patrons can watch chef James Syhabout and his team piece together creative and innovative dishes, maybe Monterey Bay abalone, soy-milk custard with chanterelles or a perfectly ripe peach topped with oats, beeswax creme and marigolds. Reservations essential.

★**BLUE BOTTLE COFFEE COMPANY**   CAFE
(☑510-653-3394; http://bluebottlecoffee.com; 300 Webster St, Oakland; ⊘7am-5:30pm Mon-Fri, to 6pm Sat & Sun; 🚌Broadway Shuttle) 🍵 Java gourmands queue at Blue Bottle's original warehouse location for single-origin espressos and what some consider the Bay Area's best coffee. Single-origin beans are roasted on-site; reserve ahead online for coffee cupping and brewing classes. Its newer **cafe** (☑510-653-3394; http://bluebottlecoffee.com; 4270 Broadway; ⊘7am-6pm; 🚌AC Transit 51A) 🍵 is north of Broadway's Auto Row.

FIELDWORK BREWING COMPANY   BREWERY
(☑510-898-1203; http://fieldworkbrewing.com; 1160 6th St, Berkeley; ⊘11am-10pm Sun-Thu, to 11pm Fri & Sat; 🚌AC Transit 12) Come to this industrial brewery taproom at the edge of town for outstanding craft beer and sit down on the outdoor patio with a tasting flight of IPAs or a glass of rich Mexican hot chocolate stout. It's dog-friendly, with racks to hang your bicycle inside the front door.

☆ ENTERTAINMENT

★**FOX THEATER**   THEATER
(☑510-302-2250, tickets 800-745-3000; http://thefoxoakland.com; 1807 Telegraph Ave, Oakland; tickets from $35; ⊘hours vary; 🅱19th St Oakland) A phoenix arisen from the urban ashes, this restored 1928 art-deco stunner adds dazzle and neon lights to Telegraph Ave, where it's a cornerstone of the happening Uptown theater and nightlife district. Once a movie house, it's now a popular concert venue for edgy and independent Californian, national and international music acts. Buy tickets early, since many shows sell out.

★**GOLDEN STATE WARRIORS**   BASKETBALL
(☑tickets 888-479-4667; www.nba.com/warriors; 7000 Coliseum Way, Oakland; tickets from $55; ⊘Oct-Apr; 🚶; 🅱Coliseum) If it's hoops you must have, then it's the Warriors for you. Originally from Philadelphia, this team moved across the bay from San Francisco in 1971. Today they play at Oracle Arena (next to the Coliseum). The Warriors caused quite a commotion when they won the NBA championship playoffs in 2015. Alas, they're moving back to San Francisco in 2019.

BERKELEY REPERTORY THEATRE   THEATER
(☑510-647-2949; www.berkeleyrep.org; 2025 Addison St; tickets $40-100; ⊘box office noon-7pm Tue-Sun; 🅱Downtown Berkeley) This highly respected company has produced bold versions of classical and modern plays since 1968. Most shows have half-price tickets for patrons under 30.

PARAMOUNT THEATRE   THEATER, CINEMA
(☑510-465-6400; www.paramounttheatre.com; 2025 Broadway, Oakland; movie/concert tickets from $7/25; ⊘hours vary; 🚌19th St Oakland) This massive 1931 art-deco masterpiece shows classic films a few times a month and is also home to the **Oakland Symphony** (www.oaklandsymphony.org) and **Oakland Ballet** (http://oaklandballet.org). It periodically books big-name concerts and screens classic flicks.

Guided tours ($5) are given at 10am on the first and third Saturdays of the month (no reservations).

YOSHI'S   JAZZ
(☑510-238-9200; www.yoshis.com; 510 Embarcadero W, Oakland; from $20; ⊘hours vary; 🚌Broadway Shuttle) Yoshi's has a solid jazz calendar, with talent from around the world passing through on a near-nightly basis. It's also a Japanese restaurant, so if you enjoy a sushi dinner before the show, you'll be rewarded with reserved cabaret-style seating. Otherwise, resign yourself to limited high-top tables squeezed along the back walls.

FREIGHT & SALVAGE COFFEEHOUSE
LIVE MUSIC

(☑510-644-2020; www.thefreight.org; 2020 Addison St, Berkeley; tickets $5-45; ☺shows daily; 🚻; 🅱Downtown Berkeley) This legendary club has almost 50 years of history and is conveniently located in the downtown arts district. It features great traditional folk, country, bluegrass and world music and welcomes all ages.

LA PEÑA CULTURAL CENTER
WORLD MUSIC

(☑510-849-2568; www.lapena.org; 3105 Shattuck Ave, Berkeley; free-$16; ☺hours vary; 🅱Ashby) Fun-loving, warmhearted community center presents dynamic dance classes and musical and visual arts events with a peace and justice bent. Look for a vibrant mural outside and the on-site Mexican cafe, perfect for grabbing drinks and a preshow bite.

924 GILMAN
LIVE MUSIC

(☑510-524-8180; www.924gilman.org; 924 Gilman St, Berkeley; tickets from $10; ☺Sat & Sun; 🚌AC Transit 12) This volunteer-run and booze-free all-ages space is a West Coast punk-rock institution. Check the online calendar for upcoming shows on weekend nights.

GRAND LAKE THEATRE
CINEMA

(☑510-452-3556; www.renaissancerialto.com; 3200 Grand Ave, Oakland; tickets $5-12.50; ☺hours vary; 🚻; 🚌AC Transit 12) Once a vaudeville theater and silent-movie house, this 1926 beauty near Lake Merritt lures you in with its huge corner marquee (which sometimes displays left-leaning political messages) and keeps you with a fun balcony and a Wurlitzer organ playing the pipes on weekends.

Muir Woods to Stinson Beach

Explore

Walking through an awesome stand of the world's tallest trees is an experience to be had only in Northern California and a small part of southern Oregon. The old-growth redwoods at Muir Woods, just 12 miles north of the Golden Gate Bridge, make up the closest redwood stand to San Francisco. The trees were initially eyed by loggers, and Redwood Creek, as the area was known, seemed ideal for a dam. Those plans were halted when congressman and naturalist William Kent bought a section of Redwood Creek and, in 1907, donated 295 acres to the federal government. President Theodore Roosevelt made the site a national monument in 1908, the name honoring John Muir, naturalist and founder of environmental organization the Sierra Club.

The Best...

➡ **Sight** Cathedral Grove (p213)
➡ **Hike** Dipsea Trail (p213)
➡ **Place to Eat** Parkside (p214)

Top Tip

To beat the crowds, come early in the day, before sunset or midweek; otherwise the parking lots fill up. Consider riding the seasonal shuttle bus to Muir Woods.

Getting There & Away

➡ **Car** Drive north on Hwy 101, exit at Hwy 1 and continue north along Hwy 1/Shoreline Hwy to the Panoramic Hwy (a right-hand fork). Follow that for about 1 mile to Four Corners, where you turn left on to Muir Woods Rd (there are plenty of signs).

➡ **Ferry & Bus** On weekends and holidays from May through October (daily between late June and mid-August), **Marin Transit** (☑415-455-2000, 511; www.marintransit.org) bus 66 ('Muir Woods Shuttle') departs Sausalito (round-trip adult/child $5/free, 50 minutes), connecting with Golden Gate Ferry (p267) service from San Francisco ($11.75, 30 minutes). On weekends and holidays, **West Marin Stagecoach** (☑415-226-0825; www.marintransit.org/stage.html) bus 61 links Stinson Beach with Sausalito ($2, 1½ hours).

Need to Know

➡ **Area Code** ☑415
➡ **Location** 12 miles northwest of San Francisco

◉ SIGHTS

★MUIR WOODS NATIONAL MONUMENT
FOREST

(☑415-388-2595; www.nps.gov/muwo; 1 Muir Woods Rd, Mill Valley; adult/child $10/free; ☺8am-8pm mid-Mar–mid-Sep, to 7pm mid-Sep–

early Oct, to 6pm Feb–mid-Mar & early Oct-early Nov, to 5pm early Nov-Jan; P 🛝) 🏊 Wander among an ancient stand of the world's tallest trees in 550-acre Muir Woods. The 1-mile Main Trail Loop is a gentle walk alongside Redwood Creek to the 1000-year-old trees at **Cathedral Grove**; it returns via Bohemian Grove, where the tallest tree in the park stands 258ft high. The **Dipsea Trail** (www.dipsea.org) is a good 2-mile hike up to the top of aptly named Cardiac Hill. Come midweek to avoid crowds; otherwise, arrive early morning or late afternoon.

Because the parking lot is often full, ride the seasonal **Muir Woods Shuttle** (Route 66F; www.marintransit.org; round-trip adult/child $5/free). You can also walk down into Muir Woods by taking trails from the Panoramic Hwy, such as the Bootjack Trail from the Bootjack picnic area, or from Mt Tamalpais'

Pantoll Station and Pantoll Campground, eventually joining the Ben Johnson Trail.

MUIR BEACH   BEACH

(www.nps.gov/goga/planyourvisit/muirbeach.htm; off Pacific Way; P 🛝) 🏊 Restored wetlands, creeks, lagoons and sand dunes provide habitat for birds, California red-legged frogs and coho salmon. In winter, you might spot monarch butterflies roosting in a small grove of Monterey pines and migratory whales swimming offshore. The turnoff from Hwy 1 is next to the coast's longest row of mailboxes at Mile 5.7, just before Pelican Inn.

STINSON BEACH   BEACH

(☎415-868-0942; www.nps.gov/goga; off Hwy 1; ⊗from 9am daily, closing time varies seasonally; P 🛝) Three-mile-long Stinson Beach is a popular surf spot, with swimming advised from late May to mid-September only. For

---

MARIN ISLANDS

The headlands rise majestically out of the water at the north end of the Golden Gate Bridge, their rugged beauty all the more striking given the fact that they're only a few miles from San Francisco's urban core. A few forts and bunkers are left over from a century of US military occupation – which is, ironically, the reason the headlands are today parklands protected as the **Golden Gate National Recreation Area** (☎415-561-4700; www.nps.gov/goga; P 🛝) FREE, free of development. It's no mystery why this is one of the Bay Area's most popular hiking and cycling destinations. As the trails wind through the headlands, they afford stunning views of the sea, the Golden Gate Bridge and San Francisco and lead to isolated beaches and secluded picnic spots.

The historical **Point Bonita Lighthouse** (☎415-331-1540; www.nps.gov/goga/pobo.htm; ⊗12:30-3:30pm Sat-Mon; P) FREE is a breathtaking half-mile walk from a small parking area off Field Rd. From the tip of Point Bonita, you can see the distant Golden Gate Bridge and beyond it the San Francisco skyline. It's an uncommon vantage point of the bay-centric city, and harbor seals haul out seasonally on nearby rocks. Call ahead to reserve a spot on one of the free monthly sunset and full-moon tours of the promontory.

For adrenaline junkies, the Marin Headlands have some excellent mountain-biking routes and it's an exhilarating ride across the Golden Gate Bridge to reach them. For a good 12-mile dirt loop, choose the **Coastal Trail** west from the fork of Conzelman and McCullough Rds, bumping and winding down to Bunker Rd where it meets **Bobcat Trail**, which joins **Marincello Trail** and descends steeply into the Tennessee Valley parking area. The **Old Springs Trail** and the **Miwok Trail** take you back to Bunker Rd a bit more gently than the Bobcat Trail, though any attempt to avoid at least a couple of hefty climbs is futile.

If you're driving to the headlands, take the Alexander Ave exit just after crossing north over the Golden Gate Bridge and dip left under the freeway. Conzelman Rd, to the right, takes you up along the bluffs; you can also take Bunker Rd, which leads to the headlands through a one-way tunnel. Arrive before 2pm on weekends to avoid traffic and parking congestion, or cycle over the bridge instead.

On Saturday, Sunday and holidays, **MUNI** (☎511, 415-701-2311; www.sfmta.com) bus 76X runs every 60 to 90 minutes from San Francisco's Financial District to the Marin Headlands Visitors Center, Rodeo Beach and the Nike missile site. Buses are equipped with bicycle racks.

updated weather and surf conditions call ☎415-868-1922. The beach is one block west of Hwy 1. There's free parking but the lot often fills up before noon on sunny days.

✖ EATING & DRINKING

MUIR WOODS TRADING COMPANY CAFE **$**
(☎415-388-7059; www.muirwoodstradingcompany.com; 1 Muir Woods Rd, Mill Valley; items $2-11; ⊙8am-5pm; ⓟ) ⚑ It's pricey, but this little cafe near the park entrance serves melty-good grilled cheese sandwiches, savory soups, baked goods and hot drinks that hit the spot on foggy days.

PARKSIDE AMERICAN, BAKERY **$$**
(☎415-868-1272; www.parksidecafe.com; 43 Arenal Ave, Stinson Beach; mains $9-28; ⊙7:30am-9pm, coffee bar from 6am; ⓘ ⓟ) ⚑ Famous for its hearty breakfasts and lunches, this cozy eatery next to the beach serves wood-fired pizzas and excellent coastal cuisine such as Tomales Bay oysters and king salmon at dinner, when reservations are recommended.

Popular with beachgoers, hikers and cyclists, Parkside's outdoor **snack bar** serves burgers, sandwiches, fruit smoothies, baked goods and ice cream.

PELICAN INN PUB FOOD **$$$**
(☎415-383-6000; www.pelicaninn.com; 10 Pacific Way, Muir Beach; dinner mains $18-36; ⊙8-11am Sat & Sun, 11:30am-3pm & 5:30-9pm daily; ⓟ) The oh-so-English Pelican Inn is Muir Beach's only commercial establishment. Hikers, cyclists and families come for pub lunches inside its timbered restaurant and cozy bar, perfect for a pint, a game of darts and warming up beside the open fire. The food is nothing mindblowing and the service is hit or miss, but the setting is magical.

Upstairs are seven cozy rooms (from $225) with half-canopy beds.

Sausalito & Tiburon

Explore

Perfectly arranged on a secure little harbor on the bay, Sausalito is undeniably lovely. Named for the tiny willows that once populated the banks of its creeks, it's famous for its colorful houseboats bobbing in the bay. Much of the well-heeled downtown has uninterrupted views of San Francisco and Angel Island, and due to the ridgeline at its back, fog generally skips it. It's the first town you encounter after crossing the Golden Gate Bridge from San Francisco, so daytime crowds turn up in droves and make parking difficult. Ferrying over from San Francisco makes for a more relaxing excursion.

Opposite Sausalito, at the end of a small peninsula pointing out into the center of the bay, Tiburon is blessed with gorgeous views. The name comes from the Spanish Punta de Tiburon (Shark Point). Browse the shops on Main St, grab a bite to eat and you've seen Tiburon. The town is also a jumping-off point for nearby Angel Island.

The Best...
➡**Sight** Sausalito Houseboats (p215)
➡**Place to Eat** Fish (p215)
➡**Activity** Sea Trek (p217)

Top Tip

Walking or cycling across the Golden Gate Bridge (p54) to Sausalito is a fun way to avoid traffic, enjoy some great ocean views and bask in that refreshing Marin County air. You can also simply hop on a ferry back to SF. The trip is about 4 miles from the south end of the bridge and takes less than an hour. Check the bridge website (www.goldengatebridge.org/bikesbridge/bikes.php) for updates.

Getting There & Away
➡**Bus** Bus 10 from **Golden Gate Transit** (☎415-455-2000, 511; www.goldengatetransit.org) runs hourly to Sausalito from downtown San Francisco ($4.75, 40 to 55 minutes).

➡**Car** Drive Hwy 101 north across the Golden Gate Bridge. For Sausalito, take the immediate Alexander Ave or main Sausalito exit; for Tiburon, exit at Tiburon Blvd/E Blithedale Ave.

➡**Ferry** Golden Gate Ferry (p267) sails from San Francisco's Ferry Building to Sausalito ($11.75, 30 minutes) and Tiburon ($11.50, 30 minutes). **Blue & Gold Fleet** (☎415-705-8200; www.blueandgoldfleet.com) sails to Sausalito ($11.50, 30 minutes) and to Tiburon ($11.50, 25 minutes) from Pier 41.

Need to Know

➡**Area Code** 📞415

➡**Location** Sausalito is 5 miles north of San Francisco; Tiburon is 12 miles north-north-east.

➡**Sausalito Chamber of Commerce Visitor Kiosk** (📞415-331-1093; www.sausalito.org; foot of El Portal St; ⊙10am-4pm)

➡**Tiburon Peninsula Chamber of Commerce** (📞415-435-5633; www.tiburonchamber.org; 96b Main St)

⊙ SIGHTS

Sausalito's main strip is Bridgeway Blvd, leading along the bay to downtown and the ferry terminal.

⭐**SAUSALITO HOUSEBOATS** ARCHITECTURE
Bohemia still thrives along the shoreline of Richardson Bay, where free spirits inhabit hundreds of quirky homes that bobble in the waves among the seabirds and seals. Structures range from psychedelic mural-splashed castles to dilapidated salt-sprayed shacks and immaculate three-story floating mansions. You can poke around the houseboat docks located off Bridgeway Blvd between Gate 5 and Gate 6½ Rds.

It's a tight-knit community, where residents tend sprawling dockside gardens and stop to chat on the creaky wooden boardwalks as they wheel their groceries home. Etiquette tips for visitors: no smoking, no pets, no bicycles and no loud noise.

BAY MODEL VISITORS CENTER MUSEUM
(📞415-332-3871; www.spn.usace.army.mil/missions/recreation/baymodelvisitorcenter.aspx; 2100 Bridgeway Blvd, Sausalito; ⊙9am-4pm Tue-Sat, extended summer hours 10am-5pm Sat & Sun; 🅿 ♿) **FREE** One of the coolest things in to see in town, fascinating to both kids and adults, is the Army Corps of Engineers' solar-powered visitor center. Housed in one of the old (and cold!) Marinship warehouses, it's a 1.5-acre hydraulic model of San Francisco Bay and the delta region. Self-guided tours take you over and around it as the water flows.

BAY AREA DISCOVERY MUSEUM MUSEUM
(📞415-339-3900; www.baykidsmuseum.org; 557 McReynolds Rd, Fort Baker, Sausalito; $14, free 1st Wed each month; ⊙9am-4pm Tue-Fri, to 5pm Sat

& Sun, also 9am-4pm some Mon; 🅿 🛜 ♿) Below the north tower of the Golden Gate Bridge, at Fort Baker, this excellent hands-on activity museum is designed for children. Multilingual exhibits include a wave workshop, a small underwater tunnel and a large outdoor play area with a shipwreck to romp around. The museum's **Bean Sprouts Café** has healthy nibbles.

RAILROAD & FERRY DEPOT MUSEUM MUSEUM
(📞415-435-1853; http://landmarkssociety.com; 1920 Paradise Dr, Tiburon; suggested donation $5; ⊙1-4pm Wed-Sun Apr-Oct) Formerly the terminus for a 3000-person ferry to San Francisco and a railroad that once reached north to Ukiah, this late-19th-century building showcases a scale model of Tiburon's commercial hub, c 1900. The restored stationmaster's quarters can be visited upstairs.

✖ EATING & DRINKING

⭐**FISH** SEAFOOD $$
(📞415-331-3474; www.331fish.com; 350 Harbor Dr, Sausalito; mains $17-36; ⊙11:30am-8:30pm; ♿) 🌿 Chow down on seafood sandwiches, BBQ oysters or a Dungeness-crab roll at redwood picnic tables facing Richardson Bay. A local leader in promoting fresh and sustainably caught fish, this place has wonderful wild salmon in season and refuses to serve the farmed stuff. It's pricey, but so worth it. Cash only, and expect a queue.

AVATAR'S INDIAN $$
(📞415-332-8083; www.enjoyavatars.com; 2656 Bridgeway Blvd, Sausalito; mains $13-20; ⊙11am-3pm & 5-9:30pm Mon-Sat; 🚪♿) Boasting a cuisine of 'ethnic confusions,' the Indian-fusion dishes here incorporate Mexican, Italian and Caribbean ingredients and will bowl you over with flavor and creativity. Think Punjabi enchiladas with curried sweet potato or spinach fettucine with mild-curry tomato sauce. All diets (vegan, gluten-free etc) are graciously accommodated.

SAM'S ANCHOR CAFE SEAFOOD $$
(📞415-435-4527; www.samscafe.com; 27 Main St, Tiburon; mains $13-25; ⊙11am-9:30pm Mon-Fri, from 9:30am Sat & Sun; ♿) Sam's has been

DAY TRIPS FROM SAN FRANCISCO SAUSALITO & TIBURON

Marin County

slinging seafood and burgers since 1920, and though the entrance looks like a shambling little shack, the area out back rewards you with fantastic waterfront views. On a warm afternoon, you can't beat a cocktail or a tasty plate of sautéed prawns on the deck.

BARREL HOUSE TAVERN CALIFORNIAN $$
(☑415-729-9593; http://barrelhousetavern.com; 660 Bridgeway Blvd, Sausalito; shared dishes $4-18, mains $16-36; ⊙11:30am-9pm Mon-Fri, 11am-9pm Sat & Sun; ➤) You can practically dangle your legs out over the water on the sunny back deck, which has spectacular

bay views. It's a short dash from the ferry terminal, and the California wine, craft beer and cocktail lists complement a raw bar, hot flatbreads and charcuterie and cheese platters.

SUSHI RAN JAPANESE $$$
(☑415-332-3620; http://sushiran.com; 107 Caledonia St, Sausalito; shared dishes $5-38; ⊙11:45am-2:30pm Mon-Fri, 5-10pm Sun-Thu, 5-11pm Fri & Sat) Many Marin residents claim this place is the best sushi spot around. If you didn't reserve ahead, the wine and sake bar next door eases the pain of the long wait for a table.

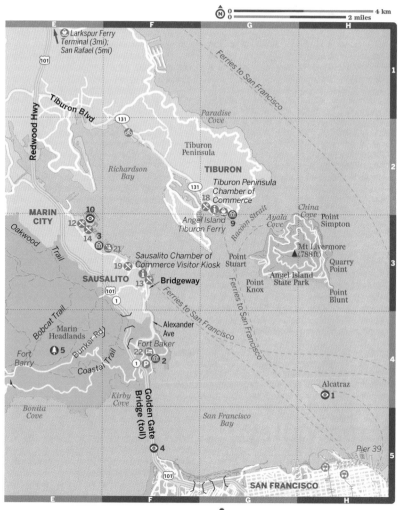

MURRAY CIRCLE   MODERN AMERICAN **$$$**

(☑415-339-4750; www.cavallopoint.com; 601 Murray Circle, Fort Baker, Sausalito; dinner mains $25-36; ⊙7-11am & 11:30am-2pm Mon-Fri, 7am-2:30pm Sat & Sun, 5:30-9pm Sun-Thu, 5:30-10pm Fri & Sat; 🖋🚻) 🖊 At **Cavallo Point lodge** (☑415-339-4700, 888-651-2003; www.cavallopoint.com; 601 Murray Circle; r from $399; 🅿🐕❄@🛜♨🚲🎈) 🖊, dine on locally sourced meats, seafood and produce – perhaps grass-fed organic beef burgers or Dungeness-crab BLT sandwiches – in a clubby dining room topped by a pressed-tin ceiling. Reservations recommended for dinner and weekend brunch.

🏃 ACTIVITIES

SEA TREK   KAYAKING, SUP

(☑415-332-8494; www.seatrek.com; 2100 Bridgeway, Sausalito; kayak or SUP set per hr from $25, tours from $75; ⊙9am-5pm Mon-Fri, 8:30am-5pm Sat & Sun Apr-Oct, 9am-4pm daily Nov-Mar) On a sunny day, Richardson Bay is irresistible. Kayaks and stand up paddleboard (SUP) sets can be rented here. No experience is necessary, and lessons and group outings are also available. Guided kayaking excursions include full-moon and starlight tours and an adventurous crossing to Angel Island. May through October is the best time to paddle.

Marin County

BAY CRUISES CRUISE
(☏415-435-2131; http://angelislandferry.com; 21 Main St, Tiburon; 90min cruise adult/child $20/10; ⊘usually 6:30-8pm Fri & Sat mid-May–mid-Oct) The **Angel Island Tiburon Ferry** (☏415-435-2131; http://angelislandferry.com; 21 Main St; round-trip adult/child/bicycle $15/13/1; ⊕) runs San Francisco Bay sunset cruises on weekend evenings in summer and fall. Reserve ahead and bring your own picnic dinner to enjoy outside on the deck.

Napa Valley

Explore

The USA's premier viticulture region has earned its reputation among the world's best. Despite hype about Wine Country style, it's from the land that all Wine Country lore springs. Rolling hills turn the color of lion's fur under the summer sun and swaths of vineyards carpet hillsides as far as the eye can see. Where they end, redwood forests follow serpentine rivers to the sea.

There are over 900 wineries in Napa and Sonoma Counties, but it's quality, not quantity, that distinguishes the region – especially in Napa, which competes with France and doubles as an outpost of San Francisco's top-end culinary scene. The valley's workaday hub was once a nothing-special city of storefronts, Victorian cot-

tages and riverfront warehouses, but booming real-estate values caused an influx of new money that's transforming downtown.

The Best...

➡**Sight** di Rosa (p219)
➡**Place to Eat** French Laundry (p220)
➡**Place to Drink** Hess Collection (p219)

Top Tip

Most vineyard wine-tasting rooms open daily 10am or 11am to 4pm or 5pm, but call ahead for appointments, especially in Napa. Fees for wine tasting range from $5 to $50, and you must be 21 to taste.

Getting There & Away

➡**Car** Downtown Napa is about an 80-minute drive from San Francisco.

➡**Public transportation** From San Francisco, public transportation can get you to Napa, but it's insufficient for vineyard-hopping. For public-transit information, dial ☏511, or look online at www.transit.511.org.

Need to Know

➡**Area Code** ☏707
➡**Location** 50 miles northeast of San Francisco
➡**Napa Valley Welcome Center** (☏707-251-5895, 855-847-6272; www.visitnapavalley.com; 600 Main St; ⊘9am-5pm; ⊕)

⊙ SIGHTS

★ **DI ROSA** ARTS CENTER
(☏707-226-5991; www.dirosaart.org; 5200 Hwy 121, Napa; $5, tours $12-15; ☉10am-4pm Wed-Sun; P) West of downtown, scrap-metal sculptures dot Carneros vineyards at the 217-acre di Rosa Art + Nature Preserve, a stunning collection of Northern California art, displayed indoors in galleries and outdoors in gardens by a giant lake.

★ **HESS COLLECTION** WINERY, GALLERY
(☏707-255-1144; www.hesscollection.com; 4411 Redwood Rd, Napa; museum free, tasting $25 & $35, tours free; ☉10am-5:30pm, last tasting 5pm, public tour 10:30am) ✐ Art lovers: don't miss Hess Collection, whose galleries display mixed-media and large-canvas works, including pieces by Francis Bacon and Robert Motherwell. In the elegant stone-walled tasting room, find well-known Cabernet Sauvignon and Chardonnay, but also try the Viognier. There's garden service in the warmer months, which is lovely, as Hess overlooks the valley. Make reservations and be prepared to drive a winding road.

★ **FROG'S LEAP** WINERY
(☏707-963-4704; www.frogsleap.com; 8815 Conn Creek Rd, Rutherford; tasting $20-25, incl tour $25; ☉10am-4pm by appointment only; P ♿ 👶)

✐ Meandering paths wind through magical gardens and fruit-bearing orchards surrounding an 1884 barn and farmstead with cats and chickens. The vibe is casual and down-to-earth, with a major emphasis on *fun*. Sauvignon Blanc is its best-known wine but the Merlot merits attention. There's also a dry, restrained Cabernet, atypical of Napa.

All wines are organically farmed.

★ **ROBERT SINSKEY VINEYARDS** WINERY
(☏707-944-9090; www.robertsinskey.com; 6320 Silverado Trail, Napa; bar tasting $40, seated food & wine pairings $70-175; ☉10am-4:30pm; P)
✐ The fabulous hillside tasting room, constructed of stone, redwood and teak, resembles a small cathedral – fitting, given the sacred status here bestowed upon food and wine. It specializes in organic Pinot Noir, plus aromatic white varietals, dry rosé and Bordeaux varietals such as Merlot and Cab Franc, all crafted for the dinner table. Small bites accompany bar tastings and seated food and wine experiences are curated by chef Maria Sinskey herself. Reserve ahead for sit-down tastings and culinary tours.

★ **TRES SABORES** WINERY
(☏707-967-8027; www.tressabores.com; 1620 South Whitehall Lane, St Helena; tour & tasting $40; ☉10:30am-3pm, by appointment; 👶) ✐ At the valley's westernmost edge, where

---

WINE COUNTRY WITHOUT A CAR

Beyond the Label (☏707-363-4023; www.btlnv.com; per couple from $995) Personalized tours, including lunch at home with a vintner, guided by a knowledgeable Napa native.

Napa Valley Vine Trail (☏707-252-3547; http://vinetrail.org) A new multiuse trail in Napa Valley that connects vineyards, wineries, downtown Napa and Yountville via 12 miles of walking and cycling paths. The trail is just a piece of ambitious 47-mile stretch that will eventually connect the Vallejo Ferry Terminal to Calistoga (in about a decade).

Active Wine Adventures (☏707-927-1058; www.activewineadventures.com; per person $125) This innovative tour company in Napa Valley pairs wine and food with scenic hikes, local art, literary adventures and, most recently, microbreweries.

Napa Valley Wine Train (☏707-253-2111, 800-427-4124; http://winetrain.com; 1275 McKinstry St, Napa; ticket incl dining from $146) A cushy, if touristy, way to see Wine Country, the Wine Train offers three-hour daily trips in vintage Pullman dining cars, from Napa to St Helena and back, with optional winery tours, in addition to six-hour journeys visiting multiple wineries with Napa Valley cuisine served between visits.

Platypus Wine Tours (☏707-253-2723; www.platypustours.com; join-in tour per person $110) Billed as the anti-wine-snob tour, Platypus specializes in backroad vineyards, historic wineries and family-owned operations. There's a daily 'join-in' tour that shuttles guests to four wineries and provides a picnic lunch, and private tours with a dedicated driver and vehicle. The Napa tours are the most popular, but Platypus also takes people to Sonoma, Russian River and Dry Creek Valleys.

sloping vineyards meet wooded hillsides, Tres Sabores is a portal to old Napa – no fancy tasting room, no snobbery, just great wine in a spectacular setting. Bucking the Cabernet custom, Tres Sabores crafts elegantly structured, Burgundian-style Zinfandel and spritely Sauvignon Blanc, which the *New York Times* dubbed a top 10 of its kind in California. Reservations are essential.

PRIDE MOUNTAIN
WINERY

(☑707-963-4949; www.pridewines.com; 4026 Spring Mountain Rd, St Helena; tasting & tour $20-30, summit experience $75; ☺by appointment only) High atop Spring Mountain, cult-favorite Pride straddles the Napa–Sonoma border and bottles vintages under both appellations. The well-structured Cabernet and heavy-hitting Merlot are the best-known but there's also an elegant Viognier (perfect with oysters) and standout Cab Franc, available only here. Picnicking is spectacular: choose Viewpoint for drop-dead vistas, or Ghost Winery for shade and the historic ruins of a 19th-century winery, but you must first reserve a tasting. Bottles cost $42 to $70.

LONG MEADOW RANCH
FARM

(☑707-963-4555; www.longmeadowranch.com; 738 Main St, St Helena; tasting $25-40, chef's table $145; ☺11am-6pm) ✐ Long Meadow stands out for olive-oil tastings ($5), plus good estate-grown Cabernet, Sauvignon Blanc, Chardonnay and Pinot Noir, served inside an 1874 farmhouse surrounded by lovely gardens. It also has a whiskey flight for $30; sells housemade products such as preserves, BBQ sauce and Bloody Mary mix; and hosts chef's tables (four- to five-course food and wine experiences) at lunch and dinner daily. Reservations for chef's table required. Bottles $20 to $50.

CADE
WINERY

(☑707-965-2746; www.cadewinery.com; 360 Howell Mountain Rd S, Angwin; tasting & tour $80; ☺by appointment only) ✐ Ascend Mt Veeder for drop-dead vistas, 1800ft above the valley, at Napa's oh-so-swank, first-ever organically farmed, LEED gold-certified winery, partly owned by former San Francisco mayor Gavin Newsom. Hawks ride thermals at eye level as you sample bright Sauvignon Blanc and luscious Cabernet Sauvignon that's more Bordelaise in style than Californian. Reservations required. Bottles cost $44 to $80.

CIA AT COPIA
CENTER

(☑707-967-2500; www.ciaatcopia.com; 500 1st St, Napa; ☺10:30am-9pm) The former food museum beside Napa's famous Oxbow Public Market has been revived as a center of all things edible by the prestigious Culinary Institute of America. In its new life as Copia, the 80,000-sq-ft campus offers wine tastings, interactive cooking demos, an innovative restaurant, a massive fork statue (composed of many thousands of smaller forks) and more food-related features.

✖ EATING

★OXBOW PUBLIC MARKET
MARKET $

(☑707-226-6529; www.oxbowpublicmarket.com; 610 & 644 1st St, Napa; items from $3; ☺9am-9pm; 🛜🍴) ✐ Graze at this gourmet market and plug into the Northern California food scene. Standouts: **Hog Island Oyster Co**; comfort cooking at celeb-chef Todd Humphries' **Kitchen Door**; great Cal-Mexican tacos at **C Casa & Taco Lounge**; the IPAs and sour beers at **Fieldwork Brewing Company**; espresso from **Ritual Coffee**; and **Three Twins** certified-organic ice cream.

BOUCHON BAKERY
BAKERY $

(☑707-944-2253; www.bouchonbakery.com; 6528 Washington St, Yountville; items from $3; ☺7am-7pm; ☑) Bouchon makes as-good-as-in-Paris French pastries and strong coffee. There's always a line and rarely a seat: get it to go.

★FRENCH LAUNDRY
CALIFORNIAN $$$

(☑707-944-2380; www.thomaskeller.com/tfl; 6640 Washington St, Yountville; prix-fixe dinner $310; ☺seatings 11am-12:30pm Fri-Sun, 5-9pm daily) The pinnacle of California dining, Thomas Keller's French Laundry is epic, a high-wattage culinary experience on par with the world's best. Book one month ahead on the online app Tock, where tickets are released in groupings. This is the meal you can brag about the rest of your life.

RESTAURANT AT MEADOWOOD
CALIFORNIAN $$$

(☑707-967-1205; www.meadowood.com; 900 Meadowood Lane, St Helena; 12-course menu $275; ☺5:30-9:30pm Tue-Sat) If you couldn't score reservations at French Laundry, fear not: Meadowood – the valley's only other Michelin-three-star restaurant – has a slightly more sensibly priced menu, elegantly unfussy dining room and lavish haute cuisine

Wine Country

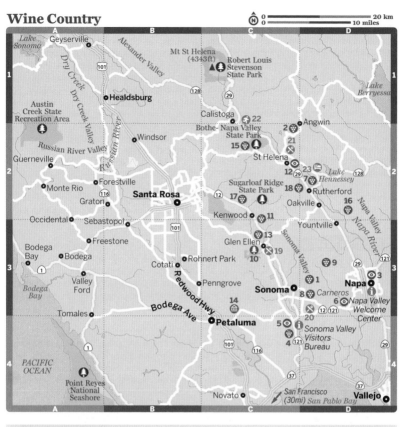

N 0 _____ 20 km
  0 _____ 10 miles

DAY TRIPS FROM SAN FRANCISCO NAPA VALLEY

Wine Country

that's not too esoteric. **Auberge** (☑800-348-5406, 707-963-1211; www.aubergedusoleil.com; 180 Rutherford Hill Rd, Rutherford; r $795-1500, ste $1525-5300; ❋🐾🛎🐾) has better views, but the food and service here far surpass it.

★**CALISTOGA KITCHEN**   CALIFORNIAN $$$
(☑707-942-6500; www.calistogakitchen.com; 1107 Cedar St, Calistoga; lunch mains $12-18, dinner $20-36; ☺5:30pm-close Thu, 11:30am-3pm & 5:30pm-close Fri & Sat, 9:30am-3pm Sun) A sparsely decorated cottage surrounded by a white-picket fence, Calistoga Kitchen is especially good for lunch in the garden. The chef-owner favors simplicity, focusing on quality ingredients in a half-dozen changing dishes, such as a delicious braised rabbit. Reservations advised, especially for the patio.

★**CICCIO**   ITALIAN $$$
(☑707-945-1000; www.ciccionapavalley.com; 6770 Washington St, Yountville; mains $25-32; ☺5-9pm Wed-Sun) The small, frequently changing menu at this family-owned Italian place is dependent on the season and likely to include just a couple of veggies, pastas, meat options and four to six wood-fired pizzas. But wow! You cannot go wrong, especially if you're lucky enough to show up when whole sea bass and garlicky pea tendrils are available.

AD HOC   CALIFORNIAN $$$
(☑707-944-2487; www.adhocrestaurant.com; 6476 Washington St, Yountville; prix-fixe dinner from $55; ☺5-10pm Thu-Sat & Mon, 9am-1:30pm & 5-10pm Sun) A winning formula by Yount-

HIGHWAY 1 SOUTH OF SAN FRANCISCO

Unspooling south of San Francisco toward the surf mecca of Santa Cruz, coastal Hwy 1 is bordered by craggy beaches, sea-salted lighthouses, organic farms and tiny towns. Spot migratory whales breaching offshore in winter or kitesurfers skimming waves like giant mosquitoes.

The beauty prize-winning beaches begin less than 10 miles south of San Francisco in **Pacifica**. After driving through the tunnels, pull over for **Devil's Slide Trail**, a paved 1.3-mile section of old Hwy 1. Five miles south of town, **Montara State Beach** (☑650-726-8819; www.parks.ca.gov; Hwy 1; ☺8am-sunset; P🐾) ꜰʀᴇᴇ is a local favorite for its pristine sand. Further south by Moss Beach, **Fitzgerald Marine Reserve** (☑650-728-3584; www.fitzgeraldreserve.org; 200 Nevada Ave, Moss Beach; ☺8am-8pm Apr-Aug, closes earlier Sep-Mar; P🐾) ꜰʀᴇᴇ protects tide pools teeming with sealife, best viewed at low tide.

Next up is 4-mile-long, crescent-shaped **Half Moon Bay State Beach** (☑650-726-8819; www.parks.ca.gov; off Hwy 1; per car $10; ☺8am-sunset; P🐾). Turn off at **Pillar Point Harbor**, packed with seafood shacks, and climb the sand dunes above **Mavericks** surf break, where in winter death-defying surfers ride 40ft-plus swells past rocky cliffs. When the bay is calm, paddle out with **Half Moon Bay Kayak Co** (☑650-773-6101; www.hmbkayak.com; 2 Johnson Pier; kayak or SUP set rental per hour/day $25/75; bicycle rental $25/50; ☺9am-5pm Wed-Mon; 🐾).

Fifteen miles further south, **Pescadero State Beach & Marsh Natural Preserve** (☑650-726-8819; www.parks.ca.gov; off Hwy 1; per car $8; ☺8am-sunset; P🐾) ꜰ attracts beachcombers and birders. Detour inland to Pescadero village for **Arcangeli Grocery Company** (Norm's Market; ☑650-879-0147; www.normsmarket.com; 287 Stage Rd; sandwiches $7-10; ☺10am-6pm; ☑🐾) bakery-deli and the cheese shop at family-owned **Harley Farms** (☑650-879-0480; http://harleyfarms.com; 250 North St; ☺10am-5pm Thu-Mon Apr-Dec, 11am-4pm Fri-Sun Jan-Mar; P🐾) ꜰ, which offers goat-dairy farm tour.

Three miles south of the Pescadero turnoff, **Bean Hollow State Beach** (☑650-726-8819; www.parks.ca.gov; off Hwy 1; ☺8am-sunset; P🐾) ꜰ ꜰʀᴇᴇ is awash in gemstone pebbles. **Pigeon Point Light Station** (☑650-879-2120; www.parks.ca.gov; 210 Pigeon Point Rd; ☺8am-sunset, visitor center 10am-4pm Thu-Mon; P🐾), one of coastal California's tallest lighthouses, stands on a windswept perch off Hwy 1. Another 5 miles south, **Año Nuevo State Park** (☑park office 650-879-2025, recorded info 650-879-0227, tour reservations 800-444-4445; www.parks.ca.gov; 1 New Years Creek Rd; per car $10, 2½hr tour per person $7; ☺8:30am-sunset Apr-Nov, tours only Dec 15–Mar 31; P🐾) ꜰ is home to an enormous colony of elephant seals. Book well ahead for a guided walking tour during the cacophonous winter birthing and mating season.

ville's culinary patriarch, Thomas Keller, Ad Hoc serves the master's favorite American home cooking in four family-style courses with no variations (dietary restrictions notwithstanding). The menu changes daily but regularly features pot roast, BBQ and fried chicken, which is also available (for takeout only) on weekends behind Ad Hoc at Keller's latest venture, **Addendum** (📞707-944-1565; www.adhocrestaurant.com/addendum; 6476 Washington St; box lunch $16.50; ⊙11am-2pm Thu-Sat; �'').

🏃 ACTIVITIES

★INDIAN SPRINGS SPA   SPA
(📞707-709-2449; www.indianspringscalistoga.com, Calistoga; 1712 Lincoln Ave; ⊙by appointment 9am-9pm) California's longest continually operating spa, and original Calistoga resort, has concrete mud tubs and mines its own ash. Treatments include use of the huge, hot-spring-fed pool. Great cucumber body lotion.

SPA SOLAGE   SPA
(📞707-266-0825; www.solage.aubergeresorts.com/spa; 755 Silverado Trail, Calistoga; ⊙by appointment 8am-8pm) Chichi, top-end spa, with couples' rooms and a fango-mud bar for DIY paint-on treatments. Also has zero-gravity chairs for blanket wraps and sex-segregated clothing-optional mineral pools.

Sonoma Valley

Explore

We have a soft spot for Sonoma's folksy ways. Unlike fancy Napa, nobody cares if you drive a clunker and vote Green. Locals call it 'Slow-noma.' Anchoring the bucolic 17-mile-long valley, the town of Sonoma makes a great jumping-off point for exploring Wine Country – it's an hour from San Francisco – and has a marvelous sense of place, with storied 19th-century historical sights surrounding the state's largest town square.

Halfway up-valley, tiny Glen Ellen is straight from a Norman Rockwell painting – in stark contrast to the valley's northern-most town, Santa Rosa, the workaday urban center best known for traffic. If you have more than a day, explore Sonoma's quiet, rustic western side along the Russian River Valley, and continue to the sea.

The Best...

→**Sight** Sonoma Plaza

→**Place to Eat** Cafe La Haye (p225)

→**Place to Drink** Bartholomew Park Winery (p224)

Top Tip

If you're not up for driving, hit downtown Sonoma's tasting rooms around shady Sonoma Plaza, where it's legal to drink wine on the grass from 11am until dark.

Getting There & Away

→**Car** From San Francisco to Sonoma Valley (90 minutes), take Hwy 101 north to Hwy 37 east. At the Hwy 37/121 split, take Hwy 121 north, then Hwy 12 north.

→**Bus** Service is infrequent and slow. From San Francisco, Golden Gate Transit (p268) buses connect twice hourly to Santa Rosa ($11.75, 2¼ hours), from where limited **Sonoma County Transit** (📞800-345-7433, 707-576-7433; http://sctransit.com) buses run to downtown Sonoma ($3.05, 70 minutes) via Sonoma Valley towns.

Need to Know

→**Area Code** 📞707

→**Location** 45 miles north–northeast of San Francisco.

→**Sonoma Valley Visitors Bureau** (📞707-996-1090; www.sonomavalley.com; 23570 Hwy 121, Cornerstone Gardens; ⊙10am-4pm)

◉ SIGHTS

Less pretentious and more laid-back than Napa, Sonoma Valley shelters more than 40 wineries alongside Hwy 12. You usually don't need tasting appointments, but call ahead to book vineyard tours. For picnicking, some wineries now charge fees and require reservations for picnic tables; otherwise, buy a bottle of your host's wine – it's only polite.

★SONOMA PLAZA   SQUARE
(btwn Napa, Spain & 1st Sts, Sonoma) Smack in the center of the plaza, the Mission Revival–style city hall, built 1906–08, has identical facades on four sides, reportedly because

plaza businesses all demanded City Hall face their direction. At the plaza's northeast corner, the **Bear Flag Monument** (Sonoma Plaza) marks Sonoma's moment of revolutionary glory. The weekly farmers market (5:30pm to 8pm Tuesday, April to October) showcases Sonoma's incredible produce.

SONOMA STATE HISTORIC PARK
HISTORIC SITE

(☑707-938-9560; www.parks.ca.gov; adult/child $3/2; ⊘10am-5pm) This park in Sonoma is comprised of multiple sites, most side-by-side. Founded in 1823, **Mission San Francisco Solano de Sonoma** (☑707-938-9560; www.parks.ca.gov; 114 E Spain St; adult/child $3/2; ⊘10am-5pm) anchors the plaza, and was the final California mission. **Sonoma Barracks** (☑707-939-9420; www.parks.ca.gov; 20 E Spain St; adult/child $3/2; ⊘10am-5pm) houses exhibits on 19th-century life. The 1886 **Toscano Hotel** (☑707-938-9560; www.parks.ca.gov; 20 E Spain St; adult/child $3/2; ⊘10am-5pm, tours 1-4pm Sat & Sun) FREE lobby is beautifully preserved – peek inside. The 1852 **Vallejo's Home** (☑707-938-9559; 363 3rd St W; adult/child $3/2; ⊘10am-5pm, tours 1pm, 2pm & 3pm Sat & Sun) lies a half-mile northwest. One ticket allows same-day admission to all, including **Petaluma Adobe State Park** (☑707-762-4871; www.petalumaadobe.com; 3325 Adobe Rd, Petaluma; adult/child $3/2; ⊘10am-5pm; P) at General Vallejo's former ranch, 15 miles away.

★BARTHOLOMEW PARK WINERY
WINERY

(☑707-939-3026; www.bartpark.com; 1000 Vineyard Lane, Sonoma; tasting $15; ⊘11am-4:30pm; P) ✦ A great bike-to winery, Bartholomew Park occupies a 375-acre nature preserve with oak-shaded picnicking and valley-view hiking. The vineyards were originally cultivated in 1857 and now yield certified-organic, citrusy Sauvignon Blanc, Cabernet Sauvignon softer in style than Napa and lush Zinfandel. There's also a new collection of reserve wines and a new private tasting experience. Bottles are $27 to $48.

★GUNDLACH-BUNDSCHU WINERY
WINERY

(☑707-938-5277; www.gunbun.com; 2000 Denmark St, Sonoma; tasting $20-30, incl tour $30-60; ⊘11am-5:30pm May-Oct, to 4:30pm Nov-Apr; P) ✦ California's oldest family-run winery looks like a castle but has a down-to-earth vibe. Founded in 1858 by a Bavarian immigrant, its signatures are Gewürztraminer

and Pinot Noir, but 'Gun-Bun' was the first American winery to produce 100% Merlot. Down a winding lane, it's a terrific bike-to-winery with picnicking, hiking, a lake and concerts, including a two-day folk-music festival in June. Tour the 1800-barrel cave by reservation only. Bottles are $20 to $50.

JACK LONDON STATE HISTORIC PARK
PARK

(☑707-938-5216; www.jacklondonpark.com; 2400 London Ranch Rd, Glen Ellen; per car $10, cottage adult/child $4/2; ⊘9:30am-5pm; P ♿) ✦ Napa has Robert Louis Stevenson, but Sonoma has Jack London. This 1400-acre park frames that author's last years; don't miss the excellent on-site **museum**. Miles of **hiking trails** (some open to mountain bikes) weave through oak-dotted woodlands, between 600ft and 2300ft elevations; an easy 2-mile loop meanders to **London Lake**, great for picnicking. On select summer evenings, the park transforms into a theater for 'Broadway Under the Stars.' Be alert for poison oak.

KUNDE
WINERY

(☑707-833-5501; www.kunde.com; 9825 Hwy 12, Kenwood; tasting $15-50, cave tours free; ⊘10:30am-5pm; P) ✦ This family-owned winery on a historic ranch has vineyards that are more than a century old. It offers mountain-top tastings with impressive valley views and seasonal guided hikes (advance reservations recommended), though you can also just stop for a tasting and a tour. Elegant, 100% estate-grown wines include crisp Chardonnay and unfussy red blends, all made sustainably. Bottles $17 to $100.

CORNERSTONE SONOMA
GARDENS

(☑707-933-3010; www.cornerstonesonoma.com; 23570 Arnold Dr, Sonoma; ⊘10am-5pm, gardens to 4pm; P ♿) FREE This roadside, wine-country marketplace showcases 25 walk-through (in some cases edible) gardens, along with a bunch of innovative and adorable shops, wine-tasting parlors and on-site Sonoma Valley Visitors Bureau (p223). There's a good, if pricey, cafe, and an outdoor 'test kitchen.'

BENZIGER
WINERY

(☑707-935-3000, 888-490-2739; www.benziger.com; 1883 London Ranch Rd, Glen Ellen; tasting $20-40, tours $25-50; ⊘10am-5pm, tram tours 11am-3:30pm; P ♿) ✦ If you're new to wine, make Benziger your first stop for Sonoma's best crash course in winemaking.

The worthwhile tour (reservations recommended) includes an tram ride (weather permitting) through biodynamic vineyards and a five-wine tasting. Great picnicking, excellent for families. The large-production wine is OK (head for the reserves); the tour's the thing. Bottles are $20 to $80.

ST FRANCIS WINERY
& VINEYARDS   WINERY
(☑707-538-9463; www.stfranciswinery.com; 100 Pythian Rd, Santa Rosa; tasting $15, wine & cheese pairing $25, wine & food pairing $68; ⊙10am-5pm) The vineyards are scenic and all, but the real reason to visit St Francis is the much-lauded food-pairing experience. The mouthwatering, multicourse affair is hosted by amiable and informative wine experts and includes things such as braised Kurobuta pork with Okinawan sweet potatoes paired with Cab Franc and American Wagyu strip loin and chanterelles paired with an old-vine Zin. Seatings at 11am, 1pm and 3pm, Thursday to Monday. Spots fill fast; book well in advance.

CLINE CELLARS   WINERY
(☑707-940-4030; www.clinecellars.com; 24737 Arnold Dr, Sonoma; tasting free-$20; ⊙tasting room 10am-6pm, museum to 4pm) 🅿 Balmy days are for pond-side picnics and rainy ones for fireside tastings of old-vine Zinfandel and Mouvedre inside an 1850s farmhouse. Stroll out back to the **California Mission Museum**, housing 1930s miniature replicas of California's original 21 Spanish Colonial missions.

LOXTON   WINERY
(☑707-935-7221; www.loxtonwines.com; 11466 Dunbar Rd, Glen Ellen; tasting $10-20, walking tour $25; ⊙11am-5pm) Say g'day to Chris the Aussie winemaker at Loxton, a no-frills winery with million-dollar views of the grapes you'll actually be tasting. The tasting room contains a small warehouse where racing cars were once designed, and there you can sample wonderful Syrah and Zinfandel; nonoaky, fruit-forward Chardonnay; and good port. Bottles cost $17 to $32.

🍴 EATING

GLEN ELLEN
VILLAGE MARKET   DELI, MARKET $
(☑707-996-6728; www.sonoma-glenellenmkt.com; 13751 Arnold Dr, Glen Ellen; ⊙5am-9pm; 🖶) Fantastic market with a huge deli, ideal for picnickers.

★ FREMONT DINER   AMERICAN, SOUTHERN $$
(☑707-938-7370; www.thefremontdiner.com; 2698 Fremont Dr, Sonoma; mains $9-22; ⊙8am-3pm Mon-Wed, to 9pm Thu-Sun; 🖶) 🅿 Lines snake out the door at peak times at this farm-to-table roadside diner. We prefer the indoor tables but will happily accept a picnic table to feast on buttermilk pancakes with homemade cinnamon-vanilla syrup, chicken and waffles, oyster po'boys, finger-licking barbecue and skillet-baked cornbread.

HOPMONK TAVERN   PUB FOOD $$
(☑707-935-9100; www.hopmonk.com; 691 Broadway, Sonoma; mains $11-23; ⊙11:30am-9pm Sun-Thu, to 10pm Fri & Sat) This happening gastropub and beer garden takes its brews seriously with over a dozen of its own and guest beers on tap, served in type-appropriate glassware. Live music Friday through Sunday, open mike on Wednesday starting at 8pm.

FIG CAFE & WINEBAR   FRENCH, CALIFORNIAN $$
(☑707-938-2130; www.thefigcafe.com; 13690 Arnold Dr, Glen Ellen; mains $12-24, 3-course dinner $36; ⊙10am-2:30pm Sat & Sun, 5-9pm Sun-Thu, 5-9:30pm Fri & Sat) The Fig's earthy California–Provençal comfort food includes flash-fried calamari with spicy lemon aioli, fig and arugula salad and *steak frites*. Good wine prices and weekend brunch give reason to return. No reservations; complimentary corkage.

★ CAFE LA HAYE   CALIFORNIAN $$$
(☑707-935-5994; www.cafelahaye.com; 140 E Napa St, Sonoma; mains $19-25; ⊙5:30-9pm Tue-Sat) 🅿 One of Sonoma's top tables for earthy New American cooking, La Haye only uses produce sourced from within 60 miles. Its dining room gets packed cheek-by-jowl and service can be perfunctory, but the simple, flavor-packed cooking make it many foodies' first choice. Reserve well ahead.

GLEN ELLEN STAR   CALIFORNIAN, ITALIAN $$$
(☑707-343-1384; http://glenellenstar.com; 13648 Arnold Dr, Glen Ellen; pizza $15-20, mains $24-50; ⊙5:30-9pm Sun-Thu, to 9:30pm Fri & Sat; 🅿) 🅿 Helmed by chef Ari Weiswasser, who once worked at Thomas Keller's French Laundry (p220), this petite Glen Ellen bistro shines a light on the best of Sonoma farms and ranches. Local, organic and seasonal ingredients star in dishes such as spring-lamb ragu, whole roasted fish with broccoli di cicco or golden beets with harissa crumble. Reservations recommended.

🛏 Sleeping

San Francisco hotel rates are among the world's highest. Plan ahead – well ahead – and grab bargains when you see them. Given the choice, San Francisco's boutique properties beat chains for a sense of place – but take what you can get at a price you can afford.

When to Book

Travelers often only consider the cost of an airline ticket when choosing the dates of their trip, but you should confirm the availability of good hotel rates before booking flights. 'City-wide sellouts' happen several times a year when there's a big convention or event in town. Check the **SF Convention & Visitors Bureau convention calendar** (www.sanfrancisco.travel/article/hotel-availability), which shows the availability 'opportunity' for meeting planners. Look for times that list 'high opportunity' – this means many rooms are available in convention hotels and, by extension, smaller hotels. But if the calendar lists a specific convention, choose other dates or pay a premium – sometimes double or triple base rates.

Room Rates & Fees

San Francisco is in a boom cycle – this is the epicenter of tech and the whole world wants to be here. There simply aren't enough beds. Between 2012 and 2017, rates at many downtown hotels jumped more than 100%. Day-to-day rates fluctuate wildly. Brace yourself. Prices reflect the average cost of a basic double room from April to October, excluding city-wide sellouts, when hotels charge 'compression rates' – a handy term when negotiating with hotels.

To get the best prices at chains, where rates change daily, call the hotel during business hours and speak with in-house reservations, rather than toll-free central reservations, for up-to-date information about inventories and specials. Some hotels have internet-only deals, but, when booking online, know that 'best rate' does not necessarily mean lowest available rate. When in doubt, call the hotel directly. Online booking engines (eg Priceline) offer lower rates but have many restrictions and may be nonrefundable.

Although hostels and budget hotels are cheapest, rooms are never truly cheap in SF: expect to pay $100 for a private hostel room, $200 at a budget motel and over $300 at mid-range hotels. Note the hefty 15% room tax on top of quoted rates. Most hotels offer free wi-fi (only luxury hotels charge, claiming it's for secured lines). Prices run higher June to August and plummet from November to April. Ask about weekly rates. At weekends and on holidays, rates for business and luxury hotels decrease, but they increase for tourist hotels; on weekdays the opposite is true.

Hotels Versus Home Rentals

Housing stock in San Francisco has been pulled off the market, as owners have decided to rent their rooms and apartments, via Airbnb and other home-rental sites, to short-term vacationers instead of long-term tenants. The downside for travelers is that you don't necessarily know what you're getting into, and if you get a bad place, you can't simply call the front desk and switch rooms. The upside is that you may get a glorious garden apartment at a great rate. *Caveat emptor.* There are ongoing fights in City Hall about regulating these sites. Stay tuned.

Lonely Planet's Top Choices

Hotel Drisco (p229) Stately boutique hotel in civilized Pacific Heights.

Argonaut Hotel (p230) Nautical-themed hotel at Fisherman's Wharf.

Hotel Vitale (p232) Contemporary downtowner with knockout waterfront vistas.

Inn at the Presidio (p229) National-park lodge in historic building surrounded by nature.

Hotel Bohème (p234) Artsy midbudget boutique charmer in the heart of North Beach.

Best by Budget

$

HI San Francisco Fisherman's Wharf (p229) Waterfront hostel with million-dollar views.

San Remo Hotel (p233) Spartan furnishings, shared bathrooms, great rates.

Pacific Tradewinds Hostel (p233) Downtown hostel with snappy design.

$$

Inn at the Presidio (p229) Small luxury inn surrounded by national-park land.

Kensington Park Hotel (p231) Spiffy Union Sq boutique hotel.

Hotel Carlton (p231) Freshly redesigned with good-value rooms.

Marker (p230) Snazzy design, useful amenities, central location.

$$$

Hotel Drisco (p229) Luxury inn atop Pacific Heights.

Loews Regency (p233) Five-star service, knockout views.

Palace Hotel (p232) Stately classical hotel, century-old landmark.

Hotel Zetta (p232) Tech-centric downtowner filled with art.

Best Views

Loews Regency (p233) Bridge-to-bridge views from a five-star skyscraper.

Sir Francis Drake Hotel (p233) Playful 1920s tower hotel above Union Sq.

Fairmont San Francisco (p235) Hilltop vistas plus SF's grandest lobby.

Mark Hopkins Intercontinental (p235) Nob Hill address for stately charm.

Best with Kids

Hotel Zephyr (p229) Games everywhere and a vast outdoor courtyard.

Hotel del Sol (p229) Colorful theme rooms, plus a heated outdoor pool.

Argonaut Hotel (p230) The Wharf's best hotel, with a giant lobby to explore.

Americania Hotel (p232) Better-than-average motel with pool.

Best for Victorian Splendor

Chateau Tivoli (p236) Legendary boarding house where Mark Twain and sundry opera divas caroused and crashed.

Inn San Francisco (p235) Antique-packed 1872 Italianate mansion with Californian flair – including a redwood hot tub.

Queen Anne Hotel (p234) An 1890 mansion and former girls' boarding school that sets the scene for novels and cozy hideaways.

Parsonage (p236) Period-perfect Italianate mansion with airy, glamorous rooms.

NEED TO KNOW

Prices

The following price ranges refer to a double room with bathroom in high season (summer); you can sometimes do better, except when there's a convention.

$	less than $150
$$	$150–$350
$$$	more than $350

Parking

Hotel parking costs $40 to $60 per night extra. The parking symbol indicates a *free* self-service lot. Hotels without parking often have valet parking or an agreement with a nearby garage; call ahead.

Reconfirming

If you're arriving after 4pm, guarantee with a credit card or your reservation may be cancelled.

Tipping

Tipping housekeepers in US hotels is standard practice; leave a few dollars on your pillow each morning and be guaranteed excellent housekeeping.

Breakfast

Breakfast is not included in rates unless specified.

SLEEPING

Where to Stay

NEIGHBORHOOD	FOR	AGAINST
The Marina, Fisherman's Wharf & the Piers	Near the northern waterfront; good for kids; lots of restaurants and nightlife at the Marina; many motels on Lombard St – with parking.	Fisherman's Wharf is all tourists; parking at the Marina and Wharf is a nightmare.
Downtown, Civic Center & SoMa	Biggest selection of hotels; near all public transportation, including cable cars; walkable to many sights, restaurants, shopping and theaters. Parts of SoMa are close to major downtown sights; great nightlife.	Downtown quiet at night; Civic Center feels rough – the worst area extends three blocks in all directions from Eddy and Jones Sts; parking expensive. SoMa: few restaurants, gritty streets at nighttime.
North Beach & Chinatown	Culturally colorful; great strolling; lots of cafes and restaurants; terrific sense of place.	Street noise; limited choice and transport; next-to-impossible parking.
Nob Hill, Russian Hill & Fillmore	Stately, classic hotels atop Nob Hill; good restaurants and shopping in Pacific Heights and Japantown.	The Hills are steep, hard on the out-of-shape; parking difficult; slightly removed from major sights.
The Mission & Potrero Hill	The Mission's flat terrain makes walking easier; good for biking; easy access to BART.	Limited choice; distance from sights; gritty street scene on main thoroughfares.
The Castro & Noe Valley	Great nightlife, especially for LGBT travelers; provides a good taste of local life; easy access to Market St transit.	Distance from major tourist sights; few choices; limited parking.
The Haight & Hayes Valley	Lots of bars and restaurants; Hayes Valley near cultural sights; the Haight near Golden Gate Park.	Limited public transportation in the Haight; gritty street scene at night on major thoroughfares; parking difficult.
Golden Gate Park & the Avenues	Quiet nights; good for outdoor recreation; easier parking.	Very far from major sights; foggy and cold in summer; limited transportation and restaurants.

🛏 The Marina, Fisherman's Wharf & the Piers

⭐**HI SAN FRANCISCO FISHERMAN'S WHARF** HOSTEL **$**

Map p292 (📞415-771-7277; www.sfhostels.com; Fort Mason, Bldg 240; dm $30-53, r $116-134; 🅿 @ 🛜; 🚌28, 30, 47, 49) Trading downtown convenience for a glorious park-like setting with million-dollar waterfront views, this hostel occupies a former army-hospital building, with bargain-priced private rooms and dorms (some co-ed) with four to 22 beds (avoid bunks one and two – they're by doorways). Huge kitchen. No curfew, but no heat during daytime: bring warm clothes. Limited free parking.

⭐**INN AT THE PRESIDIO** HOTEL **$$**

Map p291 (📞415-800-7356; www.innatthe presidio.com; 42 Moraga Ave; r $295-380; 🅿 🔄 @ 🛜 🖲; 🚌43, PresidiGo shuttle) 🏃 Built in 1903 as bachelor quarters for army officers, this three-story, red-brick building in the Presidio was transformed in 2012 into a spiffy national-park lodge, styled with leather, linen and wood. Oversized rooms are plush, including feather beds with Egyptian-cotton sheets. Suites have gas fireplaces. Nature surrounds you, with hiking trailheads out back, but taxis downtown cost $25. Free parking.

HOTEL ZEPHYR DESIGN HOTEL **$$**

Map p289 (📞415-617-6565, 844-617-6555; www.hotelzephyrsf.com; 250 Beach St; r $250-400; 🅿 🖲 @ 🛜 🖲; 🚌8, 39, 47, 🚋Powell-Mason, Ⓜ E, F) 🏃 Completely revamped in 2015, this vintage-1960s hotel surrounds a vast courtyard with fire pits and lounge chairs, modern art from nautical junk, and games like ping-pong in a tube – reminders you're here to play, not work. Rooms are fresh and spiffy, with up-to-date amenities, including smart TVs that link with your devices. Best rooms face the water. Parking costs $57.

HOTEL DEL SOL MOTEL **$$**

Map p292 (📞415-921-5520, 877-433-5765; www.jdvhotels.com; 3100 Webster St; d $259-359; 🅿 🖲 @ 🛜 🖲 🖲 🖲; 🚌22, 28, 30, 43) 🏃 The spiffy, kid-friendly Marina District Hotel del Sol is a riot of color, with tropical-themed decor. This is a quiet, revamped 1950s motor lodge with palm-lined central courtyard, one of the few San Francisco hotels with a heated outdoor pool. Family suites have trundle beds and board games. Free parking.

MARINA MOTEL MOTEL **$$**

Map p292 (📞800-346-6118, 415-921-9406; www.marinamotel.com; 2576 Lombard St; r $189-269; 🅿 🛜 🖲; 🚌28, 30, 41, 43, 45) Established in 1939 to accommodate visitors arriving via the new Golden Gate Bridge, the Marina has an inviting Spanish-Mediterranean look, with a quiet bougainvillea-lined courtyard. Rooms are homey, simple and well maintained (occasional scuffs notwithstanding); some have full kitchens (extra $10 to $20). Rooms on Lombard St are loud; request one in back. Free parking.

TUSCAN BOUTIQUE HOTEL **$$**

Map p289 (📞415-561-1100, 800-648-4626; www.tuscanhotel.com; 425 North Point St; r from $289; 🅿 🖲 @ 🛜 🖲 🖲; 🚌47, 🚋Powell-Mason, Ⓜ F) 🏃 Staying at touristy Fisherman's Wharf doesn't mean you have to settle for plain Jane chains like Sheraton. The Tuscan is just as comfortable but has more character, with spacious rooms styled with white-on-white linens and colorful accent fabrics. Kids love the in-room Nintendo; parents love the afternoon wine hour. Parking costs $55.

COVENTRY MOTOR INN MOTEL **$$**

Map p292 (📞415-567-1200; www.coventry motorinn.com; 1901 Lombard St; r $158-228; 🅿 🔄 🖲 🖲 🖲; 🚌22, 28, 30, 43) Of the many motels lining Lombard St (Hwy 101), the generic Coventry has the highest quality-to-value ratio, with spacious, well-maintained (if plain) rooms and extras like air-con (good for quiet sleeps) and covered parking. Parents: there's plenty of floor space to unpack kids' toys, but no pool.

⭐**HOTEL DRISCO** BOUTIQUE HOTEL **$$$**

Map p292 (📞415-346-2880, 800-634-7277; www.hoteldrisco.com; 2901 Pacific Ave; r $338-475; @ 🛜; 🚌3, 24) The only hotel in Pacific Heights, a stately 1903 apartment-hotel tucked between mansions, stands high on the ridgeline. It's notable for its architecture, attentive service and chic rooms, with their elegantly austere decor, but the high-on-a-hill location is convenient only to the Marina; anywhere else requires bus or taxi. Still, for a real boutique hotel, it's tops.

★ARGONAUT HOTEL   BOUTIQUE HOTEL $$$

Map p289 (☑800-790-1415, 415-563-0800; www.
argonauthotel.com; 495 Jefferson St; r from $389;
P ➔ ❋ ❋ ❋ ❋; ☐19, 47, 49, 🚃Powell-Hyde) ✐
Fisherman's Wharf's top hotel was built
as a cannery in 1908 and has century-old
wooden beams and exposed-brick walls.
Rooms sport an over-the-top nautical
theme, with porthole-shaped mirrors and
plush, deep-blue carpets. Though all rooms
have the amenities of an upper-end hotel –
ultra-comfy beds, iPod docks – some are
tiny with limited sunlight. Parking is $59.

🛏 Downtown, Civic Center & SoMa

HI SAN FRANCISCO DOWNTOWN   HOSTEL $

Map p294 (☑415-788-5604; www.sfhostels.com;
312 Mason St; dm $29-50, r $90-145; @ ❀; Ⓜ Pow-
ell, Ⓑ Powell) You've come to the right place –
a block from Union Sq, this well-managed
hostel looks fresh, clean and colorful, with
contemporary furnishings. Dorms have
four beds; private rooms sport low-slung
platform beds (beware sharp corners) and
some even have down pillows (by request).
Extras include free continental breakfast,
quiet area, social lounge, clean kitchen and
full activities calendar.

FITZGERALD HOTEL   HOTEL $

Map p296 (☑415-775-8100; www.fitzgeraldhotel.
com; 620 Post St; r $119-200; ❀; ☐2, 3, 27, 38)
Upgrade from hostel to hotel at the cheer-
ful Fitzgerald, whimsically decorated with
mismatched furniture liquidated from
fancier hotels. The old-fashioned building
(built in 1910) needs upgrades (note the
temperamental elevator) and rooms are
tiny and have occasional scuff marks and
torn curtains – but bathrooms are clean,
rooms have fridges and microwaves, and
there's a little fireplace lounge downstairs.

HI SAN FRANCISCO CITY CENTER   HOSTEL $

Map p296 (☑415-474-5721; www.sfhostels.org;
685 Ellis St; dm $33-52, r $90-155; @ ❀; ☐19,
38, 47, 49) The seven-story, 1920s Atherton
Hotel was recently remodeled into a better-
than-average hostel, with private baths in
all rooms, including dorms. All-you-can-eat
pancakes or eggs cost $1 and there's an on-
site bar – though dive bars and bargain eats
are the main selling point of this location at
the edge of the gritty Tenderloin.

USA HOSTELS   HOSTEL $

Map p296 (☑415-440-5600, 877-483-2950;
www.usahostels.com; 711 Post St; dm $46-73, r
$135-179; ❀; ☐2, 3, 27, 38) A 1909 hotel clev-
erly converted into sharp-looking hostel,
with a college-dorm vibe and international
students chilling out in the lounge. Private
rooms have fridge, microwave and TV.
Dorms have built-in 'privacy pod' screens,
reading lights and electrical outlets, and
lockers contain outlets to charge electron-
ics. Common areas include a big kitchen,
laundry and games space.

ADELAIDE HOSTEL   HOSTEL $

Map p296 (☑877-359-1915, 415-359-1915; www.
adelaidehostel.com; 5 Isadora Duncan Lane; dm
$37-50, r $120-220; @ ❀; ☐38) Down a hid-
den alley, the 22-room Adelaide has a cozy
feel, with plush furnishings and marble-
tiled bathrooms – and the odd ding and
dust bunny. Bonuses include laundry, lug-
gage storage, group activities and common
areas (one quiet). Good service; friendly
crowd. Your private room may be in the
nearby Dakota or Fitzgerald Hotels (the
Fitzgerald is the better of the two).

★AXIOM   BOUTIQUE HOTEL $$

Map p294 (☑415-392-9466; www.axiomhotel.
com; 28 Cyril Magnin St; d $189-342; @ ❀ ❀ ❀;
🚃Powell-Mason, Powell-Hyde, Ⓑ Powell, Ⓜ Powell) Of all the downtown SF hotels aiming
for high-tech appeal, this one gets it right.
The lobby is razzle-dazzle LED, marble
and riveted steel, but the game room looks
like a start-up HQ, with arcade games and
foosball tables. Guest rooms have low-slung
gray-flannel couches, king platform beds,
dedicated routers for high-speed wireless
streaming to Apple/Google/Samsung de-
vices, and Bluetooth-enabled everything.

★MARKER   BOUTIQUE HOTEL $$

Map p296 (☑415-292-0100, 844-736-2753;
http://themarkersanfrancisco.com; 501 Geary
St; r from $209; ❋ @ ❀ ❀; ☐38, 🚃Powell-Hyde,
Powell-Mason) ✐ Snazzy Marker gets details
right, with guest-room decor in bold colors –
lipstick-red lacquer, navy-blue velvet and
shiny-purple silk – and thoughtful amenities like high-thread-count sheets, ergo-
nomic workspaces, digital-library access,
multiple electrical outlets, and ample space
in drawers, closets and bathroom vanities.
Extras include a spa with a Jacuzzi, a small
gym, evening wine reception and bragging
rights to stylish downtown digs.

HOTEL CARLTON
DESIGN HOTEL **$$**

Map p296 (☑415-673-0242, 800-922-7586; www.hotelcarltonsf.com; 1075 Sutter St; r $269-309; @🛜🐾🛍; 🚍2, 3, 19, 38, 47, 49) 🌱 World travelers feel right at home at the Carlton amid Moroccan tea tables, Indian bedspreads, West African wax-print throw pillows and carbon-offsetting, LEED-certified initiatives (note the rooftop solar panels). It's not the most convenient location – 10 minutes from Union Sq – but offers good value for colorful, spotlessly clean rooms. The quietest rooms are those with suffix -08 to -19.

KENSINGTON PARK HOTEL
BOUTIQUE HOTEL **$$**

Map p294 (☑415-788-6400, 800-553-1900; www.kensingtonparkhotel.com; 450 Post St; r $234-337; ✳@🛜🛍🐾; 🚋Powell-Hyde, Powell-Mason, ⓂPowell, ⒷPowell) Arrive at the dramatic 1925 Spanish lobby to check into your dashingly handsome guest room, blending Moorish patterns, Victorian flourishes and contemporary dark-wood furnishings. What rooms lack in size they make up for in extras, like down pillows and Serta beds. Downstairs is the top-flight seafood restaurant Farallon; Union Sq is steps away.

PHOENIX HOTEL
MOTEL **$$**

Map p296 (☑800-248-9466, 415-776-1380; www.thephoenixhotel.com; 601 Eddy St; r $229-359; 🅿🛜🐾; 🚍19, 31, 47, 49) This rocker crash pad lures revelers to a 1950s motor lodge with mod paint jobs and hipster amenities (hello, Pendleton blankets). There's a courtyard pool, a happening lounge and a shrine to actor-director Vincent Gallo opposite room 43 – but Tenderloin bar crawls and Great American Music Hall shows beckon. Free parking and admission to Kabuki Springs & Spa (p143). Bring earplugs; no smoking.

HOTEL UNION SQUARE
HOTEL **$$**

Map p294 (☑415-397-3000, bookings 415-969-2301; www.hotelunionsquare.com; 114 Powell St; r $196-299; ✳@🛜🛍🐾; ⓂPowell, ⒷPowell) Cleverly stylish Hotel Union Square adds soft touches like tufted headboards and down comforters to complement the original brick walls. The main drawbacks are lack of sunlight and very small rooms, but designers compensated with concealed lighting, mirrored walls and plush fabrics. Themed suites cater to kids and Giants fans, and cable cars are right outside. Not all rooms have air-con.

HOTEL TRITON
BOUTIQUE HOTEL **$$**

Map p294 (☑800-800-1299, 415-394-0500; www.hoteltriton.com; 342 Grant Ave; r $269-389; ✳@🛜🐾🛍; ⓂMontgomery, ⒷMontgomery) 🌱 Forget boring business hotels: Triton's lobby thumps with club music and pops with comic-book color. Upstairs, splashy rooms sport shag-worthy beds with Frette linens, ecofriendly amenities (including organic snacks) and SF-centric design details like wallpaper of Kerouac's *On the Road*. Baths have limited space to primp, but there are tarot-card readings and chair massages during the nightly wine hour.

MOSSER HOTEL
HOTEL **$$**

Map p298 (☑415-986-4400, 800-227-3804; www.themosser.com; 54 4th St; r $259-289, without bath $129-159; @🛜; ⓂPowell, ⒷPowell) A tourist-class hotel in a prime location, the Mosser has tiny rooms and tinier bathrooms – but rates for rooms with shared bathrooms are (sometimes) a bargain. Service can be lackluster and the building is old, but it's centrally located and its rates are a fraction of those of the neighboring Marriott – save that budget for downtown shopping and dining.

BEST WESTERN CARRIAGE INN
MOTEL **$$**

Map p298 (☑800-444-5817, 415-552-8600; www.carriageinnsf.com; 140 7th St; r $229-349; ✳@🛜🐾🛍; ⓂCivic Center, ⒷCivic Center) A kooky motor lodge in an ersatz Victorian offers bigger-than-average rooms swathed in colorful fabrics and hung with oddly poignant portraits. The Carriage Inn offers good bang for your buck, but it's on a sometimes-sketchy street – keep your earplugs and street smarts ready. Self-parking costs $35. The pool is across the street at the Americania Hotel.

HOTEL ABRI
HOTEL **$$**

Map p294 (☑888-229-0677, 415-392-8800; www.hotelabrisf.com; 127 Ellis St; r $245-359; ✳@🛜🐾; ⓂPowell, ⒷPowell) Inside a remodeled early-20th-century building, the Abri has an updated deco sensibility, with jazz-age black-and-tan motifs, sleek wooden headboards for pillow-top beds, and flat-screen TVs hung above workstations for multitasking. Few bathrooms have tubs, but rainfall showerheads compensate. The hotel's popularity has meant wear-and-tear on the furnishings, but rooms remain comfy, and staff friendly and accommodating.

Request a quiet room away from the Subway sandwich shop to avoid the pervasive smell of baking bread.

GOOD HOTEL
MOTEL $$

Map p298 (☎800-444-5819, 415-621-7001; www.thegoodhotel.com; 112 7th St; r $199-279; @ 🎧 ⚞; Ⓜ Civic Center, Ⓑ Civic Center) 🏊 A revamped motel full of green ideas: reclaimed-wood headboards, repurposed-bottle light fixtures and soft fleece bedspreads made from recycled soda bottles. It's youthful and upbeat, like a smartly decorated college dorm. The Good Hotel is in a bad neighborhood, with street scenes and noise; book in back. Parking costs $35. There's a pool across the street at the Americania Hotel.

AMERICANIA HOTEL
MOTEL $$

Map p298 (☎415-626-0200, booking 800-444-5816; www.americaniahotel.com; 121 7th St; r $229-289; @ 🎧 ⚞ 🛅 ⚞; Ⓜ Civic Center, Ⓑ Civic Center) Retro rooms at this revamped mid-century motor lodge face a central courtyard and look sharp, with black-and-teal carpeting, studded white-vinyl headboards, Op Art linens and '60s swivel chairs. Kids love the small outdoor heated pool, while parents love the fitness center and microbrews at the downstairs burger joint – but might not be so thrilled about the gritty neighborhood and paid parking.

HOTEL DES ARTS
HOTEL $$

Map p294 (☎415-956-3232, 800-956-4322; www.sfhoteldesarts.com; 447 Bush St; r $189-239, without bath $179-219; 🎧; Ⓜ Montgomery, Ⓑ Montgomery) Welcome, art freaks: who needs red carpet when your room is painted with jaw-dropping murals by underground Bay Area artists? Service is weak, linens are thin, and some bathrooms have separate hot and cold taps – but you're basically sleeping inside a painting in the heart of downtown SF, right near Geary St galleries and SFMOMA. Bring earplugs. 'Residential' rooms with private bath require a seven-night stay.

WESTIN ST FRANCIS HOTEL
HOTEL $$

Map p294 (☎415-397-7000, 800-228-3000; www.westinstfrancis.com; 335 Powell St; r from $199; ❄ @ 🎧 ⚞; Ⓜ Powell, Ⓑ Powell, 🚋 Powell-Mason, Powell-Hyde) This is one of SF's most storied hotels – Gerald Ford was shot right outside, and Reagan was kept awake by Union Sq protests. Tower rooms offer stellar views but generic architecture, while the landmark 1904 building has old-fashioned charm, with high ceilings, crown moldings, gleaming marble and brass. Westin beds set the industry standard for comfort, but service can be lax.

⭐ PALACE HOTEL
HOTEL $$$

Map p294 (☎415-512-1111; www.sfpalace.com; 2 New Montgomery St; r from $300; ❄ @ 🎧 ⚞ ⚞; Ⓜ Montgomery, Ⓑ Montgomery) The 1906 landmark Palace remains a monument to turn-of-the-century grandeur, with 100-year-old Austrian-crystal chandeliers and Maxfield Parrish paintings. Cushy (if staid) accommodations cater to expense-account travelers, but prices drop at weekends. Even if you're not staying here, visit the opulent Garden Court to sip tea beneath a translucent glass ceiling. There's also a spa; kids love the big pool.

⭐ HOTEL VITALE
BOUTIQUE HOTEL $$$

Map p298 (☎415-278-3700, 888-890-8688; www.hotelvitale.com; 8 Mission St; r $385-675; ❄ @ 🎧 ⚞; Ⓜ Embarcadero, Ⓑ Embarcadero) When your love interest or executive recruiter books you into the waterfront Vitale, you know it's serious. The office-tower exterior disguises a snazzy hotel with sleek, up-to-the-minute luxuries. Beds are dressed with silky-soft, 450-thread-count sheets, and there's an excellent on-site spa with two rooftop hot tubs. Rooms facing the bay offer spectacular Bay Bridge views, and Ferry Building dining awaits across the street.

HOTEL ZETTA
HOTEL $$$

Map p294 (☎415-543-8555, booking 888-720-7004; www.hotelzetta.com; 55 5th St; r from $324; ❄ @ 🎧 ⚞ ⚞; Ⓑ Powell St, Ⓜ Powell St) 🏊 Opened in 2013, this savvy eco-conscious downtowner by the Viceroy group caters to overworked techies ready to play – above the art-filled lobby, there's a mezzanine-level 'play room' with billiards, shuffleboard and two-story-high Plinko wall. Upstairs, bigger-than-average rooms beckon with padded black-leather headboards and low-slung platform beds. Web-enabled flat-screen TVs link with your devices, because we invented that stuff here, mmmkay?

GALLERIA PARK
BOUTIQUE HOTEL $$$

Map p294 (☎415-781-3060; www.galleriapark.com; 191 Sutter St; r $325-369; ❄ @ 🎧 ⚞; Ⓜ Montgomery, Ⓑ Montgomery) 🏊 Exuberant staff greet your arrival at this certified-green boutique charmer, a 1911 hotel restyled with contemporary art and handsome furnishings in soothing jewel tones. Some rooms (and beds) run small, but they include Frette linens, down pillows, high-end bath amenities, free evening wine and – most importantly – good service. Rooms on Sutter St are noisier but get more light; interior rooms are quietest.

TAJ CAMPTON PLACE
HOTEL $$$

Map p294 (☑415-781-5555, 866-969-1825; www.tajhotels.com; 340 Stockton St; r from $425; ✻ @ ☎; ☐30, 45, M Montgomery) Impeccable service sets the Campton Place apart – this is where to put your fur-clad rich aunt when she wants discretion above all. Details are lavish, if beige. The cheapest rooms are tiny; pay to upgrade or be imprisoned in a jewelry box. It's in a prime Union Sq location for shopping and dining, including at the formal California-Indian restaurant on-site.

LOEWS REGENCY
HOTEL $$$

Map p301 (☑844-271-6289, 415-276-9888; www.loewshotels.com/regency-san-francisco; 222 Sansome St; r from $600; ✻ @ ☎ ☎; ☐ California, M Montgomery, B Montgomery) On the top 11 floors of SF's third-tallest building, Loews offers sweeping, bird's-eye views from every room. There's nothing earth-shattering about the classic decor, but the details are sumptuous and, oh, those vistas – you're eye level with the Transamerica Pyramid. Splash out for a 'Luxury Golden Gate King' (from $769), with floor-to-ceiling windows overlooking the Golden Gate Bridge from your bathtub. Alas, there's no pool – hence the four-star designation – but there's a spa; and service equals, sometimes beats, the city's five-stars.

SIR FRANCIS DRAKE HOTEL
HOTEL $$$

Map p294 (☑415-392-7755, 800-795-7129; www.sirfrancisdrake.com; 450 Powell St; r $269-449; ✻ @ ☎; ☐ Powell-Mason, Powell-Hyde, M Powell, B Powell) ✐ The city's most famous door-men, clad like cartoon Beefeaters, greet you at this 1920s tower. The Spanish-Moorish lobby is magnificent, but the smallish, neutral-toned guest rooms targeted to conventioneers are less glamorous than you'd expect from such a grand entrance. Still, rooms do have business-class amenities and proper beds. Book 16th-to-20th-floor rooms for expansive views. Beefeaters aside, service is lackluster.

If you can get someone's attention, ask about the secret room between elevator platforms, where during Prohibition the hotel operated a speakeasy.

⊨ North Beach & Chinatown

PACIFIC TRADEWINDS HOSTEL
HOSTEL $

Map p308 (☑415-433-7970; www.san-francisco-hostel.com; 680 Sacramento St; dm $35-45; ☺ front desk 8am-midnight; ☻ @ ☎; ☐1, ☐ California, B Montgomery) San Francisco's smartest all-dorm hostel has a blue-and-white nautical theme, a fully equipped kitchen (free PB&J sandwiches all day!), spotless glass-brick showers, a laundry (free sock wash!), luggage storage and no lockout time. Bunks are bolted to the wall, so there's no bed-shaking when bunkmates roll. No elevator means hauling bags up three flights – but it's worth it. Great service; fun staff.

SAN REMO HOTEL
HOTEL $

Map p308 (☑415-776-8688, 800-352-7366; www.sanremohotel.com; 2237 Mason St; r without bath $119-159; @ ☎ ☎; ☐30, 47, ☐ Powell-Mason) One of the city's best-value stays, the San Remo was built in 1906, right after the Great Earthquake. More than a century later, this upstanding North Beach boarding house still offers Italian *nonna* (grandma)-styled rooms with mismatched turn-of-the-century furnishings and shared bathrooms. The least-expensive rooms have windows onto the corridor, not outdoors. Family suites accommodate up to five. No elevator.

SLEEPING

WEBSITES

B&B San Francisco (www.bbsf.com) Personable, privately owned B&Bs and neighborhood inns.

Hotel Tonight (www.hoteltonight.com) SF-based hotel-search app offering discount last-minute bookings.

Lonely Planet (www.lonelyplanet.com/usa/san-francisco/hotels) Expert author reviews, user feedback, booking engine.

SLEEPING

★ORCHARD
GARDEN HOTEL BOUTIQUE HOTEL **$$**
Map p308 (☑888-717-2881, 415-399-9807; www.
theorchardgardenhotel.com; 466 Bush St; r $207-
390; P🐾❄@🤚; 🚇2, 3, 30, 45, 🅱Montgomery)
🍃 San Francisco's original LEED-certified,
all-green-practices hotel uses sustainably
grown wood, chemical-free cleaning prod-
ucts and recycled fabrics in its soothingly
quiet rooms. Don't think you'll be trading
comfort for conscience: rooms have unex-
pectedly luxe touches, like high-end down
pillows, Egyptian-cotton sheets and or-
ganic bath products. Don't miss the sunny
rooftop terrace – a sweet spot at day's end.

★HOTEL BOHÈME BOUTIQUE HOTEL **$$**
Map p308 (☑415-433-9111; www.hotelboheme.
com; 444 Columbus Ave; r $235–295; 🐾@🤚;
🚇10, 12, 30, 41, 45) Eclectic, historic and una-
bashedly poetic, this quintessential North
Beach boutique hotel has jazz-era color
schemes, pagoda-print upholstery and photos from the Beat years on the walls. The
vintage rooms are smallish, some face noisy
Columbus Ave (quieter rooms are in back)
and bathrooms are teensy, but novels beg
to be written here – especially after bar
crawls. No elevator or parking lot.

WASHINGTON SQUARE INN B&B **$$**
Map p308 (☑415-981-4220, 800-388-0220;
www.wsisf.com; 1660 Stockton St; r $209-359;
@🤚; 🚇30, 41, 45, 🅿Powell-Mason) On leafy,
sun-dappled Washington Sq, this restored
1910 inn offers European style, complete
with wine-and-cheese receptions and
continental breakfasts in bed. The taste-
ful rooms are styled with a few choice an-
tiques, including carved wooden armoires.
The least-expensive rooms don't leave much
room for North Beach shopping, but this is
a stellar location for people-watching, din-
ing and exploring. No elevator.

SW HOTEL HOTEL **$$**
Map p308 (☑415-362-2999, 888-595-9188; www.
swhotel.com; 615 Broadway; s $139, d $189-325;
❄🤚; 🚇10, 12, 30, 45) After a major overhaul,
Chinatown's former Sam Wong motel now
offers good-value rooms heavy on the beige
and air freshener. Its main selling point is location – on the Broadway axis dividing North
Beach and Chinatown, next to the buzzing
China Live food hall (p120) – but some rooms
are incredibly loud. Bring earplugs or use the
air-con (unavailable in cheaper rooms). Parking occasionally available.

🛏 Nob Hill, Russian Hill & Fillmore

GOLDEN GATE HOTEL HOTEL **$$**
Map p306 (☑800-835-1118, 415-392-3702; www.
goldengatehotel.com; 775 Bush St; r $215, without
bath $145; @🤚; 🚇2, 3, 🅿Powell-Hyde, Powell-
Mason) Like an old-fashioned *pension*, the
Golden Gate has kindly owners and simple
rooms with mismatched furniture, in a 1913
Edwardian hotel safely up the hill from the
Tenderloin. Rooms are small, clean and
comfortable, and most have private bath-
rooms (some with antique claw-foot bath-
tubs). Enormous croissants, homemade
cookies and a resident cat provide TLC af-
ter long days of sightseeing.

PETITE AUBERGE BOUTIQUE HOTEL **$$**
Map p306 (☑800-365-3004, 415-928-6000;
www.petiteaubergesf.com; 863 Bush St; r $270-
410; 🤚; 🚇2, 3, 27) Petite Auberge feels like
a French country inn, with floral-print
fabrics, sunny-yellow colors and in-room
gas fireplaces – it's among central SF's
most charming midprice stays. Alas, several rooms are dark (especially tiny 22) and
face an alley where rubbish collectors rattle
cans early (request a quiet room). Breakfast
and afternoon wine are served fireside in
the cozy salon.

WHITE SWAN INN BOUTIQUE HOTEL **$$**
Map p306 (☑415-775-1755, 800-999-9570; www.
whiteswaninnsf.com; 845 Bush St; r $289-389;
P@🤚; 🚇2, 3, 27) Like an English country
inn, the romantic White Swan is styled
with cabbage-rose wallpaper, red-plaid
flannel bedspreads and polished colonial-
style furniture. Each oversized room has a
gas fireplace – cozy on a foggy night – and
there's wine and cheese in the library. Hip-
sters may find it stifling, but if you love Tu-
dor style, you'll feel right at home.

QUEEN ANNE HOTEL B&B **$$**
Map p310 (☑415-441-2828, 800-227-3970; www.
queenanne.com; 1590 Sutter St; r $210-350;
@🤚; 🚇2, 3) The Queen Anne occupies a
lovely 1890 Victorian mansion, formerly
a girls' boarding school, long on character and architectural charm. Though the
chintz decor borders on twee, it matches
the stately house. Rooms are comfy (some
are tiny) and have a mishmash of an-
tiques; some have romantic wood-burning
fireplaces.

HOTEL KABUKI · HOTEL $$

Map p310 (☑800-533-4567, 415-922-3200; www.hotelkabuki.com; 1625 Post St; r $209-469; P @ 🛜 🐾; 🚇2, 3, 38) The Kabuki nods to Japan, with *shoji* (rice-paper screens) complementing an elegant color palette of slate grey and dark blue. The boxy 1960s architecture is plain, but rooms are spacious and had a total overhaul in 2017. Best amenity: free passes to Kabuki Springs & Spa (p143) – but only when you book directly through JDV hotels.

HOTEL REX · BOUTIQUE HOTEL $$

Map p306 (☑415-433-4434, 800-433-4434; www.thehotelrex.com; 562 Sutter St; r $289-389; ❄ @ 🛜 🐾; 🚇Powell-Hyde, Powell-Mason, Ⓜ Powell, ⒷPowell) 🐾 The Rex draws aesthetic inspiration from early-20th-century literary salons, and sometimes hosts author readings in its cozy lobby bar. Rooms feel inviting (if small) for their traditional masculine color palettes. Beds are particularly great, with crisp linens and down pillows. Caveats: rear-facing rooms lack sunlight but are quiet; street-facing rooms are bright but noisy. Request air-con.

★FAIRMONT SAN FRANCISCO · HOTEL $$$

Map p306 (☑800-441-1414, 415-772-5000; www.fairmont.com; 950 Mason St; r from $329; P ❄ @ 🛜 🐾 🐕; 🚇California) Heads of state choose the Fairmont, whose magnificent lobby is decked out with crystal chandeliers, marble floors and towering yellow-marble columns. Notwithstanding the opulent presidential suite, rooms have traditional business-class furnishings and lack the finer details of top-end luxury hotels. Still, few addresses compare. For old-fashioned character, reserve in the original 1906 building; for jaw-dropping views, go for the tower.

MARK HOPKINS INTERCONTINENTAL · HOTEL $$$

Map p306 (☑415-392-3434, 800-327-0200; www.intercontinentalmarkhopkins.com; 999 California St; r from $300; P ❄ @ 🛜 🐾; 🚇California) Glistening marble floors reflect glowing crystal chandeliers in the lobby of the 1926 Mark Hopkins, a San Francisco landmark. Detractors call it staid, but its timelessness is precisely why others (including Michelle Obama) love it. Rooms are done in business-classy style, with Frette linens, and most have knockout hilltop views, but some details miss: anticipate four-, not five-star service.

🛏 The Mission & Potrero Hill

INN SAN FRANCISCO · B&B $$

Map p302 (☑415-641-0188, 800-359-0913; www.innsf.com; 943 S Van Ness Ave; r $195-255, without bath $165-225, cottages $365-475; P 🚐 @ 🛜 🐾; 🚇14, 49) 🐾 An elegant 1872 Italianate-Victorian mansion has become a stately Mission District inn, impeccably maintained and packed with antiques. All rooms have fresh-cut flowers and sumptuous mattresses with feather beds; some have Jacuzzis. The freestanding garden cottage sleeps six. Outside there's an English garden and a redwood hot tub open 24 hours – a rarity in SF. Limited parking; reserve. No elevator.

🛏 The Castro & Noe Valley

WILLOWS INN · B&B $

Map p312 (☑415-431-4770; www.willowssf.com; 710 14th St; without bath s $130-170, d $130-175, tr $140-185, q $190-215; 🛜; ⓂChurch St) Willows has the homey comforts of a B&B without any fuss. None of the 12 rooms has a private bathroom, but all have sinks. Shared kitchenette. Rooms on 14th St are sunnier and have good street views, but, though they have double-pane glass, they're noisier; ask when you book. No elevator.

★PARKER GUEST HOUSE · B&B $$

Map p312 (☑415-621-3222, 888-520-7275; www.parkerguesthouse.com; 520 Church St; r $219-279, without bath $179-99; @ 🛜; 🚇33, ⓂJ) The Castro's stateliest gay digs occupies two side-by-side Edwardian mansions. Details are elegant and formal, never froufrou. Rooms feel like they belong more to a swanky hotel than to a B&B, with super-comfortable beds and down duvets. Bathroom fixtures gleam. The garden is ideal for a lovers' tryst – as is the steam room. No elevator.

BECK'S MOTOR LODGE · MOTEL $$

Map p312 (☑415-621-8212; www.becksmotor lodge.com; 2222 Market St; r $189-279; P ❄ 🛜; ⓂCastro St) This three-story motor-lodge motel got a makeover in 2016 and its rooms look colorful, sharp and clean. Though technically not gay oriented, its placement at the center of the Castro makes it the de

SLEEPING

facto gay favorite. Bringing kids isn't recommended, especially during big gay events, when rooms book out months ahead. Book a rear-facing unit for quiet, a room in front to cruise with your blinds open.

INN ON CASTRO B&B $$

Map p312 (☏415-861-0321; www.innoncastro. com; 321 Castro St; r $230-255, without bath $165-190, self-catering apt $230-290; ☎; MCastro St) A portal to the Castro's disco heyday, this Edwardian town house is decked out with top-end '70s-mod furnishings. Rooms are retro cool and spotlessly kept. Exceptional breakfasts – the owner is a chef. Several nearby, great-value apartments are also available for rent. No elevator.

⌂ The Haight & Hayes Valley

METRO HOTEL HOTEL $

Map p314 (☏415-861-5364; www.metrohotelsf. com; 319 Divisadero St; r $107; @☎; ☐6, 24, 71) Trendy Divisadero St offers boutiques and restaurants galore, and the Metro Hotel has a prime position – some rooms overlook the garden patio of top-notch Ragazza Pizzeria. Rooms are cheap and clean, if bland – get the one with the SF mural. Some have two double beds; one room sleeps six ($150). The hotel's handy to the Haight and has 24-hour reception; no elevator.

HAYES VALLEY INN HOTEL $

Map p316 (☏800-930-7999, 415-431-9131; www. hayesvalleyinn.com; 417 Gough St; d without bath $109-189; @☎⬢☎; ☐21, MVan Ness) Like a European *pension,* this amazingly reasonable find has simple, small rooms with shared bathrooms, a border collie in the parlor, and staff eager to mother you. Two rooms have bunks, two others have single beds; turret rooms have bay windows and accommodate three guests. Drawbacks: street noise and too few bathrooms. Bonuses: world-class dining and entertainment at your doorstep. No elevator.

★CHATEAU TIVOLI B&B $$

(☏415-776-5462, 800-228-1647; www.chateau tivoli.com; 1057 Steiner St; r $195-300, without bath $150-200; ☎⬢; ☐5, 22) The source of neighborhood gossip since 1892, this gilded

and turreted mansion once hosted Isadora Duncan, Mark Twain and (rumor has it) the ghost of a Victorian opera diva – and now you can be the Chateau Tivoli's guest. Nine antique-filled rooms and suites set the scene for romance; most have claw-foot bathtubs, though two share a bathroom. No elevator; no TVs.

PARSONAGE B&B $$

Map p316 (☏415-863-3699; www.theparsonage. com; 198 Haight St; r $220-280; @☎; ☐6, 71, MF) With rooms named for San Francisco's grand dames, this 23-room 1883 Italianate Victorian retains gorgeous original details, including rose-brass chandeliers and Carrara-marble fireplaces. Spacious, airy rooms offer antique beds with cushy SF-made McRoskey mattresses; some rooms have wood-burning fireplaces. Take breakfast in the formal dining room, and brandy and chocolates before bed. Charming owners. There's even an elevator.

SLEEP OVER SAUCE B&B $$

Map p316 (☏415-621-0896; www.sleepsf.com; 135 Gough St; d $150-195, ste $245-295; @☎; ☐21, 47, 49, MVan Ness) At this eight-room inn above a tempting Hayes Valley bar, you can almost roll out of bed and into the city's top restaurants. Simple rooms have dark-wood furniture; guests share a living room with fireplace. Bathrooms are sparkling clean with Egyptian-cotton towels, but not all are en suite. No elevator; no front desk – check in at the restaurant downstairs.

⌂ Golden Gate Park & the Avenues

SEAL ROCK INN MOTEL $$

Map p318 (☏888-732-5762, 415-752-8000; www. sealrockinn.com; 545 Point Lobos Ave; s $140-192, d $150-202; P☎⬢; ☐38) Far from downtown, this vintage 1950s ocean-side motel has big rooms Hunter S Thompson holed up in to write in the '70s. Today it's a mellow, family-friendly getaway with beach, park and coastal-hike access; ask if the pool has reopened. All rooms have refrigerators and microwaves; some have kitchenettes. Reserve for 3rd-floor rooms with views and gas fireplaces.

SLEEPING

Understand San Francisco

San Francisco Today

Congratulations: you're right on time for SF's latest tech boom, art show, green initiative, water-saving idea and (fair warning) marriage proposal. SF has its ups and downs, but as anyone who's clung on to the side of a cable car will tell you, this town gives you one hell of a ride.

Best on Film

Milk (2008) Sean Penn won an Oscar for his portrayal of America's first openly gay elected official.

Tales of the City (1993) Laura Linney unravels a mystery in SF's swinging '70s disco scene.

Harold & Maude (1971) The Conservatory of Flowers and Sutro Baths make metaphorically apt backdrops for May–December romance.

Chan Is Missing (1982) When Chan disappears, two cabbies realize they don't know Chan, Chinatown or themselves.

Best in Print

Howl and Other Poems (Allen Ginsberg; 1956) Mind-altering, law-changing words defined a generation of 'angel-headed hipsters.'

Time and Materials (Robert Hass; 2007) Every Pulitzer Prize–winning syllable is as essential as a rivet in the Golden Gate Bridge.

On the Road (Jack Kerouac; 1957) Banged out in a San Francisco attic, Kerouac's travelogue set postwar America free.

Slouching Towards Bethlehem (Joan Didion; 1968) Scorching truth burns through San Francisco fog during the Summer of Love.

Green City by the Bay

According to the North American Green Cities Index, San Francisco is the greenest of them all. Practices that are standard-setting elsewhere were pioneered here, including LEED-certified green hotels, organic cocktail bars, sustainable dining from tacos to tasting menus, and dozens of car-parking spaces that have been converted into public green oases. San Francisco mandates citywide composting and bans plastic bags – part of its initiative to become a zero-waste city by 2020.

Sanctuary City

San Francisco was the first city worldwide to declare itself a 'Sanctuary City.' In the 1980s, Central American refugees escaping civil war settled in San Francisco but were unable to obtain official refugee status. To ensure these new San Franciscans were afforded some legal protection, a 1989 'City of Refuge' ordinance prohibited SF police from detaining people based on immigration status alone. The city strengthened its Sanctuary status in 2013, with an ordinance prohibiting police cooperation with federal immigration agents – provoking criticism from Donald Trump, especially after an undocumented immigrant released from San Francisco police custody was charged with murder.

Immigration controversies are not new to San Francisco. The city upheld the racially based federal Asian Exclusion Act and Executive Order 9066 mandating internment of Japanese American citizens – even as San Franciscans mounted historic legal defenses against them. Mindful of the long arc of local and national history, the San Francisco Board of Supervisors reaffirmed San Francisco's Sanctuary City status in 2016.

Trump responded with a January 25, 2017, executive order threatening Sanctuary Cities with withdrawal of federal funds – including a projected loss to San Francisco of $1.3 billion in funding for roads, homeless shelters and other safety-net programs. San Francisco promptly filed a lawsuit against the order – and, in February, a bill declaring all of California a 'Sanctuary State' passed the California Assembly. Meanwhile, Sanctuary City pride has hit San Francisco streets at City Hall rallies and on San Franpsycho T-shirts bearing the city's latest motto: 'Build bridges, not walls.'

Boomtown Living

The Bay Area currently leads the nation in job creation: mobile apps and social media are booming SF industries, with restaurants, bars, clubs and performance spaces flourishing as the tech money flows in.

But the economic upturn does have downsides. Longtime San Franciscans struggle to keep pace with rising house and food prices. Private buses whisking SF-based tech workers to Silicon Valley jobs have come to symbolize a growing income divide, as service workers commute long distances into SF via floundering public transit.

Art Attack on Market Street

Through tech booms and busts, San Francisco prides itself on creativity. So when Mayor Ed Lee offered Twitter tax incentives to keep its headquarters in San Francisco, artists demanded to know: what would the city do to keep arts in SF?

Good question. The city's top real-estate owner is Academy of Art College – but warehouses that formerly housed galleries, rehearsal spaces and performance venues are increasingly occupied by start-ups. The city has more art-school grads than ever, but fewer places for them to make and show work.

But the arts community is rallying. Nonprofits cut a deal with the city enabling them to buy buildings on a blighted stretch of Market St at subsidized rates. A gallery district has taken root in Potrero Flats, and performance venues have sprouted up mid-Market. To ensure artists have places to make and show their work in SF, techie arts patrons bought a Dogpatch warehouse to create the Minnesota Street Project arts center. Now no matter when you arrive in SF, it's showtime.

Marriage Equality

San Francisco was the first city to authorize same-sex marriages, back in 2004 – but some 4036 honeymoons ended abruptly when their marriages were legally invalidated by the state. Court battles ensued, and California voters narrowly passed a measure to legally define marriage as between a man and a woman.

But for star-crossed San Francisco couples, there is a happy ending. Countersuits were initiated and, in 2013, the US Supreme Court upheld California courts' ruling in favor of state civil rights protections, setting a nationwide precedent. Upon further appeal, the Supreme Court declared laws prohibiting same-sex marriage unconstitutional nationwide in 2015. The day of the decision, many longtime partners got hitched at City Hall – some for the second or third time, to the same person.

population per sq mile

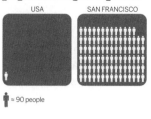

USA   SAN FRANCISCO

≈ 90 people

politics
(% of population)

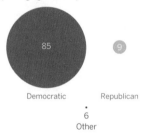

85 Democratic
9 Republican
6 Other

if San Francisco were 100 people

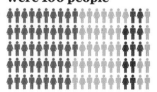

48 would be Caucasian
33 would be Asian
6 would be Latin
6 would be African American
7 would be other

History

Native Californians had found gold in California long before 1849 – but it hardly seemed worth mentioning, as long as there were oysters for lunch and venison for dinner. Once word circulated, San Francisco was transformed almost overnight from bucolic trading backwater to gold-rush metropolis. Over 160 years of booms, busts, history-making high jinks and lowdown dirty dealings later, SF remains the wildest city in the west.

Cowboys on a Mission

When Spanish cowboys brought 340 horses, 302 head of cattle and 160 mules to settle Misión San Francisco de Asís (Mission San Francisco) in 1776, there was a slight hitch: the area had already been settled by Native Americans for over 14,300 years. There was plenty of shellfish and wild foods to go around, so the arrival of Captain Juan Bautista de Anza, Father Francisco Palou and their livestock initially met with no apparent resistance – until the Spaniards began to demand more than dinner.

The new arrivals expected the local Ohlone to build them a mission and to take over its management within 10 years. In exchange, the Ohlone were allowed one meager meal a day, if any, and a place in God's kingdom – which came much sooner than expected for many. Smallpox and other introduced diseases reduced the Ohlone population by almost three quarters during the 50 years of Spanish rule in California.

As the name suggests, Mission Dolores ('mission of the sorrows') settlement never really prospered. Spain wasn't especially sorry to hand over the troublesome settlement to the newly independent nation of Mexico, but Mexico soon made this colony a profitable venture with a bustling hide and tallow trade at Yerba Buena Cove, where the Financial District now stands.

Meanwhile, US–Mexico relations steadily deteriorated, and things were made worse by rumors that Mexico was entertaining a British buy-out offer for California. The Mexican–American War broke out in 1846 and dragged on for two years before ending with the Treaty

Top Five Sites for Native History

Mission Dolores (The Mission)

Alcatraz

The Presidio

Rincon Center Murals (Financial District)

San Francisco Historical Society (Downtown)

TIMELINE	June 1776	1835	1846
	Captain Juan Bautista de Anza and Father Francisco Palou arrive in SF with cattle and settlers. With Ohlone conscripts, they build the Misión San Francisco de Asís (now Mission Dolores).	President Andrew Jackson's emissary makes an offer of $500,000 to buy Northern California. Mexico testily refuses and tries to sell California to Britain.	The Mexican–American War breaks out and drags on for two years, with much posturing but little actual bloodshed in California.

of Guadalupe Hidalgo. This treaty formally ceded California and the present-day southwestern states to the USA – a loss that was initially reckoned by missionizing Church fathers in souls but within months could be counted in ingots.

'Gold! Gold! Gold!'

In 1848 Sam Brannan, the San Francisco real-estate speculator and tabloid founder, published rumors of a find 120 miles away near Sutter's Mill, where sawmill employees had found gold flakes in the water. Hoping to scoop other newspapers and maybe sell swampland to rubes back East, Brannan published golden gossip as solid fact. When San Franciscans proved skeptical, Brannan traveled to Sutter's Fort and convinced fellow Mormons to entrust him with a vial of gold for the church, swearing to keep their secret. Brannan kept his word for about a day. Upon his return to San Francisco, he ran through Portsmouth Sq, brandishing the vial and shouting, 'Gold! Gold! Gold on the American River!'

But Brannan's plan backfired. Within weeks San Francisco's population shrank to 200, as every able-bodied individual headed to the hills to pan for gold. Brannan's newspaper folded; there was no one around to read, write or print it. Good thing Brannan had a backup plan: he'd bought every available shovel, pick and pan, and he opened a general store near Sutter's Fort. Within its first 70 days, Brannan & Co sold $36,000 in equipment – almost a million bucks in today's terms.

Other newspapers around the world hastily published stories of 'gold mountains' near San Francisco. Boatloads of prospectors arrived from Australia, China, South America and Europe, while another 40,000 prospectors trudged overland, eager to scoop up their fortunes on the hillsides.

Lawless, Loose & Lowdown

By 1850, the year California was fast-tracked for admission as the 31st state in the Union, San Francisco's population had skyrocketed from 800 a year earlier to an estimated 25,000. But for all the new money in town, it wasn't exactly easy living.

Most of the early prospectors (called '49ers,' after their arrival date) were men under the age of 40, and to keep them entertained – and fleece the gullible – some 500 saloons, 20 theaters and numerous venues of ill repute opened within five years. A buck might procure whiskey, opium or one of the women frolicking on swings over the bar on San Francisco's 'Barbary Coast.'

On November 20, 1969, 79 Native American activists defied Coast Guard blockades to symbolically reclaim Alcatraz as native land. Hundreds of supporters joined the protest, until FBI raids ousted the protestors on June 11, 1971. Public support for the protesters strengthened self-rule for Native territories, signed into law by Richard Nixon.

1848	1850	1851	1861–65
Gold is discovered near present-day Placerville. San Francisco's newspaper publisher Sam Brannan spills the secret, and the gold rush is on.	With hopes of solid-gold tax revenues, the US hastily dubs California the 31st state.	Gold discovery in Australia leads to cheering in the streets of Melbourne – and panic in the streets of San Francisco as the price for California gold plummets.	While the US Civil War divides North from South out East, SF perversely profits in the West, as industry diverted from factories burdened by the war effort heads to San Francisco.

Wise prospectors arrived early and got out quick. As gold became harder to find, backstabbing became more common, sometimes literally. Successful Peruvians and Chileans were harassed and denied renewals to their mining claims, and most left California by 1855. Native Californian laborers who had helped the 49ers strike it rich were also denied the right to hold claims. Despite San Francisco's well-earned reputation for freewheeling lawlessness, crime was swiftly and conveniently blamed on Australian newcomers. Along with Australians, Chinese – the most populous group in California by 1860 – were on the receiving end of misplaced resentment.

View from Gold Mountain

Within a year of the 1849 gold rush, Chinatown was already established in San Francisco – better known in Cantonese as Gam Saan ('Gold Mountain'). At first Chinatown wasn't exclusively Chinese at all but a bachelor community of Mexican, American, European, African American and Chinese miners who bunked, prospected and caroused side by side. But when gold prices came crashing down with the discovery of gold in Australia, miners turned irrational resentments on resident Australians and Chinese. Australian lodging houses were burned to the ground, anti-Chinese riots broke out and Chinese land claims were rendered null and void. In 1870, San Francisco officially restricted housing and employment for anyone born in China.

The 1882 US Chinese Exclusion Act prevented new immigration from China, barred Chinese from citizenship until 1943 and spurred the passage of 100 parallel ordinances limiting rights for Japanese San Franciscans. Not coincidentally, anti-Chinese laws served the needs of local magnates looking for cheap labor to build the first cross-country railroad. With little other choice of legitimate employment, an estimated 12,000 Chinese laborers did the dangerous work of dynamiting rail tunnels through the Sierra Nevada.

After the 1906 fire, city officials planned to oust Chinese residents altogether and develop the prime property of Chinatown, but the Chinese consulate and rifle-toting Chinatown merchants persuaded the city otherwise. Today Chinatown is a major tourism boon to the city, yet many residents scrape by on less than $10,000 a year – not exactly a Gold Mountain. Upwardly mobile residents tend to leave Chinatown, new arrivals move in, and the cycle begins anew.

Keeping the West Wild

As gold, silver and railroad money flowed into San Francisco, the city grew. It didn't exactly blossom at first, though – public works were com-

May 1869	1870	1882	April 18, 1906
The Golden Spike completes the first transcontinental railroad. The news travels via San Franciscan David Brooks' invention: the telegraph.	William Hammond Hall sees the development of the Golden Gate Park through to completion from 1870 to 1887.	The US Chinese Exclusion Act suspends new immigration from China; these racially targeted laws remain until 1943.	A massive earthquake levels entire blocks of SF in 47 seconds, setting off fires that rage for three days. Survivors start rebuilding while the town is still smoldering.

pletely neglected, and heavily populated sections of the city were mired in knee-high muck. Eventually the debris-choked waterfront filled in, and streets were graded and paved. As soon as Andrew Hallidie's invention of the cable car made the formidable crag accessible in 1873, Nob Hill sprouted mansions for millionaires, including the 'Big Four' railroad-magnate 'robber barons': Leland Stanford, Collis P Huntington, Mark Hopkins and Charles Crocker. Real-estate speculators saw greenbacks, cleverly repackaging even flea-plagued cattle pastures of the Mission District and Cow Hollow as desirable residential districts. The land rush was on.

Naturalist John Muir came through San Francisco in 1868, but he soon left with a shudder for greener pastures in Yosemite. The early environmentalist organization he founded, the Sierra Club, would eventually find its major backers in San Francisco. The unspoiled wilderness that Muir and his organization successfully lobbied to protect includes one of San Francisco's most popular escapes: Muir Woods.

San Franciscans determined to preserve the city's natural splendors pushed to establish the city's first park in 1867, when squatters were paid to vacate the area now known as Buena Vista Park. With a mandate from San Francisco voters to transform sand dunes into a vast city park, tenacious engineer William Hammond Hall saw the development of Golden Gate Park through to completion from 1870 to 1887 – despite developers' best attempts to scuttle park plans in favor of casinos, amusement parks, resorts, racetracks and an igloo village. Populist millionaire Adolph Sutro decided that every working stiff should be able to escape downtown tenements for the sand dunes and sunsets of Ocean Beach, accessible for a nickel on his public railway. By way of thanks, he was elected mayor in 1894.

Double Disaster

By the 20th century, San Francisco had earned a reputation for scandal, corruption, earthquakes and other calamities – none of it good for business. To redirect attention from its notorious waterfront fleshpots to its comparatively underexposed urban assets, the city commissioned Chicago architect Daniel Burnham to give San Francisco a beaux-arts Civic Center to rival Baron Haussmann's Paris. This elaborate plan had just been finalized when disaster struck...twice.

On April 18, 1906, a quake estimated at a terrifying 7.8 to 8.3 on today's Richter scale struck the city. In 47 seconds, San Franciscans discovered just how many corners had been cut on government contracts. Unreinforced buildings collapsed, including City Hall. The sole functioning downtown water source was a fountain donated to the city

William Hammond Hall briefly quit his job building Golden Gate Park in 1886 over proposals to convert the park into a racetrack lined with tract homes. When a casino and carnival were established for the 1893 Midwinter's Fair, Hammond Hall fought to get the park returned to its intended purpose.

1910	1913	1915	1927
Angel Island opens as the West Coast immigration station. Over 30 years, 175,000 arrivals from Asia are subjected to months or years of interrogation and prison-like conditions.	California's Alien Land Law prohibits property ownership by Asians, including Japanese, Koreans and Indians. Lawyer Juichi Soyeda immediately files suit; he wins in 1952, 23 years after his death.	Post-quake San Francisco hosts the Panama–Pacific International Exposition. The city cements its reputation as a showplace for new technology, outlandish ideas and the arts.	After a year of tinkering, 21-year-old Philo Farnsworth transmits the first successful TV broadcast of...a straight line.

by opera prodigy Lotta Crabtree. Assembly lines were formed to haul buckets of water from Lotta's Fountain, but the water couldn't reach the crest of steep hills fast enough. Chinatown burned for days and, even further uphill, Nob Hill mansions were reduced to ashes. Survivors fled to Potrero Hill and Buena Vista Park, and for three days they watched their city and its dreams of grandeur go up in smoke.

Second Acts

Built in 1907, soon after the earthquake, the Great American Music Hall shows the unabashed flamboyance of post-earthquake San Francisco. Carved gilt decor recalls the city's gold-rush heyday, and scantily clad frescoed figures hint at other possible backstage entertainments – this music hall once did double duty as a bordello.

Yet San Francisco had learned one thing through 50 years of booms and busts: how to stage a comeback. All but one of the city's 20 historic theaters were completely destroyed by the earthquake and fire, but theater tents were soon set up amid the rubble. Surviving entertainers began marathon performances to lift the city's spirits. Soprano Luisa Tetrazzini ditched New York's Metropolitan Opera to return to San Francisco and sang on Market St to an audience of 250,000 – virtually every surviving San Franciscan.

San Franciscans rose to the occasion and rebuilt their city at an astounding rate of 15 buildings a day. In a show of popular priorities, San Francisco's theaters were rebuilt long before City Hall's grandiose Civic Center was completed. Most of the Barbary Coast had gone up in flames, so the theater scene and most red-light entertainments decamped to the Tenderloin, where they remain.

But San Francisco's greatest comeback performance was the 1915 Panama–Pacific International Exposition, held in celebration of the completion of the Panama Canal. Earthquake rubble was used to fill 635 marshy acres of the Marina, where famous architects built elaborate pavilions showcasing San Francisco's Pacific Rim connections, exotic foods and forward thinking. Crowds gasped at displays of the latest, greatest inventions, including the world's first steam locomotive, a color printing press and an early typewriter (at 14 tons, not exactly a laptop). When the party ended, Bernard Maybeck's Palace of Fine Arts plaster folly was the one temporary exhibit San Franciscans couldn't bear to see torn down, so the structure was recast in concrete.

The Left Coast

San Francisco's port thrived in 1934, but when local longshoremen protested dangerous working conditions, shipping tycoons sought dockworkers elsewhere – only to discover that San Francisco's longshoremen had coordinated their strike with 35,000 workers along the West Coast. After 83 days, police and the National Guard broke the strike, killing two strikers and hospitalizing 85 protestors. Public sympathy forced concessions from shipping magnates. Coit Tower frescoes completed

1934	1937	February 1942	1957
A West Coast longshoremen's strike ends with strikers and sympathizers shot by police. A mass funeral and citywide strike follow; longshoremen win historic concessions.	After four years of dangerous labor in treacherous riptides, the Golden Gate Bridge is complete.	Executive Order 9066 mandates internment of 120,000 Japanese Americans. The Japanese American Citizens League files civil rights claims.	City Lights wins a landmark ruling against book banning over the publication of Allen Ginsberg's *Howl*, and free speech and free spirits enjoy a reprieve from McCarthyism.

in 1934 capture the pro-worker sentiment that swept the city – known henceforth as America's 'Left Coast.'

When WWII brought a shipbuilding boom to town, women and 40,000 African American arrivals stepped into key roles in San Francisco's workforce. But with misplaced anxiety about possible attacks from the Pacific, Japanese San Franciscans and Japantown became convenient targets for public animosity. Two months after the attack on Pearl Harbor, President Franklin D Roosevelt signed Executive Order 9066, ordering the relocation of 120,000 Japanese Americans to internment camps. The San Francisco–based Japanese American Citizens League (JACL) immediately challenged the grounds for internment and lobbied tirelessly for more than 40 years to overturn the executive order, gain symbolic reparations for internees, and restore the community's standing with a formal letter of apology signed by President George HW Bush in 1988. By setting key legal precedents from the 1940s onward, JACL paved the way for the 1964 Civil Rights Act.

Free Speech, Free Spirits

Members of the armed services dismissed from service for homosexuality and other 'subversive' behavior during WWII were discharged onto the streets of San Francisco, as if that would teach them a lesson. Instead, the new arrivals found themselves at home in the low-rent, laissez-faire neighborhoods of North Beach and the Haight. So when the rest of the country took a sharp right turn with McCarthyism in the 1950s, rebels and romantics headed for San Francisco – including Jack Kerouac. By the time *On the Road*, chronicling his westward journey, was published in 1957, the motley crowd of writers, artists, dreamers and unclassifiable characters Kerouac called 'the mad ones' found their way to like-minded San Francisco.

San Francisco didn't always take kindly to the nonconformists derisively referred to in the press as 'beatniks,' and police and poets were increasingly at odds on the streets of North Beach. Officers tried to fine 'beatnik chicks' for wearing sandals, only to be mercilessly taunted in verse by self-described African American Jewish voodoo anarchist and legendary street-corner Beat poet Bob Kaufman. Poet Lawrence Ferlinghetti and bookstore manager Shigeyoshi Murao of City Lights were arrested for 'willfully and lewdly' printing Allen Ginsberg's magnificent, incendiary epic poem *Howl*. But artistic freedom prevailed in 1957, when City Lights won its landmark ruling against book banning.

The kindred Beat spirits Ginsberg described in *Howl* experimented with art, radical politics, marijuana and one another, defying 1950s social-climbing conventions and Senator Joe McCarthy's alarmist call

Top Five Beat Scenes

City Lights (North Beach)

Beat Museum (North Beach)

Vesuvio (North Beach)

Li Po (Chinatown)

Bob Kaufman Alley (North Beach)

1959	January 1966	October 1966	January 1967
Mayor George Christopher authorizes measures against gay citizens. Openly gay WWII veteran José Sarria runs for public office – in drag.	Trips Festival is organized by techno-futurist Stewart Brand, with author Ken Kesey, the Grateful Dead, Native American activists and an Olympic trampolinist, plus Bill Graham handling promotion.	In Oakland, Huey Newton and Bobby Seale found the Black Panther Party for Self-Defense, demanding 'Land, Bread, Housing, Education, Clothing, Justice and Peace.'	The Summer of Love kicks off with the Human Be-In, with draft cards used as rolling papers, free Grateful Dead gigs and Allen Ginsberg naked, as usual.

to weed out 'communists in our midst.' When McCarthy's House Un-American Activities Committee (HUAC) convened in San Francisco in 1960 to expose alleged communists, UC Berkeley students organized a disruptive, sing-along sit-in at City Hall. After police turned fire hoses on the protesters, thousands of San Franciscans rallied and HUAC split town, never to return. It was official: the '60s had begun.

Flower Power

How to Revive the Summer of Love
....
Give a free Haight St concert
....
Commune with nature in Golden Gate Park
....
Take the Haight Flashback walking tour

San Francisco was a testing ground for freedom of expression in the 1960s, as comedian Lenny Bruce uttered the F-word on stage and burlesque dancer Carol Doda bared it all for titillated audiences in North Beach clubs. But neither jokes nor striptease would pop the last button of confining 1950s social norms – no, that was a job for the CIA. In a pronounced lapse in screening judgment, the CIA hired local writer Ken Kesey to test psychoactive drugs intended to create the ultimate soldier. Instead, they inspired Kesey to write the novel *One Flew Over the Cuckoo's Nest*, drive psychedelic busloads of Merry Pranksters across country, and introduce San Francisco to LSD and the Grateful Dead at the legendary Acid Tests. San Francisco's 1966 Trips Festival yielded revelations for co-organizer and veteran CIA tester Stewart Brand: vast computing machines ought to shrink to fit into our hands...a wild hallucination, obviously.

After the Civil Rights movement anything seemed possible, and for a while it seemed that the freaky force of free thinking would stop the unpopular Vietnam War. At the January 14, 1967, Human Be-In in Golden Gate Park, trip-master Timothy Leary urged a crowd of 20,000 to dream a new American dream and 'turn on, tune in, drop out.' Free music rang out in the streets, free food was provided by community activists the Diggers, free LSD was circulated by Owsley Stanley, free crash pads were all over the Haight and free love transpired on some very dubious free mattresses. For the duration of the Summer of Love it seemed possible to make love, not war.

But a chill soon settled over San Francisco. Civil rights hero Martin Luther King Jr was assassinated on April 8, 1968, followed by the fatal shooting of Robert Kennedy on June 5 after he'd won California's presidential primary. Radicals worldwide called for revolution, and separatist groups like Oakland's Black Panther Party for Self-Defense took up arms. Meanwhile, recreational drug-taking was turning into a thankless career for many, a distinct itch in the nether regions was making the rounds of Haight squats, and still more busloads of teenage runaways were arriving in the ill-equipped, wigged-out Haight. Haight Ashbury Free Clinic helped with the rehabbing and the itching, but

1969	November 1969	April 1977	1977
A computer link is established between Stanford Research Institute and UCLA via ARPANET, and an unsolicited group message is sent: email and spam are born.	Native American activists reclaim the abandoned island of Alcatraz as reparation for broken treaties. The occupation lasts 19 months, until FBI agents forcibly oust the activists.	The Apple II is introduced in SF at the first West Coast Computer Faire and stuns the crowd with its computing speed (1MHz).	Harvey Milk becomes the first openly gay man elected to US public office. Milk sponsors a gay-rights bill and trend-setting 'pooper-scooper' ordinance before his murder.

disillusionment seemed incurable when Hells Angels beat protestors in Berkeley and turned on the crowd at a free Rolling Stones concert at Altamont.

Many idealists headed 'back to the land' in the bucolic North Bay, jump-starting California's organic-farm movement with Stewart Brand's *Whole Earth Catalog* for a DIY natural farming resource. A dark streak emerged among those who remained, including young Charles Manson, the Symbionese Liberation Army (better known post-1974 as Patty Hearst's kidnappers) and an evangelical egomaniac named Jim Jones, who would oblige 900 followers to commit mass suicide in 1978. By the time Be-In LSD supplier Stanley was released from a three-year jail term in 1970, the party seemed to be over. But in the Castro, it was just getting started.

Pride

By the 1970s, San Francisco's gay community was fed up with police raids, done with hetero Haight communes and ready for music with an actual beat. In 1959, after an opponent accused then-mayor George Christopher of allowing San Francisco to become 'the national headquarters of the organized homosexuals,' Christopher authorized crackdowns on gay bars and started a blacklist of gay citizens.

Never one to be harassed or upstaged, WWII veteran and drag star José Sarria became the first openly gay man to run for public office, in 1962, on a platform to end police harassment of gay San Franciscans. He won 5600 votes. Undaunted, he declared himself Absolute Empress of San Francisco, the widow and true heir of Emperor Norton. When local media echoed the Empress' criticism of the continuing raids, police crackdowns stopped.

By the mid-1970s, the rainbow flag was flying high over gay businesses and homes in the out-and-proud Castro, and the sexual revolution was in full swing at gay clubs and bathhouses on Polk St and in SoMa. The Castro was triumphant when Castro camera-store owner Harvey Milk was elected the city's Supervisor, becoming the nation's first openly gay elected official – but as Milk himself eerily predicted, his time in office would be cut short by an act of extremist violence. Dan White, a washed-up politician hyped on Hostess Twinkies, fatally shot Milk and then-mayor George Moscone at City Hall in 1978. The charge was reduced to manslaughter due to the infamous 'Twinkie Defense' faulting the ultra-sweet junk food, sparking an outpouring of public outrage dubbed the 'White Riot.' White was deeply disturbed, and committed suicide a year after his 1984 release.

How to Celebrate Gay Pride

....

Join the Pride Parade

....

Meet fabulous, fearless pioneers at the GLBT Museum

....

Peruse petitions at Human Rights Campaign

....

Binge-watch at the LGBTQ Film Festival

November 1978	1981	1989	October 17, 1989
After moving his People's Temple from SF to Guyana, Jim Jones orders the murders of a congressman and four journalists and the mass suicide of 900 followers.	The first cases of AIDS are identified. The disease has since taken 30 million lives, but early intervention in SF instituted key prevention measures and set global treatment standards.	Hundreds of sea lions haul out on the yacht slips near Pier 39. State law and wildlife officials grant them squatters' rights, and the beach bums become San Francisco mascots.	The Loma Prieta earthquake hits 6.9 on the Richter scale; a freeway in SF and a Bay Bridge section collapse in 15 seconds, killing 41.

By then San Francisco had another problem. A strange illness began to appear at local hospitals, and it seemed to be hitting the gay community especially hard. The first cases of AIDS reported in San Francisco were mistakenly referred to as GRID (Gay-Related Immune Deficiency), and a social stigma became attached to the virus. But San Francisco health providers and gay activists rallied to establish global standards for care and prevention, with vital early HIV/AIDS health initiatives funded not through federal agencies but with tireless local efforts – the Empress herself organized pioneering fundraisers.

Civil rights organizations, religious institutions and LGBT organizations increasingly popped the question: why couldn't same-sex couples get married too? Early backing came from the Japanese American Citizens League, which publicly endorsed marriage for same-sex couples as a civil right in 1994. Just 45 days after taking office in 2004, San Francisco mayor Gavin Newsom authorized same-sex weddings in San Francisco. The first couple to be married were Phyllis Lyon and Del Martin, a San Francisco couple who had spent 52 years together. California courts ultimately voided their and 4036 other San Francisco same-sex marriage contracts, but Lyon and Martin weren't dissuaded: they married again on June 18, 2008, with Mayor Newsom personally officiating. Martin passed away two months later at age 83, her wife by her side.

California courts struck down laws prohibiting same-sex marriage as unconstitutional in 2010. Upon appeal, the US Supreme Court upheld California's state ruling in July 2015, effectively legalizing same-sex marriage nationwide.

San Francisco 3.0

Industry dwindled steadily in San Francisco after WWII, as Oakland's port accommodated container ships and San Francisco's Presidio military base was deactivated. But onetime military tech contractors found work in a stretch of scrappy firms south of San Francisco, an area known today as Silicon Valley. When a company based in a South Bay garage called Hewlett-Packard introduced the 9100A 'computing genie' in 1968, a generation of unconventional thinkers and tinkerers took note.

Ads breathlessly gushed that Hewlett-Packard's 'light' (40lb) machine could 'take on roots of a fifth-degree polynomial, Bessel functions, elliptic integrals and regression analysis' – all for the low, low price of $4900 (about $29,000 today). Consumers didn't know what to do with such a computer, until its potential was explained in simple terms by Trips Festival co-organizer and techno-futurist Stewart Brand. In a 1969 issue of his DIY-promoting *Whole Earth Catalog*, Brand

March 2000	2003	2004	February 2004
After the NASDAQ index peaks at double its value a year earlier, the dot-com bubble pops. Share prices drop dramatically, and the 'dot-bomb' closes businesses across SF within a month.	Republican Arnold Schwarzenegger is elected governor of California. Schwarzenegger breaks party ranks on environmental issues and wins 2007 reelection.	Google's IPO raises a historic $1.9 billion at $85 per share. By 2015, shares were worth more than seven times that amount, and the company's worth had reached $368 billion.	Defying a Californian ban, SF mayor Gavin Newsom licenses 4037 same-sex marriages. Courts declare the marriages void, but the civil-rights challenge is upheld.

reasoned that the technology governments used to run countries could empower ordinary people. That same year, University of California, Los Angeles, professor Len Kleinrock sent the first rudimentary email from his computer to another at Stanford. The message he typed was 'L,' then 'O,' then 'G' – at which point the computer crashed.

The next wave of California techies was determined to create a personal computer that could compute and communicate without crashing. When 21-year-old Steve Jobs and Steve Wozniak introduced the Apple II at San Francisco's West Coast Computer Faire in 1977, techies were awed by the memory (4KB of RAM!) and the microprocessor speed (1MHz!). The Mac II originally retailed for the equivalent today of $4300 (or, for 48KB of RAM, more than twice that amount) – a staggering investment for what seemed like a glorified calculator/typewriter. Even if machines could talk to one another, pundits reasoned, what would they talk about?

A trillion web pages and a couple of million mobile apps later, it turns out machines have plenty to communicate. By the mid-1990s, the dotcom industry boomed in SoMa warehouses as start-up ventures rushed to put news, politics, fashion and, yes, sex online. But when venture-capital funding dried up, multi-million-dollar sites shriveled into online oblivion.

The paper fortunes of the dot-com boom disappeared on one nasty NASDAQ-plummeting day, March 10, 2000, leaving San Francisco service-sector employees and 26-year-old vice-presidents alike without any immediate job prospects. City dot-com revenues vanished; a 1999 FBI probe revealed that a windfall ended up in the pockets of real-estate developers. But today San Francisco is again booming with start-ups aiming to succeed just like San Francisco–based Twitter, Pinterest, Instagram, Airbnb, Yelp, Uber and Lyft – and, just south of the city, Facebook, LinkedIn, Apple, Google, eBay, YouTube, Netflix, Adobe and hundreds more top tech companies.

Meanwhile, inside shiny new glass towers at SoMa's Mission Bay, biotech start-ups are putting down roots and yielding research. Biotech is nothing new here: since Genentech was founded over beer at a San Francisco bar in 1976, the company has cloned human insulin and introduced the hepatitis B vaccine. California voters approved a $3-billion bond measure in 2004 for stem-cell research, and by 2008 California had become the nation's biggest funder of stem-cell research. With so many global health crises demanding researchers' attention and funding, many cures still seem a distant, if not impossible, dream – but if history is any indication, the impossible is almost certain to happen in San Francisco.

Top Five for Weird Technology

Exploratorium (Fisherman's Wharf)

San Francisco Museum of Modern Art (SoMa)

Audium (Japan-town)

The Interval (Fort Mason)

Internet Archive (Richmond)

2010	2014	2016	2017
After SF couples file suit, California courts declare laws prohibiting same-sex marriage unconstitutional. In 2015, the US Supreme Court upholds this, making same-sex marriage legal nationwide.	The San Francisco Giants win their third World Series title in five years. 'Fear the Beard' and 'Rally Thong' become SF cheers.	San Franciso aims to become a zero-waste city by 2020, and to that end mandates citywide composting and bans plastic bags.	Trump's executive order threatens Sanctuary Cities; San Francisco stands by its 1989 'City of Refuge' and 2016 Sanctuary City ordinances, slapping the federal government with a lawsuit.

Literary San Francisco

San Francisco has more writers than any other US city and hoards three times the national average of library books. Anachronistic though it may seem in the capital of new technology, San Franciscans still buy more books per capita than residents of other US cities. But the truth of San Francisco is even stranger than its fiction: where else could poetry fight the law and win? Yet that's exactly what happened in City Lights Books' 1957 landmark anti-censorship ruling in *People v Ferlinghetti*.

Poetry

San Francisco's Kenneth Rexroth popularized haiku here back in the 1950s, and San Franciscans still enjoy nothing more than a few well-chosen words. When the city has you waxing poetic, hit an open mike in the Mission. Key titles:

➡ *Howl and Other Poems* (Allen Ginsberg) Each line of Ginsberg's epic title poem is an ecstatic improvised mantra, chronicling the waking dreams of the Beat generation and taking a stand against postwar conformity. Publisher Lawrence Ferlinghetti was taken to court for 'willfully and lewdly' publishing *Howl* – resulting in a landmark free-speech triumph.

➡ *Time and Materials* (Robert Hass) Every word in these Pulitzer Prize–winning poems by the Berkeley-based US poet laureate is as essential and uplifting as a rivet in the Golden Gate Bridge.

➡ *Native Tongue* (Alejandro Murguía) San Francisco's latest poet laureate is a master interpreter of San Franciscan behavior, rhythmic performance poet and charismatic co-founder of Mission Cultural Center.

Best for Readings
....
City Lights (North Beach)
....
Booksmith (The Haight)
....
San Francisco Main Library (Civic Center)
....
Adobe Books (The Mission)
....
Green Apple Books (The Avenues)

Fiction

Many San Franciscans seem like characters in a novel – and after a few days here, you'll swear you've seen Armistead Maupin's corn-fed Castro newbies, Dashiell Hammett's dangerous redheads, Philip K Dick's sci-fi subversives and Amy Tan's American-born daughters explaining slang to Chinese-speaking moms. Key titles:

➡ *Tales of the City* (Armistead Maupin) The 1976 *San Francisco Chronicle* serial follows classic San Francisco characters: pot-growing landladies of mystery, ever-hopeful Castro club-goers and wide-eyed Midwestern arrivals. See also the mini-series version, which broke PBS ratings records.

➡ *The Joy Luck Club* (Amy Tan) The stories of four Chinese-born women and their American-born daughters are woven into a textured tale of immigration and aspiration in San Francisco's Chinatown. Director Wayne Wang's film version is charming, but the novel is more richly nuanced.

➡ *The Man in the High Castle* (Philip K Dick) The bestselling Berkeley sci-fi author presents a trippy parallel-universe scenario: imagine San Francisco c 1962, if the US had lost WWII to the Axis powers and California has become a Japanese-German colony. But there's a twist: an underground novel begins circulating, describing a world where California is free.

Nonfiction & Memoir

People-watching rivals reading as a preferred San Francisco pastime, and close observation of antics that would seem bizarre anywhere but here pays off in stranger-than-fiction nonfiction. Key titles:

➡ *Slouching Towards Bethlehem* (Joan Didion) Like hot sun through San Francisco summer fog, Didion's 1968 essays burn through the hippie haze to reveal glassy-eyed teenagers adrift in the Summer of Love.

➡ *On the Road* (Jack Kerouac) The book Kerouac banged out on one long scroll of paper in a San Francisco attic over a couple of months of 1951 shook America awake.

➡ *The Electric Kool-Aid Acid Test* (Tom Wolfe) His groovy style may seem dated, but Wolfe had extraordinary presence of mind to capture SF in the '60s with Ken Kesey, the Merry Pranksters, the Grateful Dead and Hells Angels.

➡ *Cool Gray City* (Gary Kamiya) Longtime SF taxi driver Kamiya explores his 7x7-mile city block by block in this 2015 book, capturing 49 poetically true tales of San Francisco – an outlandish city 'only borrowed from the sea,' and audaciously reimagined each time the fog rolls back.

Graphic Novels

Ambrose Bierce and Mark Twain set the San Francisco standard for sardonic wit, but recently Bay Area graphic novelists like R Crumb and Daniel Clowes have added a twist to this tradition with finely drawn, deadpan behavioral studies. Key titles:

➡ *Meanwhile in San Francisco* (Wendy MacNaughton) The San Franciscan illustrator captures the city's stories as they unfold on street corners and public spaces, with a pen finely attuned to the city's ironies and poetry.

➡ *Ghost World* (Daniel Clowes) The Oakland-based graphic novelist's sleeper hit follows Enid and Rebecca as they make plans, make do, grow up and grow apart.

➡ *American Born Chinese* (Gene Luen Yang) Chinese Monkey King fables are interwoven with teenage tales of assimilation – no wonder this won the Eisner Award for best graphic novel, plus the Harvey comic-art award for SF cartoonist Lark Pien.

'Zines

The local 'zine scene has been the underground mother lode of riveting reading since the '70s brought punk, DIY spirit and V Vale's groundbreaking *RE/Search* to San Francisco. The SF Public Library has been collecting local 'zines since 1966 – check out historic examples in the Little Maga/Zine Collection on the 6th floor of the SF Main Library. For 'zines you can take with you for eye-opening airplane reading, check out the wide-ranging selection at Needles & Pens.

Currently the most successful local 'zine is *McSweeney's*, founded by Dave Eggers, who achieved first-person fame with *A Heartbreaking Work of Staggering Genius* and generously used the proceeds to launch 826 Valencia, a nonprofit writing program for teens. Besides 'zines written by kids, McSweeney's also publishes an excellent map of literary San Francisco, so you can walk the talk.

Spoken Word

San Francisco's literary tradition doesn't just hang out on bookshelves. Beat authors like Kerouac freed generations of open-mike monologuists from the tyranny of tales with morals and punctuation. Allen Ginsberg's ecstatic readings of *Howl,* commemorated at the Beat Museum, continue to inspire slam poets at Litquake (p21) and at regular, raucous open mikes in the Mission, Tenderloin and North Beach.

Best for Comics & Graphic Novels

Mission Art & Comics (The Mission)
....
Isotope (Hayes Valley)
....
Kinokuniya Books & Stationery (Japantown)
....
Cartoon Art Museum (Fisherman's Wharf)
....
Bound Together Anarchist Book Collective (The Haight)

Best for 'Zines

Needles & Pens (The Mission)
....
826 Valencia (The Mission)
....
Adobe Books (The Mission)
....
Bound Together Anarchist Book Collective (The Haight)
....
The Magazine (Tenderloin)

Visual Arts

Art explodes from frames and jumps off the pedestal in San Francisco, where murals, street performances and impromptu sidewalk altars flow from alleyways right into galleries. Velvet ropes would only get in the way of SF's enveloping installations and interactive new-media art – often provocative, sometimes overwhelming, but never standoffish.

Media, Methods & Mayhem

San Francisco has some unfair artistic advantages: it's a photogenic city with a colorful past, with 150-year-old photography and painting traditions to prove it. Homegrown traditions of '50s Beat collage, '60s psychedelia, '70s punk, '80s graffiti, '90s skater graphics and 2000s new-media art keep San Francisco's art scene vibrant.

Photography

Pioneering 19th-century photographer Pirkle Jones saw expressive potential in California landscape photography, but it was SF native Ansel Adams' photos of Northern California's sublime wilds and his accounts of photography in Yosemite in the 1940s that would draw generations of camera-clutching visitors to San Francisco. Adams founded Group f/64 with pioneering street photographer Imogen Cunningham and still-life master Edward Weston, who kept a studio in SF and made frequent visits from his permanent base in nearby Carmel.

Adams and Cunningham taught at the San Francisco Art Institute alongside the definitive documentarian of the Great Depression, Dorothea Lange. Among her many poignant photographs are portraits of Californian migrant farm laborers and Japanese Americans forced to leave their San Francisco homes for WWII internment camps. Many of Lange's internment photographs conflicted with official propaganda and were impounded by the Army, not to be shown for 50 years.

After the censorship of her photographs, Lange co-founded the groundbreaking art-photography magazine *Aperture* with Adams and fellow photographers in San Francisco. Today her legacy of cultural critique continues with the colorful Californian suburban dystopias of Larry Sultan and Todd Hido. *Aperture* still publishes, and SF Camerawork continues the proud San Franciscan tradition of boundary-pushing photography shows and publications. Photography fans should book SFMOMA tickets even before air travel – this world-class collection continues to redefine photography past, present and future with landmark shows.

Social Commentary

The 1930s social-realist movement brought Mexican muralist Diego Rivera and vivid surrealist painter Frida Kahlo to San Francisco, where Rivera was invited to paint a cautionary fresco of California on the San Francisco Stock Exchange Lunch Club and Kahlo painted some of her

Best for Photography

....

SFMOMA
(Downtown)

....

SF Camerawork
(Civic Center)

....

de Young Museum
(Golden Gate
Park)

....

Fraenkel Gallery
at 49 Geary
(Union Sq)

....

Chinese Historical
Society of America
(Chinatown)

first portrait commissions. In over a decade spent working on projects in the city and hosting open-studio parties in North Beach, the modern-art power couple inspired bold new approaches to public art in San Francisco. Starting in the 1970s, their larger-than-life figures and leftist leanings have been reprised in works by Mission *muralistas,* as seen on the Women's Building and along Balmy Alley.

The Depression-era Work Projects Administration (WPA) sponsored several SF muralists to create original works for the Rincon Annex Post Office, Coit Tower, Aquatic Park Bathhouse and Beach Chalet. When the murals at Rincon Post Office and Coit Tower turned out to be more radical than the government-sponsored arts program had anticipated, censors demanded changes before the murals could be unveiled. But the artworks outlasted the censors and today are celebrated national landmarks.

Offsetting high-minded revolutionary art is gutsy, irreverent SF satire. Tony Labatt's 1970s video of disco balls dangling from his nether regions sums up SF's disco-era narcissism, while Lynn Hershman Leeson's performances as alter ego Roberta Breitmore chronicled 1970s encounters with feminism, self-help and diet fads. San Francisco provocateur Enrique Chagoya invents archaelogical artifacts from a parallel universe in which Mexico colonized America – he borrows a page from Philip K Dick's alternative-reality novel *The Man in the High Castle* and turns it into a fascinating Mayan codex.

Best for Provocation

....
Catharine Clark Gallery (Potrero Hill)
....
Luggage Store Gallery (Civic Center)
....
Galería de la Raza (The Mission)
....
Yerba Buena Center for the Arts (SoMa)
....
Anglim Gilbert Gallery (Financial District & Dogpatch)

VISUAL ARTS ABSTRACT THINKING

Abstract Thinking

Local art schools attracted major abstract expressionists during SF's vibrant postwar period, when Clyfford Still, David Park and Elmer Bischoff taught at the San Francisco Art Institute. Still and Park founded

PUBLIC SCULPTURE

San Francisco owes its sculpture tradition to a nude sculptor's model: 'Big Alma' Spreckels. Her 'sugar daddy' Adolph Spreckels left her sugar-plantation fortunes, which she donated to build the Legion of Honor and its Rodin sculpture court. The next benefactor was the WPA, whose government-funded Aquatic Park Bathhouse commissions included the totemic seal by Beniamino Bufano and a sleek green-slate nautical frieze by pioneering African American artist Sargent Johnson.

Bufano also sculpted Chinese revolutionary Sun Yat-sen's statue in Chinatown and San Francisco City College's 1968 *St Francis of the Guns,* made of 1968 guns collected in a San Francisco gun-buyback scheme. St Francis' mosaic robe features four assassinated leaders: Abraham Lincoln, Dr Martin Luther King Jr, John F Kennedy and Robert Kennedy.

But the sculptor who made the biggest impact on the San Francisco landscape in terms of sheer scale is Richard Serra, whose contributions range from the lobby sculpture maze at SFMOMA to the University of California San Francisco's Mission Bay campus. Serra's massive, rusted-metal minimalist shapes have been favorably compared to ship's prows – and, less generously, to Soviet factory seconds.

Public sculptures have been favorite San Franciscan subjects of debate since 1894, when vigilante art critics pulled down the statue of dentist Henry D Cogswell over a public drinking fountain he'd donated. Claes Oldenburg and Coosje van Bruggen's 2002 *Cupid's Span* represents the city's reputation for romance with a giant bow and arrow sunk into the Embarcadero. But the city wasn't smitten: a recent poll ranks it among SF's most despised public artworks. Tony Bennett's musical anthem 'I Left My Heart in San Francisco' inspired the SF General Hospital's Hearts in San Francisco fundraising project, but the cartoon hearts are regularly graffitied, denounced as eyesores and marked by territorial canine critics.

the misleadingly named Bay Area Figurative Art movement, an elemental style often associated with San Francisco painter Richard Diebenkorn's fractured, color-blocked landscapes. Diebenkorn influenced San Francisco Pop artist Wayne Thiebaud, who tilted Sunset District street grids into giddy abstract cityscapes.

High Concept, High Craft

San Francisco's peculiar dedication to craft and personal vision can get obsessive. Consider *The Rose,* the legendary painting Beat artist Jay DeFeo began in the 1950s and worked on for eight years, layering it with 2000lb of paint – until a hole had to be cut in the wall of her apartment to forklift it out. Sculptor Ruth Asawa started weaving not with wool but with metal in the 1950s, following a childhood behind barbed wire in Japanese American internment camps. Her legacy includes de Young Museum sculptures that look like jellyfish within onion domes within mushrooms, and Union Sq's beloved bronze San Francisco fountain, incorporating figures by more than 200 San Franciscans. SF's most famous obsessive is San Francisco–raised new-media artist Matthew Barney, who made his definitive debut at SFMOMA with *Cremaster Cycle* videos involving vats of Vaseline.

Street Smarts

With Balmy Alley murals as inspiration, SF skateboard decks and Clarion Alley garage doors were transformed in the 1990s with boldly outlined, oddly poignant graphics, dubbed 'Mission School' for their storytelling *muralista* sensibilities and graffiti-tag urgency. The Mission School's professor emeritus was the late Margaret Kilgallen, whose closely observed character studies blended hand-painted street signage, comic-book pathos and a miniaturist's attention to detail.

Clare Rojas expanded on these principles with urban folk-art wall paintings, featuring looming, clueless California grizzly bears and tiny, fierce girls in hoodies. Street-art star Barry McGee paints piles of found bottles with freckled, feckless characters, and still shows at the Luggage Store Gallery. Some Mission School art is fairly derided as the faux-naive work of stoned MFAs – but when its earnestness delivers, it hits you where it counts.

New Media

For 40 years, the Bay Area has been the global hub for technical breakthroughs – and local artists have been using technology creatively to pioneer new-media art. Since the '80s, Silicon Valley artist Jim Campbell has been building motherboards to misbehave. In one famous Campbell 'anti-interactive' artwork, a running figure freezes as soon as it senses viewers approaching, like a deer in the headlights – and resumes activity only if you stand still. Rebecca Bollinger's grouped sketches are inspired by images found through web keyword searches, while Kota Ezawa created special cartoon-image software to turn the OJ Simpson trial into the multichannel cartoon animation it actually was.

San Francisco's interactive artists invite you to burp the art and change its DNA. At Catharine Clark Gallery, John Slepian programmed a hairy rubber nub swaddled in blankets to sob disconsolately until you pick it up and pat its posterior. New-media artist Scott Snibbe created an app that allows users to not only remix but alter the musical DNA of Björk's *Biophilia* compositions, attacking songs with visual viruses and splicing new riffs into the melodies. The app is now in MoMA's permanent collection.

San Francisco Music

Only an extremely eclectic DJ can cover SF's varied musical tastes. Symphonies, bluegrass tunes, Latin music and both Chinese and Italian opera have lifted San Franciscan spirits through earthquakes and fires, booms and busts. Music trends that started around the Bay never really went away: '50s free-form jazz and folk; '60s psychedelic rock; '70s disco bathhouse anthems; and '90s west-coast rap and Berkeley's pop-punk revival. Today, DJ mash-ups put SF's entire back catalog to work.

Classical Music & Opera

Since conductor Michael Tilson Thomas (MTT) was wooed away from the London Symphony Orchestra to take the baton here in 1995, the San Francisco Symphony has stacked up international accolades. Under MTT, the SF Symphony has won more Grammys than the Beatles – 16 and counting. You can see why: Thomas conducts on the tips of his toes, enthralling audiences with full-throttle Mahler and Beethoven and some genuinely odd experimental music.

The San Francisco Opera is the USA's second-largest opera company after New York's Metropolitan Opera, but it's second to none with risk-taking. You'd never guess that San Francisco's opera roots go back to the 19th century, from avant-garde productions like *Harvey Milk* and Stephen King's *Dolores Claiborne* to the Chinese courtesan epic *Dream of the Red Chamber*.

> Classical music is accessible and often free in San Francisco – a local tradition started when opera divas performed gratis to raise SF's spirits after the 1906 earthquake and fire. For listings of free concerts around town, see www.sfcv.org.

Rock

Lately, San Francisco's rock of choice is preceded by the prefix alt- or indie-at music extravaganzas like Outside Lands, Noise Pop and Napa's **Bottle Rock** (www.bottlerocknapavalley.com). SF acts like Rogue Wave, Peggy Honeywell and Joanna Newsom add acoustic roots stylings even when they're not playing Berkeley's twangy Freight & Salvage Coffeehouse or Golden Gate Park's Hardly Strictly Bluegrass festival. Vintage SF sounds become new again with local bands playing any given night at Public Works, Brick & Mortar, Bottom of the Hill, the Independent or Hotel Utah.

But San Francisco rock isn't all sunshine and acoustic twang. Black Rebel Motorcycle Club and Deerhoof throw Mission grit into their walls of sound., and metalheads need no introduction to SF's mighty Metallica. The city also has the ignominious distinction of being a world capital of rocker overdoses. In the Haight, you can pass places Janis Joplin nearly met her maker; 32 Delmar St, where Sid Vicious went on the heroin bender that finally broke up the Sex Pistols; and the Grateful Dead flophouse, where the band was drug-raided. Grateful Dead guitarist Jerry Garcia eluded the bust and survived for decades, until his death in rehab in 1995.

But baby boomers keep the sound of San Francisco in the '60s alive, and much of it stands the tests of time and sobriety. After Joan Baez and Bob Dylan had their Northern California fling, folk turned into folk rock, and Jimi Hendrix turned the American anthem into a jam suitable for an acid trip. When Janis Joplin and Big Brother & the Holding Company applied their rough musical stylings to 'Me and Bobby McGee,' it was like taking that last necessary pass of sandpaper to the

> **Best for Classical & Opera**
>
> ....
> *San Francisco Symphony (Civic Center)*
> ....
> *San Francisco Opera (Civic Center)*
> ....
> *Stern Grove Festival (Golden Gate Park)*
> ....
> *Zellerbach Hall (Berkeley)*
> ....
> *SoundBox (Hayes Valley)*

SF ECLECTIC HITS PLAYLIST

→ 'Take Five' by the Dave Brubeck Quartet (1959)

→ 'Make You Feel That Way' by Blackalicious (2002)

→ 'Everyday People' by Sly and the Family Stone (1968)

→ 'Evil Ways' by Santana (1969)

→ 'Restless Year' by Ezra Furman (2015)

→ 'Uncle John's Band' by the Grateful Dead (1970)

→ 'Stay Human (All the Freaky People)' by Michael Franti & Spearhead (2007)

→ 'San Francisco Anthem' by San Quinn (2008)

→ 'Welcome to Paradise' by Green Day (1992)

→ 'The American in Me' by The Avengers (1979)

→ 'Come Back from San Francisco' by Magnetic Fields (1999)

→ 'Go Go Go' by Panic Is Perfect (2015)

→ 'California' by Rogue Wave (2005)

→ 'Me and Bobby McGee' by Janis Joplin (1971)

→ 'Lights' by Journey (1978)

sometimes clunky, wooden verses of traditional folk songs. Jefferson Airplane held court at the Fillmore, turning Lewis Carroll's opium-inspired children's classic into the psychedelic anthem 'White Rabbit.'

The '60s were quite a trip, but the '70s rocked around the Bay. Crosby, Stills, Nash & Young splintered, but Neil Young keeps his earnest, bluesy whine going from his ranch south of San Francisco. Since the 1970s, California-born, longtime Sonoma resident Tom Waits has been singing in an after-hours honky-tonk voice with a permanent catch in the throat. SF's own Steve Miller Band turned out stoner hits like 'The Joker,' Van Morrison lived in Marin and regularly played SF clubs in the '70s, and the Doobie Brothers have played bluesy stoner rock around the Bay since the 1970s. But SF's most iconic '70s rocker is Mission-born Carlos Santana, who combined a guitar moan and a Latin backbeat in 'Black Magic Woman,' 'Evil Ways' and 'Oye Como Va.' Santana made a crossover comeback with 1999's Grammy-winning *Supernatural* and 2005's *All That I Am,* featuring fellow San Franciscan Kirk Hammett of Metallica.

The ultimate SF rock anthem is an '80s power ballad by San Francisco supergroup Journey: 'Lights.' Giants fans also warm up for games by air-guitar-rocking to Journey's 'Don't Stop Believing,' the unofficial theme song of the Giants' World Series championships.

Best for Funk & Hip-Hop

Mezzanine (SoMa)

Outside Lands (August; Golden Gate Park)

Independent (Haight/NoPa)

Boom Boom Room (Japantown)

Warfield (Union Sq)

Funk & Hip-Hop

If there's anything San Francisco loves more than an anthem, it's an anthem with a funky groove. The '60s were embodied by freaky-funky, racially integrated San Francisco supergroup Sly and the Family Stone, whose number-one hits are funk manifestos: 'Everyday People,' 'Stand' and 'Thank You (Falettinme Be Mice Elf Agin).' The '70s sexual revolution lives on in disco anthem 'You Make Me Feel (Mighty Real)' by Sylvester – the Cockettes drag diva who was tragically lost to the HIV/AIDS epidemic, yet still brings SF crowds to the dancefloor.

San Francisco's '70s funk was reverb from across the bay in Oakland, where Tower of Power worked a groove with taut horn arrangements. All this trippy funk worked its way into the DNA of the Bay Area hip-hop scene, spawning the jazz-inflected Charlie Hunter, free-form Broun Fellinis, and the infectious wokka-wokka baseline of rapper Lyrics Born. Oakland's MC Hammer was an '80s crossover hip-hop hit maker best known for inflicting harem pants on the world, though his influence is heard in E-40's bouncing hyphy sound.

Political commentary and pop hooks became East Bay hip-hop signatures with Michael Franti and Spearhead, Blackalicious and the Coup. But the Bay Area is still best known as the home of the world's most talented and notorious rapper: Tupac Shakur, killed in 1996 by an assailant out to settle an East Coast–West Coast gangsta rap rivalry. Today, San Francisco rappers are less pugnacious and more tech savvy, as you hear in SF MC San Quinn's tech-name-checking 'San Francisco Anthem.'

Punk

London may have been more political and Los Angeles more hardcore, but San Francisco's take on punk was way weirder. Dead Kennedys frontman Jello Biafra ran for mayor in 1979 with a platform written on the back of a bar napkin: ban cars, set official rates for bribery and force businessmen to dress as clowns. He received 6000 votes, and his political endorsement is still highly prized. But for oddity, even Jello can't top the Residents, whose identities remain unknown after 60 records and three decades of performances wearing giant eyeballs over their heads.

Today, punk's not dead in the Bay Area. The Avengers played with the Sex Pistols the night they broke up in San Francisco and, by all accounts, lead singer Penelope Houston upstaged Johnny Rotten for freakish intensity – and, unlike the Pistols, the Avengers are still going strong. In the '90s, ska-inflected Rancid and pop-punk Green Day brought punk staggering out of Berkeley's 924 Gilman into the mass-media spotlight. Hardcore punks sneered at Green Day's chart-topping hits, but the group earned street cred (and Grammys) in 2004 with the dark social critique of *American Idiot* – at least until that album became a Broadway musical.

Landmark clubs like Bottom of the Hill, Hemlock Tavern and Slim's keep SF punk alive and pogoing. Following the early success of *Punk in Drublic,* SF-based NOFX recorded an impressively degenerate show at Slim's called *I Hear They've Gotten Worse Live!* Punk continues to evolve in San Francisco, with queercore Pansy Division, glam-punk songwriter Ezra Furman and the brass-ballsiness of Latin ska-punk La Plebe.

Jazz

Ever since house bands pounded out ragtime hits to distract Barbary Coast audiences from barroom brawls, San Francisco has echoed with jazz. SFJAZZ Center is a magnet for global talents as artists-in-residence. But jazz will find you all around town, from the Mission's stalwart Revolution Cafe, to the Tenderloin's Black Cat, to North Beach's experimental Doc's Lab and the Haight's swinging Club Deluxe.

SF played it cool in the 1950s with West Coast jazz innovated by the legendary Dave Brubeck Quartet, whose *Time Out* is among the best-selling jazz albums of all time. Bebop had disciples among the Beats, and the SF scene is memorably chronicled in Jack Kerouac's *On the Road*. Billie Holiday and Miles Davis recorded here, and today John Coltrane is revered as a saint at the African Orthodox Church of St John Coltrane.

During the '60s, the SF jazz scene exploded into a kaleidoscope of styles. Trumpeter Don Cherry blew minds with Ornette Coleman's avant-garde ensemble, while Dixieland band Turk Murphy kept roots jazz relevant.

Today, at newer venues like SFJAZZ and the Chapel, tempos shift from Latin jazz to klezmer, acid jazz to swing. So where are the jazz traditionalists? Playing the Hardly Strictly Bluegrass festival, and mixing with Afrofunk at Bissap Baobab. But you can't miss SF jazz at Christmas: San Franciscan Vince Guaraldi wrote the jazzy score for *A Charlie Brown Christmas,* the beloved antidote to standard Christmas carols.

Search & Destroy was San Francisco's shoddily photocopied and totally riveting chronicle of the '70s punk scene as it happened from 1977 to 1979, starting with an initial run financed with $100 from Allen Ginsberg and Lawrence Ferlinghetti, and morphing into V Vale's seminal 'zine RE/Search in the 1980s.

Best for Rock & Punk

....
Fillmore Auditorium (Japantown)
....
Warfield (Union Sq)
....
Bottom of the Hill (Potrero Hill)
....
Great American Music Hall (Tenderloin)
....
Slim's (SoMa)
....
Hardly Strictly Bluegrass (October; Golden Gate Park)

San Francisco Architecture

Superman wouldn't be so impressive in San Francisco, where most buildings are low enough for even a middling superhero to leap in a single bound. The Transamerica Pyramid and Ferry Building clock tower are helpful pointers to orient newcomers, and Coit Tower adds emphatic punctuation to the skyline – but SF's low-profile buildings are its highlights, from Mission adobe and Haight Victorians to wildflower-covered roofs in Golden Gate Park. Amid it all are Western storefronts, their squared-off rooflines as iconic as a cowboy's hat.

The Mission & Early SF

Not much is left of San Francisco's original Ohlone-style architecture, beyond the grass memorial hut you'll see in the graveyard of Mission Dolores and the wall of the original Presidio (military post) – both built in adobe with conscripted Ohlone labor. When the gold rush began, buildings were slapped together from ready-made sawn-timber components, sometimes shipped from the East Coast or Australia – an early precursor to postwar prefab.

In SF's Barbary Coast days, City Hall wasn't much to look at, at least from the outside: it was housed in the burlesque Jenny Lind Theater at Portsmouth Sq. Most waterfront buildings from SF's hot-headed Wild West days were lost to arson, including San Francisco's long-lost waterfront neighborhoods of Sydneytown, Manilatown and Chiletown, named for early gold-rush arrivals. Eventually, the builders of Jackson Sq got wise and switched to brick.

But masonry was no match for the 1906 earthquake and fire. The waterfront was almost completely leveled, with the mysterious exception of the Italianate 1866 AP Hotaling's Warehouse – which at the time housed SF's largest whiskey stash. The snappiest comeback in SF history is now commemorated in a bronze plaque on the building: 'If, as they say, God spanked the town/For being over-frisky/Why did He burn His churches down/And spare Hotaling's whiskey?'

Uphill toward North Beach, you'll spot a few other original 1860s to 1880s Italianate brick storefronts wisely built on bedrock. Elevated false facades are capped with jutting cornices, straight rooflines and graceful arches over tall windows.

Best for Early Architecture

Mission Dolores (The Mission)

Presidio

Cottage Row (Fillmore)

Jackson Square (Downtown)

Old St Mary's Cathedral & Square (Chinatown)

Octagon House (Cow Hollow)

Victoriana

To make room for new arrivals with the gold, railroad, lumber and shipping booms, San Francisco had to expand fast. Wooden Victorian row houses cropped up almost overnight, with a similar floor plan but eye-popping color schemes and outrageous ornament. San Francisco prospectors styled themselves as conquering heroes, flaunting newfound wealth in mansions with design details lifted from the back catalogs of ancient Rome, Egypt and the Italian Renaissance. All these eclectic embellishments gave fresh-out-of-the-box San Francisco a hodge-podge instant culture.

Although the city's signature architectural style is called 'Victorian,' it's a cheerfully inauthentic Californian take on a vaguely Anglo-Continental style. Few of the older buildings you'll see in SF were actually built during Victoria's 1837–1901 reign, apart from a few rather stern, steeply gabled Gothic Revivals. Most San Francisco Victorians fall into three basic architectural categories: Queen Anne, Stick and Edwardian.

Queen Anne

Architects pulled out all the stops on flamboyant Queen Anne mansions, adding balconies, chimneys, bay windows, rounded corner turrets and gables galore. Alamo Square (p181) has several exuberant examples lavished right up to the roofline with fish-scale shingles, toothy dentil details, gilt ornament and dizzying spindle-work trim.

Stick

In the Lower Haight, the Mission and Pacific Heights, you'll notice squared-off Victorians built to fit into narrow lots side by side, typically with flat fronts and long, narrow windows. Some of the ornamental flourishes of hilltop Queen Anne mansions were added to hillside Stick row houses in Japantown and Pacific Heights, blurring neighborhood boundaries and class lines among self-made San Franciscans.

Best for Victorians

Alamo Square (The Haight)

Haas-Lilienthal House (Pacific Heights)

Conservatory of Flowers (Golden Gate Park)

Columbarium (Golden Gate Park)

Palace Hotel (Downtown)

SAN FRANCISCO ARCHITECTURE VICTORIANA

SF'S SCANDALOUS PAINTED LADIES

When San Francisco prospectors struck it rich, they upgraded from downtown tenements to hilltop 'Painted Lady' mansions, embellished to the eaves with woodwork and gilding. These ornaments served a practical purpose: rows of houses were hastily constructed using a similar template, and San Francisco's newly upstanding citizens sometimes needed reminding which stairs to stumble up after wild Barbary Coast nights.

Demure Queen Victoria would surely blush to see the eccentric architecture perpetrated in her name in San Francisco – including rococo flourishes that made mansions and bordellos look alike. Local legend has it that to help visitors tell the difference between over-the-top San Francisco homes and actual houses of ill repute, theater masks were incorporated into garland decorations on bordellos. You'll spot many masks grinning and frowning above windows and doors around Alamo Square – if those walls could talk, San Francisco might scandalize the world even more than it already does.

From the late 19th to the early 20th century, California's lumber boom produced rows of 'Painted Lady' homes with candy-color palettes, gingerbread woodwork under peaked roofs, and gilded stucco garlands swagging wraparound, look-at-me bay windows. The 1906 quake and fire destroyed many historic buildings east of Van Ness Ave – and much of San Francisco's kitschy, colorful charm went up in smoke. Since Alamo Sq mansions were built on bedrock away from downtown, several Painted Ladies were spared.

But gold-rush tastes have proved garish enough to bring down modern property values, so many Painted Ladies are now painted historically incorrect but blandly marketable beige. (Alamo Sq mansions currently go for $3 million to $8 million, in case you're in the market.) Miraculously, many Painted Ladies have stood the test of tremors and trends in the Haight and the Mission, and remain just as staunchly colorful as your average San Franciscan.

Edwardian

Most of the 'Victorians' you'll see in San Francisco are actually from the post-1906-earthquake Edwardian era – art-nouveau, Asian-inspired and California arts-and-crafts details are the giveaways. You'll spot original Edwardian stained-glass windows and false gables in the inner Richmond, Haight and Castro neighborhoods.

Pacific Polyglot Architecture

A trip across town or even down the block will bring you face to facade with San Francisco's Spanish and Mexican heritage, Asian ancestry and California arts-and-crafts roots. Italianate bordello baroque was the look of choice for San Francisco dance halls like the 1907 Great American Music Hall, while Chinatown merchants designed their own streamlined, pagoda-topped Chinatown deco to attract tourists to Grant St. San Francisco's cinemas and theaters dispense with all geographical logic in favor of pure fantasy, from the scalloped Moorish arches of Thomas Patterson Ross' 1913 Exotic Revivalist Alcazar Theater (at 650 Geary St) to the chinoiserie deco elements inside Timothy Pflueger's 1925 Pacific Telephone & Telegraph Company Building.

Some Victorian mansions are now B&Bs, so you too can live large in swanky San Francisco digs of yore: look for places in the Haight, Pacific Heights, the Mission and Castro.

Mission & Meso-American

Never mind that Mexico and Spain actually fought over California, and missionaries and Aztecs had obvious religious and cultural differences: San Francisco's flights of architectural fancy paved over historical differences with cement, tile and stucco. Meso-American influences are obvious in the stone-carved Aztec motifs on Sansome St banks, not to mention the 1929 Mayan deco gilt reliefs that add jaw-dropping grandeur to architect Timothy Pflueger's 450 Sutter St – surely the world's most mystical dental-office building.

San Francisco's 1915 to 1935 Mission Revival paid tribute to California's Hispanic heritage, influenced by the 1915 Panama–Pacific International Exposition held in San Francisco. Spanish baroque fads flourished with the 1918 construction of a new *churrigueresque* (Mexican-style Spanish baroque) Mission Dolores basilica, replacing the earlier brick Gothic cathedral damaged in the 1906 earthquake.

The look proved popular for secular buildings, including Pflueger's Mexican baroque Castro Theatre marquee. Pflueger also invited the great Mexican muralist Diego Rivera to San Francisco to create the 1931 *Allegory of California* fresco for San Francisco's Stock Exchange Lunch Club – sparking a mural trend that continues in Mission streets today.

Chinatown Deco

Chinatown was originally hastily constructed by non-Chinese landlords from brick, which promptly collapsed into rubble in the 1906 earthquake. Fire swept the neighborhood, warping bricks into seemingly useless clinker bricks. But, facing City Hall plans for forced relocation, Chinatown residents ingeniously repurposed clinker bricks and rebuilt their neighborhood.

Clinker brickwork became a California arts-and-crafts signature, championed by Chinatown YWCA architect Julia Morgan. The first licensed female architect in California and the chief architect of over-the-top Spanish-Gothic-Greek Hearst Castle, Morgan showed tasteful restraint and finesse, combining cultural traditions in her designs for the pagoda-topped brick Chinatown YWCA (now the Chinese Historical Society of America) and the graceful Italianate Emanu-El Sisterhood Residence (now home to San Francisco Zen Center).

To attract business to the devastated neighborhood, Chinatown mounted a redevelopment initiative. A forward-thinking group of Chinatown merchants led by Look Tin Eli consulted with a cross section of architects and rudimentary focus groups to create a signature Chinatown art-deco architectural style in the 1920s and '30s. Using this approach, they reinvented brothel-lined Dupont St as tourist-friendly, pagoda-topped Grant Ave, with dragon lanterns and crowd-pleasing modern chinoiserie buildings.

California Arts-&-Crafts

California arts-and-crafts style combines Mission influences with Englisharts-and-crafts architecture, as seen in Bay Area Craftsman cottages and earthy ecclesiastical structures like San Francisco's Swedenborgian Church.

Berkeley-based architect Bernard Maybeck reinvented England's arts-and-crafts movement with the down-to-earth California bungalow, a small, simple single-story design derived from summer homes favored by British officers serving in India. Though Maybeck's Greco-Roman 1915 Palace of Fine Arts was intended as a temporary structure, the beloved but crumbling fake ruin was recast in concrete in the 1960s – and it continues to serve as San Franciscans' favorite wedding-photo backdrop.

Modern Skyline

Once steel-frame buildings stood the test of the 1906 earthquake, San Francisco began to think big with its buildings. The city aspired to rival the capitols of Europe and commissioned architect Daniel Burnham to build a grand City Hall in the neoclassical Parisian beaux arts, or 'city beautiful,' style. But City Hall was reduced to a mere shell by the 1906 earthquake, and it wasn't until 1924 that Pflueger built San Francisco's first real skyscraper: the Gothic deco, 26-story 1924 Pacific Telephone Building at 140 New Montgomery St. Recently restored, the telecom megalith is now the headquarters of Yelp and home to Mourad restaurant.

Flatirons

Chicago and New York started a trend raising skylines to new heights, and San Francisco borrowed their flatiron skyscraper style to maximize prime real estate along Market St. The street cuts a diagonal across San Francisco's tidy east–west grid, leaving both flanks of four attractive, triangular flatiron buildings exposed to view.

Among the head shops and XXX dives around 1020 Market St at Taylor, you'll find the lacy, white flatiron featured as broody Brad Pitt's apartment in the film *Interview with a Vampire*. On a less seedy block above the Powell St cable-car turnaround is the stone-cold silver fox known as the James Flood Building, a flinty character that has seen it all: fire, earthquakes and the Gap's attempts to revive bell-bottoms at its ground-floor flagship store. The Flood's opulent cousin is the 1908 Phelan Building at 760 Market St, while that charming slip of a building at 540 Market St is the 1913 Flatiron Building.

Streamline Moderne

San Francisco became a forward-thinking port city in the 1930s, introducing the ocean-liner look of the 1939 Streamline Moderne Aquatic

---

Top Low-Profile SF Landmarks

California Academy of Sciences (Golden Gate Park)

....

de Young Museum (Golden Gate Park)

....

Swedenborgian Church (Pacific Heights)

....

Chinese Historical Society of America (Chinatown)

....

Frank Lloyd Wright Building – VC Morris Store (Union Sq)

Park Bathhouse and SF's signature art-deco Golden Gate Bridge. But, except for the exclamation point of Coit Tower, most new SF buildings kept a low, sleek profile. Until the '60s, San Francisco was called 'the white city' because of its vast, low swaths of white stucco.

Skyscrapers

SF's skyline scarcely changed until the early 1960s, when seismic retrofitting and innovations made upward mobility possible in this shaky city. The 1959 Crown Zellerbach Building at 1 Bush St became a prototype for downtown buildings: a minimalist, tinted-glass rectangle with open-plan offices. The Financial District morphed into a Manhattanized forest of glass boxes, with one pointed exception: the Transamerica Pyramid. High-rises are now springing up in SoMa, with slots for 'urban village' shops, condos, restaurants and cafes. This latest attempt at instant culture is consistent with the city's original Victorian vision – only bigger and blander.

Prefab

Amid Victorian prefab row houses in San Francisco neighborhoods, you might also spot some newcomers that seem to have popped right out of the box. Around Patricia's Green in Hayes Valley, shipping containers have been repurposed into stores, cafes and a beer garden. San Francisco's *Dwell* magazine championed architect-designed, eco-prefab homes innovated in the Bay Area, and you can spot some early adopters in Diamond Heights and Bernal Heights. The exteriors can seem starkly minimal, but their interior spaces make the most of air and light.

Adaptive Reuse

Instead of starting from scratch, avant-garde architects are repurposing San Francisco's eclectic architecture to meet the needs of a modern city. Daniel Libeskind's design for the 2008 Contemporary Jewish Museum turned a historic power station into the Hebrew word for life, with a blue-steel pavilion as an emphatic accent.

Once the Embarcadero freeway collapsed in the 1989 earthquake, the sun shone on the Embarcadero at last – and the potential of the waterfront and its Ferry Building was revealed. San Francisco's neglected, partly rotten Piers 15 and 17 sheds were recently retrofitted and connected with Fujiko Nakaya's Fog Bridge to form a stunning, solar-powered new home for the Exploratorium. SFMOMA's new addition envelops the original Mario Botta–designed brick box with undulating white sails constantly poised for launch.

But raising the roof on standards for adaptive reuse is the 2008 LEED–certified green building for the California Academy of Sciences. Pritzker Prize–winning architect Renzo Piano incorporated the previous building's neoclassical colonnaded facade, gutted the interior to make way for a basement aquarium and four-story rainforest, and capped it all with a domed 'living roof' of California wildflowers perforated with skylights to allow air to circulate.

Survival Guide

Transportation

ARRIVING IN SAN FRANCISCO

The Bay Area has three international airports: San Francisco (SFO), Oakland (OAK) and San Jose (SJC). Direct flights from Los Angeles take 60 minutes; Chicago, four hours; Atlanta, five hours; New York, six hours. Factor in additional transit time – and cost – to reach San Francisco proper from Oakland or San Jose, and note that what you save in airfare you may wind up spending on ground transportation. However, if schedule is most important, note that SFO has more weather-related delays than OAK.

If you've unlimited time, consider taking the train, instead of driving or flying, to avoid traffic hassles and excess carbon emissions.

Flights, cars and tours can be booked online at lonelyplanet.com/bookings.

San Francisco International Airport

One of America's busiest, **San Francisco International Airport** (SFO; www.flysfo.com; S McDonnell Rd) is 14 miles south of downtown off Hwy 101 and accessible by BART.

BART

BART (www.bart.gov) has direct rides to/from downtown ($8.95, 30 minutes). The SFO BART station is connected to the International Terminal; buy tickets from machines inside stations.

Bus

SamTrans (☑800-660-4287; www.samtrans.com) Express bus KX runs to reach Temporary Transbay Terminal, in the South of Market (SoMa) area ($30 to 45 minutes). (The permanent Transbay Transit Center is scheduled to open in late 2017; journey time from the airport will be similar.)

Airport Express (☑800-327-2024; www.airportexpressinc.com) Runs a scheduled shuttle every hour from 5:30am to 12:30am between San Francisco Airport and Sonoma ($34) and Marin ($26) Counties.

Shuttle

Airport shuttles (one way $17 to $20 plus tip) depart from *upper-level* ticketing areas (not lower-level baggage claim); anticipate 45 minutes to most SF locations. For service to the airport, call at least four hours before departure to reserve pickups from any San Francisco location. Companies include **SuperShuttle** (☑800-258-3826; www.supershuttle.com), **Quake City** (☑415-255-4899; www.quakecityshuttle.com), **Lorrie's** (☑415-334-9000; www.gosfovan.com) and **American Airporter Shuttle** (☑415-202-0733; www.americanairporter.com).

Taxi & Ride-Share

Taxis to downtown San Francisco cost $45 to $55 plus tip and depart from the lower-level baggage-claim area of SFO. Ride-share services such as Lyft also operate in SF.

Car

The drive between the airport and the city can take as little as 20 minutes with no traffic, but give yourself an hour during the morning and evening rush hours. If you're headed to the airport via Hwy 101, take the San Francisco International Airport exit. Don't be misled by the Airport Rd exit, which leads to parking lots and warehouses.

Oakland International Airport

Travelers arriving at **Oakland International Airport** (OAK; www.oaklandairport.com; 1 Airport Dr; ☎; ⒷOakland International Airport), 15 miles east of downtown San Francisco, have a longer trip to reach San Francisco, but OAK has fewer weather-related flight delays than SFO.

BART

The cheapest way to reach San Francisco from the Oakland Airport. BART people-mover shuttles run every 10 to 20 minutes from Terminal 1 to the Coliseum station, where you connect with BART trains to downtown SF ($10.20, 25 minutes). Service operates 5am to midnight Monday to Friday, 6am to midnight Saturday, and 8am to midnight Sunday.

Bus

Airport Express (☑800-327-2024; www.airportexpressinc.com) Runs a scheduled shuttle every two hours (from 5:30am to 9:30pm) between Oakland Airport and Sonoma ($34) and Marin ($26) Counties.

Taxi & Ride-Share

Taxis leave curbside from OAK and average $35 to $50 to Oakland, $70 to $90 to SF.

SuperShuttle (☑800-258-3826; www.supershuttle.com) Offers shared van rides from OAK to downtown SF for $57 for up to four people (reservation required).

Norman y Mineta San Jose International Airport

Fifty miles south of downtown San Francisco, **Mineta San Jose International Airport** (SJC; ☑408-392-3600; www.flysanjose.com; 1701 Airport Blvd) is the least convenient of SF's airports, but by car it's a straight shot to the city via Hwy 101; expect heavy traffic during peak times. The **VTA** (Valley Transit Authority; ☑408-321-2300; www.vta.org) Airport Flyer (bus 10; free, runs 5am to 11:30pm) makes a continuous run every 15 to 30 minutes between the Santa Clara Caltrain station (Railroad Ave and Franklin

St) and the airport terminals. From Santa Clara station, Caltrain (one way $9.75, 90 minutes) runs northbound trains to the SF terminus at 4th and King Sts from 5am to 10:30pm weekdays, 7am to 10:30pm Saturday and 8am to 9pm Sunday.

Train

Easy on the eyes and light on carbon emissions, train travel is a good way to visit the Bay Area and beyond.

Caltrain (www.caltrain.com; cnr 4th & King Sts) connects San Francisco with Silicon Valley hubs and San Jose.

Amtrak (☑800-872-7245; www.amtrakcalifornia.com) serves San Francisco via stations in Oakland and Emeryville (near Oakland), with free shuttle-bus connections to San Francisco's Ferry Building and Caltrain station, and Oakland's Jack London Sq. Amtrak offers rail passes good for seven days of travel in California within a 21-day period (from $159).

Most departures from Oakland are short hops to Sacramento, but several daily departures are long-haul trains, with coach service, sleepers and private rooms. The **Coast Starlight** makes its spectacular 35-hour run from Los Angeles to Seattle via Emeryville/Oakland.

The **California Zephyr** (www.amtrak.com) runs from Chicago, through the Rockies and snow-capped Sierra Nevada, to Oakland (51 hours); it's almost always late.

Bus

Until the new terminal is complete in late 2017, SF's intercity hub remains the **Temporary Transbay Terminal** (Map p298; cnr Howard & Main Sts; ☐5,38,41,71). From here you can catch the following buses:

AC Transit (☑510-891-4777;

www.actransit.org) Buses to the East Bay.

Greyhound (☑800-231-2222; www.greyhound.com) Buses leave daily for Los Angeles ($39 to $90, eight to 12 hours), Truckee near Lake Tahoe ($35 to $46, 5½ hours) and other major destinations.

Megabus (☑877-462-6342; http://us.megabus.com) Low-cost bus service to San Francisco from Los Angeles, Sacramento and Reno.

SamTrans (☑800-660-4287; www.samtrans.com) Southbound buses to Palo Alto and the Pacific coast.

Arriving by Car

Driving within San Francisco is a nightmare of traffic and stress, except in the middle of the night. If you arrive by car or motorcycle, plan to park your car until it's time to leave, and take taxis or public transit to get around.

GETTING AROUND SAN FRANCISCO

When San Franciscans aren't pressed for time, most walk, bike or ride Muni instead of taking a car or cab. Traffic is notoriously bad at rush hour, and parking is next to impossible in center-city neighborhoods. Avoid driving until it's time to leave town – or drive during off-peak hours.

For Bay Area transit options, departures and arrivals, call 511 or check www.511.org. A detailed *Muni Street & Transit Map* is available free online.

BART

The fastest link between downtown and the Mission District also offers transit to SF airport (SFO; $8.95), Oakland ($3.45) and Berkeley ($4). Four of the system's five lines pass through SF before terminating at Daly City or SFO. Within SF, one-way fares start at $1.95.

Tickets

Buy tickets at BART stations: you need a ticket to enter – and exit – the system. If your ticket still has value after you exit turnstiles, it's returned to you, with the remaining balance for later use. If your ticket's value is less than needed to exit, use an Addfare machine to pay the appropriate amount. The Clipper Card (p267) can be used for BART.

Transfers

At San Francisco BART stations, a 25¢ discount is available for Muni buses and streetcars; look for transfer machines before you pass through the turnstiles.

Bicycle

Contact the **San Francisco Bicycle Coalition** (☑415-431-2453; www.sfbike.org) for maps, information and legal matters regarding bicyclists.

Bike sharing is new in SF: racks for **Bay Area Bike Share** (☑855-480-2453; www.bayareabikeshare.com; 30-day membership $30) are located east of Van Ness Ave, and in the SoMa area; however, bikes come without helmets, and biking downtown without proper protection can be particularly dangerous. Bicycles can be taken on BART, but not aboard crowded trains, and never in the first car, nor in the first three cars during weekday rush hours; folded bikes are allowed in all cars at all times. On Amtrak, bikes can be checked as baggage for $5.

Boat

With the revival of the Embarcadero and the reinvention of the Ferry Building as a gourmet dining destination, commuters and tourists alike are taking the scenic ferry across the bay.

Alcatraz

Alcatraz Cruises (Map p290;☑415-981-7625; www. alcatrazcruises.com; tours day adult/child/family $37.25/23/112.75, night adult/child $44.25/26.50; Ⓜ E, F) has ferries (reservations essential) departing Pier 33 for Alcatraz every half-hour from 8:45am to 3:50pm and at 5:55pm and 6:30pm for night tours.

East Bay

Blue & Gold Fleet Ferries (Map p301;☑415-705-8200; www.blueandgoldfleet.com) operates from the Ferry Building, Pier 39 and Pier 41 at Fisherman's Wharf to Jack London Sq in Oakland (one way $6.65). During baseball season, a Giants ferry service runs directly from the landing at AT&T Park's Seals Plaza entrance to Oakland and Alameda. Ticket booths are located at the Ferry Building and Piers 39 and 41.

San Francisco Bay Ferry (☑415-705-8291; http:// sanfranciscobayferry.com) operates from both Pier 41 and the Ferry Building to Oakland/Alameda. Fares are $6.60.

BIKING AROUND THE BAY AREA

Within SF Muni has racks that can accommodate two bikes (only) on the front of most buses.

Marin County Bikes are allowed on the Golden Gate Bridge, so riding north to Marin County is no problem. You can transport bicycles on Golden Gate Transit buses, which usually have free racks (three bikes only; first come, first served). Ferries also allow bikes on board.

Wine Country To transport your bike to Wine Country, take Golden Gate Transit or the Vallejo Ferry. Within Sonoma Valley, take Arnold Dr instead of busy Hwy 12; through Napa Valley, take the Silverado Trail instead of busy Hwy 29. The most spectacular ride in Wine Country is sun-dappled, tree-lined West Dry Creek Rd, in Sonoma's Dry Creek Valley.

East Bay Cyclists can't use the Bay Bridge. Ride BART. Bikes are allowed on uncrowded BART trains, but during rush hours special limits apply: between 6:30am and 9am and from 4pm to 6:30pm, bikes can't board the first three cars. (Folded bikes are allowed in all cars at all times.) During commuting hours, you can carry your bike across the Bay via the **Caltrans Bay Bridge Bicycle Commuter Shuttle** (Map p298; ☑510-286-6945; www.dot.ca.gov/dist4/shuttle.htm; cnr Main & Bryant Sts; ◷6:40-8:10am & 3:50-6:15pm Mon-Fri), which operates from the northwest corner of Main and Bryant Sts in San Francisco, and from MacArthur BART station in Oakland (on 40th St, between Market St and the BART entrance); shuttles fill – arrive early; tickets are $1.

Marin County

Golden Gate Transit Ferries
(Map p301; ☑415-455-2000;
www.goldengateferry.org;
☺6am-9:30pm Mon-Fri,
10am-6pm Sat & Sun) runs
regular ferry services from the
Ferry Building to Larkspur and
Sausalito (one way $11.75).
Transfers are available to Muni
bus services and bicycles are
permitted. Blue & Gold Fleet
Ferries also operate to Tiburon
or Sausalito (one way $11.50)
from Pier 41.

Napa Valley

Get to Napa car free (weekdays only) via the **Vallejo
Ferry** (Map p301; ☑707-643-
3779, 877-643-3779; http://
sanfranciscobayferry.com),
with departures from the
Ferry Building docks about
every hour from 6:30am to
7pm weekdays and roughly
every 90 minutes from 10am
to 9pm on weekends; bikes
are permitted. However,
the connecting bus from
the Vallejo Ferry Terminal –
Napa Valley Vine bus 29 to
downtown Napa, Yountville,
St Helena or Calistoga – operates only on weekdays.
Fares are $13.80.

Bus, Streetcar & Cable Car

Muni (Municipal Transit
Agency;☑511; www.sfmta.
com) Operates bus, streetcar
and cable-car lines. Buses and
streetcars are referred to inter-
changeably as Muni, but when
streetcars run underground
beneath Market St, they're
called the Muni Metro. Some
areas are better connected
than others, but Muni spares
you the costly hassle of driving
and parking – and it's often
faster than driving, especially
along metro-streetcar lines J,
K/T, L, M and N.

Schedules

For route planning and
schedules, consult http://
transit.511.org. For real-
time departures, see www.
nextmuni.com, which synchs
with GPS on buses and
streetcars to provide best
estimates on arrival times.
This is the system tied to
digital displays posted inside
bus shelters. It's accurate for
most lines, but not always for
the F-line vintage streetcars
or cable cars. Nighttime
and weekend service is less
frequent than on weekdays.
Owl service (half-hourly
from 1am to 5am) operates
only on a few principal lines;
for schedules, see http://
allnighter.511.org.

System Maps

A detailed *Muni Street &
Transit Map* is available free
online (www.sfmta.com).

Tickets

The standard fare for
buses or streetcars is $2.50;
buy tickets on buses and
streetcars from drivers
(exact change required) or
at underground Muni sta-
tions (where machines give
change). Cable-car tickets
cost $7 per ride, and can
be bought at cable-car-
turnaround kiosks or on
board from the conductor.
Hang onto your ticket even if
you're not planning to use it
again: if you're caught without one by the transit police,
you're subject to a $100 fine
(repeat offenders may be
fined up to $500).

Transfers

At the start of your Muni
journey, free transfer tickets
are available for additional
Muni trips within 90 minutes
(not including cable cars or
BART). After 8:30pm, buses
issue a Late Night Transfer
good for travel until 5:30am
the following morning.

Discounts & Passes

MUNI PASSPORTS
A **Muni Passport** (1/3/7
days $21/32/42) allows
unlimited travel on all Muni
transport, including cable
cars. It's sold at the Muni
kiosk at the Powell St cable
car turnaround on Market
St, SF's Visitor Information
Center, the TIX Bay Area
kiosk at Union Sq and shops
around town – see www.sfm-
ta.com for exact locations.
One-day (but not multiday)
passports are available from
cable-car conductors.

CLIPPER CARDS
Downtown Muni/BART sta-
tions have machines that
issue the Clipper Card, a
reloadable transit card with
a $3 minimum that can be
used on Muni, BART, AC
Transit, Caltrain, SamTrans
and Golden Gate Transit
(but not cable cars). Clipper
Cards automatically deduct
fares and apply transfers –
only one Muni fare is deduct-
ed per 90-minute period.

FAST PASS
The **Muni Monthly Pass**
(adult/child $73/36) offers
unlimited Muni travel for the
calendar month, including
cable cars. Fast Passes are

BUSES AROUND THE BAY

Three public bus systems connect San Francisco to the rest of the Bay Area. Most buses leave from clearly marked bus stops; for transit maps and schedules, see the bus-system websites.

AC Transit (☎510-891-4777; www.actransit.org) East Bay bus services from the Temporary Transbay Terminal. For public-transportation connections from BART in the East Bay, get an AC Transit transfer ticket before leaving the BART station for 25¢ off your connecting fare, both to and from BART.

Golden Gate Transit (☎511, outside Bay Area 415-455-2000; http://goldengatetransit.org) Connects San Francisco to Marin (tickets $5.50 to $8) and Sonoma Counties (tickets $11.75 to $13); check schedules online, as service is erratic.

SamTrans (☎800-660-4287; www.samtrans.com) Connects San Francisco and the South Bay, including bus services to/from SF airport (SFO). Buses pick up/drop off from the Temporary Transbay Terminal and other marked bus stops within the city.

available at the Muni kiosk at the Powell St cable-car turnaround, and from many businesses around town; for exact locations, see www.sfmta.com.

Bus

Muni buses display their route number and final destination on the front and side. If the number is followed by the letter A, B, X or R, then it's a limited-stop or express service.

KEY ROUTES

22 Fillmore From Dogpatch (Potrero Hill), through the Mission on 16th St, along Fillmore St past Japantown to Pacific Heights and the Marina.

33 Stanyan From San Francisco General Hospital, through the Mission, Castro and Haight, past Golden Gate Park to Clement St.

38 Geary From the Temporary Transbay Terminal, along Market to Geary Blvd, north of Golden Gate Park through the Richmond district to Ocean Beach.

7 Noriega From the Temporary Transbay Terminal, along Market and Haight Sts, along the southeast side of Golden Gate Park through the Sunset District and to the Great Hwy at the beach.

Streetcar

Muni Metro streetcars run 5am to midnight on weekdays, with limited schedules at weekends. The K, L, M, N and T lines operate 24 hours, but above-ground Owl buses replace streetcars between 12:30am and 5:30am. The F-Market line runs vintage streetcars above ground along Market St to the Embarcadero, where they turn north to Fisherman's Wharf; the E-Embarcadero runs the same cars along the waterfront. The T line heads south along the Embarcadero through SoMa and Mission Bay, then down 3rd St. Other streetcars run underground below Market St to downtown.

KEY ROUTES

F Fisherman's Wharf and Embarcadero to the Castro.

J Downtown to the Mission, the Castro and Noe Valley.

K, L, M Downtown to the Castro and the western neighborhoods.

N Caltrain and SBC Ballpark to the Haight, Golden Gate Park and Ocean Beach.

T The Embarcadero to Caltrain and Bayview.

Cable Car

In this age of seat belts and airbags, a rickety cable-car ride is an anachronistic thrill. There are seats for about 30 passengers, who are often outnumbered by passengers clinging to creaking leather straps.

KEY ROUTES

California Street Runs east–west along California St, from the downtown terminus at Market and Davis Sts through Chinatown and Nob Hill to Van Ness Ave. It's the least-traveled route, with the shortest queues.

Powell-Mason Runs from the Powell St cable-car turnaround past Union Sq, turns west along Jackson St, and then descends north down Mason St, Columbus Ave and Taylor St toward Fisherman's Wharf. On the return trip it takes Washington St instead of Jackson St.

Powell-Hyde The most picturesque route follows the same tracks as the Powell-Mason line until Jackson St, where it turns down Hyde St to terminate at Aquatic Park; coming back it takes Washington St.

Caltrain

From the depot at 4th and King Sts in San Francisco, **Caltrain** (www.caltrain.com; cnr 4th & King Sts) heads south to Millbrae (connecting to BART and SF airport (SFO); 30 minutes), Palo Alto (one hour) and San Jose (1½ hours). This is primarily a commuter line, with frequent departures during weekday rush hours and less frequent service between nonrush hours and at weekends.

Car & Motorcycle

If you can, avoid driving in San Francisco: heavy traffic is a given, street parking is harder to find than true love, and meter readers are ruthless.

Traffic

San Francisco streets mostly follow a grid bisected by Market St, with signs pointing toward tourist zones such as North Beach, Fisherman's Wharf and Chinatown. Try to avoid driving during rush hours: 7:30am to 9:30am and 3:30pm to 6:30pm, Monday to Friday. Before heading to any bridge, airport or other traffic chokepoint, call 511 for a traffic update.

Parking

For real-time details on how to find parking in the city, and also how to pay your parking meter by telephone or smartphone (so you don't have to return to the car if your meter expires), see SF Park (http://sfpark.org). Parking is tricky and often costly, especially downtown – ask your hotel about parking, and inquire about validation at restaurants and entertainment venues.

GARAGES

Downtown parking garages charge from $3 to $8 per hour and $25 to $50 per day, depending on how long you park and whether you require in-and-out privileges. The most convenient downtown parking lots are at the Embarcadero Center; at 5th and Mission Sts; under Union Sq; and at Sutter and Stockton Sts. For more public parking garages, see www.sfmta.com; for a map of garages and rates, see http://sfpark.org.

PARKING RESTRICTIONS

Parking restrictions are indicated by the following color-coded sidewalk curbs:

Blue Disabled parking only; placard required.

Green Ten-minute parking zone from 9am to 6pm.

Red No parking or stopping.

White For picking up or dropping off passengers only; note posted times.

Yellow Loading zone during posted times.

TOWING VIOLATIONS

Desperate motorists often resort to double-parking or parking in red zones or on sidewalks, but parking authorities are quick to tow cars. If this should happen to you, you'll have to retrieve your car at **Autoreturn** (☏415-865-8200; www.autoreturn.com; 450 7th St, SoMa; ☺24hr; ⓜ27, 42). Besides at least $73 in fines for parking violations, you'll also have to fork out a towing and storage fee ($208 for the first four hours, $58.50 for the rest of the first day, $27.75 for every additional day, plus a $28 transfer fee if your car is moved to a long-term lot). Cars are usually stored at 450 7th St, corner Harrison St.

Rental

Typically, a small rental car might cost $55 to $75 a day or $175 to $300 a week, plus 8.75% sales tax, plus various licensing fees and tourism taxes that add another $10 to $30 beyond the tax. Unless your credit card or personal car insurance covers car-rental insurance, you'll need to add $10 to $20 per day for a loss/damage waiver. Most rates include unlimited mileage; with cheap rates, there's often a per-mile charge above a certain mileage.

Booking ahead usually ensures the best rates. Airport rates are generally lower than city rates, but they carry a hefty facility charge of about $20 per day. As part of SF's citywide green initiative, rentals of hybrid cars and low-emissions vehicles

from agencies at SF airport (SFO) are available at a discount.

To rent a motorcycle, contact **Dubbelju** (☏415-495-2774, 866-495-2774; www.dubbelju.com; 274 Shotwell St; per day from $99; ☺9am-6pm Mon-Sat). **Go Car** (www.gocartours.com; per hour $56) rents mini-cars with audio GPS instructions to major attractions in multiple languages.

To get around town techie style, you can rent a Segway from **Segway SF Bay** (www.segwaysfbay.com; per 90min $45) for use on bike lanes and trails (they're banned on sidewalks). Rates include free lessons and map. Guided Segway tours are available from **City Segway Tours** (http://citysegwaytours.com; 2hr from $70).

Major car-rental agencies include the following:

Alamo Rent-a-Car (☏800-327-9633, 415-693-0191; www.alamo.com; 750 Bush St; ☺7am-6pm Mon-Fri, to 5pm Sat & Sun; ⓡPowell-Mason, Powell-Hyde, ⓜ2, 3, 30, 45)

Avis (☏800-352-7900, 415-929-2555; www.avis.com; 675 Post St; ☺6am-6pm; ⓜ2, 3, 27, 38)

Budget (☏800-527-7000, 415-433-3717; www.budget.com; 675 Post St; ☺6am-6pm; ⓜ2, 3, 27, 38)

Dollar (☏866-434-2226; www.dollar.com; 364 O'Farrell St; ☺7am-6pm; ⓜ38, ⒷPowell)

Hertz (☏800-654-3131, 415-771-2200; www.hertz.com; 325 Mason St; ☺6am-6pm; ⓜ38, ⒷPowell)

Thrifty (☏800-367-2277, 415-788-8111; www.thrifty.com; 350 O'Farrell St; ☺7am-6pm; ⓜ38, ⒷPowell)

Car-Share & Ride-Share

Car sharing is a convenient alternative to rentals, and spares you pick-up/drop-off

CLIMATE CHANGE & TRAVEL

Every form of transportation that relies on carbon-based fuel generates CO_2, the main cause of human-induced climate change. Modern travel is dependent on airplanes, which might use less fuel per kilometer per person than most cars but travel much greater distances. The altitude at which aircraft emit gases (including CO_2) and particles also contributes to their climate change impact. Many websites offer 'carbon calculators' that allow people to estimate the carbon emissions generated by their journey and, for those who wish to do so, to offset the impact of the greenhouse gases emitted with contributions to portfolios of climate-friendly initiatives throughout the world. Lonely Planet offsets the carbon footprint of all staff and author travel.

and parking hassles: reserve a car online for an hour or two, or all day, and you can usually pick up/drop off your car within blocks of where you're staying. Sharing also does the environment a favor: fewer cars on the road means less congestion and pollution. Lyft and Uber are available in San Francisco, but licensed taxis have greater access, specifically to dedicated downtown bus and taxi lanes, notably along Market St.

Zipcar (☑866-494-7227; www.zipcar.com) Rents various car types by the hour, for flat rates starting at $8.25 per hour, including gas and insurance, or per day for $89; a $25 application fee and $50 prepaid usage are required. The maximum damage-loss insurance coverage, which brings the deductible to $0, is strongly recommended. Drivers without a US driver's license should follow instructions on the website. Once approved, cars can be reserved online or by phone, provided you have your member card in pocket. Check the website for pick-up/drop-off locations. Other current Zipcard holders may also drive the car; if you want to share the driving with someone, both of you should sign up.

Roadside Assistance

Members of **American Automobile Association** (AAA; ☑415-773-1900, 800-222-4357; www.aaa.com; 160 Sutter St; ☺8:30am-5:30pm Mon-Fri; ⒷMontgomery, ⓂMontgomery) can call the 800 number any time for emergency road service and towing. AAA also provides travel insurance and free road maps of the region. A greener alternative: **Better World Auto Club** (www.betterworldclub.com).

Taxi

Taxi fares start at $3.50 at flag drop and run about $2.75 per mile. Add 15% to the fare as a tip ($1 minimum). For quickest service in San Francisco, download the Flywheel app for smart phones, which dispatches the nearest taxi.

DeSoto Cab (☑415-970-1300; http://flywheeltaxi.com/)

Green Cab (☑415-626-4733; www.greencabsf.com) Fuel-efficient hybrids; worker-owned collective.

Homobiles (☑415-574-5023; www.homobiles.org) Get home safely with secure, reliable, donation-based transportation for the LGBT community: drivers provide 24/7 taxi service – text for fastest service.

Luxor (☑415-282-4141; www.luxorcab.com)

Yellow Cab (☑415-333-3333; www.yellowcabsf.com)

Directory A–Z

Customs Regulations

Each person over 21 years is allowed to bring 1L of liquor and 200 cigarettes duty-free into the USA. Non-US citizens are allowed to bring $100 worth of duty-free gifts. If you're carrying over $10,000 in US and foreign cash, traveler's checks or money orders, you must declare the excess amount – undeclared sums in excess of $10,000 may be subject to confiscation.

Dangers & Annoyances

Keep your city smarts and wits about you, especially at night in the Tenderloin, South of Market (SoMa) and the Mission.

➡ Avoid using your smart phone unnecessarily on the street – phone-snatching is a crime of opportunity and a problem in SF.

➡ The Bayview–Hunters Point neighborhood (south of Potrero Hill, along the water) is plagued by crime and violence and isn't suitable for wandering tourists.

➡ After dark, Mission Dolores Park, Buena Vista Park and the entry to Golden Gate Park at Haight and Stanyan Sts are used for drug deals and casual sex hookups.

Discount Cards

Some green-minded venues, such as the de Young Museum, the California Academy of Sciences and the Legion of Honor, also offer discounts to ticket-bearing Muni riders.

City Pass (www.citypass.com; adult/child $89/69) Covers cable cars, Muni and entry to four attractions, including the California Academy of Sciences, Blue & Gold Fleet Bay Cruise, the Aquarium of the Bay and either the Exploratorium or the de Young Museum.

Go Card (www.smartdestinations.com; adult/child one day $65/49, two days $90/62, three days $115/85) Provides access to the city's major attractions, including the California Academy of Sciences, the de Young Museum, the Aquarium of the Bay, the Conservatory of Flowers, the Beat Museum and Go Car tours, plus discounts on packaged tours and waterfront restaurants and cafes.

Electricity

Electric current in the USA is 110 to 115 volts, 60Hz AC. Outlets may be suited for flat two-prong or three-prong plugs. If your appliance is made for another electrical system, get a transformer or adapter at Walgreens.

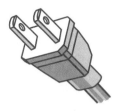

Type A
120V/60Hz

Type B
120V/60Hz

Emergency

Emergency	☑911
Non-emergency	☑311

Legal Matters

San Francisco police usually have more urgent business than fining you for picking a protected orange California poppy on public land (up to $500), littering ($250 and up), loitering on sidewalks against the Sit/Lie law ($100 to $500), jaywalking (ie crossing streets outside a pedestrian crosswalk; $75 to $125) or failing to clean up after your puppy ($50, plus shaming glares from fellow dog owners).

Drinking alcoholic beverages outdoors is not officially allowed, though beer and wine are often permissible at street fairs and other outdoor events. You may be let off with a warning for being caught taking a puff on a joint, but don't count on it – possessing marijuana for personal use is still a misdemeanor in this lenient city, but it's legal with a medical-marijuana prescription. In recent years the police have also cracked down on park squatters and illegal camping.

If you are arrested for any reason, it's your right to remain silent, but never walk away from an officer until given permission or you could be charged with resisting arrest. Anyone arrested gets the right to make one phone call. If you want to call your consulate, the police will give you the number on request.

LGBT+ Travelers

Information for LGBT+ travelers can be found on p37.

Medical Services

Before traveling, contact your health-insurance provider to learn what medical care they will cover outside your hometown (or home country). Overseas visitors should acquire travel insurance that covers medical situations in the US, where nonemergency care for uninsured patients can be very expensive.

For nonemergency appointments at hospitals, you'll need proof of insurance, or credit card or cash. Even with insurance, you'll most likely have to pay up front for nonemergency care and then wrangle afterward with your insurance company to get reimbursed. San Francisco has excellent medical facilities, plus alternative medical practices and herbal apothecaries.

San Francisco City Clinic (☑415-487-5500; www.sfcityclinic.org; 356 7th St; ◷8am-4pm Mon, Wed & Fri, 1-6pm Tue, 1-4pm Thu) Low-cost treatment for sexually transmitted diseases (STDs), including emergency contraception and post-exposure prevention (PEP) for HIV.

Drug & Alcohol Emergency Info Line (☑415-362-3400; www.sfsuicide.org)

Trauma Recovery & Rape Treatment Center (☑24hr hotline 415-206-8125, business hours 415-437-3000; www.traumarecoverycenter.org)

University of California San Francisco Medical Center (☑415-476-1000; www.ucsf-health.org; 505 Parnassus Ave; ◷24hr; ◻6, 7, 43, Ⓜ︎N) ER at leading university hospital.

San Francisco General Hopsital (Zuckerberg San Franciso General Hospital and Trauma Center; ☑emergency 415-206-8111, main hospital 415-206-8000; www.sfdph.org; 1001 Potrero Ave; ◷24hr; ◻9, 10, 33, 48) Best ER for serious trauma.

Health Insurance

Make sure your health-insurance policy covers travel to California. If it does not, consider a travel-insurance policy that covers emergency medical services.

Recommended Vaccinations

No specific vaccinations are required for travel to the US, though it is always sensible to ensure that your routine vaccinations are up to date.

MEDIA

San Francisco has plenty of print information sources:

San Francisco Chronicle (www.sfgate.com) City's main daily newspaper.

SF Weekly (www.sfweekly.com) Free weekly with local gossip and entertainment.

San Francisco Examiner (www.sfexaminer.com) Free daily with news, events, opinions and culture.

For local listening in San Francisco and online via podcasts and/or streaming audio, check out these stations:

KQED (8.5 FM; www.kqed.org) National Public Radio (NPR) and Public Broadcasting (PBS) affiliate offering podcasts and streaming audio.

KALW (91.7 FM; www.kalw.org) Local NPR affiliate: news, talk, music, original programming.

KPOO (89.5 FM; www.kpoo.com) Community nonprofit radio with jazz, R&B, blues and reggae.

KPFA (94.1 FM; www.kpfa.org) Alternative news and music.

Money

ATMs widely available; credit cards accepted at most hotels, stores and restaurants. Many farmers-market stalls and food trucks and some bars are cash only.

ATMs

Most banks have 24-hour ATMs, except in areas where street crime is a problem (such as near the BART stop at 16th and Mission Sts). You can withdraw cash from an ATM using a credit card (service charge applies); check with your bank about fees and immediately applied interest.

Changing Money

Though there are exchange bureaus at airports, the best rates are generally in town. You can change money downtown at **Currency Exchange International** (☑415-974-6600; www. sanfranciscocurrencyexchange. com; level 1, Westfield Center, 865 Market St; ☺10am-8:30pm Mon-Sat, 11am-7pm Sun; Ⓜ Powell, Ⓑ Powell) and **Bank of America** (☑415-837-1394; www.bankamerica. com; 1 Powell St, downstairs; ☺9am-5pm Mon-Thu, to 6pm Fri, 10am-2pm Sat; Ⓜ Powell, Ⓑ Powell).

Australia	A$1	$0.76
Canada	C$1	$0.73
Europe	€1	$1.09
Japan	¥100	$0.90
New Zealand	NZ$1	$0.69
UK	UK£1	$1.29

For current exchange rates, visit www.xe.com.

Traveler's Checks

In the US, traveler's checks in US dollars are virtually as good as cash; you don't necessarily have to go to a bank to cash them, as some establishments – particularly hotels – will accept them like cash. The major advantage of traveler's checks in US dollars over cash is that they can be replaced if lost or stolen.

Tipping

Tipping is *essential*, as most workers in service-industry jobs make only the minimum wage and rely almost entirely on tips for their income. However, if service is truly terrible, tip nothing – or else reduce the following standard amounts:

➡ Bartenders – $1 to $2 per drink, or 15% of the bill. Note: Good tippers get stronger drinks.

➡ Bellhops, airport skycaps – $2 per bag, plus $5 to $10 extra for special service.

➡ Concierges – nothing for simple information (like directions); $2 to $20 for securing restaurant reservations or concert tickets, or for providing exceptional service.

➡ Housekeeping staff – $2 daily, left on the pillow each day; more if you're messy.

➡ Parking valets – $2; extra for special service.

➡ Restaurant servers – 15% to 20% of the pretax bill.

➡ Taxi drivers – 10% to 15% of the metered fare.

Opening Hours

Typical opening hours in San Francisco:

Banks 9am to 4:30pm or 5pm Monday to Friday (occasionally 9am to noon Saturday).

Offices 8:30am to 5:30pm Monday to Friday.

Restaurants Breakfast 8am to 10am; lunch 11:30am to 2:30pm; dinner 5:30pm, with last service 9pm to 9:30pm weekdays or 10pm weekends; Saturday and Sunday brunch 10am to 2pm.

Shops 10am to 6pm or 7pm Monday to Saturday, though hours often run 11am to 8pm Saturday and 11am to 6pm Sunday.

Post

Check www.usps.com for post-office locations throughout San Francisco.

Public Holidays

Most shops remain open on public holidays (with the exception of Independence Day, Thanksgiving, Christmas Day and New Year's Day), but banks, schools and offices are usually closed. Holidays that may affect business hours and transit schedules include the following:

New Year's Day January 1

Martin Luther King Jr Day Third Monday in January

Presidents' Day Third Monday in February

Easter Sunday (and Good Friday and Easter Monday) in March or April

Memorial Day Last Monday in May

Independence Day July 4

Labor Day First Monday in September

Columbus Day Second Monday in October

Veterans Day November 11

Thanksgiving Fourth Thursday in November

Christmas Day December 25

Smoking

Smoking is prohibited almost everywhere. Some hotels have smoking rooms, but most have lately become entirely nonsmoking. Bars with outdoor patios allow smoking in these areas; otherwise, you must go outside to the sidewalk and stay away from the doorways of open businesses.

Taxes

SF's 8.75% sales tax is added to virtually everything, including meals, shopping and car rentals; the hotel-room tax is 14%. Groceries are about the only items not taxed. Unlike the European Value Added Tax, sales tax is not refundable.

In response to city laws mandating health-care benefits for restaurant workers, some restaurants pass those costs on to diners by tacking an additional 3% to 4% 'Healthy SF' charge onto the bill – it's usually mentioned in the menu's fine print.

Telephone

The US country code is 1. San Francisco's city/area code is 🖉415. To place an international call, dial 🖉011 + country code + city code + number (make sure to drop the 0 that precedes foreign city codes or your call won't go through). When calling Canada, there's no need to dial the international access code (🖉011). When dialing from a landline, you must precede any area code by 1 for direct dialing, 0 for collect calls and operator assistance (both expensive); from cell phones, dial only the area code and number. As of 2015, when calling local numbers in San Francisco you must dial the area code; thus, all local numbers now begin with 🖉1-415.

Area Codes in the Bay Area

East Bay 🖉510
Marin County 🖉415
Peninsula 🖉650
San Francisco 🖉415
San Jose 🖉408
Santa Cruz 🖉831
Wine Country 🖉707
Local calls from public pay phones usually start at 50¢. Hotel-room telephones often carry heavy surcharges, but local calls may be free: ask before you dial. Toll-free numbers start with 🖉800, 855, 866, 877 or 888; phone numbers beginning with 🖉900 usually incur high fees.

Cell Phones

Most US cell phones besides the iPhone operate on CDMA, not the European standard GSM – check compatibility with your phone-service provider. North American travelers can use their cell phones in San Francisco and the Bay Area but should check with their carriers about roaming charges.

Operator Services

International operator 🖉00
Local directory 🖉411
Long-distance directory information 🖉1 + area code + 555-1212
Operator 🖉0
Toll-free number information 🖉800-555-1212

Phonecards

For international calls from a public pay phone, it's a good idea to use a phone card, available at most corner markets and drug stores. Otherwise, when you dial 0, you're at the mercy of whatever international carrier operates that pay phone.

Time

San Francisco is on Pacific Standard Time (PST), three hours behind the East Coast's Eastern Standard Time (EST) and eight hours behind Greenwich Mean Time (GMT/UTC). March through October is daylight-saving time in the US.

Tourist Information

SF Visitor Information Center (www.sanfrancisco.travel/ visitor-information-center) Muni Passports, activities deals, culture and event calendars.

For further tourist information, see the following websites:

Lonely Planet (www.lonely-planet.com)
SFGate.com (www.sfgate.com)
SFist (www.sfist.com)

Travelers with Disabilities

All Bay Area transit companies offer wheelchair-accessible service and travel discounts for travelers with disabilities. Major car-rental companies can usually supply hand-controlled vehicles with one or two days' notice. For people with visual impairment, major intersections emit a chirping signal to indicate when it is safe to cross the street. Resources:

San Francisco Bay Area Regional Transit Guide (https://511.org/transit/accessibility/overview) Covers accessibility for people with disabilities.

Muni's Street & Transit (www.sfmta.com/getting-around/accessibility) Details wheelchair-friendly bus routes and streetcar stops.

Independent Living Resource Center of San Francisco (🖉415-543-6222; www.ilrcsf.org; ⊘9am-4:30pm Mon-Thu, to 4pm Fri) Provides further information about wheelchair accessibility on Bay Area public transit and in hotels and other local facilities.

Environmental Traveling Companions (Map p292; 🖉415-474-7662; www.etctrips.org) Leads excellent outdoor trips – whitewater rafting, kayaking and cross-country skiing – for kids with disabilities.

Visas

Canadians

Canadian citizens currently only need proof of identity and citizenship to enter the US – but check the US Department of State for updates, as requirements may change.

Visa Waiver Program

USA Visa Waiver Program (VWP) allows nationals from 38 countries to enter the US without a visa, provided they are carrying a machine-readable passport. For the updated list of countries included in the program and current requirements, see the **US Department of State** website (http://travel.state.gov).

Citizens of VWP countries need to register with the **US Department of Homeland Security** (https://esta.cbp.dhs.gov/esta) three days before their visit. There is a $14 fee for registration application; when approved, the registration is valid for two years.

Visas Required

You must obtain a visa from a US embassy or consulate in your home country if you:

➡ Do not currently hold a passport from a VWP country.

➡ Are from a VWP country but don't have a machine-readable passport, aka an e-passport.

➡ Are planning to stay longer than 90 days.

➡ Are planning to work or study in the US.

Work Visas

Foreign visitors are not legally allowed to work in the USA without the appropriate working visa. The most common, the H visa, can be difficult to obtain. It usually requires a sponsoring organization, such as the company you will be working for in the US. The company will need to demonstrate why you, rather than a US citizen, are most qualified for the job.

The type of work visa you need depends on your work:

H visa For temporary workers.

L visa For employees in intra-company transfers.

O visa For workers with extraordinary abilities.

P visa For athletes and entertainers.

Q visa For international cultural-exchange visitors.

Volunteering

➡ **VolunteerMatch** (www.volunteermatch.org) Matches your interests, talents and availability with a local nonprofit where you could donate your time, even if only for a few hours.

➡ **Craigslist** (http://sfbay.craigslist.org/vol) Lists opportunities to support the Bay Area community, from nonprofit fashion-show fundraisers to teaching English to new arrivals.

Women Travelers

SF is excellent for solo women travelers: you can eat, stay, dine and go out alone without anyone making presumptions about your availability, interests or sexual orientation. That said, women should apply their street smarts here as in any other US city, just to be on the safe side.

The **Women's Building** (Map p302; ☑415-431-1180; www.womensbuilding.org; 3543 18th St; ♿; 🚌14, 22, 33, 49, Ⓑ16th St Mission, ⓂJ) has a Community Resource Room offering information on health care, domestic violence, childcare, harassment, legal issues, employment and housing.

Behind the Scenes

SEND US YOUR FEEDBACK

We love to hear from travelers – your comments keep us on our toes and help make our books better. Our well-traveled team reads every word on what you loved or loathed about this book. Although we cannot reply individually to your submissions, we always guarantee that your feedback goes straight to the appropriate authors, in time for the next edition. Each person who sends us information is thanked in the next edition – the most useful submissions are rewarded with a selection of digital PDF chapters.

Visit **lonelyplanet.com/contact** to submit your updates and suggestions or to ask for help. Our award-winning website also features inspirational travel stories, news and discussions.

Note: We may edit, reproduce and incorporate your comments in Lonely Planet products such as guidebooks, websites and digital products, so let us know if you don't want your comments reproduced or your name acknowledged. For a copy of our privacy policy visit lonelyplanet.com/privacy.

OUR READERS

Many thanks to the travelers who used the last edition and wrote to us with helpful hints, useful advice and interesting anecdotes: Badong Abesamis, Lynn Gervens, Michelle Harrison, Michelle Jeffers, Scott Sminkey

WRITER THANKS

Alison Bing

Thanks to Cliff Wilkinson, Sarah Sung, Lisa Park, DeeAnn Budney, PT Tenenbaum, and above all, Marco Flavio Marinucci, for making a Muni bus ride into the adventure of a lifetime.

John A Vlahides

Thanks to destination editor Clifton Wilkinson and co-author Alison Bing, with whom it's always lovely to work. And most of all, thanks to you, dear reader – you make my life so joyful and I'm grateful for the honor of being your guide through the cool grey city of love.

ACKNOWLEDGEMENTS

Cover photograph: twilight over the Golden Gate Bridge, Danita Delimont/AWL ©

Illustration on pp52-3 by Michael Weldon.

THIS BOOK

This 11th edition of Lonely Planet's *San Francisco* guidebook was researched and written by Alison Bing and John A Vlahides, with contributions from Sara Benson and Ashley Harrell. The previous two editions were also written by Alison Bing, John A Vlahides and Sara Benson. This guidebook was produced by the following:

Destination Editors Clifton Wilkinson, Sarah Stocking
Product Editors Vicky Smith, Tracy Whitmey
Senior Cartographer Alison Lyall
Book Designer Jessica Rose
Assisting Editors Sarah Bailey, Andrew Bain, Judith Bamber, Michelle Coxall, Andrea Dobbin, Carly Hall, Shona Gray, Kate James, Kellie Langdon, Jodie Martire, Anne Mulvaney, Maja Vatric
Assisting Cartographer Julie Dodkins
Assisting Book Designer Virginia Moreno
Cover Researcher Marika Mercer
Thanks to William Allen, Kate Kiely, Jenna Myers, Susan Paterson, Mazzy Prinsep, Kirsten Rawlings, Tony Wheeler

Index

See also separate subindexes for:

✗ EATING P281

🍷 DRINKING & NIGHTLIFE P282

☆ ENTERTAINMENT P283

🛍 SHOPPING P284

🏃 SPORTS & ACTIVITIES P285

🛏 SLEEPING P285

✕ EATING

**DRINKING &
NIGHTLIFE**

San Francisco Maps

Sights

- Beach
- Bird Sanctuary
- Buddhist
- Castle/Palace
- Christian
- Confucian
- Hindu
- Islamic
- Jain
- Jewish
- Monument
- Museum/Gallery/Historic Building
- Ruin
- Shinto
- Sikh
- Taoist
- Winery/Vineyard
- Zoo/Wildlife Sanctuary
- Other Sight

Activities, Courses & Tours

- Bodysurfing
- Diving
- Canoeing/Kayaking
- Course/Tour
- Sento Hot Baths/Onsen
- Skiing
- Snorkeling
- Surfing
- Swimming/Pool
- Walking
- Windsurfing
- Other Activity

Sleeping

- Sleeping
- Camping
- Hut/Shelter

Eating

- Eating

Drinking & Nightlife

- Drinking & Nightlife
- Cafe

Entertainment

- Entertainment

Shopping

- Shopping

Information

- Bank
- Embassy/Consulate
- Hospital/Medical
- Internet
- Police
- Post Office
- Telephone
- Toilet
- Tourist Information
- Other Information

Geographic

- Beach
- Gate
- Hut/Shelter
- Lighthouse
- Lookout
- Mountain/Volcano
- Oasis
- Park
- Pass
- Picnic Area
- Waterfall

Population

- Capital (National)
- Capital (State/Province)
- City/Large Town
- Town/Village

Transport

- Airport
- BART station
- Border crossing
- Boston T station
- Bus
- Cable car/Funicular
- Cycling
- Ferry
- Metro/Muni station
- Monorail
- Parking
- Petrol station
- Subway/SkyTrain station
- Taxi
- Train station/Railway
- Tram
- Underground station
- Other Transport

Routes

- Tollway
- Freeway
- Primary
- Secondary
- Tertiary
- Lane
- Unsealed road
- Road under construction
- Plaza/Mall
- Steps
- Tunnel
- Pedestrian overpass
- Walking Tour
- Walking Tour detour
- Path/Walking Trail

Boundaries

- International
- State/Province
- Disputed
- Regional/Suburb
- Marine Park
- Cliff
- Wall

Hydrography

- River, Creek
- Intermittent River
- Canal
- Water
- Dry/Salt/Intermittent Lake
- Reef

Areas

- Airport/Runway
- Beach/Desert
- Cemetery (Christian)
- Cemetery (Other)
- Glacier
- Mudflat
- Park/Forest
- Sight (Building)
- Sportsground
- Swamp/Mangrove

Note: Not all symbols displayed above appear on the maps in this book

MAP INDEX

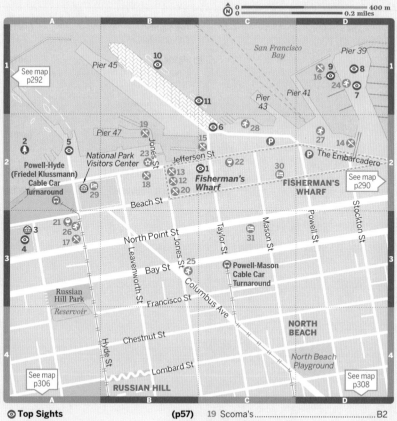

FISHERMAN'S WHARF

THE PRESIDIO

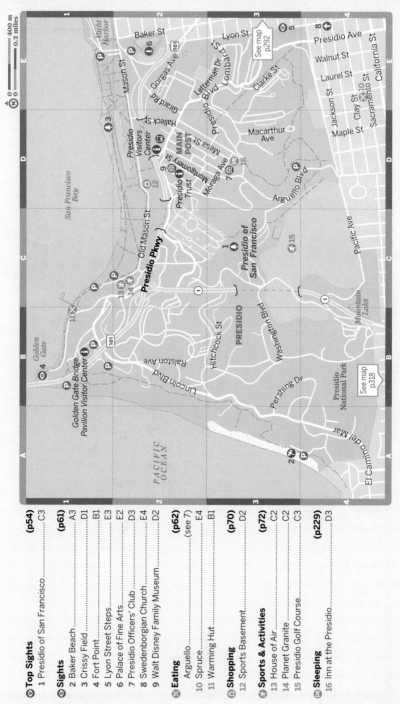

THE MARINA

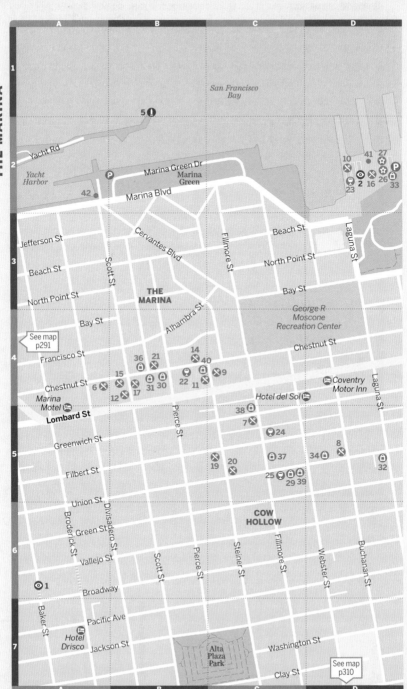

San Francisco Bay

Yacht Harbor

Yacht Rd

Marina Green Dr
Marina Green

Marina Blvd

Jefferson St

Cervantes Blvd

Beach St

North Point St

Bay St

Filmore St

Scott St

THE MARINA

Alhambra St

Beach St

North Point St

Bay St

George R Moscone Recreation Center

Laguna St

Laguna St

See map p291

Francisco St

Chestnut St

Chestnut St

Coventry Motor Inn

Marina Motel

Lombard St

Hotel del Sol

Pierce St

Greenwich St

Filbert St

Union St

Broderick St

Divisadero St

Green St

Vallejo St

Scott St

Pierce St

Steiner St

COW HOLLOW

Filmore St

Webster St

Buchanan St

Broadway

Baker St

Pacific Ave

Hotel Drisco

Jackson St

Alta Plaza Park

Washington St

See map p310

Clay St

THE MARINA

UNION SQUARE

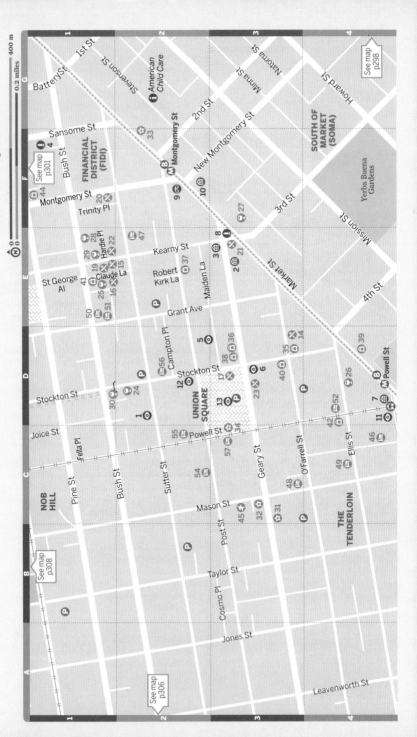

0 0.2 miles
0 400 m

See map p301

See map p298

See map p308

See map p306

Battery St
1st St
Stevenson St
Sansome St
Bush St
Montgomery St
FINANCIAL DISTRICT (FIDI)
Trinity Pl
2nd St
Montgomery St
New Montgomery St
Minna St
Natoma St
Howard St
American Child Care
SOUTH OF MARKET (SOMA)
Yerba Buena Gardens
3rd St
Mission St
4th St
St George Al
Hardie Pl
Claude La
Kearny St
Robert Kirk La
Maiden La
Market St
Grant Ave
Campton Pl
Stockton St
Powell St
Stockton St
UNION SQUARE
Geary St
O'Farrell St
Ellis St
Powell St
NOB HILL
Pine St
Fella Pl
Bush St
Joice St
Sutter St
Post St
Mason St
Taylor St
Cosmo Pl
Jones St
Leavenworth St
THE TENDERLOIN

See map
p296

San Francisco Visitor
Information Center

Eddy St

Turk St

Jessie St

5th St

Minna St

Folsom St

Sights (p81)
1 450 Sutter St.	D2
2 49 Geary	E3
3 Anglim Gilbert Gallery	E3
4 Diego Rivera's Allegory of California Fresco	F1
5 Frank Lloyd Wright Building	D2
6 I Magnin Building	D3
7 James Flood Building	D4
8 Lotta's Fountain	E3
9 One Montgomery Terrace	F2
10 Palace Hotel	F2
11 Powell St Cable Car Turnaround	D4
12 Ruth Asawa's San Francisco Fountain	D2
13 Union Square	D3

Eating (p90)
14 Bio	D3
15 Boxed Foods	E1
16 Cafe Claude	E1
17 Emporio Rulli	D3
18 Farmerbrown	C5
19 Gitane	E1
20 Golden West	F1
21 Hakkasan	E3
22 Sushirrito	E1
23 Tout Sweet	D3

Drinking & Nightlife (p95)
24 Burritt Room	D2
Gaspar Brasserie & Cognac Room	(see 47)
25 Irish Bank	E1
26 John's Grill	D4
27 Local Edition	E1
28 Pagan Idol	D3
29 Rickhouse	E1
30 Tunnel Top	D1

Entertainment (p102)
31 American Conservatory Theater	C3
32 Biscuits & Blues	C3
33 Commonwealth Club	F2
34 TIX Bay Area	C3

Shopping (p108)
35 Barneys	D3
36 Britex Fabrics	D3
37 Gump's	E2
38 John Varvatos	D3
39 Levi's Flagship Store	D4
40 Macy's	D3
41 Margaret O'Leary	E1
42 Uniqlo	D4
43 Westfield San Francisco Centre	D5
44 Wingtip	F1

Sports & Activities (p111)
45 Blazing Saddles	C3

Sleeping (p230)
46 Axiom	C4
47 Galleria Park	E2
48 HI San Francisco Downtown	C3
49 Hotel Abri	C4
50 Hotel des Arts	E1
51 Hotel Triton	E1
52 Hotel Union Square	D4
53 Hotel Zetta	D5
54 Kensington Park Hotel	C2
Palace Hotel	(see 10)
55 Sir Francis Drake Hotel	C2
56 Taj Campton Place	D2
57 Westin St Francis Hotel	C3

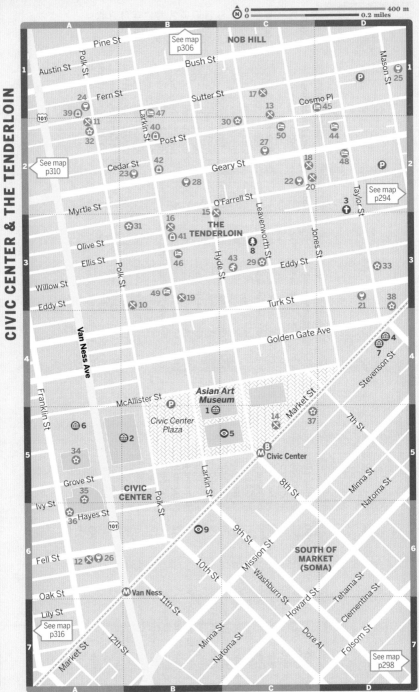

CIVIC CENTER & THE TENDERLOIN

CIVIC CENTER & THE TENDERLOIN

CIVIC CENTER & THE TENDERLOIN

Key on p300

See map p306

See map p292

See map p294

See map p310

See map p296

See map p308

See map p316

See map p302

Jackson St

Washington St

Mini Park

Clay St

NOB HILL

Sacramento St

Stockton St

Grant Ave

California St Cable Car Turnaround

California St

Pine St

Taylor St

Mason St

Powell St

Bush St

Austin St

Fern St

Polk St

Larkin St

Hyde St

Leavenworth St

Bush St

Sutter St

Post St

UNION SQUARE

Union Square

Stockton St

Franklin St

Van Ness Ave

Cedar St

Geary St

Myrtle St

O'Farrell St

Olive St

Willow St

Eddy St

Jones St

THE TENDERLOIN

Ellis St

Powell St

Powell St Cable Car Turnaround

Hallidie Plaza

5th St

Jessie St

Larch St

Polk St

Turk St

Market St

20

36

Jessie St

Mission St

Mary St

56

44

Golden Gate Ave

CIVIC CENTER

McAllister St

Civic Center Plaza

Larkin St

United Nations Plaza

Grove St

Stevenson St

Minna St

6th St

Harriet St

Russ St

47

Fulton St

Gough St

Grove St

Ivy St

Hayes St

Polk St

Ivy St

Jessie St

Civic Center

69

67

7

68

61

Natoma St

Langton St

Moss St

46

53

49

27

Page St

HAYES VALLEY

Fell St

8th St

Sumner St

35

Victoria Manalo Draves Park

31

Hickory St

Oak St

Octavia Blvd

Lily St

Page St

Rose St

Haight St

Van Ness

12th St

S Van Ness Ave

Mission St

Grace St

Washburn St

Minna St

Natoma St

Howard St

Dore Al

10th St

Folsom St

52

Tehama St

Clementina St

34

Ringold St

Heron St

62

Gough St

Otis St

11th St

45

48

Harrison St

Sheridan St

80

10

McCoppin St

Otis St

12th St

59

Juniper St

30

54

57

33

9th St

Dore Al

14

Duboce Ave

Brosnan St

THE MISSION

58

101

Isis St

39

24

Erie St

14th St

43

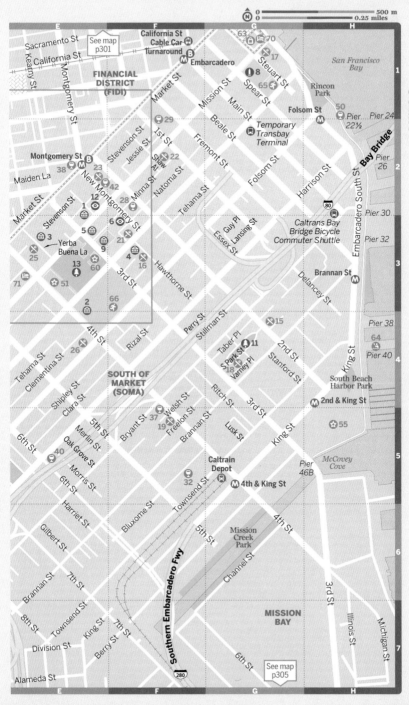

0   500 m
0   0.25 miles

Sacramento St
California St
Kearny St
Montgomery St

See map p301

California St
Cable Car
Turnaround
Embarcadero

63
70

17

San Francisco Bay

FINANCIAL DISTRICT (FIDI)

Market St

Steuart St

8

Rincon Park

65

Spear St

Mission St
Main St
Beale St
Fremont St

Folsom St

50
Pier 22½
Pier 24

29

Temporary Transbay Terminal

Montgomery St
38
23
22
42
28
12
1
6
5
21
9
13
60
2
66
4
16
51
71
25
3

Maiden La
Market St
Stevenson St
New Montgomery St
Jessie St
Shaw
Minna St
Natoma St
Tehama St
Stevenson St
Yerba Buena La
3rd St
Hawthorne St

1st St

Folsom St
Harrison St

Bay Bridge

Pier 26

Pier 30

Pier 32

Guy Pl
Essex St
Lansing St

Caltrans Bay Bridge Bicycle Commuter Shuttle

Embarcadero South

80

Brannan St

Delancey St

Pier 38
64
Pier 40

Tehama St
Clementina St
26

4th St
Rizal St
Perry St
Stillman St

15

Taber Pl
11
S Park St
18
Varney Pl

2nd St
Stanford St

King St

South Beach Harbor Park

SOUTH OF MARKET (SOMA)

Shipley St
Clara St
5th St
Merlin St
Oak Grove St
6th St
Morris St

Bryant St
Welsh St
37
19
Freelon St
Brannan St
Ritch St
Lusk St
3rd St
King St

2nd & King St

55

McCovey Cove

40

Harriet St

Bluxome St
Townsend St

Caltrain Depot
32
4th & King St

Pier 46B

Gilbert St
7th St
Brannan St
8th St
Townsend St
King St
7th St
Berry St

5th St

4th St

Mission Creek Park

Channel St

MISSION BAY

3rd St
Illinois St
Michigan St

Division St
Alameda St

Southern Embarcadero Fwy

280

See map p305

SOMA *Map on p298*

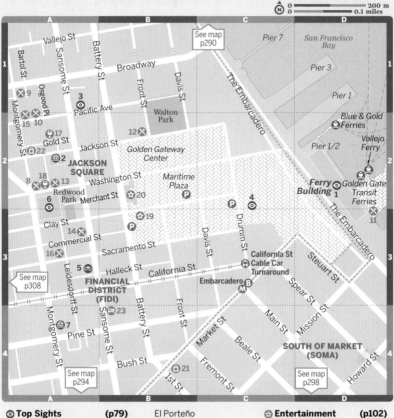

N 0 ————— 200 m
0 ————— 0.1 miles

THE MISSION

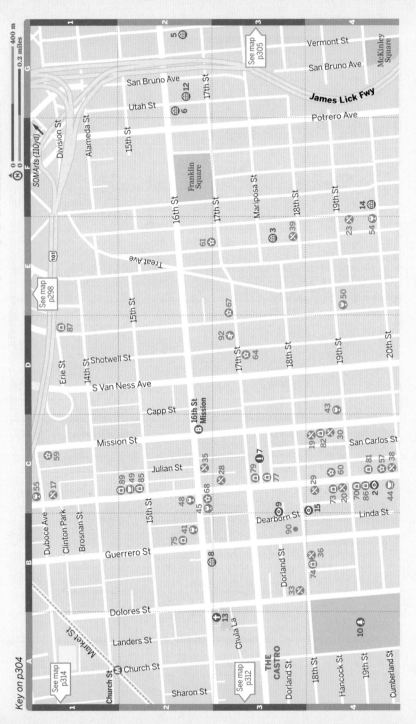

Key on p304

See map p314

See map p298

See map p305

See map p312

THE CASTRO

SOMArts (110yd)

0   400 m
0   0.2 miles

James Lick Fwy

16th St Mission

Vermont St
San Bruno Ave
McKinley Square
San Bruno Ave
Utah St
Potrero Ave
Alameda St
Division St
Erie St
15th St
16th St
17th St
Franklin Square
Mariposa St
18th St
19th St
Treat Ave
15th St
14th St
Shotwell St
S Van Ness Ave
Capp St
17th St
18th St
19th St
20th St
Mission St
Julian St
Duboce Ave
Clinton Park
Brosnan St
15th St
Guerrero St
San Carlos St
Linda St
Dearborn St
Dolores St
Landers St
Chula La
Church St
Market St
Sharon St
Dorland St
18th St
Hancock St
19th St
Cumberland St
Dorland St
17th St

5
12
6
14
3
39
23
54
61
87
67
50
92
64
43
59
17
55
89
49
85
48
45
68
35
28
79
77
7
19
82
30
81
57
38
29
73
60
20
70
86
2
44
9
15
90
8
75
41
74
36
33
13
10

US 101

22nd St

San Francisco General Hospital

San Bruno Ave

Utah St

25th St

Potrero del Sol Park
94

Potrero Ave

Hampshire St
21

58

York St
26 1

11

Bryant St

23rd St

York St

Bryant St

Florida St

Florida St

Alabama St

21st St

Alabama St

Harrison St
95

Harrison St

25

71

4

Treat Ave
Garfield Square

Treat Ave
83

Lucky St

Folsom St
65

Folsom St

69

Shotwell St

THE MISSION

22nd St

Shotwell St

S Van Ness Ave

Precita Park

Precita Ave

97

18 96
52

Cesar Chavez St

Wild Side West (0.8mi)

46

Capp St
37

27 32

42

Mission St
91

93

34

22
56

24

24th St Mission

25th St

16

Mission St

47

31 66
62

Bartlett St

Valencia St

72

88

80 40

76

84

San Jose Ave

78

63

63

53

Liberty St

21st St

Hill St

23rd St

Guerrero St

Ames St

Fair Oaks St

Fair Oaks St

Quane St

Dolores St

Jersey St

Clipper St

26th St

NOE VALLEY

Mitchell's Ice Cream (0.2mi);
Rock Bar (0.2mi)

Chattanooga St

Church St

27th St

Cesar Chavez St

Vicksburg St

Sanchez St

See map p311

51

POTRERO HILL

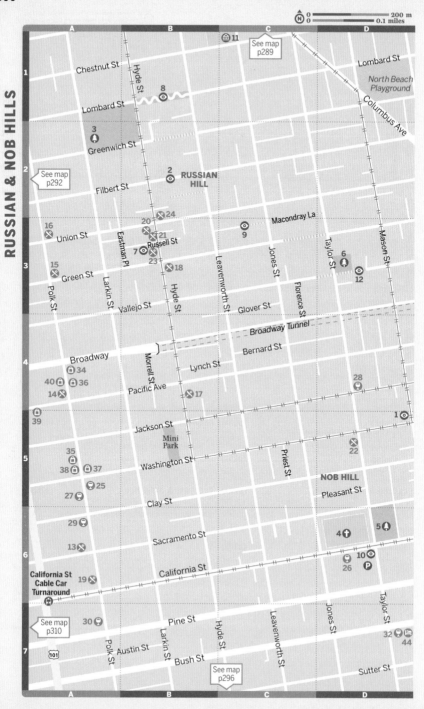

RUSSIAN & NOB HILLS

See map p289

See map p292

See map p310

See map p296

Chestnut St

Lombard St

Greenwich St

Filbert St

RUSSIAN HILL

Union St

Green St

Vallejo St

Broadway

Pacific Ave

Jackson St

Mini Park

Washington St

Clay St

Sacramento St

California St Cable Car Turnaround

California St

Pine St

Bush St

Lombard St

North Beach Playground

Columbus Ave

Macondray La

Broadway Tunnel

Bernard St

Lynch St

Pleasant St

NOB HILL

Sutter St

Hyde St

Polk St

Larkin St

Eastman Pl

Russell St

Morrell St

Leavenworth St

Jones St

Florence St

Glover St

Taylor St

Mason St

Priest St

Austin St

Taylor St

NORTH BEACH & CHINATOWN

See map p289

N 0 ————— 200 m
0 ————— 0.1 miles

← Basically Free Bike Rentals (130yd)

Powell-Mason Cable Car Turnaround

Francisco St

Water St 73

54

Pfeiffer St

Chestnut St

13

Kearny St

Montgomery St

55

Jansen St 65

Mason St

Powell St

Stockton St

Lombard St

Grant Ave

Greenwich St

Pioneer Park/ Telegraph Hill

Greenwich St

Coit 1 Tower

North Beach Playground

Telegraph Hill Blvd

NORTH BEACH

12

Taylor St

Valparaiso St

Columbus Ave

67

Greenwich St

Filbert St

Filbert St

32 31

Filbert St

3

59

Genoa Pl

Varennes St

Kearny St

Sonoma St

22

75

Jasper Pl

24

Union St

Powell St

33 38

51

28

57

RUSSIAN HILL

53

Green St

70

58

37

16

See map p306

Ina Coolbrith Park

P

Vallejo St

14

35 44 49 42 2 36

25

27 50

30

Broadway

8

74

15 52

39

48 60

56

45

Broadway Tunnel

Bernard St

Pacific Ave

29

9

62

CHINATOWN

40

41

Jackson St

63

19

Stockton St

Grant Ave

46

43

4

68 5

7

18 69

Washington St

20

23 66

21

34

10

Jones St

Taylor St

Mason St

NOB HILL

Clay St

6

61

72

Priest St

Sacramento St

Joice St

17

Huntington Park

California St

St Mary's Square

Quincy St

P

47

See map p294

Pine St

See map p298

71

Bush St

11

See map p290

Sansome St

Battery St

Alta St

Levi's Plaza

Union St

Bartol St

Osgood Pl

JACKSON SQUARE

Montgomery St

Sansome St

Mark Twain St

Redwood Park

Commercial St

Spring St

FINANCIAL DISTRICT (FIDI)

See map p301

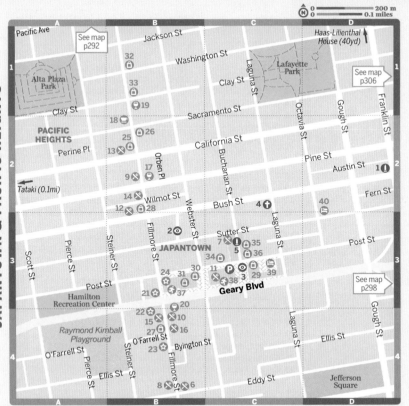

JAPANTOWN & PACIFIC HEIGHTS

THE CASTRO

See map
p314

See map
p311

N
0 — 200 m
0 — 0.1 miles

Park Hill Ave
Buena Vista Tce
Alpine Tce
Divisadero St
Castro St
Noe St
Walter St
Sanchez St

Roosevelt Way

14th St
14th St

15th St

Henry St

THE
CASTRO

Beaver St
Flint St

Museum Way

States St

16th St

17th St

Market St

18th St

Castro St

Collingwood St

LYRIC

20th St

Douglass St
Eureka St
Diamond St
Collingwood St
Castro St
Liberty St
Noe St
Rayburn St

Noe Valley

21st St
21st St

THE
CASTRO

Hancock St

Ford St

Hartford St

Pond St
Prosper St

Market St

Noe St

Sanchez St

Castro St M

Castro St

20th St

◎ Sights (p169)

1 Barbie-Doll Window....................C5
2 Castro Theatre....................C4
3 Corona Heights Park............A2
4 GLBT History Museum........B5
5 Golden Gate Model
   Railroad Club.....................A3
6 Harvey Milk & Jane Warner
   Plazas B4
7 Human Rights Campaign
   Action Center C5
8 Rainbow Honor Walk...........C5
   Randall Junior
   Museum .... (see 5)

✕ Eating (p172)

9 Anchor Oyster Bar...............C5
10 Dinosaurs.............................. D3
11 Finn Town Tavern D2
12 Frances................................. C4
13 La Méditerranée.................. C3
14 L'Ardoise C2
15 Mekong Kitchen C5
16 Myriad D2
17 Poesia.................................... C4
18 Starbelly C3
19 Super Duper Burger C3
   Thai House Express......(see 9)

◎ Drinking & Nightlife (p173)

20 440 Castro............................ B4
21 Badlands B5
22 Beaux..................................... C3
23 Blackbird E1
24 Cafe Flore............................. C3
25 Edge..B5
26 Hearth Coffee Roasters...... C4
27 HiTops D2

Lookout........................(see 13)
28 Midnight Sun........................C5
29 Mix C4
30 Moby Dick.............................C5
31 Swirl..B5
32 The Cafe................................C4
33 Toad Hall................................B4
34 Twin Peaks Tavern C4

◎ Entertainment (p175)

35 Cafe du Nord/Swedish
   American Hall....................D2
   Castro Theatre............. (see 2)

◎ Shopping (p176)

Castro Farmers
   Market......................(see 24)
   Cliff's Variety...............(see 29)
   Dog Eared Books........(see 29)
   Giddy ....(see 18)
   Human Rights
   Campaign Action
   Center & Store .... (see 7)
36 Kenneth Wingard.................C3
37 Local Take C4
38 Sui Generis C3
39 Unionmade.............................D4
40 Worn Out West......................C3

◎ Sports & Activities (p177)

41 Seward Street Slides A6

◎ Sleeping (p235)

42 Beck's Motor Lodge D2
43 Inn on Castro.........................C3
44 Parker Guest House.............E4
45 Willows Inn.............................E1

Market St

45 🛏
23 🚇
Ⓜ Church St

15th St

Sharon St
Church St
Church St

16th St

Chula La

See map
p302 ▷

17th St

44 🛏

Dorland St

18th St

Church St

19th St

Cumberland St

20th St

Liberty St

21st St

Hill St

THE HAIGHT

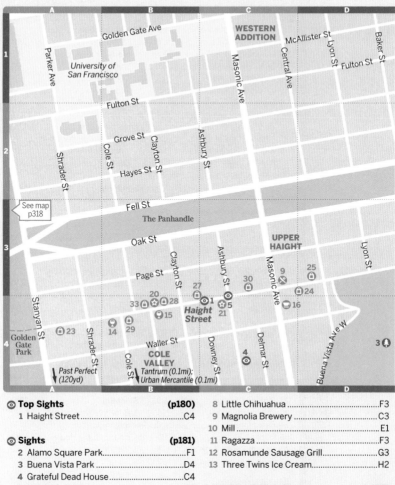

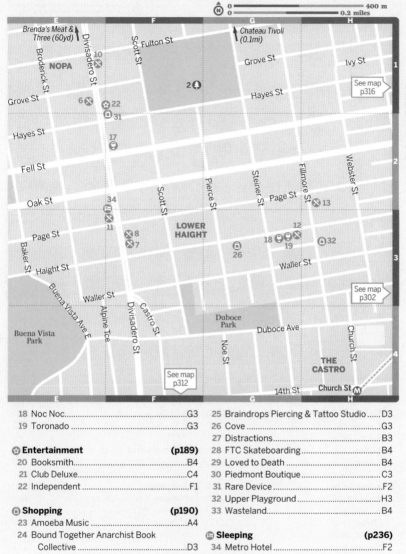

HAYES VALLEY

GOLDEN GATE PARK & THE AVENUES *Map on p318*

HAYES VALLEY

Key on p317

GOLDEN GATE PARK & THE AVENUES

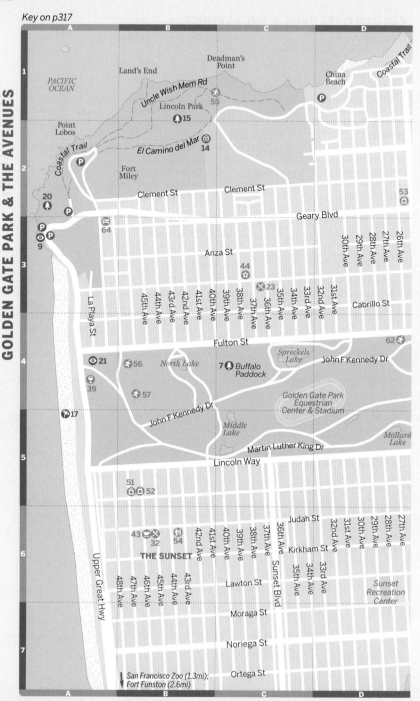

Deadman's Point

Land's End

China Beach

Coastal Trail

PACIFIC OCEAN

Uncle Wish Mem Rd

Lincoln Park

55

15

Point Lobos

El Camino del Mar

14

Coastal Trail

Fort Miley

20

Clement St

Clement St

Geary Blvd

53

64

9

Anza St

44

23

30th Ave
29th Ave
28th Ave
27th Ave
26th Ave

45th Ave
44th Ave
43rd Ave
42nd Ave
41st Ave
40th Ave
39th Ave
38th Ave
37th Ave
36th Ave
35th Ave
34th Ave
33rd Ave
32nd Ave
31st Ave

Cabrillo St

La Playa St

Fulton St

Spreckels Lake

62

21

56

North Lake

7 Buffalo Paddock

John F Kennedy Dr

39

57

Golden Gate Park Equestrian Center & Stadium

17

John F Kennedy Dr

Middle Lake

Mallard Lake

Martin Luther King Dr

Lincoln Way

51

52

Judah St

32nd Ave
31st Ave
30th Ave
29th Ave
28th Ave
27th Ave

43

32

54

THE SUNSET

42nd Ave
41st Ave
40th Ave
39th Ave
38th Ave
37th Ave
36th Ave

Kirkham St

35th Ave
34th Ave
33rd Ave

Sunset Blvd

48th Ave
47th Ave
46th Ave
45th Ave
44th Ave
43rd Ave

Lawton St

Sunset Recreation Center

Upper Great Hwy

Moraga St

Noriega St

Ortega St

↓ San Francisco Zoo (1.3mi);
↓ Fort Funston (2.6mi)

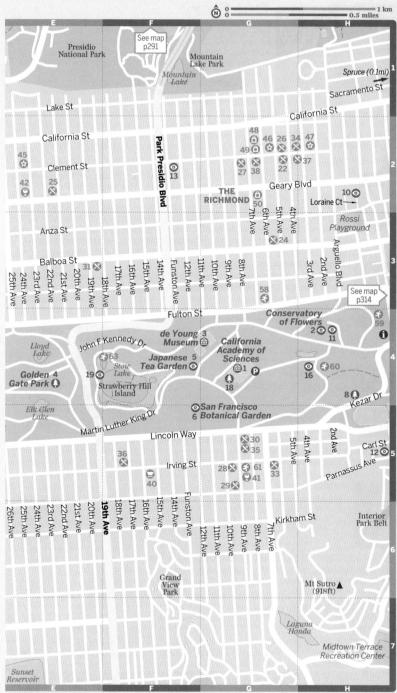

0 — 1 km
0 — 0.5 miles

See map p291

Presidio National Park

Mountain Lake Park

Mountain Lake

Spruce (0.1mi)

Sacramento St

Lake St

California St

California St

Clement St

Park Presidio Blvd

13

THE RICHMOND

Geary Blvd

Loraine Ct

Rossi Playground

Anza St

Balboa St

Fulton St

See map p314

Conservatory of Flowers

de Young Museum

California Academy of Sciences

Japanese Tea Garden

Golden Gate Park

Stow Lake

Strawberry Hill Island

Lloyd Lake

Elk Glen Lake

San Francisco Botanical Garden

Martin Luther King Dr

Lincoln Way

Carl St

Irving St

Parnassus Ave

Kirkham St

Interior Park Belt

Grand View Park

Mt Sutro (918ft)

Laguna Honda

Midtown Terrace Recreation Center

Sunset Reservoir

25th Ave
24th Ave
23rd Ave
22nd Ave
21st Ave
20th Ave
19th Ave
18th Ave
17th Ave
16th Ave
15th Ave
14th Ave
12th Ave
11th Ave
10th Ave
9th Ave
8th Ave
7th Ave
6th Ave
5th Ave
4th Ave
3rd Ave
2nd Ave
Arguello Blvd

Funston Ave

26th Ave

John F Kennedy Dr

Our Story

A beat-up old car, a few dollars in the pocket and a sense of adventure. In 1972 that's all Tony and Maureen Wheeler needed for the trip of a lifetime – across Europe and Asia overland to Australia. It took several months, and at the end – broke but inspired – they sat at their kitchen table writing and stapling together their first travel guide, *Across Asia on the Cheap*. Within a week they'd sold 1500 copies. Lonely Planet was born. Today, Lonely Planet has offices in Franklin, London, Melbourne, Oakland, Dublin, Beijing and Delhi, with more than 600 staff and writers. We share Tony's belief that 'a great guidebook should do three things: inform, educate and amuse'.

Our Writers

Alison Bing

Downtown, Civic Center & SoMa; North Beach & Chinatown; The Mission & Potrero Hill; Golden Gate Park & the Avenues; The Haight, NoPa & Hayes Valley Alison has done most things travelers are supposed to do and many you definitely shouldn't, including making room for the chickens, accepting dinner invitations from cults, and trusting the camel to know the way. She has survived to tell tales for Lonely Planet, NPR, BBC Travel, the *Telegraph*, *New York Times* and other global media. Alison also wrote the Plan Your Trip and Understand San Francisco sections.

John A Vlahides

The Marina, Fisherman's Wharf & the Piers; Nob Hill, Russian Hill & Fillmore; The Castro & Noe Valley John A Vlahides has been a cook in a Parisian bordello, luxury-hotel concierge, television host, safety monitor in a sex club, French-English interpreter, and he is one of Lonely Planet's most experienced and prolific guidebook authors. A native New Yorker living in San Francisco, John has contributed to 18 Lonely Planet guidebooks since 2003, ranging from California and the western United States to the Dubai guide. He is co-host of the TV series Lonely Planet: Roads Less Travelled (National Geographic Adventure).

Sara Benson

Day Trips from San Francisco After graduating from college in Chicago, Sara jumped on a plane to California with one suitcase and just $100 in her pocket. She landed in San Francisco, and today she makes her home in Oakland, just across the Bay. She also spent three years living in Japan, after which she followed her wanderlust around Asia and the Pacific before returning to the USA, where she has worked as a teacher, a journalist, a nurse and a national park ranger. To keep up with Sara's latest travel adventures, read her blog, The Indie Traveler (indietraveler.blogspot.com) and follow her on Twitter (@indie_traveler) and Instagram (indietraveler).

Ashley Harrell

Day Trips from San Francisco After a brief stint selling day spa coupons door-to-door in South Florida, Ashley decided she'd rather be a writer. She went to journalism grad school, convinced a newspaper to hire her, and starting covering wildlife, crime and tourism, sometimes all in the same story. Fueling her zest for storytelling and the unknown, she traveled widely and moved often, from a tiny NYC apartment to a vast California ranch to a jungle cabin in Costa Rica, where she started writing for Lonely Planet. From there her travels became more exotic and farther flung, and she still laughs when paychecks arrive.

Published by Lonely Planet Global Limited
CRN 554153
11th edition – Dec 2017
ISBN 978 1 78657 354 4
© Lonely Planet 2017   Photographs © as indicated 2017
10 9 8 7 6 5 4 3 2 1
Printed in China